The Blackwell Guide to

Medical Ethics

Blackwell Philosophy Guides

Series Editor: Steven M. Cahn, City University of New York Graduate School

Written by an international assembly of distinguished philosophers, the *Blackwell Philosophy Guides* create a groundbreaking student resource – a complete critical survey of the central themes and issues of philosophy today. Focusing and advancing key arguments throughout, each essay incorporates essential background material serving to clarify the history and logic of the relevant topic. Accordingly, these volumes will be a valuable resource for a broad range of students and readers, including professional philosophers.

The Blackwell Guide to
Medical Ethics

Edited by
Rosamond Rhodes, Leslie P. Francis,
and Anita Silvers

Blackwell
Publishing

BLACKWELL PUBLISHING
350 Main Street, Malden, MA 02148–5020, USA
9600 Garsington Road, Oxford OX4 2DQ, UK
550 Swanston Street, Carlton, Victoria 3053, Australia

The right of Rosamond Rhodes, Leslie P. Francis, and Anita Silvers
to be identified as the Authors of the Editorial Material in this Work has been asserted
in accordance with the UK Copyright, Designs, and Patents Act 1988.

First published 2007 by Blackwell Publishing Ltd

1   2007

Library of Congress Cataloging-in-Publication Data

The Blackwell guide to medical ethics / edited by Rosamond Rhodes,
Leslie P. Francis, Anita Silvers
    p.   cm. — (Blackwell Philosophy Guides; 21)
Includes bibliographical references and index
ISBN-13: 978-1-4051-2583-3 (hardback: alk. paper)
ISBN-10: 1-4051-2583-7 (hardback: alk. paper)
ISBN-13: 978-1-4051-2584-0 (pbk.: alk. paper)
ISBN-10: 1-4051-2584-5 (pbk.: alk. paper)
1. Medical ethics. I. Rhodes, Rosamond. II. Francis, Leslie, 1946– III.
Silvers, Anita. IV. Title: Guide to medical ethics. V. Series = 20
[DNLM: 1. Ethics, Medical—ethics. 2. Bioethical Issues—legislation & jurisprudence.
3. Patient Rights—ethics. 4. Public Policy. W 50 B632 2007]
R724.B515 2007
174.2—dc22   2006027510

A catalogue record for this title is available from the British Library.

Set in 10/13 pt Galliard
by The Running Head Limited, Cambridge, www.therunninghead.com
Printed and bound in Singapore
by Fabulous Printers Pte Ltd

The publisher's policy is to use permanent paper from mills that operate a sustainable
forestry policy, and which has been manufactured from pulp processed using acid-free and
elementary chlorine-free practices. Furthermore, the publisher ensures that the text
paper and cover board used have met acceptable environmental accreditation standards.

For further information on
Blackwell Publishing, visit our website:
www.blackwellpublishing.com

Contents

Notes on Contributors

Felicia Nimue Ackerman PhD is Professor of Philosophy at Brown University, Providence, Rhode Island, USA. Her essays on bioethics have appeared in the *Hastings Center Report*, the *Oxford Handbook of Bioethics* (2007), and elsewhere. Her short stories on bioethical themes are published in *Prize Stories 1990: The O. Henry Awards, Commentary*, and elsewhere. Her poems on bioethics are in *Ragged Edge Online* and elsewhere. She is preparing *Bioethics Through Fiction*, a volume of her stories and essays that will be published by Rowman & Littlefield.

Rachel A. Ankeny PhD is Senior Lecturer of the Unit for History and Philosophy of Science, University of Sydney, Australia. Her research interests include the history and philosophy of the biomedical sciences, particularly epistemological and ethical issues; the philosophy of medicine; the public understanding of biomedical sciences; and ethical issues associated with transplantation, genetics, reproductive technologies, and pharmaceuticals.

Margaret P. Battin MFA, PhD is Distinguished Professor in the Department of Philosophy and Adjunct Professor in the Division of Medical Ethics, Department of Internal Medicine at the University of Utah. She is the author or editor of a dozen books, most recently, *Ending Life: Ethics and the Way We Die* (Oxford, 2005). Her current areas of interest and research include suicide, physician-assisted suicide and euthanasia, ethics and infectious disease, and reproductive issues.

Rebecca Bennett PhD teaches in The Centre for Social Ethics and Policy, School of Law, University of Manchester, Manchester, UK. Dr Bennett has taught bioethics for 12 years and has published widely on diverse issues in bioethics. Her particular area of interest is the ethics of human reproduction including antenatal HIV and genetic testing, pre-limplatation genetic diagnosis, cloning, stem cell research, ectogenesis, and paternal rights. She is also responsible for devising, developing, and running the innovative distance learning MA/Postgraduate Diploma in Health Care Ethics and Law.

Dýrleif Bjarnadóttir MA, MS is a Senior Research Fellow at the Alden March Bioethics Institute in Albany NY, and is currently completing a dissertation in reproductive ethics. Her recent research has included newborn screening, the obligations of parents to their children, and the significance of cultural variances in the invocation of parental autonomy in treatment decisions for neonates.

Troyen Anthony Brennan MD is the Chief Medical Officer at Aetna. He was previously Professor of Medicine at Harvard Medical School.

Dan W. Brock PhD is the Frances Glessner Lee Professor of Medical Ethics at Harvard Medical School. He is the author (with Allen Buchanan) of *Deciding for Others: The Ethics of Surrogate Decision Making* (Cambridge University Press, 1989) as well as (with others) *From Chance to Choice: Genetics and Justice* (Cambridge University Press, 2000). His current research focuses on resource prioritization in the health sector.

David R. Buchanan DrPH, MA, is Research Fellow at the National Cancer Institute, Bethesda, Maryland, USA. Dr Buchanan has written extensively about the ethics of health promotion, public health ethics, and research ethics from a public health perspective. His most recent books include *An Ethic for Health Promotion* (Oxford University Press, 2000), and *Ethical and Legal Issues in Research with High Risk Populations* (APA Press, in press).

Leonard M. Fleck PhD, Professor of Philosophy and Medical Ethics, Michigan State University, East Lansing, Michigan, USA, has written extensively on the role of rational democratic deliberation in more justly addressing problems of health care rationing and priority-setting as well as ethical and policy issues related to genetics and reproductive decision-making.

Leslie P. Francis PhD, JD is Professor of Philosophy and the Alfred C. Emery Professor of Law, Adjunct Professor of Political Science at the University of Utah, and Adjunct Professor in the Division of Medical Ethics, Department of Internal Medicine at the University of Utah School of Medicine. Current areas of interest and research include bioethics and the law of bioethics, health law, the philosophy of law, and research ethics.

John Harris FMedSci is Sir David Alliance Professor of Bioethics, School of Law, University of Manchester and is joint Editor-in-Chief of *The Journal of Medical Ethics*. He has been a member of The United Kingdom Human Genetics Commission since its foundation in 1999. Recent books include *Clones, Genes and Immortality* (Oxford University Press, 1998); John Harris (ed.), *Bioethics*, Oxford Readings in Philosophy Series, (Oxford University Press, 2001); Justine C. Burley and John Harris (eds.), *A Companion To Genethics: Philosophy and the Genetic Revolution*, Blackwell's Companions to Philosophy series (Blackwell, 2002); and *On Cloning*, (Routledge, 2004).

Roger Higgs MBE, MA, FRCP, FRCGP is a physician and ethicist. He is Professor Emeritus at King's College London, specializing in general (family) practice and primary care, and ethics. He retired from active primary medical care in 2004 after 30 years as a physician, educator, and innovator in south London. He has published on psychological issues, health care development, and clinical ethics.

Douglas N. Husak PhD, JD is Professor of Philosophy at Rutgers University, New Jersey, USA. He works in legal philosophy generally, and in the philosophy of criminal law in particular. He is the author of *Philosophy of Criminal Law* (Rowman & Littlefield, 1987), *Drugs and Rights* (Cambridge University Press, 1992), and *Legalize This* (Verso, 2002).

Jay A. Jacobson MD is Professor of Internal Medicine, Chief of the Division of Medical Ethics, and a member of the Division of Infectious Disease at LDS Hospital and the Department of Medicine at the University of Utah School of Medicine. Current areas of interest and research include clinical and classroom teaching of medical ethics, infectious diseases, sub-specialty consultation and patient care, end of life care, and informed consent and medical decision-making.

F. M. Kamm PhD is Littauer Professor of Philosophy and Public Policy, Kennedy School of Government, and Professor of Philosophy, FAS, Harvard University, Massachusetts, USA. She specializes in normative ethical theory and practical ethics. Professor Kamm is the author of *Creation and Abortion* (Oxford University Press, 1992), *Morality, Mortality* , vols. 1 and 2 (Oxford University Press, 1993 and 1996), *Intricate Ethics* (Oxford University Press, 2006), and numerous essays in ethical theory and practical ethics.

Gerrit Kimsma, MD, drs Phil, is a general practitioner and fellow of the Center of Ethics and Philosopy, at Vrije Universiteit Medisch Centrum in Amsterdam, the Netherlands. His writing has focused on death and dying and the professional ethics of physicians. He is a member of the Euthanasia Committee of South-Holland and co-editor of *Asking to Die: Inside the Dutch Euthanasia Debate* (Kluwer, 1998).

Kenneth Kipnis PhD is a professor in the Department of Philosophy at the University of Hawaii at Manoa. His publications touch on ethical issues across a range of fields – law, medicine, early childhood education, engineering, and research on human subjects – and he has been writing about confidentiality for more than 25 years.

Stephen R. Latham JD, PhD is Professor of Law and Director of the Center for Health Law and Ethics at the Quinnipiac University School of Law in Hamden, Connecticut, USA. He was a former research fellow at the University of Edinburgh's Institute for Advanced Studies in the Humanities. His writings on bioethics, the history of medical ethics, and health law have appeared in numerous medical and bioethics journals, university press books, and law reviews.

Glenn McGee PhD is the John A. Balint Chair in Medical Ethics, Professor of Medicine, and Director of the Alden March Bioethics Institute at Albany Medical College/Center, Albany, New York, USA. His research has focused on showing the connections between our moral lives, medicine, and the biomedical sciences. He has published *The Perfect Baby: A Pragmatic Approach to Genetics: Beyond Genetics* (2004), *Who Owns Life?* (2002), *Pragmatic Bioethics: A New Theory of Bioethics* (1999, 2nd edn. 2002), and *The Human Cloning Debate* (4th edn., 2005), and many essays in journals of medicine, science, and bioethics such as *Science, Journal of the American Medical Association*, and *Nature Genetics*. He is the Editor-in-Chief of *The American Journal of Bioethics*.

Paul Menzel PhD is Professor of Philosophy at Pacific Lutheran University, Tacoma, Washington, USA, specializing in social philosophy and biomedical ethics. His scholarly writing has focused largely on health policy, particularly the proper role of health care economics. He has authored two books, most recently, *Strong Medicine: The Ethical Rationing of Health Care* (Oxford, 1990). He is currently examining moral issues in models for health care cost-effectiveness analysis, questions of justice in the structure of a health care system, and making the moral case for universal access to basic care from various political perspectives.

Franklin G. Miller PhD serves as a bioethicist in the Department of Clinical Bioethics at the National Institutes of Health, Bethesda, Maryland, USA. Dr Miller has published widely in bioethics and medical journals. His principal current research interest is the examination of ethical issues in clinical research, including placebo-controlled trials, placebo surgery, use of deception, informed consent, and the ways in which clinical research differs from medical care.

Ann E. Mills MSc (Econ.), MBA is Assistant Professor in the Center for Biomedical Ethics at the University of Virginia where she is co-director of the Program on Ethics and Policy in Healthcare Systems. She has written on the health care system with specific attention to the role of organization ethics. She is co-author or co-editor of *Organization Ethics in Health Care* (Oxford, 2000), *Developing Organization Ethics in Healthcare: A Case-Based Approach to Policy Practice and Compliance* (University Publishing Group, 2001), and *Professionalism in Tomorrow's Healthcare System* (University Publishing Group, 2005).

Robert T. Pennock PhD is Professor on the faculty of the Lyman Briggs School of Science, the Department of Philosophy, and the Center for Ethics and Humanities in the Life Sciences at Michigan State University, East Lansing, Michigan, USA. His research interests include issues involving epistemic and ethical values in science, especially in biology. He is the author of *Tower of Babel: The Evidence* *against the New Creationism*, (MIT Press, 1999) and many articles on philosophy of biology, and on science ethics, education, and public policy.

Janet Radcliffe Richards holds degrees in philosophy. She is a reader in Bioethics at University College London and Director of the Centre for Ethics and Philosophy of Biomedicine, UCL. Her work has focused mainly on philosophy of science, ethics, and applied ethics. Her publications include: *The Sceptical Feminist: A Philosophical Enquiry* (Routledge, 1980, Penguin, 1982), *Human Nature after Darwin* (Routledge, 2000), and numerous papers.

Rosamond Rhodes PhD is Professor of Medical Education and Director of Bioethics Education at Mount Sinai School of Medicine and Professor of Philosophy at The Graduate School, CUNY, in New York City, USA. She writes on a broad array of issues in bioethics and moral and political philosophy. She is co-editor of *Physician Assisted Suicide: Expanding the Debate* (Routledge, 1998), *Medicine and Social Justice: Essays on the Distribution of Health Care* (Oxford, 2002), and this volume.

Mary V. Rorty PhD, MA writes on practical and theoretical issues in clinical and organization ethics. She was Director of Advanced Studies at the University of Virginia's Center for Biomedical Ethics and is currently a Clinical Associate Professor at the Stanford University Medical Center in Palo Alto, California. She is co-author with E. Spencer, A. Mills, and P. Werhane of *Organization Ethics in Health Care* (Oxford, 2000), and co-editor with L. Frankel, A. Goldworth, and W. Silverman of *Ethical Dilemmas in Pediatrics* (Cambridge, 2005).

Julian Savulescu, BMedSci, MB, BS, MA, PhD holds the Uehiro Chair in Practical Ethics at the University of Oxford, UK, where he is also Director of the Oxford Uehiro Centre for Practical Ethics and Director of the Program on Ethics and the New Biosciences in the 21st Century. He is qualified in medicine, bioethics, and analytic philosophy. He has worked broadly in the ethics of science and medicine and he has published over 100 journal articles. Previously, he was Editor of the *Journal of Medical Ethics*, Director of the Ethics of Genetics Unit at the Murdoch Children's Research Institute, Royal Children's Hospital, Melbourne, Australia, Director of the Bioethics Program at the Centre for the Study of Health and Society at the University of Melbourne, and Chair of the Department of Human Services, Victoria, Ethics Committee.

Anita Silvers PhD is Professor of Philosophy at San Francisco State University. She has published seven books, including *Medicine and Social Justice* (Oxford University Press, 2002), *Americans With Disabilities: Exploring Implications of the Law for Individuals and Institutions* (Routledge, 2000), *Disability, Difference, Discrimination: Perspectives on Justice in Bioethics and Public Policy, Sociobiology and Human Nature* (Rowman & Littlefield, 1998), *Physician-Assisted Suicide: Expanding the Debate* (Routledge, 1998), and *The Recombinant DNA Controversy*

(NEXA, 1978). She has written more than 100 book chapters and articles on ethics and bioethics, social philosophy, aesthetics, law, feminism, and disability studies. In 2002, Silvers co-directed a National Endowment for the Humanities Summer Seminar on "Justice, Equality, and the Challenge of Disability."

Charles B. Smith MD is currently Emeritus Professor of Medicine at the University of Utah. He has held positions as Associate Chairman for the Department of Medicine and Chief of the Division of Infectious Diseases at the University of Utah School of Medicine. His current academic interests include clinical research on improved methods for diagnosis and treatment of tuberculosis in developing countries and ethical issues related to infectious diseases.

Evert van Leeuwen PhD, Prof. dr is Professor of Philosophy and Medical Ethics and Chair of the Center of Ethics and Philosophy at Vrije Universiteit Medisch Centrum, in Amsterdam, the Netherlands. His work has focused on the assessment of competence and issues related to death and dying and genetic screening.

Patricia H. Werhane PhD is the Wicklander Chair of Business Ethics in the Department of Philosophy and Director of the Institute for Business and Professional Ethics at DePaul University, Chicago, USA, with a joint appointment as the Peter and Adeline Ruffin Professor of Business Ethics and Senior Fellow at of the Olsson Center for Applied Ethics in the Darden School at the University of Virginia, USA. Professor Werhane has published numerous articles and is the author or co-editor of 15 books including *Ethical Issues in Business* (Prentice Hall, 1996), *Adam Smith and His Legacy for Modern Capitalism* (Oxford University Press, 1991), and *Organization Ethics in Health Care* (Oxford University Press, 2000). She is the founder and former Editor-in-Chief of *Business Ethics Quarterly*, the journal of the Society for Business Ethics.

Introduction

Rosamond Rhodes, Leslie P. Francis,
and Anita Silvers

Biomedical technology developed at an amazingly rapid rate throughout the twentieth century, and at breakneck speed during the last half of the twentieth century. Whereas previous technological advances occurred slowly enough to be accommodated into reigning moral views, the accelerated technological advances of modern medicine created moral questions that challenged accepted ethical thinking and required urgent answers. Basic concepts such as "life," "death," and "mother" had to be redefined and new definitions and distinctions had to be constructed, such as the difference between pluripotent stem cells and multipotent stem cells. Scientists, physicians, theologians, lawyers, and philosophers became involved in sorting through the ethical problems raised by the new technology in medicine and also by the new models for health care delivery that developed with post-World War II work-related medical insurance programs and government supported insurance systems. Those who contributed to the dialog offered approaches and solutions that generated a proliferation of journal articles, monographs, edited volumes, and textbooks and inspired a variety of policies and practices. Consequently, the medical ethics literature developed in many disciplines and directions at once. This volume is designed to serve as a guide through this rich and complex literature. *The Blackwell Guide to Medical Ethics* organizes the literature into a coherent structure and provides a new framework for understanding medical ethics and guiding future work in the field. In both respects, *The Guide* is intended to be useful as a text for teaching medical ethics and as a reference for anyone who wants to understand the state of medical ethics today.

This book includes the full range of topics covered by standard textbooks in medical ethics. Most textbooks in medical ethics organize this material by issues or by groups of related issues. Their structures pick up on topical themes but they fail to consider important conceptual categories that are more fundamental in understanding the complex debates that medical ethics involves. By adopting an innovative organizational principle this *Guide* both clarifies and explains medical ethics issues and arguments and provides the reader with a framework for understanding ongoing debates and sorting out the threads of discussions that they encounter not only in the bioethics literature but in the media and in public debates as well.

This volume is divided into two parts. The first part is devoted to questions that are decided primarily by individuals. The second part addresses social policy issues that are decided at the legislative or judicial level. In itself, this partition clarifies issues that are frequently confused and confusing because the ambiguities are unrecognized or ignored, and, consequently, several different questions are being considered as if they were one question. For instance, many papers address "abortion." Yet, frequently the discussions conflate three distinct questions, answering one question by highlighting factors that are relevant to answering a totally different question. For example, an individual might ask herself the question, "Should *I* terminate this pregnancy?" The factors that she would need to consider are significantly different from those that should be taken into account by someone who was trying to reach a decision about the question of whether public policy should restrict access to abortion services.

The organizing concept of this volume derives from John Rawls's important distinction between principles that follow from individuals' personal comprehensive views (i.e., the domain of personal morality) and the basic principles for governing a society that all reasonable people can endorse so long as they have reasonable and rational comprehensive views (i.e., the political domain). Questions that individuals have to answer for themselves belong to the moral realm. Questions that have to be answered for an entire society made up of individuals with different comprehensive moral views belong to the political realm. The first half of this volume is devoted to the moral, the second half to the political. Each part of the volume is further divided into two sections. Part I is divided into a section about patient decisions – the kinds of questions that individuals have to answer for themselves as they or their families or friends contemplate their health or the care they receive – and a section about decisions of physicians and other health care professionals, the questions of professional responsibility that individual health professionals have to answer in the context of their clinical practices.

The chapters in the patients' decision section discuss how the recipients of medical interventions, and their families, conceptualize their health care choices, and especially how their choices relate to personal ideas about their own good. These chapters illustrate ways in which decision-making should be informed by patients' perspectives on broad questions about the beginning and end of life, and their views on the connections between their health and their happiness. Although the bioethics literature sometimes portrays patients as independent, indeed as isolated choosers, in fact they and their families deliberate within a context already informed and shaped by professional and social policy considerations. Thus, the succeeding sections of this volume are concerned with distinctive or characteristic evaluative aspects of these other perspectives on medical decision-making.

The authors writing about professionals' decision-making address more specialized questions such as, should an obstetrician perform an abortion when her patient requests it? This perspective on the distinctiveness and priority of professional responsibilities reflects Rawls's claim in *Political Liberalism* that "the distinct purposes and roles of the parts of the social structure . . . explains there being different principles for distinct kinds of subjects."[1] Bioethicists such as Edmund Pellegrino and David Thomasma consider medicine to be just such a distinct part of the social structure, and we agree. The argument implicit in this second section is that the ethics of medicine is distinctly different from common morality and that the principles and the reasons that justify the distinctive principles of medical ethics are also significantly different from those considerations that justify decisions in private life and in public policy.

Part II of the volume is devoted to legislative and judicial decisions about social policy. It is divided into two sections that reflect the two basic commitments of democratic societies, namely, liberty and justice. The chapters in these sections examine issues by placing them in the contexts of court decisions, existing or proposed legislation, and public policy. The chapters in the section on liberty address the political questions of when and why some infringements on personal freedom are justified and when and why other governmental infringements on personal freedom are unjustified. In the section on justice, chapters address overall questions of distributive justice in health care, as well as a range of conflicts between the social good and the good of individuals.

Sorting the chapters in this volume into these four sections is intended to make two significant points. The first is that different questions get different answers. The second is that conflating different questions (e.g., a question about personal morality with a question about public policy) leads to confusion. For both reasons, clear thinking about matters of medical ethics requires clearly identifying the question that is being asked and keeping one's answers and arguments focused on that specific topic. To illustrate that point, this volume contains some chapters on the same topic considered from the point of view of different questions. For example, end of life decisions are discussed in the sections on patient decisions, professional decisions, and liberty as a matter of public policy. Similarly, reproduction and drug use are discussed both as matters for personal decisions and as matters for public policy. Many issues in medical ethics can, in fact, be framed as a question about personal morality, and as a question about professional responsibility, and as a question of liberty, and as a question of justice. Although we considered it important to illustrate how different questions about the same issue can produce very different kinds of answers, once that point was made, it did not seem crucial to do this with every issue. Some topics are most pressing as matters for one domain or another. For example, issues such as truth telling and confidentiality are particularly important as matters of professional responsibility. Issues such as the legalization of drugs and the control of science and technology are most significant as matters of public policy and liberty. Other topics, such as chronic illnesses and disabilities, human subject research, and public health, which lend themselves to discussion in all four of our sections, were allotted to the section on justice because of the special fresh insight that such a focused discussion provides.

It is worth commenting on one revealing difficulty that arose in the preparation of this volume. Over the recent history of medical ethics, authors have become accustomed to running different questions into each other and ignoring the telling differences that turn on the kind of question that is being asked. Conflating matters that should have been carefully distinguished has led to a good deal of confusion. It has also engendered a significant amount of avoidable disagreement and talking at cross purposes when authors focused on different questions without clearly identifying their specific topic and domain. The pervasiveness of ignoring important distinctions in the kind of question being considered made writing for this book particularly difficult for the contributing authors. When we asked authors to confine their chapter to discussion of a single domain it was, at first, a hard restriction for some to appreciate. Crafting the chapters to fit their defined territory required repeated communication, clarification, and manuscript revision. In the end, our sustained effort produced fresh thinking on old topics, as well as interesting and illuminating analyses of new topics.

Part I

As we have indicated, Part I, devoted to individual decisions about clinical issues, is divided into two sections. The first section takes up questions that are primarily about patient decisions. The chapters in this section focus on the place of personal conceptions of what counts as being good and bad, and personal comprehensive views (issues that Ronald Dworkin has described as religious with a lower-case "r"). The chapters in this section discuss issues from the perspective of patients as autonomous individuals, as members of families, and as participants in a variety of cultures. This section is entirely focused on the personal pronoun "I," in that it responds to the questions "What should *I* do?" and "how should *I* live?" The three chapters in this section consider three major areas of personal decision-making as they relate to medicine: an individual's view of what is good and worthwhile with respect to health, an individual's choice to reproduce or not, and decisions that can be made with respect to prolonging life or hastening death.

The first chapter in this section, "Autonomy, the Good Life and Controversial Choices" by Julian Savulescu, sets the stage for this part of the volume by exploring how individuals' decisions about their health and medical treatment are related to their views about their happiness and perfection. This topic is relevant to questions such as whether there is a duty to promote or preserve one's own health or to promote one's own health perfection. Is it morally required to keep fit and vigorous, or is it acceptable to devote one's free time, energy, and resources to helping one's children with homework, or to tending one's garden, or to the advancement of one's career, or to creating great works of art? If I see these other activities as contributing significantly to my happiness and well-being, must I sacrifice them for the sake of furthering my health? Is it ethically acceptable to engage in activities that put my life or future function at risk, activities such as riding motorcycles, missing sleep, indulging in ice cream or unprotected sex with strangers, or straining my eyes by reading small print? What factors should I consider in reaching my personal answers, and how do my other personal priorities relate to my use, abuse, or refusal of medical interventions?

In his chapter, Savulescu considers these questions primarily in the context of controversial choices, the decisions relating to health and medical interventions that others are likely to find unusual and therefore challenge. Specifically, he discusses requests for optional medical interventions (e.g., cosmetic surgery), medically questionable interventions (e.g., healthy limb amputation), interventions for the benefit of others (e.g., living organ donation), requests for intervention that serve no purpose, and refusals of treatment.

Chapter 2, "Individual Responsibility and Reproduction" by Rachel Ankeny, takes up a central area of choices affecting individual happiness, questions individuals struggle with about reproduction. Ankeny discusses such issues as whether the ability to reproduce is a necessary element of human flourishing and the kinds of factors that may be at the core of making personal reproductive decisions. She applies these considerations to questions such as whether anyone has a duty to procreate, what duties someone assumes with a procreative decision, and how someone should consider the status of the embryo or fetus. From the point of view of the individual decision-maker, the chapter discusses issues such as contraception, sterilization, pregnancy termination, embryo selection, age of reproduction, and continuation of multiple-fetus pregnancies.

Chapter 3 in this section, "Family and Patient Decisions about Life-Extension and Death," considers both the factors that make decisions about life preservation and death rational and the factors that make end of life decisions moral. Felicia Nimue Ackerman answers questions such as: "Do I have a right to live as long as possible?" And: "Do I, at some point, have a duty to die?" In the course of her discussion, she examines the factors that an individual might take into account, such as dignity, pain, the need for services, the dying process, relationships with physicians, burdens on others, nursing home placement, and advance directives, all from the perspective of personal comprehensive views and individual priorities.

The second topic of Part I is the special responsibilities of physicians and other health care professionals and how questions should be answered from their perspective. Unlike the chapters in the initial section of the volume, the chapters in this section do *not* ask "What should *I* do?" Instead they ask the question "What should any health professional in a situation such as this do?" Although the focus is still on individual moral responses, these chapters focus on the differences between approaching an issue in terms of an individual's own personal values and commitments and approaching the same issue in terms of an individual's professional responsibilities. Hence this group of chapters examines professional responsibilities and distinguishes them from personal comprehensive views and political principles. The chapters in this section explain the foundation of the distinctive responsibilities of medical professionals and the priority of principles of medical ethics in the decisions of health care professionals. The chapters in this section also discuss problems that arise when physicians do not understand or accept their patients' ideas about their own good.

This section includes chapters on a broad range of topics but each issue is addressed from the perspective of professional responsibility. The first chapter in this section, "The Professional Responsibilities of Medicine," by Rosamond Rhodes, provides a framework for understanding the other chapters in this section by arguing that the ethics of medicine is distinct and different from common morality. The six other chapters in this section address specific components of the medical professional's special obligations.

Chapter 5, "Truth Telling," by Roger Higgs, discusses dilemmas, temptations, and pitfalls of communicating with patients in the clinical setting. Higgs is sensitive to the need for paternalistically choosing the way in which information is communicated and also sensitive to the importance of honest communication with patients. He explains how the clinical task is complicated by awareness of both important duties and the learning that goes into fulfilling the medical professional's distinctive responsibilites. He also discusses the reasons for the particular truth-related professional responsibilities which reflect autonomy and kindness and the special considerations that require attention in talking to the dying and with patients who have diminished understanding.

Kenneth Kipnis, the author of Chapter 6 on "Medical Confidentiality," discusses a particular case in which the physician involved could, understandably, want to violate the medical obligation to safeguarding confidentiality. Kipnis, however, argues for confidentiality as a distinctive and crucial professional obligation. He specifically addresses the difficult conflicts that the commitment to safeguarding confidentiality can present to medical professionals whose personal values conflict with those of a patient, or when a physician can foresee that maintaining confidentiality could have some negative impact on others. Kipnis also discusses the steps that should be taken to explain the limits of confidentiality and, thereby, to minimize the circumstances in which confidentiality may be set aside.

One of the most radical differences between common morality and the distinctive ethics of medicine turns on the issue of competence. Whereas common morality requires that we take a very generous attitude toward the actions of others and view them as autonomous, physicians are required to assess decisional capacity. The issue certainly arises with patients but it also arises when surrogates are making decisions for patients who cannot make decisions for themselves. Chapter 7, "Patient Competence and Surrogate Decision-Making" by Dan Brock, explores the professional responsibilities involved in the assessment of patients' decisional capacity. Brock considers issues such as why a patient's refusal of treatment standardly triggers an assessment of decisional capacity, and the factors that clinicians should consider when surrogate decision-makers are involved.

F.M. Kamm's Chapter 8, on "Ending Life," discusses the kinds of issues that clinicians need to consider in making decisions about terminating life-saving treatment, suicide, euthanasia, assisted suicide, and responding to advance directives. She discusses the doctor's duty with respect to an array of critical conceptual issues, such as differences between withholding and withdrawing treatment, killing and letting die, foreseeing and intending, the patient's best interest, and when death can be a lesser evil. Kamm's account provides a useful structure for medical professionals to use in sorting through the complex dilemmas related to end of life care.

The final chapters of this section explore issues for professionals functioning in social and institutional settings. "Discrimination in Medical Practice: Justice and the Obligations of Health Care Providers to Disadvantaged Patients" is the title of Chapter 9 by Leslie Francis. She discusses health professionals' distinctive responsibilities of justice in the face of life-cycle differences, sex, disability, and economic and immigrant status. She also considers the obligations professionals have to each other to bear their fair share of treating disadvantaged patients, and the possibility that professionals might be obligated to engage in advocacy to benefit their patients or patients more generally.

Chapter 10, "Institutional Practices, Ethics, and the Physician" by Mary Rorty, Ann Mills, and Patricia Werhane discusses the largely overlooked issue of how institutional policy affects physician and patient choices and how institutional decisions can create moral conflicts for health professionals. These authors address professional responsibility in regard to such matters as hospital mergers, clinician relationships with institutions, and the dilemmas created for individual practitioners when institutions change their goals or priorities. They also address a variety of ethical issues that relate specifically to the professional responsibility of individual physicians in matters relating to costs, resource limitations, and health insurance.

Themes such as role responsibilities and power relationships loom large in the discussions found in this section. This treatment, from the perspective of professional responsibility, can be compared with the social perspectives employed in the discussions of resource allocation and health care financing in this volume's last section on justice and public policy. For example, Francis focuses on the responsibilities of providers who are faced with disputes about justice, whereas Menzel's discussion treats society's responsibilities with respect to the allocation of care. Rorty, Mills, and Werhane consider the professional's responsibilities in responding to health care institutions' policies, whereas Brennan weighs how the overall design of the system of malpractice litigation interferes with the physician–patient relationship. Rorty, Mills, and Werhane detail how institutional design creates conflicts of interest for the individual practitioner; Brennan explains how our system of malpractice litigation creates similar conflicts of interest.

Part II

Part II of the volume is devoted to legislative and judicial decisions about social policy. As already indicated, it has sections on liberty and justice.

Chapters in the section on liberty are about tolerating, protecting, or prohibiting individual choices where personal liberty may conflict with social values.

The section contains discussions of criteria for constraining individual liberty. In one way or another, most of these chapters also challenge the social regulation of medical materials or skills that constrict individuals' freedom to do what they want with their bodies. The last two chapters, however, address more general issues about ways of conceptualizing debates about personal and social liberty.

Chapters in the section on justice take up a variety of questions about the distribution of access to care and about conflicts between equal treatment of all and the overall social good. Some are about classic problems in the allocation of health care and public health resources. Others present contemporary conflicts about compromising individuals' interests in the name of social goods. Still others consider complex questions of public policy such as medical mistakes and malpractice, or the structure of insurance markets and the use of genetic information.

Reproductive choice poses agonizing questions for individuals and contentious questions for societies. In Part I, Ankeny explored reproductive issues as a matter of individual choice. In the section on Liberty in Part II, Rebecca Bennett and John Harris's Chapter 11 considers social policies that affect the freedom to make reproductive choices, for example, access to birth control, abortion, and assisted reproduction services. They focus on how social decisions that control the allocation of medical services related to reproduction change people's lives. A fundamental question is whether ensuring freedom and choice for some people threatens or harms others. In the context of this chapter, the question is whether such other-regarding social considerations should be given weight to the extent that they govern individuals' reproductive choices. For example, should prospective parents be free to obtain prenatal diagnoses for disabilities and terminate pregnancies on this basis, regardless of any discriminatory implications for people with disabilities generally? Should they be denied access to reproductive technology if their purpose is sex selection, but have access if their purpose is to save an older child's life? And should the lifestyles of prospective parents – for instance, not being in a heterosexual, legally sanctioned relationship – figure in offering or denying them reproductive medical treatment?

In Chapter 12, "Public Policy and Ending Lives," Evert van Leeuwen and Gerrit Kimsma discuss whether patients should be free to have their doctors bring their lives to a close (and whether doctors should be free to offer this service to their patients). They argue that public policy should be shaped by Rawlsian ideas about public reason, thereby allowing people to have a range of views about the good and permitting them to choose among diverse well-considered approaches to death. Policies must protect genuine choice, while at the same time preventing the ill, elderly, and disabled from being coerced or induced to end their lives for the sake of other people's interests. Drawing on experiences of assisted dying practice in Belgium, the Netherlands, and the state of Oregon in the US, van Leeuwen and Kimsma contend that with proper public oversight, individuals can have the freedom to secure medical assistance in ending their lives without endangering the lives of those who do not or should not desire to exercise this freedom.

Douglas Husak investigates familiar reasons for strictly controlling people's access to drugs such as opiates that have medical applications but also are sought for recreational use. Is there a clear boundary that signals when access to such drugs is bad for people? In Chapter 13, on "Drug Legalization," Husak claims that the contrast between medical and recreational drug use is at best fuzzy, especially in an era in which more and more anomalous behaviors, conditions, and inclinations have been medicalized and therefore deserve treatment. Consequently, he argues, we should abandon making the distinction between treatment and recreation a cornerstone of US drug policy.

But even were the distinction sharper than it is, justifying prohibition through punishment requires a theory of criminalization. We do not criminalize people's imprudent behavior if only their own health or happiness is risked or harmed. In general, Husak observes, reasons that people should not use drugs are not reasons for the state's punishing drug users. In a related discussion in Chapter 20 in the succeeding section on justice, Anita Silvers identifies the (in)justices that current drug prohibitions impose on patients with certain kinds of chronic impairments and explores whether these are made acceptable by appeals to the common good.

More complex questions about whether the common good would be compromised if people are at liberty to sell or rent their body parts are discussed in Chapter 14. In "Selling Organs, Gametes, and Surrogacy Services," Janet Radcliffe Richards develops a methodology for thinking these questions through. To illustrate her approach, she examines the propriety of permitting live donors to sell their kidneys and, concomitantly, permitting dialysis patients to buy the kidneys.

Presumably, both buyer and seller expect immediate benefits from the transaction. Radcliffe Richards draws out resemblances between organ selling and nonmedical commercial transactions, and argues that it would be unthinkable for the state to prevent these latter very similar transactions. She also disposes of objections to organ selling, such as that a commercial enterprise necessarily advantages the rich, or that selling parts of one's self is like selling one's self into slavery.

She then turns to claims that permitting a practice of organ selling would on balance result in more harm than good. Assessing these harm-to-benefit claims calls for systematic risk analysis of a sort that rarely is done. Because it is unlikely that organ commerce is categorically harmful, she says, fairness calls for our making serious attempts to refine the practice, keeping the good elements but jettisoning the bad. Yet although logical reasons for opposing organ selling seem weak to nonexistent, Radcliffe Richards points out that we nevertheless recoil from this idea. To condemn commercial transactions in human organs, we invoke ideals such as altruism, human dignity, and not commodifying the body. Radcliffe Richards goes on to consider whether these appeals are merely expressions of strong feelings, or whether instead they access a moral bedrock sufficient to ground public policy prohibiting buying and selling organs.

Protecting the public from infectious diseases is another health care context where curtailing some peoples' liberty in the name of other people's good is commonplace. In Chapter 15, "The Patient as Victim and Vector: The Challenge of Infectious Disease for Bioethics," Margaret Battin, Leslie Francis, Jay Jacobson, and Charles Smith point out that the issue about infectious disease most frequently discussed in bioethics – HIV transmission – is unusual because HIV transmission is almost always within the control of infected agents. But most infections are transmitted casually or through routes such as aerosolization or by intermediate vectors.

To contract an infectious disease may turn a person into a victim who dies, but at the same time the person can be a vector who kills. People can be reservoirs of disease without being aware of the threat they are to others, so their reflective self-control is insufficient to safeguard against their transmitting their illnesses to the rest of the population. Does this mean that personal choice and privacy must be sacrificed to the public good?

Battin, Francis, Jacobson, and Smith contend that casting the issue this way, as a choice between liberty or coercion, distorts the issue by artificially isolating the victim and vector roles from each other. Rather, we should recognize each other as being vulnerable to infection by others. All of us are susceptible to being vectors who make each other victims, and also to being the victims of our fellow vectors. The authors reject the idea that responsibility should be achieved either by society's imposing regulation of individual choices or by individuals self-regulating their own choices. They prefer that our choices be shaped collectively in recognition of our sharing both the benefits and the burdens of our biological roles in the process of infection.

In Chapter 16, the last in this section, Glenn McGee and and Dýrleif Bjarnadóttir offer an analysis of policy discourse directed at prohibiting or promoting either expansion of scientific knowledge intended to enable medical procedures, or the procedures themselves. They begin by pointing out that all contemporary debates in medical ethics invoke premises claiming to represent the relevant scientific facts. Often, proponents on either side of a debate about ethics accuse each other of misunderstanding, ignoring, oversimplifying, twisting, or otherwise misrepresenting the scientific facts. Such charges distract attention from difficult questions about ethical and political values by suggesting that the point of contention is about which side has the scientific truth.

But, McGee and Bjarnadóttir argue, interdisciplinary innovation and conceptual boundary-crossing are prominent in today's science, and therefore there is no clarity in science itself about such matters as fertilization, potency, and viability. Nor, for example, is there uniformity among scientists about what is a human embryo, let alone about how to designate a part-bovine, part-human, embryo-like thing. McGee and Bjarnadóttir then explore what they take to be a paradigm of how different claims about the scientific facts influence public debate about the ethics of a medical procedure: the abortion debate. More generally, they consider various approaches to political theory that might sanction public policy constraints on research and the application of medical technology, but for different reasons and in different circumstances and degrees. They characterize the debates between these theories as differences about where to draw the line between the public and private spheres.

Another example of policy being anchored in shifting sands rather than bedrock by the invocation of scientific fact is the way that the aims of both medicine and public policy about access to health care depend on the characterizations of health and disease. Rawlsian theorists typically justify their prescriptions about health care policy by presupposing a value-free epidemiological account of healthy functioning, one that elides statistical species-typicality into criteria of normality or with other normative claims. But such a presupposition is dubious, as are the exaggerated claims of opponents of embryonic stem cell research who proclaim that adult stem cells factually are less risky and more beneficial for medical purposes than embryonic stem cells, and of proponents of embryonic stem cell research who promise speculative undemonstrated medical benefits. All these examples suggest to McGee and Bjarnadóttir a need for stricter rules of discourse governing appeals to scientific fact in ethical and public policy debate about the propriety of medical procedures.

Chapters in the section on justice take up questions about the allocation of resources to health care. They also treat a more general range of conflicts between the protection of individuals and the overall social good from the perspective of public policy. In the chapters of this section, readers confront tensions between utilitarian – that is, good-maximizing – approaches to justice and approaches that emphasize equality or the rights of individuals.

An egalitarian theme that occurs frequently in this section can be traced historically to John Rawls – that inequalities are arbitrary unless they work to the advantage of the least well off. The presupposition is that we will see this if we conceptualize justice in terms of a thought experiment in which we ask what framework for social policies we would agree to abide by if we had no knowledge of our biological or social advantages. Norman Daniels's application of this thought experiment to health care – that we would accept a system in which people received care aimed to support the normal opportunity range over an ordinary lifespan – has been highly influential in discussions of justice in health care. As we shall see in this section, however, this approach is by no means the last word on justice in health care.

Paul Menzel, well known for his writing on health care rationing, begins the section with a discussion of the allocation of scarce resources. Menzel emphasizes that we are making decisions about rationing health care even when we do not notice them; markets, insurance structures, and other methods for financing health care clearly provide resources for some and restrict them for others. Tensions between the role responsibilities of individual providers to their patients – the kinds of questions taken up by Francis in Part I – and justice as viewed from the social perspective are difficult to reconcile.

In his Chapter 17 on "Allocation of Scarce Resources," Menzel explains his view that we should approach decisions to prioritize care with fuller awareness of the principles we are using than we now do. When we attempt to articulate principles, we will find a good deal of agreement on the justice of a decent minimum of care, even from conceptions of justice that appear to be radically opposed, such as efficiency and libertarianism. Menzel explores a number of more-or-less egalitarian reasons for departing from strict efficiency in allocation decisions: the relevance of age, severity of illness, the special value of care in the face of death, the reluctance to discriminate against persons with reduced health potential, maintenance of hope and the assurance of treatment, and a tendency to discount duration of life for one person in comparison to shorter gains in lifespan for a number of people.

The next chapter in this section, "Just Caring: The Challenges of Priority-Setting in Public Health," by Leonard Fleck, takes up questions of justice from the perspective of public health needs. Traditional concerns of public health – infectious disease, toxic waste, public safety – have been joined by more recent attention to conditions that affect a significant portion of the population: obesity, smoking, alcohol abuse, and the like. Fleck focuses his Chapter 18 discussion of the justice of public health practice on the traditional issues, although suggesting that public health research might be broader in scope. Should these basic public health concerns – immunization, sanitation, motor vehicle safety, and the like – take precedence over far more expensive and individualized "rescue medicine"?

The answer, Fleck suggests, is not at all obvious. Although some public health investments yield great benefits at low costs – think of polio vaccination – we may have already identified and implemented these investments and now face far more expensive ones – think of the costs of reducing the marginal cancer death from pollution or the costs of treatment that might be recommended as a result of more aggressive screening programs for elevated cholesterol levels. Widespread transfers of resources from individual patient care to public health initiatives, Fleck argues, raise significant questions of justice like those identified by Menzel. Fleck concludes by explaining why judgments that people are responsible for their health behaviors and their health conditions cannot be used to mitigate these concerns of justice.

In his contribution, "Justice and the Financing of Health Care," Stephen Latham agrees with Fleck that individuals' health status is largely arbitrary from a moral point of view, Latham uses Chapter 19 to point to the impact of ill health on quality of life and on opportunities. Just health care is thus a social, not an individual, responsibility; libertarian objections to publicly funded health care are subject to a wide range of objections, which Latham explores. Utilitarianism, Latham agrees with both Menzel and Fleck, fails to account for the special role of health care in individual welfare. Systems for financing health care, Latham contends, should pay greater attention to the social determinants of health and to the role of health as a basic human capability.

Moving to a more specific issue in Chapter 20, Anita Silvers shines the light of these more general treatments of justice on the evaluation of health care for persons with chronic illnesses or disabilities. In "Judgment and Justice: Evaluating Health Care for Chronically Ill and Disabled Patients" Silvers explains that standards for prioritizing care too often focus on judgments about "quality" of life made from the perspectives of people who are, for the present, in states of more-or-less "normal" health. But this perspective is both myopic and transient.

Chronic illness, moreover, should not be equated with disability; and models for funding treatment of acute episodes of illness are not applicable to either chronic illness or disability. While from a social perspective, the focus on life-preserving interventions may predominate as Menzel avers, from the perspective of individual persons, ameliorations in their social opportunities may be just as significant. Although there is surely reason to question adaptive values that result from oppression or resignation, people who live with disabilities or with chronic illnesses may quite rightly argue that social judgments about their good are deeply flawed epistemologically. With this point, Silvers links the argument of Part II to the questions with which the volume began: individuals' judgments about their good may not be the same as social judgments – but social judgments should take individuals' judgments as the starting point.

Systematic efforts to set international ethical standards for research with human subjects, such as the Nuremberg Code or the World Medical Association's Declaration of Helsinki, or the Belmont Report in the US, initially focused principally on the protection of the rights of individual subjects. More recently, attention has been turned to questions of justice in research ethics. In their chapter, "Justice in Research on Human Subjects," David Buchanan and Franklin Miller explore three levels of questions about justice in research: Does the state have an obligation to fund research? Which research should it fund, from the perspective of justice? What does justice require in the conduct of the research?

Their Chapter 21 discussion addresses the conduct of research within liberal democratic societies, and argues that support for research can be justified from the perspective of justice as fairness. The distribution of research funds should coincide roughly with the burden of disease, understood both in terms of substantive criteria such as morbidity and urgency of disease spread and in terms of procedural criteria such as open discussion of priorities. Justice within research requires articulating and applying a complex set of standards to protect individual subjects from exploitation. Buchanan and Miller conclude by applying their discussion on all three levels to the controversial example of research by the Kennedy-Krieger Institute (Johns Hopkins University) on alternative methods of lead abatement in poor minority neighborhoods in Baltimore, Maryland.

Community standards play a role in Buchanan and Miller's account of the protection of research subjects; such standards also are critical to Troyen Brennan's discussion of "Ethics of Disclosure Following a Medical Injury: Time for Reform?" in Chapter 22. Brennan's starting point is the data that show surprisingly high levels of patient injuries owing to substandard medical practice. Yet these injuries, and the underlying failures in patient care that they receive, are discussed infrequently with patients; and the overall picture presented to the public about health care has been that mistakes are infrequent lapses rather than endemic to current practice. The system of malpractice litigation, moreover, encourages cover ups rather than frank disclosures, Brennan contends. As an alternative, Brennan suggests a system of health courts that would encourage open disclosure and provide a far fairer compensation regime for patients.

In "Pre-existing Conditions: Genetic Testing, Causation, and the Justice of Medical Insurance," the final chapter of the volume, Robert Pennock examines the justice of another institutional system: medical insurance. Pennock's specific question is whether insurers should be permitted to exclude from coverage people with diagnosed genetic anomalies that might later result in disease. As genetic testing becomes more frequent, it may be increasingly possible to identify individuals' risks for later disease.

The justification for pre-existing condition exclusions in insurance is that they prevent individuals from turning what should be a gamble on unknown risks into the choice of protection against certain disease. But genetic diagnoses do not function in this way; presence of a gene that may result in later disease is more like the presence of an environmental risk than like the presence of a direct, ineluctable causal relationship. It is not already existing disease as in a pre-existing "condition"; it is one among other causal factors, singled out for the purposes of insurance as salient. Thus the analogy with pre-existing conditions cannot be used to argue that it is just to single out a genetic test result in denying coverage, Pennock contends. Nonetheless, genetic testing will reveal increased risks; if insurers are allowed to price differently for such increased risks, the genetically "unlucky" may be unable to purchase insurance at all. The implications of increased availability of genetic testing, Pennock concludes, are yet another reason that supports universal coverage of health care.

This volume thus offers a rich array of perspectives from which to view the ethics of medicine. From individuals' accounts of their own values, to the values of professionals working with patients, to social perspectives on liberty and justice, the volume approaches both more traditional issues in bioethics such as confidentiality and much newer issues such as infectious disease or medical mistakes. By identifying and exploring these different perspectives, the volume encourages deeper analysis and more sophisticated and nuanced resolutions of some of the most persistent debates in contemporary medical ethics.

Note

1   J. Rawls, *Political Liberalism*, New York: Columbia University Press, 1993, p. 262.

Part I.1

Individual Decisions about Clinical Issues

Patient Decisions

Chapter 1

Autonomy, the Go[...]
and Controversial [...]

Julian Savulescu

Introduction

Individuals have different values. They prioritize their values in different ways. Controversial choices are choices which are perceived by many to be either irrational or against a person's interests, such as engaging in harmful or excessively risky activities. When the medical profession is involved in such choices, the basic medical principle of acting in a person's best interests is challenged. Often doctors refuse to respect controversial choices on paternalistic grounds. We should all respect and facilitate the controversial choices of competent individuals, subject to resource limitations, our own and others' well-being and autonomy, and the public interest. But more importantly, sometimes such choices make for a better, more autonomous life. Sometimes, such choices reflect considerations of global well-being or altruism, or idiosyncratic attitudes to risk. Sometimes, they reflect unusual values. However, in some other cases, controversial choices are irrational and are not expressions of our autonomy. We have an obligation to make rational if controversial choices. I distinguish between Kantian and Millian conceptions of autonomy and the place of controversial choices within these. On both accounts, there is an important place for controversial choices in leading the autonomous life. Indeed, where rational, they should be encouraged as they increase the richness of the tapestry of human living, what Mill called "originality." Where irrational, we should aim to help people make better and more rational choices about their lives. Our controversial choices should be the result of decision and evaluation and capable of withstanding critical, normative challenge. Though at times destructive and corrosive, they can also be the essence of the good and self-constructed life.

Consider the following examples of controversial choices.

Case 1 Sado-masochism

The appellants belonged to a group of sado-masochistic homosexuals who over a 10-year period willingly and enthusiastically participated in the commission of acts of violence against each other for the sexual pleasure engendered in the giving and receiving of pain. The group activities took place at different locations, including rooms equipped as torture chambers. Video cameras recorded the activities and tapes were copied and distributed among members. The activities included branding a victim with a wire heated with a metal blowlamp, use of a cat o'nine tails, and genital torture and violence to the buttocks, anus, penis, testicles, and nipples. All the activities were done with the consent of the passive partner or victim and were carried out in private. There was no permanent injury; no infection of wounds; no evidence of any medical attention being sought; and no complaint was made to the police, who discovered the activities by chance.

(R v. Brown, 1994)

In this case, the House of Lords ruled that the practice of sado-masochistic sexual activities constituted a crime, notwithstanding the consent of all parties involved. The grounds for interference in such choices is the public interest.

Case 2 Amputation for apotemnophilia

A Scottish surgeon, Mr Robert Smith, amputated the healthy legs of two patients suffering from apotemnophilia, a body dysmorphic disorder in which the patient feels incomplete with four limbs. The patients had received psychiatric and psychological treatment prior to the operation, but had failed to respond to these methods. Both operations were carried out privately and not publicly funded, and the patients were satisfied with the results. The NHS Trust responsible for the hospital banned further amputations (Dyer, 2000).

Case 3 Requests for "futile" medical treatment

Mr Leslie Burke was 45 years old. He had been diagnosed in 1982 with cerebellar ataxia, a degenerative brain disease. He was wheelchair-bound and his speech was affected, though his mental capacity was intact. Owing to the progressive nature of Mr Burke's disease, he would require artificial nutrition and hydration at some point. He sought a court ruling that artificial nutrition and hydration be provided if he became incompetent. Mr Burke sought a declaration that the rights enunciated in Articles 2, 3, 8 and 14 of the European Convention on Human Rights pursuant to the Human Rights Act 1998 (UK) were breached by the General Medical Council's guidance entitled, *Withholding and Withdrawing Life-Prolonging Treatments: Good Practice in Decision-Making* (*R (Burke) v. The General Medical Council*, 2004).

Justice Munby ruled in favor of Mr Burke, and declared that parts of the guidance were unlawful, as a competent person pursuant to Articles 3 and 8 is able to demand artificial nutrition and hydration in accordance with the rights of dignity and autonomy which enable a person to die in a manner in accordance with their desires.

However, the decision was appealed. The Court of Appeal ruled that Justice Munby erred in law. The Court of Appeal ruled that the guidance was lawful and that it did not contravene Articles 2, 3, or 8 of the Convention and set aside the six declarations made by Munby (*R (Burke) v. General Medical Council* (Official Solicitor and others intervening), 2005).

How far should people be allowed to pursue choices which are not judged to be in their best interests?[1] The questions I want to ask are: Should these people act in such controversial ways? How should we act? How should we respond to people's controversial choices? The answer, I will argue, turns on how these people arrive at such controversial choices. People often have values which diverge from the dominant social values. These values lead them to make choices which are judged by some to be imprudent or irrational.

Controversial choices can be divided into three categories: refusal of assistance to which one has a legitimate entitlement, requests for assistance for enhancement or for assistance to which one does not have a clear legitimate entitlement, and requests for liberty to engage in activities which may result in future requests for assistance. These three categories overlap and map roughly onto the three more specific categories listed below.

Controversial Choices

Here are some examples of the three categories of controversial choice:

1 Refusal of medical intervention

1.1 Refusal of medical intervention which is in the person's interests

Refusal of life-saving blood transfusion
Refusal of life-saving cesarean section for obstructed labor

1.2 Refusal of medical intervention which is possibly in the person's interests

Some blood transfusions, for example, an elective blood transfusion following surgery where bleeding has been controlled and hemoglobin is stable
Some tests, e.g. refusal of a blood test for diagnosis of a non-life-threatening condition, spinal tap for the exclusion of an unlikely cause of a headache, or painful nerve function test where treatments for the likely disorder have little effect

Interventions with non-demonstrated efficacy, e.g., surgical removal of advanced metastases

Interventions with little effect, e.g. chemotherapy for metastatic disease which extends life by a couple of months

2   Requests for interventions[2]

2.1   Requests which appear to oppose a person's interests

Assisted suicide and euthanasia
Second best interventions:
    General anaesthesia instead of local or regional anaesthesia, e.g., for a cesarean section
    Antibiotic treatment for an inflamed appendix instead of appendectomy
Useless interventions:
    Antibiotics for a viral sore throat
    Vitamin injections

2.2   Requests for enhancements, especially those with significant risk for the purposes of enhancement of normal features or some relatively worthless goal

Normal breasts made very large
Penis enlargement of a normal penis
Viagra for improved sexual performance in normal people
Amputation of a healthy limb
Extreme body modification
Laser eye surgery to achieve hawk-like vision
Sex change or body nullification
Artificial nutrition and hydration when permanently unconscious

3   Engaging in activities with a high risk of injury requiring medical intervention

Excessive dieting
Smoking
Using recreational drugs (alcohol, heroin, ecstasy, etc.)
Serving as a live organ donor (e.g., donating or selling two healthy kidneys)
Engaging in extremely risky sports (e.g., high-altitude mountaineering, extreme skiing, real fighting and, arguably, boxing)
Engaging in high-risk work (e.g., skyscraper construction, tunnel construction, coal mining, race-car driving, being a mercenary)
Risky sexual practices, e.g., "bare backing"
Passive risky lifestyles – gluttony, sloth, etc.

So that the discussion that follows includes a broad array of the kinds of cases listed above, I shall employ the term "humping" as the generic term for describing acting controversially. I stipulate "humping" to include all three categories of controversial action, although the examples in Category 1.1 could also be described as omissions.

The answer to the question of how we should respect controversial choices lies in whether people have good reasons for these choices, and how strong these reasons are. By "good reasons" I mean good normative reasons.

The critical question to ask when evaluating a person's choice to hump is to ask "Is there a good reason, in these circumstances, for that person to hump?"

A reason for acting is a fact or circumstance forming a sufficient motive to lead a person to act. Knowing a person's reasons allows us to understand why a person acted as he did. Imagine John has suffered a serious injury and would significantly benefit from a blood transfusion. He refuses. John's reason for refusing a blood transfusion is a desire to recover his health together with the belief that receiving a blood transfusion will cause AIDS. This reason explains why he acted as he did. It has been called an explanatory or motivating reason.

Good reasons for action are normative or justifying reasons for action. A reason for action is good if it meets a standard, that is, if it conforms to a set of norms governing that behavior. In one sense, John had a good reason to act as he did: if his beliefs were true, not receiving blood would be an effective way of avoiding AIDS. If the blood transfusion was not essential, this would be a rational course of action.

However, John's action is based on an irrational belief. The chances of his contracting HIV from a blood transfusion are very very low. He is more likely to recover his health by having a transfusion. Overall, he has most reason to accept a blood transfusion. While he has a motivating reason to refuse a transfusion, he has no good reason to refuse a blood transfusion.

Kinds of Normative Reasons for Action

There are different kinds of normative reasons for action. Two kinds of reasons frequently account for or are relevant to controversial choices: prudential reasons and moral reasons.

Prudential reasons

Prudential reasons are reasons to do with a person's well-being or best interests. Prudential reasons can constitute good reasons for action. Indeed, medical practice is currently based on a principle of offering interventions which are in a person's best health or medical interests. The *Burke* case illustrates the principle that doctors are only obliged to provide treatments which are in the best interests of the patient.

In many cases, whether there is a good reason to hump turns on whether there is a prudential reason to hump. There are many points at which a doctor and patient may disagree about whether there is a prudential reason (that is, whether an intervention is in the patient's best interests) for some action.

Three theories of well-being

There are three main theories of well-being. Many modern philosophers advocate a combination of all three theories, on the grounds that each highlights relevant values not captured by the other two.

Mental state or hedonistic theories

Hedonistic theories of well-being are defined in terms of mental states. The simplest view is that happiness, or pleasure (understood broadly as a mental state) is the only intrinsic good and unhappiness or pain the only intrinsic bad. More complex views include a greater plurality of states of mind as contributing to well-being. Freud is reputed to have refused analgesia when dying of cancer, although in pain, on the grounds that he preferred to think in torment than not to be able to think clearly (cited by Griffin, 1986).

A central issue for pluralistic accounts is which mental states are to be included in an account of well-being. Two types of answer have been given: one is *preference hedonism* (or subjective hedonism) in which the valuable mental states are those that are desired. Sidgwick wrote:

> I propose therefore to define Pleasure . . . as a feeling which, when experienced by intelligent beings, is at least implicitly apprehended as desirable, or – in cases of comparison – preferable.
>
> (Sidgwick, 1963 p. 127)

The second way in which mental states might be ascribed a value is to propose that some mental states are objectively valuable. Objectively valuable mental states might include fulfillment, calm, peace, hope, the experience of love and friendship, happiness, and a sense of achievement. Each of the main alternate theories of well-being picks up on one of these ideas.

On hedonistic theories, the pleasure or happiness that we derive from some risky activity is a strong reason for action.

Desire fulfillment theories

According to desire fulfillment theories, well-being consists in having one's desires fulfilled. These theories give weight to individual values and they account well for the plurality of values. Economic theory commonly employs a related notion of value, and such accounts are widespread in philosophy and the social sciences in general. On the most plausible desire fulfillment theories, desires should be informed (of the relevant facts) and freely formed to count towards our well-being.

A strong, informed desire to engage in some harmful or risky activity grounds a prudential reason, on this account of well-being.

Objective list theories

According to objective list theories of well-being (sometimes called substantive good or perfectionistic theories) certain things can be good or bad for a person and can contribute to well-being, whether or not they are desired and whether or not they lead to a "pleasurable" mental state. Examples of the kinds of things that have been given as intrinsically good in this way are gaining knowledge, having deep personal relationships, rational activity and the development of one's abilities. Examples of things that are bad might include being betrayed or deceived, or gaining pleasure from cruelty. High-altitude mountaineering, though extremely risky, might provide great objective achievements which ground a reason to take the risks.

Composite theories

Each of the three theories of well-being outlined above seems to identify something of importance but all have problems. Because of this many philosophers opt for a composite theory in which well-being is seen as requiring aspects of all the theories. Well-being is constituted by engaging in objectively worthwhile activities which we desire and which provide us with pleasure.

These three theories and the composite theory have some practical implications for controversial choices.

Implication 1 Health v. other components of well-being

The first point to note is that our well-being includes much more than our health. Indeed, arguably, health is an instrumental good which facilitates our engagement in worthwhile activity that we desire and which gives us pleasure. Cancer is bad because it stops us from completing our projects, seeing our children grow, doing what we planned with our partner, and so on. A symptomless disease, which does not affect length or quality of life, is of no practical importance.

Whereas doctors may be concerned to promote health, patients may be concerned to promote their well-being more globally conceived. Thus, the fact that not humping is healthier does not settle the question for the potential humper of whether there is good reason to hump. Indeed the (apparent) problem of risky activity (Category 3), such as masochism, is that people trade health for other components of well-being, like pleasure. Enhancements are often sought by people at the expense of risk to their health to improve their well-being in other ways (Category 2). Apotemnophilia is classified as a psychiatric disorder. But equally, it could be seen as an example of people believing they are better off without their limbs. Amputation of healthy legs (Dyer, 2000) is not in a person's best medical interests in terms of physical health. But if the person will be depressed and psychologically dysfunctional with two legs, and there is nothing you can do about that, then amputation may be justified because of the improvement in their global well-being that will result (Fisher and Smith, 2000), even without classifying it as a disease, though classification as a psychiatric disease facilitates the deployment of medical resources.

While a person may have good reason to hump, even if humping is unhealthy, doctors might believe they *qua* doctors should not facilitate unhealthy humping. Should health or well-being be the primary goal of medicine? This is a difficult question to answer. It may be that the primary goal of a health service should be health and not well-being. The reason for this may be that by concentrating on the local goal of health, services can be most efficiently deployed. Specialization may be the most cost-effective use of resources.

Even if this argument is correct (and it is not clear that it is correct), it will not rule out respecting many controversial choices. Refusal of medical care involves forgoing medical services. There is a well established legal right of patients to refuse medical treatment, even life-saving medical treatment (*In Re T* (Adult: Refusal of Treatment), 1993). By the same principles, we should all allow people to act in controversial ways. Engaging in risky activities does not immediately involve use of medical resources.

Implication 2   Differences in conceptions of the good and estimations of risk

According to decision theoretic consequentialism, we have a prudential reason to choose a course of action when that action maximizes our own expected value. In general terms, the expected value of adopting any course of action can be given by:

> *Probability* (good outcome given that course taken) × *Value* (good outcome) + *Probability* (other outcomes given that course taken) × *Value* (other outcomes)

Consequentialism instructs the agent to:

1   list all the relevant possible courses of action
2   list the possible outcomes of each action (this strictly includes *all* possible outcomes or consequences that stem from this action, no matter how far in the future)
3   estimate the probability that each outcome of each action will occur, given that the action in question is taken
4   assign values to each possible outcome

5 calculate the expected value of each possible outcome. This is the p
   the value of that outcome and the probability of it eventuating, given
   particular action is taken
6 calculate the expected value of each action. This is the sum of expected values
   of each of the possible outcomes (or consequences) of that action
7 choose the action with the greatest expected value.

Given the different ways of conceptualizing the good or what is of value, there
will be legitimate disputes about which course of action maximizes expected
value. On more objective conceptions there will be a greater divergence between
our autonomous choices and what is best for us. On desire fulfillment theories,
what we desire defines our good, at least in terms of our informed desires. For
example, it can be rational for a person to engage in risky sexual or sporting practice if she accords greater value to sex or sport than most of us and that value is
justifiable.

In a world of incomplete information, apparently irrational choices may reflect
different probability estimations, as well as different value estimations. I fractured
my leg badly, rupturing the artery to my leg and developing a compartment syndrome. My hemoglobin dropped to about 5. The normal is 14–18 g/dL. This is
severe anemia – death may occur around 3. Transfusion is normally performed
when the hemoglobin falls below 8. Because my bleeding had ceased, the ruptured
artery was repaired and I was stable, I did not want a blood transfusion. I made
a judgment that I did not want to incur the risks of transfusion. Although these
are small, they are present. There are transmissible agents which cannot be tested
for. There is also the possibility of error in testing or in giving blood. There was
surprisingly little evidence as to the risks of blood transfusion or to the chances
it would benefit me in this situation. Having spoken to a number of experts, my
rational estimate was that the risks were not worth taking; most doctors disagreed
(Savulescu, 2003).

True imprudence

There will be cases of true imprudence which are not disputes about the value
of non-health-related well-being, different conceptions of the good, or different
weighting of risk. Instances of true imprudence may be fewer on some desire-
fulfillment conceptions of well-being. For example, on the most basic conception
of desire-fulfillment theory, the informed desire account, a person who knows
all the relevant facts and most wants to hump consequently has most reason to
hump. However, more plausible accounts take into consideration not merely satisfaction of present desires, but also future desires. On such global theories, the
harm and frustration of future desires are relevant. Examples of true imprudence
include dying for the sake of natural childbirth, dying for the sake of a (likely false)

ιe taking of blood, and refusal to act on information about
imprudent choices result from weakness of will or a com-
on of the activity concerned. The person who drunkenly
ιrse, for no other reason than he has lost all control of

ρrudent choices reflect a rational process of according
ated well-being or different but justifiable conceptions
:s of risk. But how should we evaluate truly imprudent

Kantian autonomy and controversial choice

The right of a patient either to consent to or to refuse medical treatment (and more generally the right of persons to exercise free choice) is grounded in the long-established principle of respect for autonomy, that is, the right to self-determination (Beauchamp and Childress, 1989). The legal validity of consent to treatment rests on those elements necessary to establish the patient's competence to make autonomous choices: broadly, provision of information regarding the treatment, understanding of such information, and the ability to appreciate the consequences of decisions regarding treatment (see Brazier, 1987, pp. 121–5). Similarly, the test in English law as to whether a patient is capable of validly refusing treatment requires only that they possess (and can utilize in the decision-making process) sufficient information regarding the "nature, purpose and effects" of the proposed treatment (*Re C* (Adult: Refusal of Treatment), 1994). Subject to this, the patient has an "absolute right to choose." This right is upheld in law "notwith-standing that the reasons for making the choice are rational, irrational, unknown or even non-existent" (*In Re T* (Adult: Refusal of Treatment), 1993), a principle that has been reiterated a number of times (*Re C* (Adult: Refusal of Treatment), 1994; (*Re MB* (Caesarean Section), 1997).

This implies that others – neighbors, friends, counselors, family – should respect the final choices of competent individuals. It also implies that there is a requirement to ensure that people making controversial choices are competent to make such decisions.

Importantly, whether an individual's decision is ultimately respected (by doctors, family, and friends) turns on whether that individual is competent or incompetent, and sufficiently informed of the consequences of the decision, not on whether the decision is rational or irrational. Thus whether doctors should amputate a healthy limb, or whether advance directives to provide artificial nutrition in persistent vegetative states should be respected, turns on whether the individual is competent, not whether he/she is rational. (There are limits related to distributive justice, harm to others and the public interest which I briefly discuss below.)

However, we must distinguish between a decision made by a competent person and a fully autonomous decision. According to the German philosopher, Immanuel Kant, our autonomy is tied to our rational nature (Kant, 1964). What separates human beings from other animals is rationality and the capacity to act on the basis of normative reasons. Choice is an expression of autonomy, on a Kantian conception, only when it is rational.

There are compelling independent ethical arguments to suggest that the exercise of full autonomy requires some element of rationality in addition to those elements of information and understanding identified by the courts (Harris, 1985; Savulescu and Momeyer, 1997). These arguments are based on the concept of self-determination. The idea of self-determination is not mere choice but an evaluative choice of which of the available courses of actions is better or best. The reason that information is important is to enable an understanding of the true nature of the actions in question and their consequences. But if information is important, so too is a degree of at least theoretical rationality to draw correct inferences from these facts and to fully appreciate the nature of the options on offer. More importantly, fully autonomous action reflects normative deliberation about the value of the choices on offer. We must not merely consider the relevant facts about the nature of the consequences of the actions on offer, but the value of these states of affairs.

We should therefore distinguish between two kinds of true imprudence:

Moral reasons and rational imprudence

Rational imprudence is imprudence based on a proper and rational appreciation of all the relevant information and reasonable normative deliberation. Some other reason grounds the action beside prudence – this is typically the welfare of others. Thus we should respect decisions to donate organs or participate in risky research, if these are based on a proper appreciation of the facts. However, merely citing a normative reason is not sufficient to make some action, all things considered, rationally defensible. To donate one's healthy kidney to a sick relative would not be rationally defensible if the chances of rejection were very high. There must be a reasonable appreciation of the values in question.[3]

Irrational imprudence

Irrational imprudence is imprudence where there are no good overall reasons to engage in the imprudent behavior. The explanation might be that the person is not thinking clearly about information at hand or holds mistaken values or wildly inaccurate estimates of risk. We should attempt to reason with and try to dissuade the irrationally imprudent.[4]

The appropriate response to irrational imprudence is not paternalism but an attempt not merely to provide information but to facilitate the proper reasoning about that information. More importantly it may require challenging a person's values and the reasons for holding those values (Savulescu, 1995). As individuals, we must try to construct coherent defensible lives according to what we judge as best. We discover such lives by being challenged in our values and by defending them. To achieve full autonomy, we require normative dialogue with others.

Sometimes, a case is made that where "an autonomy interest is minimal and a medical benefit maximal," paternalistic intervention can be justified (Beauchamp, 2003). Medical practice nowadays tends towards the incorporation of rationality as a criterion for respecting patient choice (see, for example, American Psychiatric Association, 1998; Del Carmen and Joffe, 2005) even if recent legal decisions have not done so. While it may be the case that "[i]n modern law medical paternalism no longer rules," (*Chester v. Afshar*, 2005), based on a principle of respecting the choices of competent persons, a richer construction of the concept of autonomy of the person is in order (Stauch, 1995), and greater concern to promote greater understanding and normative dialogue between doctors and patients.

I have argued that to be truly autonomous, one must strive to act on the basis of reasons, to strive to be rational. Whether a choice to hump is fully autonomous turns on the reasons that individual has in the particular circumstances. While there may be reasons in general not to hump, an individual may have most reason to hump, given a particular history and set of circumstances.

Consider, for example, the controversy over amputation of healthy limbs. Bioethicists Bayne and Levy (2005) argue that an alternative explanation of the request for amputation is not that it is a psychosexual disorder (apotemnophilia) involving sexual attraction to amputees, but it represents "a mismatch between their body and their body as they experience it," or Body Integrity Identity Disorder. They argue that this condition is poorly studied and treatments for it are typically ineffective. Individuals are often driven to destructive and dangerous practices (such as self-amputation by placing the limb over a rail track). When no other more effective treatments are available, surgeons ought to be permitted, they argue, to amputate such healthy limbs (ibid.).

Wesley J. Smith responded: "That this kind of article is published in a respectable philosophical journal tells us how very radical and pathologically non-judgmental the bioethics movement is becoming" (Smith, 2005).

However, I believe Bayne and Levy's conclusions are rather timid. A stronger conclusion is possible. It may be that some individuals, given their psychology, upbringing, and circumstances, will not respond to any other less invasive measures. Such individuals might have *most reason* to seek amputation. Thus not only might amputation be permissible in some situations, it might be desirable. While it is a tragedy for nearly all of us to lose a limb, there might be good reasons for certain rare individuals to choose this fate. We must be open to such radical possibilities.

Millian autonomy

There is another conception of autonomy which, while it gives consideration to reason, accords more weight to the exercise of choice. The British philosopher John Stuart Mill was the most famous proponent of autonomy, or as he called it, individuality. He was also a strong advocate of originality.

> I have said that it is important to give the freest scope possible to uncustomary things, in order that it may appear in time which of these *are fit to be converted into customs*. But independence of action, and disregard of custom, are not solely deserving of encouragement for the chance they afford that better modes of action, and customs more worthy of general adoption, may be struck out; nor is it only persons of decided mental superiority who have a just claim to carry on their lives in their own way. There is no reason that all human existence should be constructed on some one or small number of patterns. If a person possesses any tolerable amount of common sense and experience, his own mode of laying out his existence is the best, not because it is the best in itself, but because it is his own mode.
>
> (Mill, 1910, p. 125)

What Mill means here is "his own *chosen* mode" of existence. A true commitment to freedom implies supporting people's "original" choices. Indeed, there is value, on Mill's argument, just in making one's choices. Madder has described this as "existential autonomy" (Madder, 1997). Sometimes those active choices or decisions will be not to act. But on this account, there is value to decision and choice, even an active decision not to act. What subverts autonomy is laziness and passive acceptance. In this way, those who make controversial choices may be more autonomous than the herd that passively and unreflectively live their lives according to custom.

> He who lets the world, or his own portion of it, choose his plan of life for him, has no need of any other faculty than the ape-like one of imitation. He who chooses his plan for himself, employs all his faculties. He must use observation to see, reasoning and judgment to foresee, activity to gather materials for decision, discrimination to decide, and when he has decided, firmness and self-control to hold to his deliberate decision . . . It is possible that he might be guided in some good path, and kept out of harm's way, without any of these things. But what will be his comparative worth as a human being? It really is of importance, not only what men do, but what manner of men they are that do it. Among the works of man, which human life is rightly employed in perfecting and beautifying, the first in importance is surely man himself.
>
> (Mill, 1910, p. 117)

> Individuality is the same thing with development, and . . . it is only the cultivation of individuality which produces, or can produce, well-developed humans.
>
> (Ibid., p. 121)

This quote comes from the chapter from *On Liberty* entitled, "Of Individuality, as One of the Elements of Well-being." Mill clearly believes that individuality is one of the goods of life. The value of individuality for Mill is intrinsic. For although a person may "be guided in some good path," that is, achieve good, something very important will be lacking: that life will not be his own. Mill elsewhere criticizes subjugation of oneself to custom and fashion, indifference to individuality and lack of originality (Mill, 1910, pp. 119–20, 123).

On a Kantian account, a controversial choice promotes autonomy if there are good normative reasons for that choice. On a Millian account, controversial choices are valuable insofar as they promote a better life, a life of more well-being. But they are also independently valuable when they are expressions of active decision and deliberation about one's life and how to live. There is a value in just deciding to be.

Limits on Respect for Autonomy

There are limits on the exercise of autonomy, whether prudent or imprudent, rational or irrational.

Distributive justice

Distributive justice requires that our limited medical resources be allocated fairly (Wikler, 1978; Veatch, 1980; *R v. North West Lancashire HA Ex p A*, 2000). Doctors can legitimately disconnect a person who has a very poor prognosis from a ventilator, even though that patient was expecting a miracle, if a better prognosis patient requires the ventilator. The cost of providing artificial nutrition and hydration, and the use of those resources for other patients with better quality of life, provide a reason to withhold life-prolonging artificial nutrition and hydration. Such reasons provide limits on how others – friends, family, and others – should respond to controversial choice.

Harm to others

On Mill's liberalism, two "maxims" determine the limits of state interference in individual action:

> The maxims are, first, that the individual is not accountable to society for his actions, in so far as these concern the interests of no person but himself. Advice, instruction, persuasion, and avoidance by other people if thought necessary by them for their own good, are the only measures by which society can justifiably express its dislike or dis-

approbation of his conduct. Secondly, that for such actions as are prejudicial to the interests of others, the individual is accountable, and may be subjected either to social or legal punishment, if society is of opinion that the one or the other is requisite for its protection.

(Mill, 1900, pp. 150–1)

Harm to others may take many forms. The psychological harm to doctors from performing euthanasia is one reason against it. The increase of a tendency to violence by refusing to take some medication or by taking some drug are strong reasons for coercion.

There have been many cases where pregnant women have been incarcerated for engaging in behavior dangerous to their fetus. Some competent women have been forced to undergo cesarean sections for the sake of their fetus. Such decisions have been widely criticized on the basis of a woman's right to control her own body and the lower moral status which a fetus has in law (*Re S* (Adult: Refusal of Treatment), 1993; *Re MB* (Caesarean Section), 1997; *St George's Healthcare NHS Trust v. S*, 1998; Crafter, 1994; Draper, 1996; Cahill, 1999). However, where a fetus will survive in a damaged state, there is a reason to intervene in dangerous maternal behavior not for the sake of saving the fetus's life, but on the basis of preventing harm to a future individual (Savulescu, forthcoming (a)).

Public interest

There are other public interest considerations, such as those cited in the case of sado-masochism that may justify interfering in individual liberty or failing to facilitate autonomy. The archaic crime of maim is one example:

> A **maim** was bodily harm whereby a man was deprived of the use of any member of his body which he needed to use in order to fight but a bodily injury was not a **maim** merely because it was a disfigurement. *The act of maim was unlawful because the King was deprived of the services of an able-bodied citizen for the defence of the realm.*
>
> (*R v. Brown*, 1994, at p. 47)

However, in a liberal state with a commitment to autonomy and freedom, public interest should only be invoked in most unusual circumstances. We no longer have kings who need human fodder to be slaughtered in some irrational defense of the realm. Morally, it is hard to see the basis for interfering in consensual sado-masochism.

Indeed, while doctors may not be under a *legal* obligation to provide what are claimed by others to be "futile" treatments, there is a moral reason for them to offer such treatments in some circumstances. Leslie Burke's conception of his own best interests diverged from those of his doctors. Burke preferred artificial nutrition and hydration at the end of life. Some people accord value to being kept alive in a permanently unconscious state, even when doctors and courts (*Airedale NHS Trust v. Bland* [1993]) judge that it is of no benefit. Others prefer to be kept alive in marginal states, hoping for a miracle. The liberal commitment to enable people to form and act upon their own conception of a good life provides a moral provision for providing such interventions.

Children and Controversial Choice

Parents make all sorts of controversial choices about their children and we give considerable freedom to parents (Wikler, 1978) bringing up their children. Examples include:

- health habits (e.g., diet, work, training, sleep, hobbies, exercise, etc.)
- risk exposure (e.g., sports, such as motocross, horse riding, off-piste skiing, bush walking, etc.)
- culture (e.g., vegan diet, circumcision, body piercing, tattooing).

It is clear that parents, doctors, and others must act in incompetent children's best interests, based on a plausible and defensible account of those interests, even when those interests diverge from parental values (*Gillick v. West Norfolk and Wisbech Area Health Authority*, 1986; *Re R (A Minor) (Wardship: Consent to Treatment)*, 1991; *Secretary, Department of Health and Community Services v. JWB and SMB* (Marion's case), 1992; *Re W (A Minor) (Medical Treatment: Court's Jurisdiction)*, 1993; *Royal Alexandra Hospital for Children Trading as Children's Hospital at Westmead v. J and Ors*, 2005; McLean, 2000).

When parents make controversial choices for their children, these choices must meet higher standards before they are respected (Savulescu, forthcoming(b)):

1   It must be *safe* enough, compared to other interventions children are exposed to.
2   The parent's choices must be based on a *plausible conception of well-being* and a better life for the child and not on some idiosyncratic, unjustifiable conception of the good life. In addition, the choice must be based on a good enough expectation of realizing a good life. For this reason, while competent adults can refuse life-saving blood transfusions for themselves, parents cannot refuse life-saving blood transfusions for their children on any grounds.
3   It must be *consistent with development of autonomy and a reasonable range of future life plans for the child*. For example, while adults may be allowed and even have good reason to have one of their healthy limbs amputated, parents could never have the healthy limb of their child amputated for many reasons, including the fact that it removes a range of possible good futures from the child's grasp. Female circumcision, and the removal of an organ of female

sexual pleasure, severely constrain the range of possible good lives for that child, stunting the possibility of full sexual satisfaction. It should not be permitted. Male circumcision is different precisely because the possible consequences are more mixed and more uncertain. The reasons for accepting male circumcision include social and cultural considerations, as well as medical considerations such as reduced risk of disease (e.g., penile cancer) and infection (e.g., HIV and HPV). The reasons against accepting the parental choice include the possibility of surgical mishap and reduced penile sensation (see Short, 2004; Hutson, 2004; and Viens, 2004).

Controversial Choices and the Duty to Strive Toward Perfection and Full Autonomy

When faced with some choice to engage in some controversial activity which I have called humping, we should ask: "Is there a good reason, in these circumstances, for that person to hump?"

The controversial choices of competent individuals should be respected. But, at the same time, we each have a duty to be better and to make our decisions with thought and care. Physicians and public policy can promote the achievement of this goal through rational engagement (Savulescu, 2001; 2002) and not through coercion or denial of the only means for competent people to express their conceptions of the good life.

For example, requests for what is judged to be futile medical care may be denied outright on the grounds of justice and scarcity of resources, but where there are no relevant considerations of distributive justice, then doctors have an obligation to engage with patients requesting such care and examine their reasons for such care. In some circumstances, such care may be central to their conception of the good life and there would be reasons to provide it. Similarly, refusal of beneficial medical care, such as life-saving transfusions or important diagnostic tests, should be addressed through rational engagement seeking to understand the reasons for refusal and the relation of that choice to the patient's conception of a good life for himself or herself. Doctors should try to persuade patients to revise their conceptions of the good life or their choices in relation to their conceptions, but they must also be open to the possibility of radical and justifiable diversity in plausible conceptions of the good life.

As persons, we should aim to lead autonomous lives, to be individuals. On a Kantian conception, to be an individual is to respond to the circumstances and to act on the basis of reasons. But reasons pertain to different individuals at different times and in different circumstances. We must exercise our practical judgment in deciding what we have most reason to do in these particular circumstances. For some people who request amputation of a healthy limb, there may be no better alternative at this point in time. If they have failed any attempt at psychological readjustment, there may be good reasons to accede to their requests. Similarly for requests for cosmetic and body modification. Not everything goes. But we must answer the question: what is there good reason for me or this person to do, given history, the nature of the person and the particular set of circumstances at this time. It may be wrong for one person to have her breasts enlarged, because it will not bring her what she wants; however, another may have very good reason to enlarge her breasts and may be entirely happy with the result.

There can be very good reasons for engaging in risky or harmful activity. I remember a television documentary on a man who donated one of his kidneys to his son with kidney failure owing to the inherited condition Alport's syndrome. His second son also had kidney failure because of the same condition and a cadaveric kidney could not be found. He wanted to donate his remaining kidney to his second son so the son could live without the burden of dialysis. His justification for imposing dialysis on himself was that his life was over and his son's life was still ahead of him. Surgeons refused to remove his healthy remaining kidney and transplant it to his son. I believe there may have been good reasons to support this man's choice and, if the chances of his son obtaining a satisfactory result were high, good reason to provide the procedure.

On a Millian conception of autonomy, or existential autonomy, there is value in active choice, in originality. Not only should we be allowed or facilitated in forming and acting on our own conception of the good life, we have an obligation, rational and moral, to form and act on our own conception of the good life. A life is like a work of art. We should not forge a counterfeit, but rather aim to construct our own masterpiece, or at least our own creation. Active choice, commitment to one's own goals, perserverance, a sense of excellence and a vision are the ingredients of the self-constructed life. Controversial or different choices, far from being alien to self-constructed life, are an important ingredient, often recognized later as genius. We should not fear the different or distant, but be prepared to embrace it.

Life involves risk. Many of the greatest lives have involved the greatest sacrifices. The fact that an activity or lifestyle involves risk to health is only one reason against it. It is important, especially from a Millian perspective, to consider how risky activity is central to a self-constructed conception of the good life. Many people seek risk and the activities associated with risk bring the greatest rewards. Risky work or sporting activities may be central to the development of a sense of identity. While in general there appear to be good overall reasons not to smoke or take harmful recreational drugs, in certain doses and in certain circumstances, such activities may play a defensible part of a good life. Smoking a pipe in one's library while reading after dinner may provide enough pleasure to justify the risk. Similarly, occasional use of marijuana or other recreational drugs may be defensible in the context of a certain conception of a good life. After all, alcohol has established its place as a legitimate part of a reasonable conception of the good life. Some people abuse alcohol, but many use it in a way which they rationally believe makes their lives go better.

When doctors or others disagree with people's values or probability estimates, they should reason with them and engage them in normative dialogue. But if the patient is competent, the best reasons for not respecting their choices are not that the choice is imprudent or irrational, but on the basis of justice considerations and the fair allocation of medical resources, or on the basis of harm to others. The importance of freedom to construct our own conception of the good life, and to act on it, requires that doctors respect irrational choices, and, where resources allow, facilitate the originality and diversity of human existence.

> I must live my life according to what I think is good, not according to what others think is good.

Acknowledgments

Thanks to Sarah Chan for invaluable assistance and to the 21st Century School Seminar Group, Philosophy Faculty, University of Oxford, for helpful comments. The Uehiro Chair in Practical Ethics and the Oxford Uehiro Centre for Practical Ethics are supported by the Uehiro Foundation on Ethics and Education.

Notes

1 This is a queston of justifiable coercion and how far society respects personal autonomy, the subject of this volume's section on liberty.
2 The topics in Category 2 are discussed further in Chapters 4–10 of this volume's section on decisions of physicians and other health professionals.
3 Some people would not describe altruistic self-sacrifice as imprudent. I am using the term imprudence to include all acts which are against self-interest, including altruism.
4 If they are incompetent, the law allows their choices to be overridden.

References

Cases

(Burke) v. General Medical Council (Official Solicitor and others intervening): [2005] EWCA Civ 1003.
Airedale NHS Trust v. Bland [1993] 1 All ER 821 HL.
Chester v. Afshar [2005] 1 AC 134.
Gillick v. West Norfolk and Wisbech Area Health Authority [1986] AC 112.
In Re T (Adult: Refusal of Treatment) [1993] Fam 95.
R (Burke) v. The General Medical Council [2004] EWHC 1879.

R (Burke) v. The General Medical Council (Official Solicitor and others intervening) [2005] EWCA Civ 1003.

R v. Brown [1994] 1 AC 212.

R v. North West Lancashire HA Ex p A 2000 [2000] 1 WLR 977.

Re C (Adult: Refusal of Treatment) 1994 1 All ER 819.

Re MB (Caesarean Section) [1997] 8 Med LR 217.

Re R (A Minor) (Wardship: Consent to Treatment) [1991] Fam 11.

Re S (Adult: Refusal of Treatment) [1993] Fam 123.

Re W (A Minor) (Medical Treatment: Court's Jurisdiction) [1993] Fam 64.

Royal Alexandra Hospital for Children Trading as Children's Hospital at Westmead v. J. and Ors [2005] NSWSC 465.

St George's Healthcare NHS Trust v. S [1998] 3 WLR 936.

Secretary, Department of Health and Community Services v. JWB and SMB (Marion's case) 1992 175 CLR 218.

Books and journal articles

American Psychiatric Association (1998), Guidelines for assessing the decision-making capacities of potential research subjects with cognitive impairment, *American Journal of Psychiatry* 155 (11): 1649–50.

Bayne, T. and Levy, N. (2005), Amputees by choice: body integrity identity disorder and the ethics of amputation, *Journal of Applied Philosophy*, 22 (1): 75–86.

Beauchamp, T.L. (2003), Methods and principles in biomedical ethics, *Journal of Medical Ethics* 29 (5): 269–74.

Beauchamp, T.L. and Childress, J.F. (1989), *Principles of Biomedical Ethics*, New York: Oxford University Press.

Brazier, M. (1987), *Medicine, Patients and the Law*, London: Penguin Books.

Cahill, H. (1999), An Orwellian scenario: court ordered caesarean section and women's autonomy, *Nursing Ethics* 6 (6): 494–505.

Crafter, H. (1994), Forcible caesarean: a new direction in British maternity care? Thoughts on the case of Mrs S, *Nursing Ethics* 1 (1): 53–5.

Del Carmen, M.G. and Joffe, S. (2005), Informed consent for medical treatment and research: a review, *The Oncologist* 10 (8): 636–41.

Draper, H. (1996), Women, forced caesareans and antenatal responsibilities, *Journal of Medical Ethics* 22 (6): 327–33.

Dyer, C. (2000), Surgeon amputated healthy legs, *British Medical Journal* 320 (7231): 33225.

Fisher, K. and Smith, R. (2000), More work is needed to explain why patients ask for amputation of healthy limbs, *British Medical Journal* 320 (7242): 1147.

Griffin, J. (1986), *Well Being*, Oxford: Clarendon Press.

Harris, J. (1985), *The Value of Life*, New York: Routledge and Kegan Paul.

Hutson, J.M. (2004), Circumcision: a surgeon's perspective, *Journal of Medical Ethics* 30: 238–40.

Kant, I. (1964), *Groundwork of the Metaphysic of Morals* (trans. H.J. Paton), New York: Harper and Row (originally in Kant, I. *Gesammelte Werke*, Berlin: Akademie Verlag, 1911).

McLean, K. (2000), Children and competence to consent: Gillick guiding medical treatment in New Zealand, *Victoria University of Wellington Law Review* 3: 551–76.

Madder, H. (1997), Existential autonomy: why patients should make their own choices, *Journal of Medical Ethics* 23: 221–5.

Mill, J.S. (1900), *Principles of Political Economy*, New York: P.F. Collier and Sons.

Mill, J.S. (1910), *Utilitarianism, On Liberty and Considerations on Representative Government*, London: J.M. Dent and Sons.

Savulescu, J. (1995), Rational non-interventional paternalism: why doctors ought to make judgments of what is best for their patients, *Journal of Medical Ethics* 21 (6): 327–31.

Savulescu, J. (2001), Procreative beneficence: why we should select the best children, *Bioethics* 15 (5–6): 413–26.

Savulescu, J. (2002), Education and debate: Deaf lesbians, "designer disability," and the future of medicine, *British Medical Journal* 325 (7367): 771–3.

Savulescu, J. (2003), Editorial, Festschrift edition of the *Journal of Medical Ethics* in honour of Raanan Gillon, *Journal of Medical Ethics* 29: 265–6.

Savulescu, J. (forthcoming (a)), Future people, involuntary medical treatment in pregnancy and the duty of easy rescue, *Utilitas*.

Savulescu, J. (forthcoming (b)), Genetic interventions and the ethics of enhancement of human beings, in B. Steinbock (ed.), *Oxford Handbook on Bioethics*, Oxford: Oxford University Press.

Savulescu, J. and Momeyer, R.W. (1997), Should informed consent be based on rational beliefs? *Journal of Medical Ethics* 23 (5): 282–8.

Short, R. (2004), Male circumcision: a scientific perspective, *Journal of Medical Ethics* 30: 41.

Sidgwick, H. (1963), *The Methods of Ethics*, London: Macmillan.

Smith (2005), *Should Doctors Be Allowed to Amputate Healthy Limbs?* http://www.cbc-network.org/enewsle ter/index_7_13_05.htm#article1). Accessed 7/2/2006.

Stauch, M. (1995), Rationality and the refusal of medical treatment: a critique of the recent approach of the English courts, *Journal of Medical Ethics* 21 (3): 162–5.

Veatch, R.M. (1980), Voluntary risks to health: the ethical issues, *Journal of the American Medical Association* 243 (1): 50–5.

Viens, A. (2004), Value judgment, harm, and religious liberty, *Journal of Medical Ethics* 30, 241–7.

Wikler, D. (1978), Persuasion and coercion for health: ethical issues in government efforts to change life-styles, *Health and Society* 56 (3): 303–33.

Chapter 2

Individual Responsibility and Reproduction

Rachel A. Ankeny

Sociocultural and technological changes have produced unprecedented conditions under which individuals can make choices about when, how, and whether to reproduce. Reproductive and genetic technologies, ranging from relatively basic techniques such as contraception, abortion, and ultrasound, to more complex practices including *in vitro* fertilization and pre-implantation embryo screening, seem to allow individuals to exert much more precise control over their procreative decisions and practices, particularly those who are economically advantaged enough to be able to make use of these technologies. However such developments have been accompanied by increased pressures and moral conflicts for individuals who seek to make these decisions, especially with regard to individual responsibilities and reproductive choices.

Debates associated with responsibilities and rights to procreate relate to some of our most fundamental values and our basic moral and legal rights, for instance privacy (e.g., access to and use of contraception); freedom of religion (which relates to marriage and decisions about childrearing); and bodily integrity (including decisions about carrying a pregnancy to term or aborting it). In this chapter, moral questions about *individual* responsibilities and duties to reproduce will be examined. Do we have rights to reproduce? If we do, what sorts of rights are these, and what sorts of limits (if any) can be imposed on these rights? Are there duties to avoid having certain kinds of children? And why do we place such a high moral value on reproductive choice?

Why Is Reproductive Choice Important?

Respect for individual autonomy is a core principle in current-day bioethics, and arguably is central to ethical debates about decision-making with regard to reproduction (e.g., Robertson, 1994). There is a general presumption in favor of not interfering with individual autonomous decisions. Individual autonomy is furthered when people are able to control their own lives through their choices and actions. Claims to autonomy have greatest weight when individuals' decisions primarily affect themselves and do not harm others (Buchanan et al., 2000).

Decisions about reproduction also relate closely to our identities as human beings, our well-being, and our deepest relationships with others. Choices about whether we reproduce, and with whom, often reflect our most closely held values about how we wish to live our lives, and what makes something a "good" life. Some traditions view the parent–child relationship as being at the very foundation of human virtues and morality (Tao, 2004). In addition, reproductive freedom can be claimed to have its moral basis in equality, particularly equality of opportunity between the sexes (Brock, 2005). Choices about reproduction allow us to have freedom of choice about when to take on the various burdens and responsibilities associated with pregnancy, childbearing, and childrearing, which is especially important for women who often assume most of these responsibilities. Some authors, particularly feminists, express concern about whether such choices are actually free, particularly those associated with the use of reproductive technologies, which they argue are subtly coercive. Many practices which purport to further reproductive autonomy (such as *in vitro* fertilization techniques and surrogacy arrangements) can be viewed as commodifying women's bodies, and when examined more closely reveal a variety of built-in sexist, class, and economic biases (Corea, 1985; Brazier, 1998).

In summary, the ability to control what happens to one's body is vital to the exercise of autonomy, as it allows each of us to pursue our understandings of what makes life valuable and good. Thus bodily integrity is often argued to be a necessary pre-condition for an individual to have autonomy in any meaningful sense: acts such as rape or battery (including medical interventions without consent) are morally repugnant because they violate our fundamental right to bodily integrity. Respect for autonomy requires respect for individual decisions about reproduction, particularly for women whose bodies are significantly affected by decisions about whether to conceive, to carry a pregnancy to term, and to rear a child, even though in many societies the balance of childrearing responsibilities recently has been shifting along with changes in patterns of work within and outside of the household.

Is There a Right to Reproduce?

The general right to procreate (and avoid procreation) is widely recognized within bioethics and more generally within the medical, sociopolitical, and legal frameworks that govern reproductive practices. These include international codes which explicitly define the right "to marry and found a family" as a fundamental human right (e.g., United Nations, 1948). However, even if such a basic right exists, it seems insufficient to view reproductive autonomy merely in a negative sense, as a right to be left alone. This is especially true because many people cannot enact their rights without certain infrastructures (such as access to condoms, birth control pills, *in vitro* fertilization clinics, or legal structures governing surrogacy, gamete disposition, and so on). In addition, although such a right is fundamental, it is not absolute in the sense that there are circumstances in which it might be infringed, particularly when there are conflicts between other rights and interests.

There is a range of views regarding the extent of the right to reproduce. Liberal views focus on the "harm principle," which holds that we can act as we wish so long as we do not harm others (Dworkin, 1993). Just because certain actions are offensive to others or conflict with their preferred way of life, this does not justify infringing fundamental rights. Hence advocates of this view strongly value autonomy as well as equality. Some who favor this position thus argue that there should be equal treatment of all with regard to reproduction, including publicly funded access to assisted reproduction for those who cannot conceive owing to medical or social infertility (e.g., lesbian couples) (Harris, 1998; cf. Warnock, 2002). Others argue for a more limited right, which does not require that others provide or fund assisted reproductive technologies but only that those who seek to use these technologies should not be prevented from doing so (Brock, 1996). As long as no one is harmed and all individuals involved provide consent, no behaviors should be restricted (including, for instance, surrogacy arrangements). Some critics of this position hold a more restricted liberal view, and express concern about creating incentives and institutionalizing practices which may have non-beneficial effects if everyone makes similar choices. Thus this sort of liberal position provides a cautious endorsement of reproductive autonomy; some of its advocates accept restrictions on behavior, including what many would view as coercive population policies such as licensing of parents (Bayles, 1979; LaFollette, 1982; Tittle, 2004).

At the other end of the spectrum, one of the most conservative schools holds that procreation is a natural process. In this view, reproductive choices gain meaning and value only within their social, community context. Thus reproduction should not be interfered with, nor should technology be used to intervene in or achieve reproduction. Aside from some of those who write from a theological perspective, these critics do not oppose (married heterosexual) couples making autonomous decisions about using contraception, but they do not view abortion, assisted reproductive technologies, or other "unnatural" arrangements as morally permissible (e.g., Marquis, 1989). Relatedly, some Confucian commentators claim that any non-conjugal reproduction weakens the blood ties between family members and leads to moral and social instability (Qiu, 2002). Hence although there is a right to reproduce, those who support these types of conservative views do not hold that there is a right to reproductive autonomy as such.

Still others deny that rights should serve as a starting point for understanding moral arguments about reproduction. Instead they suggest that there may be moral arguments to support the freedom to have children, such as those based on the desire to have a child, that outweigh any arguments that people should not be allowed to do so (Chadwick, 1987). Finally, some argue that "rights talk" fails to capture what is essential about reproductive choices and relationships in families (Murray, 1996). Using rights and justice as the primary way to understand the values and desires associated with the creation of children and families seems to overemphasize certain sorts of claims, such as rights to noninterference. Emphasizing rights also may cause us (mistakenly) to view children as akin to property. There is a need to recast debates in this domain to take account of the values that are furthered by having children, and also to provide a more appropriate context within which to weigh decisions about uses of new reproductive technologies, without risking viewing them merely as another service or product to be bought by consumers on demand.

Is There a Duty to Reproduce?

There has been some discussion in the philosophical literature about the idea that the choice not to reproduce could be considered morally wrong, and hence that there may in fact be duties to procreate. For instance, it can be argued that a duty to procreate is supported by considering what it would mean to universalize (in a Kantian manner) existing persons' preferences in favor of having been born. The core notion here is that since persons who already exist value their lives and would not prefer that they hadn't been born, there is a duty to produce these potential lives of value that would not exist if we did not procreate.

These arguments, however, are undermined by those in favor of respect for autonomy and not forcing conception on those who do not wish to conceive or termination on those who are opposed to it. Arguments based on potential persons who would not exist, unless we engage in procreative activities, seem to expand our positive duties beyond what typically would be considered to be valid impositions on our bodily integrity. They also seem to be mistaken in terms of what sorts of rights or claims these "potential persons" might have. Theories about future generations and our duties to them must be impersonal and general, rather than focused on responsibilities or duties toward particular individuals (Parfit, 1984). Though considerable debate continues about the moral status of the embryo, there are few who would support the right of a potential person to be conceived and to interpret this right as thus creating a strong, positive duty to reproduce.

Most religions have traditionally maintained that there is such a duty. For instance in Judaism and many Christian faiths, reproduction represents the culmination of one's fulfillment of marriage vows as captured in popular religious dictum, "be fruitful and multiply." Natural law approaches stress that sex is naturally linked to procreation, and hence those engaging in sex should be doing so in order to reproduce. Various cultural beliefs promote the idea that individuals have duties to reproduce in order to promote the well-being of the family and to allow the blood line to continue. Some accounts of Confucianism, for instance, consider reproduction to be the only purpose of sexual intercourse and also that the primary role of the woman in society is to bear children (Qiu, 2002; cf. Tao, 2004).

Social and political forces also may encourage individuals to view themselves as having "duties" to reproduce. In some cultures, there is implicit promotion of genetic understandings of family, such that many people use assisted reproductive technologies in order to have biologically related children rather than pursuing adoption or other alternative forms of parenting. Some countries have promoted a sort of "pro-natalism" in response to concerns about declining populations (or at least declines in the traditional, majority populations). Public arguments are made in favor of increasing the birthrate in order to increase the prosperity of the nation (e.g., on current-day Australia, see Kevin, 2005). These ideas are promoted not only through rhetoric, but also by taxation and other economic policies that reward those who have children, and in health care policies which provide for assisted reproduction but often do not fund contraception or abortion. Similarly, some minority groups are concerned about boosting their numbers relative to the majority, and accordingly encourage individuals to view it as their duty to their community to reproduce.

However customary or politically expedient it may be to consider reproduction to be an individual duty, contemporary accounts of responsibilities to one's self and others typically reject these views. Most bioethics commentators see choices about whether to conceive as private matters to be decided by the individuals involved, particularly the woman who is to carry the pregnancy and those who will rear the child. In many cultures, marriage is no longer the sole or even primary framework for reproduction, but instead the basis for an intimate relationship within which adults can make consensual decisions about their life goals.

Might there be other circumstances which could create a duty or responsibility to reproduce? The creation of so-called savior siblings (Belkin, 2001), in cases where an existing child has a medical condition that requires a hematopoietic stem cell transplant (preferably from a well-matched donor), is often presented as morally well-justified, particularly when the parents are willing to raise additional children. The combination of pre-implantation genetic diagnosis and human leukocyte antigen (HLA) typing (or tissue typing) allows couples to have an unaffected child who can serve as a donor for the ill sibling. Those who support the creation of savior siblings argue that these parents, in fact, may be on higher moral ground than those who procreate for more common, self-interested reasons (e.g., to have a boy with whom to play baseball or a child to save a marriage) or who get pregnant without having planned to do so (Robertson, 2003; Fost, 2004). However, commentators typically do not regard the possibility of creating a savior sibling as presenting a moral duty to reproduce. Although assisting the existing child and relieving suffering are part of the normal responsibilities that we ascribe to parents, it is unlikely that we would claim this was a duty where the parents were not willing to have additional children or where the newly created child might be harmed in the process.

Are There Duties Not to Reproduce?

The issue of whether we owe certain responsibilities to our offspring, particularly so that they do not inherit genetic disease conditions, has been extensively debated in the bioethics literature (e.g. Asch, 1989, Bennett and Harris, 2002). Some bioethicists have argued in favor of a position that many members of the general public would find obvious: in cases where there is a family history of risk for genetic disease, couples should refrain from having offspring (Purdy, 1978). The goal of not creating children with genetic disease can be attained through avoiding conception altogether by abstaining from sex, practicing contraception (if termination of pregnancy is not an acceptable option), using prenatal testing and selective abortion, or using pre-implantation screening of embryos and *in vitro* fertilization to implant non-affected embryos. This argument for a duty to prevent passing on serious genetic diseases typically begins from the idea that we should try to provide every child with a "normal opportunity" for health. Every child has a right to an open future, which means that she has a right not to be raised in a manner that closes off a reasonable range of opportunities particularly for future autonomous choices (Feinberg, 1992). Some authors argue that a normal range of opportunity (particularly for genetics) could be negotiated through a form of deliberative democracy among members of the society (Buchanan et al., 2000). If we also accept the premise that it is not wrong to prevent possible children from existing (since possible persons do not yet have the rights or moral standing that we give actual, existing persons), then it follows that our duty to provide a normal opportunity for health may require us to refrain from childbearing.

A more extreme position holds that termination of pregnancy is required when a woman learns she is pregnant with a fetus which has a serious problem and will develop into a child who will experience considerable pain and suffering. In some such cases, termination of pregnancy may be a duty (Robinson, 1996). This argument may also apply to selective reduction of multiple pregnancies to increase the chances of healthy births among the remaining offspring, as multiple births are associated with low birth weight and significantly increased mortality. This argument relies on the idea that it is wrong to deliberately inflict suffering, and that a life of suffering is in fact a harm to the child and thus not in its best interests. Although the parents or the woman might suffer psychologically from having a termination, these costs are less weighty than the potential costs to the child who would experience severe impairment and suffering.

Others argue that there is no moral duty to have a termination even in cases of genetic or other disease conditions, particularly where potential parents view the fetus as a potential child (Vehmas, 2002). Some authors claim that prospective parents are not required to find out about their genetic constitution when planning to reproduce. Ignoring genetic information can, in fact, be reconciled with some views of responsible parenthood, such as those that take parenthood to be essentially an unconditional project in which parents ought to commit themselves to nurturing (nearly) any kind of child (Vehmas, 2001). Some have concluded that a pregnant woman has a right to remain in ignorance of any genetic conditions present in the fetus she is carrying. Although the information that can be gained by prenatal or other forms of genetic testing may be useful when making decisions about pregnancy, it does not prevent harm to actual, future children (Bennett, 2001). Others claim that a child with a disabling genetic condition is not harmed by being born because the only other option for that child was not to have been born, and thus never to have existed (e.g., Chadwick, 1982; Macklin, 1994).

Conversely, other scholars claim that although future children do not have current moral standing, potential parents have obligations to consider the likely effects of their actions on future people. Thus potential parents must commit to the "project of parenthood" and to the well-being of their children, including any future children (Pellegrino and Thomasma, 1993). Decisions to conceive therefore are accompanied by strong, positive duties to promote health, not to any particular individual child who might result from the conditions present at the moment of conception, but to any future child (e.g., Vehmas, 2002). Note that these accounts do not make it morally obligatory to force or coerce a woman to carry a pregnancy to term. Instead, they rely on the idea that certain duties arise from the very decision to procreate, including the need to rear the resulting child and to provide a life that is normal at least in terms of societal norms (O'Neill, 1979). Some claim further that those prospective parents who are in a position to prevent harm from coming to a child have special moral duties to the child to mitigate or prevent such harms and suffering (Blustein, 1979).

All of these arguments implicitly rely on a core ideal about a relatively objective notion of acceptable quality of life, upon which most or all could agree, and which individuals could use to assess their duties and responsibilities. However, individuals' experiences of various disease conditions and life experiences differ dramatically, particularly in families that have a history of a genetic condition such as congenital deafness, or those with a spectrum of symptoms, such as Down syndrome (e.g., see Shakespeare, 1998). It can be argued that these individual family experiences and understandings should determine individuals' senses of duties regarding childbearing. If a family is willing to raise a child with mental retardation, a condition with highly variable manifestations, there is no strong moral basis for claiming that a duty not to reproduce exists. Part of having a normal range of life opportunities includes having and raising children (if individuals wish to do so), and it is an important determinate of the good life for many people. This argument particularly applies to those with genetically based illnesses where the disease condition may form part of one's identity or culture (e.g., deafness) or pose particular physical limitations to the kind of child that one could support within the family household (e.g., achondroplasia or congenital dwarfism).

Some would argue that no one would want a loved one to suffer any of the conditions related to serious genetic diseases, and that may well be the case. Nonetheless, we still place a high priority on allowing reproductive autonomy, but most importantly on allowing individuals and couples to shape their own life plans.

Perhaps most importantly, we generally reject public policy that would compel individuals not to reproduce (e.g., through sterilization or forced abortion). This view does not require endorsing an unalienable right to genetically reproduce, as there may well be severe conditions that cause suffering and early illness and death which could be argued to warrant avoiding reproduction under most circumstances.

Given diverse opinions and beliefs about the moral legitimacy of termination under various sorts of circumstances, and the ways in which termination may well be a socially constructed response (e.g. on selective termination, see Overall, 1990), it is difficult to maintain that there are objective duties to (or not to) reproduce. This is especially the case because of the wide range of medical conditions and psychosocial issues that might arise when making these types of decisions. It is problematic to claim that children have a "right" to be born healthy, as it is impossible to say what such a right involves. More importantly, even if we might be able to outline the basis for such a rights claim, enforcing it could well infringe on the mother's most basic rights and also is likely to undermine the maternal–fetal relationship (Hornstra, 1998).

A further argument explores the details of the sorts of duties which parents have when planning to reproduce, particularly with regard to the characteristics that a child is likely to inherit. As some non-disease genetically associated conditions (such as intelligence or sex) affect the likelihood of whether one's child is able to lead a good life, some claim that we should use the available genetic information and technologies to guide our reproductive decision-making. Thus it is argued that couples should select embryos (via pre-implantation genetic diagnosis) or fetuses (using prenatal diagnosis techniques) which are most likely to have the best life, based on the concept of "procreative beneficence." Couples (or single women) should select the child (from among the possible children that they could have, say from among the embryos available for implantation) who is expected to have the best life (or at least as good a life as the other possible children might have), based on the relevant, available information (Savulescu, 2001). This rather controversial argument makes an indirect claim about the duty not to have certain types of children, where other options are available. Critics of this sort of position argue that selecting offspring with certain desirable traits will undermine our views of human life as a gift to be unconditionally accepted, which can be defended from both religious and secular points of view (President's Council on Bioethics, 2004). However, in many senses, parents have always had considerable, but not unlimited, authority to shape their children's lives, through choices about education, upbringing, and so on. Thus new genetic technologies do not in fact represent unprecedented ways of shaping future offspring, though they may raise more pressing policy issues (Brock, 2005).

The issue of sex selection is particularly controversial. The practice is banned in many jurisdictions, seemingly because it is considered to be a morally problematic and discriminatory choice (or potentially because it results in gender imbalance in the broader population). It does, however, remain popular in cultures where having a child of a particular sex, or having a "balanced" family (i.e., some boys and some girls), is an important social norm. Children created with such techniques may be harmed by their parents, as they may have expectations imposed upon them because they have "selected for" particular traits: the tomboy whose mother chose a girl with the expectation that she would enjoy shopping and ballet classes may well experience considerable parental pressure. Currently, however, there is little moral consensus about these practices and about whether individuals should be permitted to make these sorts of decisions. Given the wide range of options we currently leave open to potential parents, choosing the genetic traits of our children could be viewed as a clear expression of our reproductive autonomy which should be allowed. If we aspire to respect reproductive autonomy, unless there is good evidence that these procedures or their outcomes would have likely considerable and concrete harmful effects to individuals or to the community, such decisions would need to be respected or at least not legally prohibited.

Responsibilities in Reproductive Decisions

In undertaking procreation, do potential parents take on responsibilities to ensure the future child a good (or minimally decent) life? One view is that the rights, obligations, and privileges of parenthood come not from simply being biologically related to a child, but from a social agreement made between the prospective parent and the moral community in which the parent lives (Scales, 2002). Thus there should be a category of minimally competent, willing, and able care providers who are "good enough" parents, and who are certified by society as such (Tittle, 2004). Good parenting, or the principle of parental responsibility, requires individuals to refrain from having children until certain minimal conditions can be met, notably those conditions necessary to allow their children to have good and fulfilling lives (Freeman, 1997).

The arguments made with regard to selecting certain types of children can also be extended more generally to reproductive decision-making. Although one assumes a range of responsibilities in making a decision to reproduce, including consideration of the conditions that should be in place to bear and rear a child, there are no obvious objective norms for ideal childrearing conditions. Empirical evidence suggests that "alternative" parenting has increased markedly in recent years in many societies. Whether a child is likely to have a happy and healthy upbringing cannot be gauged directly by the sexuality, gender, age, or marital status of her rearing parents. Although responsible procreation can be argued to require thoughtful decision-making about the right time and conditions for having children, once again there is no strong duty to refrain from reproducing (and certainly not one that can be coercively enforced), except perhaps under extreme conditions where a potential child is likely to experience considerable suffering.

Are there some people who do not have a right to reproduce, or even may have a duty to refrain from reproduction, for instance because of their own medical or other conditions? This question arises with respect to procreation by adults with intellectual disabilities and drug-addicted women, among other groups. It has been argued that even severely developmentally disabled persons have positive procreative autonomy, at least in the sense of genetic replication. Procreation is an important part of having a good life for many individuals, and deserves protection as a right because it is the usual way to establish a family. Furthermore, various institutional structures which allow people to have children without genetic replication (e.g., adoption or various genetic technologies) are often not available to those with such disabilities. However, if these types of individuals lack the mental or social capacities to rear children, they might be viewed as not having a right to reproduce, and perhaps even as having duties to refrain from reproduction (Steinbock, 1994). Once again, these duties should be seen as individual responsibilities. Current-day approaches to these issues generally reject using coercive means, such as sterilization or birth control (including implantable contraception) to enforce such responsibilities. These individuals have other pressing interests that must be respected, including health (which may be adversely affected particularly by certain forms of birth control) and bodily integrity. If it is in the individual's own best interest to be temporarily (chemically) or permanently (surgically) sterilized, such claims must be substantiated and rigorously tested against these general assumptions about their range of interests (Neville, 1981; cf. Kluge, 1989). The threshold for coercive interventions is high, and must focus on the individual's interests rather than society's ideas of what is best.

A final set of considerations about when it is required for us to refrain from reproduction relates to considerations associated with the so-called "population problem." Given that much of the world is currently overpopulated, we may well have duties not to reproduce, for instance for the good of our community or the environment. Thus our generally held rights to reproductive autonomy can be outweighed by more pressing obligations, such as our duties not to overburden the environment. Reproductive rights can also be viewed in a broader context of other rights and duties (such as those owed to the environment and future generations). For instance, there may be rights that are weightier than the right to reproduce, such as the right to a minimally good quality of life (Bayles, 1979), and it could be claimed that such a life requires that we not contribute to overpopulation.

Again, although arguments are available both for and against this position, it is difficult to come to any clear, generalizable moral conclusion that is not culturally particular or situation-specific. For many, having a genetically related family is an essential part of what it means to be human and is essential to the pursuit of a good life. It is therefore difficult to argue that people's desires to parent should be utterly trumped by population issues or long-term environmental concerns, but there may well be moral duties to carefully consider one's personal and local circumstances and broader social and environmental conditions when making reproductive decisions. Certain societies may create disincentives to having large families (McKibben, 1998), such as discriminatory taxation schemes, or even encourage population control and place limits on the number of children any one family can have (Hesketh and Zhu, 1997). More coercive policies that compelled people not to reproduce (e.g., forced sterilization or obligatory termination of pregnancy) would not be likely to be warranted, given our basic shared moral values of reproductive autonomy and bodily integrity.

Are There Rights to Rear Children?

An essential correlate of the right to reproduce is what happens to children after they are born. Should one have the right to rear one's biological child, and what are the limits of this right? This question is central to custody disputes, but also to conflicts between children and their parents. It is commonly believed that parenthood brings with it not only rights, but responsibilities. A more extreme position holds that one can only make claims to having parental rights when one's core parental responsibilities are fulfilled (Archard, 1990). Others hold that although parents can prove themselves to be unfit, they generally have custodial rights which allow wide latitude within which to carry out their responsibilities as they wish and to the best of their abilities (Page, 1985). On this view, parents have authority to rear their children because they have created and given birth to them, and so have a claim to rear them unless they somehow disqualify themselves. But in modern moral terms, a child clearly does not "belong" to its parents in the sense of being property. Instead, the relationship is closer to a fiduciary one where parents have the responsibility and authority to make decisions for the child so long as those decisions are in its best interests (Brock, 2005).

Conclusions

This chapter has reviewed some of the key issues associated with our duties to engage in, or refrain from, reproduction. The approach has been to outline various ethical arguments associated with key questions about rights and reproduction. Most of these arguments are made against the backdrop of a general presumption in favor of respecting reproductive autonomy and the pursuit of diverse visions of the good life. Many of these issues are currently morally divisive, particularly those associated with termination of pregnancy and various medical or social conditions that might result in what some feel are less than ideal conditions for procreation and rearing of children. As this chapter has shown, however, there is no moral consensus on most of these issues, beyond basic agreement that the threshold for interfering with reproductive autonomy is high indeed.

With regard to individual responsibilities for reproduction, individuals should carefully consider the details and moral issues associated with various reproductive decisions as outlined in this chapter. However, given our general presumption in favor of respecting individual autonomy and bodily integrity, it is difficult to maintain that failure to come to the "right" moral decisions (i.e., those that many other members of society would find acceptable) warrants any coercive measures. In most societies, forced sterilization or punitive measures to discourage reproduction would be difficult to legislate or enforce.

Although this chapter has discussed the general presumption that an individual has the right to reproduce, it also has revealed that merely asserting such a claim typically does not allow us to explore many of the most difficult questions associated with duties to reproduce (or to refrain from reproduction) and limits that might be placed upon us. Simply casting the debate in terms of what kind of right people have, fails to provide us with a deeper understanding of the various issues and values that are at stake in such decisions. Choices about reproduction are deeply relational, as they are related to our most fundamental understandings of who we are and what kinds of lives we wish to have. Hence philosophical investigations of reproduction and the creation of families may well need to look beyond traditional, rights-based accounts in order to capture more fully the values at stake in these decisions.

References

Archard, D. (1990), Child abuse: parental rights and the interest of the child, *Journal of Applied Philosophy* 7: 183–94.

Asch, A. (1989), Can aborting "imperfect" children be immoral? In J.D. Arras and N.K. Rhoden (eds.), *Ethical Issues in Modern Medicine*, 3rd edn., Mountain View, CA: Mayfield Press, pp. 317–21.

Bayles, M.D. (1979), Limits to a right to procreate, in O. O'Neill and W. Ruddick (eds.), *Having Children: Philosophical and Legal Reflections on Parenthood*, New York: Oxford University Press, pp. 13–24.

Belkin, L. (2001), The made-to-order savior: producing a perfect baby sibling, *NYT Magazine*, July 1: 36.

Bennett, R. (2001), Antenatal genetic testing and the right to remain in ignorance, *Theoretical Medicine and Bioethics*, 22: 461–71.

Bennett, R. and Harris, J. (2002), Are there lives not worth living? When is it morally wrong to reproduce? In D. Dickenson (ed.), *Ethical Issues in Maternal–Fetal Medicine*, Cambridge: Cambridge University Press, pp. 321–34.

Blustein, J. (1979), Child rearing and family interests, in O. O'Neill and W. Ruddick (eds.), *Having Children: Philosophical and Legal Reflections on Parenthood*, New York: Oxford University Press, pp. 115–22.

Brazier, M. (1998), Reproductive rights: feminism or patriarchy? In J. Harris and S. Holm (eds.), *The Future of Human Reproduction: Ethics, Choice and Regulation*, Oxford: Clarendon Press, pp. 66–76.

Brock, D.W. (1996), Funding new reproductive technologies: should they be included in health insurance benefit packages? In C. Cohen (ed.), *New Ways of Making Babies: The Case of Egg Donation*, Bloomington: Indiana University Press, pp. 213–30.

Brock, D.W. (2005), Shaping future children: parental rights and societal interests, *The Journal of Political Philosophy*, 13: 377–98.

Buchanan, A., Brock, D.W., Daniels, N., and Wikler, D. (2000), *From Chance to Choice: Genetics and Justice*, Cambridge: Cambridge University Press.

Chadwick, R.F. (1982), Cloning, *Philosophy*, 57: 201–9.

Chadwick, R.F. (1987), Introduction, in R.F. Chadwick (ed.), *Ethics, Reproduction, and Genetic Control*, London: Croom Helm, pp. 3–43.

Corea, G. (1985), *The Mother Machine*, New York: Harper and Row.

Dworkin, R. (1993), *Life's Dominion: An Argument about Abortion, Euthanasia, and Individual Freedom*, New York: Knopf.

Feinberg, J. (1992), *Freedom and Fulfillment: Philosophical Essays*. Princeton, NJ: Princeton University Press.

Fost, N.C. (2004), Conception for donation, *Journal of the American Medical Association*, 291: 2125–6.

Freeman, M. (1997), *The Moral Status of Children: Essays on the Rights of Children*, The Hague: Kluwer Law International.

Harris, J. (1998), Rights and reproductive choice, in J. Harris and S. Holm (eds.), *The Future of Human Reproduction: Ethics, Choice and Regulation*, Oxford: Clarendon Press, pp. 66–76.

Hesketh, T. and Zhu, W.X. (1997), Health in China: the one child family policy: the good, the bad, and the ugly, *British Medical Journal* 314: 1685.

Hornstra, D. (1998), A realistic approach to maternal–fetal conflict, *Hastings Center Report*, 28 (5): 7–12.

Kevin, C. (2005), Maternity and freedom: Australian feminist encounters with the reproductive body, *Australian Feminist Studies* 20: 3–15.

Kluge, E.W. (1989), Sterilization of the mentally severely handicapped: a violation of the right to have children? *Ethical Problems in Reproductive Medicine* 1: 12–15.

LaFollette, H. (1982), Licensing parents, *Philosophy and Public Affairs* 9: 183–97.

McKibben, B. (1998), *Maybe One: A Personal and Environmental Argument for Single-Child Families*, New York: Simon and Schuster.

Macklin, R. (1994), Splitting embryos on the slippery slope: ethics and public policy, *Kennedy Institute of Ethics Journal* 4: 209–26.

Marquis, D. (1989), Why abortion is immoral, *Journal of Philosophy* 86: 183–202.

Murray, T.H. (1996), New reproductive technologies and the family, in C. Cohen (ed.), *New Ways of Making Babies: The Case of Egg Donation*, Bloomington: Indiana University Press, pp. 51–69.

Neville, R. (1981), Sterilizing the mildly mentally retarded without their consent, in R. Macklin and W. Gaylin (eds.), *Mental retardation and sterilization*, New York: Plenum Press, pp. 181–93.

O'Neill, O. (1979), Begetting, bearing, and rearing, in O. O'Neill and W. Ruddick (eds.), *Having Children: Philosophical and Legal Reflections on Parenthood*, New York: Oxford University Press, pp. 25–38.

Overall, C. (1990), Selective termination of pregnancy and women's reproductive autonomy, *Hastings Center Report* 20 (3): 6–11.

Page, E. (1985), Donation, surrogacy, and adoption, *Journal of Applied Philosophy* 2: 161–72.

Parfit, D. (1984), *Reasons and Persons*, London: Oxford University Press.

Pellegrino, E.D. and Thomasma, D.C. (1993), *The Virtues in Medical Practice*, New York: Oxford University Press.

President's Council on Bioethics (2004), *Beyond Therapy: Biotechnology and the Pursuit of Happiness*, Washington, DC: President's Council on Bioethics.

Purdy, L.M. (1978), Genetic diseases: can having children be immoral? In J.J. Buckley (ed.), *Genetics Now: Ethical Issues in Genetic Research*, Washington, DC: University Press of America, pp. 25–39.

Qiu, R.-Z. (2002), Sociocultural dimensions of infertility and assisted reproduction in the Far East, in E. Vayena, P.J. Rowe, and P.D. Griffin (eds.), *Current Practices and Controversies in Assisted Reproduction: Report of a Meeting on Medical, Ethical and Social Aspects of Assisted Reproduction, 17–21 September 2001*, Geneva: World Health Organization, www.who.int/reproductive-health/infertility/12.pdf. Last accessed January 15, 2006.

Robertson, J.A. (1994), *Children of Choice: Freedom and the New Reproductive Technologies*, Princeton, NJ: Princeton University Press.

Robertson, J.A. (2003), Extending pre-implantation genetic diagnosis: the ethical debate, *Human Reproduction* 18: 465–71.

Robinson, B.E.S. (1996), On a woman's obligation to have an abortion, in J.M. Humber (ed.), *Reproduction, Technology, and Rights: Biomedical Ethics Reviews*, Totowa, NJ: Humana Press, pp. 25–39.

Savulescu, J. (2001), Procreative beneficence: why we should select the best children, *Bioethics* 15: 413–26.

Scales, S. (2002), Intergenerational justice and care in parenting, *Social Theory and Practice*, 28: 667–77.

Shakespeare, T. (1998), Choices and rights: eugenics, genetics and disability equality, *Disability and Society* 13: 665–81.

Steinbock, B. (1994), Reproductive rights and responsibilities, *Hastings Center Report* 24 (3): 15–16.

Tao Lai Po-Wah, J. (2004), Right-making and wrong-making in surrogate motherhood, in R. Tong, A. Donchin, and S.M. Dodds (eds.), *Linking Visions: Feminist Bioethics, Human Rights and the Developing World*, Lanham, MD: Rowman & Littlefield, pp. 157–79.

Tittle, P. (ed.) (2004), *Should Parents Be Licensed?* Amherst, NY: Prometheus Books.

United National General Assembly (1948), *Universal Declaration of Human Rights*, General Assembly resolution 217A (III), December 10, Article 16.

Vehmas, S. (2001), Just ignore it? Parents and genetic information, *Theoretical Medicine and Bioethics* 22: 473–84.

Vehmas, S. (2002), Is it wrong to deliberately conceive or give birth to a child with mental retardation? *Journal of Medicine and Philosophy* 27: 47–63.

Warnock, M. (2002), *Making Babies: Is There a Right to Have Children?* Oxford: Oxford University Press.

Chapter 3

Patient and Family Decisions about Life-Extension and Death

Felicia Nimue Ackerman

"Well," said the good man, "thou were better to be counselled."

(Malory, 1969, 2, p. 309)[1]

This is for my grandmother, Carolyn Colby.
"Terminal cancer," the doctor said. His eyes filled with tears.
"I'll get you the best hospice care in Boston." He put his arm around her.
My grandmother's eyes were cloudy but dry.
She said, "I'm 84, I've had a good life, so I don't want to die.
I want experimental treatment."
"That would ruin the time you've got left," the doctor said.
My grandmother said, "I'll risk it," and she did
And died of a stroke
On her 93rd birthday.

(Ackerman, 2006)[2]

Death is said to be a taboo subject in America, but if this claim were true, it could hardly be so hackneyed in the American popular media. Such media offer the following conventional wisdom about death and dying. Terminal patients are kept alive far too long through last-ditch, high-tech procedures. This serves only to prolong dying. It harms patients, who die in needless pain, with no quality of life and robbed of their dignity. It harms patients' families both emotionally and financially. It harms society by squandering resources on futile treatment. The solution is to recognize that "[h]umane care costs less than high-tech care and is what patients want and need" (Spiegel, 1994) and that hospice is "the most effective and least expensive route to a dignified death" (Shavelson, 1996). After all, "few could argue with the powerful message that it is better to leave wrapped in the love of family and care givers than locked in the cold, metallic embrace of a machine" (Goldberg, 1996).

The popular media are not homogeneous, nor is contemporary bioethics. But Daniel Callahan is not far off the mark in saying that high-tech life-prolonging medical treatment for the dying is "universally derided these days" (Callahan, 1995a, p. S34). Should such derision influence patients and families who are making practical decisions about life-extension and death? Such decisions, like all decisions, should be constrained by rationality (which can include a rational choice not to subject certain aspects of one's life to rational scrutiny)[3] and morality. I will focus on these factors in turn.

Rationality

Clearly, different people choose to pursue different ends, and there can be more and less rational means of attempting to achieve one's ends, i.e., means that are more and less likely, given the available evidence, to bring about one's ends. Criticizing the rationality of the ends that people choose is more controversial, yet many have done so. One such criticism is especially relevant here. This is the criticism that someone's ends manifest her failure to think through crucial issues, possibly because she has unreflectively adopted ideas from her society. Such criticism is familiar in social and political philosophy. For example, Thomas E. Hill, Jr. speaks of a deferential wife whose "socially fostered ignorance of her own talents and alternatives is responsible" (Hill, 1991, p. 10) for her belief "that the proper role for a woman is to serve her family" (p. 6). While a general account of rationality is far beyond the scope of this chapter, three points should be noted. First, rationality does not preclude emotionality. On the contrary, taking into account one's (often intense) feelings about pain, disability, and death is essential to rational decision-making about one's own life-extension and death. Second, although most patients may have common values such as independence, life-extension, dignity, and freedom from pain, they often rank-order these values differently.[4] This difference is part of why different choices about life-extension and death are rational for different people. Third, conformity as uncritical as that of Hill's "deferential wife" can affect patient and family decisions about life-extension and death.

Dignity

Thus, consider the concept of dignity. The word "dignity" is a staple of popular as well as professional bioethical discussions, where it frequently follows the words "death with." People unfamiliar with these discussions might expect "death with dignity" to apply to one's manner of dying – for instance, a stately exit involving ceremonial farewells. Instead, conventional usage holds that "death with dignity" prevents or ends life without dignity. Common examples of dignity-depleters include dementia, incontinence, and being "dependent on machines" or on other people. Those who believe "dependence [has a destructive] impact . . . on their own dignity" (Dworkin, 1994, p. 210) think they have what Ronald Dworkin calls a critical interest in independence, i.e., an interest "that it does make their life genuinely better [i.e., more successful, more meaningful, non-wasted] to satisfy" (p. 201). Dworkin contrasts critical interests with experiential interests, which are interests in having certain experiences because we "find them pleasurable or exciting *as experiences*" (p. 201, italics in original). He adds that "a person's critical interests seem very much to depend on his personality" (p. 206). Of course, they will also be affected by his religion (if any), social class, culture, and ethnicity, although how these factors affect one's critical interests also depends on one's personality.

Dworkin grants that "one may be *mistaken* about what is really important in life" (p. 206, italics in original). But although denying that "every kind of dependent life under severe handicaps is not worth living" (p. 210), he offers little critical scrutiny of the view that illness, disability, and dependence reduce human dignity. Such scrutiny can benefit patients making decisions about life-extension and death. Susan Wendell notes that "independence" is "defined according to a society's expectations about what people 'normally' do for themselves and how they do it" (Wendell, 1996, p. 145). She adds that few people in her city would consider her a dependent person because she buys her food from others instead of producing it herself, but that most would consider her highly dependent if she needed someone else's help getting out of bed. Similarly, few people consider me dependent because I rely on a refrigerator, but most would consider me highly dependent if I relied on a ventilator. As Wendell points out, "The philosophical arbitrariness of our ideas concerning which of us is 'independent' seems obvious" (Wendell, 1996, p. 146). Anita Silvers adds that independence need not "be compromised by having others execute, on one's behalf, physical activities one cannot or does not wish to engage in one's self [provided that this does not involve] being controlled by the caregiver" (Silvers, 1998, p. 123). Such views are more logical than the view that the "dependence" of physical disability inherently reduces one's own human dignity.

Such views are also more humane, since holding that the dependence of physical disability reduces one's own human dignity implicitly impugns the human dignity of others in the same situation. This illustrates a connection between morality and rationality, as there are moral objections to views that irrationally impugn the dignity of one's fellow humans. Note also that the glorification of youth, health, and physical independence embodied in such judgments is inappropriate from the standpoint of traditional cultures that respect the elderly.

Similar points apply to incontinence, which is also commonly said to impair human dignity, as if human dignity resided in the bladder or the rectum. Patients can consider such questions as the following. If inability to control one's urine or feces impairs one's human dignity, why not say the same of inability to control one's menstrual bleeding? And why is there more indignity involved in having another person wipe one's behind than in having another person pull or fill one's teeth (another intimate, messy activity)?

The crucial difference lies in the attitudes of other people. Disparagement of menstruating women is widely recognized as sexist. Virtually no one loses social esteem for getting dental care, but people do lose such esteem for being disabled and/or incontinent. Like racism, disrespect of the disabled and/or incontinent is relevant to those who have a critical interest in being respected by others.

Such disrespect is also relevant to those who have an experiential interest in being respected. Many people find it excruciatingly unpleasant to be treated disrespectfully.[5] Some disabled and/or incontinent people have the comfort of belonging to a traditional culture that does not glorify youth, health, and independence. Others, finding themselves in a hostile culture, can investigate the possibility of companionship and solace "in a better world, where there is neither young nor old, healthy nor crippled . . . On the Internet" (Ackerman, 2005, p. 43)[6] or in online relationships with people who have chosen to identify themselves online as ill and/or disabled.

Pain

Another experiential consideration is pain. Almost everyone has an experiential interest in avoiding pain, and many have some level of pain-intensity and frequency that they find experientially unacceptable. Hence, they may rationally prefer death. But Christians often represent suffering as a way of identifying with Christ on the cross, which serves their critical interest as Christians. While the rationality of Christian beliefs is beyond the scope of this chapter, one can, as I have mentioned, make a rational choice not to subject certain aspects of one's life to rational scrutiny. Religious beliefs may provide solace that one is rationally loath to risk losing. For instance, many people value religion as a source of strength. Also, many have a critical interest in faith as a virtue.

Even for the non-religious, it can be rational to choose pain over death or the reduced consciousness resulting from pain medication. Many people with illnesses that are extremely painful but not life-threatening (such as rheumatoid arthritis) rationally choose to stay alive and alert in order to partake of the life benefits that pain does not preclude. This choice can also be rational for the terminally ill.[7] The choice between comfort, on the one hand, and alertness and/or life-extension, on the other, is sometimes required by the effects of pain medication. But it has also been forced on patients by hospice ideology. Recently some "open access" hospices have begun to allow patients, insofar as possible, to combine the comforts of hospice with life-prolonging medical treatment. This choice is rational for many, despite Robin Marantz Henig's claim that such patients are "indulg[ing] the fantasy that dying is somehow optional" (Henig, 2005, p. 28). Henig offers no evidence that they are indulging this irrational fantasy rather than pursuing the rational goal of living longer without sacrificing comfort care.

Availability of support services

Pain and disrespect are not the only experiential reasons a patient might choose death. Dworkin sympathetically discusses Nancy B., a Canadian quadriplegic who successfully sued to have her respirator turned off because, as she put it, "The only thing I have is television and looking at the walls" (Dworkin, 1994, p. 184).[8] Rational quadriplegics, realizing that the narrowness of such a life arises from a lack of support services such as those available to famed quadriplegic physicist Stephen Hawking, can investigate the availability of support services in their own lives. Some will use this information in making their own life-and-death decisions. Others will choose to engage in political activism to increase the availability of such services. Rational patients can also see the false dichotomy between being "locked in the cold, metallic embrace of a machine" and being "wrapped in the love of family and care givers" (Goldberg, 1996). Obviously, there is nothing intrinsically incompatible with being kept alive by machines and being wrapped in the love of family. Patients should also be aware that many of the terminally ill who desire to die suffer from treatable clinical depression (Chochinov et al., 1995 and Brody, 1997).

Prolonging the dying process

The cliché that life-support for the terminally ill merely "prolongs dying" also cries out for critical examination. A dying person who enjoys or otherwise rationally values continuing his life has a rational interest in prolonging it by "prolonging dying" and in not letting himself be swayed by the biased language that appears even in some documents that purport to be purely informative. For example, a page headed "Commonly Used Life-Support Measures" at the end of the Rhode Island Durable Power of Attorney for Health Care says, "For the dying patient, however, mechanical ventilation often merely prolongs the dying process until some other body system fails." This statement should be recognized as advocacy for a personal view that dying quickly is better than dying over a longer period of illness and disability. Rational people can disagree about this matter.

Relationships with physicians

What advice, if any, is it rational for patients to seek from doctors about end of life decisions? Ezekiel J. Emanuel and Linda L. Emanuel identify four models of the physician–patient relationship: the paternalistic model, in which "the physician presents the patient with selected information that will encourage the patient to consent to the intervention the physician considers best"; the informative model, in which the doctor provides "all relevant information" and the patient uses this information to make decisions according to his own values; the interpretative model, in which "[t]he aim of the physician–patient interaction is to elucidate the patient's values . . . and to help the patient select the available medical interventions that realize these values"; and the deliberative model, in which "[t]he aim of the physician–patient interaction is to help the patient determine and choose the best health-related values that can be realized in the clinical situation . . . The physician's objectives include suggesting why certain health-related values are more worthy and should be aspired to" (Emanuel and Emanuel, 1995, pp. 68, 69).

The Emanuels' article deals with how doctors should behave. Here I will consider what sort of doctor–patient relationship it is rational for patients to seek. Although acknowledging that different models may be appropriate under different circumstances, the Emanuels favor the deliberative model as "the shared, paradigmatic reference [exceptions to which] would require justification based on the circumstances of a particular situation" (Emanuel and Emanuel, 1995, p. 74). They pay insufficient attention to the fact that it is not just situations that vary; patients vary as well. Patients vary enormously in cultural and religious commitments (and in willingness to question such commitments), medical knowledge, interest in acquiring medical information, respect for medical authority, rigidity of values, and desire for guidance. The Emanuels defend the deliberative model on the grounds that "physicians should . . . promote health-related values" (p. 75) and "our society's image of an ideal physician . . . is a caring physician who integrates the information and relevant values to make a recommendation, and . . . attempts to persuade the patient to accept this recommendation" (pp. 74–5). This generalization overlooks the diversity of American society. While many patients reasonably seek a doctor who follows a deliberative model, those who have well-defined values and value independence of judgment reasonably regard such a doctor as intrusive. Even the informative model may reasonably seem unacceptably authoritarian to the present-day patient who gets medical information from the Internet. Furthermore, when it comes to such matters as home care v. institutional care or palliative care v. high-tech life-prolonging and/or experimental curative care, there is often no single way of promoting "the best health-related values." Such choices are lifestyle choices, about which rational, health-valuing people may vary. Accordingly, a patient who feels the need for help clarifying, but not fundamentally questioning, his own values might do well to seek guidance from people who need not be health professionals but who are in sympathy with the inchoate values he feels the need to clarify. For example, a patient who chooses not to question his religious or cultural tradition can seek guidance from those within that tradition.

These considerations are particularly important in view of the danger that a doctor who sees himself as caring and compassionate will guide patients to make decisions in accord with his own contestable values about life-extension and death and will discount patients' decisions that do not so accord. For instance, Sherwin B. Nuland, in a prizewinning and bestselling book, criticizes medical specialists for urging last-ditch, high-tech treatment upon the terminally ill. He says, "[O]ur own choices should be allowed, insofar as possible, to be the decisive factor in the manner of our going" (Nuland, 1994, p. 264). But he dismisses terminal patients who want "major resuscitative efforts" (p. 229) as being in "denial" (p. 228). His blanket castigation of the sort of doctor who "indulges a very sick person" by "a course of [aggressive] action whose odds of success seem too small to justify embarking on it" (p. 224) invites such questions as: Too small by whose standards? What if (as the term "indulges" suggests) the patient's choice is to go for a long shot? Despite his proclamation about "our own choices," Nuland's humanitarian objection to medical specialists who push their pro-intervention ideology at patients is unaccompanied by similar reservations about his own ideology to "always try to guide [patients] in making decisions that . . . will lead to relief of their suffering" (p. 249) – even if it means earlier death and the patient considers that a poor trade-off.[9]

In addition to having contestable values, health professionals generally have vested interests in patient choices. Nuland says, "The satisfaction of [providing diagnosis and cure] is . . . the fuel that drives the clinical engines of medicine's most highly trained specialists" (Nuland, 1994, p. 248). The same point applies to palliative-care providers with respect to the satisfaction of providing a peaceful death. Moreover, all health professionals have a financial interest in attracting business. Possible bias of these sorts is worth taking into account when receiving advice from any health professionals.

Morality

What do patients owe their families and vice versa? Here, too, a particular viewpoint dominates bioethics and the popular media in America. For example, a recent *New York Times* column argues that a terminally ill person owes her loved ones "a good death" (i.e., one that is easy on them) even at the price of forgoing a chance to prolong her own life (Zaroff, 2005),[10] and Daniel Callahan says, "A family member should reject [a technologically extended death] for the sake of the family's welfare after he or she is gone" (Callahan, 1993, p. 219).[11] John Hardwig goes further. He thinks people can have a duty to kill themselves (even before they become terminally ill) when their failing health makes them a burden to their families. Although very few people advocate patients' sacrificial suicide, Hardwig's views are well in the mainstream when it comes to forgoing life-prolonging medical treatment. So I will focus on these views.

One way Hardwig seeks to support his views is by pointing out that "[m]any older people report that their one remaining goal in life is not to be a burden to their loved ones" (Hardwig, 2000, p. 122.) He holds that this reflects "moral wisdom" (p. 82). He overlooks the possibility that it reflects our society's devaluation of the old, ill, and disabled, a devaluation many old people accept uncritically, just as many women, like the "deferential wife" mentioned earlier, used to accept the idea that woman should be subordinate to men and should avoid having careers that would burden their families. But few people (or at least, few liberals) in our society nowadays would think this latter attitude reflects moral wisdom. Just as we now recognize the bias in seeing women's careers but not men's as a burden to their families, patients making decisions about life-extension and death can question why a sick old person's care should count as a burden to his family when a teenager's college tuition and the reluctance of an "adult child" to reciprocate the care and/or financial support he was given do not.

What sort of burden might a sick old person seek to avoid being? Hardwig praises a list of "Responsibilities of Those Facing the End of Life" formulated by a group of retirees in a discussion he led. The list includes (2) "Die in a way that will leave your family in the best position" and (5) "Don't live so long that your loved ones will wish you were dead" (Hardwig, 2000, p. 198). A literal reading of these strictures places so little value on the lives of the elderly that it is hard to take seriously. Stricture (2) entails that any improvement, however small, in the family's position calls for any sacrifice, however great, from the old person. What if that person's forgoing radiation and chemotherapy will put his family in the "best position" of being able to buy a long-desired yacht? Even a less extreme formulation invites the question of why the family's "position" should outweigh an old person's life. Stricture (5) treats life as a dinner party where the loved ones are hosts and the elderly are guests who should not be so rude as to overstay their welcome. The lack of qualification entails that the elderly should honor *any* reason their loved ones may have for wishing them dead. What if the loved ones wish this so they can inherit money to buy a Rolls-Royce? Both strictures are also wildly inappropriate for adherents to traditional cultures that respect the elderly.

Elsewhere I have introduced what I call "the paradox of the selfless invalid" (Ackerman, 1997, p. 318), which in its most extreme form goes as follows: If a patient's family members would welcome the sacrifice of his life for their sake, how can they be worth his sacrifice? If they would not welcome his sacrifice, how can he show respect for them by sacrificing what they want him to keep? This extreme view is open to objections. Just as it is outrageous to suppose one has a duty to forgo life-prolonging medical treatment in order to bequeath money for one's family to buy a yacht, it is preposterous to expect a family to sell everything it owns, in order to give the patient a minute of extra life. Where should we draw the line? A precise answer is impossible. But (although his use of the phrase "duty to die" reflects his controversial view that committing suicide and forgoing life-prolonging medical treatment are morally on a par)[12] the guidelines Hardwig offers reflect conventional wisdom about when patients should forgo life-prolonging treatment. Hardwig says, "If [the mainstream bioethicists who contributed commentaries to his book] can admit there can be a responsibility to decline all life-prolonging treatments, they can go with me perhaps 90 percent of the way to my conclusion" (Hardwig, 2000, p. 173). Certainly the following guidelines (pp. 129–30) are hardly unconventional if we replace "duty to die" with "duty to forgo life-prolonging medical treatment."[13]

1   A duty to die is more likely when continuing to live will impose significant burdens – emotional burdens, extensive caregiving, destruction of life plans, and . . . financial hardship – on your family and loved ones. This is the fundamental insight underlying a duty to die.

2   A duty to die becomes greater as you grow older. As we age, we will be giving up less by giving up our lives, if only because we will sacrifice fewer remaining years of life and a smaller portion of our life plans . . . To have reached the age of, say, 75 or 80 years without being ready to die is itself a moral failing, the sign of a life out of touch with life's basic realities.[14]

3   A duty to die is more likely when you have already lived a full and rich life. You have already had a full share of the good things life offers.

4   There is a greater duty to die if your loved ones' lives have already been difficult or impoverished, if they have had only a small share of the good things that life has to offer (especially if through no fault of their own).

5   A duty to die is more likely when your loved ones have already made great contributions – perhaps even sacrifices – to make your life a good one. Especially if you have not made similar sacrifices for their well-being or for the well-being of other members of your family.

6   To the extent that you can make a good adjustment to your illness or handicapping condition, there is less likely to be a duty to die . . . Still, we must also recognize that some diseases . . . will eventually take their toll on your loved ones no matter how . . . you manage to face that illness.

7   There is less likely to be a duty to die if you can still make significant contributions to the lives of others, especially your family . . .

8   A duty to die is more likely when the part of you that is loved will soon be gone or seriously compromised. Or when you soon will no longer be capable of giving love . . .

9   There is a greater duty to die to the extent that you have lived a relatively lavish lifestyle instead of saving for illness or old age . . .

I suggest we re-conceptualize the problem by asking how these and related conditions affect the duty to make sacrifices in order to extend or improve the life of a seriously ill loved one. I call this "a duty to aid," a term covering both financial aid and caregiving. Here are nine guidelines parallel to Hardwig's.

1   A duty to aid is more likely when failing to aid will impose significant burdens, when the ill loved one very much wants to go on living (or remain at home or enter a costly assisted living facility) and needs your help. This is the fundamental insight underlying a duty to aid.

2   Perhaps a duty to aid becomes greater as you grow older, because you will be sacrificing a smaller portion of your life plans. Perhaps a duty to aid is greater when you are young, because you have more stamina and more life ahead of you, with more opportunity to recoup your losses. At any rate, to have reached adulthood without being ready to make major financial contributions

and changes in lifestyle in order to aid a seriously ill loved one is itself a moral failing, the sign of a life out of touch with life's basic realities.

3   A duty to aid is more likely when you are living a full and rich life that will provide you with substantial goods and pleasures to counterbalance the burden of aiding.

4   There is a greater duty to aid if your ill loved one's life has already been difficult or impoverished, if he has had only a small share of the good things that life has to offer (especially if through no fault of his own).

5   A duty to aid is more likely when your ill loved one has already made great contributions – perhaps even sacrifices – to make your life a good one. Especially if you have not made similar sacrifices for his well-being. This imbalance frequently exists between "adult children" and the parents who raised them.[15]

6   To the extent that your loved one can get appropriate aid elsewhere, there is less you have a duty to do. To the extent that you cannot make a good adjustment to aiding, there is less of a duty to aid. Still, we must also recognize that unwillingness to make a good adjustment does not entail inability to do so, nor does making a good adjustment mean you must enjoy aiding.

7   There is less of a duty to aid if you have significant obligations elsewhere. But your obligations to your children do not automatically outweigh your obligations to your parents. The popular slogan "The best thing you can do for your parents is to take good care of their grandchildren" is obviously false if your father needs and wants radiation and chemotherapy, which he cannot afford without your help, and your son "needs" and wants four years at Yale without incurring student loans.

8   A duty to aid is more likely when your loved one is agonizingly aware that the part of him that was loved will soon be gone or seriously compromised and is terrified that his loved ones will abandon him.

9   There is a greater duty to provide physical care to the extent that you have lived a relatively lavish lifestyle that has prevented you from saving enough to provide financial help.

These guidelines are not formally incompatible with Hardwig's. He grants that families "must be prepared to make significant sacrifices to respond to an illness in the family" (Hardwig, 2000, p. 124), although his examples of what can constitute an intolerable family burden (such as living "with a spouse who is increasingly distant, uncommunicative, unresponsive, foreign, and unreachable" [p. 123]) raise the question of just what sort of "significant sacrifices" he has in mind. His statement, "I cannot imagine that it would be morally permissible for me . . . to impoverish [my sons] or compromise the quality of their children's lives simply because I wish to live a little longer"(p. 127) highlights this question. What deprivation could *not* be said to compromise the quality of one's grandchildren's lives? Going without private schooling? Going without summer camp?

Finally, consider the source of the money that would be sacrificed for the patient's care. Like most bioethicists who write on this topic, Hardwig focuses on cases where a sick person's care impoverishes his family by depleting their savings and/or depriving the caregiver of a source of income. But what if the money is the patient's and prolonging his life would deprive his children and grandchildren of an inheritance? Here I think it is appropriate to take a hard line. Unless the patient is a thief, an heir, or a lottery winner, his accumulated funds are likely due in considerable part to his prudence, ingenuity, and/or hard work. Moreover, he has probably already supported his offspring through childhood, possibly including an expensive private-school education and even a young-adult subsidy as well. Except under extraordinary circumstances, no one owes his solvent and/or able-bodied "adult children" an inheritance, let alone at the cost of his own life, nor is he ever obliged to forgo life-prolonging medical treatment in order to provide his grandchildren with luxuries. Here the paradox of the selfless invalid seems least problematic. Someone who would welcome an inheritance received at the cost of his parent's life clearly values the former above the latter. Such an "adult child" deserves from his unfortunate parent neither love nor money.

Advance Directives

What if a patient is no longer competent to make decisions about treatment? Advance directives are a way of providing for this possibility. These include instruction directives (also referred to as "living wills"), stating what procedures are or are not to be performed on oneself and (since instruction directives cannot cover all possibilities) proxy directives (also referred to as "durable powers of attorney for health care") designating a proxy (also referred to as a "surrogate agent" or "health care agent"). A proxy directive empowers the proxy to make treatment decisions that would accord with the patient's wishes or, if these wishes are unclear, with the patient's best interest.

The relation between critical and experiential interests is important in connection with advance directives. Consider the case of dementia. Dworkin stresses that many people are "repelled by the idea of living demented, totally dependent lives, speaking gibberish, incapable of understanding that there is a world beyond them." He suggests that such people consider signing advance directives specifying that they be denied medical treatment "except to avoid pain" or, if possible, even killed once they become demented (even if they seem happy with what Dworkin belittles as "meager childish pleasures") so that their dignity will not be marred (Dworkin, 1994, p. 231). I have argued that a conception of dignity that stigmatizes physical disability, dependence, and/or incontinence will not withstand rational scrutiny. Can a similar argument be made here? The answer is less clear. As J. David Velleman points out,

> When Kant speaks . . . of the dignity that belongs to persons by virtue of their rational nature, and that places them beyond all price . . . he is not invoking any-

thing that requires the ability to walk unaided, to feed oneself, or to control one's bowels. Hence the dignity invoked in discussions of medical ethics – a status supposedly threatened by physical deterioration and dependency – cannot be the status whose claim on our moral concern is so fundamental to Kantian thought.

(Velleman, 1992, p. 666)

Dementia, however, threatens to undermine this rational nature, thereby undermining the core of human distinctiveness and personality. Yet patients making advance directives should be aware that recent evidence indicates that the demented may possess previously unsuspected reserves of thought and feeling; "a viable, even if crippled self may endure far later into the [Alzheimer's] disease process than was earlier believed" (Callahan, 1995b, p. 25). Patients can also ask themselves whether their human dignity was marred by their having been babies and toddlers, and if not, why cognitive inabilities in the last stage of life would mar their dignity more than those in the first stage. Note that this problem will not arise for patients who choose to be guided by a religion that holds that "even" the cognitively impaired have human dignity as children of God.

Advance directives have many limitations. As Carl E. Schneider points out, patients' "preferences are often undeveloped, weak, and conflicting." Furthermore, "there is considerable empirical evidence that some substantial proportion of patients do not yearn to make their own medical decisions" (Schneider, 1995, p. S26). Advance directives may be particularly unattractive to adherents of cultures that do not place "great importance on individualism and self-determination – or autonomy" (Hallenbeck and Goldstein, 1999, p. 25). Adherence to such a culture can be rational. Another problem is that studies yield varying, and sometimes discouraging, results as to whether advance directives make much difference in the medical treatment patients actually receive (Callahan, 1995a, p. S36). Accordingly, patients who designate a proxy should be careful to choose someone willing and able to put in the time and effort necessary to do the job effectively. What other traits will a rational patient seek in a proxy? Obviously, the proxy should know the patient well enough to judge what sort of care would be most likely to accord with his wishes. Ideally, the proxy will have neither practical vested interests nor ideological commitments that would interfere with his effectively serving as the patient's agent.

The first condition may be attainable by patients with ample resources. These can be either family and friends or funds to hire a good lawyer. The relation between the latter two conditions is problematic. People most likely to know the patient well enough to make informed decisions about what would accord with his wishes are often least likely to lack any vested interest in the matter (Hardwig, 2000, p. 46). Friends and family may have self-interested reasons for wanting a loved one to stay alive, such as not wanting to lose him or fear of feeling guilty after his death. They may also have self-interested reasons for desiring his prompt demise. This is especially true of the family, who may find the patient a financial burden as well as an emotional one. Moreover, relatives are frequently the patient's heirs. A recent survey found that 60 percent of baby boomers believe they deserve to inherit money from their parents (Birnbaum, 1995). Of course, it is possible for a patient to make a rational choice to adhere to a culture that has a "family-centered model of decision-making" (Hallenbeck and Goldstein, 1999, p. 27), to be self-sacrificing, and/or to eschew being suspicious of her family. But in the absence of such choices, it is in a patient's interest to avoid choosing a proxy who has a vested interest in her self-sacrifice.

To ignore this point is to conflate the interests of the patient with those of the family. Thus, Dworkin denigrates the wish of a demented patient to remain "at home, rather than living in an institution, though this would impose very great burdens on his family" (Dworkin, 1994, p. 221). He justifies this denigration on the grounds that "we all agree that *people lead critically better lives when they are not a serious burden to others*" (ibid., italics added). He overlooks those of us who believe that a demented old person deserves some reciprocal care from the "adult children" she raised and for whom she made sacrifices and/or that the "in sickness and in health" part of the marriage vows should count against institutionalizing one's spouse against her will. Dworkin's bias is further illustrated by his failure to recognize that the words I have italicized cut both ways. After all, if people lead critically better lives when they are not a serious burden to others, then family members lead critically better lives when they do not make their own comfort and convenience a serious burden to a patient who is institutionalized against her will in order to serve that comfort and convenience.

Mainstream American society recognizes vested interests, especially financial ones, as impediments to unbiased judgment. That is why judges and jurors are disqualified from serving in cases where their own interests are involved. Of course, patients know their own loved ones and may reasonably believe that these loved ones would not deny them care in order to preserve an inheritance. But patients may also unreasonably believe this. My claim is not that many people would explicitly reason, "I should pull the plug on Mom while there's still lots of money left for me." Financial concerns can manifest themselves in more subtle ways, corrupting the proxy's judgment about what the patient would want. For some patients, it is rational to consider this possibility and perhaps see whether a relative or friend who is neither a potential caregiver nor financially connected to the patient might be available as a proxy.

Conclusion

When Daniel Callahan approvingly remarks that high-tech life-prolonging medical treatment for the dying is "universally derided these days" (Callahan, 1995a, p. S34), he is not far off the mark when it comes to the facts. But his approval does not withstand critical examination. While some terminal patients have values that make palliative care the best option for them, other terminal patients opt for aggressive life-extending and/or experimental curative care, and it is altogether fitting and proper that they should do this.

Notes

1 The hermit who says this to Gawain on the quest of the Holy Grail has a definite ideology about what is best for Gawain. Thus, he resembles many who counsel dying people nowadays.
2 This poem, which is not autobiographical, first appeared in *Ragged Edge Online* and is reprinted by permission.
3 I discuss this point in Ackerman 1998, p. 188.
4 I owe this point to Rosamond Rhodes.
5 Of course, an incontinent and/or disabled person may have a critical interest in not letting others' disrespect sway him, just as a black person may have a critical interest in not knuckling under to racism.
6 This description comes from a short story about a disabled octogenarian who does just that.
7 Bioethicists often fail to recognize this. Linda L. Emanuel points out that a prominent recent study's bias "in favor of palliative care" (Emanuel, 1995, p. S15) underlies its use of pain reports as a criterion for assessing end of life care and that "a better outcome measure than simple pain reports would be the proportion of patients who felt their pain was optimally controlled, given the side effects of medication" (Emanuel, 1995, p. S15). Similarly, see Moskowitz and Nelson (1995, p. S5).
8 Dworkin represents this attitude as a critical interest (Dworkin, 1994, p. 210), but it can also be an experiential interest.
9 For discussion of additional examples of such behavior from doctors, see Ackerman (2003).
10 Zaroff (2005) describes his dying mother's exemplary attitude as follows: "For her to cause her family any inconvenience [even the inconvenience of a second cross-country trip to visit her!] was out of the question." He claims, "My mother was liberated when she was 80" by the death of her controlling, "patriarchal" husband. But a woman who deems her *life* less important than her family's *convenience* hardly seems liberated from the view of the "deferential wife," cited earlier, "that the proper role for a woman is to serve her family" (Hill, 1991, p. 6).
11 Space limitations prevent me from discussing whether patients have a duty to avoid burdening society through excessive use of health care resources, but see Battin (2000), Kissell (2000), Menzel (2000), and Ackerman (2001).
12 For criticism of this view, see Callahan (1990).
13 Not all bioethicists would accept them, however. Exceptions include Drebushenko (2000), Kissell (2000), and Overall (2003).
14 This claim invites the objection that it is itself "the sign of a life out of touch with life's basic realities," which include an increasing number of nonagenarians.
15 The general issue of what "adult children" owe their parents has many complexities I cannot go into here, but see Sommers (1986) and English (1996).

References

Ackerman, Felicia (1997), Goldilocks and Mrs Ilych: a critical look at the philosophy of hospice, *Cambridge Quarterly of Healthcare Ethics* 6: 314–24.

Ackerman, Felicia (1998), Flourish your heart in this world: emotion, reason, and action in Malory's *Le Morte D'Arthur*, in Peter French and Howard K. Wettstein (eds.), *Midwest Studies in Philosophy XXII: The Philosophy of Emotions*, Notre Dame, IN: University of Notre Dame Press, pp. 182–226.

Ackerman, Felicia (2001), Review of John Hardwig, *Is There a Duty to Die? and Other Essays in Bioethics* and James M. Humber and Robert F. Almeder (eds.), *Is There a Duty to Die? American Philosophical Association Newsletter on Philosophy and Medicine* 1 (1): 173–8.

Ackerman, Felicia Nimue (2003), Letter to editor, *American Philosophical Association Newsletter on Philosophy and Medicine* 3 (1): 154.

Ackerman, Felicia Nimue (2005 and forthcoming), We gather together, *East Side Monthly*, May: 42–3, Reprinted in Felicia Nimue Ackerman, *Bioethics Through Fiction*, Lanham, MD: Rowman & Littlefield.

Ackerman, Felicia Nimue (2006), This is for my grandmother, *Ragged Edge Online*, http://www.raggededgemagazine.com/departments/poetry/000772.html, accessed June 29, 2006.

Battin, Margaret P. (2000), Global life expectancies and the duty to die, in James M. Humber and Robert F. Almeder (eds.), *Is There a Duty to Die?* Totowa, NJ: Humama Press, pp. 1–21.

Birnbaum, J. (1995), Of inheritance and ruptured relations: a final accounting, *New York Times*, July 9: F8.

Brody, Jane E. (1997), Personal health, *New York Times*, June 18: C11.

Callahan, Daniel (1990), *What Kind of Life?* New York: Simon and Schuster.

Callahan, Daniel (1993), *The Troubled Dream of Life: In Search of a Peaceful Death*, New York: Simon and Schuster.

Callahan, Daniel (1995a), Once again, reality: now where do we go? *Hastings Center Report*, 25 (6): S33–6.

Callahan, Daniel (1995b), Terminating life-sustaining treatment of the demented, *Hastings Center Report* 25 (6): 25–31.

Chochinov, H.M., Wilson, K.G., Enns, M., et al. (1995), Desire for death in the terminally ill, *American Journal of Psychiatry* 152 (8): 1185–91.

Drebushenko, David (2000), How could there be a duty to die? In James M. Humber and Robert F. Almeder (eds.), *Is There a Duty to Die?* Totowa, NJ: Humana Press, pp. 159–76.

Dworkin, Ronald (1994), *Life's Dominion: An Argument About Abortion, Euthanasia, and Individual Freedom*, New York: Vintage.

Emanuel, Ezekiel J. and Emanuel, Linda L. (1995), Four models of the physician–patient relationship, in John D. Arras and Bonnie Steinbock (eds.), *Ethical Issues in Modern Medicine*, 4th edn., Mountain View, CA: Mayfield, pp. 67–76.

Emanuel, Linda L. (1995), Structured deliberation to improve decisionmaking for the seriously ill, *Hastings Center Report* 25 (6): S14–18.

English, Jane (1996), What do grown children owe their parents? In Hugh La Follette (ed.), *Ethics in Practice*, Cambridge, MA: Blackwell, pp. 174–8.

Goldberg, Vicki (1996), Looking straight into the eyes of the dying, *New York Times*, March 31: H34 and H37.

Hallenbeck, James and Goldstein, Mary K. (1999), Decisions at the end of life: cultural considerations beyond medical ethics, *Generations* 33 (1): 24–9.

Hardwig, John (2000), *Is There a Duty to Die? and Other Essays in Bioethics*, New York: Routledge.

Henig, Robin Marantz (2005), Will we ever arrive at the good death? *New York Times Magazine*, August 7: 26–35, 40, 68.

Hill, Thomas E., Jr. (1991), Servility and self-respect, in Thomas E. Hill, Jr., *Autonomy and Self-Respect*, Cambridge: Cambridge University Press, pp. 4–18.

Kissell, Judith Lee (2000), Grandma, the GNP, and the duty to die, in James M. Humber and Robert F. Almeder (eds.), *Is There a Duty to Die?* Totowa, NJ: Humana Press, pp. 191–203.

Malory, Sir Thomas (1969), *Le Morte D'Arthur*, London: Penguin.

Menzel, Paul (2000), The nature, scope, and implications of a personal moral duty to die, in James M. Humber and Robert F. Almeder (eds.), *Is There a Duty to Die?* Totowa, NJ: Humana Press, pp. 95–113.

Moskowitz, Ellen H. and Nelson, James Lindemann (1995), The best laid plans, *Hastings Center Report* 25 (6): S3–6.

Nuland, Sherwin B. (1994), *How We Die*, New York: Knopf.

Overall, Christine (2003), *Aging, Death, and Human Longevity: A Philosophical Inquiry*, Berkeley: University of California Press.

Schneider, Carl E. (1995), From consumer choice to consumer welfare, *Hastings Center Report* 25 (6): S25–8.

Shavelson, Lonny (1996), What the dying really need, *New York Times*, March 8: A31.

Silvers, Anita (1998), Review of Susan Wendell, *The Rejected Body: Feminist Philosophical Reflections on Disability, American Philosophical Association Newsletter on Philosophy and Medicine* 97 (2): 122–5.

Sommers, Christina Hoff, (1986), Filial morality, *Journal of Philosophy* 83 (8): 439–56.

Spiegel, David (1994), Compassion is the best medicine, *New York Times*, January 10: A17.

Velleman, J. David (1992), Against the right to die, *Journal of Medicine and Philosophy* 17: 665–81.

Wendell, Susan (1996), *The Rejected Body: Feminist Philosophical Reflections on Disability*, New York: Routledge.

Zaroff, Larry (2005), One last recipe from mother, for the good death, *New York Times*, August 30: F5.

Suggested Further Reading

Blackhall, Leslie J., Murphy, Sheila, Frank, Geyla, Michel, Vicki, and Azen, Stanley (1995), Ethnicity and attitudes toward patient autonomy, *Journal of the American Medical Association* 274 (10): 820–5.

Blustein, Jeffrey (1982), *Parents and Children: The Ethics of the Family*, New York: Oxford University Press.

Callahan, Daniel (1995), *Setting Limits: Medical Goals in an Aging Society*, Washington, DC: Georgetown University Press.

Humber, James M. and Almeder, Robert F. (eds.) (2000), *Is There a Duty to Die?* Totowa, NJ: Humana Press.

Kübler-Ross, Elisabeth (1969), *On Death and Dying*, New York: Simon and Schuster.

Kübler-Ross, Elisabeth (1974), *Questions and Answers about Death and Dying*, New York: Macmillan.

McKerlie, Dennis (forthcoming), Justice and the elderly, in Bonnie Steinbock (ed.), *Oxford Handbook of Bioethics*, Oxford: Oxford University Press.

Momeyer, Richard (1988), *Confronting Death*, Bloomington, IN: Indiana University Press.

Nagel, Thomas (1979), Death, in Thomas Nagel, *Mortal Questions*, Cambridge: Cambridge University Press, pp. 1–12.

Schneider, Carl E. (1994), Bioethics with a human face, *Indiana Law Journal* 69: 1075–1104.

Individual Decisions about Clinical Issues

Decisions of Physicians and Other Health Care Professionals

Chapter 4

The Professional Responsibilities of Medicine[1]

Rosamond Rhodes

It is now commonplace to view medical ethics as the application of traditional ethical theory to questions of ethics that arise in medicine. That well-entrenched view is reflected in the vast bioethics literature of the past 30-odd years. Starting with that assumption, authors discuss autonomy in Kantian terms, allocation of scarce resources in utilitarian terms, access to health care in terms of rights theory, and professionalism in terms of virtue theory. This dominant view was articulated by K. Danner Clouser in his *Encyclopedia of Bioethics* article on "Bioethics" where he explained that "bioethics is not a new set of principles or maneuvers, but the same old ethics being applied to a particular realm of concerns,"(Clouser, 1978). The strategy is further explained by Clouser and colleagues Bernard Gert and Charles M. Culver in *Bioethics: A Return to Fundamentals* when they identify ten moral rules as the crux of ordinary morality (Gert et al., 1997). It is also the approach most prominently expounded by Tom Beauchamp and James Childress in the five editions of their *Principles of Medical Ethics* (Beauchamp and Childress, 2001). In those volumes they identify the four principles of respect for autonomy, beneficence, nonmaleficence, and justice as the common features of prominent moral theories, and they show how to apply these principles to the practice of medicine.

The primary aim of this chapter is to challenge that common assumption and to make the case for the distinctiveness of medical ethics. This is not a claim about the uniqueness of the medical profession or an idea that originates with me. Here I follow John Rawls who notes that "the distinct purposes and roles of the parts of the social structure . . . explains there being different principles for distinct kinds of subjects" (Rawls, 1993: 262). Perhaps every profession has its own set of moral rules and requires a distinctive sort of character from its members. Perhaps there are areas of the social world in addition to the professions that also have distinctive sets of moral rules. Exploring those questions goes beyond my limited scope which is only to challenge the common view that medical ethics is just ordinary morality applied to the complex issues that arise as dilemmas in clinical medicine, largely as a response to remarkable technological advances in the field.

To make my case, I first present an argument for holding that medical ethics is different from the common morality of everyday life. After showing just how distinctive the ethics of medicine is, I construct an account to explain the core set of distinguishing principles of medical ethics and the medically specific uncommon justifications for them. Finally, I highlight important moral implications of this dramatic new view of the ethics of medicine.

The Distinctiveness of the Ethics of Medicine

Clouser expressed the reigning view in his sweeping claim that "bioethics is not a new set of principles or maneuvers, but the same old ethics being applied to a particular realm of concerns." This is a universal claim that reports the widely shared position that there is nothing distinctive about the moral principles of medicine or the moral virtues of a physician. According to the laws of logic, a single counter-example refutes such a universal claim. While logically speaking, one counter-example should be enough, because the belief that the ethics of medicine is just ordinary morality has come to be so generally accepted, I invite readers to consider a number of examples that should amount to a compelling argument for the distinctiveness of medical ethics.

Today, I have not killed anyone. I have not stolen anything. As far as I can tell, I have not inflicted any harm on anyone. And, so far, I have not spoken more than perhaps a little white lie. In the eyes of most observers, my actions today would be judged rather well. After all, the bulk of our moral responsibility in ordinary life is negative. We must refrain from harming others by not killing, stealing, injuring, or deceiving. Yet, a doctor who merely did what I did and sat in the Emergency Department reading her own newspaper and drinking her own coffee would not be taken to have acted well. That is because in medicine, doctors and other health professionals have a positive duty to respond to patient needs and actively promote their good.

In ordinary life, we are free to associate with whomever we choose. In fact, we were taught, and we teach our children, to be careful in the choice of friends. We are supposed to attentively distinguish between people based on their character and reputation. We are supposed to avoid the unsavory and those who might have a bad influence on us, and to seek out those who are likely to be good role models. But in medicine, doctors are supposed to be non-judgmental and to minister to every patient's medical needs without discrimination.

In our everyday lives, we are free to care most about those who are closest to us. We bestow gifts on those who are nearest and dearest. We invite those whose company we enjoy to our homes. We are expected to give our love only to a select special few. In medicine, however, doctors are supposed to care about the well-being of each patient and bestow their caring attention on each. In fact, doctors are required to avoid the intrusion of special personal attachments to favorite patients and to allocate the scarce resources at their disposal such as intensive care beds, transplant organs, their time, their energy, and their comforting smiles with fellow-love for every patient, (Rhodes, 1995).

In ordinary relationships we expect those nearest and dearest to act on behalf of their loved ones who cannot make decisions for themselves. Parents select the names for their children, they choose whether or not to inculcate religious beliefs, they decide on where to raise them, what to feed them, and the schools they should attend. Family members typically make decisions on behalf of elderly relatives who have lost their decisional capacity. We count on spouses, offspring, and siblings to choose where demented family members should reside, to make decisions about their health care, and to oversee the management of their finances. In medicine, however, doctors are expected to refer family members to the care of other clinicians precisely because their strong feelings can interfere with clinical judgment.

In the course of ordinary social interactions, we freely share our experiences. We tell one another about what we learn in the course of our daily lives, what we do, and what we discover about others. We convey information about who can and who cannot be trusted to repay a loan, about which restaurants serve good food, which teachers grade fairly, who is speaking with whom, whose relationships are on the rocks, which doctor was hours late for an appointment, and which dentist has a gentle touch. This sharing of information is useful and entertaining, and it is very much a part of the fabric of our lives. We are free to impart what we learn, and exceptions actually require explicit requests for keeping divulged information in confidence (e.g., making promises, signing non-disclosure agreements) or some special understanding arising from the details of an intimate relationship. In medicine, at least since the time of Hippocrates, confidentiality is presumed, although some exceptions can be justified.

Most people today consider sexual activity among consenting adults to be ethically acceptable. Unless force, deception, or indecent exposure is involved, sexual interactions between adults are morally acceptable. In medicine, however, disclosure and consent do not legitimize a physician's sexual involvement with a patient. We expect that a patient's invitation for a tryst will be declined and that one would not be issued to a patient by a doctor even when all of the parties are adults and no force or deception is involved.

In ordinary social situations, it is considered rude to ask probing and personal questions. I have heard that in Texas you never ask a man how much money he has or how much land he has. But in reality, the boundaries on polite conversation are far more constraining. We do not usually inquire about the details of other people's sex lives, their constipation, their drug use, or even their diet. Many people don't speak about death or disease or emotions, and lots of people studiously avoid discussion of politics. Yet, taking a complete and detailed patient history includes asking about a patient's diet, bowel habits, sexual practices, drug use, previous illnesses, and fears.

The morality of ordinary life requires us to consider others as autonomous and to respect their choices. Immanuel Kant instructs us to "cast a veil of philanthropy over the acts of others" (Kant, 1983, p. 466). This injunction amounts to asking us to see the acts of others as if they were chosen with thoughtful consideration and for reasons that the other actually endorses. For the most part, the Kantian attitude of respect commands that we leave others alone and that we allow them to advance their own conception of the good. And even doctors observe this rule when they are outside of their clinical setting. When they see others smoking cigarettes, they walk by with respectful disregard even though they worry about cancer. They hold their tongues when they observe others sporting multiple tattoos or numerous items of body piercing jewelry, even though they are concerned about hepatitis. They even remain silent as overweight others indulge in decadent desserts, but think all the while about the dangers of obesity and high cholesterol diets. Nevertheless, in a visit to the doctor's office, it is hard to imagine that a good doctor would fail to admonish a patient about the risks of cancer, hepatitis, or obesity. Physicians are not allowed to presume that their patients are acting autonomously. Instead, they are responsible for the vigilant assessment of patients' decisional capacity, and they are sometimes required to take steps to oppose patients' stated preferences (e.g., the patient who refuses an appendectomy for a ruptured appendix out of fear that her body will be invaded by aliens through the incision).

Such considerations suggest that the ethics of everyday life is significantly different from the ethics of medicine in dramatic and important ways. Together these examples show that the reigning view of medical ethics as ordinary morality applied to high-tech medicine should be set aside. If we do that, however, we need a new framework for understanding the special responsibilities of medicine that can fill the role of the anachronistic displaced accounts of medical ethics and provide a structure for reasoning about questions of how to proceed ethically in matters of clinical practice. Allow me to offer an account that explains the distinctive principles of medical ethics and the reasons why they must be so.

The Distinctive Ethics of Medicine

Imagine yourself in a strange city overcome with vomiting and abdominal pain. You are taken by ambulance to a hospital where you know no one. A stranger in a white coat pries you with detailed questions about your symptoms, your personal and family history, your sexual and drug history, and when you last had a bowel movement. You disclose information that you might not be willing to share with even your most intimate relations. Then the stranger asks you to disrobe and begins to handle and probe your body, even touching sexually sensitive areas and fingering you in ways that hurt. After a while, the stranger declares that you will have to submit to tests that you never would have otherwise sought (e.g., barium enema) or ingest some medication (i.e. a chemical that is likely to have toxic properties). Imagine further, that the next morning the stranger announces that you will have to allow yourself to be made unconscious so that your body can be invaded by knives and body parts will be removed. It is very hard to imagine that you would submit to this treatment from anyone but a doctor. And for a doctor to be permitted to do any of these things, albeit for your own good, the doctor must, to some degree, be *trusted*.

This little vignette demonstrates that trust is at the core of medicine. Society allows physicians to develop special knowledge and skills that could be particularly dangerous to members of society if physicians were not constrained by medicine's powerful professional morality. Doctors are allowed to learn about anatomy and physiology, pharmacology, and biochemistry. Doctors are also permitted extraordinary powers and privileges that could be a hazard if used carelessly, recklessly, or without goodwill. Physicians are allowed to ask probing questions and examine nakedness (i.e., invade privacy), they are given license to prescribe medications (i.e., poisons), they are granted the privilege to perform surgery (i.e., assault with deadly weapons when performed by anyone else). Although medicine is granted these uncommon commissions, society provides them on the condition that medicine can be trusted to wield them for the good of patients and society.

People appreciate their susceptibility to injury and disease. So, with respect to medical need, they would want attention from skilled and knowledgeable practitioners who could cure disease, alleviate symptoms, restore function, and ease suffering. These realizations create a broadly accepted consensus that the distinctive knowledge, skills, powers, and privileges that society allows to doctors must be used for the good of patients and society. This is the core of medicine's *fiduciary responsibility*, and it requires doctors to put their patients' good before their own.

Misplaced trust can be dangerous to people's health, and a lack of trust impedes medicine's ability to provide services. Yet, to the extent that medicine provides care, patients have to invest doctors with role-based trust. Combining these insights about trust and medicine makes a further point, that a foundational principle of the ethics of medicine is "trust." It is essential for clinicians and the institutions of medicine to be trustworthy and to seek the trust of patients and society in all of their actions. Every physician who considers the context of medical practice cannot fail to acknowledge it. No patient who vividly imagines what is being undertaken would want it any other way. All prospective patients – everyone, that is – want doctors to be trustworthy.[2] And so, all doctors must accept *seek trust and deserve it* as their moral law. In deciding what to do and how to do it they must pay attention to promoting trust and not eroding it. And in molding themselves as physicians they must focus on making themselves trustworthy practitioners.

Furthermore, we must recognize that patients need to trust, and actually do trust, doctors who are total strangers to them (e.g., think of the emergency room setting).[3] They trust because a history of doctors (for the most part) acting for their patients' good has made medicine trustworthy.[4] Physicians today are the heirs of trust that was engendered by those who came before them, and their actions today create the legacy for those who will come after. As beneficiaries of their pre-decessors' trustworthiness, and as those who create the reputation which the next generation of physicians will inherit, doctors also have the responsibility of acting to ensure that the profession of medicine will deserve its necessary trust.

Because the profession and institutions of medicine are social goods and social artifacts, and because individuals make themselves vulnerable by trusting medical institutions and clinicians based on their social role, medicine's basic principles require broad endorsement from the profession. In other words, patients need to trust their doctors from the first moment of their first visit. They know little about medical science and medical procedures, yet they yield to the advice of their physicians. They can hardly know enough about their individual doctors for their requisite trust to be earned as an individual achievement. Trust is extended by patients and their families because the doctor wears the white coat and carries the professional title. Similarly, society extends a monopoly for the authority to assure the trustworthiness of individual practitioners and medical institutions to the over-sight of the profession with the expectation that medical institutions can be trusted to meet their needs. In sum, patients and society rely upon medicine to be trust-worthy. Their reliance and the conditions of medicine's monopoly over medical practice explain the importance of trust and the importance of clinicians conforming with "the standard of care." The role-based trust of medicine means that doctors are not counted upon for their personal judgment but for providing treatment accord-ing to medical science and the well-accepted principles of medical practice.

Several further specific principles of medical ethics can be explained as features of medicine's fiduciary responsibility, or as necessary means to achieving or maintaining trust, or as derivations from an understanding of trust. In these ways, the fiduciary responsibility of medicine and the commitment to trust generate the moral force of the most commonly recognized ethical duties of physicians. The account of the ethics of medicine is, therefore, markedly different from the common justification of ordinary morality. Allow me first to explain several principles that are common to most accounts of medical ethics, but here as deductions from the two foundational principles of medical ethics rather than as features of ordinary morality.

Caring (aka beneficence)

Because patients are more inclined to trust a doctor who they believe genuinely *cares* about their good, doctors must also be compassionate. For everyone, ethical conduct involves an emotional component. Beyond the psychological appeal of a caring doctor, physicians, in particular, need to feel caring concern for their patients' well-being in order to be trustworthy. Caring is a prophylactic against the ethical danger of making clinical judgments that reflect self-interest rather than patient interest, and it also protects against the moral hazard of finding good excuses rather than doing what one should. Furthermore, in order for patients to trust their doctors and accept their medical recommendations, patients need to believe that their doctors are acting from caring rather than selfishness (Rhodes, 1995).

Respect for autonomy (aka respect)

To be trusted, doctors have to pay serious attention to the patient's view of what is good. People like to have their own way, and when decisions are intimately concerned with the patient's own body and life, differences between alternatives can be tremendously important to them. Sometimes a doctor's view of what is best can be at odds with a patient's view. In some circumstances a patient will actually consider the doctor's choice to be no good at all. Because doctors need their patients' trust and because patients need to feel confident that their doctors will not impose their personal values or priorities and thereby, in the patient's eyes, cause harm, the patient's ranking of goods, or respect for patient autonomy, has to be incorporated into the professional commitments of the physician.

Respect for patient autonomy also requires that doctors commit themselves to truth telling. Patients who want to make treatment decisions or choices about other matters in their own lives require information about their diagnosis and prognosis to reach informed conclusions. Furthermore, for patients to trust that their situation is as described and not actually worse than described, they need to be able to rely upon their physician's word. Hence, truth telling is part of the ethics of medicine as an aspect of showing respect.

Whereas ordinary morality allows people to distance themselves from the unpalatable choices of others, that luxury is incompatible with the practice of medicine. Medicine's fiduciary responsibility requires physicians to use their knowledge and skills to promote their patients' good. Respect for autonomy in this sense requires physicians to accept their patients' view of the good life and their patients' ranking of values. This commitment, for instance, requires a doctor to accept a Jehovah's Witness's refusal of a blood transfusion even when the commitment appears irrational and silly to a non-believer, and to provide what the physician takes to be the second-best treatment option when that is the choice of a competent patient.

Clinical justice (aka justice)

Although most philosophic treatments of the ethics of medicine endorse principles of justice, they typically fail to appreciate the distinctiveness of clinical justice. In many life activities different principles for the allocation of resources are employed. For instance, in civic elections everyone gets one vote, that is, an equal amount. When it comes to allocating tickets for a blockbuster movie, we rely upon the first come/first served principle of distribution. Honors are distributed according to past achievements. Respect is often accorded to the aged and protection to the young. Research grants are awarded to those who promise the greatest future contribution. Places around our holiday dinner table go to family members and our closest friends. While these allocation principles may each be just in particular contexts, only a distinctive few principles of justice are acceptable for the allocation of medical care. Consider the emergency room. There, in the allocation of limited medical resources, urgency matters, need matters, and in circumstances of extraordinary scarcity, efficacy matters. Then, for those who are similarly situated with respect to urgency, need, and efficacy, patients are treated similarly. Giving the same to each is explicitly not the rule in medicine. Neither do other such considerations like age, past contribution to society, promise of future contribution, or personal attachment, which may be appropriate for other distributions, play a part in the allocation of clinical resources. Hence, allocations according to principles of clinical justice (i.e., urgency, need, efficacy, and treating all similarly situated patients similarly) is a distinctive part of medical ethics.

The importance of these principles in the ethics of medicine is relatively uncontroversial. The content of these principles, however, is somewhat transformed by this derivation. Also, their justification, in terms of medicine's fiduciary responsibility and the need for trust in the doctor–patient relationship, is a significant departure from the usual accounts of medical ethics as common morality. Beyond these principles which appear in other accounts, consider some further principles of medical ethics that do not appear in common morality but are special features of the ethics of medicine.

Professional competence

To be trustworthy the doctor must, of course, be knowledgeable and skilled, be fully informed of the most recent clinical studies, and be able to assess their strengths, weaknesses, and implications. Without professional competence, the physician is not deserving of trust. Competence, therefore, is more than a matter of competitive pride, personal curiosity, ambition, or prudence. Being knowledgeable and skilled is essential to trustworthiness and, hence, a moral obligation of physicians. Someone who assumes the title "doctor" and pretends to practice medicine without competence is a charlatan and a quack. "Be competent" and "Be a lifelong learner" are, therefore, principles of medical ethics.

Assess decisional capacity

As part of their fiduciary responsibility, the ethics of medicine requires physicians to constantly assess a patient's decisional capacity so as to determine when, and to what extent, paternalistic intervention may be required. Because life and future function may be on the line, and because disease, medication, and psychological distortions (e.g., fear, denial) can all impede patients' judgment, doctors are expected to assess decisional capacity and to intervene with patients whose impaired preferences threaten health. Sometimes the intervention requires repeating a warning (i.e., unwelcome remedial education), sometimes cajoling, sometimes involving family members to ratchet up the level of guilt, sometimes going so far as taking a judgment-impaired patient to surgery over objection. Such judgments require first accepting the responsibility for the assessment of decisional capacity and then adopting the attitude of making such determinations about patients' capacity as a matter of professional responsibility. Hence, assess capacity is a principle of medical ethics.

Confidentiality

Since doctors need their patients to divulge intimate personal details about their behavior and their history, patients must be able to trust their doctors to keep that information as private secret matters that are only shared within the medical context on a need to know basis. Without the assurance of confidentiality, patients would be far less likely to share personal information with their doctors. Confidentiality is different from the ordinary morality concept of "privacy." "Privacy" is an individual's protected domain of activity that is shielded from the intrusion of others. "Confidentiality" is the means for creating an additional, distinctive, socially protected space for sharing specific information among a cohort of others who are committed to using that information in the service of that individual.[5] We find such protected space in medicine, but also in law and the ministry. Maintaining confidentiality is, therefore, a very high priority of medical ethics. In medicine, trust provides a direct justification for ranking confidentiality as one of the most essential moral commitments of the profession. This perspective makes it clear that individual physician's violations of confidentiality put the public's general trust of medicine in jeopardy, and it shows that confidentiality has significant moral weight for medicine as a profession.

Non-sexual regard

Everyone knows that sexual abuse is a horror. When a doctor engages in sexual abuse, however, the offense seems much more significant. In ordinary morality the wrongness of sexual abuse comes from the violation of autonomy. In medicine, the wrongness of physician sexual involvement with patients comes from the breech of the fiduciary relationship. Doctors are allowed special license, powers, and privileges that are denied to others. They are trusted to use that set of liberties only for their patients' good. So, for a doctor to take advantage of opportunities to acquire knowledge of intimate details about a patient's life, or to capitalize upon occasions for observing nudity or for sexual touching, or to exploit the effect of drugs on a patient is an abuse of the fiduciary relationship. Doctors need their patients to trust that the intimacy of the doctor–patient relationship has no sexual overtones in spite of the revelation, the nudity, and the touching. Anxiety or suspicion about a doctor's sexual intentions would seriously undermine the doctor's ability to provide patient care. The well established practice of carefully draping a patient during examinations and procedures expresses the importance of non-sexual regard as well as commitments to caring, respect, and confidentiality.

Non-judgmental regard

Great wits are often especially adapt at identifying flaws in others and making them the butts of jokes and the objects of derision. In times of war, people feel free to hate the enemy. And, frequently, we think that others should be held accountable for their own misfortune. Yet, when it comes to medical care, we want doctors to attend to our loved one's needs regardless of whether or not they were somehow at fault and regardless of their worth in the eyes of others. In fact, we expect physicians to provide excellent medical care to prisoners with medical needs and to wounded enemy soldiers. Because we never know how unworthy we or our loved ones may appear in the eyes of others, or where or how disheveled one of us is likely to be when we happen to need medical attention, we expect doctors to promote the good of those with medical needs without first judging their worth. Physicians have to be non-judgmental in their allocation of caring concern and medical attention, and they have to try hard to avoid feeling frustrated by patient non-compliance or angered by patient deception, disrespect, or demandingness.

Response regulation

Although being spontaneous and carefree may be desirable qualities in social relationships, doctors have to studiously consider and choose their responses. When most people see blood gushing or physical injuries, they pull away in horror and fear of causing further harm. Doctors have to learn to respond in exactly the opposite way – they are required to apply pressure to stop the bleeding and to explore the injuries in order to repair them. Others may freely display their reactions to the behavior and character of others. As part of their commitment to non-judgmental regard, doctors must not. One colleague explains that he gets a relatively accurate picture of a patient's behavior by framing questions with exaggerated expectations. "So, how much do you drink a day, about a case of beer and a quart of booze?" Putting the question that way shows a patient that even an excessive response will be accepted. It allows him to shrug and reply, "No, not so much, only a six pack and about a pint." Doctors have to contain their revulsion to the sights, smells, and touches that others can freely express and they have to act as if they are not fearful when they are. The doctor also has to convey bad news and compassionately share the grief with one family, then step into the corridor, compose herself, before walking in to the next room to share the joy of a good outcome with a patient who is now well and leaving the hospital. Being present in the moment and adopting the appropriate demeanor is part of the job. In one sense, these required reactions may seem disingenuous; in another sense, they resemble standard human interactions. Yet, it is the degree to which composure is required and the extent to which unnatural responses have to be incorporated into the medical response that makes regulated responses a principle of medical ethics.

Peer responsiveness

Poets and sculptors can do their work on their own. Medicine, however, requires collaboration and cooperation. Patients who are seriously ill require daily around-the-clock care. No single individual can meet that need. Patients with complicated conditions require expertise from a variety of specialties. No single individual has all of that knowledge and skill. Because the profession has the broad responsibility for meeting the medical needs of patients, and because each medical professional has a fiduciary responsibility to her patients, and because no medical professional can do the job alone, each has the responsibility to do his share in assisting colleagues to meet their patient responsibilities. This requires responding to requests from others for assistance (e.g., a consult, collaboration in a surgery) and being generous to peers with advice, education, and training.

Peer communication

Communicating what other medical professionals need to know in order to carry the torch of responsibility when it is their turn to take over is a closely related principle of medical ethics. Clinical findings (e.g., study results) and treatment plans all have to be communicated fully and honestly in order for other professionals to be able to do their jobs. Furthermore, the rationale for a treatment decision that may be unusual or controversial has to be explained to other members of the treatment team so that they are not left in the difficult position of either cooperating with a plan that appears to violate medical ethics or overriding the orders of a col-league. Sometimes such controversial decisions require peer discussion so that all of those who are engaged in the collaborative activity have an opportunity to raise their questions, to offer reasons for their positions, and to achieve a team consensus on how to proceed. Fulfilling the duty to communicate adequately with peers is particularly salient when orders are written (e.g., they must be legible), when shifts change, when different services are overseeing different aspects of a patient's care, and when a patient is transferred between institutions or discharged back to the oversight of a primary care physician. This responsibility can be discharged in face-to-face conversation, by phone, by relaying the information through other members of a team, or in some printed or electronic form. But it is not discharged until the message has been received and correctly understood.

Peer scrutiny

When a patient comes to see a doctor s/he typically has inadequate information for trusting and allowing the license that s/he does. A patient is seldom in a position to make competent judgments about a physicians' knowledge, skill, or character, and, in many medical situations, there is no appreciable opportunity for selecting a doctor (e.g., there is only whoever is on staff in the intensive care unit, or there is only one retina specialist in the region). Yet patients need to and do trust their doctors, and when the trust is undermined by unscrupulous behavior the profession's ability to deliver good care is impeded. So, for the profession to be able to continue to do its good work, medical professionals have to assure that their colleagues are trustworthy. That is to say, doctors have to take up, as a serious professional obligation, the duty to be their brothers' keepers and to keep their brothers to the profession's lofty standards. Peer scrutiny, peer criticism, and peer discipline are, therefore, required of individuals and the profession.

Together, these distinctive principles of medical ethics comprise the Ethical Standard of Care for medicine (Rhodes, 2006).[6] They are the profession-endorsed principles that should be used to guide medical behavior.[7] And just as the ethics of medicine is markedly different from the ethics of everyday life, the character of physicians must be similarly distinctive to enable them to act in accordance with their special duties. Virtues are the habitual inclinations to act and to feel as one should with respect to an object or a situation. They are the attitudes that dispose a person to choose and behave the right way. Because the principles of medical ethics are so markedly different from the principles of common morality, when doctors accept and endorse the Ethical Standard of Care they have to also commit themselves to developing the habitual inclinations and attitudes to dispose them to fulfill their professional responsibilities (Rhodes and Smith, 2006).

The Priority of Professional Ethics over Personal Morality

According to the account I have presented, medicine is not defined by a particular perfectionist conception of the good (e.g., health), or by naturalist concepts (e.g., disease, normal species function) or by teleological realism (e.g., *the* goal of medicine). Although a good deal of medicine involves preventing or healing disease and/or restoring function, defining medicine narrowly in those terms leaves out numerous medical roles. For example, we call upon medicine for the provision of prenatal care and birth control, even when no one is ill. We call upon medicine to ameliorate a dying patient's suffering, even when the disease cannot be healed nor function restored.

To understand the social role of medicine and its ethics, it is important to recognize that the medical profession is a social artifact created by giving control over a set of knowledge, skills, powers, and privileges exclusively to a select few who are entrusted to provide their services in response to the community's needs and to use their distinctive tools for the good of patients and society. Medicine is very much like other professions in this respect. Consider that firemen are called to rescue cats and children from tall trees and policemen are called to subdue escaped tigers even when no fire or law enforcement issues are involved. They have the wherewithal, so they get the job. Similarly, the special knowledge, powers, and privileges of medicine explain why assisted reproduction as well as birth control, pain management, and cosmetic surgery are included within the domain of medicine.

This account of the ethics of medicine brings a frequently overlooked issue to the floor, namely the place of personal morality or individual conscience in the practice of medicine. Again, the problem is not unique to the medical profession. In the military, soldiers owe obedience to the chain of command. Those in the military are not free to make their own judgments about which military actions are justified and how much force is appropriate. Instead they are obliged to follow the orders of higher ranking officers, who, in turn, must follow the direction of their political authorities. Similarly, lawyers and judges are not free to make decisions based on their own values and personal conscience. They are committed to following the rule of law even when their personal values dictate a different conclusion. Whereas the fact that professional responsibility overrides personal values is well accepted in other fields, those who write about the ethics of medicine typically ignore this element in their discussions, while some who consider the matter offer no justification but champion personal conscience over professional responsibility (Pellegrino, 1987; Pellegrino and Thomasma, 1993). The account of the ethics of medicine based on fiduciary responsibility and trust, leads, however, to the opposite conclusion.

As explained above, doctors are primarily trusted by patients because of their role. Patients and society expect doctors to act in accordance with the Ethical Standard of Care, and they rely upon them to meet that shared standard in all that they do. In other words, a patient who arrives in an emergency department does not expect Catholic medicine from a Catholic physician, Jehovah's Witness medicine from a Jehovah's Witness physician, self-centered medicine from an egoist physician, or the laying-on of hands from a physician who happens to believe in their power. Patients reasonably expect good medical practice in accordance with the standard of care from every physician. This means that medical practice is not a matter of private judgment. Rather, medical decisions should be the ones that any competent physician facing a comparable clinical situation would endorse as a matter of professional judgment.

Just as disagreements over treatment decisions have to be resolved by turning to the available evidence and the standard of care, conflicts between principles of medical ethics that arise in individual cases have to be resolved in terms of principle-related reasons that other medical professionals would also find compelling. Deviations from the Ethical Standard of Care have to be justified to peers in terms of principles of medical ethics or by special considerations about the patient's anatomy or values that colleagues from the profession would endorse as relevant reasons for a departure given the particular circumstances. In other words, we expect physicians to consult the clinical and ethical standards of care, rather than their individual heart of hearts in making medical decisions.

Although this all seems obvious when the focus is on the technical features of medicine, the point needs to be made explicit with respect to the ethical features of medical care. Individual physicians are not entitled to make individual, personal judgments about the dangers of treating HIV-positive patients or responding to a disaster. When it comes to providing treatment for patients who are HIV positive, each individual physician must provide treatment because, according to the judgment of the profession, the means for protection are effective and the risk of infection is not significant enough to defeat the professional duty to provide treatment. During a disaster, unless expert medical judgment determines that a situation is too dangerous for anyone to approach, physicians are required to assume the risk and provide the needed medical attention. In other words, personal priorities and personal assessment of risk have no place in the response of the medical professional. Individuals who have committed themselves to uphold the professional responsibilities of medicine, have, in essence, endorsed the Ethical Standard of Care, rather than personal conscience as their principles for making medical decisions.

Consider some additional instances in which an individual might want to refuse to provide medical care as a matter of personal judgment. Is it ethically acceptable for a doctor to refuse to provide life-preserving surgery to a Jehovah's Witness who refuses to accept blood transfusion because of the desire to avoid the personal pain of losing a patient who could have been saved? Is it morally acceptable to pass on the job to some willing but less experienced surgeon who is more likely to lose the patient during the course of the procedure? Is personal conscience a sufficient justification for refusing to provide pain medication to a suffering patient? Does personal discomfort or discretion justify refusing to disconnect the ventilator of a competent dying patient who has decided that he wants it no more?

When a physician chooses to act on his own values instead of honoring his patient's, the physician puts his own interest in ease of conscience above the fiduciary responsibility that is the defining feature of the ethics of medicine. The doctor who chooses to avoid personal psychic distress, declares his willingness to impose burdens of time, inconvenience, financial costs, and rebuke on his patients so that he might feel pure. Someone who places his own interests above his patients' departs from medicine's standard of promoting the patient's good and violates a crucial tenet of medical ethics that every physician is duty bound to observe.

Conclusion

This chapter argued that the ethics of medicine is different and distinct from the ethics of everyday life. In making my case, I challenged the common view of medical ethics as merely an extrapolation of the principles of ordinary morality. Instead, I offered an account of the basic moral principles for guiding the practice of medicine which should be seen as the Ethical Standard of Care.

Seeing medical ethics from the perspective of a commitment made to society to guide medical practice by profession-wide standards of care has two important consequences. First, it implies that clinician decisions must be informed by professional judgment, not personal judgment. Although peer judgment is largely irrelevant in personal morality, peer judgment is crucial in medical ethics. Patients and society rely upon physicians to provide treatment according to that standard and, for the most part, they cannot know enough about their doctors' personal values to choose them on any other basis. Thus, when a patient with decisional capacity requests, for instance, that a life-sustaining ventilator be disconnected, or desires a surgical procedure that an individual physician finds too disfiguring (e.g., Van Ness rotationplasty, translumbar amputation), or asks for birth control or pregnancy termination, the doctor is required to set aside personal values and refer to the Ethical Standard of Care in deciding how to proceed.

The second implication is that becoming a doctor is a moral commitment to give priority to the Ethical Standard of Care over personal values. Becoming a doctor is, therefore, also ceding authority to professional judgment over personal preference. Someone who is not prepared to make that commitment and practice medicine according to the professional standard should choose another livelihood in which such conflicts will not arise. Appropriately, the conscientious objector who takes seriously both her personal values and the obligations of medicine would be willing to pay the price of her commitments rather than ask others to bear the weight of her convictions.

Notes

1 This chapter weaves together arguments and themes from several previous works (Rhodes, 1995, 2001, 2006).

2 Unfortunately, medical treatment is sometimes delivered without a climate of trust. Patients have learned to be distrustful because of unfortunate experiences with untrustworthy physicians and our untrustworthy system of health care delivery. Distrustful patients do accept treatment when there is no better option. Yet, examples of distrust do not refute the claims that patients would prefer to be able to trust their doctors, that most doctors would prefer to be trusted by their patients, and that society grants special license to the profession of medicine on the expectation of trust.

3 Stell (1999) calls this "status trust" which he distinguishes from earned trust.

4 Baier (1994) focuses on trust that is earned through interaction. Her concept is illustrated by the example of rowers learning to trust one another by cooperating in rowing across a river together.

5 This language was provided by Alan D. Schlechter MD, in conversation.

6 I do not mean to claim that this list of responsibilities is complete. There may be some principles of medical ethics that I have overlooked. There are also other ways of identifying and describing them so that other lists may be longer or shorter, more detailed or more general.

7 Most accounts of medical ethics contain an account of a principle of non-maleficence (e.g., Beauchamp and Childress, 2001) or moral rules that require doctors not to cause death, pain, disability, loss of pleasure of loss of freedom (Gert et al., 1997). In medicine, doctors frequently speak of the "do no harm" principle which is taken as a gloss of the Hippocratic standard of medical ethics. I do not include a separate discussion of such a concept for two reasons. In one sense, it is merely a rule that expresses the negative content of ordinary morality. Hence, it is not a specific feature of the ethics of medicine. In another sense, it is an expression of medicine's fiduciary responsibility and its content is explained in other sections on fiduciary responsibility, caring, and respect for autonomy. Some consequences of a medical intervention are beneficial, others, however, are harmful. It is always important for physicians to assess and compare both sorts of consequences and their likelihood in determining a course of treatment. Nevertheless, because what we call "good" is highly subjective, for the most part, the ethics of medicine also requires incorporating the perspective of the patient and accepting the patient's view of the good or the patient's rankings of goods.

References

Baier, A. (1994), *Moral Prejudices*, Cambridge, MA: Harvard University Press.

Beauchamp, T.L. and Childress J.F. (2001), *Principles of Biomedical Ethics*, 5th edn., New York: Oxford University Press.

Clouser, K.D. (1978), Bioethics, in W. Reich (ed.) *Encyclopedia of Bioethics*, 1st edn., New York: The Free Press, pp. 532–42.

Gert, B., Clouser, K.D., and Culver, R. (1997), *Bioethics: A Return to Fundamentals*, New York: Oxford University Press.

Kant, I. (1983), *The Metaphysical Principles of Virtue*, (Part II of *The Metaphysics of Morals*) translated by James W. Ellington in *Ethical Philosophy*, Indianapolis, IN: Hackett Publishing Company.

Pellegrino, E.A. (1987), Toward a reconstruction of medical morality, *The Journal of Medical Humanities* 8 (1): 7–18.

Pellegrino, E.D. and Thomasma, D.C. (1993), *Virtues in Medical Practice*, New York: Oxford University Press.

Rawls, J. (1993), *Political Liberalism*, New York: Columbia University Press.

Rhodes, R. (1995), Love thy patient: justice, caring and the doctor–patient relationship, *Cambridge Quarterly of Healthcare Ethics* 4 (4): 434–47.

Rhodes, R. (2001), Understanding the trusted doctor and constructing a theory of bioethics, *Theoretical Medicine and Bioethics* 22 (6): 493–504.

Rhodes, R. (2006 in press), The ethical standard of care, *American Journal of Bioethics*, 2006.

Rhodes, R. and Smith L.G. (2006), Molding professional character, in N. Kenny and W. Shelton (eds.), *Lost Virtue: Professional Character Development and Medical Education*, Advances in Bioethics, vol. 10, Oxford: Elsevier, pp. 99–115.

Stell, L.K. (1999), Diagnosing death: what's trust got to do with it? *The Mount Sinai Journal of Medicine* 66 (4): 229–235.

Chapter 5

Truth Telling

Roger Higgs

Telling the truth is one of life's basic rules. Why should this subject still be of concern in medicine? One answer was provided by a recent discussion in a post-graduate seminar. Looking back at some of the perplexities of her early medical training, a specialist now in middle life described her first day as a junior in a surgical team in the UK in the 1980s. Exhausted after a night of emergency admissions, she was flustered by the irascible style of her new boss on the next day's ward round, and was unclear about whether some important tests had been performed or not. The senior, in response, suggested she was covering up an inadequate performance, and warned her not to tell lies on his unit. A few minutes later, as the team round reached an elderly man with widespread metastases, she was instructed by the same senior not to tell the patient how near death he was. At the end of the round, brushing past some bedside lilies in his expensive suit, her boss left for his private office with a big yellow pollen stain on the sleeve of his jacket. She decided to stay silent.

Bullying behavior is never acceptable, but that was not the point of her story. She was presenting the struggle to reconcile three common strands of thinking deeply embedded in the tradition of most societies. Lying is unacceptable behavior, but doctors seem to have been allowed from time long past to "treat truth like a medicine" when difficult news was to be given to a patient. Beyond this, to add to the confusion, in most cultures politeness (sometimes combined, as above, with less honorable motives) prevents people from being immediately or totally sincere in their day-to-day conduct, in personal areas such as emotional feelings, deep motivation, or reactions to other people's appearance. Different social settings may change the way a balance is struck in these three areas of human behavior, but the central issues remain. Are there times when being less than truthful is justifiable? Is this particularly so in medical practice? If it is, what might these justifications be? Do clinicians really have a special dispensation from telling the truth to their patients, and if so why and in what circumstances? More broadly, are all deceptions tantamount to lies, or are other ways in which truth is withheld from other people more acceptable? Should the practice of health care be conducted under a rubric of openness, as is the stated aim (whether achieved or not) of many public services in western democratic societies, or are there good reasons for holding back?

The Clinical Task

In attempting to provide a response to some of these questions, it will be important for both reader and writer to keep their feet firmly on the ground of the real world (or real ward). The scene painted by the physician above contained some important contextual features. There are many conflicting demands on a professional's time and attention. There must be very few clinicians who have not forgotten to do something in the pressure of normal practice. If the omission appears to make no difference to the outcome, most will feel a strong temptation not to own up but just move on to the next pressing task. The anxious newcomer to a task, it could be claimed, might cause dangerous disruption to the flow of the business in hand by constant checking or by over-meticulous explanation. Yet, any leader of a clinical team has the multiple tasks of reviewing activity, maintaining standards and training new staff: they would expect to be kept in the picture and told the truth.

Just as the first clash was understandable, so was the second. Even if patients nowadays in many countries expect their physicians to be more straightforward with them than used to be the case, there are still many, from an older generation or from other cultures, who might want to be approached differently. In situations of uncertainty where the medical condition is probably untreatable (or the consequences of a misunderstanding in communication so dire) there is a temptation for physicians to avoid the issue. At least, many would say, it still makes sense to think twice before the worst prognosis is voiced. Where a patient is very anxious, depressed or just not in an emotional state to take difficult information on board, it seems unkind or quite wrong to add to their distress. Yet this clearly leaves the most important person involved in the dark, unable to make a decision perhaps because he is not aware there is a decision to be taken. A person cannot consent if they do not know what they are consenting to. The standards covering consent are both professional and legal.

It would be strange if personal standards were not as high as professional ones but they might be different. We all like to be thought of as truthful, and to lose the trust of people we admire would always be a personal tragedy. To be called a liar, as the young doctor thought she was, is a deep insult. But there is a point for everyone where they would not think they were expected to be open, marking the boundaries of a "private space" which no one should expect to visit uninvited, as it were. Someone could be reticent, silent, or evasive about their own thoughts or their private lives: though they risk being thought dull, distant, or very deep, no one would lose trust in them. Everyone is a person at work as well as in their home life, and physicians are also expected, in some sense, never to be totally off duty. So the boundary between personal and professional lives is one to which health professionals should give special and careful attention.

It would be a relief if the problems of truth telling in medical practice were to stop there, as there is more than enough, it may seem, to be thinking about. But clearly they do not. Emergency work may appear to have its own "rules of engagement" but similar problems appear in everyday encounters between patient and professional, however routine these may appear to be. Where a possible new and serious diagnosis presents itself, a clinician must think when and how this should be voiced. A diagnosis is usually not absolutely certain but a matter of probability, and a prognosis even more so. Both require care so that the way they are expressed makes sense to a lay person. All drugs have side effects. Some are important, some trivial or well known. No doctor could manage routine clinical work and talk about them all. Choices have to be made.

Where there are more than two in a clinical encounter, the plot inevitably thickens. A different professional may make a different evaluation. A relative may be even more conscious of the distress the patient may suffer, and may urge the clinician to make light of the situation, perhaps, very understandably, saying that an untruth should be told "to keep hope alive."

Sometimes routine tests may reveal to the physicians something totally unexpected, whose relevance and importance are hard to assess: they might wonder when, if ever, this should be shared with the patient. Perhaps the notes of previous encounters reveal a colleague's error. If this error amounts to malpractice, or the news may be of potential financial benefit to the patient, there might be disagreement as to whose side the physician should be on. If, in the reverse situation, an agency or individual is not taking a vulnerable patient's case seriously enough, people differ about where the line is to be drawn between advocacy and invention in "improving" the patient's story.

Truth and Truthfulness

Every walk of life and every branch of medicine must have its own peculiar dilemmas, temptations or pitfalls. The discussion is potentially endless. How can we bring some sense of order to such an array? Most people respond to decisions about whether to tell the truth in their private lives quite rapidly, perhaps apparently almost instinctively. Can the discussion in medicine be cut short too? There are two possible strategies to achieve this, one of which reframes the problem and "exports" it, as it were, and one which takes it head on. The first was perhaps most clearly enunciated in an article by Lawrence Henderson (1955). "It is meaningless to speak of telling the truth, the whole truth and nothing but the truth to a patient . . . because it is a sheer impossibility." It is all too complex, too much is uncertain. If telling the truth were in this way impossible, he argued, there could be no hard and fast distinction between what might be true and what could be false, and so the question would no longer be important. This view strikes a chord with many doctors, particularly early in their careers. The volume of factual information required to practice medicine is huge, and mastery is a matter of years of training, however bright the student is. It would be impossible to get all this across to someone who has no medical experience, particularly if their mind is untutored or clouded by anxiety or illness. Most doctors in training also struggle themselves with conceptual issues: the medical facts, told from different angles, simply do not come together as a whole, until a moment, perhaps when something "clicks." (In some areas of the subject maybe it never does, and so the medical student quietly closes off these options of work, and decides, say, that psychiatry or neonatology is simply "not for me.") In the face of such complexity, especially once the concepts of uncertainty and probability enter the field, it becomes difficult to know what one is trying to put across, let alone whether and how it should be done.

But this response involves both elements of special pleading – medicine, after all, is not the only, or even the most, complex area of thinking affecting ordinary people – and conceptual confusion. In questions of truth telling in medicine, the issue at stake, as Bok (1980) made clear, is not usually one of "truth" as an abstract entity, but of *truthfulness*. It is not about whether some statement or artifact actually represents the world as it is (or whether such a world exists) but more simply about whether the speaker or actor *intends to deceive*. This response returns the issue from the philosophical debate to the motives of the agent and her skills in communication. Factual accuracy is vital, here as elsewhere, but what is at issue is what the professional intends to get across to her patient.

An Absolute Duty?

Leaving aside for the moment the question as to whether all deceptions are the equivalent of lies, the argument is then thrown back to the opposite pole. We were all taught as children to tell the truth. Wherever this rule to us comes from (or for whatever reason it has force for us all), the question arises as to why we should not simply make this an inviolable and absolute rule. Although everyone is regularly tempted, the moral injunction would thus be clear, and not to be broken under any circumstances. Everyone would know where they stood. Immanuel Kant, the German philosopher, writing in the eighteenth century, made this point by suggesting that such injunctions only made sense if they were seen as universal or "categorical" imperatives (O'Neill, 1991). They were to be seen as rules that were not negotiable: they were to be obeyed *whatever*. In this view, anyone who did otherwise risked manipulating other people, treating them differently from how one expected to be treated oneself (in defiance of the Golden Rule), and so using them possibly as a means to an end, rather than respecting them as ends in themselves.

Such a direct and simple rule seems to fit well with some aspects of modern health care, but its unwavering clarity in some senses is its undoing. One of the problems lies in the absolute nature of the claim. If the word "absolute" means anything, it must be the only such claim: if there is a second but different absolute claim – for instance to save saveable lives – then it is only a matter of time before the two conflict, and one must trump the other. For instance, if it were thought that the sole survivor of a road accident were in such a delicate state of cardiovascular health that the distress of the truth about the other deaths might threaten survival, it would be hard to argue that the full story should be revealed and the truth told at that point. (Avoiding telling lies might be another matter.) Kant was aware of this problem of his approach, which has been debated at length by supporters and critics since. One refinement, which seems strangely not to have occurred to the philosopher himself, is to define the universal rule more narrowly, to cover the obvious and important clashes. But the importance of the style of thinking that Kant articulated probably lies elsewhere, in two main areas.

Giving Reasons, Respecting Autonomy

The first is Kant's insistence (echoed in philosophical thought before and since but given great emphasis in his work) on the prime importance of *reason*. The moral rules we live by should not be handed down unquestioned but should be backed by good and consistent reasons (Rachels, 1995, p. 125). The second, however, bears perhaps even more closely on medical practice. There can be no doubt that deceiving people will in some sense always diminish them. To treat people as an end in themselves, rather than as means to some else's end, must mean that their own views of those ends – in the sense of aim and purpose – must be paramount when it comes to decisions about things that are theirs and that matter to them. If they are able to make choices for themselves in matters of their own welfare, if they are in other words autonomous people, they must be allowed to do so. Specifically, if there is a difficult decision to be made about treatment, the final arbiter must be that person to be treated, the patient. No one could make such a decision without being appropriately informed about the options, and their consequences, and the reasons for and against each, so the professional must give that person as accurate a picture as can be given, on which she can make her decision. Anything less means that the professional is set up as more powerful than the patient, and indeed *more of a person* than the patient: if the patient's choice is abrogated, she is reduced to a means to the physician's (perhaps perfectly laudable) ends. The choices might even include whether or not to continue as a patient at all. It is hard to see how an autonomous person's choice could possibly be respected in health care unless they were told the truth about their condition.

Codes of Conduct

From this it follows that honest communication is at the heart of every modern statement in western countries about the duties of physicians. This wasn't always the case: the original Hippocratic oath mentioned nothing about the matter, and although it had long been an important area of debate it was probably first fully codified in 1973 (American Hospital Association): "The patient has the right to obtain from his physician complete current information concerning his diagnosis, treatment, and prognosis in terms the patient can reasonably be expected to understand." However, even this clarion call is less helpful than may initially appear. While "complete current information" may sometimes seem to expand beyond what is manageable, the onus is still left with the patient to demand, rather than with the physician to offer. Perhaps the problem is in what can be expected from codes: these are by definition stark, unnuanced statements that may offer strong guidance in direction of travel, but less help in the manner of the journey itself, or much of a clue about how to judge when the destination has been reached. What can be said, though, is that the justification for veracity, the underlying concept of respect for an autonomous individual's wishes, has become so central to medical care that it is also part of general law in every jurisdiction known to me, and underpins the modern relationship between doctor and patient worldwide.

So if telling the truth in medicine is a stringent requirement, both made by regulating bodies and backed by the law in many countries, in two circumstances this might be considered an absolute, or so near an absolute as makes little difference in practice. One would be when a physician is in court under oath. To deceive a court would be to run the risk of perjury, a criminal act in itself. A strong commitment to absolute confidentiality continues to pose problems for doctors: once again, here there are two apparent absolutes in conflict, and only one can triumph. It should remind us that a modified promise of confidentiality might, in practice, be best; that is one that has the rider (perhaps amongst others) "unless a legitimate court orders me to do otherwise." Also this reminds us once again that there may be other ways of answering questions truthfully than simply telling everything one knows. An obligation to tell the truth may be different from an obligation to reveal. If a doctor declared herself to be under a professional obligation not to say anything in response to a question, a court would have to take a view as to whether the issue was serious enough to warrant compelling a disclosure.

The second circumstance in medicine where truthfulness is clearly an overriding concept is in medical research. Though deception might be an element in the process of gathering data, where, for instance, a research subject had willingly agreed to a deception if necessary, or, more controversially, where a clinical area could not be studied without some deceptive element, nevertheless the reporting of the data gathered must be under an entirely different rubric. To be inaccurate would be bad enough, but to deliberately falsify data would mean that the researcher had broken the trust between science and the community it served. It is likely that the researcher would be dismissed from any scientific society worthy of the name, and would be stripped of his or her degree and license to practice medicine as well.

One of the answers from a scientific group asked to justify these reactions might help us to see truthfulness and deception from a slightly different angle. Most scientists do not give promises before they start work (though that might be implied by an application to a research ethics committee) nor do they take an oath. Trust in science in the community at large is always vulnerable to the negative influence of media reports and such like. So the discussion of scientific veracity is likely to include concerns about the perversion of outcomes: that false information would do harm directly by, say, suggesting a medication was more effective than it really was, or indirectly, by diverting the attention of other scientific work. Without attempting to cover the whole field, it could be said that some of the seriousness of deception in reporting scientific work lies in the bad *consequence*: and often specific, identifiable consequences rather than a general loss of trust. This opens the door, if only a crack, onto the idea of the reverse: that the *consequences* of truthfulness might also need to be taken into account sometimes. We have already seen that there might need to be a trade-off with saving life or confidentiality in some extreme circumstances. Could consequences of telling the truth, desirable or undesirable, modify the overall approach in medicine? Are physicians afraid of causing some harm, or hoping to achieve something better, when they avoid being open with patients?

Harm and Benefit

Many people still fear that they may come to more harm than good in doctors' hands. No one actually wants to receive bad news, any more than they want to have an anesthetic or an appendectomy. That doctors have to do unpleasant things on the way to curing people is axiomatic. It is the aim and intention of overall benefit that is crucial. The shock of bad news in itself has to be set against the need for the patient to understand, choose, or consent to the way forward. Information presented badly, without a plan of action, or without an explanation of how the professional would like to proceed, could be devastating. Without a long-term view, without discussion or follow-up, not only is the job half done but the harmful effects may ensue without the benefit of professional support, guidance, and review. What do patients themselves think?

To some investigators' surprise, when the question was asked initially in studies conducted in anglophone countries in the second half of the last century, the majority of correspondents, whether actually sick or being asked to imagine themselves as having a serious illness, wanted to know clearly from their physician what was the matter with them (Veatch, 1978). This has if anything become more marked over time, although it is by no means replicated in all cultural settings. Most studies, however, do also demonstrate that there is a minority who vote the other way. Circumstances may alter the views even of someone previously well known to the medical team. Mindful that a patient may be what Engelhardt (1996) called a "moral stranger," a physician must gain some impression, perhaps even by asking directly, of which camp the patient is in, or how much they wish to be involved. In some circumstances, where, say, the illness carries public or family risk, an explanation is mandatory. But a simple introduction may be all that is needed to begin a sensitive and satisfactory interaction. "In my experience, patients have different views about how they want me to manage information about their care. Would you prefer me to communicate directly with you, or with you and someone else, or is there some particular person you would like to have the information instead of you?"

The Physician Herself

An overview of medical practice, however, would probably still reveal that many physicians even today misunderstand their patients' needs and desires in this area. Why might this be? It may be that physicians want to save time: this may be short-sighted in its own terms, as well as a misunderstanding of their role. It may be that they mistakenly believe that their job is only to solve technical or physical problems in health care. These views contain their own solution: these are people either in the wrong job or needing to acquire relevant skills as a priority before a major complaint terminates their careers. My unproven hypothesis is that some physicians' reluctance to communicate bad news reflects their concerns about how such news would impact not on their patients but on *them*. Physicians make difficult patients, often displaying either "denial" or "panic." The old joke in medical school is that no doctor graduates without suffering from at least three lethal diseases. Even in the unimaginative, fear can work overtime. No one would wish the future generation of physicians to be less empathetic (were that possible, as the cynic might say) with their patients; but equally every clinician should be clear where personal boundaries lie. It is the patient's disease, from beginning to end, and the patient's reactions and choice that matter. If physician anxiety distorts the response, that problem should receive attention in its own right.

Accuracy and Trust

In my view, however, the issue of harm in truth telling is real, and needs evaluation. Yet the problem may lie in a very different place from that expected. Many patients have been disabled by careless medical talk which had no proper warrant: people told about asymptomatic murmurs, given prejudiced psychiatric diagnoses, or faulty gynecological assessments have been unnecessarily, and sometimes permanently, disabled not by a disease but by a physician's words. Second opinions are part of the routine of medical work. Perhaps second thoughts before giving a potentially damaging opinion should be as well. This said, the harms of not being honest may be greater. Were it to be widely thought that physicians would never share their concerns about a patient with that patient, it might be a short step to generalized loss of trust in the medical profession. Trust and confidence in the physician are necessary before the doctor can begin work, and may be on occasion the only effective tool available. At present in most western countries, doctors remain amongst the most trusted professionals or public servants. Yet errant individual professionals squander the profession's trust. Trust in a physician remains a precious but scarce source for increasingly fragmented and changing societies, and its benefits extend beyond individual care. It is something more to be earned than expected: its origins in each individual patient lie in a good experience of the doctor–patient relationship.

Talking to the Dying

Nowhere does trust in honest disclosure matter more than in the medical management of the process of dying, and yet this remains an area of moral confusion for many physicians (Higgs, 1999). In the nineteenth century and before, when very little of real benefit could be done for most patients by today's standards, physicians were nevertheless reported speaking openly to their patients about a poor prognosis and imminence of death (Beatty, 1998). Nowadays, although patients' fears of death are unlikely to be less (and may, with the waning of consolatory religious faith, if anything be greater) such conversations, or their modern counterpart, are not routinely heard. Aside from units which make special provision for care of the dying, the tendency is for physicians to present, or pretend they present, a continuing struggle to achieve cure, even as the chances of such an outcome reduce to zero. Some of this reluctance to discuss dying may be understandable: prognosis remains an inexact part of medical science, and the ways it is expressed professionally (whether framed as a percentage death rate or a survival rate) can make little or no sense to an individual sufferer. What doctors put across at this stage may have a different significance from what they say at other times. To a frightened individual what they say may seem more like a curse, or an extreme form of challenge, than a cool assessment of probable outcome. Nevertheless, a physician who cannot at least engage in discussion of dying (for reasons related to her attitude, communication skills, or work schedule) often condemns her patient to unpleasant isolation. He remains alone with his worst thoughts, and is desperately unprepared for some of the difficult but key decisions about changing therapeutic aims or methods as care succeeds cure in the final stages of his disease. Though some individuals might, in their imaginations, choose a sudden death for themselves, this is neither the likely mode for most people in the western world in the twenty-first century nor the aim of public health programs. We are at a point where all physicians, while enquiring sensitively about the patient's anxieties, need to be able to discuss prognosis openly and should be prepared to handle appropriately the facts and fears of a slowly approaching death.

There will be many occasions in this stage of work when a physician will be tempted or even asked to withhold the truth. The latter request, in my practice as a physician, has often come from relatives, who may even attempt to instruct the doctor not to discuss with the patient that he or she is dying. This may be understandable, given their own anxiety and grief, but the physician needs to be gentle but firm in her reminder about whose death it really is and, therefore, whose choices take precedence when it comes to communication, and indeed in all the decisions at this final stage of life. I reported (Higgs, 1982) a case where a patient was kept in a strange form of limbo by being denied by relatives an open discussion with her physician; when she created an opportunity for the exchange, she seems then to have made her mind up to die peacefully and with dignity.

Diminished Understanding

Many studies have indicated (such as Sullivan et al., 2001) that the more educated patients are the more they express a wish to be informed. Less happily, other work shows that the more a physician can identify with a patient, the more time (in settings like family practice) is allowed for the exchange. While the profession should not be proud of this apparent discrimination, it probably is quite predictable: everyone spends more time talking to people they like or identify with. But this issue gives particular concern when it is pushed the other way. Colleagues working in elderly care recently suggested that elderly patients in hospital *without* photographs of themselves in their youth or without obvious evidence of the quality of their former lives seem to get *less* attention from the care team. This report creates the impression of a sliding scale of open communication which is very different from the declared intentions of the medical and nursing professions to serve patients equally, to respect individual autonomy, and to inform. A study in the UK (Marzanski, 2000) with a small cohort of patients with definite dementia showed that the patients themselves, while often having adequate insight into their condition, had received very poor or even misleading information about what was wrong with them. While most wished to know more, nearly one third of these patients "preferred not to be informed . . . and their motives seemed to be diverse." On the one hand, routine disclosure might seem to be needed, but on the other hand, a formula might swiftly lead to the sort of openness that could be cruel or abusive. There seems little option but to make an individual assessment of what a particular person in his or her own individual circumstances wants, wherever possible appropriately in advance, while being aware that their views might change, and giving time to the follow-up work that might be required.

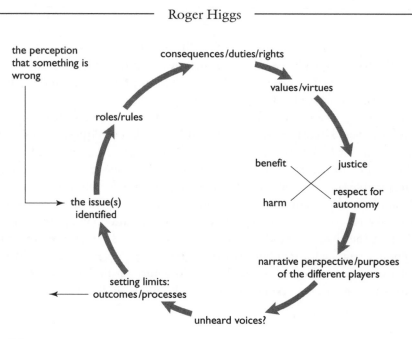

the perception that something is wrong

consequences/duties/rights

values/virtues

roles/rules

benefit

justice

harm

respect for autonomy

the issue(s) identified

narrative perspective/purposes of the different players

setting limits: outcomes/processes

unheard voices?

Figure 5.1

Increasing Complexity

Decisions in a context where the usual markers have become worn or are beginning to drift will always be difficult, and those concerned with whether or how much to tell are no exception. The passing of crucial information, like the breaking of confidentiality or the loss of a life, allows no turning back, and so where the best way forward is not clear the widest possible assessment is suggested. Individual philosophers may make their reputations by espousing and explaining a particular approach, but the best practice will require examination in as many ways and from as many different points of view as is possible in the context. Once the issue is identified, the type of pathway outlined in Figure 5.1 may help to assure the ground has been covered.

It may be that an individual person involved in the decision has a particular role to play which is less familiar but has its own special rules or responsibilities, like being a researcher, teacher, or team manager. This may require a particular approach, or the law may have detailed requirements of people playing these roles. It would be important then, broadly but in as much detail as possible, to define possible outcomes, important duties, and appropriate rights. As well as getting to know the moral stranger, the expressed and real values of the organization concerned may need to be examined. Balancing the four well-known principles may offer enlightenment, but as Campbell and I have maintained (Campbell and Higgs, 1982), a fully rounded picture is unlikely to be obtained unless the stories of those involved are heeded, the narrative which tries to encompass individual and group experience or expectations is heard, and the issue is examined for the different perspectives of all those who may be involved in the decision. In spite of this there may still be individuals, issues, or aspects of an organization whose voice is not properly being attended to: such "unheard voices" should be sought wherever possible. What is causing a problem may not be the difficulty of making the central decision but the concerns of another participant in the drama or worries about how to deal with the possible "side effects" of an otherwise good decision that may impede progress. For instance, where relatives of a dying patient ask strongly that a patient is not informed, they may well be saying something about their own distress or their own ability to cope. This distress may well need to be managed in its own right by the team: when it is addressed the original decision, say, correctly to inform a patient who wants information, may go ahead. The voice of the relatives' distress, unlistened to, may otherwise lead to complaints or continuing antagonism. We have seen above how a physician's own views about herself may color the picture, and a bad outcome elsewhere, say in the family of a member of the medical team or in the history of the institution, may continue to resonate unhelpfully unless acknowledged and dealt with.

Good resolution of a difficult decision may not be a quick process, any more than complex surgery can be performed at speed and without preparation. But decisions in heath care are usually time-limited. Something has to be done, and events will force a decision if one is not reached in appropriate time. So there will be limits to the amount of deliberation that is possible in most circumstances of health care. A "good enough" decision may well have to suffice to cover the requirements of the moment, but the team must remember that it needs to come back, in a cool time of reflection, to consider whether and how decisions might have been improved. The cycle suggested is one way of looking at a decision, which may not necessarily end with a change in decision outcome, but may improve – and speed up, rather than necessarily put the brake on – the process by which a decision is reached.

However complex and initially unwieldy such an approach may seem, a problem like whether to tell a patient about an incidental abnormal finding on a series of routine tests will require to be visited from many of the angles shown above. The particular *role* that the professional is in, for instance, may entail a prior commitment: the professional may be a teacher, researcher or manager, rather than a clinician. There may be clear claims by way of obvious *rights* to being informed that could be enunciated. The *consequences* of different lines of action may need to be explored. The openness of the *relationship* and the existence or not of trust are relevant, and the balancing of the *four principles* (particularly remembering the often forgotten issue of justice) undertaken with as much care as possible. Professionals, patients, and the organization itself may already have a background or declared aims which form part of "the story so far," but equally may involve the suppression of a point of view which needs to be brought out. None of the considerations raised by Figure 5.1 challenges the patient-centered dynamic of modern best practice, but many of these considerations may need to be addressed in order that such practice be sensitive and safe in the broadest terms.

Being Prepared

To have time to think deeply through all the aspects of a problem, however, is not a common experience in medicine. Often clinicians are confronted by something unexpected, which may catch them off their guard. For the junior intern whose story began this chapter, this meant that she was unnecessarily hesitant and so wrongly accused of lying. But the senior, while leaping to the wrong conclusion and behaving like a bully, was shrewd enough to realise that people are often tempted to lie when they are caught out unprepared. Most of us were taught at our mother's knee not to lie, and that lying is wrong, precisely because the temptation so often arises. Nothing that has been discussed here so far makes a lie less objectionable because it occurs in health care. The situation is quite the reverse: the harms stack up one after the other. A deceived person cannot take her own proper decisions about her future. Trust may be lost between individuals, and this may extend to the team or the system itself. A patient may decide to change to another doctor, discharge herself from care, go to a lawyer, or simply give up. The young intern might well be upset to be wrongly accused, but if her senior was sincere in his accusation it is hard to see how he could sleep easily at night knowing that a member of his team might not be honest to him on the ward.

If the temptation to lie should be resisted at all costs, however, it does not necessarily mean that the whole truth should be told without question. We have seen that there may be a clash because of the promise of confidentiality. The person asking for information may not have a right to it, or the person asked may not be the one who can or who should give a response. The time or place or company might be wholly inappropriate. Clinicians and others in health care should have responses ready to deal with such situations, and equally must have strategies to offer to make sure that the issue is properly followed up and resolved.

In human interaction the wise clinician acts not with robotic consistency but with skilled communication and sensitivity. A desperately ill patient may suddenly grab the physician's hand: "I will be all right, doctor, won't I?" To interpret this as a moment for telling the whole truth may well be to misunderstand what the question means. Panic and distress call initially for human comfort – holding hands, calm companionship, assurances of continuing concern and professional presence – not a dispassionate discussion of survival rates and chances. The latter may be needed, but it is very unlikely that the right message will be heard by someone so distressed. An appeal is being made for human kindness and companionship, not distant professionalism, even if professional competence and calmness is called for too. A response is needed which will work at a human level without telling a lie. "I'm here. I'm looking after you, and we'll help you in everyway we can." A promise to come back with the appropriate person to discuss things will probably be needed, but if there is time for this, it should be given *proper time.* When that is arranged, honesty will be needed to preserve and deepen the trust. If someone clearly or repeatedly makes the request, it is no longer our job to parry with further interpretations. The questions is not whether, but how and how much to disclose: it is now a professional question which depends on concepts of good care in that given situation. Prudence, kindness, evidence base and so on may all join with respect for the patients' wishes in providing a map of what is to be said. There is no place for false reassurance or unfulfillable promises. It is a question of proper judgment; disclosure to a different person, in different circumstances, may call for a different response.

Gaining Skills

Being frank in distressing situations isn't necessarily easy, though, and the ability to be so comes more naturally to some people than to others. The culture of a professional's family or group may encourage or discourage it. As well as personality, experience plays a crucial part. Being deceived for apparently benevolent reasons remains (sadly, in my view) a common experience in childhood. By this, I don't mean the deceptions of stories or acting: children enjoy fantasy, and can distinguish it from reality at an early age. But there are many for whom as children the experience of deception was real but not a kindness, and this may not be clearly recalled nor have been properly digested and may cause difficulties: human beings have an alarming propensity for offering to others as adults the behavior they experienced when young. If a young doctor now knows what she should do, but finds she cannot, then this is something which needs to be addressed, first by assessing the problem and then by practicing the necessary skills, with videos, role plays, group discussion, or professional help as necessary. Not to do so allows for the possibility that an otherwise kind and skilful clinician may be ambushed when under pressure by responses which are normally repressed. Medicine offers all too many opportunities for inhuman behavior under pressure, and there is such a thing, as we have seen, as inappropriate and cruel truth telling as well as cruel lying or perversions of the truth. If any readers think that is or could be their response under pressure, they need to set aside time to work on it and get help. Giving information appropriately and carefully is a moral, practical, and professional skill. Few musicians find that every scale can be played with ease: difficult tasks always need practice.

Summary

The rubric of modern health care prescribes honesty in giving information wherever possible, because without being appropriately informed, patients cannot make good decisions about their health care. This means that if they want to be told what is happening to them, as well as the treatment choices they face, this should be done. Lies destroy trust, and trust is a crucial component of good treatment in health care. Being truthful to patients about themselves, as well as avoiding unnecessary deception, treats them as proper persons and respects their autonomy: being treated in this way is likely to be a component of best possible recovery. Total and automatic openness, however, is no more appropriate in medicine than in any other walk of life. Both patient and professional have private lives, which under normal circumstances they have the liberty to reveal or conceal as they chose. The limits to information to be given by a clinician to patients about themselves are judged part of good clinical care, and should be carefully considered within the framework of what is required or requested. The time given, the timing and the circumstances will all be important. Clinicians should be truthful and trustworthy, which implies not some type of informative incontinence but the skill to assess the patients' requests and respond appropriately. How this is done is crucial. In particular they should not tell lies, and if they find this difficult they should seek help and training in truth-telling skills. On those few occasions when there is an appropriate justification for withholding information, it should be carefully and kindly done in a way which looks to strengthening the doctor–patient relationship and to minimizing the distress that any deception will inevitably cause between people who need each other and need to trust each other.

References

American Hospital Association (1973), Statement on a patient's bill of rights, *Hospitals* 47: 41.

Beatty, W. (1998), The Battle of Trafalgar: the death of Lord Nelson, in J.E. Lewis (ed.), *The Mammoth Book of How it Happened*, London: Robinson.

Bok, S. (1980), *Lying: Moral Choice in Public and Private Life*, London: Quartet.

Campbell, A. and Higgs, R. (1982), *In That Case: Medical Ethics in Everyday Practice*, London: Darton, Longman and Todd.

Engelhardt, H.T., Jr. (1996), *The Foundations of Bioethics*, New York: Oxford University Press.

Henderson, L.J. (1955), Physician and patient as social system, *New England Journal of Medicine* 212: 819–23.

Higgs, R. (1982), Truth at the last – a case of obstructed death? *Journal of Medical Ethics* (8): 48–50.

Higgs, R. (1999), The diagnosis of dying, *Journal of the Royal College of Physicians of London* 33: 110–12.

Marzanski, M. (2000), Would you like to know what is wrong with you? On telling the truth to patients with dementia, *Journal of Medical Ethics* 26: 108–13.

O'Neill, O. (1991), Kantian ethics, in P. Singer (ed.), *A Companion to Ethics*, Oxford: Blackwell.

Rachels,R. (1995), *The Elements of Moral Philosophy*, New York: McGraw-Hill.
Sullivan, R., Menapace, L. and White, R. (2001), Truth-telling and patient diagnoses, *Journal of Medical Ethics* 27: 192–7.
Veatch, R. (1978), Truth-telling I, in W.T. Reich (ed.), *Encyclopedia of Bioethics*, New York: Free Press.

Further Reading

Benn, P. (2001), Medicine, lies and deceptions, *Journal of Medical Ethics* 27: 130–4.
Cliffe, L., Ramsay M., and Barttell, D. (2000), *The Politics of Lying: Implications for Democracy*, New York: St Martin's Press.
Fadiman, A. (1997), *The Spirit Catches You and You Fall Down*, New York: Farrar, Straus and Giroux.
Jackson, J. (2001), *Truth, Trust and Medicine*, London: Routledge.
Williams, B. (2002), *Truth and Truthfulness*, Princeton, NJ: Princeton University Press.

Chapter 6

Medical Confidentiality

Kenneth Kipnis

The Infected Spouse

The following fictionalized case is based on an actual incident.

1982: After moving to Honolulu, Wilma and Andrew Long visit your office and ask you to be their family physician. They have been your patients since that day.

1988: Six years later the couple decide to separate. Wilma leaves for the mainland, occasionally sending you a postcard. Though you do not see her professionally, you still think of yourself as her doctor.

1990: Andrew comes in and says that he has embarked upon a more sophisticated social life. He has been hearing about some new sexually transmitted diseases and wants to be tested. He is positive for the AIDS virus and receives appropriate counseling.

1991: Visiting your office for a checkup, Andrew tells you Wilma is returning to Hawaii for a reconciliation with him. She arrives this afternoon and will be staying at the Moana Hotel. Despite your best efforts to persuade him, he leaves without giving you assurance that he will tell Wilma about his infection or protect her against becoming infected.

Do you take steps to see that Wilma is warned?

If you decide to warn Wilma, what do you say to Andrew when, two days later, he shows up at your office asking why you revealed confidential test results?

If you decide not to warn Wilma, what do you say to her when, two years later in 1993, she asks how you, her doctor, could possibly stand idly by as her husband infected her with a deadly virus. She now knows she is positive for the virus, that she was infected by her husband, and that you – her doctor – knew, before they reconciled, that her husband could infect her.

The ethical challenges here emerge from an apparent head-on collision between medical confidentiality and the duty to protect imperiled third parties. Notwithstanding Andrew's expectation of privacy and the professional duty to remain silent, it can seem unforgivable for anyone to withhold vital assistance in such a crisis, let alone a doctor. The case for breaching confidentiality is strengthened by at least five circumstances. First, the doctor knows, to a medical certainty, that Andrew is both infected with HIV and infectious. Second, knowing Wilma as a patient, the doctor reasonably believes (let us suppose) that she is not infected. (Wilma cannot be at risk of contracting the disease if she is infected already.) Third, Wilma's vulnerability is both serious and real. HIV infection is both debilitating and, during those years, invariably fatal. Moreover the couple's sexuality makes eventual infection highly likely. Fourth, it is probable that, were Wilma to be told of Andrew's infection, she would avoid exposing herself to the risk. This is not a trivial condition: many people knowingly risk illness and injury out of love and other honorable motivations. Molokai's Father Damien contracted and died from Hansen's disease while caring for patients he knew might infect him. Soldiers and firefighters expose themselves to grave risk. It is not enough that a warning would discharge a duty to Wilma, merely so she could make an informed choice. Plainly the paramount concern is to save Wilma's life. Finally, Wilma is not a mere stranger. Instead she has an important relationship with her doctor – you – that serves as a basis for special obligations. You have a special duty to look out for her health.

In the light of these five considerations, it should not be a surprise that the conventional wisdom in medical ethics overwhelmingly supports either an ethical obligation to breach confidentiality in cases like this one or (occasionally and less stringently) the ethical permissibility of doing so.[1] *The Infected Spouse* is paradigmatic of the type of case where the duty to protect endangered parties overrides the duty of confidentiality. Notwithstanding this consensus, it is my intention to challenge this received view. Broadly, I will argue in what follows that confidentiality in clinical medicine is far closer to an absolute obligation than it has generally been taken to be; more narrowly, that doctors should honor confidentiality even in cases like this one. Although the focus here is on this one case, the background idea is that, if it can be demonstrated that confidentiality should be scrupulously honored in this one case, where so many considerations support breaching it, confidentiality should be presumed as binding in virtually all other cases as well.[2] I shall not, however, argue for that broader conclusion here.

To avoid misunderstanding, I emphasize that this essay is not offered as a defense of absolute confidentiality in medical practice. In taking *The Infected Spouse* as paradigmatic of the circumstance when the professional obligation of confidentiality is taken to be overridden, I do aim at blowing a hole in the conventional wisdom about protecting the vulnerable. Wilma Long is exactly the type of endangered party contemplated by the duty to breach. So if the standard argument for qualified confidentiality fails in this single paradigmatic case – as I shall try to show – it is high time to rethink the conventional wisdom. It can no longer be taken for granted.

Although this essay specifically addresses the professional obligations of doctors, its approach applies more broadly to all professions that take seriously the responsibility to provide distressed practitioners with authoritative guidance.[3] While the focus is on confidentiality in the clinical setting, the intellectual strategies used in what follows can be employed to map the ethical dimensions of practice in a number of fields. In taking professional obligations seriously, this approach also represents something of a challenge to conventional thinking in medical ethics.

Background: The Concept of Information Management

Within medical ethics, the topic of medical confidentiality is best understood as a part of a broader area of inquiry: what can be called "information management." Clinicians routinely encounter prodigious amounts of information about patients (medical histories, complaints, names and addresses, etc.) and assorted items from which information about patients can be derived (x-ray films, tissue samples, surgically removed organs, cadavers, stomach contents, extracted bullets and other foreign objects, etc.). The concept of information management calls attention to certain ethical standards that are applicable to this body of material.

Consider a medical chart for a single hospitalized patient. This is a folder of documents (either paper or electronic) that contains a clinical narrative. There may be recounted conversations, an advance directive, a medical history, addresses and telephone numbers, test results, reports from consultants, hour-by-hour nurses' notes, and so on. As the primary repository of the most solid and current information about the patient, the chart is essential for doctors, residents, and nurses coming onto the hospital floor. What is this patient's problem? What is the current treatment plan? What is happening now? The medical chart allows all this information to be updated constantly, to circulate freely among the caregivers and to facilitate an empowering interdisciplinary teamwork. Omissions and errors in the chart can be fatal. Even for doctors who work alone, the chart protects a patient from the physician's sudden death or incapacity. Responsibility for patient care can be transferred to another provider should the need arise.

But even as health-related information must circulate freely among caregivers, the medical chart contains information that may not be capriciously revealed beyond that narrow circle. Some special justification is always required, usually involving either the patient's permission or restrictions on the scope of what is disclosed.

Although – legally – the physical pages belong to the hospital, the information on them belongs to the patient. For that reason the chart's contents must generally be withheld from any who are not directly involved in the patient's care. Reporters, relatives, researchers, private detectives, acquaintances, employers, lawyers, gossips, co-workers and busybodies – to name a few – may want access. But their purposes can conflict with the patient's interests and wants and even, as we shall see, with the deepest obligations of health care professions. Accordingly a patient's willingness to make available sensitive information to a doctor may be predicated on a grounded expectation that personal and potentially embarrassing facts will not be publicized or disclosed to others. To the extent that patients are worried about the release of sensitive information, they may be reluctant to share it with health care professionals who might disclose it. The quality of care can suffer if those who need it withhold medically relevant information or, worse yet, if they delay or avoid seeing physicians when prompt medical attention is essential. Trustworthiness (being worthy of patients' trust) is a core value of medicine. Any novice who failed to appreciate the importance of this fidelity to the patient has likely made an error in career choice.

It is important to note the difference between privacy and confidentiality. Privacy is sometimes spoken of as a contested legal right under the United States Constitution; sometimes as a consideration in the realm of personal morality. Just as most of us protect personal aspects of our lives from the gazes and intrusions of others, so we allow others the same space and latitude that is important to them. As an interest that most people cherish, privacy can be protected by both law and social convention. Confidentiality, on the other hand, is a distinct ethical duty observed by a number of different professions: lawyers, librarians, accountants as well as doctors. Though patients can sometimes find it difficult to bare their souls and bodies to medical examination, they commonly do this in order to obtain essential benefits that cannot be secured otherwise. The information so received by doctors comes with restrictions. In general it can only be used for the patient's health-related benefit or for other purposes to which the patient specifically consents.

In addition to being confidential, such information is also commonly "privileged." While a court of law can generally compel witnesses to testify, those occupying certain roles and receiving information in certain ways can be immune to this judicial power. Doctors, lawyers, priests, and spouses all possess such a privilege. Courts are limited in their ability to compel them to testify as regards certain information they may receive.

Notice that the obligation of confidentiality is collective rather than individual. The health care team bears the obligation together. A minor patient who wants to tell a medical resident "a secret" is making a mistake. The resident lacks the standing to withhold pertinent information from her attending physician. She should say "You can trust all of us on the health care team to honor confidentiality" instead of "You can trust me." Everyone caring for the patient needs to be on the same page.

Accordingly, a health care professional's ability to establish patient trust may entail a duty to sequester what is learned. Classically, the Hippocratic Oath has served as a public solemnizing of this obligation:

> And about whatever I may see or hear in treatment, or even without treatment, in the life of human beings – things that should not ever be blurted out outside – I will remain silent, holding such things to be *arreta* [unutterable, sacred, not to be divulged].[4]

But confidentiality is only one dimension of information management. There are also duties of communication and disclosure. The patient is plainly entitled to information about his or her medical condition and about the options for treatment. And there may be additional duties to disclose medical information to others besides the patient: to other caregivers (as already noted), to the public on occasion, to consultants, to those the patient has designated as proxy decision-makers, etc. Consulting physicians who examine patients have duties to disclose their findings to attending physicians. There are also common legal obligations to report child abuse, gunshot and knife wounds, certain infectious diseases, and loss of consciousness in drivers. Doctors in the military, in occupational medicine, and correctional health services can have institutional duties of disclosure to officers, to corporate executives, and prison wardens. Similarly, forensic psychiatrists may have to report their findings to the court. There are the concerned parents of juvenile patients, court orders, police investigations, public health crises, and other special circumstances. There are third-party insurers who require information prior to covering medical services. Finally confidential materials are commonly given to clerks, secretarial staff and medical transcriptionists, and the hospital's medical records office. The task for medical ethics (and this essay) is to develop justified standards that best inform this dimension of clinical practice.

In the face of all of these "exceptions," some have thrown up their hands and declared confidentiality a "decrepit concept."[5] Though this despair seems premature, it is evident – as in *The Infected Spouse* – that arguments can pull in both directions. Clinicians may be hard-pressed to determine whether some fact must be disclosed or kept confidential. As blurred and faded as the lines are, doctors may be ethically at risk regardless of their choice. Clarity here, if it could be achieved, would be valuable.

Clearing the Ground: What Professional Obligations are Not

Among philosophers, it is commonplace that if people are not asking the same questions, they cannot arrive at the same answers. It may be that the main reason doctors have difficulty reaching consensus in ethics is that, in general, systematic discussion about professional responsibility is commonly confused with three other types of conversation. When one asks whether one should call the hotel to warn Wilma, one can be asking what the law requires, what one's personal morality requires (as an Orthodox Jew, a Roman Catholic, etc.) or what is required by one's most deeply held personal values (preventing deaths or honoring other obligations), or what would be required by sound professional standards. Discussions can mindlessly meander over all four areas without attending to boundary crossings. More to the point, deliberation about professional obligations, as I will try to show, differs importantly from all three of the discussions considered immediately below. I have found it necessary to identify and bracket these three other perspectives in order to mark off the intellectual space within which practitioners can productively reflect on questions of professional responsibility. What follows is an examination of importantly different conversations. I am not claiming that these norms are a complete list – there may be more. Nor do I set them out in order of priority. It is, in my view, a sad fact of life that obligations can conflict and, even more sadly, that there are no cookbook directions for resolving such dilemmas once we are facing them.

Law

The conventional wisdom on the ethics of medical confidentiality has been largely shaped by a single legal case: *Tarasoff v. Regents of the University of California*.[6] In 1969 Prosenjit Poddar, a student at Berkeley, told a university psychologist he intended to kill a Ms Tatiana Tarasoff, a young woman who had been spurning his affections. The psychologist dutifully reported him to the campus police who held him briefly and then set him free. Shortly afterwards, Poddar did as he said he would, stabbing the young woman to death. The Tarasoff family sued the University of California for their daughter's death, eventually prevailing in their contention that the psychologist (and, by implication, the university) had failed in their duty to protect. Today it is hard to find discussions of the ethics of confidentiality that do not appeal to this parable and, occasionally, to its California Supreme Court moral: "The protective privilege ends where the public peril begins."

Taking its cue from *Tarasoff*, the prevailing standard in medical ethics now holds that the obligation of confidentiality will give way when a doctor is aware that a patient will seriously injure some identified other person. (One might ask why disclosure should not also be required when a patient will seriously injure many unidentified persons. Under this standard, there is no ethical duty to alert others to an HIV-infected prostitute who neither warns nor protects a very large number of anonymous clients.)

Under *Tarasoff*, a warning (or other protection) is required only when professionals know that injuries will likely occur. If there is no warning and no subsequent injury, there will be no liability. But if there is no warning and an injury ensues, there may be liability if the professional knew that a patient would likely cause serious harm to some identified third party. Obviously a key question involves the accuracy of professional predictions of dangerousness. If professionals are usually wrong in predicting injury, it would follow that they do not know who is dangerous even if they often think they do. What would be useful would be empirical research investigating the accuracy of professional predictions of dangerousness. The best study would track those who had been predicted to be dangerous to determine how accurate the predictions were. Obviously the persons professionally deemed to be dangerous would have to be allowed to circulate freely, so we could tell when serious injuries were caused. But just as obviously, few would be willing to permit such a study.

Remarkably, a confluence of events permitted such a study following the Supreme Court's decision in *Baxtrom v. Herold*.[7] The case involved 967 "criminally insane" patients who had been confined in two New York State institutions: Mattewan and Dannemora. These patients had been evaluated annually for dangerousness but were not receiving treatment for mental illness. In addition, they had already spent more time in confinement than they would have spent in prison had they been convicted instead of adjudicated as criminally insane. The *Baxtrom* patients were released from mandated confinement and tracked for four years by Steadman.[8] Among the conclusions of the study were: of the 967 deemed dangerous by reason of insanity, only 21 (about 2 percent) were returned to Mattewan and Dannemora over the following four years, an error rate of 98 percent.

This dramatic overprediction of dangerousness probably has its roots in the payoff schedule applicable to those who must make these predictions. Health care professionals may make two types of error. There are false positives, when one predicts dangerousness for a truly non-dangerous patient. And there are false negatives, when one predicts non-dangerousness for a truly dangerous patient. Errors of the first kind are typically masked by unnecessary preventive incarceration. Unless there is a lawsuit, these mistakes may never see the light of day. However errors of the second kind can appear on the front pages of the newspapers – "Lunatic Runs Amok in Library: Psychiatrist Said He Was Normal" – and they can be career-ending. Given that the risk of these adverse consequences to doctors can carry great weight and affect judgment, it seems likely that *anyone* placed in such a position will overpredict dangerousness. The conflict of interest is clear: clinicians can be expected to behave more to shield themselves from lawsuits and damaging publicity, than to protect patients from unnecessary confinement. So it would seem that clinicians seeking to avoid *Tarasoff* liability may become too willing to breach confidentiality. If the *Baxtrom* experience is representative, most predictions of harm will be inaccurate.

Although many states have not adopted the California rule, either judicially or legislatively, *The Infected Spouse* plainly falls under the *Tarasoff* standard. We will, for now, assume that the physician knows Andrew is seropositive, that Wilma is likely seronegative, that the two will likely engage in activities that will transmit the virus, that breaching confidentiality will probably result in those activities not occurring and Wilma's not becoming infected. We accept that a warning will mean that Wilma is highly likely to remain infection-free and that the failure to warn allows the risk of death to remain high.

In legal cases like *Tarasoff*, it is useful to distinguish between "special legal duties" and "general legal duties." Special duties apply to individuals occupying certain roles. A parent, but not a bystander, has a (special) duty to rescue an imperiled daughter; firefighters and police officers have (special) duties to take certain occupational risks on behalf of endangered others, and doctors have many (special) duties to their patients: confidentiality is a good example. In contrast, virtually everyone has a (general) duty to be scrupulously careful when handling explosives, to pay taxes on income, to respect others' property, and so on. It is notable that the

Tarasoff duty to protect is a special duty, applicable only to certain people occupying special roles. So if my neighbor assures me he is going to kill his girlfriend tomorrow, the *Tarasoff* ruling does not require me to warn her.

It is surprising to many that the default standard in Anglo-American jurisprudence is that there is no general duty to improve the prospects of the precariously placed, no legal obligation to undertake even an easy rescue. As first-year law students discover, one can stand on a pier with a lifeline in hand and, with impunity, allow a stranger to drown nearby. Although we will pass over it, it is notable that, in general, the parties who are legally obligated to warn are those who are otherwise ethically obligated not to disclose. One should reflect on the absence of a general duty to warn.

The easy transition from law to ethics reflects an error that infects much of the writing on this topic. The mistake is to move from the premise that some action is legally required (what the *Tarasoff* opinion establishes in the jurisdictions that have followed it) to the conclusion that the action is ethically required. But of course ethical obligations can conflict with legal ones. Journalists, for example, are sometimes ordered by the courts to reveal the identities of their confidential sources. Although law demands disclosure, professional ethics requires silence. Reporters famously go to jail rather than betray sources. Practitioners who find themselves in such a quandary face a dilemma. While good citizens obey the law and good professionals honor their professional codes, laws requiring journalists to violate their duties to confidential sources force a tragic choice between acting illegally and acting unethically. Conscientious persons should not have to face such decisions.

Similarly in pediatrics, statutes may require doctors to report suspicions of abuse. But where protective agencies are inept and overworked, and foster care is dangerous or unavailable, a doctor's report is more likely to result in termination of therapy and further injury to the child instead of protection and care. To obey the law under these appalling but too common circumstances is most likely to abandon and even harm the child, both of which are ethically prohibited in medicine. To assume that legal obligations always trump or settle ethical ones is to blind oneself to the possibility of conflict. Professions have to face these dilemmas head-on instead of masking them with language that conflates legal standards and ethical ones. They must conceive professional ethics as separate from the law's mandate. And when law requires what professional responsibility prohibits (or prohibits what professional responsibility requires), professional organizations must press the public, legislatures, and the courts to cease demanding that conscientious practitioners dishonor the duties of their craft. This is one of the most important responsibilities of professional organizations. It can be a mistake to configure professional obligations to mirror the law's requirements. Rather the law's requirements must be configured so that they do not conflict with well-grounded professional obligations. Law is a human artifact. In a well-ordered society it will be configured so no one has to choose between legality and professional integrity.

Since the law can require conduct that violates ethical standards (and ethical standards can require conduct that violates the law), it cannot be the case that legal obligations automatically create ethical obligations. As the tradition of civil disobedience shows, it can be ethically permissible (though not legal) to break the law. But even though laws cannot create ethical obligations by fiat, professions need to distinguish between the state's reasonable interests in the work of doctors – e.g., preventing serious harm to children – and the specific legal mandates a state imposes – e.g., requiring doctors to report suspicions of child abuse to an incompetent state agency. Just as patients can make ill-considered demands that should not be satisfied, so too can the state and its courts.

Accordingly it is assumed in what follows both that the state has a legitimate interest in preventing harm to people, and that doctors have an ethical obligation to further that important public objective. The focus in this essay is narrowly on the shape of the ethical obligation to prevent harm, as it applies narrowly to health care professionals facing cases like those involving Wilma Long and Tatiana Tarasoff. We set aside situations involving (1) children brought in by parents,[9] (2) patients referred for independent medical evaluation, (3) mentally ill or retarded patients in the custody of health care institutions, (4) health care that is the subject of litigation, (5) gunshot and knife wounds and the like, (6) workers' compensation cases, and a few others. A much longer discussion would be needed to cover these areas.

Though I will not discuss them, institutional policies (hospital procedures, for example) function very much like laws. Both involve standards that can be imposed externally upon practitioners. Both can be formulated knowledgeably and wisely, or with a disregard for essential professional responsibilities.

Personal morality

We will understand a "morality" as a set of beliefs about obligations. There are plainly many such sets of beliefs: the morality of Confucius has little in common with the moralities of George W. Bush and Thomas Aquinas. For most of us, morality is uncritically absorbed in childhood, coming to consciousness only when we encounter others whose beliefs differ.

There are still parts of the world in which virtually all members of a community are participants in a common morality. But moral pluralism now seems to be a permanent part of the social order. Consider a Jehovah's Witness physician who is opposed, on religious grounds, to administering blood transfusions. If this doctor were the only physician on duty when his patient needed an immediate transfusion, a choice would have to be made between being a good Jehovah's Witness and being a good doctor. Personal moral convictions can be inconsistent with professional obligations. It follows that clarity about personal morality is not the same as clarity about medical ethics. Professionalism can require that one set aside one's personal morality or carefully limit one's exposure to certain professional responsibilities. Here the rule has to be that doctors will not take on responsibilities that might conflict with their personal morality. Problems could be sidestepped if the Jehovah's Witness doctor specialized in dermatology, or always worked with colleagues who would administer transfusions. If I am morally against the death penalty, I shouldn't take on work as an executioner. If I am deeply opposed to the morning-after pill, I shouldn't counsel patients at a rape treatment center. To teach medical ethics in a pluralistic professional community is to try to create an intellectual space within which persons from varied backgrounds can agree upon responsible standards for professional conduct. Participants in such a conversation may have to leave personal morality at the door. For some, it may be a mistake to choose a career in medicine.

If ethics is critical reflection on our moralities, then the hope implicit in the field of medical ethics is that we might some day reach a responsible consensus on doctors' obligations. While medicine has dozens of codes, it is not hard to observe commonalities: the standards for informed consent, for example. At a deeper level, there can also be consensus on the justifications for those standards. One role for the philosopher is, as in this essay, to assess the soundness of those arguments. The problem for a profession is to move beyond the various personal moralities embraced by practitioners and to reach a responsible consensus on common professional standards.

Personal values

Values are commonly a part of an explanation of personal conduct. It is always reasonable to ask of any rational action, What good was it intended to promote? While some wear shoes to avoid hurting their feet (embracing the value of comfort) others think they look better in shoes (embracing aesthetic values). Where we have to make personal decisions, often we consider how each option furthers and erodes our values and try to decide among the good and bad consequences.

This strategy can work well when the question is "What should I do?" But the question, "What should a good doctor do?" calls for a different type of inquiry. For while I have many personal values, the "good doctor" is an abstraction. He/she is not Protestant or Buddhist, doesn't prefer chocolate to vanilla, and doesn't care about money more than leisure time. Questions about professional ethics cannot be answered in terms of personal values.

A second difficulty appears when we consider that one can give perfect expression to one's most deeply held personal values, and still act unethically. Hannibal Lecter in *Silence of the Lambs* and Mozart's Don Giovanni are both despicable villains who give vigorous effect to deeply held but contemptible personal values. While personal values can determine action, they do not guarantee that the favored actions are ethical.

Accordingly we cannot appeal to our personal values to inquire about what physicians in general ought to do. Medicine has no personal values: only individual physicians do. When a physician must decide whether or not to resuscitate a patient, personal values should have nothing to do with the issue. Whether you like the patient or detest him, whether you are an atheist or a fundamentalist believer in a joyous here-after: none of this should weigh in the balance. A key part of professionalism involves being able to set personal values aside. While medical students have much to gain by becoming clear about their personal values, it must be remembered that that clarity, no matter how precious, is not the same as responsible certainty about professional obligations.

To summarize the argument so far, discussion about professional obligations in medicine is not the same as discussion about legal and institutional obligations, personal morality or personal values. If a responsible consensus is to be achieved by a profession, it is necessary for physicians to learn to bracket, to some degree, their personal moral and value commitments and to set aside, at least temporarily, their consideration of legal or institutional rules and policies. The practical task is to create an intellectual space within which responsible consensus can be achieved on how physicians, as professionals, ought to act. I will now describe one way in which this might be done.

The Concept of a Professional Obligation[10]

Professional ethics involves disciplined discussion about the obligations of profes-sionals. One place to begin is with a distinction between personal values, already discussed, and what can be called "core professional values." A physician can prefer (1) pistachios to Brazil nuts and (2) confidentiality to universal candor. While the preference for pistachios is merely personal, the preference for confiden-tiality is a value doctors ought to possess. The distinction between personal values and "core professional values" is critical here. There is what this flesh-and-blood doctor happens to care about personally, and what the good doctor ought to care about. The "good doctor" is a social construction, a determinate social role, an integral element of medical professionalism. Our idea of a good doctor includes a certain technical/intellectual mastery and a commitment to certain social values. As with the Jehovah's Witness doctor, personal and professional values may be in conflict. As part of an appreciation of the ethical claims of professionalism, phys-icians must be prepared to set aside their personal values and morality, to set aside what the legal system and their employers want them to care about, and to take up instead the question of what the responsible physician ought to care about. Core values inform those purposes that each medical professional should have in common with colleagues. In discussing the professionally favored resolution of ethically problematic cases (*The Infected Spouse*, for example) physicians can ask – together – how medicine's core professional values ought to be respected in those circumstances.

We have alluded to some of these core professional values. Trustworthiness needs to be on the list. Beneficence toward the patient is essential. Respect for patient autonomy is a third. Others might be collegiality (duties to colleagues), and perhaps a few others: nondiscrimination and due deference to families are among the most commonly mentioned candidates. If we were to leave out that doctors should care about the well-being of the public, the argument for confidentiality would be easy. But it too properly goes on the list.

Each of these values has two dimensions. Along one vector, they define the aspirations of a profession. At any time, for example, medicine's ability to benefit patients will be limited. It is a part of the profession's commitment to push its envelope, to enlarge its collective competency. It is a part of every professional's commitment to be a lifelong learner. Those who stretch the profession's knowledge and skills are exemplary contributors, but practitioners do not discredit themselves by failing to serve in this estimable way.

Along the second vector, values define a bottom line beneath which practitioners shall not sink. Paraphrasing Hippocrates, although you may not always be able to benefit your patients, it is far more important that you take care not to harm them. Knowingly to harm patients (on balance) is not merely a failure to realize the value of beneficence. It is a culpable betrayal of that value, a far more serious matter.

All the values above can be understood in this way. Trustworthiness, for example, entails (among other things) that I not lie to patients, or deliberately withhold information they have an interest in knowing. Respect for patient autonomy can require that I not use force or fraud upon them. And the concern for the well-being of the public requires that that interest somehow appear prominently upon every practitioner's radar screen, that doctors not stand idly by in the face of perils the profession can help to avert and, as a lower limit, that they not do anything to increase public peril. The overutilization of antibiotics, producing new drug-resistant infectious micro-organisms, is a good example of the latter.

Ethical problems arise when two core values appear to be in conflict, as with *The Infected Spouse*. At issue are trustworthiness toward Andrew on one side, and beneficence and trustworthiness toward Wilma, and perhaps also a concern for the well-being of the public, all on the other. If the conflict is real, what is required is a priority rule. For example, the concept of decisional capacity is part of a priority rule resolving the well-studied conflict between beneficence and autonomy: when do physicians have to respect a patient's refusal of life-saving treatment? There is what the patient wants and what the patient needs. But when a patient is decisionally capacitated and informed, his or her refusal trumps a doctor's recommendation. The best arguments support that conclusion at the present time.

Problems can also arise when it is unclear what a core professional value requires one to do. Though we can all agree that doctors should avoid harming their patients, there is no professional consensus on whether deliberately causing the deaths of certain patients – those who are experiencing irremediable and intense suffering – is always a betrayal of beneficence. Likewise, although doctors may be in a position to prevent harm to third parties – as with Wilma – it is not completely clear how far they should go out of respect for that value. When core values conflict, what is required is a priority rule. When they are unclear, what is required is removal of ambiguity: what philosophers call "disambiguation." These two tasks – prioritizing and disambiguating core professional values – need to be carried out with a high degree of intellectual responsibility.

I do not think there is much that is controversial about the above list of core values. Propose a toast to them at an assemblage of physicians and all can likely drink with enthusiasm. What is less clear is why such a consensus should obligate professionals. A criminal organization can celebrate a shared commitment to its oath of silence. But it doesn't follow that mobsters who cooperate with the police are unethical. In addition to this "celebratability," three additional elements are required to establish a professional obligation.

The first element is that attention to core values has to be a part of the professional's education. Most medical education is aimed at beneficence. The procedures used in informed consent express a commitment to respect for patient autonomy and trustworthiness. If the profession wholly fails to equip its novices to further its core values, it can be argued that it is not serious about those professed values. Its public commitments are likely intended to convey an illusion of concerned attention. In replicating itself, the medical profession must replicate its commitment to its intrinsic values. Students of medicine must come to care about the goods that doctors ought to care about. Because justice is rarely explored as a topic in medical education, it cannot be counted as a core professional value. However some aspects of justice – nondiscrimination and disaster triage for example – are routinely covered.

The second element is critical. The core values are not just goods that doctors care about and that doctors expect other doctors to care about. They are also goods that the rest of us want our doctors to care about. I want my doctor to be trustworthy, to be intent on benefiting me, to take my informed refusals seriously, and so on. And we want our doctors to look out for the well-being of the public. The core professional values are also social values. (Consider that it is not reasonable to want our mobsters to respect their oaths of silence.)

The third element flows from the second: exclusive social reliance upon the profession as the means by which certain matters are to receive due attention. We mostly respect medical competence. But it is precisely because, as a community, we have also come to accept that doctors are reliably committed to their values (our values), that we have, through state legislatures, granted the medical profession an exclusive monopoly on the delivery of medical services. The unauthorized practice of medicine is a punishable crime. If, like the medical profession, one were to make a public claim that, because of unique skills and dedication, some important matter ought to be entrusted to you, and the public believes you and entrusts those important matters to you, incidentally prohibiting all others from encroachment upon what is now your privilege, you would have thereby assumed an ethical obligation to give those important matters due attention. Collectively, the medical profession has done exactly this in securing its monopoly on the delivery of certain types of health care. Accordingly the profession has a collective obligation to organize itself so that the responsibilities it has assumed in the process of professionalization are properly discharged by its membership.

A sound code of ethics consists of a set of standards that, if adhered to broadly by the profession's membership, will result in the profession as a whole discharging its responsibilities. Where physician behavior brings it about that a public loses that essential trust, society may have to withdraw the monopolistic privilege and seek a better way of organizing health care. Professionalization is but one way of organizing an essential service. There are others.

Summarizing, the medical profession has ethical obligations toward patients, families, and the community because of its public commitment to certain social values and because of society's exclusive reliance on the profession as its means of delivering certain forms of health care. With privilege comes responsibility. We can now turn our attention to medicine's responsibility to diminish public perils.

The Duty to Diminish Risks to Third Parties

There is an implication for the way in which we must now understand the problem in *The Infected Spouse*. The opening question "Do you take steps to warn Wilma?" has to be understood as a question about medical ethics and not about "you." We want to know what the "good doctor' should do under those circumstance. Each doctor is ethically required to do what a responsible doctor ought to do: to properly respect the core values of the profession. To become a doctor without a proper commitment to respect the profession's ethical standards is to be unfit for the practice of medicine. So how are trustworthiness and confidentiality to be understood in relationship to medicine's commitment to diminish risks to third parties?

It will be useful to begin by distinguishing among three distinct circles of disclosure and the standards applicable to each. We have already considered the narrowest circle: those directly involved in patient care. Residents who work in emergency departments do not have any automatic right to track what happens to patients after they are taken to the floor for further treatment. Doctors may get into serious trouble if they read the charts of their family members. The principle here is that those directly involved in patient care must have access to the chart, but others beyond that circle are not entitled to it.

Certain patient needs can enlarge the circle somewhat. When a clinician is uncertain about a patient's medical condition, experts not involved with the patient might be able to provide advice. In order to get needed advice, the puzzled clinician must disclose information about the patient. The expert's more extensive knowledge and experience can help to fill out a murky or incomplete picture and improve patient care as a result. While no one with an interest in safe and effective treatment would want to impede these consultations, it is rarely necessary to reveal identifying information about the patient in order to obtain what one needs to know. Those who consult with caregivers, but who are not directly involved in the patient's care, should receive the information they need to provide an informed opinion, but no more than that. Consultations of this sort are extremely common. But the restriction mentioned here is not always explicitly acknowledged.

Public needs enlarge the circle still further. Occasionally a medical condition appears that is of broader social importance. A backpacker shows up at an emergency department with plague. There is a need to alert doctors and members of the public about this new risk of an unfamiliar illness. Doctors may have to refresh their diagnostic and treatment skills and ordinary citizens may need to know whether they are at risk and what to do if they develop symptoms. Information must be disseminated quickly, broadly, and publicly, but these messages need contain even fewer identifying references than communications within the second circle. "A camper who had been hiking in the forest west of Springfield has been diagnosed with plague. Call your doctor or go to an emergency department if you are experiencing any of the following symptoms . . ." Such announcements are an effective way to protect the public.

Because it is based on an actual case, my use of *The Infected Spouse* involves disclosure at this third level. It seems there is a public interest in grasping the issues the case raises. But not only have the identifying references been omitted: some of the facts are invented. Wilma and Andrew are in that way even more anonymous than the unnamed backpacker. Medical journals commonly carry case histories that elevate professional competence. Suitably edited, these reports do not compromise a properly understood obligation of confidentiality. Readers cannot link the narrative descriptions to identified persons. (Indeed, as a personal matter, I do not know who "Wilma" and "Andrew" really were, although I know the doctor who treated "Andrew.")

But unlike those anonymously imperiled in the case of the unnamed backpacker, Wilma Long is an identified person at risk of infection from a second identified person. Here generic public announcements are not sufficient to protect her.

A strategy called "contact tracing" is sometimes employed. When a patient is diagnosed with a sexually transmitted disease, he or she can be asked to provide a list of the names and addresses of all sexual contacts who might have been infected. A public health worker knocks on the door and says "We have received a report that you may have had sexual relations with a person who has been diagnosed with a venereal disease." The goals are to encourage the contact to be treated and to prevent further transmission. While this approach is useful when patient confidentiality can be preserved despite the warning, sometimes this is impossible: "What do you mean I may have been exposed to a venereal disease? I have only had sex with my husband!" In *The Infected Spouse*, Wilma and Andrew have not yet seen each other so "contact tracing" would not as yet apply. And any subsequent warning to Wilma would convey that Andrew is infected.

The Infected Spouse poses its question in 1991, after the doctor–family relationship has been in place for a decade. The dilemma arises during a single office visit, forcing a choice between having to explain to Andrew, in two days, why you disclosed his infection to his wife; or having to explain to Wilma, in two years, why you did not disclose Andrew's infection to her. Each option has a bad outcome: the betrayal of Andrew's trust or the fatal infection of Wilma. Either way, you will need to account for yourself.

Infection seems a far worse consequence for Wilma than betrayal is for Andrew. Much of the literature on confidentiality has been shaped by this fact and perhaps the standard strategy for resolving the apparent dilemma in favor of disclosure calls attention to the magnitude and probability of the bad outcomes associated with each option. While predictions of harm can be wrong, it can be evident that Tatiana Tarasoff and Wilma Long are at grave risk and, accordingly, it can seem honorable to diminish the danger to extremely vulnerable parties like these two. Justice Tobriner appeals to a version of this consequentialist argument in *Tarasoff*:

> Weighing the uncertain and conjectural character of the alleged damage done the patient by such a warning against the peril to the victim's life, we conclude that professional inaccuracy in predicting violence [or deadly infection] cannot negate the therapist's duty to protect the threatened victim.

Beauchamp and Childress, in their widely read *Principles of Biomedical Ethics*, urge clinicians to take into account "the probability that a harm will materialize and the magnitude of that harm" in any decision to breach confidentiality.[11] (While they also urge that clinicians take into account the potential impact of disclosure on policies and laws regarding confidentiality, they do not describe how this assessment is to be carried out.) In brief, the very bad consequences to Wilma – disease and death and the betrayal of her trust – outweigh the not-that-bad consequence to Andrew.

The preferred argument for breaching confidentiality would go something like this: The state's interest in preventing harm is weighty. Medicine has an obligation to protect the well-being of the community. Because the seriousness of threatened grave injury to another outweighs the damage done to a patient by breaching confidentiality, the obligation of confidentiality must give way to a duty to prevent serious harm to others. Accordingly, despite confidentiality, warning or reporting is obligatory when it will likely avert very bad outcomes in this way. Of course clinicians should try to obtain waivers of confidentiality before reporting, thereby avoiding the need to breach. But failure to obtain a waiver does not, on this argument, affect the overriding obligation to report.

A Defense of Unqualified Confidentiality

As powerful as this justification is, there are problems with it. Go back to 1990, when Andrew comes in to be tested for sexually transmitted diseases. Suppose he asks "If I am infected, can I trust you not to disclose this to others?" If, following the arguments set out in the previous paragraphs, we are clear that confidentiality might have to be breached in order to protect identified third parties like Wilma, then the only truthful answer to Andrew's question is 'No. You can't trust me." If the profession accepts that its broad assurance of confidentiality must sometimes be breached, then any unqualified assurances are fraudulent and the profession should stop making them. If there are exceptions, clinicians have a duty to be forthcoming about what they are and how they work. Patients should know up front when and how they can trust doctors, and when they can't. To withhold this important information is to betray the value of trustworthiness.

Accordingly, the argument for breaching confidentiality has to be modified to support a qualified confidentiality rule, one that carves out an exception from the very beginning, acknowledging an overriding duty to report under defined circumstances. (In contrast, an unqualified rule contemplates no exceptions.) Instead of undertaking duties of confidentiality and then violating them, doctors must qualify their expressed obligations so they *can* honor them. Commentators who have walked through the issues surrounding confidentiality have long understood the ethical necessity of "Miranda warnings."[12] A clinician could say: "Certain things that I learn from you may have to be disclosed to . . . under the following circumstances: . . . and the following things might occur to you as a result of my disclosure . . ." filling in the blanks as required. If doctors are ethically obligated to report, they need to say in advance what will be passed along, when, to whom, and what could happen then. They should never encourage or – more important – even accept trust, only to betray their patients afterwards. To do so is to betray the value of trustworthiness.

But now a second problem emerges. If prospective patients must understand in advance that a doctor will report evidence of a threat to another, they will only be willing to disclose such evidence to the doctor if they are willing to accept that others will come to know. If it is important to them that the evidence not be reported, they will have a weighty reason not to disclose it to those who are obligated to report it.

Some have questioned this proposition, arguing that there is no empirical evidence that prospective patients will avoid or delay seeking medical attention or conceal medically relevant information if confidentiality is qualified in this way. Despite widespread reporting practices, waiting rooms have not emptied and no one really knows if people will stop talking openly to their doctors if confidentiality is breached.

Three immediate responses are possible regarding this claim. First, there is a serious difficulty doing empirical research in this area. How, for example, do we determine the number of child-abusing parents who have not brought their injured children to doctors out of a fear that they will get into trouble with the authorities? How many HIV+ patients avoid telling their doctors about their unsafe sexual practices? How many us would provide unflattering truthful answers to direct questions on these and other shameful matters? It is notoriously difficult to gather reliable data on the embarrassing, criminal, irresponsible things people do, and the steps they take to avoid exposure, especially if those are wrongful too. I don't want to suggest that these problems are insurmountable, but they are decidedly there and they make it hard to study the effects of these betrayals.

Second, despite the problems, certain types of indirect evidence can emerge. Here are two anecdotal examples from Honolulu, both confirming that patients avoid clinicians who cannot be trusted to keep confidences. There was a time, not long ago, when military enlistees who were troubled by their sexual orientations knew that military doctors and psychologists would report these problems to their officers. Many of these troubled soldiers obtained the services of private psychologists and psychiatrists in Honolulu, despite the free services available in military clinics. The second example emerged from the failure of the Japanese medical system to keep diagnoses of HIV infection confidential. Those Japanese who could afford it often traveled to Honolulu for diagnosis and treatment, avoiding the clinics where they lived. At the same time Japanese data on the prevalence of HIV infection were unrealistically low, especially given the popularity of Japanese sex tours to the HIV-infected brothels of Thailand. Evidence of this sort can confirm that the failure to respect confidentiality can impair the ability of doctors to do their job.

And third, there is an argument based on the motivational principle that if one strongly desires that event E does not occur, and one knows that doing act A will bring about event E, then one has a weighty reason not to do act A. Consider the care exercised on a crowded subway platform. The criminal justice system is based on this idea. We attach artificial and broadly unwelcome consequences (imprisonment and other forms of punishment) to wrongful, harmful conduct with the expectation that, even if inclined, most people will decide against the conduct in order to avoid the unwelcome consequence. If I don't want to go to prison, and if a career in burglary will likely result in my going to prison, then I have a weighty reason to choose a different career. If I don't want my marriage to be destroyed by my wife's discovery that I am HIV+, and I know that telling my doctor about reconciliation will result in her discovering just that, then I have a weighty reason not to tell my doctor. If there is a burden of proof, it falls to those who challenge the principle that, characteristically and for the most part, people try to avoid immediate harm to themselves when they can. The presumption must be in favor of the truth of this nearly self-evident principle. If critics allege that it is false or otherwise unworthy of endorsement, the burden of proof belongs to them. It seems it would be their job to come up with disconfirming evidence.

It is often argued, in rebuttal, that people still commit burglary and, despite reporting laws, people still go to doctors for HIV testing, even knowing that confidentiality has its limits. But no one would maintain that punishing convicted criminals completely prevents crime and that breaching confidentiality results in all people avoiding or delaying obtaining medical treatment, or remaining silent about aspects of their lives. Clearly the situation is more complicated than that.

Consider that Andrew belongs to one of two groups of prospective patients.[13] Members of the first group are willing enough to have reports made to others while members of the second are deterred from disclosure by the fear of a report that will be harmful to them. Of course we can't know in advance which type of patient Andrew is, but if both groups are treated alike, that uncertainty will not be a problem.

Consider the first group, patients who would be willing to have a report made. Recall that the physician in *The Infected Spouse* tried to obtain assurance that Wilma would be protected. Under an unqualified confidentiality rule – no exceptions – if the patient were willing to have reports made to others, the doctor should be able to obtain a waiver of confidentiality and Wilma could then be informed. Once permission to report is given, the ethical dilemma disappears. Notice that for this group of patients an exceptionless confidentiality rule works just as well as a rule requiring doctors to set aside confidentiality when necessary to protect identified endangered third parties. The at-risk party will be warned just the same, but with appropriate permission from the patient. In these cases there is no need to trim back the obligation of confidentiality since patients in this first group are, by definition, willing to have a report made.

Difficulties arise with the second type of patient: those who will not want their medical condition reported to others. Notice that these prospective patients are in control of the evidence doctors need to secure protection for any parties at risk. If these patients cannot be drawn into a therapeutic alliance – a relationship of trust and confidence – then doctors will not receive the information they need to protect imperiled third parties (at least so long as patients have options). As a result, doctors will not be able to mobilize protection for imperiled third parties. When one traces out the implications of a reporting rule on what needs to be said in 1990 (when Andrew asked to be tested and the doctor disclosed the limits to confidentiliaty), it becomes evident Wilma will not be protected if Andrew does not want her to know and understands that disclosure to his doctor will result in Wilma's knowing. Depending on his options and the strength of his preferences, he will be careful about what he discloses to his doctor, or will go without medical advice and care, or will find another physician who can be kept in ignorance about his personal life. None of these strategies will help Wilma. Nor will they be optimal for Andrew.

My argument for unqualified confidentiality in *The Infected Spouse* could be summarized as follows. For those who are not deterred by the threat of disclosure – those who now knowingly present at clinics where doctors report – it is unnecessary to qualify confidentiality. They can agree to disclose. But for those who expect to be seriously harmed if others learn of their health-related problems, they will try to keep sensitive information secret: i.e., not consulting or confiding with doctors who are duty-bound to make unwanted reports. For patients like Andrew, who want to avoid harm to themselves, a reluctance to be forthcoming will neither protect patients like Wilma nor serve themselves very well. In contrast, unqualified confidentiality encourages unimpeded access to health care for this second group of patients, and allows health care professionals to counsel them and – more important – thereby protect some Wilmas who could not otherwise be protected. In this specific way unqualified confidentiality provides more protection for the Wilmas of the world than qualified confidentiality can.

We began by characterizing *The Infected Spouse* as an apparent head-on collision between the doctor's duty of confidentiality and the duty to protect imperiled third parties. If the argument just set out is sound, there is, despite initial appearances, no collision. The obligation to warn third parties does not provide added protection to at-risk parties. In particular, an unqualified confidentiality rule has a better chance of getting the facts on the table, at least to the extent that honest promises of confidentiality can make it so. To be sure, clinicians would have to set aside the vexing "Should I report?" conundrum and search for creative solutions instead. These strategies will not always prevent harm, but they will sometimes. Some Wilmas can be protected; others can't. The nub of the matter is that these strategies can never work if they can't be implemented. And they can't be implemented if the fear of reporting deters patients from disclosure. Accordingly there is no justification for trimming back the obligation of confidentiality in these cases since doing so *actually reduces protection to endangered third parties, increasing public peril.*

The argument advanced here is that – paradoxically – ethical and legal duties to report make it less likely that endangered parties will be protected. Depending on the prospective patient, these duties are either unnecessary (when waivers can be obtained) or counter-productive (when disclosure to the doctor is deterred and interventions other than disclosure are prevented).

In part, the conventional wisdom on confidentiality errs in focusing on the decision of the individual clinician. Perhaps little will be lost if one doctor betrays a single patient one time, or if betrayals are extremely rare. But medical ethics is not about a single decision by an individual clinician. The consequences of a rule governing professional practice may be quite different from the consequences of a single act. Better to ask: What if every doctor did that?[14]

While it is accepted here that doctors have an overriding obligation to prevent public peril, it has been argued that they do not honor that obligation by breaching or chipping away at confidentiality. This is because the protective purpose to be furthered by reporting is defeated by the practice of reporting. The best public protection is achieved where doctors do their best work and, there, trust is probably the most important prerequisite. Physicians damage both their professional capabilities and their communities when they compromise trustworthiness.

If the argument above is sound, and if, accordingly, confidentiality must be respected in this case, we can now return to the question of what the doctor must say to Wilma when, now infected, she returns to the office two years after the reconciliation. Though this question has to be faced in 1993, it is on the table well before her return to Honolulu. It is there even before Andrew asks to be tested and you have to decide whether to live out the trust he has placed in you or disabuse him of it. In fact, the problem is on the table even in 1982, when the couple asks you to become their physician. As a doctor, you have obligations of beneficence and confidentiality and you owe both to each. Now – having read this far – you are aware that something can happen that you cannot control; and, if it does, you will face those apparently conflicting obligations: you can only provide what you owe to one if you betray your obligation to the other. That is the choice you will have to make in 1993, unless you (and, more to the point, the medical profession) contour professional responsibilities.

If, in choosing a governing ethical principle, the end-in-view is to protect vulnerable third parties; and if this can be done best, as I have tried to show, by honoring confidentiality and doing one's best to protect imperiled third parties within that framework; then what you must say to Wilma and Andrew, when they first walk into your office in 1982, should be something like this:

> There is an ethical problem physicians sometimes face in taking on a married couple as patients. It can happen that one partner becomes infected with a transmissible disease, potentially endangering the other. If the infected partner won't share information with me because he or she fears I will warn the other, there will be no protection at all for the partner at risk. There may, however, be something I can do if I can talk with the infected partner. What I promise both of you is, if that were to happen, I will do everything I possibly can to protect the endangered partner, except for violating confidentiality, which I will not do. You both need to remember that you should not count on me to guarantee the wholesomeness of your spouse, if doing this means betrayal.

It is in these words that the final explanation to Wilma can be found. If Wilma understands from the beginning that medical confidentiality will not be breached; if she (and the public generally) understand that the precariously placed are safer under unqualified confidentiality, she will have final responsibility for her choices. If you are clear enough about it, she will grasp that she can't depend on you to protect her at all costs, and that she is better off because of that. Both the doctor and the medical profession collectively need to work through these issues and fully disclose the favored standard to prospective patients long before the occasion arises when a doctor must appeal to it. The view defended here is that doctors should continue to make an unqualified pledge of confidentiality to their patients, and they should mean it.

It is also appropriate to consider what one should say to Andrew, as he leaves your office in 1991 to prepare for a romantic dinner with Wilma. I once spent part of an afternoon with a health care professional who had served in the Vietnam War. His job had been counseling married enlistees who had just returned from visits with their wives but had been diagnosed with a venereal disease that was probably contracted before they left: they may have infected their wives. This former clinician had become quite skilled in convincing these young men to agree to disclosure. He stressed that their wives would likely find out eventually and that the emotional and medical consequences would be far more severe because of the delay. Most importantly – given the young soldiers' tentative decisions not to let their at-risk spouses know – he would ask whether this was a marriage they really wanted to preserve? I recall that he claimed a near perfect record in obtaining permission to notify the at-risk spouses. It would be useful if there were skilled allied caregivers, bound by confidentiality, who could routinely conduct these counseling sessions. While this is not the place to set out the full range of options for a profession reliably committed to trustworthiness, it will suffice to point out a direction for professional and institutional development.

Final Thoughts

Even if the foregoing is accepted, what may trouble doctors still is a painful fear that they will learn about an endangered person and be barred by this no-exceptions confidentiality rule from doing anything. (Actually there is only one thing they cannot do: disclose. All other paths are open.) Even if a reporting rule keeps many prospective patients out of the office, or silences them while they are there, the rule protects doctors from the moral risk of having to allow injury to third parties when a simple disclosure would prevent it. This distress is significant and has to be faced.

Here we must return to an error discussed earlier: the conflation of personal morality and professional ethics. Like law, personal morality can also conflict with professional responsibility. We considered a Jehovah's Witness surgeon, morally prohibited from administering blood transfusions to patients needing them. Like-wise a Catholic doctor may be unable to discuss certain reproduction-related options. And despite understandable moral misgivings, doctors everywhere must be prepared to administer risky treatments they know will cause the deaths of some of their patients. Paradoxically, the personal inability to risk killing one's patients can disqualify one for the practice of medicine. While personal morality should play a decisive role in career choice, it shouldn't play a decisive role within medical ethics.

Many enter medicine believing that good citizens must prevent serious injury to others, even if that means violating other obligations. But the task of professional ethics in medicine is to set out principles that, if broadly followed, will allow the profession to discharge its collective responsibilities to patients and society. Confidentiality, I have argued, is effective at getting more patients into treatment more quickly, more effective in bringing about better outcomes for more of them and – counter-intuitively – most likely to prevent harm to the largest number of third parties. Now it is ethically praiseworthy for honorable people to belong to a profession that, on balance, diminishes the amount of harm to others, even though these same professionals must sometimes knowingly allow – and even cause – harm to occur. Although doctors may feel guilty about these consequences of their actions and inactions, they are not guilty of anything. They are acting exactly as it is reasonable to want doctors to act.

It is hard enough to create therapeutic alliances that meet patients' needs. But if doctors take on the added duty to mobilize protective responses without waivers of confidentiality, their work may become impossible in too many important cases. And all of us will be the worse for that. The thinking that places the moral comfort of clinicians above the well-being of patients and their victims is in conflict with the requirements of professional responsibility, properly understood. While it will be a challenge for many honorable physicians to measure up to this standard, no one ever said it was easy to be a good doctor.[15]

Notes

1 Bernard Lo, *Resolving Ethical Dilemmas: A Guide for Clinicians*, Baltimore, MD: Williams and Wilkins, 1995, pp. 44–55.

2 M. Kottow, Medical confidentiality: an intransigent and absolute obligation, *Journal of Medical Ethics* 12 (1986), pp. 117–22.

3 Mark Wicclair, A shield right for reporters *vs.* the administration of justice and the right to a fair trial: is there a conflict? *Business and Professional Ethics, Journal* 4 (2) (winter 1985–6); Kenneth Kipnis, Confidentiality in criminal practice, in *Legal Ethics*, Englewood Cliffs, NJ: Prentice-Hall, 1986, pp. 63–79.

4 H. von Staden, "In a pure and holy way": personal and professional conduct in the Hippocratic oath, *Journal of the History of Medicine and Allied Sciences* 51 (1996): 406–8, quoted in Steven H. Miles, *The Hippocratic Oath and the Ethics of Medicine*, New York: Oxford University Press, 2004. p. 149.

5 Siegler, Mark. Confidentiality in medicine: a decrepit concept, *New England Journal of Medicine* 307 (24) (December 8, 1982): 1518–21.

6 *Tarasoff v. Regents of the University of California*, Supreme Court of California, *Tarasoff* I, 529 P.2d 553 (Cal. 1974); *Tarasoff* II, 551 P.2d 334 (Cal. 1976).

7 *Baxtrom v. Herold*, 383 US 107, 1966.

8 H.J. Steadman and J.J. Cocozza, The prediction of dangerousness – Baxtrom: a case study, in G. Cooke (ed.), *The Role of the Forensic Psychologist*, Springfield, Il.: Thomas, 1980, pp. 204–15; J.J. Cocozza and H.J. Steadman, The failure of psychiatric predictions of dangerousness: clear and convincing evidence, *Rutgers Law Review* 29 (1976): 1081–101.

9 K. Kipnis, Gender, sex, and professional ethics in child and adolescent psychiatry, *Child and Adolescent Psychiatric Clinics of North America* 13(3) (2004): 695–708.

10 K. Kipnis, The concept of professional responsibility, in *Legal Ethics*, Englewood Cliffs, NJ: Prentice-Hall, 1986, pp. 1–14.

11 T.L. Beauchamp and J.F. Childress, *Principles of Biomedical Ethics*, New York: Oxford University Press, 2001, p. 309.

12 A. Goldman, *The Philosophical Foundations of Professional Ethics*, Totowa, NJ: Rowman & Littlefield, 1980, p. 135; S. Bok, *Secrets*, New York: Pantheon Books, 1983, p. 121.

13 This division is somewhat oversimplified, but the qualifications needed would take us too far afield. One issue: patients' situations, knowledge, and attitudes can be indeterminate and subject to change.

14 Those with philosophical backgrounds will notice that the strategy used in my essay is, in part and at a certain level, rule-utilitarian. For cases like *The Infected Spouse*, the practice of unqualified confidentiality has better consequences over the long run. That is why health care professionals, legislators, and judges should adopt an unqualified rule. But there is a second, Kantian, stage of my argument. It is that the act of becoming a doctor places one under the distinctive professional obligations attaching to the clinical role. It is a role-related obligation of stewardship with deontological foundations. I think Christine Korsgaard (*The Sources of Normativity*, Cambridge, MA: Harvard University Press, 1996) is right in judging that many of our obligations are rooted in our identities or, as I would prefer, our normatively rich social roles. Ideally, professions sustain a collective process of reflection and education that is calculated to elicit a shared endorsement of evolving standards. These norms can be captured in a formal

code of ethics. If a profession is healthy, it will sustain a robust and responsible debate on the values implicit in its work and the practices in virtue of which those values can be respected, furthered, and secured. Entry into a profession would therefore involve a proper commitment to defensible professional norms.

15 An earlier version of this essay appeared as A defense of unqualified medical confidentiality, in *The American Journal of Bioethics* 6(2) (2006): 7–18. I am grateful to many whose comments and suggestions have, in my judgment, improved this paper. Among these are Leslie Francis, Rosamond Rhodes, John Banja, Alex Capron, Michael Boylan, Joan McGregor, Robert Klitzman, Jacob Kurlander, and Leanne Logan.

Chapter 7

Patient Competence and Surrogate Decision-Making

Dan W. Brock

A settled principle of medical ethics, the law, and medical practice is that physicians may not render medical care to competent patients without their informed consent (Faden and Beauchamp, 1986). This places a responsibility on physicians to ensure that patients have given valid consent before proceeding with treatment. Valid informed consent is standardly understood to have three components. First, patients must have been *informed* about their diagnosis, available alternative treatments for their condition including their rationale and likely prognoses with those treatments as well as with no treatment, and the risks and benefits of the alternative treatments. Physicians are responsible for providing this information to patients in an understandable form. Second, patients' choices must be *voluntary*. This means that the choice must have been made without coercion, manipulation, or undue influence by others, such as physicians or other family members. Physicians are responsible for ensuring that patients' choices are voluntary, which can mean helping to free patients from coercive pressure when necessary. The third requirement for valid consent is that patients have decisional capacity or *competence* to give or withhold valid consent to the treatment in question. I shall use here the concept of competence for the status of having sufficient capacity to make one's own health care decisions and the concept of decisional capacity for the underlying capacities that support the determination of competence. This third informed consent requirement of competence and how decision-making should proceed when the patient is not competent are the subjects of this chapter.

While in contested cases a patient's competence may ultimately have to be decided by the courts, in the vast majority of cases the assessment remains within the health care system. Physicians have the moral and legal responsibility to secure their patients' valid informed consent before proceeding with treatment. Since ensuring the patient's competence is one component of that consent, the patient's physician typically has the initial responsibility for assessing the patient's decisional capacities, even if in some cases others such as psychiatric consultants may be called in to aid in the assessment. How should that assessment be made? As we shall see, that assessment is both more complex and more controversial than it might at first seem. If a patient has been judged to be incompetent to make the treatment choice in question, the physician is then responsible for selecting a surrogate to act for the patient and to ensure that the surrogate is both competent and making a decision for the patient in accordance with appropriate surrogate decision-making standards. Finally, the physician may be responsible for initiating the removal of the surrogate from that role if the surrogate fails to act as required by standards for surrogacy. How then should physicians carry out these various responsibilities?

While physicians are responsible for ensuring that the patient is competent whenever decisions about treatment arise and the patient's consent is sought, this does not mean that a formal competence evaluation is required in all cases. In medical care, as elsewhere, adults are presumed to be competent unless and until they have been determined not to be. In most cases of medical decision-making, there is little or no reason to question the patient's competence to make a treatment decision, and so the presumption that the patient is competent is not seriously questioned. But when that competence does come into question, physicians need clarity about what capacities are needed for competence to give or refuse valid consent (President's Commission, 1982).

The first necessary capacity is for understanding information and communicating a choice. Some skeptics about informed consent argue that patients rarely have the necessary medical and scientific background and training to understand all the medical facts relevant to treatment choices (Ingelfinger, 1972). In its most extreme form, the skeptic holds that patients would need the same medical training as physicians have to fully understand the information relevant to the choice. But this extreme skepticism is unwarranted. Patients need not understand all the underlying biological and scientific information that their physicians understand in order to make an informed choice. What patients need to understand is how their lives will be affected by their medical conditions if untreated, and how their future life prospects may be improved by possible treatments, together with the possible risks to them of those treatments. It is the physicians' job to use their scientific and medical training and experience to explain to their patients how their life is likely to be affected by their medical condition if it is not treated, and how various possible treatments may affect those prospects. While the average patient may lack the necessary training to understand the underlying scientific basis of their diagnosis and prognosis, or of their physician's assessment of what treatments might improve that prognosis and what their risks and benefits are, that is not necessary for valid consent. If physicians fulfill their responsibility to use their medical knowledge to explain how patients are likely to be affected by their medical conditions and possible treatments, then patients are generally capable of understanding the information they need to make informed choices.

Besides the capacity to understand relevant information, decision-making competence requires the capacity to use that information in a process of reasoning and deliberation. That process largely consists of "if/then" reasoning – if I choose this, then these will be the consequences. Also required is the capacity to entertain at once or serially, and to compare the consequences of, alternative choices or courses of action. These are capacities that ordinary people regularly exercise in going about their everyday lives, and so they will be available for medical decision-making unless special circumstances impair them.

Finally, patients require values, preferences, plans, and purposes for their lives that they can use to evaluate the desirability of the consequences of alternative treatments, including the alternative of no treatment, and to select the one that will be best for them. This is not to say that people must already possess artic-ulated values with determinate relative weights that could then be applied in a straightforward and mechanical way to yield a decision about treatment. Serious medical choices often confront patients with new and difficult choices that go beyond their previous experiences. What is then necessary is the capacity to decide what value to place on various alternative consequences and outcomes so as to be able reach a decision about a course of action. This too is a capacity that ordinary people also exercise in non-medical circumstances when they are faced with new and unfamiliar choices. It is important to distinguish this third capacity to have and apply values because some accounts of competence require only capacities for understanding and reasoning. These accounts are defective, however, because a patient's values can be impaired as well. Perhaps the most important example is when severe depression distorts patients' values so that they no longer care about the harm, even including death, that may come to them without treatment. There may be no failure in their understanding or reasoning about this outcome, but they "no longer care" about the harm that will come to them. Here, mental illness that distorts what they value from what it would otherwise be can result in incom-petence to decide about treatment.

The general point is that none of these capacities necessary for competence are typically beyond ordinary people. They are all exercised continually in everyday life and do not include or require special training or expertise unavailable to typical patients. Barring special circumstances, there will be no reason to question the competence of most patients to make most treatment decisions.

Nevertheless, sometimes the effects of illness, treatment, age, or other special circumstances may impair any of these capacities. If they are fully or virtually fully impaired, as with a comatose patient, then no uncertainty or dispute will exist that the patient is not competent to make decisions about treatment. The difficult cases are those in which there is significant, but not complete, impairment of the decision-making capacities delineated above. In those cases, the physician will have to evaluate the patient's competence. In many contexts, competence is used as a global assessment of people's abilities – a competent auto-mechanic, mathemati-cian, or musician. To say that a person is competent in a particular domain is to say that she meets some general standard of ability to perform in that domain. As already noted, in many cases decision-making capacity works this way as well – the typical patient has the competence to make treatment decisions and the coma-tose patient lacks it. But in borderline cases, no general or global assessment of competence can be relied upon. Instead, the patient's capacity to make the particular treatment decision in question must be evaluated. A variety of factors, such as general confusion in their thinking, particular delusions, and severe depression, may call into question the competence of patients who have some capacity to participate in decision-making but undoubtedly the most common trigger calling patients' competence into question is their refusal of their physicians' treatment recommendations (Appelbaum et al., 1987). (This is not to say that patients' competence should not sometimes be questioned and evaluated when they agree to treatment recommendations, particularly if there are substantial differences between alternative possible treatments.) Moreover, if we assume, as seems not unreasonable, that physicians' treatment recommendations are more often than not, though certainly not always, in their patients' best interests, then refusals can often be a basis for evaluating the patient's competence. In fact, a common cause of initial refusal is patients' failure to understand the nature of recommended treatment or the reasons for the recommendation of it. That means that the most important first response to a patient's treatment refusal should be to re-explain the reasons for the recommendation. Clarifying the recommendation with the patient will usually lead to withdrawal of the refusal, but if it does not, then reconsideration of whether the recommendation was well founded is called for. When the recommendation is reaffirmed and the refusal persists, the patient's competence should often be evaluated. How is that done?

An initial point of considerable importance is that while the refusal may often serve as a reasonable trigger for the evaluation of the patient's competence, it does not constitute evidence for the patient's incompetence. Rather, the evaluation should be of the patient's decision-making process regarding the treatment in question and evidence for incompetence should consist of impairments and shortcomings in that process. Various short mini-mental status exams are sometimes used as a part of a competence evaluation, but in cases of borderline decision-making capacities, they cannot determine competence. Rather, they are best understood as somewhat crude cognitive screening devices suggesting areas of reasoning, understanding, or thinking that may be significantly impaired (Folstein et al., 1975). They can then often be useful in directing the competence evaluator to particular decision-making deficits that may be affecting the decision now in question. The competence evaluator's principal task is to understand the patient's reasoning and how she has arrived at her conclusion. The approach to the patient is often an informal one: "Help me understand why you don't want this treatment." The task is to elicit the patient's understanding of her medical condition and of the reasons for the physician's treatment recommendation, and to understand why the recommendation has been rejected.

In many cases this will allow for correction of remaining misunderstandings. In other cases it may clarify that the patient has made a choice that is in accord with her values and should be respected as a competent choice, even if different from what most people would want. But in some other cases serious impairments in the patient's decision-making may be uncovered that resist correction. For example, the patient seems unable to fully understand relevant information, is in denial about her condition or its likely prognosis without treatment, is in the grip of fear about a treatment such as surgery or about pain that may follow the treatment, and so forth. In a variety of ways, the patient's decision-making in the case in question may exhibit impairments or limitations that cannot be fully removed. The crucial question then will be: is the patient's decision-making sufficiently impaired that she should be judged to be incompetent? Or, is her understanding and reasoning good enough that her competence should be affirmed? An important complexity in the competence evaluation is that ineliminable uncertainty often remains about the patient's decision-making process – exactly what does the patient understand, exactly how did he get to the conclusion that he did, exactly what values did he use to arrive at that conclusion? – and so forth. This raises an analogous question about how much uncertainty about the patient's decision-making is compatible with affirming his competence.

It is common when a patient's competence has been called into question to get a psychiatric, or sometimes neurologic, consult about the patient's competence. Some health care institutions have liaison psychiatric services or individual psychiatrists or psychologists on staff who have built up considerable experience and clinical expertise in evaluating patients' competence. They can often be very helpful in competence evaluations, especially in evaluating the effects of medical conditions, including mental illness, on cognitive and deliberative processes. But as can be seen in the brief description above of the competence evaluation process, the evaluation need not always involve or require special psychiatric expertise and so a psychiatric consult is not a necessary component of a competence evaluation. The physician responsible for the patient's care is typically the first evaluator of the patient's competence when it has come into question, and often he or she is able to resolve the issue without need for additional consultation or involvement. When the patient's competence remains contested, with or without additional consultation from psychiatry or elsewhere, and it is important that it be resolved, appeal to the courts for a final resolution can be necessary.

In understanding the competence evaluation it is essential to understand that while the decision-making capacities delineated above as necessary for competence come in different degrees, in a particular patient on a particular occasion the status of competence for making that decision is "all or nothing," not a matter of degree. This point is compatible with the fact that a patient even at one time may be competent to make some decisions and not others, for example because of differences in their complexity, how focal delusions might affect some decisions and not others, and so forth. Moreover, a patient may not be competent to make a particular treatment decision, but nevertheless competent to select a surrogate to act for him. The all or nothing character of competence for a specific treatment decision follows from the medical and legal function of the competence determination to allocate decisional authority about the patient's treatment. If the presumption that an adult patient is competent to make his or her own decisions is affirmed, then the patient retains the authority to do so and others must respect the patient's choice. If, on the other hand, the patient is determined not to be competent to make the choice in question, then decision-making authority must be transferred to another to decide for the patient. That does not imply that the patient's preferences will always be overridden, but only that the decision no longer rests with the patient. Nor does it imply that a surrogate should always ignore an incompetent patient's preferences. Once a surrogate is in place to decide for the patient, the surrogate may or may not make a different decision than the patient had made. Likewise, for the physician there are two judgments to be made – is the patient competent to make the decision in question, and what treatment is justified?

If the patient's competence to make a particular treatment choice is a yes/no matter, and should be based on the patient's decision-making capacities as exercised in the choice in question, which are a matter of degree, then what degree of decision-making capacities should be required for competence? Or, conversely, how much decision-making impairment is sufficient for a finding of incompetence? An artificial example may help clarify the question. Suppose we had a scale of decision-making capacities as exercised on a particular occasion from zero to 100, with zero representing no capacity whatever and 100 representing ideal or perfect decision-making capacity; of course we do not now and never will have such a scale. But imagining such a scale, the question of competence is what should be a passing score for competence. We need a principled answer to this question so that competence determinations do not depend in an arbitrary way on the preferences, values, and idiosyncrasies of different competence evaluators. Setting aside cases in which the patient's medical condition may constitute a serious public health threat to others, where decision-making authority is not determined entirely by the patient's competence, the principal impact of the competence evaluation is on the patient – the patient either retains or loses the right to make his or her own decision about treatment.

What are the principal values or interests at stake for the patient in whether he or she retains or loses this decisional authority? The first is the patient's interest in self-determination or autonomy (Dworkin, 1988). This is the interest of people in making significant decisions about their lives for themselves according to their own values or conception of a good life. It is important to understand that this interest does not depend on an assumption that individuals will always make the decision that is best for them, according to either their own or anyone else's conception of what is best for them; that assumption would be false. We want to make our own decisions because that is the way we exercise some measure of control over and take responsibility for our lives, even recognizing that we will not always make the best decision. The general requirement of informed consent is based in large part on recognition of this interest of ordinary people in self-determination. Sometimes the moral principle concerning self-determination is characterized as a right to self-determination, but whether characterized as a moral right or an interest, it is not absolute in the sense that it always trumps all other rights or interests. If it was, then in the context of consent to medical care, patients' choices would always have to be respected, whether or not they were competent to make those choices.

The second value or interest of patients in whether they retain treatment decision-making authority or that authority is instead transferred to a surrogate is their own well-being (Griffin, 1989). In some cases patients' refusal of their physicians' treatment recommendations could have a great and harmful impact on their well-being, including in some cases leading to their preventable death. Sometimes not refusing all treatment, but insisting on a far from optimal treatment, can also have serious adverse effects on patients' well-being. Individuals' reasonable and near universal concern for their own well-being supports steps to protect it when their seriously impaired decision-making capacities result in a treatment choice that would be seriously harmful to them. This is not an imposition that most patients would not want, though they may be resisting it at the time. Most patients would want others to act to protect their well-being if their decision-making is seriously impaired and has resulted in a choice likely to be seriously harmful.

Usually, patients' treatment choices will be in accord with their own well-being and there will be no conflict between respecting their self-determination and protecting their well-being. Their decisional authority and treatment choices should then be respected. But when the patient's decision-making capacities are seriously impaired resulting in a harmful choice, then these two values will be in conflict and must be balanced. It is not possible to state precisely how they should be balanced or traded off, and the proper balancing is ethically controversial in any case. Different people give different relative weight or importance to their own self-determination and well-being. Perhaps the most important point about this balancing is that the weight the two values should receive will vary significantly depending on the circumstances of the choice in question. In particular, given the same degree of decision-making impairment, the consequences for the patient's well-being of accepting his or her choice can range all the way from highly positive to highly negative. If the consequences are positive, then there is no need to limit the patient's self-determination in order to protect his or her well-being. However, the more serious the negative effects on the patient's well-being of accepting his or her choice, the more weight should be given to the value of protecting the patient's well-being. The value properly accorded to the patient's self-determination can vary as well, though not generally to the same extent. For example, most people give greater value to having their self-determination respected the more far-reaching and enduring the consequences of a choice on their lives – whom to marry versus what to have for lunch – and the more their decision-making capacities remain intact and adequate to the decision at hand.

Other things being equal, the more serious the negative consequences of accepting the patient's choice, the higher the level of decision-making capacities as exhibited in the decision at hand that is reasonably required; for example, the higher the level of understanding of the consequences of the choice that should be required. Another way of putting the balancing issue is that competence evaluators should seek to avoid two possible mistakes – on the one hand, failing to adequately respect the patient's self-determination when the patient has sufficient decision-making capacity, and, on the other hand, failing to protect the patient's well-being when the patient's seriously impaired decision-making capacity has led to a seriously harmful choice. The necessary balancing will seek to avoid both of these errors. I noted earlier that there is sometimes significant ineliminable uncertainty about the patient's decision-making – just what the patient understands, how his or her reasoning led to the choice that was made, etc. Again, other things being equal, the more serious the adverse consequences for the patient of accepting his choice, the higher the level of certainty reasonably required about his decision-making capacity as exercised in the decision in question.

One consequence of this view about the values to be balanced in setting a standard of competence is that the standard is properly a variable one, and so the patient's competence is a choice-specific evaluation (Buchanan and Brock, 1989). It is uncontroversial that at least in borderline cases the patient's competence should not be understood as a global property of the patient – holding in all cases or in none. Rather, a patient's decision-making capacities can vary over time from effects of the disease, of its treatment, from whether the patient is in familiar or unfamiliar surroundings, and so forth. As a result, an important responsibility of the physician is to take whatever steps may improve and optimize the patient's decision-making capacities, such as tapering or temporarily stopping medications that interfere with those capacities. As already noted, patients may also be competent even at any one time to make some decisions but not others; for example, some decisions may be very simple while others may require fairly difficult balancing of complex alternatives.

The more controversial implication of this account of the balancing required in making a determination of competence is that a patient might be properly found to be competent to consent to a treatment, but not to refuse it, or vice versa. That is principally because the consent and the refusal could and often do have radically different consequences for the patient's well-being, and so the balancing of self-determination and well-being could come out differently in the case of consent and refusal. For example, compare a patient in the Emergency Room (ER) with classic signs of meningitis who refuses to have a diagnostic lumbar puncture (LP) and instead wants to leave the ER without further diagnostic or treatment measures versus the same patient who consents to the LP; accepting the first choice has life-threatening implications for the patient's well-being, while accepting the second choice serves the patient's well-being.

Suppose a patient has been determined to be incompetent to make the treatment decision at hand. How then should the physician proceed? Some time ago, when physicians often made treatment decisions without significant involvement of even competent patients, it was common for physicians also to make treatment decisions for incompetent patients. With shared decision-making between physicians and competent patients having largely replaced that earlier practice of physician paternalism, it is now accepted in ethics, the law and medical practice that a surrogate should be selected to act for an incompetent patient in shared decision-making with the physician (Buchanan and Brock, 1989). How should that surrogate be selected? In some cases, the patient may remain competent to select a surrogate even if he is not competent to decide about treatment, and then he should be permitted to do so. In other cases, one respect in which patients' self-determination can be respected when they are incompetent and unable to decide about treatment for themselves is to select as surrogate the person they would have wanted to act in that role for them. Sometimes patients will have executed a Health Care Proxy or Durable Power of Attorney for Health Care, formally appointing a surrogate for them (Emanuel et al., 1991). In that case, that person should be the surrogate so long as he or she is competent. In most cases, however, patients will not have formally selected a surrogate by such means. Physicians are then responsible for working with available family members and/or close friends of the patient to select an appropriate surrogate. The goal should still be to select whom the patient would have wanted as surrogate, and this will usually be a close family member. Health Care Decision Acts, which now exist in most states, authorize physicians to use available family members as surrogates without going to court for their formal appointment as surrogates or guardians, and typically designate the order of priority of family members to be surrogates (Menikoff, Sachs and Siegler, 1992). Some of these statutes also authorize physicians, in the absence of an available family member, to select another adult who has exhibited special care and concern for the patient and who is familiar with the patient's personal values. Such a friend who is reasonably available may act as surrogate.

However, sometimes there is evidence that the family member with priority under these legal rules is not the appropriate surrogate; for example, the patient is estranged from his or her spouse but has close adult children, or is estranged from his or her legal family, but has a long-time same-sex partner. In these cases, the physician's responsibility is to negotiate with the involved parties to seek agreement on the appropriate surrogate, which can require supporting an appeal to the courts for a formal designation of the surrogate if necessary. In other cases, there may be several possible surrogates, for example several adult children of the patient, and no evidence that the patient would have preferred any one of them to be surrogate and no other obvious reason to prefer one to the others. Then the physician can seek to work with the family group so long as it is able to function effectively in the surrogate role as a group; if it is not, the physician can ask the family to decide who among them will act as surrogate. In all these cases, the aim is to select a surrogate whom the patient would have wanted and who knows the patient well and is concerned for the patient's well-being. When a possible surrogate has serious conflicts of interest with the patient that could affect the decisions to be made, then another surrogate should be sought.

In some cases, there may be no appropriate person, either family or friends, to act as surrogate for an incompetent patient. Here, practice varies significantly across different institutions and for different kinds of decisions. The responsible physician will often make relatively uncontroversial decisions. For more controversial or consequential decisions, such as the issuance of a Do Not Resuscitate order or the withholding or withdrawal of other life support, some institutions require consultation with the chief of service or with an ethics committee. Sometimes, an institution will go to court to have a surrogate appointed with formal legal authority to make such decisions. What is most important is that institutions have developed a decision-making procedure for such cases so that decision-making does not become paralyzed by the absence of a surrogate and the patient's care suffer as a result.

Once a surrogate has been selected, the issue arises of what standard the surrogate should try to apply in making treatment decisions for the patient. This might seem to be only a question for the surrogate and not for the physician, but that would be a mistake for at least two reasons. First, the surrogate will be making decisions together with the responsible physician and will typically seek the physician's guidance about decisions to be made. This can be guidance about the particular choice at hand, or more general guidance about how to approach decision-making. Physicians often are able and should seek to help surrogates understand their proper role as surrogates. That not only will often make decision-making go more smoothly, but also will generally lead to better decisions. Second, since surrogates' decision-making authority should not be understood to be absolute, physicians will sometimes have to make judgments about whether surrogates' decisions are within the proper bounds of their authority, and about how to proceed if they are not; to make these judgments physicians must understand the proper role of surrogates.

We can start by distinguishing three ordered guidance principles for surrogates' decisions, although this simple picture will have to be complicated later (Buchanan and Brock, 1989). The principles are ordered in the sense that the first should be applied if possible, if it cannot be then the second should be applied, and if the second cannot be applied, then the third should be applied. These different principles are not competitors for use in the same circumstances, but rather are to be applied in different circumstances. The Advance Directives principle directs the surrogate to follow the instructions in the patient's advance directive. Quite obviously, this can only be used when the patient has an advance directive, either a so-called living will or a Durable Power of Attorney for Health Care. Despite extensive efforts over three decades to increase the use of advance directives, most Americans still do not have them. Even when patients have them they often do not get into the medical record so that surrogates and physicians can make use of them. Finally, even when available they usually lack explicit directions that clearly apply to the decision at hand (Teno et al., 1997). Since they must be executed by patients while still competent and often well in advance of when they are needed, individuals will generally not have anticipated either their current medical condition or the treatments about which decisions must be made. In the case of progressive or chronic diseases with relatively predictable courses, this problem is reduced, but clear and precise instructions are still difficult to formulate and are uncommon. The result is that advance directives typically require significant and often difficult interpretation by the surrogate and physician.

When no advance directive exists with clear instructions about the decision at hand, the Substituted Judgment principle directs the surrogate to attempt to make the decision that the patient would have made in the circumstances if competent. Since surrogates will usually be a close family member or friend of the patient, their job will be to use their knowledge of the patient to attempt to decide what the patient would have wanted in the circumstances. Sometimes this will be relatively clear as a result of previous explicit discussions with the patient about the patient's treatment wishes, although these too will usually have been relatively general and so require some interpretation by the surrogate for the decision at hand. In other cases, in the absence of explicit prior discussions, surrogates will have to use their general knowledge of the patient's values and desires to make a judgment about what the patient would likely have wanted. In either case, surrogates will often have to make judgments in the face of some uncertainty about what the patient would have wanted.

A number of studies have shown that family members are incorrect at least a quarter of the time in their judgments about what their incompetent family members would have wanted, though no less inaccurate than patients' physicians are (Sulmasy et al., 1998). If making the decision the patient would have made were the only ground for the family member being the surrogate, this might seem to call the family member's authority as surrogate decision maker into question. Even on this ground, however, it would do so only if there were someone else who would generally do a more accurate job of determining the patient's wishes; research has not identified any such party. But as already noted above, this is not the only ground of the surrogate's authority, indeed not even the most important ground (Brock, 1997). The most important ground is that a close family member or friend is typically the person the patient would have wanted to act as surrogate, recognizing that that person will not always accurately reflect the patient's wishes. Physicians must be prepared to accept within limits some decisions by surrogates that they believe are not likely what the patient would have wanted both because they are not better than surrogates at knowing that and because making the most accurate substituted judgment decisions is not the sole or even the principal ground of the surrogate's decision-making authority.

Finally, when the surrogate has no relevant knowledge about what the patient would have wanted, then the Best Interests guidance principle should be used. This directs the surrogate to make the decision in the patient's best interests, which means in a more practical sense the decision that most reasonable persons would make in the circumstances. This is the appropriate guidance principle because it is to be used only in circumstances in which the surrogate lacks any relevant information or evidence about how the patient's wishes would likely have been different from those of most people.

As noted above, these three guidance principles are to be used in different circumstances: Advance Directives when there is an advance directive with relevant and clear instructions; Substituted Judgment when there is no such advance directive, but the surrogate has sufficient relevant knowledge of the patient and his or her values and desires to make a judgment about what the patient would have wanted; Best Interests when there is no advance directive and no surrogate with knowledge of the patient's relevant preferences and values. Probably the most important respect in which this ordering, with each principle to be applied in different circumstances, requires qualification is that real circumstances do not divide as neatly as it suggests. Sometimes there is an advance directive with instructions that provide some evidence, but unclear or indecisive evidence, of what the patient wanted; sometimes a surrogate similarly has some, but indecisive evidence of the patient's likely wishes. In these cases, more than one of the three guidance principles may be used at the same time; for example, the less clear the instructions in an advance directive, the more the surrogate may have to rely as well on substituted judgment reasoning, and the more substituted judgment reasoning may remain indecisive, the more it may have to be supplemented by best interests reasoning. A second qualification to this ordering is that it is not uncontroversial. Some commentators have defended the Best Interests principle even when it is in conflict with an advance directive or with substituted judgment (Dresser, 1986).

For the physician, perhaps the most important use of these guidance principles is in helping surrogates understand their proper role, how they should be trying to make decisions. So, to take a crude but unfortunately still familiar example, the physician's question to the surrogate should not be, "Do you want us to give this treatment to your mother?" but rather, "Use your knowledge of your mother to help us decide together whether she likely would have wanted this treatment." This framing by the physician of the surrogate's decision-making role helps the surrogate to arrive at the right decision by having asked the right question, but also has the added benefit of often making decision-making psychologically and emotionally easier for the surrogate by properly shifting the burden of responsibility off of the surrogate and back to the patient to the extent possible in the circumstances.

The second important lesson here for physicians from these guidance principles is that there are limits to the surrogate's decision-making authority. Typical Durable Powers of Attorney for Health Care explicitly deny to the surrogate any authority to make decisions in conflict with the patient's known wishes or, if they are not known, in conflict with the patient's fundamental interests. One aspect of physicians' responsibility to their incompetent patients is to ensure that those limits have not been exceeded. This is not to say that it will always be either clear or uncontroversial whether they have been – for example, whether the surrogate is reasonably interpreting the advance directive, whether a conflict of interest is motivating the surrogate to make a decision in conflict with the patient's wishes or interests, and so forth. It should not always be assumed that surrogates should never give weight to their own interests, since in some cases there may be good reason to believe that the patient selected this surrogate in order for the surrogate to be able to do that. Particularly within families, it is common for family members to give substantial weight to the interests of other family members in a wide range of their decisions, including medical decisions. When there is a serious question about the appropriateness of the surrogate's decision, the physician should re-explore the decision with the surrogate and other family members. If that does not resolve the issue, consultation with an ethics committee or, if necessary, appeal to the courts to seek to have a different surrogate appointed will help the physician protect the patient's interests.

This chapter has provided an ethical framework for the determination of patients' competence to give or withhold consent, and for surrogate decision-making for incompetent patients. But more should not be expected from an ethical framework than it can provide. An ethical framework can help guide involved parties through these often difficult determinations and choices, but it cannot eliminate all emotional burdens that come with them, avoid the need for sensitive judgment, or eliminate all ethical controversies about patients' competence and surrogate decision-making.

References

Appelbaum, P.S., Lidz, C.W., and Meisel, A. (1987), *Informed Consent: Legal Theory and Clinical Practice*, New York: Oxford University Press.

Brock, D.W. (1997), What is the moral authority of family members to act as surrogates for incompetent patients? *The Milbank Quarterly* 74 (4): 599–618.

Buchanan, A.B. and Brock, D.W. (1989), *Deciding for Others: The Ethics of Surrogate Decision-Making*, New York: Cambridge University Press.

Dresser, R. (1986), Life, death, and incompetent patients: conceptual infirmities and hidden values in the law, *Arizona Law Review* 28: 373–405.

Dworkin, G. (1988), *The Theory and Practice of Autonomy*, New York: Cambridge University Press.

Emanuel, L.L., Barry, M.J., Stoeckle, J.D., Ettelson, L.M., and Emanuel, E.J. (1991), Advance directives for medical care – a case for greater use, *New England Journal of Medicine* 324: 889–95.

Faden, R.R. and Beauchamp, T.L. (1986), *A History and Theory of Informed Consent*, New York: Oxford University Press.

Folstein, M.F., Folstein, M.E., and McHugh, P.R. (1975), "Mini-mental state." A practical method for grading the cognitive state of patients for the clinician, *Journal of Psychiatric Research* 3: 189–98.

Griffin, J. (1989), *Well-Being: Its Meaning, Measurement, and Moral Importance*, Oxford: Oxford University Press.

Ingelfinger, F. (1972), Informed (but uneducated) consent, *New England Journal of Medicine* 287: 465–6.

Menikoff, J.A., Sachs, G.A., and Siegler, M. (1992), Beyond advance directives – health care surrogate laws, *New England Journal of Medicine* 327 (16): 1165–9.

President's Commission for the Study of Ethical Problems in Medicine and Biomedical and Behavioral Research, (1982), *Making Health Care Decisions*, Washington, DC: US Government Printing Office.

Sulmasy, D.P., Terry, P.B., Weisman, C.S., et al. (1998), The accuracy of substituted judgments in patients with terminal diagnoses, *Annals of Internal Medicine* 128 (8): 621–9.

Teno, J.M., Licks, S., Lynn, J., et al. (1997), Do advance directives provide instructions that direct care? *Journal of the American Geriatrics Society* 45 (4): 519–20.

Additional Reading

Brock, D.W. (1989), Children's competence for health care decisionmaking, in J. Moskop and L. Koppelman (eds.), *Children and Health Care: Moral and Social Issues*, Dordrecht/Boston: D. Reidel Publishing.

Cantor, N.F. (2005), *Making Medical Decisions for the Profoundly Mentally Disabled*, Cambridge MA: MIT Press.

Grisso, T. and Appelbaum, P.S. (1998), *Assessing Competence to Consent to Treatment: A Guide for Physicians and Other Health Professionals*, New York: Oxford University Press.

Grisso, T. and Appelbaum, P.S. (1998), *MacArthur Competence Assessment Tool for Treatment (MaccatT)*, Sarasota, FL: Professional Resources Press.

King, N.N.P. (1996), *Making Sense of Advance Directives*, Washington, DC: Georgetown University Press.

Roth, L.H., Meisel, A. and Lidz C.W. (1977), Tests of competency to consent to treatment, *American Journal of Psychiatry* 134: 279–84.

Weithorn, L.A. and Campbell, S.B. (1982), The competency of children and adolescents to make informed consent treatment decisions, *Child Development* 53: 1589–98.

White, B.C. (1994), *Competence to Consent*, Washington, DC: Georgetown University Press.

Chapter 8

Ending Life

F.M. Kamm

In this chapter, I shall discuss several approaches to the issues of terminating life-saving treatment, suicide, euthanasia, and assisted suicide. I shall also consider the issue of giving advance directions for end of life decisions.[1] I shall be presenting key concepts and arguments that bear on a health care provider's making end of life decisions for and with patients.

Conceptual Issues

Suicide (S) involves one intending one's death either as an end itself or as a means to some further end. Assisted suicide (AS) involves someone helping another person commit suicide. Sometimes, we can help people accomplish their goals without sharing their goals. Hence, it remains open that someone who assists a suicide does not intend that the patient kill himself, only, perhaps, that he be able to do whatever he wants to do. Often, it is the physician assisted suicide (PAS) that people are most interested in. Euthanasia (E) involves someone doing something to bring about someone else's death – in particular, killing or letting die – with the intention that the person die because the death is in the best interests of the person who will die. (Unlike S and AS, death being in the person's interests is involved in the definition of E.)

How can death be overall in someone's interest? Suppose death shortens a person's life so that the life has fewer bad things in it and does not deprive him of any significant good things because there would not have been any. Then death might be in someone's interest because his shorter life is a better thing than his longer life would have been. For example, we could imagine, independently of any question of active termination, that someone could prefer, because it would be better for him, that he was created to a life of 60 years with no pain in it than to be created to a life of 61 years where the last year was full of pain. This could be so even if death is bad not only when it deprives us of goods but also because it puts an end to us as persons. Prolonging our life may not be worth every misery, especially since we cannot be immortal in any case. Someone does not have to continue on experiencing good things (e.g., relief from pain) in order for the shorter life to be better for him.

It is possible that there are alternative ways of deciding whether death would be best for someone besides weighing the forthcoming goods and bads. For example, some insist that we must consider how the future goods and bads connect psychologically with the interests of the person at the time the death would occur. (These are known as time-relative interests.) For, it is argued, even if future goods would belong to the person in question, the fact that he now would not have even an indirect psychological connection to himself in the future (e.g., if he were to undergo radical dementia) makes the person now have no stake in remaining alive to get those future goods. It is also suggested that we must consider how what will happen from now on completes the life the person has already had – the same future attached to different pasts might render one life, but not another, bad overall.[2] But, in addition, it may be that some near future event will be so bad that even if it would eventually be followed by an outweighing degree of good that satisfies current time-relative interests, one should not have to go through it. There is a deontological quality to this reasoning – for just as the deontologist says that there are some things one need not do to promote best consequences in general, the reasoning claims that there are some things a person might reasonably not go through even to promote the best consequences for himself.

S, AS, and E need not be involved in actions that bring about death. For example, if we disconnect a patient from life support simply because he does not want invasive treatment, or if we give pain relief via morphine that as a side effect kills the patient, our acts will bring about death but will not involve S, AS, or E.

Discussion of S, AS, and E, and terminating treatment (TT) for other reasons, are complicated by the fact that many subtle distinctions in how these might be brought about are often thought to have moral relevance. In this section, I shall describe some of these distinctions, without yet judging how they affect moral permissibility.

S and E involve intending death. This is to be distinguished both from doing something foreseeing, even with certainty, that death will come about as a side effect, and from doing something because (that is, on account of the fact that) it will cause death. For example, one could give a drug to reduce a patient's pain only on condition that it also has a side effect of causing his death, this being the only way to avoid a side effect of the drug that is worse than pain or death. Doing this would not imply that one intended the death, I think.

S, AS, and E may each have what are called passive (p) and active (a) versions. Active suicide (S_a) involves inducing death by, for example, shooting oneself. Active assisted suicide (AS_a) could involve a doctor giving a patient death-inducing pills. Active euthanasia (E_a) involves someone inducing death by, for example, injecting a death-causing drug. Passive versions of S, AS, and E may involve *acts* or *omissions*. Hence, in this discussion, the distinction between passive and active is not the same as the distinction between omission and act. For example, a doctor could perform E_p by actively pulling a plug on life-saving treatment he was providing to a patient, if pulling the plug does not introduce a cause of death but allows the underlying disease to kill the patient. He could perform PAS_p by pulling the plug on sedation of a patient so that sleepiness does not interfere with a patient's killing himself. E_p, AS_p, and S_p could take place by omission as well. For example, a patient may omit taking his life-saving drug with the intention that death occurs. As noted above, one could terminate treatment that is life saving without an intention that death come about and without the patient having an intention to die. For example, a patient may simply not want invasive or expensive treatment, even though he foresees that he will die without it. Or an agent might terminate treatment on one patient in order to provide treatment to another merely foreseeing the death of the first.

Which of these behaviors is killing and which letting die? This question is not settled by considering the agent's intentions. One can omit life-saving aid, intending death, without this being a killing. And one can kill by injecting a person with a pain-killing drug that has a later side effect of causing his death, even though one did not intend to kill him but only to relieve his pain.

It seems that all active S and E involve killings. TT by an act could be a killing if, for example, it triggers an electrical discharge that causes the patient's death. (Active AS does not involve a killing by the agent who is the provider of the death-inducing substance.) E_p that involves someone acting to terminate treatment that is life saving and that they (or an agent they represent) did not provide can be a killing, for example, when such a person does not have the consent to terminate treatment of the person who will die. This is true even though there is no inducing of death. It is true even though a doctor who terminates aid she is providing only lets die, as much as if she did not start the aid, even if the patient objects to TT. (Perhaps, however, it can be said that the doctor helps someone die only when she terminates aid but not when she does not begin providing life-saving assistance.) Why does consent sometimes matter and sometimes not matter to whether TT is a killing? If one removes what one is providing that helps make life-saving treatment possible, then one either lets another or oneself die. One lets oneself die when one removes one's body from the treatment, or denies consent to interference with one's body, and the doctor lets die when she removes her (hospital) resources. If one is a representative of those who either provide treatment or their own bodies to the treatment process, one will, in TT, let die. One becomes a representative of someone who provides his body for treatment if one receives his consent. Hence, a treating doctor providing treatment may not require patient consent in order to be performing a letting die in TT, but some other agent may require patient (or doctor) consent in order to be performing a letting die rather than a killing in TT. (None of this speaks to the permissibility of the letting die or killing.)

This role of consent leads us to the next distinction: that between the voluntary (V), the nonvoluntary (NV), and the involuntary (IV) in the context of S, AS, and E. V just means willed by the party either killed or let die, IV means against the will of the party killed or let die, and NV means killing or letting die takes place in the absence of there being a determination by the person killed or let die as to what he or she wills. (It may also refer to acting without knowledge of his or her willing, when an attempt has been made to ascertain the choice. In the case of AS, the object of choice is the assistance of another rather than the death.) That one's act or choice is voluntary does not ensure that it is a fully autonomous choice of a rational agent. Someone could be irrational, uninformed, or even coerced when he makes a voluntary choice. Suicide seems, by definition, to be voluntary, but it is not necessarily always a fully autonomous choice. TT, E, and AS could be V, IV, or NV. While someone may choose against E, AS, or TT, making it IV were it to occur, this choice too may not be fully autonomous.

The last distinctions I shall point to are those among the morally permissible, impermissible, and dutiful. None of the previous distinctions we have discussed has been assumed to be equivalent to, or to serve as conclusive evidence of, the permissibility or impermissibility of conduct. So, the fact that some behavior would be a killing or an involuntary withholding or termination of treatment should not be assumed to settle the question of whether the behavior is permissible or impermissible. For example, a doctor refusing to provide treatment, against the will of the patient, when not providing treatment is in the patient's best interests, might be permissible. A doctor's TT that constitutes a letting die against the will of the patient may be impermissible, even if it is not a killing. Killing someone who autonomously chooses to be killed may sometimes be permissible. *Not* refusing treatment to a patient or *not* killing him could sometimes be *im*permissible, for all that has been said so far, and then one would have a duty to not treat or to kill. In the next part, we shall consider whether certain killings and lettings die are permissible, impermissible, or dutiful.

Arguments concerning AS, E, or TT

We shall consider two types of arguments in favor of AS and E and objections to them.

1

In the work known as "The philosophers' brief on assisted suicide,"[3] it is argued that it is sometimes permissible to omit or terminate treatment with the intention that the patient die, and that if this is permissible, it is sometimes permissible to assist in killing with the intention that the patient die, at least when the patient consents. One reason that is given for this conclusion is that there is no intrinsic moral difference between killing and letting die and that "the 'common-sense' [moral] distinction . . . is not between acts and omissions, but between acts and omissions that are designed to cause death and those that are not."

Objections

This is a defense of PAS on the assumption that the doctor does intend the patient's death. Let us assume this is true in the following discussion of the defense. I agree that the *act/omission* distinction will not bear much moral weight in this setting, but this does not mean that if intending versus foreseeing death matters, it alone matters. For killing versus letting die, which is not the same as act versus omission, may matter. When doctors remove life-sustaining treatment by pulling a plug at time t, they act (though do not necessarily kill) and their act could be as permissible as not starting treatment at time t (an omission). As I argued above, if doctors are terminating treatment at time t that they (or the organization whose agent they are) have been providing, then in certain cases they *let* die rather than kill, and their act is as permissible (or as impermissible) as not starting treatment at time t would be. The doctors let die, even though they act, because (1) the patient dies of some underlying cause whose effects the life support was counter-acting[4] and (2) the patient loses out only on life he or she would have had with the support the doctors (or organization whose agent they are) are providing.

Is there always a moral difference between letting die (by act or omission) and killing? I do not think so. Some TT could be killings that would be no more difficult to justify than cases of letting die (that involve omissions or acts). Hence, if killing versus letting die sometimes matters morally, this does not mean it must always matter. For example, suppose that one particular hospital in a community is known to have faulty electrical wiring. If the doctors at that hospital accede to a patient's request to terminate treatment by pulling the plug on the life-support machine, they and the patient know that he will get a painless electric shock and die (Faulty Wiring Case I). In another hospital, if we would terminate treatment on the same patient, she would die immediately of her underlying condition. I think that in these cases it is no harder to justify TT when this kills than to justify TT that just lets the patient die; it is not true that if the patient is in one hospital, we may not TT, but if she is in the other hospital, we may. In Faulty Wiring Case I, the patient is killed by the shock, he does not die because some underlying medical condition he has is the cause of death; but the fact that the patient loses out only on life he would have had with the doctor's help – a factor like that present in letting die cases and present in this particular killing case – helps render the killing on a moral par with letting die.

There are also other commonly accepted instances in which doctors kill their patients, and doing so is morally permissible. When a doctor gives morphine to ease pain, foreseeing that it will also cause death, the doctor also acts, and kills (though without intending to kill). Yet, it is often permissible to do this, at least if the patient permits it.

However, I part company with the authors of "The philosophers' brief" when they argue that, once patients have consented, we can *always* move from the permissibility of letting the patient die while intending his death to the permissibility of PAS that involves patients killing themselves. Killing and assisting killing are not always on a moral par with letting die. Let me explain by reference to some cases.

(a) In all the first type of cases, doctors act *against* their patients' wishes to live. Suppose doctors may permissibly deny a life-saving organ to a patient who wants it, in order to give it to another, but *not* kill a nonconsenting patient in order to get that patient's organ for another. Some hold that this is not because of a moral difference between letting patients die and killing them, but because the doctors merely foresee death in the first case, whereas they intend it in the second. Intending the patients' death, against their wishes, it is said, makes the behavior impermissible.

But suppose that a doctor who denied an organ to a patient and gave it to another person who needs it more did this because the person denied the organ was his enemy whose death he intended; giving the organ to the needier person was only a pretext. (Call this the Enemy Case.) Though we can conclude that the doctor has a bad character, I do not think that we should conclude that he acted impermissibly in giving the organ to the needier patient. This shows that intending a patient's death when it is against his wishes does not necessarily make not aiding impermissible.[5]

Now I shall defend the claim that killing versus letting die can make a moral difference in the absence of intending death against a patient's wishes. If it were intending death and not killing that makes a moral difference in the case where doctors kill patients in order to get their organs for others, it should be as permissible to kill patients when their death is *not intended* as it is to let them die when their death is not intended. Suppose that a doctor, in order to transplant organs (innocently gotten) into several needy patients, uses a chemical that he *foresees* will seep into the next room where another patient lies, killing that patient. In this case, the doctor does not intend the death of the patient in the other room, but only foresees that patient's death as a side effect of the chemical. Presumably, though, transplanting when this effect will occur is wrong, even if it cannot be done otherwise, because it is a killing. Yet, letting the patient next door die simply because one is busy transplanting into several needy patients is permissible. So, in cases in which we merely foresee death, killing may be wrong, even if letting die is not. This shows that there is a per se moral difference between killing and letting die that can lead to differential moral judgments in at least some cases.

It can be claimed that a doctor who lets patients die of asphyxiation against their will, intending that they die so that their organs are available for use in others, has done something wrong, as has a doctor who kills the same sort of patients, intending them to die. When the letting die and the killing are both wrong, as in these cases, I would say that this is because both doctors violate their patients' rights. The first doctor violates the positive right to treatment without this denial being the immediate alternative to doing something else more important (such as saving two other people); the second doctor violates the negative right against being killed. But this does not always imply, as "The philosophers' brief" states, that a "doctor violates his patient's rights whether the doctor acts or refrains from acting *against the patient's wishes* in a way that is designed to cause death." We have already discussed a counter-example in the Enemy Case. For another example, suppose that patients do not want to die, but it would be in their interest to die. If a treatment is experimental, or in general something to which the patients have no positive right, it may be permissible to deny it to them even when one does this only because death would be in their own best interest. I do not believe that the patient acquires a right to have the experimental therapy merely because the doctors' reason for refusing it is that they aim at a death which is in the patient's interest but which the patient does not want. But it would violate a patients' rights and be morally wrong to kill those patients if they did not want to die, even if it were in their best interests to die and the doctors acted for their best interests. Once again, we see a case where a moral difference between killing and letting die surfaces.

(b) Next, consider the second type of case in which the patient consents to death. These are the cases that bear directly on whether the killing/letting-die distinction is morally relevant in AS contexts. Does the distinction between killing and letting die make a moral difference when deciding on the *scope* of permissible refusal of treatment versus the scope of permissible assistance to killing? Some suggest that the scope should be the same, saying that if doctors can turn off a respirator, intending death, they can prescribe lethal pills. Prescribing pills is a way to assist patients to kill themselves, even when they are not currently receiving life support, and it is this sort of AS that some think is permissible. In addition, by turning off a respirator, they have in mind, I believe, cases where the patient is then left to die. It is these sorts of cases of killing and letting die that I shall compare first.

Mentally competent patients may legally refuse treatment, intending to die, even when it is *against their best interests* to do so and, on many occasions, even when they could be cured. Presumably, in many of these cases, they could also insist on the doctor terminating treatment, even if their intention is to die. Furthermore, even if the doctors themselves in these cases improperly intend that the patients die, the treatment must be terminated. *This is because the alternative to letting the patients die is forcing treatment on them.* We think that the right of mentally competent patients not to be physically invaded against their will is typically stronger than our interest in the patients' well-being (even if the right could be overridden for considerations of public safety). But if such patients ask for assistance in killing themselves when it is against their medical interest to die, it might well be morally *impermissible* to assist in killing them. This is, at least in part, because the alternative is not forcing treatment on them. So, contrary to what some think, doctors might in some cases be permitted and even required to turn off a respirator, even when the doctors intend death, but not be permitted to give pills that will cause death.

The argument against the general moral equivalence of AS and TT, even when the patient consents to these, also helps us see that sometimes killing or assisting in killing will have the same moral standing as TT. For example, in Faulty Wiring Case I, we will kill a patient (or assist in killing him), if we help the patient disconnect himself. This is because he dies of the electric shock from disconnection. But since the patient will continue to be interfered with against his will if we do not do this, we should terminate treatment even when we know that the shock will ensue.

In sum, I have argued that the claim that whenever terminating life saving treatment while intending death is permissible, then AS while intending death is also permissible is not correct. A further argument would be needed in order to show the permissibility of AS.

2

We have considered an argument that if we may let die (including TT) while intending death, then we may kill or assist killing while intending death. By contrast, we could argue that if we may treat a patient, when he consents, though we *foresee* that this treatment will rapidly kill him, then we may kill or assist in killing a patient, when he consents, while *intending* his death, even when our behavior has no other good effects for him besides ending his life.

Consider the following four-step argument below. Assuming patient consent:

1   Doctors may permissibly relieve pain in a patient (e.g., by giving morphine), even if they know with certainty that this will cause the death of the patient as a foreseen side effect, when death is a lesser evil and pain relief is a greater good and only the morphine can stop the pain. Call this the Morphine for Pain Relief (MPR) Case.
2   Doctors may permissibly intentionally cause other lesser evils to patients when these are the means to patients' medically relevant greater good (e.g., a doctor might permissibly intentionally cause them pain temporarily, if only this would keep them from falling into a permanent coma).
3   When death is a lesser evil for a person, it is not morally different from other lesser evils.[6]
4   Therefore, when death is a lesser evil and pain relief is a good for the same person (just as it is in step 1), it is also permissible to intentionally cause death, or assist in its being intentionally caused, when it alone can stop pain. (For example, we could give morphine, which itself no longer relieves pain, in order to induce death.)

Here is the alternative four-step argument. Assuming patient consent:

1a Doctors may permissibly relieve pain in a patient (e.g., by giving morphine), even if they know with certainty that *this will cause the death of the patient as a foreseen side effect* (and even if death is a greater evil than pain), when death is unavoidably imminent in any case (e.g., in a terminal patient) and the morphine alone can stop pain.

2a Doctors may permissibly intentionally cause other (greater) evils to patients, if the evils are unavoidably imminent anyway, when these evils are the means to the patients' medically relevant (lesser) goods. (For example, suppose that it is worse to be blind than to be deaf. If a patient will shortly be blind anyway, it would be permissible to intentionally cause the blindness, if only this would prevent the patient from also going deaf.)

3a When death is an imminent evil for a person, it is not morally different from other imminent evils.

4a Therefore, doctors may permissibly intentionally cause death, or assist in its being intentionally caused, when death is imminent anyway and it alone can stop pain in the same patient (even if death is a greater evil and relief of pain is a lesser good).

In the alternative four-step argument, we need not assume that a shorter life with less suffering can be better for someone than a much longer one with more suffering, only that it is in one's interest to die somewhat sooner when death would come soon anyway and only dying sooner can reduce suffering.

The general structure of the two four-step arguments is to show that in some carefully circumscribed cases, if we may permissibly kill people or assist in causing their death where we foresee the death as a side effect, we may also kill them, intending the death, or assist them in intentionally causing their own death, when the death is the means to a greater good. Note that the arguments do not *merely* say that the doctors in the first step of each argument may give the morphine for pain relief (MPR) even if they also intend their patients' deaths, though this is true. In such a case, the morphine they give would still relieve the patients' pain, even if that is not the doctors' reason for giving them the morphine. (In this way, the pain relief provides a pretext because it could justify the act of giving morphine.) Rather, the arguments are concerned in their conclusions with more than this; for their conclusions are concerned with a doctor who (it is reasonable to think) could have no other reason for giving morphine besides killing, since the morphine itself no longer relieves pain but it does cause the death that is the means to pain relief. (Furthermore, even a bad doctor who does not intend that the patient not be in pain, but only wants to have the experience of intentionally killing (or assisting in killing) may permissibly proceed, if the killing will in fact relieve the pain and pain relief can justify the killing or assisted killing.)

The four-step arguments are directed against the common use of the Doctrine of Double Effect (DDE) to rule out S, AS, and E. The DDE says that it is impermissible to intend lesser evil, even as a means to a greater good, but it can be permissible to pursue greater good by innocent means, even foreseeing that lesser evil will certainly occur as a side effect. One need not agree with the more radical claim that the distinction between intending and foreseeing evil never makes a moral difference, in order to hold that sometimes the distinction makes no moral difference to the permissibility of an act. It makes no such difference, for example, in cases mentioned in premise 2 in the first four-step argument, when the lesser evil is A's pain, when we have A's consent and the greater good is A's life: we may act merely foreseeing the pain or intending it.[7]

Objection

An objection to the four-step arguments is that premises 3 and 3a are not true; that is, eliminating the person as a means to the person's own greater good is not morally the same as eliminating some part of him as a means to his greater good while he survives. There are at least three ways to put this objection.

1   First, some have held that the person does not have a right to dispose of himself because he belongs to God. But then why is it permissible for someone to take MPR to relieve his pain when it is known that it will destroy what belongs to God? To reject the four-step arguments because we belong to God seems to require us to reject MPR, which is commonly thought to be morally permissible.

2   The second way in which to make the objection is said to rest on Kant's views. In PAS, but not in MPR, it is said, a person is treated as a mere means, and this violates the Categorical Imperative of Morality to always treat persons also as ends-in-themselves. How might PAS treat a person as a mere means, if the person himself consents to death and death is (assumed to be) overall in his best interest?

    Perhaps meeting these two conditions is insufficient for treating a person also as an end in himself, if we treat rational humanity in the person as a mere means to what is good for him merely as a sentient being (e.g., pain relief). But when does this occur? It occurs in one sense if we see rational humanity in ourselves as merely an instrument for getting a positive balance of sentient good over evil in our life, and we are willing to eliminate rational humanity when the balance is evil over good. We do not attribute intrinsic worth to being a rational agent.[8] But if this is an objection to PAS, it can also be an objection to MPR. This is because if we give too little weight to the value of being a rational agent in itself, the evil of pain will too quickly serve as a justification for taking morphine even when it causes death as a side effect. Hence, this sense in which we could see rational humanity as a mere means does not distinguish between death as a means and death as a mere side effect. Likewise, if we treat rational humanity as having intrinsic value so that only a great deal of pain could override the worth of its continuing, we will not have treated rational humanity as a mere means (in the sense we are now examining) in either PAS or MPR.[9]

3   But if we allow pain to override the intrinsic weight of continuing rational humanity, perhaps we do not give rational humanity in the person and the person himself unconditional and incomparable value. To have unconditional value is to have value always, but that does not yet mean to have overriding value, which meaning is transmitted by incomparable value.[10] So now we should consider that we may be treating the person as a mere means if we do not give him *qua* rational being incomparable value relative to things that are merely good for him. Possibly this point might be made by the following reductio-type argument: Bringing about something good for some being, merely because it is good for it, is important only if the being is important (i.e., is really worth caring for). Its worth grounds the worth of its not being in pain. But if it is permissible to dispose of a being (independent of concern for any other worthwhile thing) while the being retains the characteristics that supposedly make it important that it have what is good for it, the being does not matter. If the being does not matter, that it gets what is good for it because it is good for it does not matter. So, if the being matters, we should not eliminate it to stop its pain, and if we may eliminate it, its pain does not give us any reason to eliminate it.[11]

One concern about this argument is raised by considering its implication for cases: it seems to imply that we would not be morally justified in euthanizing a cat to stop its pain. For it seems reasonable to me to say that a cat's being out of pain matters just because it would be good for the cat. According to the argument, this can be true only if a cat matters. I suggest a cat matters intrinsically, not just because it matters to someone. But according to the argument, the permissibility of destroying the cat to stop its pain would imply that it does not matter. Hence, its being out of pain would not matter. But this seems wrong; it is not impermissible to euthanize cats when we are trying to achieve what is good for them because we think they matter intrinsically to some degree.

This cat example suggests that we should distinguish between the value of something and the value of its continuing to exist. It can be that a person's (or a cat's) not being in pain does not have greater value than the person (or cat) does, but it has greater value than the *continuing existence of the person (or cat)*. In the light of the nonovershadowed value of a person, because a person continues to have worth, we might decide that it is not only important that a person be out of pain but that it would be permissible for the person not to live on in pain. In this sense, killing or letting the person die can respect the incomparable worth of the person, even if it eliminates him. Hence, the permissibility of eliminating the entity for the sake of its good does not show that it lacks overriding worth. Nor does it show that we are not acting in response to this worth by responding to its autonomous request to end its pain by death.

An additional argument to support the claim that one cannot respect a person if one eliminates her to stop pain is what I shall refer to as the *exchange argument*.[12] It claims that suicide is immoral when committed on the ground that life is not worth living and it is in one's interest to die, for then one is trading one's person for benefits or for relief from harms. David Velleman says (1999, pp. 614–16): "I think Kant was right to say that trading one's person in exchange for benefits, or relief from harms, denigrates the value of personhood . . . The objection is not even to suicide per se, but to suicide committed for a particular kind of reason – that is, in order to obtain benefits or escape harms."

But when we give morphine in MPR, when morphine will shortly kill the person, do we not also exchange a person for his pain relief? If so, the Kantian argument will rule out MPR that is widely thought to be morally (and legally) permissible. Further, consider terminal sedation, which is currently employed when painkillers do not work and which is legally permissible. By "terminal sedation," I mean putting a patient to sleep as long as he is in pain until the underlying disease kills him. In terminal sedation, we deliberately seek the cessation of rational agency distinctive of persons as the intended means of stopping pain. Hence, if aiming against the continued existence of rational agency for pain relief is an impermissible exchange of a person for his good, terminal sedation will be ruled out by the Kantian objections to AS or E we are considering, even if it does not hasten death. But is it really wrong? I do not think so. If it is not wrong, then this would be reason to think that the Kantian objections to AS and E are not correct.

Doctors and Ending Life

Some claim that patients have a right to AS only from a willing physician. They do not claim that a doctor has a duty to provide AS. But perhaps there is yet another four-step argument for such a duty. Assuming patient consent:

1   Doctors have a *duty* to treat pain (e.g., with morphine), even if they foresee with certainty that it will make them cause the patient's death soon, when death is a lesser evil and pain relief is a greater good, or when death is unavoidably imminent (even if it is a greater evil) and only morphine can stop the pain.
2   Doctors would have a *duty* to intentionally cause evils (e.g., pain, blindness) for a patient's own medical good, when the evils are lesser and the goods to be achieved by them greater, or when the evils are unavoidably imminent anyway (even if greater) and they are the only way to achieve a medically relevant good.
3   When death is a lesser or imminent evil for a person, it is not morally different from other lesser evils.
4   Therefore, doctors have a *duty* to intentionally cause the patient's death or

assist in its being intentionally caused, when death is a lesser evil (or imminent anyway) and pain relief is a (greater) good for the patient and only death can bring it about.

Call this last four-step argument the Doctor's Duty Argument. This argument, as well as arguments showing that it is morally permissible for a doctor to perform AS or E, are limited to the achievement of medically relevant goods, whatever they are. By contrast, suppose it would be in a patient's best interest to be killed in order to achieve posthumous glory. The good of posthumous glory is not a good a doctor is called upon to help patients achieve.

The Doctor's Duty Argument is important because some have claimed that doctors' *professional ethic* in particular implies that they may not engage in PAS. By contrast, this argument suggests that doctors' professional ethic allows them and even calls for them to perform PAS. It is also important because it shows that a doctor's conscientious objection to, for example, killing a fetus in abortion could be permissible while such an objection to PAS might not be. This is because a doctor could also conscientiously refuse to intentionally cause such evils as blindness in a fetus for the sake of helping a woman in whose body the fetus lies. But harming people for their own greater good (either by causing them blindness or death) is morally different from harming some being for the sake of the good of another being. If one continues to believe that doctors may conscientiously refuse to assist in suicide, one will have to show what is wrong with the Doctor's Duty Argument for the opposite conclusion.

The Doctor's Duty Argument says that it is at least permissible and perhaps a doctor's duty to participate in AS or E, because sometimes these behaviors are analogous to other interventions it is permitted or obligatory for doctors to perform. But this argument does not tell us the ground of doctor's duties and is compatible with several grounds. The degree of moral responsibility that a doctor has for the patient's death may vary depending on what is the ground of the doctor's permission or duty to intervene. Consider two possible grounds.

The first takes the view that doctors have a duty of medical beneficence. That is, one of the projects to which they commit themselves is the good of patients including relief of the misery of their patients. The second view emphasizes the patient's autonomy. In certain contexts, it is said, patients may decide what is best for them. It is then either a doctor's duty to serve the patient's will, at least when it is not obviously against the patient's interests to do so, or it is permissible for a doctor to serve the patient's will, at least when it is not obviously against the patient's interests to do so. Hence, on the second view, the doctor should act as a patient's agent in carrying out her wishes when doing so is not obviously against her interests.

On the second view, the doctor commits himself to the project of being the patient's agent, at least so long as this is not obviously against the patient's interests, rather than to the project of doing what is best for the patient, so long as this is not against the patient's wishes. There is a reversal of emphasis in these two accounts. Only the second view *need not imply* in PAS either that the doctor agrees with the patient's decision to die or that the doctor is fulfilling his own project to do what is best for the patient, in seeking the patient's death or giving him the option to choose death. It can be argued that in prescribing a lethal drug, the doctor's intention is to give the patient a choice about ending her life; simply because this serves the patient's will.

Intending in this way that the patient have a choice can also lead a doctor to actively kill a patient when the patient decides that he wants to die but he is unable to kill himself. Yet, if the doctor does not in this case kill for the patient's good, but only to carry out the patients' wishes when it is not obviously against the patient's interests, then this active killing is *not* appropriately called E. (This is not a judgment of its moral permissibility, only of its type.) This is because E involves killing the patient intending his own good. Hence, there is a form of active killing of the patient to which the patient consents that may be permissible even though it is not E. In this form of killing, unlike PAS by provision of lethal drugs to be used by the patient, the doctor causes the patient's death and does the patient's bidding, when it is not obviously against the patient's interests that he do so.

My central claim is that only on the agent model of the doctor does positive moral responsibility and accountability for all positive and negative consequences of killing the patient or provision of lethal substances lie at the patient's doorstep. What is true on the beneficence model of the doctor who either performs VE_a or AS? On the beneficence model, seeking the death because it is good for the patient is at least a project of the doctor's. Let us assume the patient also seeks his good (though he could seek his death, even when it is good for him, for some other reason). Then both decide the patient's death best fulfills their individual projects. But the doctor cannot fulfill his project without the patient's consent. Even though this is true, it seems to me that the doctor is more than the patient's agent once he gets the consent. Doctor and patient are like two people who set up a project on the land of one of them. For this reason, doctor and patient may share positive moral responsibility and accountability for negative and positive consequences.

I suggest that if complete positive moral responsibility for any negative consequences of AS or VE would be at the patient's doorstep in the agent model, this might be a reason for the doctor to act as an agent when she otherwise would be reluctant to act from beneficence. This includes cases where she thinks that the patient is doing the overall right thing in choosing death, but the doctor herself does not act in order to bring about death as a good.[13]

Advance Directives

Someone might make a decision for or against TT, S, AS, or E while he is judged legally competent to make such decisions, and carry the decision out (or have it carried out) while he is competent as well. However, at least with respect to decisions for or against TT and E, someone might have to decide now, while competent, about what should be done at a later point in time when he will not be available to give valid consent. For example, later he might be unconscious or deranged. One mechanism to allow a person to make decisions for himself about the future is known as a living will. In such a document, a person enumerates what he would like done should various circumstances arise. For example, would he want a life-saving antibiotic given to him if he is in a persistent vegetative state? One problem with a living will is that circumstances might arise that one had never contemplated in the will. A second problem is that one might not have enough knowledge about a possible condition prior to being in it to know what one would want done. For example, prior to being disabled, one might think one would not want to go on living with a disability, but once one had experienced the disability, one might decide that it was worth going on (or vice versa).

An answer to the first problem is known as an advance directive. One part of this document is a living will. But this is supplemented with the designation of another person as a substitute decision-maker (SD), who will have the legal power to make decisions in the event that one cannot make them oneself. There are at least two types of reasoning an SD can employ. In "substituted judgment," the SD tries to decide as the person himself would have in the circumstances. This requires knowing the values and commitments of the person. It does not necessarily result in doing what is in the best interests of the person, if she herself would not have decided in her best interests. It is a way of respecting the person's autonomy. The second type of reasoning the SD might engage in when he does not know what values or commitments someone had that pertain to the circumstances of choice, is simply deciding what would be in the person's best interest.

Ronald Dworkin has argued[14] that there are two types of interests that a person has. There are "experiential interests" in having good experiences and the absence of bad experiences (such as pain and frustration) in one's life. But there are also "critical interests" in having one's life be an objectively good life, a meaningful, worthwhile life. It is possible that a life that is not high on experiential goods is a better life. (For example, the life of a creative artist who is often in torment might be better than the life of someone who is always having pleasant experiences.) One's values will lead one to have a certain view about what really is a good life, but one's view could be mistaken. One's critical interest in really having a good life could then come into conflict with one's autonomous choices, even when they reflect one's values. An SD might, therefore, not only have to think about respecting someone's autonomy and values, but also sometimes to pursue someone's true experiential and critical interests.

Particular problems arise for the use of living wills or advance directives when a person's values and interests change (or seem to change) from the time these devices are put in force. One type of case involves temporary derangement. Consider a Jehovah's Witness whose values require that he not have blood transfusions even to save his life. Suppose that when he is ill, he becomes temporarily deranged and in this state he requests a transfusion. (Notice that he might make the request and then become unconscious at the very time we had to give the transfusion, but the problem would remain when he is unconscious of whether to follow his most recent request [to have the transfusion] or the one made when he was sane.) Should he be given the transfusion?

If he is deranged, it is thought that he is not competent to make decisions relating to this matter and his choice may not reflect his real values. It may also be said that if he were to live on as a result of the transfusion and regain sanity, he would regret having had the transfusion. He is unlike a sane person who undergoes a real change in his values. Hence, if respect for autonomy influenced by underlying values takes precedence, an SD should decide as the Jehovah's Witness would have decided when making a competent autonomous choice. This case shows the importance of a person's history in how we act toward him. Had the deranged person never been sane, it might very well be right to heed his request when deranged for the transfusion, given that this is also in his interests.

It might be argued, however, that attending to values someone last held when sane is correct only in cases where this person will again become sane and be committed to the same core values, as was imagined in the Jehovah's Witness case. This is because, some argue, it is important whether the person will have to "live with" the results of his decisions made when deranged, in the sense that involves his being aware whether they are consistent with his deep values.[15] Therefore, a second case that is important for considering this issue involves permanent derangement, as in late-stage dementia.[16] Suppose a person when competent agrees in a living will that when he is in late-stage dementia, he should be left to die. As he understands it, his life will be a better one if it ends without a period of dementia, even if it is thereby shortened and deprived of some simple pleasures. However, when he is demented, he resists, expressing a wish to go on living because he gets experiential goods from simple activities in his life. What should be done?

Some have analyzed this case as involving two different persons diachronically occupying the same body.[17] The first person, it is said, has no right to control the fate of the second person. This second person is demented, incapable of considered judgments and the formulation of values, He has no autonomous will. Nevertheless, he has a desire to remain alive and is having positive experiences in his life. So, staying alive is in his experiential interest and at least not inconsistent with any deep will or values he has. However, some might counter-argue that it is worse to be an adult human being in a demented state (especially if one has been nondemented previously) than to be dead, even if experientially his life is no different from that of a happy rabbit for whom life is not a worse option than death. If the objectively true critical interests of an adult human are defeated by his staying alive in this condition, this might trump actual desires and experiences, even on the two-person view that tells us to ignore the first person's living will.

Alternative analyses of this case[18] insist that there is only one person who has lived through a competent stage and is now in a demented stage. (Those who believe dementia is a form of withering away of the self and the person (understood as a self-conscious being) may speak of the same individual rather than the same *person* in two stages.) Only the person in his competent stage has a will that should be taken very seriously and is owed great respect, and because he is only deciding for himself in his later stage, there is no improper attempt to decide for someone else. If there is only one person throughout, what are the interests of that person? The opinion of the person when he was capable of having opinions was that a demented end would be inconsistent with his critical interests by comparison to an earlier death. The time-relative interests he has when nondemented in having future pleasant experiences while demented are weak and get trumped, according to this view, by his critical interests. Furthermore, these critical interests are said to be the same when he is demented and nondemented for he is the same person. Though he could still be wrong about what is in his critical interests, when he has made a choice when competent, respect for his autonomy should govern our treatment of him, on this alternative view.

Let us assume the one-person (or individual) view is correct. The question we are asking is whether the fact that the person will not return to sanity and will not have to, as a sane person, "live with" the results of his being kept alive when demented should affect our views? Someone who thought it should might deal differently with the case of permanent derangement and, by contrast, with the following two hypothetical cases: (1) The demented person regains his sanity one day every year. While he does not have any awareness of having been demented, he always repeats the request he made before becoming demented, not to be kept alive when demented. (2) We know that at the very end of his life, the dementia will lift and the person will regain his sanity. Though he will not remember, first-personally, having been demented, he expresses the view that it would have been wrong to have kept him alive after he became demented. In these cases, the person-as-sane does not disappear forever. Hence, some may think that, due to this, there is someone who can be wronged by our decision to keep him alive when demented.

The important point to grasp, however, is that even when the person could never again form the view that he should not be kept alive when demented or that he would be wronged in not having wishes when competent carried out (because he remains demented), we can wrong the person and harm him in keeping him alive. Similarly, we can wrong and harm someone after his death, by not carrying out his last will and testament or destroying his unpublished life's work. (In the dementia case, of course, the person (or individual) still exists, unlike what is true of death.) This strengthens the case for heeding the advance directive over the desire to live of the individual when demented.[19]

The case for respecting the directive of the person when sane is also strengthened, I think, by considering the following hypothetical case. An elderly parent, competent to decide, wants to give an organ to save his child's life. The medicine that must be given the parent a few days prior to surgery to make possible the removal of his organ will, unfortunately, cause permanent dementia. The parent knows this and consents nevertheless. When demented, however, the parent refuses to allow the removal of his organ for transplantation (Dementia Transplant Case). Suppose the parent is morally permitted to make the dual sacrifice of organ and reason. Further, suppose that if he did not object to the transplant when demented, we would follow the instructions he gave when competent. Then, I believe, one should follow these instructions, even when he resists when demented. It would certainly be a cruel waste of the sacrifice of reason not to follow those instructions, and I think it is a poor reason not to allow the competent parent to make this sacrifice solely on the grounds that we will have to heed the wishes of the person when demented, which will interfere with the organ donation. (In this case, of course, the child will benefit if we do *not* heed the wishes of the person when demented. But we would not ordinarily take organs from a demented person, especially when he resists, in order to save his child's life. So, it is the instructions of the person when competent, overriding his objections when demented, that play a crucial role in making the transplant permissible.)

Practically speaking, it may be wise for a person who strongly wishes not to live through predictable end-stage dementia to forego some period of still worthwhile life, in order to end his life while he is still in a competent state. Then there will be no question of decision-makers having to consider the desires and experiences of himself when demented. If such a person's concern in seeking death is only that his experiences when demented will be bad, he should become well informed about whether this is likely to be true, on the basis of other people's experience. If a person's concerns are, rather, that in the light of his values, the state is demeaning whether or not it is pleasant, becoming well informed about experiences is irrelevant. However, if only such particular characteristics as becoming violent to others are considered demeaning, then he should become informed about whether this is likely to occur.

Notes

1 This chapter draws on material in Kamm, 1998, 1999, and 2004.

2 On these suggestions see McMahan, 2003.

3 Rawls et al., 1997.

4 Note that this underlying cause need not be the original illness from which the patient suffered. It could be some dependence on life support that he did not originally have but has acquired.

5 Judith Jarvis Thomson, one of the coauthors of the brief, argues similarly in Thomson, 1999.

6 I thank Michael Otsuka for suggesting that I bring out this suppressed premise in the three-step argument presented in Kamm, 1997.

7 The first four-step argument speaks of death as a lesser evil. Is death an evil at all if one's future will contain only bad things in it? If death were no evil at all but actually good for the patient, the DDE could not be used to raise an objection to PAS. I am willing to say that death is an evil, even if one's future contains only bad things, because I think that the elimination of the person is something bad in itself, even if it has as a part the elimination of the person's pain. And it is the elimination of the person that is being intended. (Note also that in the MPR Case where the morphine relieves the pain, the death is most clearly

an evil, because the elimination of the person does not involve as a part of itself elimination of pain, the pain having already been eliminated by morphine.)

8 This is how I understand Thomas E. Hill, Jr's version of the Kantian objection to S (Hill, 1991).

9 It is a problem with the account of Kantian objections to S given by Hill, 1991 that none of the objections really aim at S per se (i.e., they do not distinguish between death as means or end (required for suicide) and death as a mere side effect). In a sense, Hill's discussion is not really about suicide per se at all.

10 On the distinction, see Hill, 1980. I thank Richard Arneson for calling this discussion to my attention.

11 This is how I construe David Velleman's argument in Velleman, 1999.

12 I believe this argument is also found in Velleman, 1999.

13 The distinction I have drawn between two ways of conceiving the doctor's behavior is sometimes not recognized in discussions of these topics. For example, Dan Brock says: "Both physician and family members can instead be helped to understand that it is the patient's decision and consent to stopping treatment that limits their responsibility for the patient's death and that shifts responsibility to the patient" (Brock, 1996). Brock, however, also says in discussing AS: "Seeking a physician's assistance, or what can almost seem a physician's blessing, may be a way of trying to remove that stigma and show others that . . . The decision for suicide was . . . justified under the circumstances. The physician's involvement provides a kind of social approval." But I believe what makes the first claim true may make the second claim false. For it is only when the doctor is merely an agent that moral responsibility for the killing lies completely with the patient, and then helping the patient or killing him does not imply that the doctor has blessed the patient's decision or shown that it is justified under the circumstances. Could it also be that what makes the second claim true makes the first claim false? For if a doctor acts only because he approves of the patient's choices, then he may also be acting for the sake of his own goal to do good for the patient, as the patient acts for her goal, and this could give the doctor a share in moral responsibility for both the negative and the positive aspects of the death. But it is also possible that Brock's particular scenario allows one to imagine that the doctor is still only an agent whose own preferences for the patient's good are fortuitously achieved without his committing himself to a goal of beneficence.

14 Dworkin, 1993.

15 Seana Shiffrin, 2004 seems to emphasize such a factor.

16 We might also consider a case in which having the transfusion will cause a permanent change in the Jehovah's Witness' values, but not through any autonomous reflection or choice. There will then be no regret at having had the transfusion. Should this affect our judgment of what to do? I think not, as I will argue.

17 For a view like this, see Dresser, 1995.

18 Provided by, for example, Dworkin, 1993.

19 It is also problematic to focus too much on whether the sane person will have to live with what the insane person does for another reason. Suppose it were, for some reason, in the interests, and consistent with the desires, of the person *qua* deranged person not to have life-saving treatment. It would obviously be incorrect not to do what saved the person, if he would return to sanity when saved, given that that was his request when he was sane. This is so even though the person when sane would never have had to live with the decision he made when deranged because he would be dead.

References

Battin, M. (1995), *Ethical Issues in Suicide*, Upper Saddle River, NJ: Prentice Hall.

Battin, M., Rhodes, R., and Silvers, A. (eds.), (1998), *Physician-assisted Suicide: Expanding the Debate*, New York and London: Routledge.

Beauchamp, Tom L. (ed.), (1996), *Intending Death: The Ethics of Assisted Suicide and Euthanasia*, Upper Saddle River, NJ: Prentice Hall.

Brock, D. (1996), Voluntary active euthanasia, in R. Munson (ed.), *Intervention and Reflection: Basic Issues in Medical Ethics*, 5th edn., Belmont, CA: Wadsworth, pp. 180–7. (Reprinted from *Hastings Center Report*, pp. 11–12, 14–17, 19–21, March/April 1992.)

Dresser, Rebecca (1995), Dworkin in dementia: elegant theory, questionable policy, *Hastings Center Report*, 25: 32–8, November–December.

Dworkin, G., Frey, D., and Bok, S. (1998), *Euthanasia and Physician-assisted Suicide*, New York: Cambridge University Press.

Dworkin, R.M. (1993), *Life's Dominion*, New York: Knopf.

Hill, T.E. (1980) Humanity as an end in itself, *Ethics* 91: 84–99.

Hill, T.E. (1991), Self-regarding suicide: a modified Kantian view, in T.E. Hill (ed.), *Autonomy and Self-Respect*, Cambridge: Cambridge University Press, pp. 85–103.

Kamm, F.M. (1997), A right to choose death, *Boston Review*, 22: 21–3.

Kamm, F.M. (1998), Physician-assisted suicide, euthanasia, and intending death, in M. Battin, R. Rhodes, and A. Silvers (eds.), *Physician-assisted Suicide: Expanding the Debate*, New York and London: Routledge, pp. 28–62.

Kamm, F.M. (1999), Physician-assisted suicide, the doctrine of double effect, and the ground of value, *Ethics* 109 (3): 586–605.

Kamm, F.M. (2004), Ronald Dworkin on abortion and assisted suicide, in J. Burley (ed.), *Dworkin and his Critics*, Malden, MA: Blackwell, pp. 218–40.

McMahan, J. (2003), *The Ethics of Killing: Problems at the Margins of Life*, New York: Oxford University Press.

Rawls, J., Thomson, J.J., Nozick, R., Dworkin, R., Scanlon, T.M., and Nagel, T. (1997), Assisted suicide: the philosophers' brief, *New York Review of Books* 44 (March 27): 41–5.

Shiffrin, Seana (2004), Autonomy, beneficence, and the permanently demented, in J. Burley (ed.), *Dworkin and his Critics*, Malden, MA: Blackwell.

Thomson, J.J. (1999), Physician-assisted suicide: Two moral arguments, *Ethics* 109: 497–518.

Velleman, D. (1999), A right of self-termination? *Ethics* 109: 606–28.

Chapter 9

Discrimination in Medical Practice

Justice and the Obligations of Health Care Providers to Disadvantaged Patients

Leslie P. Francis

We live in a world of apparently spiraling health care costs and just as apparently spiraling health care inequalities. When the percentage of gross domestic product spent on health care approaches or passes 15 percent, as in the United States, or reaches the far loftier levels that are predicted, flexibility to spend new dollars on health care may become limited, for political if not for moral reasons. Yet when health inequalities remain impressive in at least some countries of the developed world, and outright staggering in the developing world, demands of justice are even more pressing.

One set of demands of justice take place at the level of macro-allocation: what amounts and kinds of resources should be devoted to health care?

Demands of justice take place at the level of the individual practitioner, too. Practitioners decide how to allocate their time, how to communicate with patients, and what care options to discuss with patients. In making these choices, practitioners work within a variety of structures of reimbursement or financing that set economic constraints and pose ethical problems as a result. Practitioners also decide whether to become politically active in their own countries or to participate in international organizations such as Médecins Sans Frontières.[1] This chapter is devoted to this second set of demands, the issues of justice in health care that are raised for practitioners in the developed world in treating their patients.

Arguably, it is mistaken to focus on questions of justice as encountered by individual practitioners. Questions about the distribution of health care arise purely at the level of society, it might be urged, not at the level of decisions made by individual providers of care. The provider–patient relationship should focus solely on the choices and interests of the individual patient. Health care providers must be loyal to their patients, deciding only what is best in the context of the individual relationship; rationing decisions must be made elsewhere, if they are to be made at all. To put it simply, "rationing at the bedside" is wrong. To interject considerations of the justice of the distribution – or redistribution – of health care into the individual provider–patient relationship, on this view, is to dilute or deflect providers' loyalty to their patients. Discussion of justice belongs in Part II of this volume, on this view, not in the discussions devoted to providers' choices and encounters in the clinical setting.

This chapter argues that it is naïve at best and misleading at worst to ignore questions of justice faced by individual practitioners. Encounters between individual providers and their patients do not occur in a vacuum. Patients come – or fail to come – to health care providers from their contexts of privilege or injustice. From birth and before, their health status may be significantly affected by the social situations of justice or injustice in which they have led their lives. The resources that they have available to use in paying for health care or for the adjuvant services that may make health care possible or effective (assistive devices, environmental adaptations, home care, supported living, and the like) are themselves features of the justice of the society in which they live. Health care providers need to understand how principles of justice may apply to these situations. They also need to consider their responsibilities as individual actors in the face of both justice and injustice. This chapter addresses some of the issues of justice that providers must face as they treat patients who fall into categories that place them at risk of discrimination: children, pregnant women, and the elderly; people with disabilities, including dementia; racial and ethnic minorities; and people in poverty.

The Risk of Injustice and Characterizing a Group as "Vulnerable"

The claim is frequently made in bioethics, particularly in the ethics of research, that a variety of "vulnerable" groups warrant special protection.[2] High on lists of vulnerability are children, pregnant women, racial and ethnic minorities, people with disabilities or impaired cognition, the elderly, or people in poverty. What makes these groups supposedly "vulnerable" is their reduced ability to protect themselves. In some cases, their difficulties in protecting themselves stem from the lack of decisional capacity: children or people with intellectual disabilities such as dementia might be thought to fall into this category. In other cases, a lack of resources is the problem: people in poverty may be vulnerable because they lack the resources to obtain adequate health care in the first place. In still other cases, the problem is a history of past injustice: as a residue of their history with medicine, African-Americans in particular may be suspicious of health care generally and experimentation in particular (Savitt, 1982). In yet other cases, these factors combine: persons with disabilities may be lacking in decision-making capacity, economically disadvantaged, and treated unjustly all at once.

Characterizing a group as vulnerable is fraught with peril. A label of "vulnerability" risks a judgment that members of the group are flawed or impaired. But vulnerability in the sense of comparative limitations in the ability of members to protect themselves may be a function of social rather than individual circumstances. That immigrants are "vulnerable" to deportation, for example, is a legal, not a personal, fact. That people with mobility impairments cannot access the second floors of buildings without elevators is as much a fact of building design as it is of their physical conditions. That young children cannot protect themselves is of course a matter of their developmental stages, but it is also a matter of the limited economic resources society devotes to children, of their parents' skills, and of the availability of other social support.

Recognition of vulnerability may be a call to remedy injustice, rather than a call for augmented protection. In what follows, we will need to consider a wide variety of issues of distributive justice. These will be not only questions of ideal justice, but also questions about what justice requires in circumstances of injustice or justice achieved only partially – what have been called "partial compliance" contexts.[3]

Discrimination and Distributive Justice: Some Background

"Discrimination" is a loaded term; it represents not just a judgment that someone has been treated differently, but a judgment that someone has been treated differently in a manner that is unjustified. "Discrimination," that is, is *unjustified* differential treatment, differential treatment that is impermissible *as a matter of justice*. To know that someone has been treated differently on the basis of age, race, sex, disability, or any other similar category, we need to know not only that they were categorized on this basis but also that the categorization was unjust. Driver's licenses that require corrective lenses, museum discounts that apply to people over the age of 62, pediatricians who treat children but not adults, and programs that consider race in admission decisions for medical school all differentiate on the basis of categorizations that might be regarded as problematic. Whether these differentiations are *discriminatory*, however, is a separate question that can only be answered against the background of a theory of justice.

For the past 25 years, two families of approaches to distributive justice have predominated among theorists who believe health care is at least to some extent a matter of social responsibility and not merely a matter of what people can buy on their own through whatever market mechanisms exist. These families of approaches can be roughly characterized as "egalitarian" – insisting on at least a minimum of care for each individual person – and "utilitarian" – insisting on care distributions that will be beneficial overall but not necessarily for particular individuals. Among "egalitarian" views, a predominant approach, due principally to Norman Daniels, considers what system of health care people would agree to live by over a complete lifetime, if they were positioned in ignorance of their own natural or social circumstances (Daniels, 1985, 1988, 2002). Placed in such a justificatory scheme, Daniels argues, people would agree to distributions of health care that would support the normal opportunity range for each person, understood in terms of species-typical functioning over a normal lifespan. This approach sets limits to egalitarianism that are critical for the discussion here. The approach theorizes about justice within societies, leaving aside questions of international distributive justice. The norm to be achieved by justice is species-typical functioning; on this norm, people who cannot achieve species-typical functioning or who have atypical needs may be at risk of marginalization. And the egalitarianism extends only over a normal lifespan; age-based rationing may be justified outside of this range. In what follows, Daniels's view will be referred to as "species-typical egalitarianism."

Also egalitarian to at least some extent are defenses of a "decent minimum" of health care for everyone. Decent minimum views attempt to specify the required minimum of care for everyone in many different ways, including along the lines suggested by Daniels's approach. More minimalist views may include only care that is life-saving or that avoids significant morbidity. Others specify the "decent minimum" to be an adequate level of care (Kalb, 1992). Still others observe that a decent minimum may vary with the resources of a given society and should be regarded as a matter of collective social choice (Buchanan, 1984). This group of views will be referred to as "decent minimum egalitarianism."

The other predominant family of approaches to distributive justice is utilitarian: funds should be allocated to health care, and distributed among forms of care, in accord with policies that will produce the most good on the whole. How the good is to be defined and measured, whether the focus should be policies or separate decisions, and whether the strategy should be to formulate policies for ideal or partial compliance circumstances track important theoretical differences among utilitarians. On utilitarian views, care that is extremely expensive for limited returns will be less likely to be funded than care that yields predictable success. People who are less likely to contribute socially, who have very expensive needs, or whose quality of life may remain poor no matter what care they receive will have lower priority.

Well-known controversies attend each of these approaches. With respect to Daniels's species-typical egalitarianism, the focus of criticism has been the privileging of supposed "normalcy." Concerns about "decent minimum" views are that they urge minima that are less than decent, or that it may be very difficult to specify what should be included within the minimum. With respect to utilitarianism, the focus of criticism is whether strategies to maximize overall welfare disadvantage those with lower possible levels of welfare or more costly health care needs. Critics have expressed particular concern about the fates of so-called vulnerable populations – children, pregnant women, and the elderly, racial and ethnic minorities, people in poverty, and people with disabilities – under both egalitarian and utilitarian approaches to justice.

An additional difficulty is that these principles have largely been elucidated as applying in conditions of ideal justice. Little attention has been paid to how their application might be shaped by actual circumstances of injustice. It is not at all clear, however, that the same principles that apply under circumstances of ideal justice are those that would hold under circumstances of non-ideal justice (Murphy, 2000). In circumstances of injustice, egalitarians may urge us to consider principles of compensation, perhaps within certain boundaries set by ideal justice about what are permissible grounds for compensation. If so, characteristics such as race that have been the bases of prior injustice may nonetheless provide grounds for remediation, even if these characteristics would be utterly irrelevant under circumstances of ideal justice. Utilitarians might urge us to select the rules that will have the best consequences under circumstances of present injustice, even if they would not be the rules that would obtain in a better world.[4]

Tensions within and between egalitarian and utilitarian theories provide the backdrop to contemporary clinical care. Whether a decent minimum includes organ transplants that are very expensive but potentially life-saving, whether preventive care should take priority over care to cure disease, and whether expensive interventions such as dialysis should be provided for people with significant cognitive impairments, are but a few of these tensions. The significance of persistent injustice complicates the picture, as providers encounter patients whose are sicker because they have been unable to obtain care, who lack resources to pay for care, or whose lives have been marked by poverty or abuse.

Choices for Providers

It may seem that providers have little to choose with respect to justice and their patients. Providers typically do not judge, on their own, who should have private health insurance or what care will be paid for by that insurance, or who or what is covered by social insurance programs. To a large extent, health care providers work within systems in which funding decisions are made elsewhere. This is as it should be if judgments about what to fund are to be divorced from judgments about patient care and if providers are to be able to focus on the needs of individual patients.

It is rare, moreover, that providers can simply decide independently to provide care that is free. Providers work within reimbursement schemes that may regard "free" care as encouraging over-treatment; in the United States, for example, Medicare regards waiving a patient's co-payment as an illegal "kick-back." Much of the care provided in today's world requires facilities that must be paid for, regardless of the providers' own willingness to donate their own services. Providers cannot order tests, utilize office equipment, recommend physical therapy, or perform surgery on their own; they work within systems that have made allocation decisions that constrain individual action.

Nonetheless, providers do have choices that raise questions of justice. Providers need to be aware that such choices exist. They must make such choices explicitly, not covertly. Otherwise, patterns of injustice – discrimination – may exist but go unrecognized. For example, in the United States over the last few years increasing attention has been paid to apparent racial variations in the medical care that people receive; although these variances may not be intentional, they do raise questions of justice (Institute of Medicine, 2002). A quite simple, but very important choice providers make is the amount of time they spend with individual patients. Another choice is the options they offer to the patients they see. Still another choice is what they discuss with patients – for example, whether they explore the costs or burdens of different care modalities. Still another choice is the extent to which providers are informed about the costs of different care options and work to share this information openly with patients. A further choice is whether providers strive to help patients secure resources for care. And a final choice is the extent to which providers become policy advocates for access to care, lobbying, as the American Academy of Pediatrics has done, for adequate health care coverage for children (Senate, 2005), joining Physicians for a National Health Program (2006), or going on strike in support of more resources for patient care.

As health care costs rise, it can be expected that providers will increasingly be pressed to make rationing decisions. The impacts of managed-care structures on the amount of time physicians spend with patients are well known (Peifeng Hu and Reuben, 2002). Funding for "last chance" therapies, when patients make appeals for insurance coverage of expensive but unproven care modalities, continues to be responsive to public appeals (Cerminara, 2005). Providers may play important roles such as helping patients to understand the evidence-bases on which care decisions are made – or challenging unjustified refusals to pay for care that has been shown to be effective. When providers are pushed to make decisions that take cost and efficacy into account, they should do so in a way that is well-reasoned, principled, and fully open to patients. That way, providers may differentiate but not discriminate. The least principled scenario would be to allow cost pressures to continue without recognition of the implicit rationing choices they involve, as is alleged with respect to the pricing of pharmaceuticals in the United States (Kleinki, 2004). The criticism of the British National Health Service some years ago for failing to open rationing decisions to patient and public scrutiny (Schwartz, 1985) remains pertinent to rationing decisions made today.

Life-Cycles: Children, Pregnant Women, and the Elderly

An initial set of concerns about injustice targets the life-cycle. Children are unable to care for themselves, pregnant women are thought to be at a stage where care is particularly important and where they are particularly at risk, and the elderly may be especially in need of health care. But at least in the United States these three groups present very different questions of justice.

Children

If justice in health care should be aimed at providing each person with species-typical opportunities over a normal lifespan, as Daniels suggests, then health care for children is especially compelling morally. Health care for children should include not only basic preventive care, but also services such as dental or vision care which are critical to species-typical functioning. These services matter for health itself, but also for opportunity more generally; poor vision or hearing makes it more difficult for children to learn in school. Given the benefits and costs of basic health services for children, it is quite likely that these services would be supported by utilitarian analyses as well. Yet, decent minimum views might not extend funding to care that is important for opportunity but that is not life-saving, such as vision care, depending on the level at which the minimum is set. Despite expansions of the federal-state children's health insurance program (S-CHIP) in recent years, the United States still falls far short of the minimum demanded by species-typical egalitarianism and, for the approximately ten million children who lack any health insurance at all,[5] may fall below even the most minimal decent minimum of care. Providers will face difficult choices in the light of these injustices to children.

Where all of these approaches to justice might well deviate from current practice, however, involves the treatment of seriously ill or very premature newborns. In the United States, federal law has encouraged very aggressive treatment of even extremely premature newborns; the "Baby Doe" regulations, which states must adopt to receive federal funds for the prevention of child abuse, require that treatment be continued for infants unless the infant is irreversibly comatose, the care will be futile in saving the child's life, or the care is virtually futile and under the circumstances inhumane.[6] Defenders of the regulations argue that they are necessary to prevent discrimination against infants with disabilities. Critics have argued that the regulations inappropriately restrict the possibility of physicians – with the informed consent of parents – making decisions to discontinue treatment when the child's quality of life is likely to be very poor (Doyle, 2004). The regulations arguably restrict parental choice and result in the need for expensive long-term care for children with very poor prognoses (Kopelman, 2005). Critics also argue that parents and their physicians should be able to make decisions that explicitly involve rationing judgments at the bedside (Hall, 1994). In the treatment of seriously ill newborns, physicians will continue to encounter legal pressure to make decisions to continue care at the edges of what parents view as appropriate.

From the point of view of justice, these decisions are also highly controversial. Utilitarian views counsel against aggressive interventions where costs are high and quality of life is likely to be poor. "Species-typical" egalitarianism also counsels against care where there is very little chance of recognizable approximation of species-typical functioning. This is one reason why some disability advocates regard emphasis on species-typicality as privileging problematic normalcy. "Decent minimum" views need to consider whether the minimum should prioritize survival. Any view that sets limits on care expenditures for individuals over a lifetime will need to confront the fact that very premature newborns may quickly exceed the ceiling in their first year of life.

Pregnant women

Judgments that pregnant women are especially vulnerable create unjustified stereotypes. Good prenatal, perinatal, and infant care surely would be included in any account of a decent minimum of care – given its importance to how infants and children fare. From a utilitarian perspective, this care would also be judged to be cost-effective, given the very high expenses associated with prematurity.

It is less likely that infertility treatment would be mandated by justice considerations. If reproduction were a species-typical function, then infertility treatment would be required by species-typical egalitarianism. But standards for a decent minimum that emphasize mortality and morbidity would not include infertility treatment. Whether utilitarianism would support the interventions would depend on the benefits of having biological children (and concomitant, potentially deleterious effects on adoption), as well as the risks, benefits, and costs of care. For a utilitarian, a particular concern would be fertility practices that result in multiple-birth pregnancies. These pregnancies are riskier for mothers and babies, and they are, therefore, much more expensive as well.

The elderly

Being of an advanced age, by itself, does not portent victimization. In the United States, the elderly may have more political power than other demographic groups; they vote in greater proportions than other age cohorts and are represented by a very powerful lobby, the American Association of Retired Persons.[7] In the United States, they also have higher rates of insurance coverage than other age cohorts. Despite gaps in coverage, especially for long-term care, Medicare covers a very high percentage of Americans over the age of 65.

Conditions associated with age, however – Alzheimer's and other dementias, hearing and vision loss, or mobility impairments – may disable people in protecting themselves. Confusing age with these conditions may have deeply discriminatory consequences, consequences that providers should guard against. Despite reminders, health care providers may fail to treat older people as independent actors, able to consent for themselves. The wrongful result may be paternalism or breaches of confidentiality as providers look to family members to make decisions for a fully competent patient. Health care providers may unwittingly assume that older people have poorer prognoses and make unjustifiably limited recommendations for care as a result; age is not a contra-indication for a variety of interventions, although age-associated features such as tumor aggressiveness and type, cardiac function, or cognitive status may be (Kaiser Family Foundation, 2006).

From the point of view of justice, the ultimately difficult question is whether age per se is a factor that ought to be taken into account in allocating health care. With respect to the elderly, egalitarian theories of justice are more likely to recommend limiting care; for example, species-typical egalitarianism recommends care that supports the normal opportunity range over a normal lifespan, not care prolonging extra-long life. To the extent that the elderly have already consumed more of the good of life than younger people have – and by definition they will at least have consumed more life*time* than their youngers – most forms of egalitarian theory will give them lower priority. Utilitarian theories will also assign the elderly lower priority on average because of predictably more limited benefits of care. Loyalty to their patients suggests that providers should not take age into account in limiting care in this way. On the other hand, there is some evidence that patients themselves may wish to discuss levels of resource consumption with their providers, and providers certainly should explore these issues when patients wish to do so.[8]

As a recent example, consider lung reduction surgery for emphysema, a procedure that costs approximately $50,000 in the United States. The US Medicare program pays for care that is "reasonable and necessary" for the diagnosis or treatment of illness or injury in the Medicare population, but it is not authorized to take costs into account.[9] Medicare has been petitioned repeatedly to cover expensive new treatment modalities such as lung reduction surgery, and has responded by relying on evidence-based medicine.[10] When Medicare decided in 2004 to cover lung reduction, analysts feared the cost implications. The results of the trials – funded by Medicare and used in making the coverage decision – showed 10 percent mortality from the procedure itself, an improvement in quality of life for recipients, but no improvement in long-term survival. With this information, few patients appear to be opting for the coverage. This may be as it should be. If the goal is to offer patients choices, then Medicare should cover expensive care modalities such as lung reduction surgery and providers should offer the care to their patients. Patients, however, should be given good information about what the care can – or cannot – achieve. The conclusion that this example is playing out as it should assumes the clinical trials themselves are well founded. The conclusion also assumes that physicians are offering the procedure to patients – with full information about its risks and benefits – and that patients are making choices based on how this information plays into their values about immediate risks of death, quality of life, and length of life (Kolata, 2006).

The Significance of Injustice

Defenses of life-cycle rationing are complicated by circumstances of injustice. Providers may encounter patients who have reached old age despite having suffered from persistent injustice; women who have been caregivers of children, parents, and finally spouses are especially likely to fall into this situation. Suppose that species-typical egalitarianism becomes the norm as they reach older ages; is it fair to impose limits at that point after they have been treated unfairly all along? Similar arguments might be advanced on behalf of infants with poor prognoses due to poverty – after all, survival, however impaired, is the only chance at life that they have. Women whose infertility results from rape, who have been infected with HIV/AIDS by their partners, or who seek reproductive services under circumstances of abuse may likewise argue that rules that might be just in an ideal world are grievously unjust when applied to them. Providers may find that principles about limits to care that seem appropriate on a social level or when contemplated for relatively affluent patients seem especially unjust when contemplated for patients who have been victimized. Loyalty to their patients may seem to require especially strong efforts to seek out care on their behalf.

Disability

People with disabilities historically have been subjected to economic and other forms of discrimination, thus leaving them with fewer resources to protect themselves. Such concerns about discrimination underlie opposition on the part of some disability rights activists to physician-assisted death in Oregon or to termination of treatment decisions more generally – that is, they have led some advocates to suggest that contested approaches to care should not be permitted when people have disabilities. The activist group Not Dead Yet, for example, urges that "[t]hough often described as compassionate, legalized medical killing is really about a deadly double standard for people with severe disabilities, including both conditions that are labeled terminal and those that are not."[11]

Disability discrimination in medicine has been documented extensively. From inaccessible examination tables to difficulty in consulting specialists, people with disabilities face barriers in access to health care (Anderlik and Wilkinson, 2000). Coverage decisions, too, may be influenced by stereotyping judgments about the capabilities of people with disabilities; for many years, patients with Alzheimer's dementia were routinely rejected for physical therapy or mental health visits by Medicare carriers in the United States, on the misjudgment that they could not benefit from the care. These judgments were mistaken, and the decisions based on them were discriminatory.

Considerable controversy remains, however, about whether it may ever be just to take disability into account in decisions about the allocation of health care. This controversy emerges both for species-typical egalitarians and for utilitarians. As has been suggested above, species-typical egalitarians argue that care should be provided that will give each person a reasonable chance of species-typical functioning over a normal lifespan. People who cannot achieve these norms will be disadvantaged if care is not offered to them on the ground that they cannot achieve normalcy. They may also be disadvantaged by care that is not tailored to their own needs if the goals of care are specified to be achieving normalcy to the extent possible. On this view, determining that someone should not receive care because species-typical functioning cannot be achieved for them would be to deepen the injustice they have already experienced. On this basis, it would be discriminatory.

This is not to insist, however, that care should be imposed on people with disabilities. Usual principles of autonomy or decision-making about what is in someone's good should remain paramount. People with disabilities – like anyone else – should be at liberty to accept or to turn down care. The important factor is that they should have the opportunity to choose whether or not to undertake or to continue care – and that their surrogates, when appropriate, should have the ability to choose for and with them. Practitioners should be especially careful to be sure that stereotypes about disability – for example, the judgment that the quality of life of people with disabilities is thereby inferior – are not influencing, in subtle ways, the care that is offered. This is the grain of truth in the argument of "Not Dead Yet": ensuring that impairment is neutral with respect to the care received. At the same time, conceptions of the good of people with disabilities, even people with significant intellectual disabilities, should be shaped to their own preferences and experiences, varying as these preferences and experiences do.

Utilitarian views raise equally serious problems in regard to justice and people with disabilities. To measure the comparative cost-effectiveness of care, metrics have been proposed that take disabilities into account. These measures may disadvantage people with disabilities. One such measure, "disability adjusted life years" (DALYs) was proposed by the World Bank and the World Health Organization as a comparative international measure of the burden of disease. Applied to measure the benefits of care, DALYs assess the number of years of disability-free life gained by a care intervention (Homides). Although DALYs have been defended as a way to measure the comparative importance of health interventions worldwide, it is arguably unjust to let disability function as a consideration that counts against allocation. If impairments are arbitrary from a moral point of view – the luck of nature or life – people with disabilities are potentially doubly wronged if their impairments are taken to be grounds for regarding health care that cannot "ameliorate" disability as lower in priority (Orentlicher, 1996). To let the impairment count against the care adds injustice to injury, as it were. Another widely suggested metric, "quality adjusted life years" (QALYs), which considers quality of life, raises similar problems if the quality of life of people with disabilities is downgraded stereotypically.

Contexts of injustice

People with disabilities, like the elderly, may well have been the victims of injustice during their lifetimes. Indeed, many impairments are at least partially the result of social injustice: for example, impairments attendant on prematurity that could have been prevented by adequate prenatal care, intellectual impairments resulting from high levels of lead paint in impoverished neighborhoods, or limb amputations caused by war. Metrics for the allocation of health care that lower the priority of care modalities that will be efficacious but not eliminate disability will simply compound these injustices. That disability may have been generated by injustice is an additional argument – albeit a partial compliance theory argument – for rejecting health care allocations based on metrics such as DALYs or QALYs. Health care providers should be aware of this argument when they and their patients face limitations on care options because of the patient's disability.

Race

In the United States, the topic of race and health care is plagued by the history of slavery and discrimination. The Tuskegee syphilis study has become emblematic of that sordid past. In 1997, President Clinton publicly apologized to the study subjects and their families for this abuse.[12] Any attempt to discuss racial disparities in health care in the United States must recognize this history and the impact it has had on the African-American population's distrust of medicine. Discussions must also tread carefully on whether race is viewed as a category with any biological basis, or as a social construction (Mallon, 2004; Craddock, 2005). Analyses of racial disparities in care are based on perceptions of race rather than any view about biological categorizations, however.

In 2002, the United States Institute of Medicine published a report documenting health care disparities by race in the United States (Institute of Medicine, 2002). The report, summarizing the results of over 300 studies, concluded that race was independently statistically significant in explaining the variance in health care offered to patients, as well as concomitant disparities in health status. In some studies, race explained as much as half of the variance, even when other factors such as education, income level, disease status or co-morbidities, age, or insurance status were taken into account. The report hypothesized that difficulties in communication and racial stereotyping, as well as histories of discrimination and current racial disparities, have played important roles in the disparities. Since the publication of the report, studies have continued to document racial disparities in health care in the United States,[13] with the important exception of care in the system maintained by the Veterans Administration and perhaps basic primary care. These disparities are not limited to the United States; they have been documented with respect to aboriginal people in Canada (Adelson, 2005), Australia (Couzos and Davis, 2005), and New Zealand (Bramley et al., 2005) and for racial minorities in the European Union (Stronks et al., 2001).

There is also evidence that gender disparities interact with racial and ethnic disparities in health status in the United States, particularly with respect to functional status among African-American women (Read and Gorman, 2006). There is some evidence for similar interaction between gender and racial disparities in the United Kingdom (Mirza and Sheridan, 2003).

In light of these data, health care providers cannot avoid attending to the risk that their conduct unwittingly contributes to these patterns. Just as researchers are poor judges of whether their sources of financing may bias their study results (van Kolfschooten, 2002), individual providers who, in all good conscience believe that they are not acting in discriminatory ways may nonetheless behave in ways that overall yield patterns that are problematic. They should pay particular care to how their communication skills, their comfort levels with different patients, and their patients' trust in them, may influence care interactions.

Contemporary theories of justice agree that race is a characteristic that should not influence access to health care. (Whether differences by race are physiologically significant and thus should be taken into account in the care modalities employed is a different, empirical question, not addressed here.) Race is irrelevant from a moral point of view – today, this is beyond disagreement. Where disagreement continues is over how to deal with histories of discrimination and ongoing discriminatory practices. Some argue that race is irrelevant, and so it should not matter at all, even in efforts to identify and eradicate discrimination. Arguably, this prohibition confuses a prescription of ideal justice – race is irrelevant – with a prescription for partial compliance contexts: where racial injustice has or does occur, it may be necessary to take race into account to remedy the situation. This recapitulates the debate over "affirmative action" – the idea is that we must attend to race matters in order to remedy injustice.

Narrow views of the significance of race would limit its use to compensatory justice. Only providers who have discriminated, on this view, are obligated to compensate their patients. Only people who have been refused health care on grounds of race – for example, the participants in the Tuskegee syphilis study or the pregnant African-American women in labor who were turned away from hospitals because of their color (see, e.g., *Childs v. Weis*) – are owed compensation for injuries they suffered (Noah, 1998).

A broader view of the significance of race contends that as long as racial injustice persists, race may be used in the development of strategies to correct or eventually overcome injustice. Racial categories may be used in making progress towards justice, even if benefits accrue to people who were not themselves the victims of prior injustice and thus deserving of compensation. This argument has been used to defend affirmative action in admission to medical school or special efforts to deliver medical services to underserved racial communities. It might also be used to defend public support for clinics, advertising targeted at underserved groups, or practitioners' efforts to pay special attention to whether they are engaged in subtle behaviors that disadvantage racial minorities.

People in Poverty and Immigrants

Approaches to distributive justice in health care at the macro level must confront the significance of national borders, considering whether justice requires redistribution of health care resources from richer to poorer nations (Buchanan, 2003; Institute of Medicine, 2003). National borders also present ethical questions for individual practitioners.

In facing questions of international justice, utilitarians tend to begin as universalists, arguing that individuals have obligations to act in ways that would produce the most good on the whole, or to follow rules that would produce the most good. In this vein, Peter Singer famously argued that residents of richer countries have far stronger obligations to contribute to the health care needs of impoverished nations than they are currently doing – indeed, obligations to contribute their time and resources up to the point at which overall utility falls (Singer, 1972). On Singer's view, health care providers should attempt to deliver their services where they are most needed; others who are more affluent should attempt to contribute to those who are worse off, through organizations such as Oxfam. The significance of national borders for each of us as we go about our business is pragmatic only; it may be more cost-effective for individuals to deliver care to the nearby rather than to the distant needy. Critics of Singer's utilitarianism contend that individuals have special rights to consider their own satisfactions, their families, their established patients, and others to whom they bear special relationships.

Within many societies today, providers make daily decisions about treating the impoverished. As a matter of justice, providers should work with patients to try to manage care in a cost-effective way, for example prescribing generic medications or exploring therapeutic options that may be effective and are within the patient's means. Providers should also try to find what resources might be available for patients. This is time-consuming, but advocacy on behalf of patients demands no less. Moreover, physicians who work in larger practices may be able to take advantage of combined administrative resources to help streamline this process.

As Morreim has argued, however, these obligations of justice do not extend to lying or "gaming" the system to get care for patients who are not otherwise eligible (Morreim, 1991). Leaving aside the principled concern that lying is itself wrong, "gaming" also contributes to a structure of dishonest practices and clouds observation of the true extent of needs for care. Thus while the consequences of "gaming" might seem to be beneficial in individual cases, they are likely deleterious over the longer run.

In addition, providers owe it to each other to bear their share of the profession's responsibilities to ensure that the poor receive at least minimal care. Otherwise, some providers will bear disproportionate burdens of a responsibility arguably shared by members of the profession as a matter of justice. This may include taking a fair share of patients on publicly reimbursed programs, gathering information about resources available to patients, and advocating for expansion of these public programs to cover greater numbers of the poor and medically needy.

In many nations, poor immigrants lack eligibility even for public programs and thus may present the most difficult challenges of justice for providers. In the United States, the 1996 Personal Responsibility and Work Opportunity Act (PROWRA) made most newly arriving, legal immigrants ineligible for Medicaid (Francis, 1997). Immigrants are also deterred from seeking care by threats of investigation and deportation (Bernstein, 2006). In the European Union, immigrants also may find themselves excluded from access to health care (Woolf, 2005).

Providers asked to treat immigrants without resources face difficult choices of justice. They will, in the United States at least, experience pressures to report illegal residents. There may be restrictions on the use of resources – even resources that would be helpful in preventing disease spread, such as immunizations or antibiotics. These situations present perhaps the most powerful case for political activism by health care providers. The risks at issue when immigrants are deterred from seeking care are not just individual risks. They may be risks of disease transmission, even transmission of epidemic proportions, even if avian flu is today more the subject of fear than actual disease transmission to human beings. Providers thus should be open and encouraging to immigrants in need of care. They should also seek to educate the public about the important public health reasons for extending access to basic preventive care even to people who are not legal residents of the country in which they live.

Conclusion

In facing patients who may lack resources or who may have been the victims of injustice, providers have many different choices. They have choices about whether to undertake the provider–patient relationship, how much time to spend, how to communicate, and what treatment options to offer. They have additional choices about advocacy: how to help patients learn about resources that might be available for them, whether to protest care denials, and whether to participate in political advocacy. Finally, they may have decisions about whether to engage in acts of protest or even disobedience when social policies are especially unjust or risky, and unlikely to be changed without concerted effort by health care providers themselves. The judgments providers make will differ, depending on the theory of distributive justice that is employed. Theories of justice that are roughly egalitarian in character may yield quite different conclusions about what is discriminatory than theories of justice that are roughly utilitarian. Judgments providers make also need to take into account the significance of ongoing injustice. Providers may need to pay special attention to patients who have been the victims of injustice, to work to obtain care for immigrants or others excluded from health care systems, and to be active politically in order to protect their own patients and ultimately us all.

Notes

1 For a description of the international activities of this humanitarian organization, see http://www.msf.org/ (accessed March 9, 2006).
2 This classificatory strategy is fostered by regulations of the ethics of research that focus on "vulnerable" groups. See Childress et al., 2005 for a typical discussion of such regulatory strategies. For an analysis of tensions between principles of justice and mandates to protect vulnerable subjects see Kahn et al., 1998.
3 The term is originally due to John Rawls, who noted the possibility of partial compliance theory only to set it aside in his magisterial work on ideal justice (Rawls, 1971).
4 Rule utilitarianism is the view that we ought to act in accord with principles the adoption of which would produce the most good on the whole. Considerably controversy has attended the extent to which present circumstances should affect the selection of these rules (Brandt, 1988).
5 Over 10 million children in the United States had no health insurance in 2002 (Kaiser Commission on Medicaid, 2005).

6 These regulations offer the "carrot" of federal funds for child abuse prevention to states with programs that meet the requirements of the regulations, 45 C.F.R. §1340.15 (2006).

7 http://www.aarp.org/ (accessed March 3, 2006).

8 The actual 2006 estimate for a private room is $74,095 (AAHSA, 2006) per year, per resident. The estimate for semi-private rooms is over $60,000. http://1tc-usa.com/statistics/statistics.htm (accessed March, 2006).

9 Social Security Act §1862(a)(1)(a).

10 Centers for Medicare and Medicaid Services, http://www.cms.hhs.gov/center/coverage.asp (accessed February 27, 2006).

11 http://www.notdeadyet.org/, accessed March 7, 2006.

12 http//www.cdc.gov/nchstp/od/tuskegee/time.htm, accessed November 1, 2005.

13 The literature continues to be replete with studies documenting disparities in health care and health outcomes by race in the United States. For a discussion of disparaties in chemotherapy for breast cancer, see Hershman et al., 2005; for a discussion of differences in dental care, see Gilbert, 2005; for a discussion of renal transplantation, see Young and Kew, 2005; and for end of life care, see Welch et al., 2005.

References

Adelson, N. (2005), The embodiment of inequity: health disparities in aboriginal Canada, *Canadian Journal of Public Health* 96, Suppl. 2: S45–61.

American Association of Homes and Services for the Aging (AAHSA), *Aging Services in America: The Facts*, available at http://www2.aahsa.org/aging_services/default.asp (accessed March 4, 2006).

Anderlik, Mary R. and Wilkinson, Wendy J. (2000), The Americans with Disabilities Act and managed care, *Houston Law Review* 37: 1163–248 at p. 1179.

Bernstein, Nina (2006), Recourse grows slim for immigrants who fall ill, *New York Times*, March 3: A4, p. 1.

Bramley, D., Hebert, P., Tuzzio, L., and Chassin, M. (2005), Disparities in indigenous health: a cross-country comparison between New Zealand and the United States, *American Journal of Public Health* 95 (5): 844–50.

Brandt, Richard B. (1988), Fairness to indirect optimific theories in ethics, *Ethics* 98: 341–60.

Buchanan, Allen E. (1984), The right to a decent minimum of health care, *Philosophy and Public Affairs* 13 (1): 55–78.

Buchanan, Allen (2003), *Justice, Legitimacy and Self-Determination: Moral Foundations for International Law*, Oxford: Oxford University Press.

Cerminara, Kathy L. (2005), Dealing with dying: how insurers can help patients seeking last-chance therapies (even when the answer is "no"), *Health Matrix* 15: 285–328.

Childress, James F., Meslin, Eric M., and Shapiro, Harold T. (eds.) (2005), *Belmont Revisited: Ethical Principles for Research with Human Subjects*, Washington, DC: Georgetown University Press.

Childs v. Weis, 440 S.W.2d 104 (Tx. Civ. App. 1969).

Couzos, S.and Davis, S. (2005), Inequities in Aboriginal health – access to the asthma 3+ visit plan, *Australian Family Physician* 34 (10): 837–40.

Craddock, Lee, SJ (2005), The risks of race in assessing health disparities, *Hastings Center Report* 35 (4): 48.

Daniels, Norman (1985), *Just Health Care*, Cambridge: Cambridge University Press.

Daniels, Norman (1988), *Am I My Parents' Keeper? An Essay on Justice Between Young and Old*, New York: Oxford University Press.

Daniels, Norman (2002), Justice, health, and health care, in R. Rhodes, M.P. Battin, and A. Silvers (eds.), *Medicine and Social Justice: Essays on the Distribution of Health Care*, New York: Oxford University Press, pp. 6–23.

Doyle, L.W. (2004), Neonatal intensive care at borderline viability: is it worth it? *Early Human Development* 80 (2): 103–13.

Francis, Leslie P. (1997), Elderly immigrants: what should they expect of the social safety net? *The Elder Law Journal* 5: 229–50.

Gilbert, G.H. (2005), Racial and socioeconomic disparities in health from population-based research to practice-based research: the example of oral health, *Journal of Dental Education* 69 (9): 1003–14.

Hall, Mark A. (1994), Rationing health care at the bedside, *New York University Law Review* 69: 693–780.

Hershman D., McBride, R., Jacobson, J.S., et al. (2005), Racial disparities in treatment and survival among women with early-stage breast cancer, *Journal of Clinical Oncology* 23: 6639–46.

Homides, Nuria, The Disability-Adjusted Life Year (DALY) definition, measurement, and potential use, *Human Capital Development and Operations Working Papers*, available at http://www.worldbank.org/html/extdr/hnp/hddflash/workp/wp_00068.html (accessed March 7, 2006).

Institute of Medicine (2002), *Unequal Treatment: Confronting Racial and Ethnic Disparities in Health Care*, Washington, DC: National Academy Press, available at http://www.iom.edu/CMS/3740/4475.aspx (accessed February 26, 2006).

Institute of Medicine (2003), *Improving Birth Outcomes: Meeting the Challenge in the Developing World* (2003), p. 11, available at http://www.iom.edu/CMS/3783/ 3915/ 16191.aspx (accessed March 9, 2006).

Kahn, Jeffrey P., Mastroianni, Anna C., and Sugarman, Jeremy (1998), *Beyond Consent: Seeking Justice in Research*, New York: Oxford University Press.

Kaiser Commission on Medicaid and the Uninsured (2005), Medicaid Facts 2005, available at www.kff.org/medicaid (accessed February 26, 2006).

Kaiser Family Foundation, *Prospects for Retiree Health Benefits as Medicare Drug Coverage Begins: Findings from the Kaiser/Hewitt 2005 Survey on Retiree Health Benefits* – report, http://www.kff.org/medicare/7439.cfm (accessed March 4, 2006).

Kalb, Paul E. (1992), Defining an "adequate" package of health care benefits, *University of Pennsylvania Law Review* 140: 1987–97.

Kleinki, J.D. (2004), Access versus excess: value-based cost sharing for prescription drugs; Rationing based on value, not price, offers one way to ease the tension between medical research and medical excess, *Health Affairs* 23 (1): 34–47.

Kolata, Gina (2006), Medicare says it will pay, but patients say "no thanks," *New York Times*, March 3: C4.

Kopelman, Loretta M. (2005), Are the 21-year-old Baby Doe rules misunderstood or mistaken? *Pediatrics* 115 (3): 797–802.

Mallon, Ron (2004), Passing, traveling and reality: social constructionism and the metaphysics of race, *Nous* 38 (4): 644–673.

Mirza, Heidi Safia and Sheridan, Ann-Marie (2003), Multiple identity and access to health: the experience of black and minority ethnic women, *Equal Opportunities Commission Working Paper* no. 10, available at http://www.eoc.org.uk/PDF/multiple%20identity.pdf (accessed November 1, 2005).

Morreim, E. Haavi (1991), Gaming the system: dodging the rules, ruling the dodgers, *Archives of Internal Medicine* 151 (3): 443–7.

Murphy, Liam (2000), *Moral Demands in Non-Ideal Theory*, New York: Oxford University Press.

Noah, Barbara A. (1998), Racial disparities in the delivery of health care, *San Diego Law Review* 35: 135–78.

Orentlicher, David (1996), Destructuring disability: rationing of health care and unfair discrimination against the sick, *Harvard Civil Rights–Civil Liberties Law Review* 31: 49–87.

Peifeng Hu and Reuben, David B. (2002), Effects of managed care on the length of time that elderly patients spend with physicians during ambulatory visits: National Ambulatory Medical Care Survey, *Medical Care* 40 (7): 606–13.

Physicians for a National Health Program, http://www.pnhp.org/ (accessed February 26, 2006).

Rawls, John (1971), *A Theory of Justice*, Cambridge, MA: Harvard University Press, 1971.

Read, J.G. and Gorman, B.K. (2006), Gender inequalities in US adult health: the interplay of race and ethnicity, *Social Science and Medicine* 62 (5) (2006): 1045–65.

Savitt, Todd L. (1982), The use of blacks for medical experimentation in the old south, *Journal of Southern History*, XLVIII (3): 331–48.

Schwartz, Robert L. (1985), Why Britain cannot afford informed consent, *Hastings Center Report* 15 (4): 19.

Senate Finance and House of Representatives' Energy and Commerce Committee Statement for the Record for hearings on the National Governor's Association's Medicaid Proposal (June 15, 2005) http://www.aap.org/advocacy/washing/FINALMEDICAIDSTATEMENT.pdf (accessed February 26, 2006).

Singer, Peter (1972), Famine, affluence, and morality, *Philosophy and Public Affairs* 1: 229–43.

van Kolfschooten, F. (2002), Conflicts of interest: Can you believe what you read? *Nature* 416: 360–3.

Welch, L.C., Teno, J.M., and Mor, V. (2005), End of life care in black and white: race matters for medical care of dying patients and their families, *Journal of the American Geriatric Society* 53 (7): 1145–53.

Woolf, Marie (2005), ID cards may create health underclass, MPs say, *The Independent* (London), August 5: 19.

Young, C.J. and Kew, C. (2005), Health disparities in transplantation: focus on the complexity and challenge of renal transplantation in African-Americans, *Medical Clinics of North America* 89 (5): 1003–31, ix.

Chapter 10

Institutional Practices, Ethics, and the Physician

Mary V. Rorty, Ann E. Mills, and Patricia H. Werhane

Introduction

The delivery of health care involves organizations of varying size and role, from individual practice associations of sole practitioners or several physicians operating within a particular community, to health care systems composed of many hospitals, all of which relate to other organizations within the sector, including their suppliers, payers, and regulators (Robinson, 1999b). It would be a mistake to believe that all ethical issues for physicians arise only on the individual level of the physician–patient encounter. Since physicians practice medicine in and through health care organizations, the way those organizations operate furthers or impedes their own professional activities. Recent changes in care delivery mean that excellence of practice must involve a wider range of considerations than were involved when most professional codes were developed. To protect professional integrity, the contemporary physician must carefully scrutinize the business practices associated with the delivery of medical care for possible threats to ethical medical practice.

This chapter focuses on the ethical implications for physician practice of decisions which are made on other levels of the health care system and are thus often out of the individual physician's control. We instance several ways in which organizational decisions impact the professional functions of physicians. The organizations we consider are of two sorts: practice and delivery organizations – the hospitals or health care systems in which much of physician practice occurs; and payer organizations – public and private insurers and the managed care organizations or systems that increasingly determine how physicians are reimbursed for services. The cases we present incorporate three perspectives which may also be considered tools for analysis: professional ethics, organization ethics, and stakeholder thinking.

Professional ethics

As well as knowledge, experience, and skill, physicians acquire a particular ethical perspective in the course of their professional training. The mainstay of professional ethics is the physician's commitment to the best interests of the patient. This Hippocratic tradition of medical ethics has influenced the professional codes of other health care workers, including nurses, hospital administrators and members of the allied health professions. Clinical ethics, addressing ethical conflicts arising at the bedside, is a compartmentalized function of health organizations, and ethics committees have been a condition for accreditation of US hospitals since the 1990s.

Organization ethics

Organizations too set goals, institute processes and procedures to attain them, act according to articulated values and decide how to prioritize them in particular situations. Organization ethics focuses on the alignment of interests and values within organizations, and with the implications of individual decisions for the organization's vision and culture. It is concerned with the extent to which the organization is to be counted as a moral agent, and the mutual implication in health care organizations of professional, clinical, and business ethics (Spencer et al., 2000). The organization and the individual physician in one sense share common values and have a common social role: patient health. In another sense they have different values, because they look at what it is to fill those obligations in different ways, have different priorities, or specify the situation differently. Our hypothetical cases illustrate how decisions driven by business considerations can have professional and clinical implications for affected parties.

Stakeholder thinking

Recent work in health care ethics has depended heavily upon a tool developed in business ethics for understanding organization decision-making. Under the stakeholder model it is important to consider the implications of an organizational decision on all the individuals or groups that will be affected by it, acknowledging the existence of multiple perspectives on the same decision. The stakeholders of a business include not only the stockholders, as in the traditional business model, but other affected organizations, payers, employees, the consumers of the product or service delivered by the organization, the local community and the larger society. In health care, stakeholders include care providers and patients, payers and suppliers, the local community, and the larger society that supports the social institution of health care.

Stakeholder theory assumes that the relations of the organization with all its stake-holders are to some extent reciprocal, and represent normative claims which need to be taken into consideration in calculating the consequences of a course of action. It requires evaluating and prioritizing various stakeholder claims, taking into con-sideration relationships between organizations and the various stakeholders whose interests are affected by organizational decisions (Elms, Berman, and Wicks, 2002). Our hypothetical examples illustrate organization-level decisions, often driven by business considerations, that have ethical implications for medical professionals.

The Physician and the Provider Organization

Case I From a local hospital to a health care system

Markson Valley Hospital is a 300-bed tertiary care hospital in a mid-sized city in a rural region of the northwest USA. It has served the area for 60 years but was run-ning into financial difficulties because of changing demographics and competition from the academic health center in the state capital.

When they were beginning to worry that they might have to close the hospital, their recently appointed chief executive officer suggested that a merger, a strategy proved successful in many other industries, might be a solution to their financial problems. By merging, hospitals can eliminate excess capacity, increase efficiency, and boost market share, as well as increasing their ability to bargain with insurers.

Markson arranged financing to purchase three other hospitals: two small urban hospitals that were also facing financial difficulty – one of which was quickly closed – and one thriving suburban hospital. The combined organization was renamed the Markson Valley Health System (MVHS).

Dr Abrahmson is a gastroenterologist in private practice in the town of Markson Valley. The hospital that was closed was the one most proximate to his office. He wonders what the impact of the merger will be on his practice.

Hospital mergers have been a common phenomenon in recent years. Consider-ations of economies of scale drive many mergers: by combining facilities and potential patient populations, institutions may be in a better position to negoti-ate cost savings with suppliers or obtain better reimbursement rates from insurers. Mergers can address problems like low census, turning competitors into allies, and may make it possible to better utilize available facilities by reallocating beds or services to better meet demand.

Often mergers are not successful. One source claims that the failure rate is as high as 65 percent (Ruocco, 2005). For instance, a merger between two northern California health systems that was expected to save $100 million over three years incurred losses of $173 million, leading to a hasty termination of the arrangement (Kastor, 2001; Blackstone and Fuhr, 2003). Even when a merger is financially suc-cessful, other stakeholders may be adversely affected. There may be a price to pay for the physicians practicing in a hospital that has been sold. Consolidating services may cut costs for hospitals, but increase costs and inconvenience for the physicians who practice in them, who may have increased travel time, or reduced access or decision-making power, or face greater competition for operating rooms or beds (Blackstone and Fuhr, 2003).

The hospital that was closed by Markson Valley Health System may have provided services to a group of patients that will now have no comparable facility available to them. The capacity that is eliminated may be the unit upon which Dr Abrahmson's practice depends. Bed reduction might mean that fewer patients are able to be served or that some may be sent home prematurely. Increased purchasing power may come at the cost of a reduced formulary or reduced control over equipment purchases.

The success of the new organization depends upon the support and trust of the community it serves, and that is based on the historical characteristics of its once-separate constituent institutions. In order to reap its hoped-for benefits, the integrated Markson Valley Health System must consider the perspective of the increasing number of individuals and organizations that are stakeholders in the expanded system. Combining their operations in a way that will preserve that historical advantage and further the financial security of the unified system will require forethought and a balancing of considerations. The success of the transition is a test of the organizational culture of the new Markson Valley Health System.

The organization's culture and climate

One of the most frequent reasons given for failure of health care mergers is incompatibility of the cultures of the merging institutions (Blackstone and Fuhr, 2003).[1] The way an organization operates, the pattern of its behavior, is its culture. It includes the goals it pursues, and the rules, processes, and norms for behavior by which it seeks to attain those goals. Often expressed formally in mission statements, value statements, and codes, the organizational culture expresses what the organization does and how it does it (Victor and Cullen, 1988). The ethical climate of an organization is its morale – the perception of the organization's members, its employees, and those associated with the organization, of the extent to which the expressed values are actually implemented in its daily operations.

A positive ethical climate has at least two important characteristics. First, the mission and values of the organization, which inform its expectations for professional and managerial performance, are implemented in the actual practices of the organization. Second, a positive ethical climate requires that the organization operate in the way society expects it to – the manifest organizational culture is appropriate for the organization's social role. Morale is low in an organization that is behaving in ways not in accordance with society's expectation of it, and its stakeholder's trust in the organization can be damaged. Culture and climate are particularly important in health care, an institutional sector with a particularly sensitive and strongly defined social role. Two health care organizations that share the same socially sanctioned values but prioritize them differently in their operations might fail to achieve successful merger, even if the financial pre-conditions are adequately met. The changes brought about by the combination of separate institutions into one system may present difficulties that have not been anticipated by MVHS's new administrator.[2]

> At the high point of its expansion Markson Valley offered to buy Dr Abrahmson's practice. He was tempted to accept the offer, but wondered if the sale would limit his ability to refer patients to outpatient facilities in the neighborhood that were unaffiliated with Markson Valley Health System.

The decisions made by the hospital closest to Dr Abrahmson affect his ability to refer patients to that facility, and the new system's decisions about which of their services to invest in or to upgrade affect the quality of the care he can offer his patients. If the expanded Markson Valley is going to close its facilities to non-affiliated physicians, there may be some advantage for Dr Abrahmson in accepting the offer of purchase. But as he is aware, such affiliation may preclude referrals outside the system.

The size of the organization in which a physician practices can be very important to his ability to meet his professional ethical expectations. In Independent Practice Associations (IPAs) – organizations of a small number of partners in community primary or specialty practice – close integration between professional, clinical, and business considerations may be possible. New contracts, new insurance company or governmental regulations, may be able to be accommodated between partners. New support staff can be added to handle administrative details as insurance plans proliferate; admitting agreements can be shifted from one local hospital to another as the health care organizations in the community close, consolidate, or change their target populations. The number and mix of patients in the practice can be adjusted to meet changing conditions.

If Dr Abrahmson accepts the offer of purchase of his practice, he may lose some of that flexibility. Markson Valley Health System may impose utilization quotas that determine how many patients Dr Abrahmson should have in his practice. If the number is higher than his present practice, he will have less time to spend with each. If it is lower, he may feel some relief from financial pressure that will allow him to pay more attention to each encounter. The conditions of the contract will determine the effect on his clinical encounters. For the physician who is an employee or whose area of practice is becoming tightly tied to a large organization, the practice situation can be very different than that of the individual practitioner. Depending upon the size, degree of compartmentalization, and the organizational culture of a large organization, the integration between clinical and administrative functions can be cooperative and flexible or almost non-existent. As has been noted by many commentators, any arrangement has incentives and disincentives, and physicians must scrutinize any suggested arrangement for explicit or tacit threats to professional practice (Rodwin, 2004).

Case II From non-profit to for-profit

Marymount Hospital is located in the heart of New England in what was at one time an important mill town. It was founded in the early part of the twentieth century by a local philanthropist, the wealthy owner of a majority of the mills, with a charter that charges the hospital with primary responsibility for the health and well-being of the community in which it is located. Its benefactor left a healthy endowment to sustain the hospital, devoted primarily to supporting unreimbursed care, and it thrived for a number of years, developing an excellent reputation for a number of specialty services.

Unfortunately it has recently fallen into financial difficulties and was purchased by Aleph, a large for-profit hospital corporation based in California. The parent corporation has determined to narrow the scope of several of its hospitals, including Marymount, concentrating on developing centers of excellence for specific services to attract national and international patients. They have increased the number of pediatric cardiologists and expanded their transplant services, and downsized the maternity ward and emergency room.

Local physicians are finding that there are no beds available in the intensive care units for emergency admissions, since all the beds are full of scheduled surgical patients, and Dr Wilkinson, a local obstetrician, is worried that the nearest maternity ward with a Newborn Intensive Care Unit is 40 miles away across the state line.

The community is a stakeholder in its hospital, and the consequences on the larger community of Marymount's acquisition remain to be seen. The conditions under which it will be able to continue to use its endowment for its designated purpose are subject to conditions out of its control. Few have suffered the fate of one of the hospitals purchased by the Allegheny System, which found its endowment emptied to meet shortfalls in other hospitals in the system (Massey, 1999), but "studies have demonstrated that investor-owned hospitals will not commit to providing the same level of charity care . . . as non-profits" (Kline et al., 2004, p. 354).

The history of this hospital is a snapshot of the history of the transitions across the country. Non-profit to investor-owned conversions have increased in frequency in the last few decades. Many once-charitable foundations have been forced to close, and others have been absorbed or transformed into for-profit organizations. Hospital conversions have been described as "the largest potential redeployment of charitable assets in the history of the United States" (Kline et al., 2004, p. 352). Historically, non-profit hospitals have been committed to the mission of providing charitable health care to the communities in which they are based. However, recent emphasis on cost constraint and the entry of for-profit enterprises into the business of health care delivery have transformed this expectation. All health care organizations are now under demands for efficiency and cost constraint that are increasingly incompatible with the way they used to provide services for the indigent and uninsured of their communities. The mandate to be competitive and the mandate to be compassionate are in some ways simply incompatible. "We can't ask non-profits to be more like for-profits in the ways that we like – efficient, responsive, aggressive – without expecting that they will also become more like for-profits in the ways that we don't: rapacious, hardheaded and yes, sometimes selfish" (Jacob Hacker, quoted in Cohn, 2004).[3]

In the short term Dr Wilkinson's conditions of practice have become much harder, and his (and everybody else's) community patients, for whom there is no room at the hospital, will suffer as well. The decisions that influence their practice are not made on the individual level, but impact the individual physicians because of their position within the larger system. Financial considerations have led the hospital to change its business practices in the broad sense. The mission of the hospital and its prioritization of values have changed, so what is done in it changes, and the physicians and patients who don't fit with the new model will be excluded.

Case III The incredible shrinking unit

Dr Kim is the director of a 20-bed surgical ICU in Marymount Hospital. Shortly after the purchase by Aleph, she received a memo announcing that two new cardiologists were being added to staff in order to increase the prominence of Marymount as a national and international center of excellence in cutting-edge cardiac surgery. As of next month 10 of the beds of her unit were to be designated for the scheduled surgeries of cardiac patients.

Because Dr Kim practices entirely within the hospital, the impacts of organizational decisions on her professional practice are much greater than upon Dr Abrahmson's. In this instance, the organization suffered severe disruption of the alignment of values within the organization. The coordination between the administrative decision and the clinical staff was almost non-existent. The speed of the change, the lack of consultation with affected units, and the lack of preparation for the shift in emphasis, sent ripples of consternation throughout the unit. Nursing staff clamored for re-training to deal with the expected onslaught of seriously compromised patients, but were going to have very little time to get it. Dr Kim was losing control of half of her beds, and had to scramble to find alternate sites of care for some of the patients now in her unit, many of whom required a level of care unavailable in other units of the hospital. She now dreads the monthly meetings of the county medical association, of which she has been an active member, because she faces the unpleasant task of telling her community colleagues that there is suddenly "less room at the inn" for their local patients. Morale within the hospital has plummeted; community trust in the institution, she fears, will soon follow.

Marymount, driven by decisions in the head office of Aleph, has handled this transition badly. The health care professionals who are at the crucial interface between patients and the institution have been disrespected and disregarded. Low morale in this crucial unit, often one of the central fee-generating dynamos of the hospital, will have implications throughout the organization as the word spreads and each internal stakeholder wonders if his unit will be the next to be downsized. The commitment of the organization as a whole to the primary value of excellent patient care, as trumpeted in its mission statement, has been called into question, creating a negative ethical climate. It will be bad if clinicians doubt the commitment of the organization to clinical care. It will be worse if they shrug and dismiss it as "business as usual" – no better than they have learned to expect of institutions under control of the Aleph corporation. Apathy is dangerous for the patients, and contempt is dangerous for the system.

Individual and organizational moral distress

Dr Kim is a physician whose area of practice is within a large complex organization with many goals and objectives, not all of which are easy to reconcile. A hospital is a site for the exercise of professional services, and the professional integrity of its practicing physicians can be either supported or impeded by the decisions made in furthering the hospital's various needs for financial stability, patient satisfaction, and care of high quality.

If moral *dilemmas* arise when a caregiver must choose between incompatible courses of action, each of which has ethical justification, moral *distress* arises when the agent is clear about the ethically appropriate course of action but institutional constraints make it difficult to implement. Conceptualized in the mid-1980s in the nursing literature (Jameton, 1984, p. 5), moral distress is applicable in many realms of health care. Much of the literature on moral distress focuses on the individual psychological consequences of frustrated agency: loss of self-esteem, demoralization, and guilt in individuals, reduced efficiency, lowered quality of care and increased turnover in staff in organizations. All caregivers, physicians as well as nurses, are increasingly torn between conflicting commitments: their account-ability to their patients and their accountability to the institutions in which they practice. Of particular concern to both individuals and organizations throughout the health care system is the current pressure for cost containment and continuing pressure for quality improvement. An organization committed to excellent care for reasonable cost may institute policies oriented toward cost containment that are perceived by internal constituents as constraints upon the quality of care required by their professional clinical judgment. Working conditions that impede, rather than support, actions required by the professional ethics of health care providers can be a source of moral distress.[4]

Case IV Cost over quality?

Dr Pearson recently completed his residency in a nationally recognized transplant program. In looking around for placement he chose Marymount because of their expressed intention to expand their transplant services. But last year one of the trans-plant patients spent 260 days in Marymount's ICU, at a total cost of over $4 million dollars, much of which was not able to be recovered from any source. Marymount's board is now looking again at their transplant program, and has established an inter-nal oversight committee to evaluate any proposed surgeries that are both high-cost and high-risk. Furthermore, a recently developed anti-rejection drug that Dr Pearson had good results with in his residency is not on the hospital's formulary for reasons of cost. He is wondering if he chose wisely when he opted to come to Marymount.

In Dr Pearson's case the provider organization is crucial to his practice. The extent to which the services available in that institution facilitate or impede Dr Pearson's practice is an important professional consideration for him. As a practitioner of a specialty with both high risk and high cost, he is particularly vulnerable to institutional mechanisms to control costs. At the stage he has reached in his career, his ability to further hone his own skills and to contribute to advances in transplant medicine may weigh very heavily in his choice of where to practice. The unavailability of a pharmaceutical that improves the chances of his patients for positive outcomes is worrying as well. Dr Pearson faces a conflict between his personal career goals, his ability to advance his medical specialty, his attention to his patients, and his loyalty to the organization in which he practices.

Conflicts of interest and conflicts of commitment

Most business practices in the health care sector create the possibility of conflicts of interest. It is considered a breach of professional ethics if a physician recommends an unnecessary procedure or course of action that results in financial advantage for himself. Conflicts of interest can usually be easily recognized and avoided, If Dr Abrahmson consistently refers patients for diagnostic imaging only to a lab in which he has a financial interest and the quality of their care suffers as a result, this might represent a conflict of interest. Conflicts of commitment involve the distribution of focus and effort between competing professional obligations, rather than a conflict between professional obligations and self-interest (Werhane and Doering, 1996, p. 61). Conflicts of commitment are much harder to avoid and can create moral dilemmas for conscientious professionals. Dr Kim has professional responsibilities to her fellow clinicians, her community colleagues, and the organization in which she practices. She wrestles with how she can continue to meet those competing commitments in the fact of changing conditions in her unit. Dr Pearson too faces a professional conflict between his pursuit of professional excellence and the advance of transplantation medicine, and his contractual commitment to Marymount Hospital.

What is the nature of the conflict faced by the institution? Marymount (and its parent company Aleph) have an obligation to both cost containment and care of high quality. Marymount Hospital must maintain financial viability, and may be uncertain how much financial support they can count upon from Aleph, even though it was the decision of the home office that they expand their transplant program. The hospital may be expected to heed their advice, but also to take full financial responsibility for the results. Aleph can shift financial risk to its component units. But those components are then going to have to distribute that risk to their various services – a complex balancing of short- and long-term advantages that is bound to disrupt established expectations. The ability of Marymount to support care is currently influenced by its relation to Aleph, but it may have been equally, if differently, constrained by its financial instability as the free-standing institution it was before its acquisition.

The extent to which necessary accommodations impact the physicians and patients in the hospital may be in large part a function of how the decisions are made. What is the degree of communication between the administrative and professional leadership in the hospital? Does the Board discuss, or only pronounce? Will the oversight committee include representation from the various services? Are there mechanisms for altering or supplementing the formulary when particular cases need special consideration? Will decisions of the oversight committee rely on available data about outcomes, or will cost be the only consideration? The answers to these questions speak to the organizational culture and ethical climate of Marymount Hospital.

The Physician and the Payer Organization

The majority of people with health insurance in the US are covered under some form of managed care. Following the failure of the Clinton Health Plan in 1993, managed care has become the primary business model for reimbursement for medical services. Managed care organizations have as their major rationale the containment or reduction of health care costs. Methods of cost constraint vary by plan, but usually involve some combination of the following strategies: selecting and limiting the number of providers who are authorized to provide care for plan enrollees, monitoring what services are available, requiring pre-certification for treatments or referrals, and restructuring how individuals and institutions are paid. Only 8 percent of insurance offered through employers resembles the traditional indemnity coverage of the past, and 80 percent of the insured US population is now covered by some form of managed care (Voss et al., 2005 quoting Fletcher, 1999).

While fee-for-service medicine has been accused of having the potential for encouraging overtreatment, its replacement model has the potential for encouraging undertreatment. One of the major criticisms directed toward the financial incentives introduced by some managed care contracts is that they constitute a conflict of interest for providers between their professional concern for their patients and their concern for their own financial advantage. Another concern is the dominance of for-profit entities in the field, whose commitment to profit for investors competes with their commitment to care of high quality.

Case V Whose costs? Whose problem?

Dr Abrahmson's practice serves patients covered by several different insurance plans, a few reimbursing on a fee-for-service basis, the others by capitated payment with several different capitation rates. He frequently sees patients presenting with gastro-esophageal reflux, a problem for which there are several diagnostic procedures. Depending upon which he chooses, the costs to the patient, the costs to his practice, and the cost to the medical system as a whole will be different.

The benefits of the payment mechanisms adopted by different payers accrue differently to providers, patients, and the society at large, depending upon the circumstances of each patient that Dr Abrahmson sees (Voss et al., 2005). To whose interests is he most immediately commited? As citizen, proximate agent of the wider health care system, partner in a practice, and a physician committed to the ethics of his profession, Dr Abrahmson faces complex decisions, all of which have ethical implications. If he had decided to sell his practice, some of the decisions he faces may have been pre-empted by the conditions of his relationship with the Markson Valley Health System. But even absence of choice is freighted with ethical implications.

Balancing professional obligations is not new to medicine. Physicians have obligations to their individual patients, but also obligations to the population of patients for whom they are responsible, and to the support and advancement of medical science. The most recent claim has to do with resource allocation. Insofar as they are designated or appropriate custodians of communal resources, physicians need to consider cost as well as the quality of medical care. Recent focus on cost containment as well as changes in the patterns of reimbursement have prompted a heated dialog on how, when, and whether physicians should be involved in bedside rationing (Weinstein, 2001).

Case VI To refer, or not to refer?

Dr Simms is a family practitioner in Markson Valley. She is in practice with three other doctors and her practice has a contractual relation with Markson Valley Health System. Dr Simms has just seen a patient with a painful mass in her abdomen and she thinks an ultrasound examination is necessary for diagnosis. The Health System refuses to reimburse for out-of-system referrals, and the Markson Valley facility has no appointments for 10 days. She wonders what she should do.

If Dr Simms decides to send her patient to an ultrasound facility outside the Markson Valley network in order to get timely information about the cause of her patient's inflammation, she may suffer individual financial loss or threaten the financial viability of her partnership, depending upon the conditions of her contract. The practice may have contractual provisions that penalize them for out-of-network referrals, or the additional expense might cause the contract to be cancelled. Her commitment to her patient may conflict with her commitment to her practice association.

If she decides to recommend that the patient wait for the next available appointment with the Markson facilty, she may run a risk of a different sort. While providers are held responsible for quality of care, payers are held responsible only for cost. Current law regulating health insurance (ERISA, the Employee Retirement Income Security Act of 1974) exempts many insurers for care decisions, without acknowledging that some managed care organizations deliver care as well as providing insurance. In the *Pegram* case that went to the Supreme Court, a patient for whom delayed diagnosis led to a ruptured appendix, peritonitis, and a prolonged hospitalization filed suit for negligent care against both the physician and the health maintenance organization with which she contracted. While it was arguably the HMO's rules that led to the postponement of the diagnosis, it was only the doctor, the proximate agent, who was held liable. While the doctor was sued for malpractice, it was decreed that the HMO could be held liable only for the cost of the benefit that was initially denied (Applebaum, 2000; Bloche, 2000).

Dr Simms's dilemma arises because Markson Valley Health System's strategy for financial security included purchasing practices and restricting referrals outside of the network. While there may be no specific policy of reducing the number of services available, the waiting list for a service like ultrasound serves as a tacit dissuader.

New forms of insurance and the "end of managed care"

There is good reason why early forms of managed care directed their attention to physicians, developing complex strategies to persuade physicians to prescribe less, refer less, utilize fewer expensive diagnostic technologies, discharge patients earlier, or admit them to less expensive facilities. Physicians remain the gateway to medical treatment, controlling access to pharmaceuticals, hospital admissions, and specialist referrals. But there is a wide consensus that these strategies cost more in good will than they reaped in cost savings. As one of its more sympathetic observers noted, "the managed care system has achieved considerable economic success but has proven itself a cultural and political failure" (Robinson, 2001). Narrow physician panels offend patients and disrupt long-term physician–patient relationships, while pre-admission authorizations, coverage denials, and any risk-shifting mechanisms that imposed third-party judgments between physicians and their patients were vehemently rejected by both patients and providers. As a result there has been less of a tendency in the last few years for the intermediaries between physicians and the purchasers of health plans to combine insurance and delivery. Instead, insurers stick to the area they know best, and the mechanisms of managing care – utilization review, gatekeeping, capitation – are more often mediated by the provider organizations (Robinson, 1999a, 2001).

There is some question whether this actually represents the "end of managed care" (Robinson, 2001) or just its perpetuation in a new guise. In practice, Dr Simms is as likely to have some "management" of her referral and utilization of services by her immediate practice, even if she and her partners decided to dissociate themselves from MVHS. But from her perspective, such reviews done by her practice might be less threatening to her professional integrity than utilization reviews done by agents less proximate to and less knowledgeable about the particulars of her patients.

Dealing with Systems

Although we have been speaking of payer or provider organizations, there is a sense in which it is the health care system as a whole that is both payer and provider. In almost all its dimensions health care is imbedded in a complex set of systems and subsystems, a complex network of interrelationships. To deal with ethical issues in health care from either a dyadic or even an organizational perspective often belies what is really at issue and thus ignores a number of elements that are related to the issue in question. Proper evaluation may rather require what the organizational and scientific literature calls "systems thinking," or a systems approach (Werhane, 2002, p. 293; Mills et al., 2003).

Systems thinking

The physician–patient relationship is where the social institution meets the recipients for which it exists. But to focus only on that micro level is to exclude from view many factors that explain and determine the content of that dyadic relationship. Individuals as a source of choice, decision, and action are embedded in a complex set of networks and interrelations. The micro-level of the individual, the meso-level of organizations, and the macro-level of the larger society are interdependent, and decisions on any level affect and are affected by decisions on other levels.

The importance of a systems-approach to health care in the US is becoming obvious to many people in the health care system. The prestigious Institute of Medicine has approached the problem of quality in medicine with a systems-approach (Institute of Medicine, 2001; Plsek, 2001) and recent reforms in resident education are also paying increasing attention to implications for professional practice of decisions and policies on organizational and system-wide levels (ACGME 1999, esp. Competency 6).

These considerations do not pre-empt individual professional decision-making, but do affect those judgments and their outcomes.

> A truly systemic view of current health care [in the United States] considers how this set of individuals, institutions, and processes operates in a system involving a complex network of interrelationships, and array of individual and institutional actors with conflicting interests and goals, and a number of feedback loops.
>
> (Wolf, 1999)

Because of the interrelationships of the various units and levels of the health care system, the factors that combine to produce an ethically troubling situation have their source in distant as well as proximate decisions.

Acknowledging the interdependence of the various levels of the health care system, from the dyadic relation of the physician and the patient to the macro-level of the role of the social institution of health care in the larger society, has several benefits. For one thing, it mitigates simplistic analysis and inappropriate "victim" blaming, and raises the possibility of more appropriate allocations of accountability within the system (Emanuel and Emanuel, 1996). The element of the system that is most proximate to an ethical issue is not necessarily the cause of the problem. It is not Dr Kim's fault that there are no free beds in the ICU, and Dr Wilkinson did not choose to close the maternity ward.

Further, it facilitates the ability of the stakeholders in the system to weather the unpredictable and strategize for optimal outcomes. Some things can be resisted, some changed, and some only endured. A cultured and honed sensitivity to morally problematic situations, and the moral imagination to address them, will be useful, if not always comforting, to the medical practitioner in the twenty-first century (Werhane, 1999).

Aligning values in the organization

It is no accident that the sub-field of organizations ethics, representing the intersection of business ethics, clinical ethics and professional ethics, has grown up at the same time as some of the changes in the conditions of individual physician practice instanced in our examples. When the Joint Commission for the Accreditation of Health-Care Organizations introduced the term as a requirement for the continued accreditation of health care organizations in 1995 it did so to emphasize the obligation of health care organizations to manage their business relationships in an ethical manner, while recognizing the primacy of patient care (Joint Commission for the Accreditation of Health-Care Organizations, 1996). Organization ethics directs attention to the ethical implications of the relationships health care organizations have, not only to individuals affected by or implicated in their operation, but to other organizations and to the larger society of which they are a part.

We do not consider organization ethics a replacement for professional ethics. Rather, an effective organization ethics program should protect and foster the professional ethics of its professional stakeholders, as well as serving as a forum for prospective discussion of decisions, structures, strategies, policies, or contracts that members of professional groups judge to be threats to their ethical practice (Spencer et al., 2000, p. 161). The more intimately professional practice is implicated in organizational structures, the more important it is that organizations have some mechanisms for addressing the integration of clinical and business decisions, mechanisms that allow clinical professionals a voice in organization-level decisions.

Conclusion

This chapter has focused on the impact of organization level decisions on individual professional practice, with particular attention to ethical issues raised by business decisions. Physicians practice their profession in and with organizations, within which they are not always the sole decision-maker. Decisions of those organizations have ethical import in their own right and also have ethical implications for the physicians affected by them and their patients. Some ethical conflict in medical practice is a function of the degree of alignment of values between physicians and their associated organizations, between different components of those organizations (e.g., management and clinicians), and between the health care system and the larger society. Hospitals are complex institutions, involving divergent objectives and multiple actors linked in fluid and ambiguous power relations. Because of compartmentalization, hierarchical organization and bureaucratization, integration of goals and alignment of values among various stakeholders can be hard to achieve (Denis et al., 2001).

We need to address the confusions created by the changing model of health care delivery in the US on several levels. On the level of the individual provider, the professional ethics of the physicians needs to include an imperative to deliver cost-effective medicine. On the level of the organization, we need to strengthen the support for high-quality medicine – to balance the forces within the society that are pushing for cost control without attention to its effect on quality. We cannot perpetuate a split such that one component of the provider organization, the clinician, is responsible for quality, while another component, the administration, is responsible for cost. All stakeholders need to consider both.

On a national level, the health care system is in rapid and rocky transition, driven in part by commercial interests that are foreign to the Hippocratic tradition of medicine. We commend the professional who is also an active citizen. The health care system as a whole is responsible for providing care of high quality at a reasonable cost to the population, but faces many structural impediments. It has never been more important that physicians include among their professional obligations a commitment to improve a fragmented health care system and advocate on local, regional, and national levels for their patients. While the obstacles are daunting, the objective should be achievable – but not without the active participation and advocacy of those who have the most invested in the adequate care of their patients.

Notes

1 Mergers may be complicated by explicitly incompatible ethical commitments, as when a previously secular hospital joins a Catholic system (Ikemoto, 1996), but less tangible differences in priorities, such as commitments to different populations between a suburban and a city hospital, or unwillingness to jointly operate some services, may prove equally intractable and contribute to the failure of mergers.

2 The dangers of overexpansion due to merger activity are nowhere better exemplified than in the story of Allegheny General Hospital. Under the leadership of an ambitious chief executive officer it underwent rapid expansion in hopes of consolidating and improving its financial position. Ten years later the expanded Allegheny Health Education and Research Foundation had 14 hospitals, two medical schools, "hundreds" of associated physician practices, and over 20,000 employees. But many of its strategic decisions, and some of the problematic means by which they were implemented, failed in the desired intent. In 1998 the Allegheny System declared bankruptcy, having incurred $1.4 billion in debt. At the time of its collapse it was the largest medical care provider in Pennsylvania and the largest non-profit physician-hospital organization in the United States. The collapse of the System marked the end of a blind belief in expansion as the answer to fiscal viability (Burns et al., 2000).

3 The logic of expansion decrees that services will be consolidated when a hospital joins a larger organization. Conversions have often resulted in increases in administrative costs, staffing cuts, and, as in the case of Marymount, reduction or discontinuation of vital community health services. One economy may be the outsourcing or consolidation of collection services, and thus treatment of uninsured patients can be problematic in hospital conversions. There have been reports of some hospitals requiring up to 50 percent pre-payment from uninsured patients seeking non-emergency care, and some hospitals are facing litigation for charging uninsured patients up to four times more than the same hospitals charged patients with private insurance for the same procedures (Cohn, 2004; *Patient Care Law Weekly*, 2004). Not-for-profit hospitals with a long history of community service that have outsourced their bill collection services may end up demanding the full cost of care from patients unable to pay.

4 Organizations too can suffer a form of moral distress, when external pressures from other organizations or social factors impede their capacity to fulfill their social function (Mills and Werhane, 2005). Several well known court cases provide examples of organization demoralization. In the Baby K case in Virginia in 1993, caregivers were concerned about the propriety of and professional responsibility for continuing to treat an anencephalic baby. The institution concurred with the professional judgment and took the case to court. When the courts ruled against the hospital (arguing that federal law required that anyone coming to an emergency room must be stabilized and treated) the morale and reputation of the hospital were called into question (McCarthy, 1993). A different alignment of values occurred in the case of A.C. in Washington, DC. When caregivers wished to honor the wishes of a terminally ill pregnant cancer patient to let her die without a cesarean section to save her premature baby, the hospital's lawyers, acting on behalf of what they believed to be extramural social values, injudiciously forced an unconsented cesarean section. Mother and child died, and the resulting court case went against the institution (*In re A.C.* 1990). Here too the morale and reputation of the institution suffered.

References

ACGME Outcome Project (1999), *ACGME General Competencies*, vers. 1.3, Chicago: Accreditation Council for Graduate Medical Education.

Applebaum, P.S. (2000), *Pegram v. Herdrich*: The Supreme Court passes the buck on managed care, *Psychiatric Services* 51 (10): 1225–6, 1238.

Blackstone, E.A. and Fuhr, J.P., Jr. (2003), Failed hospital mergers, *Journal of Health Law* 36 (2): 301.

Bloche, M.G. (2000), US healthcare after *Pegram*: betrayal at the bedside? *Health Affairs* 19 (5): 224–7.

Burns, L.R., Cacciamani, J., Clement, J., and Aquino, W. (2000), The fall of the house of AHERF: the Allegheny bankruptcy, *Health Affairs* 19 (1): 8–41.

Cohn, J. (2004), Uncharitable? *New York Times Magazine*, December 19, 2004: 51.

Denis, J., Lamothe, L., and Langley, A. (2001), The dynamics of collective leadership and strategic change in pluralistic organizations, *Academy of Management Journal* 44: 809–37.

Elms, H., Berman, S. and Wicks, A. (2002), Ethics and incentives: an evaluation and development of stakeholder theory in the health care industry, *Business Ethics Quarterly* 12 (4): 413–32.

Emanuel, E. and Emanuel, L.L. (1996), What is accountability in health care? *Annals of Internal Medicine* 124: 229–39.

Fletcher, R.H. (1999), Who is responsible for the common good in a competitive marketplace? *Journal of the American Medical Association* 281: 1127–8.

Fox R.C. (1976), Advanced medical technology: social and ethical implications, *Annual Review of Sociology* 2: 231–68.

Ikemoto, L.C. (1996), When a hospital becomes Catholic, *Mercer Law Review* 47: 1087–106.

In re A.C., 497 US 261 (1990).

Institute of Medicine (2001), *Crossing the Quality Chasm: A New Health System for the 21st Century*, Washington, DC: National Academy Press.

Jameton, A. (1984), *Nursing Practice: The Ethical Issues*, New York: Prentice Hall.

Joint Commission for Accreditation of Healthcare Organizations (1996), Patient rights and organizational ethics: standards for organizational ethics, in *Comprehensive Manual for Hospitals*, Oakbrook Terrace, IL: Joint Commission for Accreditation of Healthcare Organizations, pp. 95–7.

Kastor J. (2001), *Mergers of Teaching Hospitals in Boston, New York, and Northern California*, Ann Arbor: University of Michigan Press.

Kline, P., Stephan, R.T., and Holbrook, R.F. (2004), Protecting charitable assets in hospital conversions: an important role for the Attorney General, *Kansas Journal of Law and Public Policy* 13: 351–79.

McCarthy, M. (1993), Anencephalic baby's right to life? (Baby K born in Fairfax Hospital, Virginia), *Lancet* 342 (8876): 919.

Massey, S. (1999), Anatomy of a bankruptcy, Part 5: Burning down the house, *Pittsburgh Post-Gazette*, Friday, January 22, 1999, www.post-gazette.com/aherf/part5.asp (last visited 3/2/2005).

Mills, A.E. and Werhane, P.H. (2005), Organization moral distress, in P. Werhane and E. Freeman (eds.), *The Blackwell Encyclopedia of Management: Business Ethics*, 2nd edn., Oxford: Blackwell Publishing, pp. 391–4.

Mills, A.E., Rorty, M.V., and Werhane, P.H. (2003), Complexity and the role of ethics in health care, *Emergence* 5 (3): 3–21.

Ochmann, P.M. (2001), Managed care organizations manage to escape liability: why issues of quantity v. quality lead to ERISA's inequitable preemption of claims, *Akron Law Review* 34: 571–612.

Patient Care Law Weekly, Legal Issues, July 18, 2004.

Plsek, P. (2001), Redesigning health care with insights from the science of complex adaptive systems, in Institute of Medicine, *Crossing the Quality Chasm: A New Health System for the 21st Century*, Washington, DC: National Academy Press, pp. 309–23.

Robinson, J.C. (1999a), The future of managed care organizations, *Health Affairs* 18 (2): 7–24.

Robinson, J.C. (1999b), *The Corporate Practice of Medicine: Competition and Innovation in Medicine*, University of California Press.

Robinson, J.C. (2001), The end of managed care, *Journal of the American Medical Association* 285 (20): 2622–8.

Ruocco, A. (2005), Mergers and acquisitions: great planning for leveraging synergies is the key to success, available http://www.portfoliomgt.org/ForumItem.asp?itemID=930 (last visited 3/2/2005).

Rodwin, M.A. (2004), Financial incentives for doctors, *British Medical Journal* 328 (7452): 1328–9.

Spencer, E.M. (1997), Recommendations for guidelines on procedures and process to address "organization ethics" in health care organizations (HCOs), Virginia Bioethics Network, reprinted in Spencer et al. (2000), *Organization Ethics in Health Care*, pp. 211–15.

Spencer, E.M., Mills, A.E., Rorty, M.V., and Werhane, P.H. (2000), *Organization Ethics in Health Care*, New York: Oxford University Press.

Victor, B. and Cullen, J.B. (1988), The organizational bases of ethical work climates, *Administrative Science Quarterly* 33 (1): 101–25.

Voss, J.D., Nadkarni, M.M., and Schectman, J.M. (2005), The Clinical Health Economics System Simulation (CHESS): a teaching tool for systems- and practice-based learning, *Academic Medicine* 80 (2): 129–34.

Weinstein, M.C. (2001), Should physicians be gatekeepers of medical resources? *Journal of Medical Ethics* 27 (4): 268.

Werhane, P. (1999), *Moral Imagination and Management Decision Making*, New York: Oxford University Press.

Werhane, P. (2002), Business ethics, organization ethics, and systems ethics for health care, in N. Bowie (ed.), *The Blackwell Guide to Business Ethics*, Boston, MA: Blackwell, pp. 289–312.

Werhane, P. and Doering, J. (1996), Conflicts of interest and conflicts of responsibility, *Professional Ethics* 4: 47–81.

Wolf, S. (1999), Toward a systemic theory of informed consent in managed care, *Houston Law Review* 35: 1631–1749.

Legislative and Judicial Decisions about Social Policy

Liberty

Chapter 11

Reproductive Choice

Rebecca Bennett and John Harris

Technological advances now provide individuals and couples with extended choices when it comes to reproduction. The availability of contraception and abortion allows considerably enhanced choice regarding if and when we reproduce. Reproductive technologies such as *in vitro* fertilization (IVF) and intracytoplasmic sperm injection (ICSI), originally designed for those having difficulty reproducing coitally, now extend the choices of all adults who can gain access to them. Pre-implantation, and prenatal diagnosis techniques now provide prospective parents with an increased range of choices regarding what sort of child their offspring might be and in the future gene manipulation and cloning are likely to increase these choices dramatically. In this chapter we will explore the ethical issues surrounding these reproductive choices and ask the question, "What should and shouldn't constrain choice in reproduction?"

Reproductive Choice and Reproductive Autonomy

The principle of respect for autonomy is a central principle of modern medical ethics and is often considered the most important principle in this area. People are said to be autonomous to the extent to which they are able to control their lives, and to some extent their destiny, by the exercise of their own faculties (Harris, 1985, p. 195). Thus, respecting individual autonomy involves respecting and not interfering with autonomous decisions. This principle of respect for autonomy is based on a respect for what, arguably, makes human life valuable, the ability to be the author of one's own life.

Clearly the decision whether or not to reproduce is a decision that is fundamental to notions of individual autonomy. As G. Pennings. explains:

> Reproduction is an important and central part of a person's life plan. Control over one's reproductive capacities is therefore a crucial element of a person's autonomy. This control includes both a right to reproduce and a right not to reproduce.
>
> (Pennings, 2002, p. 295)

This notion, that respecting autonomous choices in the area of reproduction is important, is often referred to as the principle of "reproductive autonomy." Reproductive autonomy is the idea that there is a powerful interest or "right" in the freedom to make reproductive choices, even where these choices may be thought unwise, frivolous or contrary to the public interest. The American philosopher and legal theorist Ronald Dworkin has outlined arguments for such a right, which he defines as "a right [of people] to control their own role in procreation unless the state has a compelling reason for denying them that control" (Dworkin, 1993, p. 148). The principle of reproductive autonomy defends liberty and privacy in matters of reproduction unless especially powerful moral reasons can be demonstrated as to the wrong of a particular exercise of that liberty. If reproductive autonomy is accepted, then those who would object to a particular exercise of that autonomy must show more than the fact that such exercise would result in disutilities, either to the parents of the child or the wider society. Moreover they must show more than that the exercise in question is foolish or ill-judged or offensive to others. If respect for individual autonomy is an important moral principle then infringements of this individual autonomy must have stronger justification than mere offence or disapproval. Thus, on this view, reproductive choices may only be interfered with either if substantial and serious harm may be shown to be the likely result or if serious moral wrong is involved (Bennett and Harris, 2002).

The Limits of Reproductive Autonomy

The rest of this chapter will consider different current and possible future reproductive choices in order to explore whether such substantial and serious harm might be a risk as a result of reproductive choices. This will involve an overview of the ethical issues raised by choices not to reproduce, choices to reproduce using medical and technological assistance, choices regarding what sort of children we wish to have, and the ethics of autonomy and decision-making in pregnancy.

Choice to avoid reproduction (contraception and abortion)

There is no doubt that generally the availability of effective contraception and abortion has increased reproductive choice, particularly the choices of women. Contraceptive use is an established part of modern life. Apart from the usual issues of voluntariness and informed consent, the use of contraceptives, for most, do not raise serious ethical issues. The main ethical controversies regarding contraception question policies that may appear to administer contraception in a way which infringes reproductive autonomy rather than enhancing it. For instance, there are concerns about the level of information regarding side effects of contraceptives especially as "emergency" contraception pills are now available in the UK without prescription (Anonymous, 2000). Further, the prescribing of contraception to those under the age of consent is, for some, problematic (Gillick, 1988). And perhaps most controversial are proposed policies that require the use of long-acting contraception as a condition of welfare payments or parole (Kimelman, 1990; Moskowitz et al., 1995).

Abortion continues to provoke controversy. Traditionally the debate around the ethics of abortion focuses on the moral status of the fetus and the question of whether the fetus has a right to life. However, in additional to this well-rehearsed debate other issues relating to abortion have emerged:

- Is late abortion justified to avoid so called "minor disabilities" such as cleft palate or deafness?
- Should we use the ovarian tissue of aborted fetuses in fertility treatment?
- Is selective abortion in the case of multiple fetuses morally acceptable?

But ultimately how we answer these questions will depend on our answer to the central question of whether a fetus has a right to life.

A *right* not *to reproduce?*

Access to contraception and abortion are extremely important in terms of respect for the autonomy of women. If we accept the importance of respecting autonomy we must also accept the related importance of bodily integrity, that is, the right to decide what happens to our bodies. It would seem that allowing control over what happens to one's body is a necessary condition for respecting individual autonomy. John Robertson explains further why this right not to reproduce is fundamental to respecting the individual autonomy of women:

> If women lack the liberty to end unwanted pregnancy, they will undergo major physical, social, and psychological burdens that deprive them of control of the physical and social self in essential ways. Most immediately, the burden is felt in physical terms, as their bodies are taken over by pregnancy. But pregnancy carried to term also entails responsibility for offspring. Even if the child is relinquished for adoption, there will be powerful feelings of attachment, responsibility, and guilt that will, in many cases, last a lifetime . . . Any account of individual autonomy and respect for persons must recognize the prima facie liberty interest of women in being free of the burdens of unwanted reproduction. To deny presumptive right status to this interest is to deny that woman the fundamental right to control what is done to her body and her life.
>
> (Robertson, 1994, p. 49)

Thus, while the reproductive choices of men are important, the ultimate choice regarding whether a woman should bear a child must be the woman's choice. Men have an interest in choosing whether or not to reproduce but as long as this repro-duction involves the gestation of a fetus inside the woman's body then it must be that woman's choice whether she begins or continues a pregnancy. The alternative would be a huge affront of this woman's autonomy and bodily integrity.

The Right to Reproduce?

In this section we will consider whether there are any legitimate moral constraints on our reproductive choices. Are there some techniques that are morally unaccept-able means of expressing our reproductive autonomy? Further, do we have a positive right to reproduce, that is, a right that places an obligation on the state to assist with reproduction where such assistance is needed? And if there is such a positive right does this imply access for all to treatment to aid reproduction?

Moral constraints on reproductive choices?

While assisted reproduction itself has been the focus of controversy in the past, now that such techniques are an established part of medical care, assisting repro-duction per se is not usually seen as controversial. However, while such techniques are generally accepted it is important to recognize that there will always be those who question the morality of techniques. There are two main arguments that ques-tion the acceptability of assisted reproduction generally. The first argument is one based on the premise that the embryo has a right to life. Thus, as many forms of assisted reproduction particularly IVF inevitably involve the destruction of human embryos (more embryos are usually created than can be implanted and brought to birth), they are opposed based on the right to life of the embryos. The second kind of argument does not question the morality of the techniques of assisted repro-duction but the application of these techniques to women. The argument here is that rather than allowing a further expression of women's reproductive autonomy, the choice to use assisted reproductive techniques in many cases may undermine women's reproductive autonomy. It is claimed that women's decisions to undergo infertility treatment are often not freely chosen but are taken under pressure from society and/or from partners. Thus, it is suggested that reproductive technologies that aim to overcome infertility contribute to creating a society in which is harder to choose not to have children (Spallone and Steinberg, 1987).

Even if we reject these arguments and assume that, in principle, assisting reproduction in this way is generally acceptable, particular instances of assisting reproduction continue to raise numerous other ethical issues. The first kind of issue relates to so-called "designer babies." This issue raises the question: Should we be able to choose the characteristics of our children and if so under what circumstances is this acceptable? The second kind of issue relates to the question of who, if anyone, should be provided with assistance to reproduce and whether this assistance should be state funded? We will consider these two questions in turn.

"Designer babies"

IVF combined with pre-implantation genetic diagnosis (PGD) allows the "parents" of embryos created by IVF to choose, to some extent, what sort of children they will have. During the process of PGD one or two cells are removed by pipette for biopsy from the pre-implantation embryo at around day three of development. If the biopsy reveals severe genetic defects that embryo may be rejected and other embryos implanted. PGD can be used to avoid specific genetic or chromosomal abnormalities and avoid X-linked disorders by sex selection of embryos (Flinter, 2001). This use of PGD to avoid abnormalities is often referred to as "medical" use of PGD and is usually considered the least controversial of the possible uses of this technique. As Richard Ashcroft explains:

> These uses are somewhat controversial, in that they embroil us in debates about inter-ventions on the embryo and about arguably eugenic selection. None the less, there is reasonably broad consensus in the UK medical and regulatory world that these uses are acceptable, and merit the term "clinical indication." Although there are meta-physical complexities here, the view that these uses of PGD are acceptable because they focus on the interests of the future child has respectably broad support.
>
> (Ashcroft, 2003, p. 217)

The claim is that so-called "medical" uses of PGD are morally acceptable as they attempt to avoid the creation of children with harmful conditions and disorders. However, while this use of PGD may be considered less controversial than other uses of PGD (we will come to these in a moment), this application of the tech-nique is far from uncontroversial. It is important to be clear here about what PGD attempts to do. It does not attempt to "cure" disability in a future child but to choose to bring to birth a "healthy" child rather than a "disabled child." The "metaphysical complexities" Ashcroft refers to above are that while "medical" uses of PGD do "focus on the interests of the future child" (Ashcroft, 2003, p. 217), they do not prevent disability in any particular child but prevent children with dis-ability being brought to birth.

People with inherited disabilities may regard selecting between embryos on the basis of disability as a form of discrimination against themselves and people like them, and objections may be made to such choices on this ground (Shakespeare, 1998). It is argued that claiming that it is morally wrong to choose to implant a "disabled" embryo ultimately places a lower value on disabled lives and is there-fore discriminatory. The debate surrounding this issue is extensive and complex. However, simply put, those who claim that PGD to avoid disability is morally acceptable do so from two main positions. Where the disability to be avoided is serious and likely to result in a life dominated by suffering it would seem that PGD provides an invaluable opportunity to avoid creating such an "unworthwhile life." However, most disabilities do not involve such overwhelming suffering and it is the debate around the use of PGD to avoid these kinds of disabilities, such as deafness, that create the most controversy.

The first position on this issue argues that avoiding even "minor" disability in this way is the morally preferable option (Harris, 2000). The claim here is that it is morally wrong in such a situation to choose to bring a disabled child to birth. Thus, if a couple are attempting to reproduce by IVF and a choice will have to be made about which embryos to implant, then PGD should be used to inform this choice and avoid disability wherever possible. The nature of this alleged wrong of bringing to birth a disabled child is complex. It is not claimed that the disabled are wronged by being brought to birth, as being born in this way is their only chance of life. But the wrong suggested here might be classified as "the wrong of bringing avoidable suffering into the world" (Harris, 1998, p. 111). Thus, on this view the choice to bring to birth a "disabled" child is partly wrongful because it causes a child to be born in a "harmed" condition and partly wrongful because it creates a world which needlessly contains more suffering, hardship, or disability than would have been created by an alternative choice. It is claimed (Bennett and Harris, 2002) that to choose to have a deaf child, for instance, is analogous to not curing curable deafness in a child. Just as the deaf child denied the cure is harmed by this decision, so the child with incurable deafness is harmed by the choice to bring him to birth. Moreover, in so far as the claim is that deciding to select against a deaf child constitutes some sort of criticism of, or discrimination against, the deaf, so also must treating deafness as a medical condition. For in so far as avoiding deafness or any other disability is seen as implying that there is something wrong with deaf or disabled people, then the same must be true of treating deafness or other disabilities that would be responsive to treatment. For why is the treatment needed if there is not something wrong with being deaf or disabled. "What," so those who regard disabilities as simply "different abilities" might ask, "does treating deafness say about those whose deafness is untreatable?" It is argued that, in consistency, those who object to selecting against disabled embryos must surely, for analogous reasons, also oppose treating injury or disability in existing people.

A second alternative argument supports the use of PGD but claims that there the avoidance of disability using PGD is only the morally preferable option where it is thought that the disability avoided would be such as to render a life "unworthwhile," that is, dominated by suffering (Bennett and Harris, 2002). The argument here is that in less extreme cases where it can be supposed that the future child may be disabled but have a "worthwhile life," then the choice whether to select the "disabled" over the "non-disabled" embryo is not a moral choice. While there may be reasons for preferring a "non-disabled" child, it is argued, these are not moral reasons but reasons arising from preferences we have about what sort of children we would like to have. Choosing to implant embryos with disabilities on this view is not a morally wrong or a morally worthy decision but a morally neutral one. Thus, on this view the only morally questionable choice is to implant and bring to birth a child who will be likely to have a life that is not worthwhile, that is, a life completely dominated by suffering. In choosing to bring to birth a disabled child (providing he is likely to have a worthwhile life) no one is harmed by that decision: the resultant disabled child gains existence and a worthwhile life. Thus, it may be argued that choosing to implant an embryo with disabilities (providing this embryo is likely to have a worthwhile life) is not a morally wrong nor for that matter a morally worthy decision but a morally neutral one.

The creation of "savior" children

Other controversies involved in medical uses of PGD focus on the creation of "saviour siblings." For instance, *The Times* of London recently carried the following story:

> The path to the creation of "designer babies" was opened last night when the Government's fertility watchdog lifted its ban on selecting embryos purely to donate tissue to sick siblings . . . Fertility doctors broadly welcomed the ruling by the Human Fertilisation and Embryology Authority (HFEA), which will make it easier for couples with terminally ill children to have "saviour siblings" suitable to donate life-saving blood from their umbilical cords . . .
>
> The move relaxes strict regulations laid down by the HFEA in 2001 governing the use of a technique called pre-implantation genetic diagnosis (PGD) to screen embryos for their tissue type. This is critical to their suitability as potential donors. Under the old policy this procedure was allowed only when doctors were conducting PGD to check embryos for an inherited disease. It was forbidden to test for tissue type alone as this carried a theoretical risk of harm to the embryo, while bringing it no direct benefit.
>
> This approach was widely attacked as inconsistent. The authority allowed one couple, Raj and Shahana Hashmi, to use PGD to help their son Zain, who has the blood condition beta-thalassaemia, but rejected a similar application from Jayson and Michelle Whitaker. It argued that the cases were different: the Hashmis wanted to screen for both tissue type and the presence of the disease, but the Whitakers sought tissue tests alone as there is no PGD test for Diamond Blackfan anaemia – which afflicts Charlie Whitaker and Joshua Fletcher . . .
>
> The HFEA said that it had reversed its position because of new evidence from an unpublished study of more than 300 children born after PGD, which has found no evidence of any harm to embryos screened in this way.
>
> (Henderson, 2004)

Charlie Whitaker has now apparently been successfully treated with stem cells from his brother's cord blood. What can be said about the ethics of such "saviour siblings? It seems to us very simple. As a result of the Whitaker's having a second child chosen to be a genetic match for Charlie, there are two live healthy and happy children who are loved and cherished instead of one very sick child. This must be a real gain for all those who believe in life and prefer health to severe illness. Those who are sincerely pro-life can have no rational objection to this on pro-life grounds. Some worry about the motives of the parents or how Charlie's savior sibling brother will feel about his role in this life-saving and life-creating enterprise. As for the parent's motives – what better reason could there be for having a child than the idea of saving a life or restoring a child to health? All parents and would-be parents can perform the simple exercise of asking themselves whether their motives for having or contemplating having children are anywhere near as good as this? Charlie's brother will start life knowing he has already saved a life or restored the health of his brother. Few of us will ever have the chance of being responsible for something so wonderful. And even if it had gone wrong, Charlie's brother would still have "done his best." The alternative would be to know that "my parents could have had a child that would have had a chance of saving Charlie but they chose, or were forced to choose, to have a child with no prospect of this." Seldom in bioethics does everything speak for one conclusion and nothing for the alternative. This is surely such a case.

Non-medical use of PGD

The most controversial use of PGD would seem to be its use to create children with particular "non-medical" traits such as intelligence, a particular sexual orientation, hair color, height, gender, etc. As Ashcroft explained earlier, "medical" uses of PGD have gained broad support because such techniques appear to focus on the interests of the future child (Ashcroft, 2003, p. 217) (or in the case of "saviour siblings," the welfare of another child). However, PGD for "non-medical" reasons is not an attempt to avoid disability or suffering but an attempt to create the sort of children parents might wish to have in terms of their abilities and appearance. Objections made to this technique usually focus on two issues: possible harm to the child created and possible harm to society which permits it. Thus it is argued that the children created in this way will have unacceptable expectations put on them because they have particular traits "selected" for. For example, if it were possible to select for intelligence or musical ability, the argument would be that pressure would be put on the child to maximize these abilities. Or if the child's gender had been selected it might be argued that this selection may put pressure on that child to act in accordance with stereotyped gender roles (Berkowitz and Snyder, 1998). In terms of society, it might be argued that such a use of PGD is wrong as it wastes valuable resources and it involves "playing God" which may have disastrous consequences such as the creation of a gender imbalance if sex selection were sanctioned (HFEA, 2003).

However, choosing the traits of our children would seem to be a clear expression of reproductive autonomy and thus, unless there is good evidence that these procedures would be harmful, a strong argument could be made that if we value reproductive autonomy then they should be allowed. Is it clear that the welfare of children born as a result of PGD to select particular "non-medical" traits would be any more compromised than other children? Don't all parents have expectations of their children and put pressure on them to fulfill them? Isn't it open to all prospective parents to try to "choose" the characteristics of their offspring by choosing sexual partners with these traits? If we did not publicly fund these techniques wouldn't this remove the problem of scarce resources? What evidence is there that "playing God" in this way would lead to disastrous consequences?

Reproductive cloning

A further development in the area of "designer babies" is the prospect of human reproductive cloning. Human reproductive cloning, when it becomes possible within reasonable limits of safety (Harris, 2004), will extend the reproductive choices of some individuals. This is because cloning by nuclear somatic transfer offers hope for infertile couples who wish to have a child who is genetically related to one or possibly both of its parents.

Nuclear somatic transfer cloning involves removing the nucleus of an egg and substituting the nucleus taken from a cell either of another individual or of the egg donor herself. This can be done using cells from an adult, thus creating a "clone" of this nucleus donor. Clones produced by nuclear somatic transfer will not be identical to the nucleus donor unless she is also the egg donor. Part of our genetic material comes from the mitochondria in the cytoplasm of the egg and with nuclear somatic transfer only the nuclear DNA is transferred; as a result the genetic material of the egg donor will partly shape the clone. Thus, if the male partner's nuclear DNA were transferred into an egg from his partner not only would the child be genetically related to its father, the mother would also have contributed to its make up via the influence of the mitochondria.

While cloning may provide huge potential benefits to humanity, the possibility of human reproductive and therapeutic cloning has been met with widespread unease from all quarters including legislative bodies and the scientific community (Bennett and Harris, 2003). It has been argued that many of the statements which oppose human cloning are thin on argument and rationale (Harris, 1997). There are many distinct reasons put forward for objecting to cloning. Often arguments against reproductive cloning are similar to those used against "non-medical" uses of PGD such as the welfare of the child created and a reluctance to "play God" which we have seen do not necessarily offer strong reasons for opposing a technique. In addition arguments against cloning are also often based on notions of human rights and human dignity (The European Parliament, 1997, paragraph B; WHO, 1997) but as these statements typically provide little or no attempt to explain what these principles are, or to indicate how they might apply to cloning they also do not seem to provide the sort of evidence we might need in order to justify the prohibition of such a procedure.

Who Should Be Provided with Assistance to Reproduce?

A legal right to reproduce

In most western democracies the right to reproduce free from interference is generally viewed as a basic human right and as such is enshrined in law in many juris-dictions. For instance, Article 12 of the European Convention on Human Rights states: "Men and women of marriageable age have the right to marry and found a family according to the national laws governing the exercise of this right." This legal right is usually assumed to be a negative right, that is, "a right not to have one's reproductive capacities interfered with against one's will," (Frith, 1998, p. 818).

Such legal rights have never been interpreted as an unqualified right to reproduce or to be given assistance with reproduction but are intended to protect individu-als from coercive policies such as enforced sterilization. This negative legal right to reproduce is again based on notions of respect for individual autonomy. The choice to reproduce is a choice that is at the center of our notion of autonomy. Policies that enforce a one-child rule or compulsory sterilization constitute serious infringements of autonomy, placing respect for autonomy as secondary to other interests. Thus, it seems important to protect individual autonomy with a negative legal right to reproduce. But if we believe that the freedom to choose to have a child is a funda-mental human right then where does this leave the rights of the infertile? If having a child is to many a fundamental expression of their autonomy then do we have a moral and even a legal right to assist the infertile to have a child?

Thus, the question then remains whether this right to reproduce should be interpreted as a positive right, that is, a right that imposes a duty on states to provide fertility treatment to those who need assistance in reproduction? If it can be established that there is such a positive right to reproduce what are the limits of this right – who should be provided with assistance and is there a limit to which public funding should be used to provide this assistance?

A positive moral right to reproduce?

While human procreation is usually seen as a morally acceptable goal, and the expression of reproductive choices is seen as fundamental to respect for autonomy, there are those who argue that there is no positive moral right to reproduce and thus that the state has no responsibility to assist those who cannot reproduce without assistance. The argument here is that reproduction is not a priority and so should not be assisted in this way. Thus, while human reproduction is acceptable when it requires no assistance, funding assistance to reproduce is a waste of scarce resources.

However, this objection to using public funding to treat infertility only has force if it is accepted that the choices about reproduction are not important to the autonomy of individuals generally. As Robertson explains:

> If the moral right to reproduce presumptively protects coital reproduction, then it should protect noncoital reproduction as well. The moral right of the coitally infertile to reproduce is based on the same desire for offspring that the coitally fertile have. They too wish to replicate themselves, transmit genes, gestate, and rear children biologically related to them. Their infertility should no more disqualify them from reproductive experiences than physical disability should disqualify persons from walking with mechanical assistance. The unique risks posed by noncoital reproduction may provide independent justifications for limiting its use, but neither the noncoital nature of the means used nor the infertility of their beneficiaries mean that the presumptively protected moral interest in reproduction is not present.
>
> (Robertson, 1994, p. 32)

Thus, if we believe that the right to reproduce without assistance is important enough to warrant protection, then this is done in recognition of the importance of allowing individuals to reproduce. If it is important to enable individuals to reproduce without hindrance then whatever makes this important would seem to be equally applicable to those who cannot reproduce without assistance. To decide otherwise would seem to be discriminatory towards the infertile.

However, are there any limits to the assistance the state should provide, and should there be any further limits on who should be eligible for assisted reproductive techniques both state funded and privately funded?

Access for all?

In a world of scarce resources there does have to be some way of restricting access to fertility treatment. There are not enough resources to provide all the treatment that people may want. It may even be true that there are certain people we feel should not be assisted in producing children. But how do we decide who should get access to fertility treatment and who should have this access publicly funded?

In the UK all licensed centers offering fertility treatment must by law consider the welfare of any resulting child (including the need of that child for a father),[1] before offering any services to assist conception and pregnancy. While it is clear that the welfare of children is always an important consideration, it has been argued (Bennett and Harris, 1999 and 2001) that the welfare of the child guidelines are, in practice, often used as the main basis on which to ration scarce resources in publicly funded National Health Service (NHS) clinics. Although the Human Fertilisation and Embryology Act (HFE) (1990) which regulates fertility treatment in the UK does not specifically exclude any category of patient from treatment, access to fertility treatment is routinely restricted by individual NHS clinics to treating so-called "medical" infertility. That is, treatment is often only considered for relatively healthy heterosexual couples in a stable relationship who, if they did not have "medical" problems with fertility could conceive without assistance. While this is unlikely to have been the intention, the welfare of the child guidance is often used to justify access to fertility treatment that could be said to "restore natural function," that is, providing treatment which mimics nature. Fertility treatments potentially offer increased reproductive choices to single women, lesbians, and post-menopausal women but applications from women who do not meet the requirement of "medical" infertility are often denied treatment, especially scarce NHS or other publicly funded treatment. It has been argued (Bennett and Harris, 1999 and 2001) that a distinction is made between "medical" infertility and "social" infertility, a distinction encouraged by the requirement to consider the welfare of the resultant child and that child's need for a father. Would-be parents who are likely to have just as good a chance of technical success with IVF are restricted because of concern about the quality of parenting that they would provide for a resulting child because they will be a single parent or a single lesbian parent or an older parent. On this view, social obstacles to conception (such as a lack of a male partner) or those combined with medical obstacles should not be overcome with precious public resources. But is restricting access to publicly funded fertility treatment to "medical" infertility an ethically acceptable method of dealing with the difficult problem of scarce resources in fertility treatment?

If the welfare of the child guidelines are used to refuse potential parents access to assisted conception then this refusal is based on a view that these potential parents will somehow be "worse" parents than the average young heterosexual couple. Thus if single women, lesbians and older women are denied access to fertility treatment on this basis the implication is that their parenting skills are in question. However, there is no evidence to support the claim that the welfare of any resulting child is likely to be affected by the fact that his parent/s are single, homosexual, or middle aged (Brewaeys et al., 1997). Indeed, there appears to be no compelling evidence from which to establish criteria for adequate parenting that can be applied to potential parents rather than to actual parents who have proved their inadequacy in objective ways.

Even if reliable evidence were available to support the claim that the welfare of children born to all would-be parents, apart from young heterosexual couples, was likely to be a cause for concern it would be unjust to allow this evidence only to influence decisions involving scarce resources. If we should be concerned about assisting conception in certain individuals then this concern should apply not only when the treatment sought is licensed fertility treatment, but whenever candidates come forward for medical assistance with reproduction. Prescription drugs such as Clomiphene, for instance (probably the commonest forms of medical help with procreation) should certainly be withheld from anyone not meeting defensible criteria, as should access to fertility treatment at licensed private clinics. There appears to be no support for applying these restrictions in this more consistent way. If considering the welfare of the resulting child is deemed an important consideration then it must be an important consideration in parallel situations.

It could be argued that if it is important for people to demonstrate their adequacy as parents in advance of being permitted to procreate, then all parents should be licensed. However, if, as is evidenced by actual practice, society thinks that it matters very little whether natural parents are fit to be parents, then it seems unjust and indefensible that those who seek NHS licensed infertility treatment are singled out and required to establish their suitability in advance (Harris, 1985). Those seeking fertility treatment are not different in any relevant way from those intending to have children in circumstances in which no assistance is necessary. When a child is conceived without specialist medical help a child is created that would not otherwise have existed. The same is true when conception is achieved as a result of assisted reproduction. The welfare of a child is not maximized if access to fertility treatment is denied as no child will come into existence as a result.

What is being considered when we contemplate the welfare of a future child is whether the child created will be expected to have a life which is, all things considered, a benefit or a harm to the child him or herself. In some instances we may have good reason to believe that a child is likely to have a life so dominated by suffering that we would consider such a life one that is not a benefit. However, if we consider existence in itself to be a benefit, then it can also be assumed that in most cases existence is more of a benefit than non-existence. Even if compelling evidence existed which indicated that a child born to a single homosexual or an older parent is likely to be at more of a disadvantage than a child born to a young heterosexual couple, it is surely unlikely that this disadvantage would be so great as to make non-existence preferable.

We are not suggesting that those who developed the HFEA recommendations and those who implement them believe being born to single women, lesbians or middle-aged women is so disadvantageous that non-existence would be preferable. Rather the legislative requirement to consider the welfare of the child is at best ambiguous and unhelpful and at worst a smoke screen behind which many prejudices may flourish (Bennett and Harris, 1999 and 2001).

If the way the welfare of the child criterion is applied does not provide an ethically acceptable way to reduce demand for fertility treatment, a workable solution is required that will allow fair access to the scarce resources. In order to do this, it has been suggested (Bennett and Harris, 2001) that we have to decide what it is that we are trying to achieve in providing fertility treatment. Are we trying to enable individuals to express their reproductive choices (even where assisted conception is unsuccessful it may be that it is a valuable experience to know that all options were attempted)? Or are we trying to get the best return from our money – producing the "best" and greatest amount of children possible using the money we have?

If we decide that the ultimate aim of fertility services is to help individuals to fulfill their reproductive choices then potential parents should be treated as long as there is no reason to suppose that any resultant child will have a life that will be so dominated by suffering that it would be considered a harm not a benefit to bring him to birth. However, this would not be used to veto treatment in many cases and thus a more just and appropriate replacement rationing tool must be found, but one that does not discriminate unfairly between prospective parents on "social" reasons.

Reproductive Choices in Pregnancy

While discussions of reproductive choice often focus on assisted conception, reproductive choice does not end when pregnancy is established. Pregnant women are faced with a huge array of choices regarding the management of their pregnancies. Should she be tested for conditions such as HIV and genetic abnormalities which may affect her future child? Should she change her behavior in order to prevent injury to her developing fetus? Should she accept hugely invasive procedures such as cesarean section delivery in an attempt to prevent harm to her future child? Should she terminate a pregnancy when the fetus is shown to be "abnormal" in some way?

These are complex and difficult choices that face all pregnant women, not just the coitally infertile. These choices can be divided into two categories:

- choices concerned with the welfare of any resultant child
- choices regarding one's own autonomy – choices about what sort of child you wish to have.

It is important to recognize these two different categories of choices in pregnancy as these different focuses raise different ethical issues and moral obligations.

Pregnancy and autonomy

If we accept the importance of respecting individual autonomy then it would seem that competent individuals should be allowed to choose whether they have diagnostic tests, undergo surgery, accept drug therapy or modify their lifestyles. However, the moral situation is changed significantly if the action of an individual is likely to cause harm to a third party. Even the most liberal of commentators would argue that it may be ethically justifiable to thwart an individual's autonomous choices in order to protect a third party from harm. So, while an individual may have the right to refuse information or treatment or maintain an unhealthy lifestyle and in doing so risk her own health and happiness, it seems that this right is weakened by a risk to third parties from this decision. Thus, this section asks whether pregnant women have the right to refuse tests, treatment, or lifestyles changes which may benefit them and their future child.

The answer to this question will depend upon whether the refusal of the women will have a significant harmful effect on the welfare of their future child. There is a strong obligation not to harm the future person or seriously damage his or her welfare or other significant needs or interests. Thus, there is obviously a strong obligation to do one's utmost to protect one's future child during pregnancy. However, while this does mean that pregnant women have a moral obligation to take some measures in an attempt to protect their future child from harm this does not mean that in all cases they are no longer free to choose whether they have diagnostic tests, undergo surgery, etc. In some cases it may be acceptable to put pressure on pregnant women to undergo testing and even surgical procedures such as cesarean section but, for a number of reasons, this does not meant that pregnant women's autonomy should generally be infringed in this way in order to protect a future life. We should be extremely careful before implementing policy that infringes pregnant women's autonomy.

As we have already discussed, if it is acceptable to infringe autonomy in order to protect third parties from harm then it is reasonable to assume that this justification would require some degree of evidence that harm would indeed be avoided by this infringement.

Preventing children rather than preventing harm?

With the increase in understanding of the human genome and of genetic factors involved in a range of diseases, and with genetic testing becoming safer and cheaper to administer, there is a clear potential for a dramatic increase in prenatal genetic diagnosis. It is likely that as new techniques for identifying genetic disorders emerge they will become routine in antenatal care. The fundamental aim of routine testing is to secure the testing not only of those women who would have elected to be tested, but also of those women who would not have specifically chosen to be tested. Thus, it has been argued that such routine testing is necessarily coercive in nature and does not involve the same standard of consent as is required in other health care settings (Bennett, 2001). Are pregnant women a special case where such infringements of autonomy are acceptable?

Pregnant women who become aware that the fetus they are carrying has a genetic disorder, or (in the future) an undesirable genetic predisposition, can do little to prevent this state of affairs by a diagnosis during pregnancy.[2] Prenatal diagnosis aims to provide pregnant women (and their partners) with as much information as possible on which to make an informed choice about whether they wish to continue a pregnancy. Prenatal genetic diagnosis may provide reassurance to those whose test shows no abnormality and allows consideration of termination of pregnancy for fetuses diagnosed with genetic abnormalities. But this is not avoiding harm to third parties, either the third party (the future child) is born with abnormalities or not at all. If genetic testing is routinely recommended to pregnant women then it is done so in order that women have the choice to terminate pregnancies where problems are detected. If we accept that the existence of routine testing programs involves putting pressure on women to be tested and if the purpose of that testing is to enable the termination of pregnancy where problems occur, then it seems likely that women will feel some pressure again to follow what might appear (however implicitly) to be the recommended path towards termination.

This takes us back to the earlier discussion of the ethics of avoiding disability using PGD. If, on the one hand, we accept that it is morally wrong to choose to bring to birth a child with a disability then it seems that there are good reasons to put pressure on pregnant women to accept all genetic testing available, perhaps even making antenatal genetic testing of this kind mandatory. If, on the other hand, we believe that in most cases bringing to birth a disabled child harms no one – the child may be brought to birth in an impaired state, but it is an impaired state that cannot be avoided if this child is to be born, then genetic testing in pregnancy cannot be justified on grounds that it is in the interests of the child. Just like other instances where genetic testing may be thought to be advisable, it is advisable, on this view, in order that the individual undergoing testing be provided with information that will be of interest to her and the decisions she makes concerning her life. Where genetic disorders cannot be prevented, information about these disorders may prove important for those women who do not wish to raise an impaired child. But as, on this view, prenatal genetic testing provides information in the interests of the pregnant woman and not in the interests of any future children, pressure to be tested is not acceptable.

Thus, if a decision is concerned with the welfare of the future child, then there may be some justification to put pressure on pregnant women to make a particular decision which may involve testing, medication, surgery, or other invasive procedures. For example, the recently introduced policy in the UK of routine testing antenatally for HIV could be justified on these grounds as women who know they are HIV positive can take steps (a drug regime (Connor et al., 1994), cesarean section and avoiding breastfeeding (McGowan et al., 1999; Mandelbrot et al., 2001) to minimize the risk of infecting their future child. However, even if it can be shown that coercion may prevent harm to future children in this way we should consider such policies extremely carefully before they are adopted, asking further pertinent questions including: Could the same or similar results be reached without such coercion? Is it clear that that the recommended course of action would actually protect the future child (is this an accurate assessment, are there other side effects that should be considered)? Is the likely benefit significant enough to warrant such an affront on autonomy? Will this infringement of autonomy of pregnant women lead to a "slippery slope" where pregnant women's autonomy can always be overridden "for the sake of the future child" (Bennett, 2004)?

Future Reproductive Choices

As knowledge increases about reproduction there will be many more techniques available to enhance reproductive choices. It will become possible to identify an increasing number of genetic disorders before birth and it will become possible to "correct" disorders (either through gene therapy or fetal surgery) before birth. These developments will raise new ethical questions but questions that are closely related to the issues facing us presently.

However, there are some developments that may raise new ethical dilemmas concerning reproductive choice.

So called "synthetic gametes"

It is now theoretically possible to create both male and female gametes, eggs and sperm, from the stem cells of members of either gender. This will make possible alternative reproductive scenarios including a gay male couple having children which share half the genetic composition of each of them, just as in normal sexual reproduction. Artificial eggs would be created from one male partner's stem cells which would be refertilized *in vitro* by the sperm of the other. Until the dawn of ectogenesis a female third party would be required to gestate the resulting embryo (Dennis, 2003; Testa and Harris, 2004).

Gestation outside the female body

It is likely that at some point in the future reproduction will be possible outside the female body. Ectogenesis (Knight, 2002) and male pregnancy (Winston, 1999, p. 206) are yet to be a reality but it appears to be a matter of time and expertise before such techniques are added to our reproductive choices. The advent of human reproduction outside of a female body will change the ethics of reproductive autonomy dramatically. As we discussed earlier, while reproduction involves the gestation of a fetus inside the woman's body the ultimate choice regarding whether a woman should bear a child must be that woman's choice. However, when it becomes possible to conceive, gestate, and bring to birth human beings outside the woman's body this ultimate female choice regarding reproduction will not always be applicable.

Conclusions

This chapter has reviewed many of the most intractable problems concerning human reproduction. Its conclusions are both too specific and too varied to be susceptible of straightforward summary. Indeed the authors themselves take different views on some of the issues rehearsed. What we have tried to do however is to show the intellectual primacy of a combination of evidence and argument and we hope to suggest that where this combination of rational forces does not lead to a clear conclusion, that the most honest intellectual course is uncertainty and the best moral course is tolerance.

Notes

1 Section 13(5) of the Human Fertilisation and Embryology Act (1990).
2 There is little preventative treatment for genetic disorders at present. There are, of course, some infants with genetic disorders who will benefit significantly from early diagnosis and treatment for their disorder, for instance phenylketonuria (PKU) and congenital hypothyroidism and perhaps sickle cell disease, but even in these cases the "harm" of the genetic disorder cannot be prevented by diagnosis during pregnancy.

References

Anonymous (2000), Chemist morning-after pill closer, *BBC News Online*, Friday, May 19, 12: 36 GMT 13: 36 UK available online at: http://news.bbc.co.uk/1/hi/health/755347.stm.

Ashcroft, R. (2003), Bach to the future: response to: extending pre-implantation genetic diagnosis; medical and non-medical uses, *Journal of Medical Ethics* 29: 217–19.

Bennett, R. (2001), Antenatal genetic testing and the right to remain in ignorance, *Theoretical Medicine and Bioethics* 22 (5): 461–71.

Bennett, R. (2004), Routine antenatal HIV testing and its implications for informed consent, in Lucy Frith and Heather Draper (eds.), *Ethics and Midwifery*, 2nd edn., Edinburgh: Butterworth Heinemann, pp. 74–90.

Bennett, R. and Harris, J. (1999), Restoring natural function: access to infertility treatment using donated gametes, *Human Fertility* 2: 18–21.

Bennett, R. and Harris, J. (2001), The welfare of the child and access to infertility treatment, *Journal of Fertility Counseling* 8 (3) (autumn): 24–9.

Bennett, R. and Harris, J. (2002), Are there lives not worth living? When is it morally wrong to reproduce? In Donna Dickenson (ed.), *Ethical Issues in Maternal–Fetal Medicine*, Cambridge: Cambridge University Press, pp. 321–34.

Bennett, R. and Harris, J. (2003), Pursuing a rational analysis of cloning, in Ralph Levinson and Michael J. Reiss (eds.) *Key Issues in Bioethics: A Guide for Teachers*, London: RoutledgeFalmer, pp. 51–8.

Berkowitz, J.M. and Snyder, J.W. (1998); Racism, sexism in medically assisted conception, *Bioethics* 12 (1): 25–44.

Brewaeys, A., Ponjaert, I., Van Hall, E.V., and Golombok, S. (1997), Donor insemination: child development and family functioning in lesbian mother families, *Human Reproduction* 12: 1349–59.

Connor, E.M., Sperling, R.S., Gelber, R., et al. (1994), Reduction of maternal–infant transmission of human immunodeficiency virus type 1 with zidovudine treatment, *New England Journal of Medicine* 331: 1173–9.

Dennis, C. (2003), Developmental biology: synthetic sex cells, *Nature* 424 (July 24): 364–6.

Dworkin, R. (1993), *Life's Dominion*, London: HarperCollins.

The European Parliament (1997), *Resolution on Cloning*, motion dated March 11, 1997, passed March 13, paragraph B.

Flinter, F.A. (2001), Preimplantation genetic diagnosis, *British Medical Journal* 322: 1008–9.

Frith, L. (1998), Reproductive technologies, overview, in Ruth Chadwick (ed.) *Encyclopaedia of Applied Ethics*, vol. 3, San Diego, CA: Academic Press, pp. 817–27.

Gillick, V. (1988): Confidentiality and young people, *Ethics and Medicine* 4 (2): 21–3.

Harris, J. (1985), *The Value of Life: An Introduction to Medical Ethics*, London: Routledge and Kegan Paul.

Harris, J. (1997), Goodbye Dolly: the ethics of human cloning, *Journal of Medical Ethics* 23: 353–60.

Harris, J. (1998), *Clones, Genes and Immortality*, Oxford: Oxford University Press.

Harris, J. (2000), Is there a coherent social conception of disability? *Journal of Medical Ethics* 26: 95–100.

Harris, J. (2004), *On Cloning*, London: Routledge.

Henderson, M. (2004), Now parents can design donor babies, *The Times*, London, July 22.

HFEA (2003), *Sex Selection: Options for Regulation*, available online at: http://www.hfea.gov. uk/AboutHFEA/ Consultations.

Kimelman, D. (1990), Poverty and Norplant: can contraception reduce the under-class? *Philadelphia Inquirer*, December 12: A18.

Knight, J. (2002), Artificial wombs: an out of body experience, *Nature* 419 (September 12): 106–7.

McGowan J.P., Crane, M., Wiznia, A.A., and Blum, S. (1999), Combination antiretroviral therapy in human immunodeficiency virus-infected pregnant women, *Obstetrics and Gynecology* 94: 641–6.

Mandelbrot, L., Landreau-Mascaro, A., Rekacewicz, C., et al. (2001), Lamivudine-zidovudine combination for prevention of maternal–infant transmission of HIV-1, *Journal of the American Medical Association* 285: 2083–93.

Moskowitz, E.H., Jennings, B., and Callahan, D., (1995), Long-acting contraceptives: ethical guidance for policymakers and health care providers. (Long-acting contraception: moral choices, policy dilemmas), *Hastings Center Report*, January–February, 25 (1): S1 (8).

Pennings, G. (2002), The validity of contracts to dispose of frozen embryos, *Journal of Medical Ethics* 28: 295–8.

Robertson, J.A. (1994), *Children of Choice*, Princeton, NJ: Princeton University Press.

Shakespeare, T. (1998), Choices and rights: eugenics, genetics and disability equality, *Disability and Society* 13 (5): 665–81.

Spallone, P. and Steinberg, D.L. (eds.) (1987), *Made to Order: The Myth of Reproductive and Genetic Progress*, Oxford: Pergamon Press.

Testa, G. and Harris, J. (2004), Ethical aspects of ES cell-derived gametes, *Science* 305 (September 17): 1719.

WHO (1997), Press Release, WHO/20, March 11.

Winston, R. (1999), *The IVF Revolution: The Definitive Guide to Assisted Reproductive Techniques*, London: Vermilion.

Chapter 12

Public Policy and Ending Lives

Evert van Leeuwen and Gerrit Kimsma[1]

Should political institutions and legislation be involved in decisions about citizens' death and dying? Or should the medical profession and physicians decide when and how patients depart from life? These questions are as old as civil societies, but they have become poignant since medicine has vastly improved its technological ability to keep very ill people alive with continuous life-support measures.

Death and Democracy

In this chapter, we shall answer these questions from a Rawlsian perspective, using John Rawls's distinction between the political conception of justice and the comprehensive character of moral, religious, and philosophical doctrines. From this perspective the question becomes: is there a need for society to develop explicit rules or guidelines concerning questions of death and dying? We are convinced that the answer is affirmative. First, every society has to see to it that its members have the opportunity to prepare themselves for their death. Second, our current conception of individualism within the age of technology implies that individuals are competent to choose the place and time of their death. And third, the boundaries between medical necessity, social need, and personal desire have become porous and vague.

According to Rawls, the impact of a public conception of justice should be, at least in a constitutional democracy, removed as far as possible from controversial philosophical and religious doctrines.[2] The plurality of conceptions of the good that we find in a democracy makes it impossible to develop a moral conception of justice that would be general enough to encompass all ideologies. Therefore, we have to restrict ourselves in questions of justice to political conceptions. The political conception of justice is based on intuitive ideas that underlie our conception of a democratic society.

Political Philosophy and Choosing Death

From philosophers like John Rawls and also Tom Scanlon, we learn the importance of distinguishing between a public conception of justice and the plurality of goods that can be pursued by all free and equal democratic citizens.[3] The civil rights of citizens should not be infringed by legislative statutes that are based on a particular view of the good in human life. Instead the legislative rules of a country should arise from a plurality of rational conceptions regarding a good and well considered view of what a meaningful life is. This distinction should also hold with respect to choices in letting die. It implies that a public conception of justice requires that physicians will have to inform themselves about the patient's wishes in dying. Every patient should, whenever possible, be allowed to die according to his own beliefs and conception of the good in life, as long as the rights and liberties of other citizens are not infringed. In this way the public conception of justice is in accordance with the idea of public reason and avoids appeals to metaphysical conceptions that are not endorsed by an overlapping consensus of citizens.[4] The person who is subjected to the political conception of justice remains until death a person who has (or had) the moral power to have a conception of the good, who is (or was) a self-originating source of valid claims, and who is (or was) responsible for his/her own ends.

That said, allowing someone to die when his/her life could, instead, be prolonged, should not occur without a discussion of the matter with the patient or the representative(s) of a patient who no longer has decisional capacity. Without this step, the expert opinion of the physician becomes the only argument in favor of active life-prolonging medical treatment. Without allowing the guiding force to reside with the patient, social issues like scarcity of beds in intensive care and the physician's personal standards of quality of life can easily slip into end of life decisions. We must appreciate that members of society have their own individual conceptions of the good and individuals should be considered as self-originating sources of valid claims. Withholding effective treatment and hastening the death of a person without his/her consent ignores the fact that patients may have duties and can also legitimately make claims on others. The same remains true in the clinical setting, even in palliative care units, facilities for psycho geriatrics, and nursing homes. The only way to avoid usurping personal decisions is by instituting public policy to require that the authoritative voice in decisions about the end of life is the individual's. Valid claims that citizens have based on their own conception of the good in life or the good life should also rule in decisions about one's own death. The practices of voluntary euthanasia and physician-assisted suicide recognize this voice. The question then has to be raised whether granting the well-considered wish of a patient in unbearable pain or terminal suffering violates the rights of fellow citizens? The answers can be both negative and affirmative: No, not as long as the wish is evaluated within a political conception of justice that does not envisage a particular good of life, but recognizes that every citizen might have a personal religious or metaphysical point of view. Yes, when someone goes on to argue that allowing people to choose death confronts fellow-citizens with their own mortality and the need to make a plan for their own last days. One might see this as harm, because no one should be forced to ponder the end of his life or how to die. Both these answers fit within a Rawlsian conception of justice, if inequalities are arranged according to the difference principle. So no one should be forced or pressed into accepting some support in dying.

Belgium and the Netherlands have legalized voluntary euthanasia and the state of Oregon in the US has legalized physician-assisted suicide, based on the voluntary request of patients, thereby recognizing the valid claims of citizens based on their own conception of the good in life, while prohibiting that anyone should be forced into accepting support in dying. These governments have also instituted regulations governing the practices and organized public oversight of cases. Under such systems, the request of patients is granted because people who choose to end their lives are considered as free persons with moral power. At the same time, the regulations specify the medical conditions that must be fulfilled in order to allow a physician to assist a patient in dying. In this way public reason about justice in dying remains responsible to its principles as well as to the public without creating public offense about the practice.

Historical Roots

The solutions in Belgium, the Netherlands, and Oregon differ radically from the laws and regulations concerning death and dying in most countries of the western world. The dominant legal perspective on this issue derives from a tradition that regulates the relationship between citizens and the state. Historically, laws that criminalize killing concern the right of self-defense and the duty of states to protect the lives of their citizens.

Throughout history people have speculated about how we came to live in communities or states. Political philosophers from Hobbes to Rawls have derived their theories by positing a process that may have motivated people at a particular moment in time to establish the rules, morals, and laws that ordered communities. Anthropologists and historians of today are still searching for evidence about those origins. Irrespective of the details, it is safe to presume that the goal of protection from physical violence and external threats to life has been a common factor. Countering violence, therefore, became a necessary tool in the exercise of political power and a crucial factor in the justification of a state's existence. Today it seems beyond question that states and nations use power to protect their citizens, and human lives may be put in jeopardy or sacrificed in order to ensure the safety of the community. Although justified killing by the state is not the subject of this chapter, it is important to acknowledge that legal conceptions and public policies regarding the end of life have developed in the broader context framed ages ago from the dual perspective of protecting citizens and neutralizing possible threats. Issues of justified war and armed police belong to this category, as well as the right to have a peaceful life based on the principle of non-interference.

Two sorts of legal rules related to killing do not sit well with the justification of protection and threat to life. One is legal acceptance of the death penalty, the other is the prohibition of suicide.[5] Defensive reasoning to support the death penalty invokes retaliation ("an eye for an eye") and deterrence by setting an example of fear to those who might plan serious crimes. Although most European countries have recently rejected the death penalty as unjustifiable, the assumption that the state has the authority to decide over life and death was challenged in the past as well. Some religious leaders, like Clement of Rome and Chrysostomos in the times of early Christianity, disputed that legislative right. But a condition for the Church being accepted by political powers after 325 AD required the Church to accept killing in times of war and killing as punishment for extreme crimes as morally justifiable. The basic terms for this accommodation employed the legal concepts of guilt and innocence.[6] Adoption of the term "innocent" made it possible for religion to stand firm stand against all kinds of killing of the innocent. This religious prohibition on taking an innocent life was recently restated in the encyclical *Evangelium Vitae* of Pope John Paul II, which expressed the profound conviction that the life of an innocent human being is incomparable in worth to any other value. The conclusion that follows from this theological position is that no human institution has the right to take the life of an innocent human being.

Although introducing the notion of "innocence" and linking it closely with justified killing seems to resolve the clash between the political realities of protection and the religious commandment, "Thou shalt not kill," it introduces other difficulties. Declaring that some people and acts are innocent means that others are not, that is, they are guilty. And the determination of innocence or guilt requires judgment that some harm or wrong has been done and judgment that the act was culpable. Thus, the compromise between religion and political necessity produced the question of who is to judge guilt and innocence, political authority (i.e., legislators or courts), religious authority, or individuals. It also bequeaths us with the background religious presumption that killing someone who is not guilty is wrong. Ever since the death of Socrates and the Christian martyrs, the ethical acceptability of their acts has been argued. Were they innocents? If so, was it wrong for them to kill themselves?

This problem becomes particularly clear within the debates on suicide and assisted suicide. Today dispute about this matter continues in bioethics and in palliative care. The controversy arises over the moral acceptability of brain death criteria, terminal sedation, letting people die by withholding life-prolonging interventions, euthanasia, physician-assisted suicide, and assistance of suicide. All of these disagreements reflect moral convictions as well as confusion and uncertainty with respect to rights, innocence, and ending lives justifiably. These matters challenge public policy because they question the fundamental legal pattern of protecting innocent lives while neutralizing threats.

A few exceptional cases of letting die can be supported by the traditional protection justification. In the case of the forced isolation of someone who is infected with a highly contagious and extremely lethal virus like Ebola, the community as a whole is threatened. Then it can be argued that the government has a right to quarantine an infected person and let the person die. That decision is justified by protecting other human beings from infection. Of course these infected patients are innocent in contracting the virus, but they nevertheless pose a threat that requires a defense.

In this chapter, however, we concentrate on issues of abiding by a patient's choice to be allowed to forgo life-prolonging medical interventions within a health care setting. Should a state prohibit these specific liberties to people who choose to end their lives? Or should a state develop rules and procedures to accompany those liberties? Or should a state limit its role in protecting the innocent and the unwilling in such matters?[7]

In what follows, we shall start by considering the latter cases: the circumstances in which decisions about death are made without consent and for individuals who can be said to be innocent. We shall first discuss public policies about brain death to illustrate how public policies are developed to balance the interests of individuals – those in need of transplant organs as well as those who might be considered as brain dead according to some definition – against those of society. From there on we shall move to issues regarding newborns (neonates), to letting die and terminal sedation. We shall finish our discussion with the subject of public policies on euthanasia and physician-assisted suicide.

Brain Death

The introduction of brain death criteria has an interesting medico-legal history. In the late 1960s, it became clear that transplantation of kidneys, hearts, and livers could be effective medical interventions for end-stage organ failure. In order to acquire an adequate number of viable transplant organs a new transparent definition of brain death was needed.[8,9] Most countries have since then introduced criteria for brain death, defined as clinical, irreversible loss of all brain functions. The loss of brain functions is to be established by clinical examination and radiological investigations. After brain death is declared, heart and lung function can be maintained with technological support until the transplantable organs can be removed.[10]

Japan was one of the last countries to accept the definition of brain death. The Japanese resistance shows the importance of a cultural context for setting public policy. After at least three years of political debate, the use of the brain death standard was legalized in cases where the donor had given written consent both to the determination of brain death and to organ procurement. In practice, however, the patient's family can override the prior consent decision.[11] Sato et al. suggest a number of factors for the long delay in adopting brain death standards in Japan. One is a deep public mistrust of the medical profession. Another reason involves Japanese culture and traditional religious views which translate into the lack of a broad public consensus. These reasons apply to almost every country of the world where groups, often with religious backgrounds, have opposed the brain death criteria.

Technological intervention in the dying process, the reliance on medical knowledge, skills, and equipment, conceptions of the wholeness and integrity of the human body and human life, and the idea that people are trespassing into an area where they lack authority all contribute to family reluctance to accept brain death standards and, hence, a low rate of organ donation.

Distrust and fear continue to characterize the attitudes of populations in many countries, even those with a long-standing legal acceptance of the brain death criteria. In common experience, the dead do not breathe and their hearts do not beat. But the brain dead who are sustained on ventilators and with other artificial support do have breath and blood flow. They do not appear dead. That makes it hard for families to accept and supports the suggestion that someone who is brain dead is just not dead. How can someone be dead, while his heart (or liver or kidney) is alive?

That intuitive conviction seems to be the rule rather than the exception. According to recent research in Ohio, 36 years after its legal acceptance of the standard, the majority of the public is still puzzled about the meaning of the brain death criteria and how they are used in practice.[12] According to this survey, the public is unable to distinguish brain death from a persistent vegetative state or a coma. The authors conclude that "[w]hile brain death is the accepted legal and medical standard in the US, it does not represent a universal vision of what it means to be dead."[13]

Robert Veatch, one of the ethicists involved in defining the brain death criteria in the US, provided some interesting observations on this incongruence between medico-legal reasoning and public beliefs.[14] He claims that the main issue is the definition of death itself and the recognition of its moral and legal force. Veatch maintains that the committee members who formulated the first criteria for brain death in 1968 did not assume that fully brain-dead people are dead in the traditional biological sense.[15] Instead, they implicitly held that those who are brain dead have "lost their moral status as members of the human moral community." Therefore, these individuals do not need the normal protection by the law against homicide. In most cases, removing vital treatment from a person who is not dead could be homicide. Removing vital medical interventions from someone who is brain dead cannot be considered a homicide. In other words, by calling those who meet the brain death standards "dead," that is, through adoption of a medico-legal definition, those who disconnect ventilators or discontinue other medical interventions and even those who procure organs from brain-dead humans are exempted from criminal charges such as homicide. It comes as no surprise that this type of reasoning increases fear and distrust, especially among those who already feel that they have suffered from other injustices.

Veatch is quite clear that the definition of brain death is a medico-legal "artifact." In fact, one might go so far as to defend the idea that every "declaration of death" is a medico-legal fact. Nevertheless, many people still regard death as a natural event and invest it with romantic meaning. In that light, one has to realize also that some people see the brain death standard as a denial of inalienable moral status to members of the human community and they claim that those who are brain dead with artificially sustained breathing and circulation are (still) living.

Nevertheless, legal acceptance of the brain death standard is crucially important for the procurement of transplant organs from dead donors. Public acceptance of the standard is therefore also crucial for consensual donation of organs and to overcome the current low rates of donation. For that reason, prudence is required in the construction of public policy based on theoretical bioethical concepts and legal positions. As the 50-year history of brain death criteria has shown, projects can easily be misunderstood. Also, caution is required because a great deal is at stake when policies redefine what it means to be human and human life merits protection. And, furthermore, it is difficult to separate personal or professional interests from rational or public interests.

For example, acceptance of the brain death standard has significant consequences. Discontinuing treatment from those who are declared brain dead saves society the resources that would otherwise be spent on their continued medical care. So the criteria need to be accurate enough in order to assure that without support the person would surely die in every circumstance. Discontinuation also makes the usable organs and tissue available for transplantation. Criteria of brain death should therefore also be accurate enough to keep those organs vital. That assures a huge advantage in chances of long-term survival for would-be organ recipients, it will keep their families in peace, and it will give the medical teams and institutions that are eager to perform the transplants a higher rate of success. Given the hazards of misunderstanding, unanticipated consequences, and bias arising from self-interest, policy-makers need to proceed with caution in defining the criteria of brain death.

Confusion and ambivalence over brain death is further compromised by the fact that brain death statutes seem to challenge traditional boundaries. With the exception of today's Japan, those who are to become brain dead do not consent to the use of the standard. Furthermore, there is no reason to presume that those who are declared brain dead and disconnected from life-prolonging medical interventions are anything but innocent when they die soon after. The popular confusion over the brain death criteria therefore contributes to moral suspicion about whether these innocent people are really dead when their organs are removed for transplantation.

Abortion and Decisions for Neonates and Other Children

Another area of policy controversy involves decisions about terminating pregnancies and withholding life-prolonging interventions from neonates. Again, these human lives are innocent, and again, those who die do not participate in the life-ending decisions.

Ending the lives of fetuses has become accepted in many countries during the last 30 years. Public policies that allow abortion give women the choice about whether to terminate their pregnancy. Justifications for this intervention may be social, emotional, or medical. According to most legal reasoning, induced abortion does not conflict with the duty to protect persons because, according to law, the life of the person begins at birth. Only after birth does one become a person with inalienable rights. Traditionally, fetuses have not been legally recognized as persons.

From the perspective of individuals who comprise the moral community in a pluralistic society, an array of different feelings and conceptions may play a role in their thinking on abortion. People conceive of their fetuses in terms of their own moral vocabulary (which could include acceptance of the fetus as a full moral person) and their own expectations. The focus of public reasoning and policy on abortion in the 1960s and 1970s was the legal issue of a pregnant woman's right to choose. The legalization of abortion thus reflects a change in public policy from measures on behalf of the public good towards legal conceptions of individual rights, which give women the authority to make decisions for themselves. More generally, the shift in public policy expressed a move away from social control of personal behavior and toward support of reasonable deliberative choice.

Again we have to assess a change in moral thinking due to new biomedical technology. Unlike the case of brain death, the legalization of abortion does not seem to reflect a direct interest for society or specific social groups, although there may be social interests in population control on the aggregate level. The decision turns mainly on the interests of the woman in privacy, equal opportunity, and self-determination. Public policy in most countries has, therefore, allowed women to take their personal views on the moral status of the fetus into account, and focused primarily on the right of women to choose abortion.

Although the freedom to choose may be pivotal before birth, after birth the moral rules change. Chromosomal abnormalities may justify a woman's decision to abort a pregnancy because its moral status is left as a matter of private judgment. The decision to let a neonate die is governed instead by the young citizen's legal right to protection. In fact, the position that the lives of newborns with abnormalities may be terminated just as severely deformed fetuses are aborted has not been accepted in any public policy anywhere in the world. Only a few ethicists, such as the consequentialist thinker Peter Singer, have endorsed such a view.[16]

The moral assessment for severally impaired newborns only changes when there is significant doubt about whether medical support is beneficent or maleficent. Severe conditions, such as immaturity of the lungs or massive intra-cranial bleeding, can make it unclear whether the child's interests are best served by initiating medical treatment or by allowing the child to die as an act of medical benevolence. In these cases, as with other similar medical conditions, public policy in many countries seems to have adopted an attitude of reservation and distance. The dilemmas raised by such cases have a high emotional impact on both surrogates and caregivers. The emotions and the medical uncertainties reflect the tragedies of life and the limits of traditional medical ethics.

Policy varies somewhat between countries and legal systems. In the US, for example, the public has decided that doctors confronted with these issues should maximally act to prolong life. Decisions to forgo treatment in the best interest of the child are prohibited according to the Child Abuse Prevention and Treatment Act.[17] It appears that at least two issues are at stake in the development of public policy. First, there is the issue of public trust. Citizens want to trust that no human being or member of the moral human community shall be abandoned in a seriously hopeless situation. Second is the issue of public funding. Because public funding will have to absorb a substantial portion of the immediate and lifelong financial needs of the newborn, decisions to apply technology that makes survival possible mean that the family as well as society will have to face the consequences.

Neither of these political considerations can overrule the common medical judgment that treatment should not result in a tragedy of suffering and pain. If this medical judgment would be allowed to rule, most countries in the world would recognize the traditional medical adage, *in dubio abstine*, or letting go.[18] Yet, legal rules or public guidelines to that effect are strangely absent. Until very recently there has been little or no legal interest in dilemmas of this nature and physicians are not delegated the moral and institutional authority to make these decisions with the parents. One possible explanation for the absence of regulations to address these issues is public distrust of the motives of parents/surrogates and of the discretional power of physicians.

This type of distrust inclines states to legislate to protect newborns, such as the Baby Doe Rules in the US. In the Netherlands there has been a long debate about the criteria that should apply to these dilemmas. The aim has been to make medical judgments about life-ending decisions for children transparent to parents, the profession, and the public, based on a well supported judgment that the life of the child would be unbearable, filled with pain, immediately and in the future. Recent developments in the Netherlands illustrate the profound difficulties in dealing with severely ill neonates and other children. This story starts with the Netherlands' liberal approach to allowing adult patients to choose to die. Following the enactment of the Euthanasia Law of 2002, the establishment of a special committee made up of lawyers and physicians was proposed to recommend policy for end of life medical decisions about minors. Although the committee is soon to begin work, the proposal met political resistance. In the meanwhile, the clinicians in the neonatal intensive care units (ICUs) of university hospitals, tired of waiting for political action, decided to act on such cases and report their actions to the legal authorities. The university hospital of Groningen actually developed a protocol with procedures to evaluate and justify every step in the deliberative process. The protocol's main goal is to make the ethical deliberations and the medical judgment about withdrawing or withholding treatment or life-ending acts for children transparent and accessible to public control.[19] This procedure, now accepted by the Dutch Society of Pediatricians, intends to protect the child and to rule out improper motives for letting a child die, while allowing life ending under special and difficult circumstances. By abiding by the Groningen Protocol the public trust in medical decision-making can be enhanced, without undue political interference in the difficult dilemmas parents and physicians face.

Within societies that provide citizens with full medical coverage, as most European countries do, the financial burden of caring for severely handicapped children is assumed by the community. One might therefore be concerned that a society's financial stake generates a public interest in preventing these children from being born or surviving the tragedy of their birth. This financial interest, however, plays no role in the debates. Instead the legal duty to protect the innocent and the moral duty to be compassionate prevail. Public interest focuses on ensuring mothers a choice in whether or not to have their children and offers each newborn a fair chance in life, regardless of the economic consequences.

Public policies in this area have to address philosophical questions about the nature of human beings and the extent of their rights. But they also have to take account of the interests of third parties, including parents, caregivers, and the whole of society. These interests may include the financial risks and burdens that need to be accepted by society, insurance companies, and families. In these matters the well-being of the child still prevails. Procedures for balancing the complex medical, emotional, and financial matters in order to prevent harm to neonates and children become irrelevant when these policies refuse to admit that in some cases ending a life could be the most benevolent act. People who take such stands always see ending a life as a refusal to protect the innocent and the most vulnerable in society. They challenge all public policies on life ending by claiming that every human life deserves protection.

Letting Die and Terminal Sedation

Within the context of law and public policy, the death of an adult person through disease, illness, or old age has traditionally been called "natural." By calling a death "natural," policy recognizes that members of society will eventually die, not because of a societal decision, but as an event of and in life. Since the middle of the nineteenth century, public policies for the collection of data on death have required that the (natural) cause of death is confirmed by a physician. A death certificate is registered and the death is publicly acknowledged. In a sense, these requirements give society some control over death. At the same time society shows that natural death is outside the reach of public control and responsibility by leaving the care of the ill and dying to relatives and friends who also take charge of last rites and the disposal of the corpse.

In all past reflections on social justice, in the work of moral and political philosophers from Hobbes and Spinoza to Kant, it has been the ideal to construct a just society in which people would die from natural causes or by accident only. There should be no killing, nor should society allow people to be put to death for unjustified reasons. This ideal of a reasonable, peaceful society has ever since been an important subject in political philosophy.

According to the societal and legal points of view built on that ideal, statutes and rules create a black and white dichotomy between life and death. As long as society considers someone alive, he or she is alive, while as soon as death is declared, be it natural or not, the person ceases to exist. Someone who has disappeared is not considered dead unless a corpse is found or enough evidence is provided to prove that the person has lost life. As soon as someone is declared dead, that individual no longer has a legal identity. So the declaration of natural death is the affirmation of a contingent legal fact managed by a physician. Non-natural death requires public investigation into the cause of death. If death is not certified, someone can live forever in terms of the law.

The concept of natural death has become obsolete in many ways, but especially in hospital care since the introduction of intensive medical technology. Some 40 years ago, philosopher Ivan Illich argued that natural death itself was becoming a problem in the welfare states of affluent societies.[20] With the use of medical technology at the end of life, people in modern ICUs die under more or less meticulously controlled circumstances. At the end of life, technology can take over many crucial vital functions. In hospital ICUs it is, therefore, often possible to delay natural death for a very long time. But, in recognition of the inevitable fact of death, contemporary palliative care and end of life medical care strive not for natural death, but for a comfortable death without pain.

The effect of these developments is that many patients die of natural causes only after a medical decision. In the Netherlands it is calculated that in 2001, 43.5 percent of deaths involved some kind of medical decision. In 17.6 percent of deaths, the decision was made that no further treatment would be provided, in other words that the patient was allowed to die. This makes the procedure of allowing a patient to die normal medicine in most hospitals today.

Letting or allowing to die can be defined in several ways. It may involve:

- withholding treatment that might prolong life
- discontinuing treatment and/or withdrawal of technology necessary to keep the patient alive
- administering pain medication that might shorten life
- withholding nutrition and hydration
- terminal sedation.

Research shows that these measures are not uniformly defined nor are they uniformly applied. Procedures to forgo treatment at the end of life vary widely in Europe.[21] In most countries decisions to forgo or withdraw treatment are considered to be part of the medical professional domain. Do Not Resuscitate (DNR) codes do not, for instance, require the explicit consent of the patient. Sometimes however, as in France, there are legal prescriptions for the medical profession directed not only at withdrawal or withholding of technological interventions, but also concerning the administration of pain medication.

In most countries the justification for physicians' withdrawal or withholding of treatment is based on their professional judgment of the possible effects. A decision that a treatment will almost certainly have no effect or only a slight effect in keeping the patient alive is generally accepted as a sufficient reason for calling the treatment futile. The intervention may then be discontinued and a DNR order is issued. Medical focus then shifts from life prolongation or cure to keeping the patient comfortable.

The expected quality of life is an entirely different sort of justification for withdrawal of treatment and it clearly creates all kinds of difficult problems. Judgments about quality of life necessarily involve personal subjective opinion. Such judgments are also a source of conflict. Sometimes patients or family members desire medical treatments which, in the assessment of their physicians, are clearly futile. The diversity of views on whether or not a treatment is "futile" or whether the goals achieved by an intervention are worthwhile, can make decisions about withdrawal or withholding treatment highly contentious. The lack of uniform standards for making these decisions is also an obstacle for making explicit rules or prescriptive regulations about when medical treatment may be discontinued.

A special case of withdrawing and withholding treatment concerns withholding nutrition and hydration. In general, withholding food and water from someone who is totally dependent on others to receive it, is considered a crime. In nursing homes, patients who cannot care for themselves, receive food and water as part of standard care. In terminal care however, for instance after a period during which a patient is in a persistent vegetative state (PVS) or a deep coma, the patient may be unable to swallow. Nutrition and hydration are then provided artificially through feeding tubes. Because the provision of nutrition and hydration involves artificial means, it can be considered a medical treatment falling under the authority of the physician. Physicians (along with family members) may then decide to stop nutrition and hydration in order to let the patient die. This medical authority is legally recognized in most countries, although it is sometimes disputed.

As the case of Terry Schiavo in the US in 2005 showed, we find troubling differences in views on the acceptability of withholding or withdrawing treatment, particularly nutrition and hydration. The Schiavo case evoked intense emotions. In the eyes of the passionate objectors, removing Terry's feeding tube was killing an innocent human being. The problem was confounded by different conceptions of natural death and views about the role of medical technology in the dying process. The legal case hinged in the end on the question of whether the parents or the husband had the more accurate account of Terry's preferences in her condition. The controversy around cases like Terry's becomes deeper when a patient is still able to swallow. In those cases a decision to stop food and drink has solely to be based on a medical judgment about the patient's condition. Consider, for instance, a patient with serious dementia accompanied by serious physical co-morbidity that causes significant enduring pain. The decision to withhold feeding then requires agreement between physicians and family and a more public assessment and oversight, perhaps from an Ethics Committee's review. The public needs a clear understanding of the conditions that must be met before such medical decisions can be put into effect.

Administration of pain medication that might shorten the life of a patient has been defended for ages. Some people invoke the "principle of double effect" to justify such life-shortening comfort measures. Roughly, they argue that if an action would cause a significant good effect (e.g., pain relief) that can be achieved in no other way, and the bad effect (e.g., the foreseen death) is comparatively less bad than the harm that is to be mitigated, the action is justified by the intended good effect. This principle has been adopted by Catholic theology and it has been formally acknowledged as applicable to end of life care by Pope Pius XII. Within the medical and ethical literature the principle is still debated and not generally accepted. Using the principle of double effect to justify hastening a patient's death seems deceptive because efficient and effective palliation need not shorten life, even though it does not prevent the death of the patient. Invoking double effect is furthermore problematic because it introduces ambiguity into medical decision-making by allowing the moral acceptability of the act to turn on what the real intentions of the physician were for administering sedatives.

Terminal sedation is another variant on letting a patient die. Because of untreatable pain, a patient is deeply sedated until death occurs. Artificial nutrition and hydration are normally not provided. Criteria for these measures typically include irreversible symptoms, pain, the imminence of death, and, according to some guidelines, the consent of the patient or family.

All of these situations, where patients are allowed to die or where death is hastened by the administration of narcotics or the withdrawal of medical intervention, are controversial because an innocent's life is ended, frequently without informed consent. Some also continue to be troubled by death under such circumstances because it seems so different from their image of a natural death.

Euthanasia and Physician-Assisted Suicide

Voluntary active euthanasia (VAE) and physician-assisted suicide (PAS) differ in a crucial way from letting die procedures. In VAE and PAS the patient requests help to effect death. A patient's request to end his life fundamentally alters the standard medical situation.[22] The request breaks through the chain of professional medical reasoning about palliative and other forms of care, because a patient's request forces physicians to rethink possible interventions aimed at palliation and a natural route to death. It also changes the balance of responsibility and power. When a patient wants to manage his own death, this patient assumes responsibility for the decision and seeks medical assistance in determining the moment and circumstance of his dying.

Such requests do not relieve the physician of responsibility. A medical evaluation of the request is necessary because medical assistance in hastening death always has to be justified. Following a careful procedure to support a physician's decision to assist in a suicide is extremely important for two reasons. (1) It ensures that physicians will remain within the limits of public and professional rules. (2) It also assures the community that physicians will continue to act in accordance with society's trust.

Public rules for controlling and guiding VAE and PAS are, therefore, extremely important. First, this type of medical assistance falls outside the standard boundaries of medicine. The legal, public justification for medical interventions which violate the inviolability of the human body (e.g., surgery) is based on conceptions of the well-being of the patient and the restoration of health or continuity of life. Medical assistance in dying clearly cannot be based on this same foundation in any simple sense. Second, a patient's request for active help in dying falls outside the medical profession's common authority. In fact, such a request for active assistance in dying brings medicine into the legal arena of public deliberation about murder and manslaughter.

Two countries in the world, the Netherlands and Belgium, presently have laws and rules regarding VAE and PAS. Beyond these two, Switzerland legally accepts assistance in suicide, including PAS. And, in the US, the state of Oregon has a law allowing medical assistance in suicide. In these states that sanction assistance in death, legislation requires that the physician's intervention be in response to the patient's request to die with medical assistance. By law, specific conditions must also be fulfilled. Supporting documentation must be provided in reports that are open for official review. Legally if the required measures are not followed, the physicians involved are subject to criminal charges of murder or manslaughter. In the Netherlands and Belgium physicians are even required to self-report their involvement in PAS and VAE.

The legislation that permits PAS or VAE is complex and its application is somehow at odds with common legal thinking. No law or public rule in the world acknowledges "a right to die." In most countries today suicide attempts in themselves are not considered a criminal offense. Assisting suicide is, however, a crime, except in Switzerland. Legalization of VAE and PAS first of all legitimizes a patient's request for aid in dying and suspends the state's obligation to protect life. Legalization also legitimizes the voice of citizens in determining the circumstances of their own death. Public oversight to assure the authenticity of the request and that the medical conditions are fulfilled serves as the instrument to protect individuals from possible abuse. These legal requirements have a similar structure in all the laws that allow PAS and VAE. In the Dutch law these conditions are:

- a voluntary and well-considered request
- a situation of unbearable suffering in which no alternative for alleviating the suffering exists
- a consultation by an independent physician, who visits the patient and corroborates the legal conditions.

In Belgium the criteria are:

* a voluntary request, based on reasonable grounds
* a situation of suffering in the terminal phase of life.

In both countries a physician must report an act of euthanasia or assisted suicide to the legal authorities, either the prosecutor or the medical coroner. The reported cases are then reviewed by a committee in which legal, medical, and ethics experts participate. When the oversight committee concludes that the physician acted according to the criteria set by law, the physician is not prosecuted or subjected to further legal investigations. When a committee finds that a physician deviated from the legal standards, a legal investigation begins which may lead to prosecution.

The most remarkable point in the Dutch and Belgian procedures is that a physician must self-report. This feature is radically different from any other criminal procedure in the penal code. When physician involvement in PAS or VAE is not self-reported, the physician may be charged with falsely reporting a natural death. Similarly, when the request and unbearable suffering cannot be demonstrated, a physician runs the risk of prosecution for murder or manslaughter.

Since the enactment of enabling legislation, additional requirements have been developed in order to ensure careful compliance with the procedure. For instance, a physician must personally acquire the pharmaceuticals (i.e., euthanatics) that are used (e.g., barbiturates and derivates of curare). In the case of PAS, a physician must be present during the entire process. This requirement stands in contrast to the procedures in Oregon, where it is forbidden for a physician to be present during the act of suicide.

All of these requirements express the public's concern with VAE and PAS. Although it is commonly accepted that every competent adult has a right to choose his of her own way to die, the support by publicly authorized agents, such as physicians, is regulated by stringent fixed criteria.

Even though a very few countries allow PAS and VAE, worldwide opposition is still is the rule. This opposition frequently reflects the view that deliberately ending innocent lives can never be justified. Some opponents of PAS and VAE, who may support the death penalty or killing in war, tend to reject the idea that complying with a patient's request for help in the process of dying justifies the intervention.[23] According to these critics, decisions about ending innocent life belong to nature or to its creator, and the matter is not for a patient or a physician to decide. Others argue against PAS and VAE on the basis of fear of abuse. They are afraid that law will be not able to assure that physicians who participate do not overstep the bounds.[24] They worry that oversight and review will be inadequate, because evaluation comes after the acts and because reports may be doctored to conceal how criteria are not met. In the Netherlands an additional safeguard requires consultation with an independent physician, but deception and misrepresentation of the facts are still possible.

Although it is well recognized that in PAS or VAE neither the attending physician nor the consultant has any real interest whatsoever in ending the life of a patient, worries remain. Cases that are difficult to evaluate according to the legal requirement also continue to challenge physicians and judicial authorities, although the conditions of the law nevertheless remain. In the Netherlands challenging cases are reviewed from the perspective of professional duties in comparable cases and the integrity of a professional. Because the professional autonomy of physicians is still highly valued in the Netherlands, doctors are allowed to make medical decisions without pressure from third parties, including institutional economics, insurance, and so on. If such external pressures were allowed to play a part, the whole procedure would collapse because people would then worry that the individual choice about when and how to die would no longer be authentic or voluntary. Allowing physicians to kill patients who are denied medical support for economic or social reasons would make patients victims.

Conclusion

In his later work John Rawls acknowledged that within pluralistic democratic societies individuals invoke different moral views as they formulate public policy to optimize human freedom and show respect for individual dignity. The resulting public policies aim at promoting public good and preventing harm. On the one hand, law in western democracies is based on protecting citizens and neutralizing possible threats. On the other hand, liberty and freedom are core democratic values supported by the law.

In the introduction to this chapter we described some of the complex issues involved in public policies about death and dying. When public policy-makers turn their attention to questions of death and dying, significant differences in personal and religious views frustrate efforts to achieve a consensus that can be broadly accepted. Conflict between these basic values of protection and liberty arises when legislators try to craft public policy on death and dying. These conceptual problems are exacerbated when groups claim that their perspective on death and dying is above the law because life is sacrosanct.

Medical advances have made it imperative for societies to deal with these conflicts. We have tried to explain the controversies as clashes between legal and personal moral perspectives. As such, a path to resolution may be found in Rawls's later work. Although the definition of the good life plan is not a part of public policy, it is appropriate for policy to set limits and boundaries based on the common human aversion to pain and suffering. Within legal boundaries people are left free to make choices according to their own moral and religious perspectives. Outside the boundaries, the law has to be effective in preventing harm and crime. In the end, the law has to accept that ending pain and suffering can be a legitimate reason for allowing patients to choose death. Dying as a meaningful event of life does after all not depend on the law but on the moral stories of living beings.

Notes

1 The authors wish to thank with admiration and gratitude Rosamond Rhodes for her excellent redaction of the manuscript.

2 J. Rawls, Justice as fairness: political not metaphysical, in *Collected Papers*, ed. S. Freeman, London: Harvard University Press, 1999: 388ff.

3 T.M. Scanlon, The difficulty of tolerance, in *Toleration, an Elusive Virtue*, ed. D. Heyd, Princeton, NJ: Princeton University Press, 1996: 226–39. Rawls, *Collected Papers*, 588.

4 Rawls, *Collected Papers*, 574–5.

5 See R. Dworkin, *Life's Dominion*, New York: Knopf, 1993, pp. 49, 127.

6 J. Rachels, *The End of Life*, Oxford: Oxford University Press, 1986, p. 20.

7 See Dworkin, *Life's Dominion*, p. 127, where he argues that in the US the Fifth and Fourteenth Amendment forbid the government to take life or liberty or property without "due process of law." According to Dworkin the Supreme Court has decided that this clause imposes substantive limits on what a government could do.

8 Ad Hoc Committee of the Harvard Medical School to Examine the Definition of Brain Death, A definition of irreversible coma, *Journal of the American Medical Association* 205 (6) (1968): 337–40.

9 K.G. Gervais, *Redefining Death*, New Haven, CT and London: Yale University Press, 1986.

10 R.E. Carson, Modern technology and the care of the dying, in D.C. Thomasma and T. Kushner (eds.), *Birth to Death. Science and Bioethics*, Cambridge: Cambridge University Press, 1996, pp. 191–7.

11 H. Sato, A. Akabayashi, and I. Kai, Public appraisal of government efforts and participation intent in medico-ethical policymaking in Japan: a large scale national survey concerning brain death and organ transplant, *BMC Medical Ethics* 6 (2005): 1.

12 L.A. Siminoff, C. Burant, and S.J. Youngner, Death and organ procurement: public beliefs and attitudes, *Social Science and Medicine* 59 (2004): 2325–34.

13 Ibid.: 2332.

14 R.M. Veatch, Abandon the dead donor rule or change the definition of death? *Kennedy Institute of Ethics Journal* 14 (3) (2004): 261–76.

15 Ibid.: 267

16 P. Singer, *Writings on an Ethical Life*, New York: The Ecco Press, 2000, p. 146ff.

17 L.M. Kopelman, Are the 21-year-old Baby Doe rules misunderstood or mistaken? *Paediatrics* 115 (2005): 797–802.

18 M. Cuttini, M. Nadai, M. Kaminski, et al., End-of-life decisions in neonatal intensive care: physicians' self-reported practices in seven European countries, EURONIC Study Group, *Lancet* 355 (2000): 2112–18.

19 A.A.E. Verhagen and P.J.J. Sauer, The Groningen Protocol – euthanasia in severely ill newborns, *New England Journal of Medicine* 352 (2005): 959–62.

20 I. Illich, *Medical Nemesis*. New York: Basic Books, 1972.

21 G. Bosshard, T. Nilstun, J. Bilsen, et al., Forgoing treatment at the end of life in six European countries, *Archives of Internal Medicine* 165 (2005): 401–7.

22 David Orentlicher has stated that terminal sedation is essentially euthanasia in many cases, but can be induced without the patient's consent or even the patient's knowledge. It forces the patient to accept a dying process that is prolonged as compared with

VAE or PAS. See D. Orentlicher, The Supreme Court and physician-assisted suicide, *New England Journal of Medicine* 337 (17) (1997): 1236–9.

23 L.R. Kass, *Life, Liberty and the Defense of Dignity, The Challenge for Bioethics*, San Francisco: Encounter Books, 2002, p. 231ff.

24 E.J. Larson and D.W. Amundson, *Euthanasia and the Christian Tradition. A Different Death*. Downers Grove, IL: Intervarsity Press, 1998, p. 226ff.

Chapter 13

Drug Legalization

Douglas N. Husak

Introduction

Should drugs be legalized? Providing a thorough answer to this question involves many complex issues too large to discuss here. In this chapter, I will narrow the topic and confine myself to a specific issue. I will argue that much of the resistance to the legalization of drugs rests on a failure to distinguish the following two questions:

1   Should I use drugs?
2   Is the state justified in punishing me if I do?

Clearly, these two questions are different. The first asks what individual persons should do; the second asks what the state is justified in punishing persons for doing. But how are the answers to these questions related? I will contend that a negative answer to 1 provides virtually no support for a positive answer to 2. In other words, we should not be persuaded that the state would be justified in punishing me for using drugs simply because I shouldn't use them. The central purpose of this essay is to explain, support, and qualify my thesis that a great deal of opposition to drug legalization derives from a failure to understand the relation between the answers to these two questions.

Three preliminary matters are important before discussing each of these questions in turn. First, no "official" rationale for contemporary drug policy exists (Husak, 2002). Unlike judges, who must explain their decisions in written opinions, legislators need not provide reasons to justify the laws they enact. Legal philosophers who hope to evaluate the arguments in favor of punishing drug users must guess what these reasons are. This task is perilous; those who are skeptical of our punitive policies must guard against the tendency to attribute bad reasons to their opponents. In this chapter I examine only one of many possible reasons in favor of employing criminal sanctions against drug users. Of course, many additional reasons might exist – some of which may be more plausible than the reason I discuss here. But I do not claim to provide a comprehensive analysis of the case for drug proscriptions.

Second, I think it is indisputable that many commentators who support our current policies uncritically suppose that a negative answer to Question 1 provides powerful support for a positive answer to Question 2. Admittedly, direct evidence for this contention is hard to find. That is, few commentators explicitly say that the state is justified in punishing drug users *because* persons should not use drugs. Still, their commitment to this inference is apparent from the kinds of arguments they employ when called upon to defend the status quo. Whenever someone suggests that the criminal law should be changed so that persons are not punished for using a given drug, these commentators are bound to respond by citing some study or another that purports to show why persons should not use the drug in question. Generally, these studies allege that users of the given drug risk their health and well-being. If these studies are valid, they provide a perfectly good reason for individuals to abstain from the drug in question. All rational persons have an interest in preserving their health and well-being. The unstated assumption, however, is that these findings show why existing law should not be altered and persons who use that drug are justifiably punished. This is the assumption I will challenge here.

Third, some theorists may respond that I am discussing *criminalization* rather than *legalization*. There is remarkably little agreement among theorists about how these words should be defined. Some contend that *decriminalization* refers to the absence of state *punishments*, while *legalization* refers to the absence of state *regulations*. If so, no responsible person proposes that all drug use should be legalized. In other words, no responsible person advocates that drugs should be exempted from all state regulations. It is surprisingly difficult to find *any* item that is or ought to be entirely immune from state regulation; drugs are not good candidates for this unusual status (but see Szasz, 1992). We may disagree about what set of legal regulations should govern such matters as manufacture, sale, or use of given drugs. Some plausible examples include restrictions on age, limitations on time and place, bans on advertising, and the like. I will not attempt to describe an ideal set of regulations; trial and error are needed before anyone should be confident about what combinations of policies work best. In any event, since drug legalization *as defined above* is wildly implausible, I will suppose that the present inquiry involves what I have called decriminalization, and asks whether state punishments are justifiably imposed on drug users.

With these three preliminaries behind us, I now turn to an examination of each of the two questions I have raised. I will not be entirely successful in separating my discussion of these two issues. After all, my main reason to address Question 1 is to assess its relevance to Question 2. But I will try to examine each issue individually.

1 Should I Use Drugs?

In this section I will make three observations about Question 1: Should I use drugs? The first set of observations involve the word *should*; the second examine the nature of *drugs*; the third discuss the various *purposes* for which drugs are used. Without these observations, we have no realistic hope of answering this question, or of understanding its relation to Question 2: Is the state justified in punishing me if I use drugs?

First, the word *should* in this question is notoriously ambiguous. All uses of this word raise issues of practical reasoning. There are many different *kinds* of reasons for persons to act in one way rather than another; I will focus on two. Some uses of this word are *prudential*; they provide reasons of rational self-interest. Other uses of this word are *moral*. Philosophers locate the boundary between prudence and morality in different places, but almost no one believes the two realms coincide. Thus it is imperative to decide whether to construe the word *should* in Question 1 prudentially or morally. Clarifying this matter is important in its own right; different answers are plausible depending on how this ambiguity is resolved. Just as importantly, however, this matter must be settled before we can decide how an answer to Question 1 bears on an answer to Question 2.

Imagine a competent and rational adult sought guidance from someone more experienced and learned about how to conduct his life. He might ask such questions as: Should I complete my education? Should I exercise regularly? How often should I visit my doctor? What kinds of foods should I eat? He might also ask: Should I use drugs? The most sensible interpretation of the word *should* in these questions is prudential. If Question 1 is construed prudentially, how should it be answered? *Do* I act imprudently by using drugs? Most commentators are confident that the answer is yes. Drugs are widely thought to represent a handicap or obstacle, an impediment to just about any of our physical or intellectual goals. Despite conventional wisdom, however, empirical support for the imprudence of drug use is surprisingly hard to find. Once we move beyond anecdotes and generalizations from worst-case scenarios, what kind of data can we cite to demonstrate the folly of drug use? Obviously, drugs cause tangible harms to only a subset of persons who use them. If drug use is imprudent, it must be because of the *risks* they pose to our health and well-being. We cannot decide whether and to what extent drug use is imprudent unless we understand *how* risky drugs really are.

Epidemiological studies are the easiest and most obvious way to identify the hazards of any activity. If tobacco causes cancer, for example, one would expect that the cancer rates of smokers would be substantially higher than those of non-smokers. Of course, numerous studies confirm our worst fears about tobacco. What do epidemiological studies show about the effects of illicit drugs? If we divide the population into two groups – those who have used illicit drugs and those who have not – existing data do not uniformly reveal the former to be less healthy or well-off than the latter (Shedler and Block, 1990). From a welfare perspective, the

90 million American adults who have used illicit drugs are not readily distinguishable from the slightly greater number of Americans who have abstained throughout their lifetimes. Suppose, however, that the population is further subdivided into moderate and heavy drug users. A minority of individuals have consumed massive amounts of drugs over extended periods of time. Evidence about the health effects of heavy, long-term illicit drug use provides greater cause for alarm. This result is not surprising. Heavy drug use – like excess in just about anything else safely done in moderation – is imprudent.

Of course, all activities involve *some* risks. How can we hope to decide whether the risks of drug use are acceptable? Aggregate statistics are helpful in answering this question. According to estimates from the Office of the National Drug Control Policy (ONDCP), about 25,000 Americans die each year from using illicit drugs. This statistic is not very informative unless it is placed alongside data about the number of fatalities caused by other behaviors. Aggregate statistics about *licit* drugs provide the most obvious basis of comparison. First, consider the facts about licit drugs used for medical purposes. Approximately 100,000 people die each year from adverse reactions to their medications, making prescription drugs one of the leading causes of death in the United States (Cohen, 2001). The assumption that illicit drugs are unsafe, and prescription drugs are safe, is perhaps the greatest myth surrounding the debate about drug decriminalization.

Aggregate statistics about licit drugs used for non-medical purposes offer an even more obvious basis of comparison. Each year, tobacco kills about 430,000 people in the United States. The number of annual fatalities caused by alcohol is more controversial, but nearly all estimates exceed 100,000. By contrast, illicit drugs seem relatively benign. For example, no one has ever been known to die from smoking marijuana (Earlywine, 2002, pp. 143–4). Consider the 25,000 casualties the ONDCP attributes to illicit drugs. Few of these deaths are actually caused by drugs; a majority result from diseases like AIDS and hepatitis that are spread by sharing contaminated needles. Approximately 2,500 are caused intentionally; 1,600 are due to injuries inflicted "accidentally or purposely." Illicit drugs themselves cause remarkably few fatalities.

Of course, these aggregate figures do not give us much insight unless they take into account the fact that many more people use licit than illicit drugs. Naturally, we would expect to see more health problems caused by whatever drugs happen to be the most popular. Nonetheless, once we adjust our statistics to reflect this fact – and express the risk of various drugs by the ratio of fatalities per user – we reach the same conclusion. Nicotine is still the most lethal drug by a wide margin. About one-quarter of all persons who smoke a pack of cigarettes daily lose 10 to 15 years of their lives (Goodin, 1989, pp. 8–9). Illicit drugs are far less hazardous. If the punishment of drug offenders is designed to prevent persons from risking their lives, our society has criminalized the wrong substances.

So far, my statistics about the relative risks of licit and illicit drugs involve only fatalities. But the health problems caused by drugs also include various diseases and illnesses that lower the quality of life. Allegations about the health hazards of illicit drugs are many and varied. Drug use has been said to kill brain cells, impair memory and cognition, undermine motivation and performance, produce psychosis and insanity, destroy the immune system, hamper sex drive and reproduction, and generally contribute to hospital emergencies. Obviously, each of these allegations must be assessed drug-by-drug. How can we begin to evaluate the health hazards of illicit drugs?

Again, licit drugs used for medical purposes provide an appropriate basis of comparison. Illicit drugs tend to be less injurious than many licit drugs. Legal medications cause between one million and 5.5 million hospitalizations every year. Approximately 70,000 of these annual hospitalizations are caused by common anti-inflammatories like Advil and Tylenol. But data about licit drugs used for non-medical purposes are even more relevant. Tobacco is a major cause of coronary artery disease, peripheral vascular disease, cerebrovascular diseases, as well as many kinds of cancers. Alcohol is known to be a contributing factor to as many as 75 human diseases and conditions. Heavy drinkers increase their risk of gastrointestinal disorders, heart disease, and high blood pressure. But relatively few known mechanisms link illicit drug use to common diseases.

Admittedly, marijuana smoke is carcinogenic. But the quantity of smoke inhaled over time is the most important factor in predicting the likelihood of cancer. Since users of marijuana tend to smoke so much less than users of tobacco products, epidemiological statistics fail to show higher rates of cancer in smokers of marijuana (Earlywine, 2002, p. 156). Cocaine increases the risk of coronary artery disease, which is particularly worrisome for those with pre-existing heart problems – but is not otherwise implicated in common physical diseases. Heavy users may develop paranoia, which includes anxiety, sleeplessness, and hypertension. But many of these same symptoms are common in alcoholics; up to 85 percent of frequent cocaine users are heavy drinkers, making the effects of the two substances difficult to disentangle. Comparable problems surround attempts to measure the health risks of opiates. Contemporary heroin addicts tend to lead notoriously unhealthy life-styles, eat terrible diets, avoid doctors, and smoke large numbers of cigarettes. But opiates themselves seem to be fairly nontoxic; addicts whose lifestyles are otherwise healthy and who have a steady supply of heroin suffer primarily from constipation, with few other difficulties. In short, the use of illicit drugs is not especially high on the list of health problems in the United States today.

Thus far I have neglected to mention the most compelling prudential reason not to use illicit drugs. In the United States today, illicit drug users face arrest, prosecution, and punishment. Approximately 410,000 persons are currently imprisoned for drug offenses in the United States; 130,000 were convicted of mere possession. About 1.5 million drug arrests were made in 2003. Although these legal consequences provide an obvious prudential reason not to use illicit drugs, it is easy to see why they lend no support to the case for criminalization. These legal consequences arise only because drug use is *already* a criminal offense; they do not provide an independent justification to enact these criminal laws.

Perhaps, however, I have misinterpreted the *should* in the question: Should I use drugs? Arguably, it is better construed as raising a moral than a prudential inquiry. *Why* might drug use be morally wrongful? How *can* the act of ingesting a substance be immoral? These questions raise some of the most divisive issues in contemporary drug policy. Unfortunately, those who are convinced that illicit drug use is immoral almost never try to answer them. That is, they rarely offer a reason to support their vehement moral condemnation of illicit drug use. Many prohibitionists apparently regard this belief as self-evident. Clearly, this sort of response – or lack of response – is unhelpful. As long as conclusions about the immorality of drug use are not defended, we have no reply to people who disagree or are undecided, and do not regard this belief as obvious.

Some prohibitionists appeal to public opinion polls to try to support their belief that the use of illicit drugs is immoral (Blendon and Young, 1998). They point to surveys that indicate that roughly two-thirds of Americans agree that illicit drug use is morally wrong. Seventy-six percent report that they would continue to oppose the legalization of cocaine and heroin, even if they could be guaranteed that it would lead to less crime. For at least three reasons, however, public opinion polls fail to establish that illicit drug use is immoral. The first point is the most obvious. Moral controversies simply cannot be resolved by surveys. We could make no sense of the claim that the majority might be mistaken about morality if disputes of this kind could be resolved by a poll. Next, the answers respondents give to pollsters are greatly affected by how the question is framed. When the public is asked whether they believe that drug use is immoral, they may think that they are being asked about personal or private morality – about what they believe is right or wrong *for them*. Respondents are less likely to judge that *others* behave immorally when they use drugs. Finally and most controversially, I think these surveys lead us to exactly the opposite conclusion about drug prohibition. We had better have a very powerful consensus about the immorality of given kinds of behavior before we should feel confident about punishing those who disagree with us. But 49 percent of American respondents do *not* agree with the statement that all illicit drug use is morally wrong and intolerable. About 14 percent of Americans believe that all drugs should be legalized. No other crime – at least no other crime punished with comparable severity – gives rise to such ambivalence. When dissent is significant, we should entertain the possibility that the majority might be mistaken. Prohibitionists who defend criminalization because polls reveal drug use to be immoral should feel embarrassed rather than vindicated when the data reveal the extent to which our citizenry is so deeply divided.

Thus far, all of my attention on Question 1 has focused on how to construe the crucial word *should*. But Question 1 requires clarification for a different reason. This question asks whether I should use drugs. Unless we have a reasonably clear idea about what substances are drugs, we will be hard-pressed to provide a principled answer to it. Debates in drug policy have proceeded as though the opposed parties understand what they are talking about when they argue about drugs. Definitional issues have escaped notice because the disputants have been content to talk about particular kinds of substances like marijuana, cocaine, and heroin, with no real need to decide what makes them drugs. We *can* debate what to do about these substances. But the failure to examine why these substances are *drugs* threatens to impoverish the debate. On any sensible definition, lots of substances qualify as drugs, even though the legitimacy of their use is taken for granted. We cannot fail to be aware that different policies for different drugs are firmly in place; criminalization has always been *selective*. We do not punish adult users of alcohol or tobacco, and caffeine is permitted even for children. Are these substances really drugs? Why or why not?

Unfortunately, no entirely satisfactory definition of a drug exists. Consider the definition most frequently contained in statutes that prohibit drugs: "Any substance other than food which by its chemical nature affects the structure or function of the living organism" (Uelmen and Haddox, 1985, p. 1). What is noteworthy about this definition is what it does *not* contain. It does not purport to use the *law* to distinguish substances that are drugs from those that are not. For this reason, this definition deviates from how ordinary speakers of English tend to identify drugs. Empirical studies indicate that respondents are more inclined to classify a substance as a drug when its use is banned. Relatively few Americans regard alcohol, tobacco, or caffeine as drugs, while nearly everyone recognizes heroin, cocaine, and marijuana as drugs. But nothing in the definition of a drug provides any reason to exempt alcohol, tobacco, and caffeine from the scope of a comprehensive drug policy. Unquestionably, alcohol, tobacco, and caffeine *are* drugs according to the foregoing definition. There is no pharmacological basis for questioning the categorization of these substances as drugs. These substances are *licit* drugs.

Surely the question of whether a given substance is a drug should depend on its pharmacological properties and its effects on persons who use it, rather than on whether or how it is legally regulated. The status of a substance as a drug should not fluctuate as legal regulations are imposed and repealed. Opiates and cocaine were not suddenly transformed from non-drugs into drugs in the early part of the twentieth century, when the state first began to punish people for using them (Musto, 1999). Moreover, a drug does not magically become something other than a drug at the moment its use is legalized. Most importantly, we need to decide whether our punitive drug policies can be justified. Surely this inquiry is sensible. We should not prevent our conclusions about drug policy from being applied to licit substances simply because we have used the law to define them as something other than drugs. Once we realize that many familiar licit substances are drugs, we must find morally relevant distinctions between the drugs that should be allowed and those that should be prohibited. This task has proved daunting.

Perhaps we should decide which substances are drugs based on whether they have psychotropic effects, generally understood as an influence on mood or behavior. But this definition runs into trouble with a variety of substances, most notably sugar. An alternative suggestion, to characterize drugs in terms of their addictive properties, defines the obscure in terms of the mysterious, since there are as many different senses of addiction as there are definitions of drugs (Morse, 2000). The presence or absence of withdrawal symptoms is not a useful criterion, since withdrawal does not occur from all substances generally categorized as drugs (such as LSD), but does occur from many activities not ever classified as drugs (most notably in the case of love). Such difficulties are not merely theoretical; the problem of deciding whether given substances qualify as drugs has emerged as an important problem in public health. Any "health food store" contains a great number of substances that are alleged to be effective in treating various ailments and conditions. The manufacture and distribution of these substances often escapes most regulations – with potentially serious consequences to persons who use them (Nestle, 2002). Many of these substances are said to be "herbs" or "herbal remedies." Are herbs drugs? If not, is marijuana a drug? Return to the above definition. The only possible basis for disqualifying herbs as drugs is that herbs are foods. Are herbs foods? Can they be both foods and drugs? Are they neither foods nor drugs?

Our best definition of drugs is not very helpful in answering these straightforward questions. We do not really have a good idea of what a drug is. The plain fact is that, in many cases, we have no clear means of deciding whether a given substance is or is not a drug. If we don't know what a drug is, we may be unable to construct anything that deserves to be called a *drug policy*. Arguably, we will not make progress if we retain a concept that we don't understand. Perhaps we should abandon this concept altogether. Despite these misgivings, I will continue to pretend that we know what we mean when we ask questions – like Questions 1 and 2 – about drugs.

A final set of issues must be addressed in order to answer Question 1. We cannot hope to decide whether persons should use a drug without specifying the *purpose* for which that drug is taken. If so, the topic is not really about drug use per se, but rather about a particular *kind* of drug use – that is, a particular *reason* for using drugs. We might well decide that one and the same drug – cocaine, morphine, or Prozac – should be allowed for some purposes, but prohibited for others. Presumably, the use of these drugs should not be a criminal offense when people have a *medical* reason to take them. No one has qualms about entering a drug store to purchase a substance for a medical purpose. But attitudes, reactions, and state policies can be entirely different when that same drug is taken for a non-medical purpose. Although drugs can be used for several different kinds of non-medical purposes, one such purpose is especially significant. This use is *recreational*. It is hard to be precise in characterizing when use is recreational. Roughly, people engage in recreational activities to seek pleasure, euphoria, satisfaction, or some other positive psychological state. When a drug is used in order to attain a positive psychological state – a drug *high* – I will call that use recreational.

The contrast between medical and recreational drug use is *not* a contrast between two kinds of drugs. Again, one and the same drug might be used for either a medical or a recreational purpose. Therefore, the term "recreational drug" is potentially misleading. Since just about any drug might be used for a recreational purpose, a recreational drug can only be a drug that is *typically* or *generally* used for a recreational purpose. Alcohol is one such drug. Marijuana is another. But since these drugs can be (and are) used non-recreationally, we should not classify them as "recreational drugs." Instead, we should categorize them as drugs with a predominant recreational *use*. To be precise, we should always use the adverbial form of the word *recreational*. The word modifies the verb "use," as in "to use recreationally," rather than the noun "drug," as in "recreational drug."

Prudential and legal responses toward drug users depend on the purpose for which that drug is used. A recreational user of a given drug may face severe punishment; nothing at all is done to that person when his use of that same drug is medical. Since this distinction is so important, one would hope that the line between medical and recreational purposes would be fairly clear. If the contrast between medical and recreational use proves very hard to draw, we can anticipate that the response of the state – which depends on this contrast – will prove difficult to justify.

When *are* drugs used medically? Generally, drugs are used for a medical rather than for a recreational purpose when they are used to treat a medical condition – a *disease* or *illness*. Whether a given condition is *really* a disease cannot be answered without a theory, or a criterion, to distinguish those conditions that are diseases or illnesses from those that are not. We can evade this question by trusting doctors to draw this contrast. But how do doctors perform this function? In many cases, determining that a condition is a disease is beyond controversy. No one challenges the classification of cancer as a disease. In a growing number of cases, however, we cannot provide a satisfactory answer to this question.

The line between conditions that are diseases or illnesses and those that are not – and the corresponding distinction between medical and recreational drug use – has always been tenuous, and is becoming more difficult to draw every day. The difficulty is compounded because drugs no longer are prescribed only for the treatment of disease or illness. The conditions for which drugs are prescribed now include *syndromes* and *disorders*. Confidence in our ability to detect a medical condition when we see one evaporates in the face of the growing number of syndromes and disorders that are recognized today. What exactly *is* a syndrome or disorder? Many commentators have noted that we live in an era in which our problems tend to be *medicalized* (Peele, 1989). That is, most every problem or shortcoming is conceptualized as a medical condition, eligible for treatment with drugs. The phenomenon of medicalization is most pervasive in the United States, which leads the world in the consumption of licit drugs to change mood and behavior. Sexual conditions – and drugs used to treat these conditions – illustrate this phenomenon. Consider Viagra, for example. Does the inability to maintain an erection really qualify as a medical condition – the disease or syndrome of erectile dysfunction? How should we decide? After all, the condition this drug treats has little to do with reproduction and everything to do with sexual pleasure. Viagra is used largely by men who are beyond the age at which they want to reproduce; it is taken for purposes that seemingly qualify as recreational. At the very least, such drugs illustrate the difficulty of drawing the line between medical and recreational use.

Sex is not the only context in which the contrast between medical and recreational drug use becomes fuzzy. If a drug qualifies as medical when used to enhance sexual performance, what should we say about a drug that enhances the pleasure of other activities – such as eating, watching movies, or listening to music? How should we categorize drugs used for the many "eating disorders" that now are recognized? These questions are important, because people who use these same drugs for recreational purposes can be sent to prison. Even if some of these questions are fanciful at the present time, there is no reason to doubt that pharmaceutical companies are capable of creating substances that add to the pleasure of everyday tasks or help us to reshape our bodies. If existing drugs do not demonstrate the difficulties of drawing the line between recreational and medical use, we can be sure that new drugs are on the horizon that will blur that line to the vanishing point.

When a distinction proves virtually impossible to draw, we should review our reasons for trying to draw it. Why should it really *matter* whether a drug is used for a medical or a recreational purpose? As I have indicated, our prudential attitudes and legal responses attach enormous significance to this distinction. Persons who use opiates medically are left alone; persons who use them recreationally face severe punishments. Why does recreational drug use, as opposed to medical drug use, justify punitive measures? Ultimately, I do not believe that a satisfactory answer can be provided. The distinction between recreational and medical use, which has proved so hard to draw, is probably not worth preserving as a cornerstone of our drug policy. It makes little sense to confidently proclaim: Persons should not use drugs, except when their use is medical.

2 Is the State Justified in Punishing Drug Users?

Is the state justified in punishing me if I use drugs? Despite the interpretive uncertainties discussed above, I will construe this question to ask whether the state is justified in punishing people who use illicit substances like marijuana, cocaine, and heroin for recreational purposes.

I take questions about whether given activities should be punished to be equivalent to questions about whether these activities should be criminalized. Persons become subject to state punishment if and only if they have committed a crime. Thus it is incoherent to believe that users of a given drug should not be punished, and yet to oppose the decriminalization of that drug. Of course, someone may endorse decriminalization while advocating a variety of state responses designed to discourage drug use. Perhaps the state should deny benefits and withhold privileges from drug users. Reasonable minds may differ about whether given kinds of state responses to drug users – like mandatory treatments – are modes of punishment. But no one who supports drug decriminalization can agree that a particular response is a type of punishment and continue to believe that drug users should be subjected to it.

In order to decide whether drug use (or anything else) should be punished, we need a *theory of criminalization* – a set of principles to determine whether given kinds of conduct should be proscribed. We need such a theory to decide whether to accept some reasons frequently given in favor of imposing criminal punishments. Consider two examples. In section 1, I stated that persons who use given drugs for medical purposes are exempted from the punishments inflicted upon persons who use those same drugs recreationally. But this statement requires qualification; the fact that a drug is used for a medical purpose does not resolve all questions about whether its use should be permitted. Consider the contemporary debate surrounding the medical use of marijuana (Joy et al., 1999). Few medical practitioners still deny that marijuana is effective against diseases like glaucoma. Despite this concession, some commentators insist that *all* users should be punished. They fear that a relaxation of prohibition would "send the wrong message" and increase non-medicinal marijuana use. Their argument, then, is that some patients should be punished for using an effective medicine because others would be more likely to abuse that drug if its use were tolerated. A theory of criminalization is needed to decide whether the penal sanction is justifiably imposed for this purpose.

Second, some individuals are subject to punishment even if they have a medical reason to use a drug that is not likely to be abused by others. Many drugs are permitted for medical use only for patients who have obtained a prescription from a licensed physician. If a person somehow manages to get her hands on such a drug despite lacking a prescription – say, by using drugs prescribed to her spouse – she becomes subject to criminal liability. The rationale for punishment cannot be that such persons cannot benefit from using drugs that have not been prescribed to them. Instead, the rationale must be that criminal punishments are needed to maintain the prescription drug system, which, on balance, does more good than harm. Again, a theory of criminalization is needed to determine whether this argument justifies impositions of the penal sanction. Arguably, the prescription drug system can be preserved without the need to punish drug users.

Ultimately, then, the case for or against drug prohibitions requires a theory of criminalization. I take it to be a moral truism that all punishments must be justified. Philosophers disagree radically about *what* justifies punishment, but none suggests that a justification is not required. If so, any law that subjects persons to punishment must be justified as well. It is impossible to decide whether a given punishment is justified without attending to the content of the criminal law for which it is inflicted. That is, punishment is not justified simply because persons have broken a duly enacted criminal law; the criminal law itself must proscribe conduct for which criminal sanctions are justifiably imposed.

A theory of criminalization is not equivalent to a set of principles about the legitimate purpose or function of law generally. The state may tax, discourage, or require that persons pay compensation for given behaviors, even though it lacks a justification for punishing them. The criminal law is *different*; it is unlike other bodies of law. The most obvious difference is that criminal punishments are unique in their severity. As a type of response, penal sanctions are the most severe hardship the state can impose. In addition, the criminal law is unlike other bodies of law because criminal sanctions are uniquely designed to express censure. A civil penalty like a fine may cause a deprivation every bit as severe as a punishment, but is not intended to stigmatize. We should not criminalize drug use unless we are confident that drug users should be subjected to the deprivations and stigma inherent in punishment.

Thus we need a rationale for censuring and imposing hardship on persons who use drugs. Of course, criminalization may be selective; we might find a justification for punishing recreational users of some but not all drugs. As I have indicated, the criminal law is already selective in its drug policy; alcohol, tobacco, and caffeine are permitted. If decriminalization is to be extended beyond its present boundaries, it is apparent that marijuana – the most widely used and least dangerous illicit recreational drug – is the sensible place to begin. But the case for criminalization should not be taken for granted for *any* substance. Why should the state *ever* punish persons for using drugs?

Unfortunately, legal philosophers have reached almost no consensus about the principles in a theory of criminalization that are relevant to this question. Nonetheless, we can make progress discerning how a negative answer to Question 1 might bear on an answer to Question 2, even without a comprehensive theory about the limits of the criminal sanction. We might begin by asking how a negative answer to 1 could *possibly* support an affirmative answer to 2. In other words, how might punishments be justified by whatever reasons show that people should not use drugs? In all likelihood, the answer is that punishing users will deter some persons from using drugs, thereby causing fewer people to do what they shouldn't do.

The extent to which punishments deter is extraordinarily complex, varying from one offense to another. But most criminologists are skeptical that punishments for drug offenses are very effective as deterrents (MacCoun and Reuter, 2001). The empirical evidence for deterrence is not impressive; decades of a concerted "war on drugs" have not succeeded in curbing rates of illicit drug use. Theorists have tried to explain why deterrence for drug offenses is relatively weak. Since drug transactions are consensual and tend to lack a complaining victim, the probability of arrest and prosecution is too low to dissuade prospective offenders. The criminal justice system tries to compensate by increasing the severity of punishments, but this variable is among the least important in deterring specific behaviors.

Two mechanisms explain why punishments may actually *increase* drug use. First, prohibited behaviors are often subject to a "forbidden fruit" effect. In some populations, criminalization may add to the allure of drugs. Second, those drug offenders who are convicted and incarcerated must eventually be released. Because of the long sentences frequently imposed on them, these persons are less able to find employment, or housing, or to re-establish ties with their families. As a result, they are more likely to resort to deviance – including subsequent drug use.

Moreover, even if we concede that drugs are bad for persons who use them, it hardly follows that punishments are better. Theorists have provided many reasons to believe that drug prohibitions are counter-productive, causing more harm than good (Nadelmann, 1989). Prohibition has created black markets and removed illicit drugs from FDA supervision. As we have seen, most of the fatalities attributed to drugs are really caused by their delivery systems. In addition, buyers do not know the purity or potency of the drugs they consume, increasing risks of overdose. Regulations that are easily implemented under a regime of decriminalization would probably make drugs less hazardous to health. I emphasize these points because virtually any basis for inferring a positive answer to Question 2 from a negative answer to Question 1 seemingly presupposes that punishments will be somewhat effective in reducing the harms of drug use. If this presupposition is dubious, we are left with almost no basis to infer that the state is justified in punishing drug users from the statement that persons should not use drugs.

A few other points need not await the details of a theory of criminalization. Recall the discussion in section 1 about how to interpret the word *should* in the question: Should I use drugs? If the *should* in this question is construed prudentially, as seems likely, it would be extraordinary to believe that a negative answer to Question 1 supports a positive answer to 2. That is, we almost never think that persons are justifiably punished for their imprudent behavior. Surely it is preposterous to suppose that answers to many questions about rational self-interest (for example, should I eat vegetables, floss my teeth, or get a colonoscopy when I turn 50?) provide a good reason to inflict punishments. Whatever might be said on behalf of *paternalism* – coercion designed to protect persons from the consequences of their own decisions – *criminal* paternalism is rarely justified (Husak, 2003). In particular, severe punishments cannot plausibly be defended as good for the very persons on whom they are imposed. Even if the welfare of individuals is retarded by drug use, their welfare is diminished even more by punishment.

In section 1, I indicated that our society has criminalized the wrong substances if punishments are designed to prevent users from risking their lives, health, and general well-being. This point is not simply one of consistency. The question is not "if the state endeavors to protect us by punishing users of illicit drugs, why doesn't the state also punish people who smoke tobacco and drink alcohol?" After all, this inconsistency can be rectified in either of two ways – by repealing laws against illicit drug use, or by enacting laws against the consumption of alcohol and tobacco. The latter alternative, however, is unthinkable. No one explicitly recommends that we should throw smokers and drinkers into jail in order to reduce the personal problems caused by these licit substances. Why not? The best answer is that punishing smokers or drinkers would be unjust. The point, then, is that the criminalization of illicit drug use is unjust for the very same reason that applies to proposals to criminalize the use of licit drugs (but see Sher, 2003).

Although I have contrasted the risks of illicit drugs with those of licit drugs, we should look elsewhere – beyond drugs of any kind – to demonstrate the implausibility of using the criminal law to protect us from acting against our self-interest. As I have indicated, many behaviors that do not involve drugs are far more risky to health and welfare, even though no one would dream of using the criminal law to prohibit them. Perhaps unhealthy foods provide the best source of examples. More than half of all Americans are now overweight. The millions of obese adults far outnumber illicit drug users, and the health hazards of excessive weight are more easily demonstrated than those of illicit drugs. According to the Center for Disease Control and Prevention, obesity accounts for about 300,000 deaths a year – far more than all illicit and licit drugs (except tobacco) combined. Yet high-calorie foods that cause obesity are hardly the only examples that illustrate my point. Illicit recreational drugs do not pose significant health risks relative to any number of recreational activities that we tolerate and even applaud. Mountain climbing and competitive sports like boxing provide excellent examples. In short, no other recreational activity is singled out for severe punishments because of its risks to health and welfare. The only conceivable basis for treating illicit drugs differently from other recreational activities is that the former are more risky, by a substantial degree, than the latter. But illicit drug use is *not* more risky than any number of these behaviors.

But what if the word *should* in Question 1 is construed morally? Doesn't the (supposed) immorality of drug use provide a good reason to prohibit it? To be sure, immoral behavior is a better candidate for criminal liability than mere imprudence. *Legal moralists* believe that immorality is sufficient for criminality (Feinberg, 1984). But the legal moralist case for punishing drug users encounters two formidable hurdles. First, as I observed in section 1, no moral argument against drug use has been defended. In addition, legal moralism itself has been rejected by most criminal theorists (but see Moore, 1997). Many instances of conduct more clearly immoral than drug use are not and presumably ought not to be criminalized – breaking promises or lying, to name two prominent examples.

Admittedly, it is hard to make more progress in resolving Question 2 – or in determining how an answer to Question 1 bears upon it – without a theory of criminalization. The theory we ultimately accept, however, must be sensitive to the distinction between criminal and non-criminal legislation. As I have indicated, the criminal law is different in that it subjects persons to punishment. By definition, punishment involves the imposition of both hardship and condemnation, each of which is a clear violation of rights in the absence of a compelling justification. Thus an adequate theory will demand a higher standard of justification for criminal than for non-criminal laws. I am skeptical that a viable theory of criminalization will allow persons to be punished simply for using drugs, but we cannot be confident of this conclusion until such a theory is produced.

Conclusion

In the absence of an official defense of laws that punish drug users, commentators who are skeptical of the status quo must speculate about the reasons that might support it. Many possible rationales might be offered. The claim that persons should not use drugs, however, is not a very plausible basis for concluding that the state is justified in punishing drug users.

References

Blendon, Robert J. and Young, John T. (1998), The public and the war on illicit drugs, *Journal of the American Medical Association* 279: 827–32.

Cohen, Jay S. (2001), *Overdose: The Case Against the Drug Companies*, New York: Jeremy P. Tarcher/Putnam.

Earlywine, Mitch (2002), *Understanding Marijuana: A New Look at the Scientific Evidence*, New York: Oxford University Press.

Feinberg, Joel (1984), *Harm to Others: The Moral Limits of the Criminal Law*, New York: Oxford University Press.

Goodin, Robert E. (1989), *No Smoking: The Ethical Issues*, Chicago, IL: University of Chicago Press.

Husak, Douglas (2002), *Legalize This! The Case for Decriminalizing Drugs*, London: Verso.

Husak, Douglas (2003), Legal paternalism, in Hugh LaFollette (ed.), *The Oxford Handbook of Practical Ethics*, Oxford: Oxford University Press, (pp. 387–412).

Joy, Janet, Watson, Stanley, and Benson, John (1999), *Marijuana and Medicine: Assessing the Science Base*, Washington, DC: National Academy Press.

MacCoun, Robert J., and Reuter, Peter (2001), *Drug War Heresies: Learning from Other Vices, Times, and Places*, Cambridge: Cambridge University Press.

Moore, Michael (1997), *Placing Blame*, Oxford: Clarendon Press.

Morse, Stephen J. (2000), Addiction and responsibility, *Law and Philosophy* 19: 3–49.

Musto, David (1999), *The American Disease: Origins of Narcotics Control*, New York: Oxford University Press.

Nadelmann, Ethan A. (1989), Drug prohibition in the United States: costs, consequences, and alternatives, *Science* 245: 939–47.

Nestle, Marion (2002), *Food Politics: How the Food Industry Influences Nutrition and Health*, Berkeley: University of California Press.

Peele, Stanton (1989), *The Diseasing of America*, Boston, MA: Houghton Mifflin.

Shedler, Jonathan, and Block, Jack (1990), Adolescent drug use and psychological health, *American Psychologist* 35: 612–30.

Sher, George (2003), On the decriminalization of drugs, *Criminal Justice Ethics* 22: 30–3.

Szasz, Thomas. (1992), *Our Right to Drugs: The Case for a Free Market*, New York: Praeger.

Uelmen, Gerald F. and Haddox, Victor G. (1985), *Drug Abuse and the Law Sourcebook*, New York: Clark Boardman Company.

Further Reading

Courtwright, David T. (2001), *Forces of Habit: Drugs and the Making of the Modern World*, Cambridge, MA: Harvard University Press.

Davenport-Hines, Richard (2001), *The Pursuit of Oblivion: A Global History of Narcotics*, London: Weidenfeld and Nicolson.

Fish, Jefferson M. (ed.) (1998), *How to Legalize Drugs*, London: Jason Aronson.

Heymann, Philip B. and Brownsberger, William N. (eds.) (2001), *Drug Addiction and Drug Policy*, Cambridge, MA: Harvard University Press.

Husak, Douglas (1992), *Drugs and Rights*, Cambridge: Cambridge University Press.

Husak, Douglas (2004), Guns and drugs: case studies on the principled limits of the criminal sanction, *Law and Philosophy* 23: 437–93.

Iversen, Leslie L. (2000), *The Science of Marijuana*, Oxford: Oxford University Press.

Kleiman, Mark A. (1992), *Against Excess: Drug Policy for Results*, New York: Basic Books.

Krauss, Melvyn B. and Lazear, Edward P. (eds.) (1991), *Searching for Alternatives: Drug-Control Policy in the United States*, Stanford, CA: Hoover Institution Press.

Luper-Foy, Steven, and Brown, Curtis (eds.) (1994), *Drugs, Morality, and the Law*, New York: Garland Publishing.

Parker, Howard, Aldridge, Judith, and Measham, Fiona (1998), *Illegal Leisure: The Normalization of Adolescent Recreational Drug Use*, New York: Routledge.

Sullum, Jacob (2003), *Saying Yes: In Defense of Drug Use*, New York: Jeremy P. Tarcher/Putnam.

Zimmer, Lynn, and Morgan, John P. (1997), *Marijuana Myths, Marijuana Facts*, New York: Lindesmith Center.

Zimring, Franklin E. and Hawkins, Gordon (1992), *The Search for Rational Drug Control*, Cambridge: Cambridge University Press.

Chapter 14

Selling Organs, Gametes, and Surrogacy Services[1]

Janet Radcliffe Richards

The Problem

The exchange of goods and services for money is among the commonest of human activities, and this is not surprising. Trade is just a sophisticated form of barter – one that comes about when a society is organized enough to institute money as a means of indirect exchange – and barter is exchange that both parties involved regard as beneficial. As such, it is likely to happen spontaneously whenever one person has anything transferable that another wants, and for which the buyer is offering a high enough price to make the transfer worthwhile to the seller.

As this is a perfectly general point, it applies to even the most intimate categories of transferable goods, such as body parts or bodily services. Prostitution is the most obvious and notorious case in point, but it is not the only long-established kind. Women have always been able to suckle each other's children or bear children to give other women, and if they can give such services they can, and in at least the first case often did, receive payment for them. The same has even been true of body parts, to a limited extent. Presumably hair has always been sold, and as dentistry advanced there was certainly a market for teeth. It was inevitable, therefore, that as science developed new ways of making parts or functions of one person's body useful to others, corresponding markets would spontaneously develop – along with all the networks, organizations, and professional facilitators that characterize buying and selling in general.

Still, the fact that markets for transferable body parts and bodily services are bound to develop unless actively prevented does not mean they should be condoned or allowed, and many people have the feeling that payment in these contexts is straightforwardly wrong. When the news of kidney selling by live donors first broke, for instance, the reaction, at least in the west, was remarkable for both its immediacy and its virtual unanimity. Doctors involved were struck off the register for manifestly inappropriate conduct even though they had broken no explicit rules, professional associations pronounced the practice anathema, and governments rushed to make it illegal.

The subject of payment for body parts and bodily services is difficult to discuss in general terms because there is no clear dividing line between goods and services that involve bodies and ones that do not. There is a sense, for instance, in which all paid employment involves putting bodies at the service of others. Individuals and societies differ considerably in their views of which monetary transactions are unacceptable, and countries vary in the ones they prohibit.[2] In the case of surrogacy, for instance, the USA permits more or less normal commercial arrangements,[3] the UK forbids commercial arrangements but allows private payments between individuals,[4] while other European countries forbid payment, or even surrogacy, altogether.[5] Payment for organ donation is condemned altogether by The Transplantation Society (the international association of doctors involved in transplantation) and is now illegal in most countries, with some so determined to prevent surreptitious payments that they disallow even the payment of expenses.[6] In other countries it may be technically legal and even much practiced, but nevertheless kept in the dark (Israel). One or two countries allow it openly; others allow it under considerable restrictions.[7]

Because the range of goods and services encompassed by the vague category of ones involving the human body is so wide, and attitudes to payment for most of them so varied, anything approaching a comprehensive discussion of them would need a substantial and regularly updated book. What is most needed in a constantly shifting terrain, however, is a methodology for thinking through the issues as they arise. That is what I shall present.

I shall concentrate for illustration mainly on the issue of kidney selling by live donors, because that seems to produce the strongest and most uniform opposition. But the line of argument offered is equally applicable to all other issues of prohibited payment; and, indeed, with appropriate adjustments, to all areas of practical ethics.

The Burden of Proof

To say that buying and selling will develop as soon as people perceive the possibility of mutually beneficial exchange is not to say anything about its justifiability. The whole purpose of laws and social pressures is to change what people would do if left to their own devices. Nevertheless, the fact that any proposed transaction is seen as desirable by both parties involved is enough to establish, by just about anyone's standards, a presumption in favor of it.

In the case of kidney selling, furthermore, that presumption is strengthened by the fact that the buyer is desperately trying to avoid imminent death, or at least to escape the crippling restrictions of dialysis. It is also strengthened, paradoxically, by the very fact most often raised as an objection: the extreme poverty typical of the sellers. They presumably do not like the prospect of selling a kidney any more than do the horrified westerners who want to protect them from themselves, but if they regard kidney selling as their best option they must regard their current situation as even worse. Anyone in favor of saving life and alleviating poverty should therefore regard the presumption in favor of permitting trade as even stronger in this case than in many others.

Such a presumption, of course, still falls a long way short of providing a justification. We routinely override presumptions in favor of or against particular actions and policies because we regard them as outweighed by more important considerations. Medicine is full of such cases. There are strong presumptions against cutting people open, filling them with toxic chemicals, and causing them pain, but doctors do these things all the time because in spite of their being bad in one respect they are regarded as justified *all things considered*. Similarly, although exchanges that both parties see as beneficial should be regarded as good in that respect, some may nevertheless be unjustified all things considered, and appropriately prevented.

Nevertheless, even though the presumption in favor of allowing people to exchange money for body parts is nowhere near decisive, it is methodologically important. If the debate starts with a recognition that any sale is regarded by both transacting parties as beneficial, it puts the burden of proof on the other side. This makes no difference to the logic of the matter, since if opponents can raise objections strong enough to outweigh the presumption, those objections will work wherever the argument starts. But it makes a great deal of difference to the conduct of an argument that usually starts with the conviction that organ selling must be wrong.

Schematically, then, the challenge for opponents of kidney selling is to construct an argument that starts with a presumption in favor of allowing the sale of kidneys, but reaches the conclusion that it should nevertheless be prohibited. It would have to take the form:

> There is a (strong) presumption in favor of allowing the sale of kidneys
> But
>
> _____
>
> Therefore it should be prohibited.

The challenge is to fill the "but" premise in such a way as to support the conclusion.

Setting up the argument in this way makes it clear that there is no a priori limit to the number of candidate objections that might be attempted, and in practice the refutation of one is followed quickly by the sprouting of others. However, keeping the formal structure in mind helps to prevent the kind of blur that allows a series of bad arguments to pass as cumulatively compelling.

What follows is a selection of the most familiar attempts.

"But they are incompetent to consent"

One claim that appeared very early on in the debate was that although both parties might seem to have agreed to the transaction, the consent of at least one was not valid. In populations poor enough to be tempted by kidney selling, would-be sellers would be too uneducated to understand the risks involved and therefore incompetent to consent (Sells, 1993; Broyer, 1991).[8]

This line of argument is precarious from the start, because no one really believes the premise. A good many people from well-educated populations have said they would sell if they were allowed to and the reward were high enough, and even people from uneducated groups seem to be regarded as competent to consent when the issue is unpaid kidney donation. The idea that would-be sellers must be incompetent to consent probably depends on the question-begging assumption that wanting to sell an organ is in itself proof of incompetence.

But even if significant numbers of potential organ sellers were incompetent to consent, this would still not be enough to support the conclusion that there should be a total prohibition. To make the transition you would need to insert an additional premise, such as "if a significant number of people are incompetent to consent to a procedure, it should be forbidden to everyone." It is hard to imagine many people trying to defend such a claim. Our usual principles about autonomy and consent demand our assessing competence on a case-by-case basis and, where non-competence results from ignorance rather than incapacity, trying to provide enough information to bring about competence.

"But they are coerced into selling"

A variation on the theme of invalid consent lies in the claim that the problem is not so much the sellers' competence as their situation. It is said that they are coerced into organ selling by poverty, and that coerced consent is not genuine.[9]

Here it may perhaps be allowed that there is a (considerably extended) sense in which the first premise is likely to be true for most potential sellers. Coercion typically involves a coercer's deliberately curtailing the range of options available until the best one left is the one the coercer wants the victim to choose; and poverty, even though it has no intentions, is a severe curtailer of options. Nobody would choose to have a healthy kidney removed if better options were available.

However, even though it may be agreed that most sellers' options are severely limited by poverty, the second claim, that coerced consent is not genuine, is not true – at least in any sense that supports the conclusion that the choice should be disallowed. If a kidnapper tried to coerce money out of you by threatening to kill your child, you would not have much gratitude to a well-intentioned bystander who leapt in to prevent your handing over the money, on the grounds that your consent was not genuine, and left you with a dead child. The kidnapper would have reduced your range of options, but that would not make your consent to the best remaining option anything other than genuine (Radcliffe Richards, 1996). The same applies when people are left by poverty with an unwelcome range of choices. To remove the best remaining option is actually, in the relevant sense, to coerce them still further. The only way to improve their situation is to expand their options, typically by removing the real or metaphorical causes of coercion.

A version of this reply can also be made to the extraordinary claim sometimes heard, that organ selling should not be allowed because the poor are coerced into selling by being offered more money than they could possibly get by other means (Sells, 1991). Even if coercion – real or metaphorical – did generally invalidate consent, it would still be irrelevant to the issue of inducement by unrefusable offers. This is exactly the opposite of coercion, because it *expands* the range of available options. The original one, of keeping the kidney, still remains. The difference is only that a better one has become available, which means that any coercion by poverty is lessened. Perhaps the idea behind this argument is that such temptations are so great as to dazzle prospective sellers into incompetence, but if so the appropriate reply is the one in the previous section. Our normal standards require us to assess competence on an individual basis, not to remove an option for everyone because some cannot give valid consent.

It should be added, incidentally, that if the coercion-by-poverty argument worked it would work just as effectively against organ donation. Unpaid kidney donors do not relish the idea of nephrectomy. They are, metaphorically, coerced into it by the impending death of someone they care about, in the light of which giving a kidney seems their best option.

"But we should lift them out of poverty"

The claim that we should not remove the best option open to the poor frequently provokes a further response. Surely, it is said, it would be better to lift them out of poverty altogether than allow them to try to alleviate their situation in this particularly horrible way.

No reasonable person could dispute that; but, once again, the admirable premise provides no support at all for the conclusion that kidney selling should remain illegal. There is no connection between the ideas that we should make people less poor and that organ selling should be prohibited. In fact the implication is, if anything, in the other direction, because if everyone were well enough off to be untempted by kidney selling no one would want to sell, and prohibition would be pointless because it would have nothing to do. Conversely, as long as prohibition has anything to do, there must be people for whom selling seems a better option than any other they have, and who are therefore made worse off by prohibition.

Concern for the badly off provides a very good reason for making them better off, but none at all for the prohibition of organ selling.

"But sellers are harmed, not benefited"

Another way to expand the "but . . ." premise is to argue that even though the sellers may have given genuine consent, they are simply wrong about the transaction's being to their benefit. Paternalism is now theoretically rejected in legislative and medical circles, but that does not prevent its appearance in contexts like this. Dossetor and Manickavel, for instance, claim that "state paternalism grounded in social beneficence dictates that the abject poor should be protected from selling parts of their bodies to help their sad lot in life" (Dossetor and Manickavel 1992, p. 63). This idea has been considerably strengthened by distressing reports from campaigning journalists and various watchdogs about the fate of people who actually have sold kidneys in the expectation of improving their situation, but found themselves even worse off than before.

Even if all these reports are accurate, there are legitimate questions about how representative they are, since the failure of some people to benefit in the way they expect, which happens in all areas of trade, is not usually regarded as sufficient to justify abolishing that kind of trade altogether. More interesting, however, is the question of how, even if the reports are both true and representative, they are supposed to support the required conclusion. Prohibition is, after all, the situation we have now. If people are faring badly under the present system, the need to protect them can hardly be used as a justification for keeping things as they are.

For this argument to work it would need another premise, to the effect that things would be even worse if kidney selling were legalized. But is that plausible? Live kidney donation is now so safe that many surgeons encourage it, and losing a kidney is, in itself, the same whether it is given or sold. This means that any harms specific to selling must have to do with the surrounding circumstances. The most obvious difference in circumstances is that donation is tightly controlled and supervised, and selling, as long as it is illegal, cannot be controlled at all.

The point here is that the horror stories about exploitation, shoddy work, unfulfilled contracts, inadequate advice, lack of after care and all the rest are exactly what is to be expected when illegality forces a resort to black markets. Properly regulated selling would be as safe for sellers as for donors. As long as some people are desperate for life-saving operations and others for money, the two groups will get together by some means or other; and although a legal market might not protect everybody, without one we can protect nobody. The current abuses are among the strongest elements in the case not for prohibition, but against it.

Even with proper regulation there would of course still be some burdens and risks associated with nephrectomy, as with all surgery, but the worthwhileness of any risk depends on both the nature of the risk and the value of the anticipated reward. If the rich who take up hang-gliding or mountaineering are regarded as entitled to judge their own risks, it is difficult to see why the poor, who propose to take lower risks for higher returns, should be regarded as so manifestly irrational as to need saving from themselves. *Contra* Dossetor and Mackinavel, it would seem reasonable to claim that the poorer you were, the more rational it would be to risk selling a kidney.

"But the rich should not get benefits denied to the poor"

Another common claim is that allowing organ sales is wrong because it gives benefits to the rich that are not available to the poor. Like most of the arguments in the terrain, this one sounds attractive because it appeals to a benevolent-sounding principle, but it runs into the usual problems. In the first place, virtually nobody would be willing to defend, when pressed, a principle to the effect that unless everyone can have some benefit, no one should. It would rule out all the privileges enjoyed by the people in the rich world. In particular, it would certainly rule out all private medicine, which is allowed in nearly all the countries that have banned organ selling.

But even if the principle were acceptable, it would, anyway, be irrelevant to the issue of buying and selling as such. Kidneys could still be bought by public bodies, for distribution on the basis of need, as has been suggested by various commentators (Erin and Harris, 2003) and as happens in Iran. Once again, whatever the merits of the premise, the conclusion does not follow.

"But selling body parts is like slavery"

Another argument, frequently produced as decisive, is that selling parts of yourself is like selling yourself into slavery. Everyone now agrees that slavery is wrong, so, the argument implies, they should by parity of reasoning agree that selling parts of people is also wrong.

An argument of this kind depends on the accuracy of the analogy, and the most obvious reply is that there is an enormous moral difference between owning and selling parts of yourself and owning other people. But this reply is not necessary, because there is an even more obvious problem. Slavery *itself* is forbidden. We are no more allowed to sell – or even give – ourselves into slavery than we are other people. If anything is forbidden altogether – as are, for instance, possession and use of various drugs, or murder, or living donation of vital organs such as hearts – then the outlawing of payment for such things follows *a fortiori*. Slavery cannot provide an analogy with payment for live kidney donation because live kidney donation itself is allowed, and even actively encouraged.

This is an important general issue in the area of debates about body selling, where objections to some procedures *as such* may be offered as objections to payment for them. Many of the new processes that give rise to the possibility of selling are controversial in themselves. This already applies strongly, for instance, to the advances in reproductive technology (gamete donation and surrogacy) that lead to confusion in family relationships, and to other new possibilities such as the use of fetal tissue, pre-implantation genetic diagnosis, and genetic engineering of all kinds. Nearly all such advances allow for the possibility of buying and selling parts of bodies, but the debates about their acceptability in themselves must not be confused with the debates about selling. The payment issue arises in its own right only in contexts where giving is regarded as acceptable.

"But you can't sell your body because you don't own it"

A variant on the slavery argument is the issue of ownership. It is often said that we do not own our own bodies, and so cannot sell parts of them.

For anyone inclined to this line of argument, the first question is about the status of the claim. Is it intended as moral, religious, legal, or what? People with moral or religious objections to selling can always choose to refrain from doing so. The interesting question is about the law.

It is true that the legal status of bodies is often murky, but the relevant question here is what the law *should* be. Most people now think we should have the right to decide whether to *donate* our kidneys, and the right to give normally implies ownership. If there is a good reason for claiming that we should have a kind of legal ownership that extends to giving but not selling, it is, to say the least, not obvious what it might be.

"But there are better ways of getting organs"

Another claim made in the kidney selling context is that there are better ways of getting kidneys. Yet again, however, this is an attractive and plausible premise that provides no support at all for the conclusion that selling should be prohibited. It might just as well be argued that because it would be better if everyone had first-class health care, we should eliminate primitive clinics in the third world.

The analogy shows where the idea goes wrong. If first-class health care were known to be available everywhere there would be no need to eliminate primitive clinics, because no one would go to them. Conversely, as long as people do want them, it shows that better ones are not available – or known to be available. Of course we should try to make enough organs available by other means (ideally obviating the need for live donation of any kind); but if that happened selling would disappear because no one would want to buy. Conversely, as long as people do want to buy, not enough are available by other means.

For this argument to work it would need an extra premise, to the effect that allowing sales would actually lessen the overall availability of transplant organs. This claim is indeed frequently made, and it raises the final kind of argument to be discussed here.

"But there would be catastrophic consequences"

It is often claimed that if kidney selling were allowed people would stop donating organs, and even that the whole program of transplantation would fall into disrepute.

This line of argument is quite different from the ones discussed so far. The foregoing arguments all try to demonstrate that organ selling is ruled out directly by fundamental, generally accepted moral standards, and they fail essentially on grounds of logic. They appeal to principles incompatible with the ones their advocates accept in other contexts, or the principles do not support the conclusion, or both. But the argument just mentioned is of a quite different kind – not usually identified as different – that works not by claiming that organ selling involves something wrong in itself, but that it would lead to harms greater than any good it could achieve. Arguments of this kind have the potential to succeed where the other attempts fail outright.

The version just mentioned is only one among infinitely many possibilities, predicting disasters that would come about if kidney selling were legalized. It has been alleged, for instance, that if the sale of organs were allowed, "mutual respect for all persons [would] be slowly eroded" (Dossetor and Manickavel, 1992, p. 66), or that it would "[invite] social and economic corruption . . . and even criminal dealings in the acquisition of organs for profit" (Abouna et al., 1991, p. 171), or remove the incentive to overcome resistance to a cadaver program (Broyer, 1991), or discourage related donors from coming forward (Abouna et al., 1991, p. 167; Broyer, 1991, p. 199). The possibilities are endless. This is therefore a class of arguments rather than a single one, and it needs to be recognized as a class because the various candidates all need the same kind of discussion.

There is obviously nothing wrong with the principle of claiming that some proposed course of action should be rejected because the resulting harms would probably outweigh the benefits, and since such arguments depend essentially on empirical claims they cannot be refuted a priori. Perhaps this is why, now that so many of the early arguments in defense of prohibition have been exposed as fallacious, arguments of this second kind seem to be increasingly popular. The one about causing a decline in rates of donation and an overall lessening of the supply is particularly prevalent now.

However, although nothing can be said a priori about whether any such argument can succeed or not, there are relevant points to be made about methodology. Dealing with these arguments calls for an understanding of the difference between a genuine enquiry into the question of whether some policy would be desirable or not, and attempts to rationalize – find an excuse for holding on to – an existing conviction. Virtually all attempts to show that kidney selling should be prohibited come into the second category.

In the first place, no one who started with a serious recognition that some policy had elements in its favor – as in this case – and was considering whether to implement it, would dream of ruling it out because of the mere *possibility* of harms that might ensue. A genuine enquiry calls for a careful risk analysis, involving identifying and weighing possible goods and harms, and assessing the probability that each would come about. This involves proper empirical enquiry, ideally involving experiments and pilot studies. Anyone who rules out some project on the basis of the mere possibility of harm has almost certainly decided against it on other grounds, and is looking for persuasive ways to justify that decision.

Second, the appropriate response to real evidence of probable or even certain harm, in contexts where there is a presumption in favor of some policy, is not a rush to prohibition but serious efforts to devise ways of keeping the good elements while avoiding the bad. Nearly everything we do – including trade of all kinds – carries potential for harm, but it does not usually occur to us to abolish some activity entirely rather than try to lessen or remove its dangers. When we do have such an impulse, once again, it means that we really regard the activity in question as undesirable in itself, and are using the harms as an excuse to oppose it.

Third, it is most unlikely that *any* such evidence could reasonably support a conclusion that prohibition must be appropriate universally: at all times, in all places, and in all circumstances. Whether allowing payment for some kind of service would lead to any particular harm such as a lessening of rates of donation, for instance, might well depend on the attitudes of a particular population, or the way the issue was presented.

There is far more evidence now of serious enquiry into different ways in which payment for organ donation might be implemented than there was ten years ago, and various people have made genuine attempts to think of ways to allow the good aspects of kidney selling while lessening possible harms (Erin and Harris, 2003). But still, most of the arguments alleging its dangers are put forward as if they provided justification for total prohibition, accompanied by no suggestion of willingness to experiment or devise ways of limiting harm. The alleged harms are, furthermore, typically backed up by no evidence at all beyond the strong feelings of their allegers – which, in a context where even the most flagrant logical fallacies are overlooked, are certainly not to be relied on. They are clearly rationalizations of a conviction that organ selling should not be allowed, rather than serious attempts to balance goods and harms.

Perhaps there are indeed good reasons for never allowing organ selling, but at the moment we have no reason to believe it. The familiar arguments show no evidence even of any recognition that there is anything to be said in its favor, or any presumption to be overcome. The feeling that prohibition must be right is clearly lurking in the background, systematically undermining the standards of rationality we would take for granted in a genuine enquiry.

Feelings in Ethics

Here lies the root of the problem. The pattern of argument demonstrates a familiar phenomenon, described by John Stuart Mill:

> For if [an opinion] were accepted as a result of argument, the refutation of the argument might shake the solidity of the conviction; but when it rests solely on feeling, the worse it fares in argumentative contest, the more persuaded its adherents are that their feeling must have some deeper ground, which the arguments do not reach; and while the feeling remains, it is always throwing up fresh entrenchments of argument to repair any breach in the old.

(Mill, 1988, p. 1)

The feelings come first, and the arguments are determined attempts to justify them.

The strong feelings at the root of objections to payment show in other ways as well. They show, for instance, in the immediacy with which objections appear: the outright condemnation of payment for kidney donation came before there had been any time to consider how our usual moral principles should apply to this new phenomenon, or any anxious weighing of pros and cons. They also show in the kinds of argument employed. The mistakes so far described are not obscure, of a kind that only a logician could reasonably be expected to spot. They are simple mistakes that no one would make in neutral contexts, where a genuine enquiry was being conducted.

The strong feelings also show themselves, more subtly, in another range of familiar justifications for prohibition, invoking high-sounding ideals about altruism, human dignity, and not commodifying the human body. These ideals are introduced as though they provided independent support for the conclusion, but they all turn out to be nothing more than restatements of the point supposedly at issue, and therefore question begging.

This is most obvious in the arguments that supposedly appeal to the wrongness of commodifying the human body. Since the claim that commodification is wrong just *is* the claim that payment should not be allowed, it cannot be used as a justification of it.

Less obviously, the same is true of the endlessly repeated insistence that donation must be altruistic. On the most familiar understanding of the idea, altruism has nothing to do with the distinction between giving and selling, since many people try to sell their organs because they need the money for altruistic purposes. A Turkish man involved in the original kidney selling scandal in the UK, who was trying to buy treatment for his daughter's leukaemia, would have been regarded as altruistic beyond question if he had wanted to give his kidney directly to his daughter; obviously he was showing exactly the same selflessness in trying to sell it for her sake. Altruism can differentiate between giving and selling only if giving is actually defined as altruistic and selling as non-altruistic. But in that case the insistence that organ giving must be altruistic is just a restatement of the claim that it must not involve selling – and therefore cannot be used as part of the argument to that conclusion.[10]

The same is true of arguments about human dignity. If the conclusion that payment for donation should be prohibited is to be derived from principles about human dignity, there needs to be an independent account of what human dignity is – so that we can see whether to accept the account, and whether it really does entail the conclusion that organs should not be sold. But no such account seems to be forthcoming from people who argue in this way. The wrongness of organ selling is being treated as part of the account of what human dignity is.

All this, however, raises the most fundamental question of all. If the feelings against organ selling really are so strong, and so prevalent, is that not significant in itself? Some opponents of allowing payment for body parts and services, when they recognize the failure of the usual lines of argument, do move into the position that Mill sees as the final retreat of his non-reasoning opponents: the conviction that their feeling reflects some deeper truth, that argument cannot reach. Payment in these contexts just is wrong, and there is nothing further to be said about it.

Strong feelings do typically appear to their possessors as compelling insights into moral truth, but nobody who thinks seriously about the matter can regard mere intensity of feeling as providing the last word in matters of ethics. The fonder people are of their own moral intuitions, the more they are inclined to regard the opposing intuitions of others as prejudice and bigotry; and even religions that recommend individual conscience as the ultimate authority usually find they need other criteria to distinguish the word of God from the promptings of the devil. Anyway, nobody who thinks in detail about even their own moral intuitions can fail to discover that they are full of contradictions, and cannot all be right.

If the wrongness of payment in these areas is treated as moral bedrock, it is indeed irrelevant that it cannot be justified in terms of other moral principles. But anyone tempted to sink with relief into this apparently comfortable position must recognize what it involves. To accept the wrongness of payment as a self-standing principle, rather than as derived from other principles, involves accepting that there are many possible circumstances in which its implications will actually *conflict* with the implications of those others, and that keeping to it will involve allowing it to override them. It must be treated as *more* important than saving life and health, respecting autonomy, increasing options, and preventing the harms done by the inevitable black market.

It is clear that most people are not willing to take this line, because if they were they would not need to engage in endless attempts to justify their opposition to organ selling *in terms of* other values. If they claim that organ selling is wrong *because* it is exploitative, or *because* people are not really choosing to do it, or *because* it is too risky, or *because* it will dry up the supply of other organs, that implies an unwillingness to accept that it would be wrong irrespective of such considerations, let alone in spite of conflict with them. It seems that most people, at least in public and in theory, are not willing to recognize the wrongness of organ selling as moral bedrock, overriding other moral considerations.

Rationality in ethics is not a matter of disregarding feelings, but of being willing to recognize conflicts between feelings, and engage with the question of which should be allowed to prevail. The familiar arguments against organ selling systematically dodge this confrontation by fudging connections and compatibilities between prohibition and the very moral concerns that it overrides. In practice the feeling that organ selling must be wrong is given the position it is denied in theory, and allowed to override the familiar principles in terms of which it is justified.

Conclusion

I said at the outset that because the question of payment for body parts and bodily services was so wide, all that could be offered here was a method for engaging with the issues as they arose. The method proposed applies equally to any other case where people have strong feelings that where bodies are involved, payment should not be.

It should be stressed that the line of argument developed makes no reference whatever to libertarian principles about individual rights and unfettered markets, and comes nowhere near implying that commercial pressures should be allowed to take their course. Its starting point is only a modest *presumption* in favor of letting competent adults decide what risks to take for themselves, strengthened, in the case of kidney selling, by the intrinsic desirability of saving life and mitigating poverty. For anyone who wants to reject these starting points, the rest of the argument will be irrelevant, but these are principles that most people, including most opponents of payment in these areas, would usually accept.

This provides nothing more than a starting point, since a presumption may always be overcome by more important considerations, but it has the great methodological advantage of preventing strong feelings against payment from carrying the case unchallenged. The question from this point onwards is whether any of the arguments offered against payment are strong enough to override the starting presumptions in its favor. As Mill suggests, there is no end to the entrenchments of argument that may be thrown up in defense of strong feelings, but the ones discussed here show the kinds of mistake to look out for.

Some of the proposed objections turn out to be irrelevant because they are objections to the procedure at issue itself, rather than to payment in particular. Specific questions about the acceptability of payment arise only in contexts where the procedure itself is considered acceptable.

Other objections fail outright on grounds of logic. Some depend on principles incompatible with their advocates' own beliefs in other contexts; others fail because the premises invoked do not support the conclusion. Such arguments, as they stand, straightforwardly do not work, and can be disregarded.[11] They often reflect legitimate concerns, but that is quite different from their supporting this particular conclusion.

Finally there are the ones that invoke threats of danger. Here the point to be made is methodological. There is a difference between a serious enquiry into risks and benefits and a determination to justify an existing conclusion. The serious enquiry will involve genuine investigations and experiments, and attempts to devise ways of keeping what is good while avoiding harm. Properly pursued, they will lead to proposals for appropriate kinds of regulation and perhaps even the discovery of ways to make buying and selling irrelevant. They may occasionally lead to the conclusion that prohibition is appropriate in particular times and places. It is difficult to imagine their ever being strong enough to justify a total prohibition, appropriate to all possible times and places.

None of this suggests for a moment that payment for these things is to be recommended as an ideal means of procurement, let alone of alleviating poverty. In the case of organ selling, at least, it is most decidedly is not. Nevertheless, as long as people are dying for lack of organs or are desperate for children, and as long as both buyers and sellers suffer in the inevitable black market, the total prohibition of payment is almost certainly unjustified.

At the very least, the issue needs serious debate. At the moment much of the debate is not serious at all, and as a result it is – like many other issues in biomedical ethics – in intellectual, and therefore moral, confusion.

Notes

1 This article draws on previously published work of the author (Radcliffe Richards, 1996, 1998, 2005).
2 For a comprehensive review of the legal position in different countries, and an extensive bibliography (see Pattinson, 2003).
3 Except that in the US as elsewhere no legally binding contract is allowable. A woman who wants to keep her surrogate baby can do so.
4 Surrogacy Arrangements Act, 1985; Human Fertilisation and Embryology Act, 1990.
5 Denmark forbids payment; all surrogacy arrangements are banned in France, Austria, Switzerland, Germany, the Netherlands, Spain, Norway, and Sweden.
6 For example, Portugal.
7 In Iran kidney sales are legal and regulated, with the trade organized and controlled by two nongovernmental organizations (McLaughlin et al., 2004).
8 Some people have also argued on the same basis that the purchasers' desperation makes them incompetent to consent.
9 "Surely abject poverty . . . can have no equal when it comes to coercion of individuals to do things – take risks – which their affluent fellow-citizens would not want to take? Can decisions taken under the influence of this terrifying coercion be considered autonomous? Surely not" (Dossetor and Manickavel, 1992, p. 63). "A truly voluntary and noncoerced consent is also unlikely . . . the desperate financial need of the donor is an obvious and clear economic coercion. It is also sometimes said that the recipient has not chosen freely, either because he is coerced by the threat of death into entering the market. This is probably enough in itself to illustrate the absurdity of the idea" (Abouna et al., 1991, p. 166).

10 There is a further objection to this argument, that nobody holds a general principle to the effect that if something cannot be obtained as a gift, it must not be obtained at all. If the principle is to apply to organs when it does not apply generally, a reason needs to be given.

11 It is important to distinguish between bad arguments and incomplete evidence. Small pieces of evidence, individually inadequate, may accumulate to make a decisive case. But if they are individually wrong they cannot accumulate in this way; and the same is true of bad arguments. They carry no weight at all.

References

Abouna, G.M., Sabawi, M.M., Kumar, M.S.A., and Samhan, M. (1991), The negative impact of paid organ donation, in W. Land and J.B. Dossetor (eds.), *Organ Replacement Therapy: Ethics, Justice, Commerce*, Berlin and New York: Springer Verlag, pp. 164–72.

Broyer, M. (1991), Aspects of living organ donation with emphasis on the fight against commercialism, in W. Land and J.B. Dossetor (eds.), *Organ Replacement Therapy: Ethics, Justice, Commerce*, Berlin and New York: Springer Verlag, pp. 197–202.

Dossetor, John B., and Manickavel, V. (1992), Commercialization: the buying and selling of kidneys, in C.M. Kjellstrand and J.B. Dossetor (eds.), *Ethical Problems in Dialysis and Transplantation*, Dordrecht: Kluwer Academic Publishers, pp. 61–71.

Erin, Charles A., and Harris, John (2003) An ethical market in human organs, *Journal of Medical Ethics* 29 (2003): 137–8.

McLaughlin, Abraham, Prusher, Ilene R., and Downie, Andrew (2004), What is a kidney worth? *Christian Science Monitor*, June 9, 2004, available at www.csmonitor.com/2004/0609/p01s03-wogi.htm 8jun04.

Mill, John Stuart (1988 [1869]), *The Subjection of Women*, ed. Susan M. Okin, Indianapolis, IN: Hackett Publishing Company.

Pattinson, Shaun D. (2003), Paying living organ providers, *Web Journal of Current Legal Issues* 3, available at webjcli.ncl.ac.uk/2003/issue3/pattinson3.html

Radcliffe Richards, Janet (1996), Nephrarious goings on: kidney sales and moral arguments, *Journal of Medicine and Philosophy* 21 (4) (August): 375–416.

Radcliffe Richards, Janet (2005), Is it desirable to legitimize paid living donor kidney transplantation programmes? 1. Evidence in favour, in Robert S. Gaston and Jonas Wadstrom (eds.), *Living Donor Kidney Transplantation: Current Practices, Emerging Trends and Evolving Challenges*, London: Taylor and Francis, pp. 181–91.

Radcliffe Richards, Janet, Daar, A.S., Guttmann, R.D., et al. (1998), The case for allowing kidney sales, the International Forum for Transplant Ethics, *Lancet* 351: 1950–2.

Sells, R.A. (1991), Voluntarism of consent, in W. Land and J.B. Dossetor (eds.), *Organ Replacement Therapy: Ethics, Justice, Commerce*, Berlin and New York: Springer Verlag, pp. 18–24.

Sells, R.A. (1993), Resolving the conflict in traditional ethics which arises from our demand for organs, *Transplantation Proceedings* 25 (6) (December): 2983–4.

Chapter 15

The Patient as Victim and Vector

The Challenge of Infectious Disease for Bioethics

Margaret P. Battin, Leslie P. Francis,
Jay A. Jacobson, and Charles B. Smith

Seeing Infectious Disease as Central

Only decades ago, infectious disease was thought to be on the verge of being vanquished. Developments in public sanitation, immunization, and antibiotics, together with other public-health and scientific milestones, were thought to mean the imminent end of infectious disease. Smallpox had been eliminated; polio was nearly conquered; and diphtheria, tetanus, typhoid, yellow fever, and many other traditionally most feared diseases like leprosy and plague were largely controlled by immunization or treatment. Still others were the subjects of promising research. The US Surgeon General is reported to have said in a burst of optimism, sometime between 1969 and 1972, that it was time to "close the book" on infectious diseases.[1] That this story is quite likely apocryphal is barely relevant; the legend remains alive.

The Birth of Bioethics Amid the Decline of Infectious Disease

Meanwhile, the new field of bioethics was coming into being. Born in the 1960s, bioethics began with observations about the dilemmas physicians faced at the bedside, such as whether to tell dying patients the truth, whether to reveal confidential information, or whether to limit patients' liberties for their own good. However, during the formative period of bioethics, infectious disease played virtually no role.[2] The issues explored in bioethics's early years arose in situations like coma and terminal illness; organ transplantation and dialysis; reproductive failure, including abnormal pregnancy and neonatal deficit; and human experimentation. The conditions at issue were congenital anomalies, brain injuries, disseminated cancers, renal failure, and heart disease. These conditions largely involve deterioration, malformation, or destruction of various sorts of organ function and physical structures of individual patients. These early core issues and the clinical cases associated with them presented the challenges of life-extending technologies in already compromised persons. Problems of social justice also eventually received attention, for instance in concerns about access to health care or discrimination based on race or age.

In general, issues involving infectious disease were virtually nowhere to be seen. Only a few cases that generated extensive discussion in bioethics during its initial decades involved infectious disease.[3] These include the notorious Tuskegee studies of deliberately untreated syphilis in black men, the Willowbrook studies of institutionalized children intentionally infected with hepatitis, and end of life controversies about letting terminally ill patients succumb to pneumonia, "the old man's friend." However, in each of these controversial cases that did involve infectious disease, the discussions that consumed bioethics pointed largely away from the fact that the diseases involved could be transmitted from one person to another. Instead, matters of concern were the vulnerability of the study populations, coercion in institutional settings, civil rights, and racial discrimination and exploitation – not infectiousness per se.

Largely left aside in bioethics – unlike in public health – were problems that are more characteristic of infectious conditions: the importance of rapid diagnosis; the significance of acute onset; the risk of transmissibility to family, friends, caregivers, and even strangers; the apparent need for surveillance; the role of screening, prevention, and immunization; the constraints of quarantine and isolation; and the effects of treatment of a given patient on the health of others. Only when AIDS was recognized in the early 1980s and the cause had been identified as a virus did ethical issues begin to be widely raised in bioethics about illness where the disease could be transmitted from one person to another through contagion. By the time the AIDS epidemic had emerged, however, the field of bioethics had already been largely defined, with areas of inquiry laid out and a core set of normative principles enshrined as the prevailing philosophical approach. Whether these principles – identified in the canonical text by Beauchamp and Childress[4] as autonomy, non-maleficence, beneficence, and justice – would prove adequate for the context of transmissible disease remained largely unexplored. Frameworks for clinical decision-making, such as Jonsen et al.'s patient preference, quality of life, medical indications, and other considerations,[5] also left transmissibility virtually unexplored, even though legal requirements were included under "other considerations." Moreover, at least in part for political reasons, some of the discussions of HIV/AIDS, despite the epidemic's vast scope, treated the disease largely as an exceptional case, a point to which we shall return.

The Shifting Concerns of Public Health

Concerns about infectious disease and transmissibility might seem properly to belong to the domain of public health rather than to the problems of clinical medicine that were the focus of bioethics. Long before the mechanisms of infectious disease transmission were understood, public health originated in societal attempts to try to control the spread of disease by isolating lepers, attaching bells to plague victims, imposing quarantines on ships entering a harbor (Venetian law required ships from the east to lie 40 days at anchor, hence the term "quarantine"[6]), and similar measures. With increasing understanding of the microbial basis of infectious disease towards the end of the nineteenth century, practical public health measures became more effective, reflected in improved public sanitation, immunization, the application of the germ theory of disease in encouraging doctors to wash their hands between seeing patients, and many other public health measures aimed at reducing transmission. Indeed, at least until the mid-twentieth century, the containment of communicable infectious disease was the central concern of public health.

In more recent years, public health has increasingly turned its attention to other factors affecting the health of populations – matters like asbestos exposure, cigarette smoking, toxic waste, and obesity.[7] While human behavior plays a major role in these conditions, none of them involves biologically transmissible disease.

Public health measures have been astonishingly successful in transforming morbidity and mortality, especially for the developed world: up through the middle of the nineteenth century most people in most parts of the world died of infectious disease. By 1984, just before the outbreak of AIDS, infectious diseases – with the exception of pneumonia and septicemia – were no longer the leading causes of death in the developed world. They had been displaced by heart and circulatory disease, cancer, and various forms of degenerative organ system failure.

Throughout its history, public health has been largely population-focused rather than individual-focused, involving societal, governmental, or institutional measures aimed at protecting or improving the health of populations by containing or preventing transmission of disease rather than treating disease in individual patients. The ethical paradigms of public health have been largely utilitarian in character, looking at the overall costs and benefits of initiatives rather than the rights or liberties of individuals within them.

Bioethics and Public Health: How the Twain Didn't Meet

Bioethics developed in schools of philosophy, theology, and in medical schools. Schools of public health are often institutionally distinct from these academic homes of bioethics scholars. Perhaps as a consequence, until quite recently, public health *ethics* has not only been institutionally separate but has occupied a separate sphere of discussion from bio*ethics*, and bioethics developed with virtually no real dialogue with public health ethics. This is a point about the ethics considerations in each field, not just about practice.

The contrast is clearest between early bioethics and traditional public health. In a word, bioethics was primarily interested in the *patient as (actual) victim*, public health in *individuals as vectors* and *potential victims*. The paradigms of theoretical analysis that were developing in bioethics – particularly the emphases on patient autonomy and the interests of the individual patient – were not integrated into the more utilitarian public health analysis. The *primum non nocere* of the Hippocratic Oath was understood in bioethics to refer to the ill patient who is being treated by the physician; in contrast, public health was particularly concerned with persons who might become victims in the future; prevention is the core of public-health interest. To some extent, the concerns of the then-new field of bioethics were seen as in conflict with public health concerns, to the extent that public health concerns were considered at all. Problem cases which might have challenged the underlying normative paradigms of bioethics – for example, what to do about that icon of asymptomatic infectiousness once much in the public eye and well known to public health, Typhoid Mary – never entered the early bioethics texts. And where infectious disease actually was the focus, as in the Willowbrook experiments on hepatitis or the Tuskegee syphilis study, the consequences for others of not treating these transmissible diseases in the research subject were almost completely overlooked. The public health discussions and the field of bioethics developed so separately that the twain never really met.

Rethinking the gulf between bioethics and public health, however, is becoming ethically urgent. Far from being a closed book, infectious disease is now on the public agenda again, in deeply alarming ways. Not only HIV/AIDS, but Ebola, Marburg, SARS, multi-drug-resistant tuberculosis, West Nile virus, and avian influenza are in public view. Systemic threats like antibiotic resistance and bioterrorism have become the focus of substantial concern. Other global problems, including environmental degradation, population growth, refugee migration, and widespread poverty, feed reservoirs of infection that are transnational and international matters of concern. Infectious diseases know no borders. For example, within a few months after leaders in the Nigerian state of Kano ordered the cessation of polio vaccination efforts, the disease had spread to seven neighboring countries.[8] SARS spread from Hong Kong to Toronto via a single index patient's intercontinental flight.[9] Avian flu, moving throughout south-east Asia and beyond, is at the top of the current most-feared list.

While the problems of national and international law raised by infection are under heavy discussion, much less attention has been directed thus far to the significance of these developments for how we understand the ethics of the provider–patient relationship, the liberty of patients, and the obligations of health care institutions when the patient is not simply an individual, but also a patient-in-a-disease-relationship. In infectious disease, the patient is both *victim* and *vector*, a *person-in-need* and at the same time a *person-as-threat*.

The Case of HIV

The link between bioethics and public health ethics first began to be forged when HIV/AIDS was emerging in the early 1980s. HIV was in some respects a wake-up call for bioethics, bringing a reinvigoration of traditional public health concerns.[10] In other respects, however, HIV may have been doubly exceptional. The transmission routes of HIV – through the exchange of bodily fluids – are likely to be the subjects of both awareness and control. The politics of HIV, moreover, shaped analyses in rights-based terms. HIV thus may not have been a particularly good provoker of the challenges to traditional bioethics presented by the full range of infectious diseases.

HIV is transmissible only by routes that today can be largely brought under the control of the agent or identified others: primarily sexual intercourse, sharing of syringes in IV drug administration, and transfusions and contaminated blood products. While HIV is like many other infectious diseases in that it can be (and very often is) transmitted unknowingly, the mechanisms of transmission are nevertheless open *in principle* to the agent's control, both for the transmitter and the transmittee. There are even reported incidents of quite deliberately controlled transmission of HIV, including a web site for "bugchasers" who wish to receive or transmit HIV.[11] This is quite a different picture from diseases that are aerosolized or transmitted through intermediate vectors, like mosquitoes; here, the human agents – both transmitter and transmittee, even with the conscientious use of such measures as masks or bednets – have very much less control over whether the disease is passed along.

The picture of the human individual as a way-station, breeding-ground, and launching-pad for micro-organisms that we will develop here is not reflected very well in HIV. This is certainly not to say that there is a sharp distinction between HIV and other infectious diseases – they share many features – nor that HIV is unique. But the fact that the HIV virus is not transmitted casually or by diffuse routes such as aerosolization or intermediate vectors, but only by the limited routes of exchanges of bodily fluids normally subject to agent control is a very significant difference. Thus it may be especially telling that the first extensive efforts of modern bioethics to deal with an infectious disease were focused on HIV, one of the least instructive and least challenging cases for understanding the *theoretical* implications of infectious disease for bioethics more generally, despite its enormous and devastating global impact.

This is not to say that bioethics has not developed tremendously in response to the crisis of HIV/AIDS. Discussions of issues like personal responsibility, confidentiality, public surveillance, and the stigmatization of gay men and intravenous drug users have assumed great importance in bioethics. The growth in bioethics has been extraordinary; but these concerns have still been largely discussed within the traditional framework of bioethics, based in liberal theory and its standard constructions of autonomy and the harm principle. These discussions have not taken fully into account what we might characterize as the dual exceptionalism of AIDS: on the one hand, the conclusions reached in bioethics about HIV/AIDS have not been extended to infectious disease as a whole, and on the other hand, HIV/AIDS does not present the full range of challenges other infectious diseases might to standard liberal paradigms. Recent calls for the application of public health ethics to the case of HIV[12] are, we think, useful, but will require us at the same time to develop the more robust structures for bioethical analysis that we explore in what follows.

Bridging the Gap: Seeing Bioethics in Terms of the Patient as Victim and Vector

What is needed, then, to bridge and transcend the gap between bioethics and traditional public health? At the practical level, clearly, further attention is needed to issues such as confidentiality and privacy, for example in disease-containment strategies like mandated reporting, contact tracing, mandatory immunization, and global surveillance; or informed consent in death-and-dying contexts when the patient is dying of a rapidly fatal and highly contagious disease; or paternalism and its interaction with other-interested policies in mandated immunization or treatment for infectious disease. But bioethics also needs, we think, a revised, enhanced account of its basic ethical concepts and principles, especially those inherited from the individualist liberal tradition. Bioethics's theoretical underpinnings are still, we contend, not sufficiently developed to accommodate issues about transmissible infectious disease.

At least four aspects of traditional liberal bioethics require direct attention: the account of the individual agent, together with associated accounts of autonomy, of the harm principle, and of responsibility.

Re-understanding the individual agent

Among other things, communicable infectious disease forces us to recognize that individuals are not only socially but also physically situated in a distinctive way. They are foci of victim-hood and vector-hood in *physical* relation to others. People stand in a nexus of social relationships to each other; but they stand in a nexus of biological relationships as well, and not just those of familial ties and ancestry.

To be sure, philosophers increasingly have recognized the inadequacy of individualistic metaphysical accounts of the agent. Thomas May, for example, rejects the "impoverished, atomistic" view of the individual that characterizes earlier accounts in bioethics in favor of a view of individuals as "socially located."[13] Feminist writers have developed important accounts of relational autonomy.[14] These views emphasize familial and caring relationships: partners, parents, caregivers, and ones cared for. Such social relationships are also often physical ones, more-over, involving touching, holding, containment (as in pregnancy), penetration, and genetic continuity.

But such attention to social locatedness is not enough; "physical locatedness," to adapt May's term, is critical as well. The theoretical paradigms of liberalism typically see the individual as a physically discrete entity, however tightly differ-ent individuals may be socially related, and not as physically connected except in largely elective actions such as shaking hands, fist-fighting, undergoing surgery, and of course making love. But these paradigms are simplistic and misleading when infectiousness is taken seriously. The notion that a person is a discrete individual is not wrong, exactly, but seriously abbreviated.

When the infectious-disease patient is victim and vector, physical relationships may be personal and intimate or accidental and among strangers. Contagion may occur despite whether the victim knows the vector or not, and despite whether the victim can even identify the vector or the time of contagion. Transmission can be reciprocal, chained in a sequence of transmissions, or exponentially widespread. One can be both victim and vector at the same time, or victim of one disease but at the same time vector of another; this is particularly true where one disease affects susceptibility to or transmissibility of other infectious diseases, like HIV and tuber-culosis or gentital herpes and other sexually transmitted diseases. One individual can transmit over and over again. The feminist emphasis on relationality, while it reminds us of our sociality, our interconnectedness and even our physicality, does so in a more local and less universal way than does infectious disease.

The only possibility of being a true non-vector may seem to be hermit-like iso-lation. But even isolation will not fully protect us from the nexus of infectious diseases. Many infectious diseases are not only transmitted person to person; there may be animal reservoirs in between. If I am bitten by a mosquito, even though I have no contact with other humans, I can still transmit malaria; if I defecate near the stream even in a remote forest, I still may pass disease along. For some diseases, such as HIV/AIDS, the patient may be able to largely control transmission, in this case by not donating blood or having sex or sharing needles. For others, immu-nization may prevent transmission and isolation may reduce the likelihood. But such control is not possible for many others, such as flu, tuberculosis, and other "crowding diseases," or Creuzfeldt-Jakob ("mad cow") disease. Cultural practices are also relevant in controlling transmissibility, for example, bowing as a greet-ing rather than shaking hands. In some contemporary Asian cultures, people wear masks to avoid spreading disease. Even so, people are never in full control of their status as either victim or vector.

As physically located bodies, we are always "embedded" in potential circum-stances of exchange. One person's transmission of disease to others – to person x and x_1, and from x_1 to x_2 and from x_2 to x_3, and so on along a chain, or along these chains fanning out to perhaps many, many others – may be easy to track. But we must also understand that it, or something like it, may rebound back to that person, from x_3 to x_2 to x_1 to the original person, among many others, whether by this or by other transmission routes. Even where one episode of disease may confer immunity to that disease (and sometimes to related conditions), individuals are still at risk for transmission of other and related diseases.

Thus we all live with each other in a web of potential and actual disease, all the time, even when we are not currently overtly ill and not aware of the possibility of transmission. While many infectious diseases are comparatively innocuous and mild, some are rapid-moving, rapidly fatal illnesses. With some infectious diseases, people are literally well one day, gravely ill the next, and either dead or fully recovered the next – infections such as meningitis can move exactly this fast. In some severe conditions, contracting infectious disease may mean that we will die; transmitting infectious disease may mean that we will kill. This vulnerability is not one we can always choose to avoid by taking precautions, for instance by gloving, masking, or taking immunizations. As long as there are unpreventable, uncontained infectious diseases in the human population, this agent/patient/agent relationship will remain an ineluctable feature of our moral lives. No matter how we try, we cannot avoid the fact not just that we are at risk of infection from others but that we in turn pose risks to them and thus force them to pose risks to others – even others far distant from ourselves.

Biologically speaking, the human "individual" must be seen for what he or she is: a larger organism carrying and inhabited by a host of smaller ones that move easily from their habitat in one "person" to another. The human organism is a way-station, a breeding-ground, a launching-pad for an enormous multitude of smaller life. The "individual" human organism, after all, is colonized by billions and billions of micro-organisms, both internally and on its surfaces. This is not news, and it is not always a threat. Many of these micro-organisms are beneficial and indeed indispensable for human survival – for example, the bacteria that are involved in the digestive tract. Others, such as the chickenpox virus that can recur many years later as shingles, inhabit the individual for the most part innocuously but can become dangerous when that individual is under stress or is immune-compromised. Still others invade from outside, opportunistically, like fungal infections in the environment of the immune-suppressed host, or even when the human host is in full health. Some micro-organisms, like the staphylococcus bacterium, kill cells directly. In other cases, such as tuberculosis, it is the host's immune response to the invading organism that causes tissue damage. Many infectious disease organisms cause disease in the malnourished, the elderly, and infants. And some are most damaging to the vigorous – for instance, the flu of 1918–19 that killed 20 million people or more worldwide was most fatal in healthy young adults, those with the most active immune systems.

These biological vulnerabilities and capacities for physical threat and threatenedness evident in infectious disease must be part of our full normative account of human agency. This is why we must reassess the conventional notion of the individual. We are not the tall-standing, health-enjoying, competent, rational, individually discrete figures envisioned in many accounts in liberal normative theory, traditionally central in bioethics. Instead, we are complex and vulnerable constellations of organisms always under threat and always capable of causing threats to others, yet also dependent on some of these organisms, without which we would die. We typically dichotomize the individual and the environment; this is misleading, in that we *are* our microbial environment. That's the physical picture of the human individual we must keep in mind. This isn't metaphysical nonsense; this is biological fact.

Rethinking autonomy

But if our picture of the individual agent requires modification in the light of our social and physical situatedness with respect to infectious disease, it will force modifications in our understanding of autonomy, as well as what might follow from it such as claims about liberty or rights.

Autonomy, although characterized by early and later writers in a wide variety of differing ways, has most centrally been viewed in terms of self-determination. Yet particular characteristics of some infectious diseases undercut familiar conditions for the exercise of autonomy. For example, the acuity of some infectious diseases militates against reflective decision-making; the capacity for permanent prevention may reshape assessments of risk and benefit; and the complex infective mechanisms of communicable disease may work against some philosophical accounts of autonomy as informed by plans. Acuity can be regarded as an unusual, impaired circumstance, but prevention is an ongoing, ubiquitous issue. The prospect of communicable disease is ever-present and complex, even if not at the moment occurring. We do not deny the importance of autonomy, rights, plans, and related notions as appropriately central concepts in bioethics (and law). Our point is rather that the ideal of the thoughtful chooser, deciding in accord with his preferences and interests, is upset by our picture of the embedded agent. We must enhance our understanding of autonomy and its implications as a result.

Now, it might seem that the absence of infectious disease in bioethics is an oversight that can be corrected relatively easily within standard bioethical analysis: just add infectiousness in, as one more factor for the autonomous agent to consider. The agent in exercising autonomy then would be expected to attend in her choices to the risks of infectiousness that she experiences and constitutes. But are things so simple? Behind an easy grafting of infectiousness onto the consideration of these and other issues in bioethics lurk deeper tensions. For example, the agent who lacks time for reflection is not just an ordinary decision-maker in a hurry or under pressure who should be urged to consider choices more carefully. She is a potential risk *in herself* to others, and they are risks *in themselves* to her. These are sometimes threats of unknown urgency, gravity, or magnitude. To be sure, someone who holds a hidden bomb may also be a risk of which others are unaware. But infectiousness reminds us that we all may pose risks to each other, all of the time, whether we know it or not, not just because of a weapon we carry, but because of the very kind of organism we are. Sometimes these are direct risks of reciprocal transmission, where two parties mutually infect each other. But the far more general point holds as well, that we are always potential victims and potential vectors to each other and to the natural world.

Traditional accounts of autonomy fail to remind us of the possibilities of unknown and interlocking risks in transmissible infectious disease. These risks press important questions and suggest different options for discussion. Consider voluntary informed consent in the clinical context. If the patient is informed about his infectious-ness and still refuses treatment, what should be done? Is informed consent – and the autonomy it protects – simply to be overridden? Should liberty be curtailed directly, by measures such as isolation or quarantine? Should confidentiality be violated to protect others, even if the patient has not been informed in advance of the possibility that information will not be protected? Or consider research ethics. Should autonomy require that it be solely this individual patient's choice whether to enter an experimental study where contagion is a possibility? Would it violate the patient's autonomy for the physician to inform third parties who might be affected? Does autonomy license a patient's declining to join a study when that patient may be able to supply a crucial link in understanding a chain of transmission? Under standard accounts of research ethics and the right of autono-mous choice that regulations requiring informed consent are supposed to protect, a subject is entitled to withdraw from an experimental study at any time, for any reason; should the impact of potential infectiousness on others influence his choice concerning whether to remain in the study? These – and many more – are the kinds of questions pressed by contagious disease.

Or, consider the relationship between autonomy and justice.[15] What if there are conflicts between the choices of an autonomous, highly contagious agent to refuse treatment or to be treated in certain settings, and the achievement of justice for others? What of trade-offs with justice, such as between achieving a decent minimum of health care for everyone within a society, and the means needed to provide sufficient health care and vector management to reduce the risk of reser-voirs of infectious disease? As victim, the patient may tend to see his plight as the responsibility of others, deserving care as a result; as vector, the patient may ignore his effects on others, thus creating otherwise avoidable needs for resources by his or her individual choices.

One conclusion to draw here might be that such tensions are inevitable. Indi-vidual patient choice just may be a complex matter, both as it affects the person himself or herself, or as it conflicts with the choices or needs of others. Traditional autonomy theory treats the former as self-respecting choices, and the latter as the tension between competing actors. On this view, bioethics must simply live with these tensions, resolving them as best it can by providing patients with fuller infor-mation and other protection for the rationality of their choices, and by helping patients think through which values are most important in the solution of a given problem. Advance planning can be used to try to deal with decision-making when illness is too acute to permit reflection.

We believe, however, that this may be giving up too soon. The roots of seeing decision-making in this primarily conflictual way – the agent against others – we think, lie initially in the limited way in which the autonomous agent has been understood in bioethics. Autonomy is not simply a matter of the choices of separate and separable agents who affect one another only contingently. It is a matter of the choices of embedded agents who must take into account the ever-present possibility of their unavoidable biological connections with each other. The normative implications of these biological facts have been insufficiently developed, as discussion of the harm principle will show.

Rethinking the harm principle

Standard liberal theory has developed accounts of the permissible limits to patient autonomy and political liberty. Libertarians, who hold that people have rights to do whatever they want so long as they do not interfere with the rights of others, limit individuals' choices about how to move their fists by others' rights not to be punched. Liberals in the tradition of John Stuart Mill struggle with questions about the extent to which individuals are morally obligated to take into account the effects of their actions or omissions on others. Whether we are obligated to rescue someone who is drowning, calculate the effects of our energy use patterns on others, or refrain from taking jobs that are important to us despite the fact that we might sometimes perform them in a way that is risky to others, are sources of ongoing discussion in liberal theory and accommodation in the law. So, too, there are now some discussions of whether we have obligations not to go to work if we are contagious, not to travel if we have been exposed to certain infectious diseases, or not to reproduce if we might transmit infectious conditions to our offspring.

The "harm principle," famously set out by Mill, holds that "the only purpose for which social power can be rightfully exercised over any member of a civilized community, against his will, is to prevent harm to others."[16] Like other harms, risks of contagion may legitimate social intervention under the harm principle. Quarantine, restricting a person's liberty to move about in the world, is one of the most extreme such constraints. But also constraining are restrictions on persons that are imposed in order to control infectious disease: for example, restrictions on sexual activity (like closing bathhouses), on attending school (like requiring immunization), on keeping matters secret (like contact tracing), on refusing medical interventions (like directly observed therapy), or on getting health care treatment from one's chosen providers (like requiring mainstream medical treatment rather than alternative health care).

Discussions in bioethics and the law have typically treated the solutions to these dilemmas as a matter of taking sides in a conflict between the liberty of the individual patient and the rights of others to be protected from harm. This view treats the patient and those she might harm as ineluctably in conflict. The liberty of the one must be curtailed if others are to be protected. Or we must depend on voluntary self-restraint, reflecting, as Susan Okie suggests, on whether a person might be obligated to take an "altruistic" vaccine, such as a transmission-blocking vaccine against malaria that is designed to induce an immune response against the stage of the malaria parasite that develops inside the mosquito, a vaccine that would not protect the recipient of the vaccine but would prevent that person's blood from infecting a mosquito which could transmit the parasite to someone else.[17]

On this "either liberty or coercion" view, cases of contagion are analogized to the more standard "harm principle" cases in liberal theory, such as shooting another, stealing another's property, or shouting "fire!" in a crowded theater and causing a fatal stampede as people rush for the exits. In these cases, people are understood as actors, capable of refraining from shooting, stealing, or shouting false alarms. People "assault" each other by "delivering" their infectious micro-organisms, something they could avoid, albeit at some costs to their own preferences. Society expects people who are infected with dangerous, transmissible diseases to sacrifice their interests for the overall social good, either altruistically or as a result of coercion. Altruistic action involves the individual's sacrificing her own interests for the good of others. The constraints permitted by the harm principle are seen as arising externally from the agent who might want to shoot, steal, or shout "fire." They are not seen as connected to his agency in any deep sense; the harm principle permits limits on liberty that are imposed from outside.

On our view, however, this picture is simplistic. The contagious patient is not simply a vector-threat to victim-others. She is also a victim-other to their vector-threats.

When a patient is both victim and vector, the question of preventing harm arises not just from the outside. A person who might harm others by transmitting disease is in a position to harm them, but by the same act might also be harmed by them. People may be contagious before they are even aware that they are infected – or before currently available forms of medical diagnosis could detect their infectiousness. In some cases, the sources of harm may be unknown to anyone. The control of infectious disease may also involve the imposition of constraints on people who are not yet exposed or ill – that is, not yet either vectors of harm or victims of harm – but who are always in some sense at risk.

The challenge this picture presents is not just the problem of extending the harm principle's legitimation of interference with liberty to cases in which the harm is merely probabilistic or speculative. Rather, we all live in a surrounding environment of micro-organisms which travel from one human "individual" to another as their mode of life. We are thus non-electively related in our vulnerability, in part because we are not biologically discrete beings whose physical interactions with each other are always under our own control. "Our" interests aren't always so clearly distinct from "your" interests or from those of "society" as a whole. We must think through how to deal with these situations so that we all are protected as thoroughly as possible, and so that the burdens of protection are fairly shared.

Constraints protect the actual and potential victim as much as they constrain the actual and potential vector. But we cannot always tell who is who, and in any case we all occupy all these roles. The traditional harm principle separation between a realm of self-regarding and therefore socially-free actions, and a realm of other-regarding and therefore socially-subject actions, breaks down in the context of these features of infectious disease.

Our point here is not that liberty should be overridden to protect everyone from risks of contagion. We are not arguing that autonomy should be abandoned, or that the rights it engenders should be thought of as a nuisance, as public health sometimes seems to do. Nor do we want to ignore some of the insights in public health's population-based approach. We need an account that can serve both the view of clinical medicine – in which the patient is characteristically seen primarily as victim – and the view of public health, in which the patient is seen as potential vector. What we want is an account in which the patient can be seen as both victim *and* vector at the same time, a person simultaneously occupying both morally relevant roles.

Consider how such an account might look. The earliest accounts of autonomy in bioethics are focused around reasonable preferences, including preferences that involve other parties, are altruistic, and so on. Individuals can have interests in the interests of others – in how their children, their partners, or their friends fare. But individuals' interests start to look different when transmission is at issue. Beyond individuals' own sets of interests and subsidiary concerns about how they affect others, and beyond any possible assumptions about whether people may be motivated by altruism, people have interests in not transmitting diseases *because they are embedded among other people who, like them, are also at once victims and vectors.* To put it most simply, as rational agents accepting a plausible view of moral responsibility, *we don't want this to be the way we all live.*

To be sure, we are most likely to transmit and acquire the diseases to and from people with whom we have close, physical contact, including family members, coworkers, sexual partners, in some cases sports partners (think of wrestlers and flesh-eating strep), and perhaps also nurses and physicians treating us. We are also likely to pass disease within groups that we identify with – occupational, religious, recreational groups – primarily because they are the groups with which we have the most contact. Although we may not have contact with every member of those groups, those to whom we do transmit may pass it on among the group's internal web of contacts. Such "groups" are not necessarily residential, geographic, or interest-based; they may be stable over long periods or come together in a unique situation. A "group" may come together in a particular situation of stress but be otherwise unrelated, like passengers on an airliner with a re-circulating air system or people interned in the same refugee camp. Examples include religious groups, such as those that oppose immunization or share potato salad at church picnics. Such groups may be affiliational or behavioral – for example, gay men and HIV, or adventure travelers and malaria, or dormitory schoolmates and meningitis. A "group" might be Haitians quarantined on entering the US, or residents of a SARS-infected apartment building in Hong Kong, or poultry-farmers in Asia. And, of course, groups intersect with other groups, society-wide.

We are completely familiar with mutual disease transmission within families – one family member gets a cold and most everyone does – and we are also familiar with the way in which disease may be transmitted throughout a group even when individual members have contact with only some of the individuals composing that group. We also recognize how disease travels around the world – ordinary flu does this every year. But we rarely recognize the full moral implications for ourselves. We live in a world in which we transmit our diseases to others, often whether we want to or intended to or not – others who have already transmitted their diseases to us, whether they wanted or intended to or not.

Clearly, we have an interest in not transmitting disease not only to people who are close to us and to people in groups we identify with, but we also have an interest in not transmitting to the world more generally. Or, more exactly, we have an interest in not being part of a mutually disease-transmitting family, group, or society – or, for that matter, globe. After all, distant parts of the globe are just a plane ride away, and disease – whether mild, moderate, or lethal – can travel in a matter of hours on an airliner from the other side of the earth – from them to us, or from us to them. The moral implications of this picture do not rest simply on an enhanced or more sophisticated conception of self-interest. They rest on a modified and deepened picture of the self involved – a relational, embodied self who is unavoidably threatened by and a threat to others. This deepened picture of embedded agency also has implications for judgments not only about what we ought to do, but about ourselves as responsible agents.

Rethinking responsibility

Judgments of responsibility include both whether we can be held responsible at all and what we can be held responsible for. Suppose we start with a fairly standard picture of the responsible agent, able to control whether she exceeds the appropriate limits of autonomy by violating her obligations not to harm others. If she cannot exercise self-control, it is because of flaws in her – impairments, bad will, or lack of self control. If she causes harm because of a mental disease or defect, she may be judged not to be responsible for what she has done, because there are flaws in her understanding or in her ability to conform her conduct to the requirements of law.

With some forms of contagiousness, this control is not possible. With other forms, capacity for control may vary in many ways; it may be partial, or fluctuating, or time-dependent, as during periods of pre-symptomatic infectiousness. Compare judgments about the absence of responsibility in cases of mental illness with the partial or complete lack of control we have when our sneezing dissipates droplets. Sneezes cannot always be stifled successfully, even if we try. People can cover their mouths when they sneeze – but that may not obviate contagion. People often act inadvertently or carelessly, too – for example, someone may think to cover her mouth when she sneezes but then puts her hand on the stair railing right afterwards. But even if we are very careful about infection-control measures, the only way to completely limit our potential vector-hood would be simply to stay away from everyone else, a very costly solution over the long term. Even then, as we have seen, we may not be able fully to obviate either our vector-hood or our victim-hood.

To be sure, many aspects of infectious disease fit the picture of a person who can choose to avoid risks presented by others or to avoid imposing risks on them. Individuals do have choices about their actions in light of what they know about contagion, and they can be held responsible for those choices, at least when they knowingly infect others or put them at risk. Deliberately sneezing on one's competitor, having sex when one is aware of the possibility of transmitting disease, like chlamydia or syphilis – these are (ir)responsible acts. Similar notions of responsibility, praise, and blame apply to them, as to other reckless acts that put persons at risk: leaving toxic waste near a playground, having sex without protection against unwanted pregnancy, and so on. And they also apply to more sinister acts involving infectious agents, such as the plots of bioterrorists or the deliberate transmission of HIV as an act of revenge.

But there is more here, too, in the context of infectious disease. With communicable diseases, the situation of the individual agent in relation to others is sometimes not obviously under voluntary control, either for the victim or for the vector. People may be unaware that they are infectious or even ill or at risk of being ill, at the very point disease is most likely to be transmitted to others. Transmitting disease or not may not even be the subject of agency; with respect to some infectious diseases, spread to susceptible hosts may occur despite our very best efforts at prevention.

Long transmission chains, moreover, may compound the issues here; it may be difficult or impossible to trace these chains and thereby attribute harm to one to the acts of another. Blameworthiness for transmission may be further affected by factors such as susceptibility in downstream parties, sometimes unpredictable but sometimes comparatively easily foreseen. For example, with a simple sneeze someone might transmit an infectious agent that has no effect on herself but is utterly devastating to others, as a pneumonia might be simple to resolve in a healthy young adult but fatal in an elderly or immune-compromised person. Leaving a rainwater-filled old tire in the back yard during mosquito-breeding season in a West Nile virus-endemic area might be merely a nuisance if the neighbors are a college dormitory full of healthy young adults, but a lethal threat if a nursing home is next door.

It may be tempting to shrug these cases off as unpredictable, requiring too omniscient a capacity for foreseeing outcomes of our choices and so not a violation of our responsibilities to avoid harming others. After all, a person cannot be held responsible for what he or she cannot realistically predict. But we cannot grant this point. Our more complex metaphysical status as individuals – our physical as well as social "locatedness" – cuts against binary judgments that we are either responsible or not responsible, blameworthy or not blameworthy. We are too immersed in infectious illness too much of the time to claim that we cannot know that

Thus "source patient" imagery, the frequent picture in public health, can be misleading, especially when translated into moral-theoretical contexts for identifying agents responsible for given harms. Source patient imagery suggests a chain with a starting point, as disease moves on to others but does not further affect the originating party. Except for new mutations in emerging diseases and final eradication (like the last wild smallpox patient on earth, in Somalia in 1977), there is no one "source" patient and no end-point terminus; the disease keeps traveling from one person to another. Source patient imagery tends to fail to see the web of interlocking and interplaying mutual, multiple transmissions, especially within groups we are associated with. We may be appropriately held responsible for transmitting disease to others – that is, blamed – if we do so knowingly. But others are responsible, perhaps also blameworthy, for transmitting diseases to us. We are all implicated in a web of relationships that establish themselves without our knowing and that may be difficult to sort out in a linearly traceable way – even when it is possible to identify specific strains of a virus, for instance, that have been transmitted from one person to another. This is because it is not just single occasions of disease transmission that we are each responsible for, but a whole web of disease relationships in which we participate.

If we see ourselves as "embedded" in a physical as well as social nexus, we will see that judgments of responsibility that point fingers at blameworthy originators of harm are too simplistic. Notions of blame must take into account that although I may be blameworthy for transmitting a specific disease if I can avoid doing so, at one and the very same time I may be justified in blaming others, as are those who transmitted it to me if they could have avoided doing so. But such judgments must also take into account that I may put others in my position as they do so to me, even though none of us intend that this occur. Thus individual finger-pointing does not take into account very well what it is to be caught in – and contributing to – a web of mutual transmission, ongoing all the time. Judgments of individual responsibility, appropriate in the cases of deliberate transmission or known risks, must be supplemented by judgments about how we together are responsible for reservoirs of infectiousness and must respond fairly to these burdens.

An Ordinary Example

Let us pull these themes together in terms of a frequent and mundane example. Suppose someone has a noninfectious illness and nevertheless goes to work. He may fail to get sufficient rest or stress his body in other ways, and thus remain sicker for a longer period of time and recover more slowly. His work may be performed less well and he may be unable to meet deadlines. These are costs that he must take into account as he decides whether or not to drag himself to work. However, they are not typically thought to require him to rethink his preferences and values, to change the kind of information he considers in making a well-reasoned choice, to re-examine the standard reasoning structure of trying to select the alternative that will most realize his preferences and values, or even to reconsider the determination of what he is like as a reasoning agent. On this account of autonomy, the autonomous agent deciding whether or not to go to work acts as an individual whose relationships to others are solely contingent. Acting autonomously, he thus may or may not choose to take risks for himself or to take risks that affect others, knowing that if he does he will incur moral responsibility for those choices.

But now suppose his illness is infectious and transmissible. Of course, he also will want to factor in the costs of affecting others if he goes to work in spite of the illness, for example by disrupting the flow of activities at his workplace, or by incurring the resentment of others infected. On standard individualistic analyses, these concerns will figure in only as they affect his concerns. To be sure, these concerns may include second-order concerns for the interests of others as well as his views about obligations not to harm others. If he is a parent considering whether to take his child with the sniffles to day care – or to miss work when an important project is due – he will want to consider the likelihood that his child will get even sicker, requiring more days of absence, as well as the extent to which his child's misery affects his own happiness, the impact of his absence from the office on his co-workers and clients, and so on.

If his condition or his child's condition creates identifiable risks for others, under the harm principle it is permissible for society to constrain his behavior. He may be required to submit to fitness-for-duty examinations before he can drive a school bus or fly an airplane. His child may not be admitted to day care without proper immunizations or with signs of chickenpox. He may experience these limitations on his liberty as unwelcome intrusions that burden him purely for the benefit of others. The intervention is defended because it is likely to be successful and because he can choose to avoid these activities. It would seem less justifiable if it were unlikely to prevent the harm at issue, as well as particularly unfair if his activities were not under his control or if others could avoid the harm more readily than he could.

Sometimes the situation may be more complex, as in cases of mutual transmission. One party in a sexual relationship may transmit gonorrhea to another person, but at the same time may acquire syphilis from them – and the flu as well. Needle-sharing may transmit multiple diseases both to and from a given person. Mutual disease transmission may be particularly frequent in environmental situations that involve crowding, poor nutrition, or poor sanitation such as occur in refugee camps. For example, hepatitis may be spread from one party to others at the same time that, say, cholera is spread from others by to them. In such conditions, unknowing transmission and transmission without preventative measures may be an even greater risk: measles, cholera, diarrheal diseases, and respiratory infections may all be mutually transmitted within a given environment at one and the same time, among the same group of people who are victims of and vectors to each other's pathogens.

Consideration of infectiousness suggests there may be far more to this picture, however. Because he is positioned as victim and as vector, the risks of victim-hood and vector-hood are part of what he must recognize as very biological facts about himself. Moreover, the risks at issue – even the risks of catching a cold – are not always ones that he or others can choose to avoid – they may be uncontrollable, or even unknown.

To make judgments about whether he should go to work or what he should be held responsible for, we need to consider the overall distribution of the burdens of infectiousness. We need to consider, for example, how to support or compensate him if the judgment is that it is too risky for others for him to be on the job on a given day, or if his child must be kept at home. When the patient is both victim and vector, he cannot be seen simply as an isolated reasonable agent, deliberating about what to do – that is liberalism's picture, but a picture that, while it may be partly useful in HIV, is not fully compatible with much of infectious disease. It is not only that the patient may be sick, and hence subject to the impairments illness sometimes brings – confusion, pain, reduced memory or reasoning capacity. In addition, his or her agency must be seen as embodied – hence both vulnerable to infection and at the same time at risk of transmitting infection to others. Persons with whom he or she is in contact, directly or indirectly, also occupy this dual role. In general, with most communicable diseases, there are no parties who are in principle to be seen as agents, no parties who are never patients in a causal sense, no parties who are only victims, no parties who are only vectors. Insofar as a person is a potential patient in the sense of being affected by another person's disease-transmitting actions, that "patient" also becomes – without explicitly assuming this responsibility – an "agent" in the next series of transmission. In infectious disease, agency and patienthood are not independent, but inextricably intertwined. One person's choices as agent have the capacity to make others agents too in the next iterations of the same difficult choices. Judgments about what people ought to do, when we can restrict their liberties, and what we owe them in return must thus be seen not only as individual, but as shared distributive problems.

Summing Up: Autonomous Agency in the Context of Infectious Disease

Thus the traditional bioethics literature, more often than not, ignores our agency in transmitting disease and our potential for passing it on. On the other hand, discussions in public health have often overlooked or at least under-weighed the other side of the equation, that we are nonetheless patients, victims as well as vectors. Both the bioethics and public health literatures have overlooked the full social *and* physical character of our relationships with each other. The parties to whom we transmit disease are not just targets, harmed by us; they are our family members, our friends, co-workers, fellow passengers, members of our social networks, religious groups, our society at large, and the natural world. The parties who transmit sometimes serious, even fatal diseases to us are the same ones – our family members, our friends, co-workers, fellow passengers, members of our social networks, religious groups, our society at large. These complexities, we have argued, challenge bioethics to develop more complicated accounts of agency, autonomy, harm prevention, and responsibility. We cannot think of ourselves as individual agents whose liberties are to be restricted when we pose especially urgent threats to each other; we must think of ourselves as embedded agents who share the benefits and the burdens of these biological facts.

We can hardly suppose that the exploration of clinical and policy dilemmas involving infectious disease will be conducted in the terms we've set forth here: human "individuals" as way-stations and breeding-grounds for billions and billions of micro-organisms. Of course, public discussion will continue to use the ordinary language of bioethics. But we think that this biologically augmented view should be always in the background, since it may have dramatic consequences for how we should respond to measures intended to prevent, control, and treat infectious disease – measures that are typically seen as involving constraints on individual liberty to prevent transmission from one person to another. Our modified and deepened picture of the self – the self who is both victim *and* vector – recommends, we believe, a fuller normative view of our reciprocal obligations in an environment of infectious disease.

Notes

1 This phrase is quoted in many places. For an example, see the Department of Energy website, http://www.eh.doe.gov/health/news/infectious20040331.pdf (accessed February 22, 2006). Although the quotation is typically attributed to testimony before Congress, original references are unavailable.

2 For an account of the virtual absence of references to infectious diseases in the early bioethics texts, see Leslie P. Francis, Margaret P. Battin, Jay A. Jacobson, Charles B. Smith, and Jeffrey Botkin, How infectious diseases got left out – and what this omission might have meant for bioethics, *Bioethics* 19 (2005): 307–22, esp. pp. 308–11.

3 A compendium of cases assembled in 1982 from the *Hastings Center Report* is illustrative. Among 42 cases dealing with topics such as "the last bed in the ICU," "can the fetus be an organ farm?" or "baby making and the public interest," only two feature infectious diseases. In one, the primary question is whether to reveal a prospective husband's homosexuality to his intended wife – not whether to reveal that he has a sexually transmitted disease. In the other, the issue is whether to permit mentally retarded hepatitis B carriers to attend public school; the discussion attends to the risks of hepatitis B within the context of a discussion of the claims of people with mental retardation. Carol Levine and Robert M. Veatch (eds.), *Cases in Bioethics from the Hastings Center Report*, New York: The Hastings Center, 1982.

4 Tom L. Beauchamp and James F. Childress, *Principles of Biomedical Ethics*, Oxford: Oxford University Press, 1979, 5th edn., 2001.

5   Albert R. Jonsen, Mark Siegler, and William J. Winslade, *Clinical Ethics: A Practical Approach to Ethical Decisions in Clinical Medicine*, New York: Macmillan, 1982.

6   For a discussion of the history of quarantine, see the website of the US Centers for Disease Control, Division of Global Migration and Quarantine, http://www.cdc.gov/ncidod/dq/history.htm (accessed February 24, 2006).

7   See, e.g., Dan E. Beauchamp and Bonnie Steinbock (eds.), *New Ethics for the Public's Health*, New York, Oxford University Press, 1999. Among 29 essays devoted to such topics as human rights, access to health care, obesity, drug use, violent injury, gene therapy, and infertility, the volume devotes four chapters to infectious disease. For a criticism of the paternalism of the "new public health," see Richard Epstein, In defense of the "old" public health: the legal framework for the regulation of public health, *Brooklyn Law Review* 69 (2004): 1421–70.

8   Stephen Pincock, Poliovirus spreads beyond Nigeria after vaccine uptake drops, *British Medical Journal* 328 (2004): 310.

9   T. Svoboda, B. Henry, L. Shulman, et al., Public health measures to control the spread of the severe acute respiratory syndrome during the outbreak in Toronto, *New England Journal of Medicine* 350 (2004): 2352–61.

10 An excellent discussion of the ethical issues raised by HIV is Ronald Bayer, *Private Acts, Social Consequences*. New York: The Free Press, 1989.

11 See Bugchasers: The men who long to be HIV+, *Rolling Stone* online, available at www.solargeneral.com/pdf/BugChasers.pdf (accessed February 8, 2006).

12 Thomas R. Frieden, Moupali Das-Douglas, Scott E. Kellerman, and Kelly J. Henning, Applying public health principles to the HIV epidemic, *New England Journal of Medicine* 353 (22) (2005): 2397–402.

13 Thomas May, The concept of autonomy in bioethics: an unwarranted fall from grace, in James Stacey Taylor (ed.), *Personal Autonomy: New Essays on Personal Autonomy and Its Role in Contemporary Moral Philosophy*, Cambridge: Cambridge University Press, 2005, pp. 299–309.

14 Catriona MacKenzie and Natalie Stoljar, *Relational Autonomy: Feminist Perspectives on Autonomy, Agency, and the Social Self*, New York: Oxford University Press, 2000.

15 Rosamond Rhodes, Justice in medicine and public health, *Cambridge Quarterly of Health Care Ethics* 14 (1) (2005): 13–26.

16 John Stuart Mill, *On Liberty*, New York: Liberal Arts Press, 1956, p. 13.

17 Susan Okie, Betting on a malaria vaccine, *New England Journal of Medicine* 353 (18) (2005): 1877–81, at p. 1880.

Chapter 16

Abuses of Science in Medical Ethics

Glenn McGee and Dýrleif Bjarnadóttir

All contemporary debates in medical ethics involve arguments comprised of premises that depend, in part, on an account of the scientific facts involved in the matter at hand. A valid argument against the continuation of artificial nutrition and hydration for patients in a persistent vegetative state (PVS) would beg no questions about the conditions under which a patient could be said to be in such a state, nor about the effect of nutrition and hydration on such patients. Whatever the normative claim, and regardless of whether the facts of the matter have been correctly established from a mutually agreeable account of "good science," the facts matter.

Yet it is in the nature of political discourse that even well-established facts that have not been falsified or widely contested in the relevant, peer-reviewed scientific literature can easily be twisted to suit the arguments of disputants. Contemporary public debates about, for example environmental protection and stem cell research, are riddled with claims to the effect that those on the opposite side of the issue proceed from an insufficient understanding of the facts of the matter, or worse are guilty of deliberate misrepresentation. Such claims can be quite effective as political tools, because they detract attention from the normative question at hand, placing it instead on the skill or character of the disputant who holds the opposite view.

For example, if, in refuting the claim that embryonic stem cell research is a moral activity, I pause to argue that the claims made by my opponent are buttressed by factual inaccuracies, I divert attention to the question of who is the better scientist. If I can then point to a more elaborate scientific account that demonstrates that alternative modes of stem cell research, involving no embryos, are somehow better, I will have succeeded in turning a moral debate about stem cell research into a referendum on who is telling the truth. In most cases the candidates for "best scientist" in such a forum will neither be scientists by training nor, more importantly, have been charged with demonstrating a review of the peer-reviewed scientific literature before presenting their conclusion.

One might draw the inference that there is good science that, in this case, both sides would just as soon suppress or advance, or that both sides are at worst eluding or unaware of the good science that exists. But in many of the most complex areas of debate in medical ethics, the facts of the matter are far from clear. Just as there is nothing approaching certainty in the law on many matters at issue in jurisprudential debates about medical ethics, the science today in areas such as complex clinical trials, transplantation, and enhancement technologies, to name but a few, is subject to enormous disagreement and, more importantly, to a very high level of interdisciplinary innovation. Stem cell research, for example, relies on the science of embryology and the technological innovations of cell therapy. Yet there are no departments of embryology in the United States, and the world of "cell therapy" is a hodgepodge of academic, industry, and foundation researchers whose work may have very little in common. The very fact that those who first cultured the pluripotent human embryonic stem cell were, respectively, an obstetrician and a veterinarian by training, gives some sense of the diversity involved in unsettled areas of scientific innovation. To turn to stem cell researchers for an account of what "counts" as an embryo, or what it would mean to "destroy" one is to ask a great deal of those to whom disputants might normally turn for the facts of the matter.

To further complicate matters, a question that we will not take up in any significant way in this essay but that bears directly on bioethics's engagement with new scientific technology is the status of scientific facts more generally. For those who adopt the position that science is socially constructed, even the best informed scientific claims, having been subjected to the best peer review, are neither tests of what James (1979) and later Rorty (1991) would call "capital T truth," nor are they in principle ever removed from the social constructs that govern how science is institutionalized, funded, evaluated, published, disseminated, etc. Several social constructivists argue, then, that the best accounts of facts are those that allow scientists and those who utilize the products of their labors to predict and control things within their own experience.

Social constructivists have played a major role in debates concerning, for example, stem cell research, where a position on science and epistemology is made more plausible by the fact that so much of what is involved in the science of regenerative medicine cannot be accounted for using the previous vocabulary about such matters as fertilization, potency, or viability. What is a scientist to call a part-cow, part-human embryo-like thing? And on what basis? What sort of peer review will clarify matters, and which methods will allow scientists to ascertain the truth of the matter about when a thing is or is not an embryo? The difficulties presented by innovation in biomedical science plague not only the honest scientist who would explore these new questions about boundary conditions for the life sciences, but also the political disputant, who relies so much more today than in the past on representations of what the science "is" about such matters.

Those engaged in contemporary debates about the allocation of resources, the morality of proceeding with new areas of research, and the correct boundaries to be placed on personal or institutional freedoms in exploring new therapies all find themselves in the almost perfect storm of rapidly advancing science and biotechnology, an increasingly sophisticated and sophistical use of scientific mis-representation by those who seek to advance moral positions, and an almost impenetrable fog of uncertainty about the facts that matter or how and whether to assess their truth or falsity.

Into this storm enters an extraordinarily sophisticated and, often, organized confederation of non-scientists deeply invested in making public policy arguments about these complex issues, and frequently making those arguments not only on the national stage, where they might be subject to the scrutiny of media, but also in increasingly regional discussions of science and ethics. When science is misrepresented or otherwise misused by disputants whose methods resemble *jihad*, the storm described becomes virtually impossible to counter.

It is our purpose in this brief essay to consider some poignant examples of the uses and misuses of science in medical ethics.

Abortion and Physician-Assisted Suicide

Arguably the paradigm case of the significance of different accounts of science's facts, and its role in a public debate about medical ethics, is abortion.

In 1994 Ronald Dworkin's book *Life's Dominion* claimed that government interference in the debate about the legitimacy of abortion in the US was mis-placed. According to Dworkin's analysis the only anti-abortion argument that is not silenced by overwhelming scientific facts about fetal development is at its core a religious argument. The constitutional protection we afford citizens of this country is based on certain criteria that fetuses do not fulfill. Dworkin's claim is that the evidence available to us from embryology and obstetric science is over-whelmingly clear; fetuses do not have any of the characteristics we associate with personhood or holders of citizen rights. Thus the allocation of a right to life for the fetus as an individual does not make any sense and cannot be what opposition to abortion is all about. Once we discount the fetus as an individual holder of rights all we have left to oppose abortion is the view that all human life is sacred, regard-less of individual moral status (Dworkin, 1994).

Dworkin's argument squarely pits the judgments of science against the values and beliefs of individuals about the sanctity of human life. His argument assumes, and reasonably so, that metaphysical beliefs cannot overrule scientific evidence. Stated another way, his is a claim that one cannot choose whether or not to believe scientific evidence about objective facts in the world. One can certainly accord little importance to such knowledge in one's life, but not pretend that it is not so. Science, according to this view, has a unique status among our areas of knowledge in that it systematically and rigorously strives to discover and describe what facts are true of the world. We can choose to hold these facts in little esteem or doubt their significance in the complex web of arguments, that make up our understanding of the world but we cannot claim that they are not empirically true. This leaves issues such as the legality and availability of abortion to be debated in the realm of values, not facts. Thus the debate becomes whether or not government should regulate the fundamental values of citizens.

At the opposite end of life, Dworkin and others go so far as to claim that facts of the matter are not even in contention, in direct contradiction to those whose position was that physician–assisted suicide was clinically unnecessary and an inappropriate use of biomedical technology. In the 1996 cases of *Compassion in Dying v. Washington* and *Quill v. Vacco*, physicians brought suit against Washington state and New York state respectively, asserting the right of a doctor to help a terminally ill patient determine their time and manner of death. The case eventually ended up before the Supreme Court where the states sought and succeeded in overturning a verdict of the lower courts in favor of the physicians.

Dworkin and five other moral philosophers wrote an amicus brief to the Supreme Court describing and discussing the situation of terminally ill patients or patients in chronic untreatable pain. The philosophers suggest two principles to guide future legislation on the subject. The first principle is that there is and should be a general moral and constitutional principle that gives competent people the right to make their own momentous decisions about aspects in their own lives concerning the spiritual, philosophical, or religious meaning of life and death. The second principle deals with the special circumstances of the vulnerable population of terminally ill patients. Recognizing that people may make such momentous decisions impulsively or out of emotional depression, the brief suggests that in some circumstances the state may have the constitutional power to override that right in order to protect its citizens from mistaken but irrevocable acts of self-destruction (Rawls et al., 1997).

The claim of the brief is clear; autonomous individuals have a fundamental and constitutional right to hold and act on their own fundamental beliefs about the value of their life and the meaning of their death. But undergirding the claim of the "philosophers' brief" is a set of references to well-established scientific facts about the limits on decision-making capacity. The claim that a state should retain the right to protect its citizens from themselves when they display limited capacity to make reasonable decisions, is put forth without questioning the accepted understanding of the effects that depression, duress, dementia, to name a few, have on the decision-making capacity of the individual. The legitimacy of those facts is accepted on the basis of rigorous and well established scientific evidence. Rejecting those facts as relevant to the judgment of when self-determination is appropriate moves the discussion into the realm of values, pitting the value of having the freedom to make the choice to end one's life against the value of protecting and preserving life at all costs. The accepted facts underlying the first principle amount to the belief that, depression and the like aside, there is an absence of any good empirical facts that would limit the availability of choice for an autonomous individual when it comes to these intensely private issues.

The Philosophical Division of the Debate

Dworkin's argument against prohibitive abortion legislation relies on a secular notion of human worth that he believes is in keeping with the constitutional provision of separation of religious convictions of individuals and the regulatory powers of government. The same spirit of individual freedom that the founding fathers aimed to capture is a fundamental part of the liberal notion that the government of a pluralistic democratic society has limited say over the way its citizens conduct their private lives. On this liberal interpretation of the *public sphere* on the one hand and the *private sphere* on the other, matters of religion, reproductive choices and views about sanctity of life fall squarely within the private sphere.

Thus we can portray the dilemma that Dworkin's argument illustrates in terms of the ongoing tension between the demands of a liberal democracy for the acceptance of the diverse way in which people choose to conduct their lives, and the demands of the powerful moral doctrine of Christianity whose influence can be seen in many basic institutions and practices of western societies. Dworkin's and colleagues' use of science, on either side of either issue, is remanded to the superstructure of the argument in favor of or against the use of a technological intervention – but the scientific claims are nonetheless inextricably tied to the account given for freedom and its limits.

Liberals, libertarians, and communitarians are distinguished by their differences concerning the composition of the private and the public realm, as well as by the appropriate form of interaction among peoples, groups, and institutions. Each of these, too, is articulated most strongly when accompanied by arguments framed as science to justify their theoretical suppositions concerning the moral life.

Liberals argue for a clear distinction between the private and public spheres in society, where the public sphere only invokes values that all private conceptions of the good have in common. This clearly leaves the bulk of values that make up the identity and outlook of an individual outside of the structure and institutions of the public sphere. In the private sphere each individual is entitled to have his own conception of the good as long as it does not violate the basic principles of society.

John Locke wrote that all men have a civil interest in life, liberty, health, and property and that it was the proper role of government to protect these civil rights. In addition to these rights, continues Locke, it is also in man's individual power to choose his own road to salvation (Locke, 1955). Despite his claim that our talents and abilities are gifts from God, and that no man can take his own life or that of another for both are God's property, Locke strongly opposes the use of force by the state to get people to hold certain beliefs or practice certain ceremonies. Locke argues that beliefs are not the kind of things that can be forced upon people and anyone who tries to do so does not understand the first principle of salvation:

> A sweet religion, indeed, that obliges men to dissemble, and tell lies to both God and man, for the salvation of their souls! If the magistrate thinks to save men thus, he

seems to understand little of the way of salvation; and if he does it not in order to save them, why is he so solicitous of the articles of faith as to enact them by a law?
(Locke, *A Letter Concerning Toleration*, quoted in Mendus, 1991, p. 41)

Behind Locke's rejection of enforcement of one true religion is a recognition of the serious skeptical arguments to which religious doctrine is susceptible. Locke presents a civil government that has a minimal set of rules and limitations in order to allow a diverse group of people to come together under one social contract. Many historians maintain that the accomplishment of the French Republic and of the United States of America in the last decades of the eighteenth century are a testament to the great wisdom of Locke's vision of a truly civil government with civil laws and legislators.

In modern times John Rawls's liberal theory has provided the backdrop for further applications of the liberal principles of safeguarding the core freedoms of individuals. In very broad terms, philosophical liberals and those who accept their arguments identify a notion of the *good* of individuals as strictly defined by individuals themselves. They see public life as a distinct domain where what is *right* is defined by a shared societal notion of what is just, and that concept is used to inform decisions about the distribution of societal resources.

In keeping with his understanding of the political requirements of a pluralistic democratic society, Rawls relies on a "thin" conception of the good to support the basic structure of society. This notion is "thin" because it does not have enough detail to promote any specific conception of the good. Instead, it is designed to assign the primary goods that are essential for most conceptions of the good to individuals in a fair way so that everyone can have an equal chance to pursue their "thick" or detailed individual conception of the good life. Rawls offers two principles of justice for distributing societal resources while maintaining the distinction between public life and private life. These principles ensure the basic liberties of each individual and provide that primary goods are distributed fairly (Rawls, 1971).

It is worth noting that the basic structure of society necessarily facilitates some "thick" conceptions of the good more than others. A society that focuses on fair distribution of primary goods will, unavoidably, promote the goods of individuals who are, in their private lives, committed to a principle of justice as fairness. The basic principles of justice are, however, intended to ensure that each individual is treated fairly, not that the pursuit of each conception of the good is given an equal opportunity of being realized. The emphasis is thus on fair distribution and minimal interference, not on equal promotion of all conceivable conceptions of the good.

Rawlsian accounts of justice have received systematic attention from social scientists and moral and political philosophers. However, few make reference to the thin and the thick, which are at the core of Rawls's philosophy.

Communitarian critics of Rawlsian liberalism, however, object to the minimalist picture of the role of the public sphere and the portrayal of justice as fairness because it overemphasizes the individualistic nature of citizens who consciously choose to realize their self-identity. The communitarian model, in contrast, emphasizes the importance of community as the creating force and influence of an individual's identity. Communitarians claim that it is unreasonable to separate the individual from the roles and commitments he has in a society, as Rawls suggest we do in his theoretical starting point, "the original position." Hence, on the communitarian account, the two principles of justice that individuals in the original position come up with are not exhaustively representative of the good that it is essential to preserve and promote on a societal basis. Michael Sandel and others point not only to the importance of a communal account of the interaction of individuals in their moral lives, but also to extensive evidence from the social sciences that undermines any account of the individual in the absence of a robust moral community (Sandel, 1982).

One major point of contention between liberals and communitarians is that moral or religious convictions are important aspects of individuals' identity that the original position ignores. Communitarians insist that those kinds of convictions are too central to individuals' identity to be left at the door in the original position. Thus it follows, according to communitarian beliefs, that principles of justice formulated in the original position where the individuals are ignorant of their most salient moral and religious convictions will not address basic aspects of those individuals' needs. This is Sandel's point when he rejects the Rawlsian commitment to democratic liberalism on the basis of the conceptual failure of "the unencumbered self" that is essential for the formulation of the liberal ideal.

The third camp of political philosophy that has been concerned with the role and scope of government is comprised of another group of students of Locke. These Lockeans focus on his basic notions of individual freedoms, in particular the sanctity of private property. Libertarians' arguments for free markets and strict limitations on social or welfare services rely on claims about human nature. Specifically, they invoke a descriptive account of human interaction to the affect that moral actors can speak and act coherently with regard to property and markets and all their implications.

Libertarians therefore argue that the freedom of an individual to dispose of his own body and property as he wishes should be absolute. Thus the role of government in citizen's lives should be confined to preventing coercion (Nozick, 1977). Coercion is defined as the use of physical force, the threat of such, or deception, that alters, or is intended to alter, the way individuals would use their body or property. Libertarians would thus reject any control over science by a government as that would clearly constitute interference with how individuals disposed of their own bodies or property and with the free market of supply and demand. A government that passes a law against selling organs and thus prevents me from selling my kidney at market price is influencing in a coercive way how I use my body and thus violating my basic liberty.

Philosophy, Politics, and the Control of Science

Disputants in contemporary debates in medical ethics frequently allege that science should not be subjected to government regulation and political control, albeit by those on the other side of whatever issue is under discussion. For moral theorists writing in medical ethics, the question of science's misappropriation is often framed in terms of a debate concerning the scope of public control *v.* private conceptions of the good. Those who hold a scientific view often articulate it in terms of an epistemological claim about science's role in society that depends, in an almost circular fashion, on the degree to which the disputants trust individuals or a collective to arrive at conclusions about facts.

Proponents of government regulation of science often appeal to the communitarian claim that considerations such as religious conviction cannot be separated from identity of those individual citizens who hold them. A basic structure that strictly delegates such convictions to the private sphere is unreasonable for Sandel, who articulates this position most clearly not in his philosophical work but in the transcripts of the Presidential Commission on Bioethics (2002) where this argument becomes a lynchpin for those who would apply a communal structure to arguments against technology that might otherwise be embraced by a wide variety of individuals. And in the 1990s, communitarian philosophy produced political arguments for individual social responsibility as a prerequisite for individual freedom and tolerance of others. There is for example a Communitarian Network of nonpartisan, nonreligious individuals and organizations that advocates for a better political, moral and social environment in the US through greater acceptance of our social responsibilities. This particular coalition is a liberal secular type of comunitarianism. The following is from their website:

> The adjustment communitarians favor is not a diminution of rights, as some of their critics – most notably the American Civil Liberties Union – claim. Rather, the communitarian movement's main concern is with assumptions of responsibilities. Communitarians favor national service, for instance, to enable the young to develop their civic spirit. Communitarians seek to curb the role of special interests in Congress by stemming the flood of private money into the coffers of elected officials, thereby enabling the legislature to serve the public interest. And communitarians favor drug tests for those who directly have the lives of others in their hands (e.g., airline pilots and school-bus drivers), and see these measures as a legitimate interpretation of the Fourth Amendment's ban on "unreasonable searches and seizures" rather than as a diminution of rights. The same holds for sobriety checkpoints and other carefully crafted measures to protect the public.
>
> (The Communitarian Network)

The present US presidential administration appeals to community, and indeed to communitarianism, when identifying the role of communities in determining the most appropriate or most "American" values for the nation. This is communitarian in the sense that it appeals to values of identifiable communities, but it differs from the traditional political philosophy of communitarianism as well as from the call for increased social responsibility iterated above.

An important distinction between the two kinds of communitarianism we can identify in today's political discourse is about what social responsibility means.

The religiously based or conservative communitarians are committed to a certain kind of community and the rights and responsibilities of those that belong to that community trump other considerations. The more traditional version of communitarian theory emphasizes the need to respect community and societal obligations as a necessary premise for the survival of individual liberties.

Thus it seems that even within the communitarian camp the dispute hinges on where we draw the line between the public sphere, that is legitimately under the control of government and regulatory bodies, on the one hand, and the private pursuits of individuals of their chosen conception of the good, on the other. The essence of the debate between liberals and what we have now identified as the conservative communitarians is twofold. On the one hand it concerns the different understanding of the liberals and the communitarians of what constitutes the right and good in turn, as well as what should be their order of importance. On the other hand it deals with whether government should control the right only or if it also has authority to interfere in people's conception of and search for the good. The conservative communitarians define the good operationally, within boundaries strictly tied to that of the community as properly construed within the theory.

Are Values and Objectivity Incompatible?

Lurking in the wings of the dispute about where the private sphere ends and the public sphere begins, is another fundamental disagreement. How do we define health and disease? The significance of this question becomes clear if we consider how different understanding of health and disease can change what we consider the aim of science and medicine.

Arthur Caplan frames the concern in a 1997 article:

> [The concern] is that if health and disease are nothing more than socially determined, culturally mediated and individually subjective concepts, there is some fear that there will be little possibility of placing medicine on a firm scientific footing or of finding consensus among experts and patients about the proper limits of medical concern.
>
> (Caplan, 1997, p. 71)

It seems that without a coherently defined concept of disease it becomes difficult to shape health care policy and to structure health care systems in such a way that they can face their economic, social, and ethical challenges.

There is extensive literature about the definition of disease (Hoffman, 2001). We will mention two opposing views that mark off the outer edges of the debate.

On the one side of the debate we have the influential works of Christopher Boorse, published in 1975 and 1977. Boorse makes the argument that disease is a value free concept based solely on the statistical deviation from the species biological design. This makes the recognition of disease purely a matter of science, not an evaluative decision. This also provides us with a value-free biological function account of health. Boorse distinguishes seven accounts of health and disease from the previous literature, all of which have some connection with the notion of normal functioning but none of which capture fully the "breakdown or mal-function of the machinery" that he argues constitutes disease. These accounts are; (1) value – health is determined as something we value and disease is thus some-thing undesirable; (2) treatment by a physician – diseases are undesirable conditions that doctors treat; (3) statistical normality – disease is what is statistically abnor-mal; (4) pain suffering and discomfort – disease causes the bearer of it pain and suffering; (5) disability – any disease must at some stage cause disability or death; (6) adaptation – the species ability and success in adapting to its environment con-stitutes a measure of health; (7) homeostasis – health is maintaining an equilibrium of the body/organ, disease is a disruption of this balance (Boorse, 1977, p. 550).

Boorse's definition of disease is in tune with the accepted medical model of defining disease as the failure of an organ or system to function at or above its species-typical level. This definition can incorporate all of the above categories where appropriate to the species-typical functioning account, but avoids the prob-lems of relying on them for a definition of disease. Defining health as, for example, a state of affairs that we value, and disease the absence of, or a threat to this val-uable state, presents the problem of changing and subjective values resulting in absurd definitions of disease, such as drapetomania, the disease of slaves that are possessed with an obsessive desire to run away from their owners. Under the defi-nition of disease as failure of an organ or system to function in a species-typical way, we confine our view of disease to the physiological condition, for example, the heart fails to do what the body requires it to do. This notion of normalcy is not dependent on a majority of individuals having a well functioning heart – some diseases, such as tooth decay or minor lung irritation, are more prevalent than their absence, but they still constitute a disease since there is deviation from some account of functioning that Boorse and others embed in a biostatistical analysis of the organism population.

Peter Sedgwick's view is at the other extreme. Sedgwick argues that disease does not exist in nature but is created solely as a social construct by humans. A tiger who has fought another tiger and been wounded may be extremely uncomfortable and in great distress but only in human eyes can it be described as ill.

> Out of his anthropocentric self-interest, man has chosen to consider as illness or disease those natural circumstances which precipitate the death (or the failure to func-tion according to certain values) of a limited number of a biological species; man himself, his pets and other cherished livestock and the plant varieties he cultivates for his gain or pleasure.
>
> (Sedgwick, 1981, p. 121)

Sedgwick's view focuses entirely on the social value of a certain state of affairs that we have chosen to call health. This leaves the door open to changes in or evalua-tion of which states of affairs are desirable and which are not. The history of mental illness provides examples that support this view, particularly in the classification of masturbation, homosexuality, women's sexual desire, and the tendency of slaves to run away from their masters, which have all at some point been classified as illnesses that warranted the concern and involvement of the medical profession (Caplan, 1997, pp. 57–73). Intellectual heirs of Sedgwick's view often claim that the chosen values of our society discriminate against individuals who fall below a socially constructed ideal. The implication of their criticism is that societies have a duty to try to change these attitudes and be more inclusive of people with socially constructed "disabilities" (Parens and Asch, 2000).

Today's proponents of Boorse's view continue to want to incorporate the notion of normal species functioning into the basic structure of society. Norman Daniels has written extensively on how the right to health care, as a primary good to be distributed in society according to the principles of justice, follows from the definition of normal species functioning (Daniels, 1985). For Daniels and colleagues writing in the Rawlsian tradition, an account of the just distribution of health care depends on the possibility of providing a value-free epidemiological account of normal functioning. They fear that in the absence of such an account their argument for distributing scarce health resources or restricting personal liberty with regard to health decisions would have no justification.

From a liberal standpoint which limits the grounding of governmental interventions to a thin conception of the good, we can identify many instances on the current political landscape that count as illegitimate government attempts at controlling science and technology. In considering these examples we need to try to understand who is trying to control what and why. Powerful constituencies frequently have interests in how scientific knowledge or technology will be received by some target audience. Science is no longer the noble quest for truth that the renaissance elite professed it to be, nor are research results unbiased representations of an objective truth. A great deal of the research agenda is determined by political pressure, societal expectations or the promise of lucrative relationships to industry. Much of research in plasma cell physics is propelled by military contracts. Research on breast cancer took a huge leap forward after the neglect of women's health concerns became a political issue and signaled awareness that women were a voting force to be reckoned with. Money and public interest are driving forces behind the direction of scientific research. So are political interests and politicians often control where the money goes and where it does not. This ability to control the direction of scientific advance is not inherently abusive or manipulative. The difference between wise and benevolent direction and allocation of resources by politicians and abusive self-serving politically motivated attempts at control, lies in the root of the influence.

In his book *The Republican War on Science* Chris Mooney discusses the deliberate debunking of good scientific evidence in order to promote a particular political agenda (Mooney, 2005). Mooney's examples, taken at face value, suggest a systematic attempt (and considerable success) of Republican politicians in the US to discredit or ignore well-grounded scientific evidence about global warming and human activity causing climate changes and acid rain, the spread of HIV in the early days of the disease, the relationship between unhealthy foods and the global rise of obesity, and the need to protect endangered species. Mooney claims that the way Republican Washington interprets scientific evidence depends on its connections to the industry that will be affected by the science and occasionally on the effect it will have on future fundraising. Mooney presents evidence to show that at the outbreak of the AIDS epidemic in the early 1980s, the Reagan administration did not react to the epidemic's emergence because a response might have required educating children about safe sex and condom use, subjects that would have offended the sensibilities of the Reagan administration's conservative Christian constituency (Mooney, 2005, pp. 36–7).

We can identify a similar attitude towards scientific research in the current US presidential administration's concern for the influential conservative Christian movement. This is evident in many areas such as stem cell research, the teaching of intelligent design as science in primary and secondary schools, and sex education for teenagers in public schools.

Stem cell research, using government funding, is now allowed only on cell lines that were in existence in 2001, prior to the current administration's moratorium on the creation of cell lines. Defenders of the administration policy argue that existing lines of embryonic cells are plentiful enough to allow the research to thrive, and (with not a twinge of irony) they argue that research on embryonic stem cell is not really crucial for advances in the field of human stem cell technology. Researchers who oppose the ban claim that adult stem cells cannot take the place of embryonic stem cells in the research because at this stage we cannot know which line of research will be productive and for what results. Also, they can point to no research to support either that claim or the more important one, that the resources allocated to stem cell research are better put to use there than in other direct treatment of the relevant diseases.

The two camps dress their claims as scientific views, but, as already noted, the name of science is frequently misused by those who are unable or unwilling to draw conclusions from scientific data or even to attempt to read and interpret the scientific literature. It has been argued that, despite claims to the contrary by those who oppose embryonic stem cell research, there is no data whatsoever to support the claim that adult stem cell research, which they tout as scientifically superior, is in fact so. The question that is raised by such arguments is whether or not these disputants make improper appeals to scientific authority in their arguments, and if so, how such appeals can best be supplanted by a more genuine form of appeal to science, even where disputants disagree about the facts at hand.

When politicians embrace this way of talking about science not only as a strategy but as doctrine, the public becomes part of the attack both on science and on careful debate. The endorsement by the administration of George W. Bush of the Intelligent Design curriculum in Kansas is an embrace of fundamental metaphysical beliefs in the public sphere of state-sponsored education. The government thereby puts biology, a rigorous unbiased discipline, devoid of any appeal to supernatural non-empirically verifiable explanations, on the same level as spiritual commitment that is, by its very nature, unexplainable. Whether or not the administration is right to do so, it is not acting in the interests of, or with any regard to, science as practiced by scientists.

The same reluctance to respect the boundaries of the shared public sphere as distinct from individual private convictions and ways of life, is found in repeated government policies that ignore sound scientific data about the effectiveness of teaching abstinence as a way of avoiding STDs, HIV, and teenage pregnancies. Numerous studies have shown that teaching abstinence only as the way to deal responsibly with sex before marriage does not reduce risk behavior among teenagers (Texas A&M, 2005). In line with Dworkin's critique on the government involvement in the abortion debate, this is another vivid and dangerous example of conclusive scientific research that simply falls on the deaf ears of policy-makers. The critical point is that those who advance the abstinence-only view not only ignore scientific findings, they also embrace a view that is actually refuted by science in order to justify a moral stance on sex.

Conclusion

The spheres of science and politics are perhaps eternally intertwined. Regardless of one's view about the role of society in constructing and constraining scientific truth, the public does in fact play the crucial role in determining how science is used and what scientific findings ultimately come to mean in public discourse.

The uses and misuses of science feature prominently in the moral arguments of medical ethics. Those who argue for a just distribution of health care resources typically rest their claims on a dubious theory of normal species function. It projects conclusions based on the possibility of a value-free epidemiology within which it would be possible to know who is sick and who is typical or "functional" in a normal way. Those who decry stem cell research make claims about the moral status of a blastocyst and an early embryo without any scientific basis whatsoever, and consistently misstate the *status quo* and proclaim outright fabrications concerning the risks and benefits of adult versus embryonic cells. Similarly, those who fear that any resistance to stem cell research using embryos will energize the fight against abortion often appeal to science concerning the therapeutic potential of those cells, when efficacy has not yet been demonstrated in humans or even primate models. Science is contentious everywhere in medical ethics. It is too much to ask that those engaged in disputes about science and ethics read science in the same way, read the same literature, and evaluate conclusions through the same filter. It is not, however, unreasonable to expect that there be basic rules concerning how far those who would make moral arguments can delve into the empirical foundation for those arguments without themselves being subject to the scrutiny of those who work in the fields of science under discussion.

References

Boorse, C. (1975), On the distinction between disease and illness, *Philosophy and Public Affairs* 5 (1): 49–68.

Boorse, C. (1977), Health as a theoretical concept, *Philosophy of Science* 44 (4): 542–73.

Caplan, A.L. (1997), The concepts of health, illness, and disease, in Robert M. Veatch (ed.), *Medical Ethics*, 2nd edn., Sudbury, MA: Jones and Bartlett Publishers, pp. 57–73.

The Communitarian Network for Individual Rights and Social Responsibilities, http://www.gwu.edu/ccps/index.html.

Compassion in Dying v. Washington, 79 F.3d 790, 801 (9th Cir. 1996).

Daniels, Norman (1985), *Just Health Care*, Cambridge: Cambridge University Press.

Dworkin, Ronald (1994), *Life's Dominion: An Argument about Abortion, Euthanasia and Individual Freedom*, New York: Vintage Books.

Hoffman, Bjorn (2001), Complexity of the concept of disease as shown through rival theoretical frameworks, *Theoretical Medicine* 22: 211–36.

James, William (1979, originally published 1907), *Pragmatism*, Cambridge, MA: Harvard University Press.

Locke, John (1955), *A Letter Concerning Toleration*, New York: Liberal Arts Press.

Mendus, Susan (1991), *Locke on Toleration in Focus*, London: Routledge.

Mooney, Chris (2005), *The Republican War on Science*, New York: Basic Books.

Nozick, Robert (1977), *Anarchy, State and Utopia*, New York: Basic Books.

Parens, Eric, and Asch, Adrienne (eds.) (2000), *Prenatal Testing and Disability Rights*, Washington, DC: Georgetown University Press, Hastings Center Studies in Ethics.

Presidential Commission on Bioethics transcripts, 2002, http://www.bioethics.gov/transcripts/dec02/session4.html.

Quill v. Vacco, 80 F.3d 716 (2d Cir. 1996).

Rawls, John (1971), *A Theory of Justice*, Cambridge, MA: Harvard University Press.

Rawls, John, Jarvis Thomson, Judith, Nozick, Robert, Dworkin, Ronald, Scanlon, T.M., and Nagel, Thomas (1997), Assisted suicide: the philosophers' brief, *New York Review of Books* 44 (5) (March 27).

Rorty, Richard (1991), *Objectivity, Relativism and Truth*, Philosophical Papers, vol. I, part 1, Cambridge: Cambridge University Press, pp. 21–113

Sandel, M. (1982), *Liberalism and the Limits of Justice*, Cambridge: Cambridge University Press.

Sedgwick, P. (1981), Illness – mental and otherwise, in A.L. Caplan, H.T. Engelhardt and J.J. McCartney (eds.), *Concepts of Health and Disease, Interdisciplinary Perspectives*, Reading, MA: Addison-Wesley, pp. 99–129.

Texas A&M University, *Teen Sex Increased after Abstinence Program*, report of a study conducted by researchers at Texas A&M University, reported on MSNBC on February 2, 2005. http://www.msnbc.msn.com/id/6894568/

Legislative and Judicial Decisions about Social Policy

Justice

Chapter 17

Allocation of Scarce Resources

Paul Menzel

Resources, including health care resources, are almost always scarce, and they somehow have to be allocated. Often, though, we do not perceive them as either scarce or allocated, particularly when no person is making conscious decisions about how those resources get distributed. Instead some structure in which we work or live just handles the distribution without us having to think about it. When in the US, for example, a much greater volume of health care services is delivered to well-insured citizens than to those who are un- or under-insured, it is the structure of health insurance and financing that explains much about how the allocation comes about, without anyone making "decisions" to allocate more to the well-insured than the relatively uninsured.

A distribution like this could perhaps be regarded as still an "allocation" of health care, but the usual sense of that term involves more conscious decisions by particular persons or groups of people who direct different amounts of care to different people. This entry will focus only on allocation in this latter sense: the relatively deliberate, conscious distribution of care to different persons. Even among such consciously distributed care, however, we should notice a large segment that we still would not count as "allocated." Competent health care professionals are always consciously aiming care differentially at different patients, but that is just "good medicine." A physician's primary responsibility is to get medically appropriate care to the patients who need it for their condition and not to those for whom it is inappropriate. Accordingly, I will use "allocation" in this entry only to encompass care consciously distributed among a population of citizens and patients for reasons that go beyond professionally determined medical need.

As much as is thus eliminated from the scope of "allocation," however, much remains. In any situation of scarcity, resources are insufficient to handle all medical need. Flu vaccine ends up in short supply, for example, and someone has to determine an order of priority among all the potential patients who want or need it. Should infants, who are most susceptible to influenza but will seldom die from it, get the vaccine first, or should it go to the very elderly who, though they contract influenza at a lower rate, are more likely to die from it? Allocation of this sort is often called "rationing," but that term's harsh sound to many ears can perhaps be skirted by using the less provocative but still transparent term, "prioritizing."

Micro- *v.* Macro-Allocation, and a Quandary for Clinical Practice

Within such a meaning of allocation, bioethicists, health policy analysts, and health economists typically distinguish between micro- and macro-allocation to signify different contexts in which prioritizing decisions are made. Micro-allocations occur within a specific delivery setting rather than more population-wide; physicians in a given hospital, for example, have only so many renal dialysis beds, and more patients are referred to the unit than it can accommodate. Macro-allocations of dialysis, on the other hand, occur at the level of a regional or state coordinating agency, or in a report making recommendations about prioritizing care for potential dialysis recipients. (Note, of course, that structural elements in a situation like this may hide the fact that anything is allocated. If some kind of insurance ends up covering virtually all prescribed renal dialysis – as, e.g., Medicare in the US does – then supply may expand to accommodate demand without any further conscious decision being made to "allocate" anything. Resources are still being allocated to dialysis as a category of care, of course, in society's "act" of having Medicare cover dialysis.)

One important controversy about how and by whom prioritizing and allocating should be done can be seen as an argument about the relationship between micro- and macro-allocation: should a physician or nurse ever engage in "bedside rationing"? Such decisions by clinicians would seem to be a violation of their oath to serve the welfare and dignity of the patient they are treating, for in "bedside rationing" providers consider the relative benefits of care that might be given to whole different categories of patients before deciding whether the particular patient before them warrants provision. The issue becomes whether an intrusion of macro-level considerations into the decisions of clinicians constitutes an abdication of providers' moral duties to their patients. This question has become pervasive in an age where managed care is managed partly precisely to control costs. On the one hand, patients come to providers trusting that providers' professional fidelity is to them. On the other hand, aren't patients members of the insurance pools that have to wrestle with difficult prioritizing questions about the pools' scarce resources? Can patients legitimately expect providers not to be, at least somewhat, bedside rationers (Pellegrino and Thomasma, 1988; Menzel, 1990; Morreim, 1991; Ubel, 2000)?

Some examples of the strong moral pull in both directions of this dilemma are striking. Take the use of a temporary artificial heart or ventricular assist device (VAD) as a bridge to a hoped-for transplant for a patient on an organ waiting list. Understandably, given that the patient is at death's doorstep and has only one route to significantly longer life – a transplant – the bridge device is *urgent and necessary rescue care* for that individual. On the other hand, it is absolutely clear that given the real shortage of human organs for transplant, the *net* life-saving capacity of such bridge devices is *zero*. They only shuffle people around on the list. Instead of dying soon and allowing someone else to move up on the waiting list, the person using the device tries to find an organ, and if she does so, it will almost certainly be one that would otherwise have gone to someone else. But if bridge devices thus save no lives (net) whatsoever in the larger picture of the organ-scarce transplant world, how can one defend their use and expense? Doctors who continue to prescribe such devices are providing the world *no net life-saving at all.*

Before leaving the bedside rationing issue with the impression that it constitutes simply a knock-down, drag-out tussle between a provider's loyalty to the individual patient and consideration of the larger total good of all patients, we should recognize that "reconciliationist" views may be plausible, claiming that a wiser and more efficient use of resources can be reconciled with the moral obligations of practitioners to their individual patients. Reconciliationists come in at least three stripes.

1 *Separation of roles.* Parties more distant from the patient than the immediate clinician should make prioritizing decisions by constructing "practice guidelines." Clinicians should then ration only within those predetermined guidelines.

2 *Patients as larger, autonomous persons.* The persons who are patients are not just patients. They are also subscribers and earlier patients, and bedside rationing can be morally grounded in the consent of the patient at an earlier time to restrictions on his or her later care. In the bridge-to-transplant case, for example, imagine patients who have just come onto the transplant waiting list. If asked whether they are willing to adopt a policy of abstaining from the use of any bridge devices, won't all of them likely say that they are, once they realize that (a) their own chances of being saved by a transplant are just as high if no such devices are allowed as their chances would be were such devices allowed, and (b) resources would be "left over" for some other value-producing use (Menzel, 1990; Hall,1997)?

3 *The patient as a member of a just society.* A provider's proper loyalty to a patient, though it is not directly dictated by efficiency, is to the patient as a member of a just society. That loyalty enables the clinician to prioritize and ration with a clean conscience by basing her decisions on considerations of fairness and justice (Brennan, 1991).

Such reconciliationist views may seem an ideal way to handle the conflict between clinician loyalty to patients and societally efficient resource use, still allowing conscientious clinicians to play a major part in allocating scarce resources. These views may face great difficulties in actual use, however. The separate-roles view will involve formulating detailed, care-rationing practice guidelines in abstraction from some of the medically relevant particulars of individual patients. By contrast, more active bedside rationing in which clinicians make substantive rationing decisions may be more efficient and more artful, and therefore preferable (Ubel, 2000).

The prior-consent-of-patients view requires not only accurate readings of what restrictions people are actually willing to bind themselves to beforehand but also a willingness of subscribers and citizens to think seriously about resource trade-offs and then abide honestly by the conclusions of their prior thinking even when that places them on the short end of rationing's stick. And the patient-in-a-just-society model requires more agreement on what constitutes a just society than is possible.

Allocation and Theories of Justice

Health care systems are sometimes thought to fall on a spectrum from those that are characterized by great equity of distribution but employ considerable collective coercion to those that achieve little equity but encroach much less on individual liberty (Culyer et al., 1981). Usually systems lying in the equity-emphasizing and arguably liberty-diminishing direction are also surmised to be likely more efficient (cost-effective). More centralized, they seem better able to control costly provider behavior and insurance-distorted patient demand. Their structural paradigm is a unitary public system, either single payer insurance or national health service, and justice is usually taken to be the dominant value that they serve. The paradigm on the other, decentralized end of the spectrum is a pluralistic system of market competition that does not achieve universal access to even a basic minimum of services and is therefore regarded as leaving allocation to considerations quite other than those of justice.

Two cautions are in order, however, about these preconceived associations of various structural options for the delivery of health care with differing emphases on justice, liberty, and cost-effectiveness. First, it is highly debatable whether the stereotypical conflicts of liberty and cost-effectiveness with equity should be regarded as conflicts of liberty and cost-effectiveness with *justice*. Senses of justice vary widely across the political spectrum, and libertarians and utilitarians as well as contractarians and egalitarians have their own, different views of justice. Utilitarian theories of just allocation of scarce medical resources are likely to focus significantly on services' cost-effectiveness and costworthiness. Contractarian and egalitarian views of justice generally insist from the start on both universal access to a robust basic minimum of care and financially equitable burdens of financing (for example, community rated premiums), and they emphasize that allocations of resources in situations of scarcity must respect the equal value and dignity of every individual. Libertarians do not just speak of denying claims of justice in favor of claims of liberty; they think that justice itself requires a high respect for liberty and the pluralistic market that it generates (Engelhardt, 1996).

Second, conflict between the values of individual liberty and responsibility with the values of both equity and cost-efficiency may be less intractable than is usually assumed. If it is, the result will be to break the rigid and stereotypical association of senses of justice with the two paradigms of basic organizational structure for a health care system: libertarian-leaning senses of justice with pluralistic market systems that employ little central coercion, and egalitarian senses with unitary public systems. Critically examining and understanding better the ingredients of liberty, equity, and justice as well as the complexity of how they actually intersect in a health care system may open up different possible associations.

Here, for example, is one such different view (Menzel, 2002). Even non-egalitarian, libertarian leaning, responsibility-emphasizing views of distributive justice, this view claims, should strongly embrace compulsory, universal coverage of health care for basic care. A primary reason is the high degree of objectionable, irre-sponsible free-riding that occurs in a voluntary insurance system; those who do not insure (or pay to get their employees insured, for example) usually get basic care anyhow, paid for by cost-shifting that raises prices and premiums for those who are insured. In a complementary concession from the opposite end of the political spectrum, those who hold egalitarian views of justice ought not to regard different levels of health care coverage for people of different income levels as necessarily unjust. Such variety may reflect the varying relative values that differently situ-ated persons put on higher and lower consumption of health care, and thus a lean system of universal access to only very basic care may be just and equitable.

Cost–Utility Analysis as a Framework for Allocation

Health economists have developed a number of models for allocating care that aim at achieving efficiency – the most health benefit for the least cost. Efficiency is not just some mysterious gospel of economists. It seems commonsensical: why not see the point of prioritizing health services to be the same as the point of medicine itself – namely, to create greater health? The intuitive attraction of economic effi-ciency is rooted in its basic concept of "opportunity cost": the value sacrificed by not pursuing alternatives that might have been pursued with the same resources. When the value of any alternative use is less than the value of the current use, the current one is efficient; when the value of some alternative is greater, the current use is inefficient.

In thinking of the possible alternative uses, our sights can be set either narrowly or broadly. If we focus just on other options in *health care*, wondering whether we can get *more benefit* for our given health-care dollars, or whether we can get the *same health benefit more cheaply*, we are engaged in cost-effectiveness analysis (CEA). If, on the other hand, we are comparing an investment in health care with *all the other things* we might have done with the same time, effort, and money, we are engaged in cost–benefit analysis (CBA). CEA asks whether the money spent on a particular program or course of treatment could produce healthier or longer lives if it were spent on other forms of care. CBA involves an even more difficult query: whether the money we spend on a particular portion of health care is "matched" by the benefit. We determine that by asking in turn whether, spent elsewhere, it could produce greater value of another sort, not just healthier or longer lives.

Both kinds of analysis are important in allocation decision-making, though CBA has been less developed by health economists than CEA. CEA – getting the most health and life for a given size investment in health care – seems more feasible and less ambitious: compare different health-care services, detecting either final differences in expense to achieve the same health benefit or differences in some health benefit (added years of life, reductions in morbidity, etc.). We don't have to compare health benefits with opportunity costs having nothing to do with health. Yet even CEA – achieving efficiency *within* health care – may be very difficult. How do we really compare the values of non-life-extending hip replacement, for example, and life-extending dialysis or transplantation?

A major step taken by health economists at this point is to develop the notion of a unit of "health utility" (or "health state utility"), a common valuational currency for all losses and gains in health. The specific conceptual units developed to represent this go by various labels. Two examples are a "well-year" and a "quality-adjusted life year" (QALY, pronounced to rhyme with "holly"). The idea is to construct or discern a unit that combines mortality with quality of life considerations – "a year of healthy life" (Williams, 1985). We can then compare not only life-prolonging measures with each other but also measures that enhance quality with those that prolong life – hip replacements with kidney dialysis, for example. And then we can also track the health of a population, calculating changes in per capita "years of healthy life." In both cases, we will be doing "cost–utility analysis" (CUA).

Having available a unit of health utility that combines mortality and morbidity will be immensely useful if we are trying to maximize the "health benefit" of a given amount of resources invested in health care. Suppose dialysis patients' self-stated quality of life is 0.8 (where 0 is death and 1.0 is normal healthy life). They would gain 8.0 QALYs from 10 years on $40,000-a-year dialysis, a cost–benefit ratio of $50,000 per QALY. Suppose hip replacements improve 15 years of life from 0.9 quality ranking to 0.99. That will be a 1.35 QALY gain for the $10,000 operation, a cost of less than $7,500 per QALY. To achieve greater efficiency, we apparently should expand the use of hip replacements and look toward reducing dialysis. Similar CUAs of other health services can be done using the basic elements of size of quality improvement produced by treatment, duration of that improvement, and the number of persons who gain it.

A sizable literature of CUA has developed, not only studies of particular procedures but also intense discussions about how to construct a common unit of health benefit. Take the QALY. Questions abound. Who does one ask to discern quality-of-life rankings for different sorts of health states – patients with the problems, or other citizens and subscribers who are less dominated by their desire to escape their immediate health need? What questions do we ask them? Those building the QALY and well-year frameworks have used "time trade-off" (how much shorter a life in good health would you still find preferable to a longer lifetime with the disability or distress you are ranking?), "standard gamble" (what risk of death would you accept in return for being assured that if you did survive, you would be entirely cured?), and several others. Whatever question people are asked, it should convey as accurately as possible what might be called the "QALY bargain": their exposure to a greater risk of being allowed to die should they have an incurable, low-ranking condition, in return for a better chance of being helped to significant recovery or saved for prospectively normal health.

The moral argument for employing CUA and using some common health benefit unit like the QALY is more than just a narrow focus on aggregate economic efficiency per se. A major argument for using both quality adjustment as well as longevity extension in a serious attempt to maximize the benefit that a plan or an entire health care system produces is that it is people themselves who implicitly quality-rank their own lives and thus consent to the allocation priorities that QALYs or well-years generate.

Critics charge, however, that maximizing years of healthy life in our life-saving policies systematically fails to respect the individual with an admittedly lower quality of life (Harris, 1985). To what interpersonal trade-offs have people consented, when those might involve themselves? Suppose you yourself prefer a shorter, healthier life to a longer, less healthy one. You have now become, let us say, an accident victim who can, if saved, survive only as a paraplegic, while someone else can be saved for more complete recovery. Admittedly, you yourself prefer a life with recovery to one with paraplegia, and you would be willing to take a significant risk of dying from a therapy that promised significant recovery if it succeeded. But here is the problem: you do not admit – and you never have admitted – that, when life itself is on the line, a life with paraplegia is any less valuable to the person whose life it is than life without that disability is to someone else. Compared with death, *your paraplegic life would still likely be as valuable to you* as anyone else's "better" life is to them. That is, you want to go on living as fervently as the non-disabled person does. Conventional CUA thus raises significant questions about discrimination against the disabled and chronically ill when it is used to prioritize among various opportunities to save lives. (This consideration will surface again in the Rule of Rescue segment of the next section.)

Accounting for Specific Factors Other than Health-Related Utility

If we have thus opened up the search for *reasons* to use CUA in making allocation decisions, we may already have departed from a purely utilitarian framework within which to make allocation decisions. Not surprisingly, conventional CEA – that is, CUA – provokes many of the same ethical objections that plague utilitarianism in general: inadequate attention to the individual person in relationship to the aggregate ("common") good, and insensitivity to issues of distributive justice involving those who are less advantaged. Some will even just dismiss CUA because of the alleged weaknesses of the utilitarian philosophy that it reflects. Others have urged, however, an alternative, usually termed "cost–value analysis" (CVA): examine specific values that CUA fails to incorporate, with an eye toward reforming the methodology of CEA itself into something other than CUA (Nord, 1999 and Nord et al., 1999).

Included among the arguably non-utilitarian factors that CUA currently under-estimates are patient age (age itself, as distinct from the association of age with duration of effect), the initial severity of illness from which a treatment produces an improvement, and patients' limited potential for increased health as a long-term identifying characteristic of their lives. Consequently, important social values of justice and non-discrimination can stand at odds with recommendations generated by CUA. Regardless of whether such arguably non-utilitarian social values could be incorporated into a revised model of CEA, they are important factors politi-cally to consider in allocation decisions. What politician wants to defend policies which expose individual people to injustice in the name of an impersonal, aggre-gate good?

Although some of these factors may affect the "individual utility" dimension of value, they are mainly relevant when "societal value" is being calculated. The latter is a different kind of value. In societal value the focus is explicitly on *interpersonal* trade-offs – decisions about what services to provide among the wide array of pos-sible services that often affect *different* groups of people. Typically such trade-offs are at issue in allocating preventive or acute care services at the "budget" or "cov-erage" level for large populations, as distinct from the "admission" or "bedside" level where such interpersonal trade-offs may be more debatable.

Whether as factors transcending cost–utility analysis that health economics might incorporate into their frameworks for allocation or as independent elements having little if anything to do with health economics, several variable characteristics of all the different people who have medical need are arguably plausible grounds for allo-cating scarce resources. Six will be discussed here: age, severity of illness, urgency of rescue, health potential upon recovery, maintenance of hope and assurance of treatment, and comparative duration of benefit (regarding these and others, see Kilner, 1990 and Menzel et al., 1999).

Age

While through duration of effect age is indirectly accounted for in CUA, age per se is not. Indirectly it is, as treatments for the relatively elderly often produce ben-efits of shorter duration than treatments for the relatively young, thereby yielding priority for the young. In addition to this indirect effect of age, however, there is notable evidence that for comparisons in which duration of gain is held equal while age is varied, most people express preferences considerably at odds with CUA's disregard of age per se. For example, many people would not only agree that more than one person would have to be saved for an additional 20 years to equal the value of saving five people (of the same age as the one) for an additional four years each. Many would also say that more than one 70-year-old, for example, would have to be saved for 10 years of additional life to equal the value of saving one 30-year-old for an extra 10 years. Moreover, this preference continues when one rids respondents of any implicit presumptions that quality of life between 70 and 80 must be lower than that between 30 and 40 (Johannesson and Johannesson, 1996; Nord et al., 1996).

The moral ground for this preference for the young is undoubtedly thus egalitarian, not – or not only – utilitarian. The young should be treated first, even when their gain is smaller, so that they obtain a fairer and more equal chance of living a long life. This has been called the "fair go" or "fair innings" argument (Harris, 1985; Williams, 1997). There may, of course, be societies in which the elderly are so revered that these egalitarian considerations for at least some favoring of the young get overridden. In those contexts, CUA-recommended allocations that effectively ignore age per se may not be out of step with public preferences. For societies that do not have such strong differential reverence for the elderly, however, those allocations will be.

Societal values that favor the young, whether they be based on egalitarian fairness reasons or on utilitarian calculation, may give rise to charges of "agism." Perhaps, in fact, the societal issues are so contentious that empirical investigation will show little in the way of any predominant social value toward greater priority for the young than is already indirectly accorded by duration-of-benefit considerations. In any case, however, the conventional utilitarian treatment of age – assuming that age is relevant only through its highly variable effect on the duration of treatment benefit – is questionable on both moral and empirical grounds.

Severity of illness

Utilitarian analysis incorporates the severity of the illness that a procedure treats only insofar as it is one of the two variables needed for determining the size of the treatment effect (initial health and treatment end point). It does not accord any weight to the severity of illness per se – the initial health-related quality of life. Both public official statements and population preference data, however, suggest that people often wish to give greater priority to those who are worse off before treatment, above and beyond any priority they may achieve by health benefit calculation (Nord, 1993a; Core Services Committee of New Zealand, 1994; Ubel, DeKay, et al., 1996; Ubel, Scanlon, et al., 1996; Nord, 1999).

For example, in one study of 150 Norwegian politicians accountable for health policy at the county level, subjects were presented with a dilemma: provide treatments for a severe illness A that would bring "a little" help, or treatments for a moderate illness B that would help "considerably." They had three choices: divide resources evenly between the two illnesses and their treatments, allocate most to illness A (the most severe), or allocate most to B. Nearly half (45 percent) chose equal division, and 37 percent chose priority for A. Only 11 percent chose priority for B (Nord, 1993a).

The key to severity's ethical relevance is captured by the fact that treating the more severely ill is helping those who are in greater need. Notable treatises in social philosophy have articulated a fundamental general priority for helping "the worst off" – those whose life prospects are the most disadvantaged (Rawls, 1971; Daniels, 1985). We reduce inequality if we give priority to patients with more severe illness. For example, if two treatments can raise one person's health-related quality of life from 0.5 to 0.9 and another's from 0.3 to 0.6, treating the less severe illness leaves a greater difference between the two persons' health states (0.3 and 0.9). Treating the more severe illness reduces inequality of health and leaves the two individuals with more nearly equal health quality rankings of 0.5 and 0.6.

Preference data suggesting an independent concern for severity would thus appear to have an ethical basis. To be sure, critics might challenge the data themselves. Did the study respondents really understand the hypothesized treatment effect to be smaller for those whose initial illness is more severe? Perhaps respondents accord extra priority to the most severely ill not because they see them as more ill, but because they believe that the increments in individual utility obtained from treatment are actually larger than those accruing to those whose baseline health is better. Some studies, however, have used examples that conveyed particularly clearly that the more severely ill were benefiting from smaller treatment effects; it, too, yielded distinct preference for giving priority to those with the more severe illnesses (Nord, 1993a).

Life-saving and treatment in the face of death – the "Rule of Rescue"

The most severe illnesses, of course, put people face to face with death. The propensity to regard situations where identifiable patients face great risk of avoidable death as holding a unique call on resources has been called the "Rule of Rescue" (Jonsen, 1986). Rooted in the Kantian tradition of considering the individual to whom one is relating as an ultimate end-in-herself, this "rule" resists the usual maximize-benefit calculation. Critics of conventional CEA such as Hadorn, for example, have argued that "any plan to distribute health care services must take [this Rule of Rescue aspect of] human nature into account if the plan is to be acceptable to society" (Hadorn, 1991).

The actual actions that people take provide ample evidence that we will expend great effort and large resources to avert death (the girl down the well, astronauts in space, sailors lost at sea, etc.). We also have examples from public life such as the state of Oregon, where all life-saving services rose to a separate high priority category in the state Medicaid plan's eventual rationing list after having been treated in the conventional efficiency manner earlier (Hadorn, 1991).

It is possible, of course, that such disproportionate investments in immediate life-saving are irrational, the result of a weakness in our mental judgment that suppresses the greater aggregate gain in quality improvement or life-saving that results if the same total investment is made in a larger number of less urgent but still health threatening situations. Compare, for example, saving two lives by eliminating 1: 50 risks of death for 100 people with saving one life by trying to save two people threatened by certain death if we do nothing but who each have a 50 percent chance of recovery if we act. The former action will likely save two lives, the latter action only one. The latter, though, takes place in a "death's doorstep" situation. It is in fact irrational to invest in the latter before the former *if* the value of a life that is discerned by willingness to reduce only a statistical risk can properly be equated with the value of a life saved on death's doorstep. But can it be?

This is, in fact, the problem at the heart of all claims to place a monetary or resource value on life based on people's distinctly limited willingness to sacrifice to reduce moderate or low risks. Of what relevance are differences in perspective by degree of risk? One critic of claims to discern a limited monetary value of life has argued that in principle only valuations of life made directly in the face of death are correct reflections of the actual economic value of life (Broome, 1982). Another contributor to this discussion has noted that he does not know of anyone "who would honestly agree to accept any sum of money to enter a gamble in which, if at the first toss of a coin it came down heads, he would be summarily executed" (Mishan, 1985, pp. 159–60). Some conclude from this that there is no rational limit on what to do or spend to save a life because no particular finite amount of effort or money is adequate to represent the real value of life.

Even if this point about the actual value of a life is correct, however, it may not render estimates of a limited monetary value of life irrelevant for use in health policy. In the context of setting policy about whether to include a certain service in our package of insurance, we cannot just assume that the later perspective of an individual immediately in the face of death is the correct one from which to make decisions. Such a perspective may be proper for the legal system to adopt in awarding compensation for wrongful death, for there we are trying to compensate people for losses actually incurred. Arguably, however, health-care decisions ought to be made from an earlier perspective. In modern medical economies most people either subscribe to private insurance plans or are covered by public ones. Once insured, whether in private or public arrangements, subscribers and patients as well as providers find themselves with strong incentive to overuse care and underestimate opportunity costs. Why should we not address the problem of controlling the use of care in the face of these value-distorting incentives at the point in the decision process, *insuring*, where the major cost-expansion pressure starts? In health policy, while it may not be necessary to claim that willingness to risk life shows us the "value of life," willingness to risk may still be appropriate to use.

In any case, regardless of these basic considerations for and against thinking in terms of a monetary value of life, we need to keep in view the possibly broader context of any special value of life-saving. The special value of treatment in the face of death involved here may pertain to more than life-saving services. Widespread attitudes toward hospice and other non-life-saving terminal care also suggest the same special value of care in the face of death. Putting up with severe pain for a six-month period when one expects to live for many years is one thing; having to put up with it at the end of one's life is another. People generally, not just patients facing death, have a special concern that life not end in pain. Thus, palliative measures for patients with terminal conditions may produce an extra value. Perhaps the "Rule of Rescue" is more appropriately expressed as the special value of "Care in the Face of Death."

Level of health potential

The societal value of priority for treatment of those with more severe illnesses focuses independently on a patient's start point, as distinct from the size of treatment effect. Analogously, the end point may have independent relevance that is not accounted for in a utilitarian calculation of the size of treatment effect. Call this factor the "level of potential." The social value it expresses is a reluctance to discriminate against patients who happen to have lower potential for overall health, or do anything that would reduce the priority given to their care.

Suppose that on a subjective utility scale, treatment can move one person from 0.6 to 0.8 and another from 0.6 to 1.0, and that the first person's end point of 0.8 represents her maximum prospective health potential. Should we really regard the second person's treatment effect as having twice the value of the first person's? Treatment can, after all, "fully cure" the first within the perspective of her life. Her health potential defines the life she can lead. Since a life with that health potential is the only life that she will in any case have, it would seem plausible to say that reaching her 0.8 level counts as more than half the value of another person's move from 0.6 to full health. The essential ethical claim here is that where people are "located" in life in relation to their realistic potential is an important factor to take into account.

The same study of Norwegian politicians involved in health care decision-making previously mentioned in connection with severity of illness, also provides suggestive empirical support for this level-of-potential factor (Nord, 1993a). Perhaps the empirical data confirming consideration of returning to a previous level of limited health potential as an important societal value are less clear than those available to confirm severity of illness or urgent life-saving as prioritizing factors, but they still point to societal values that conflict with conventional CUA (Nord, 1993b).

A relatively simple thought experiment confirms this intuitive power of an individual's maximum health potential against the results of conventional utilitarian calculation. Imagine two groups of patients stricken with a life-threatening illness. The first group were previously in full health and can be returned to full health with treatment. The second group previously had paraplegia and, with treatment of their life-threatening condition, will continue to have it. Both, if treated, will live the same number of additional years. Assume that the health-related quality of life with paraplegia is 0.8, as calculated from "time trade-off" responses in which persons with paraplegia themselves expressed a willingness to sacrifice 20 percent of their remaining life extension to obtain a complete cure of their condition. CUA would recommend priority for saving the first group to full health and would shift to priority for the paraplegia group only if the number of lives saved there for the same total cost was at least 25 percent greater than in the other group saved to normal health. Yet few among us, reflecting seriously about the value of continuing to live, honestly believe that it is less important for society to save the lives of persons with paraplegia than the lives of others to full health (Nord, 1993b). The equal value of life-saving regardless of final health state appears to dominate.

These societal preferences to save lives regardless of total health benefit may be based in more individual reasoning, too, and arguably they reveal special concerns about discrimination against the disabled and the chronically ill (Hadorn, 1992). Suppose, again, that the disabled person has ranked her individual quality of life at 0.8. This willingness to accept a 20 percent shorter remaining life in order to be cured from a permanent disability does not in any way indicate that she thought that her *life*, in relation to the prospect of *death*, was any less valuable and important to save than *another* fully healthy person's life (Menzel, 1990, p. 84). The 0.8 that expresses willingness to trade time *within* a life does not constitute a judgment about the relative value of saving *different persons'* lives.

Note that the independent relevance for both the end and the start points of treatment – level of potential and severity of illness – above and beyond their role in determining the size of treatment effect, does not require us to dismiss the importance of size of treatment effect. It is only that gains in health-related quality of life need supplementing by independent consideration of severity of illness and level of potential.

Maintenance of hope and assurance of treatment

Conventional utilitarian analysis views societal benefit as directly proportional to the combination of the average improvement in quality of life and the number of people benefited. Two other factors, however, may qualify this simple linear relationship between numbers of people and total value.

One of them is "maintenance of hope." Suppose we can allocate resources to one program, administered to a smaller segment within a larger group, that will yield a certain level of beneficial outcome for a finally greater number of beneficiaries, or to another program that generates that same individual outcome for what turns out to be a smaller number of actual beneficiaries though the segment of people *treated* is larger. The efficient allocation would be to devote *all* of the available pool of resources to the former program. Several studies, however, reveal that many people would wish to preserve for each individual the hope that they still may receive treatment; to accomplish this, they prefer to use some resources inefficiently (Ubel and Loewenstein, 1995).

Another factor disrupting the linear relationship between numbers of people and total value is "assurance of treatment." Many people prefer extending entitlement for a treatment from some to all in a disease or treatment category even when such extension is inefficient (Ubel, DeKay, et al., 1996; Ubel, Scanlon, et al, 1996). They consider it inequitable to exclude some from treatment that most others receive, regardless of the increase in cost per benefit when treatment is extended to all. To satisfy desires for assurance of treatment, we might offer a treatment to everyone in an illness category despite the diminished odds of cost-effective outcomes for many of those added at the margin. In either case, we will have contradicted the outcome-efficiency orientation of conventional economic analysis.

Duration discounting

Conventional calculation of value achieved takes duration of health effect into account by multiplying the value of one year of a treatment effect by the number of years for which the effect lasts, usually with one important additional step: each year past the first is discounted for time preference back to its present value. Empirical studies, however, suggest a different pattern in people's valuations of the importance of duration – perhaps a different pattern when they are evaluating different potential durations in their own lives, and very likely a different pattern when they consider duration in the context of interpersonal comparisons.

In the latter context, for example, respondents in Australia thought that saving 10 people for 10 years each would be equivalent to saving 7 people for 20 years each (Nord et al., 1996). That is, it took 140 total years accumulated in 20-year spans to equal in value 100 total years accumulated in 10-year spans, a reduction of 57 percent in the average value of a year of life in the last 10 years of each 20-year span (Menzel et al., 1999).

There are at least three possible reasons for such discounting beyond the pure time-preference used in conventional economic analysis.

1   At the level of individual utility, there may be a "quantity-effect" similar to the phenomenon of diminishing marginal utility generally: because of the benefits already achieved, the last year of life in a 10-year span of experience is not seen to be as valuable as any one of the earlier years.

2   At the level of societal value, people may have an aversion to inequality that leads them to value duration less then proportionately. It seems more equitable, for example, to extend two persons' lives for 10 years each than one person's life for 20.

3   Also at the level of societal value, an element may operate that is similar to the ethical basis of the level-of-potential factor: patients' shorter life potential should not be held against them.

Regardless of what explanation dominates, it appears safe to say that to adequately capture people's values, allocation decision-makers may need to discount the value of longer spans of life or health gained more, and perhaps considerably more, than is already occurring as a result of what economists call people's "pure time preference." Health policy and health economics need to embark on a wide range of future studies of duration, keeping pure time preference of the individual distinct from the other elements which may arise in social values. Such empirical research will hopefully reveal the relative importance of these different elements in people's discounting of the value of longer durations of health benefit. More-over, a possible outcome from such research is the acceptance of the relevance of duration discounting for some reasons but its rejection for others.

Other influential factors

Undoubtedly there are other factors that can arguably be considered relevant to allocating scarce health care resources. Among them are personal responsibility, citizenship and nationality, compensation for those who are generally socially dis-advantaged, health effects on others, non-health effects on others, and the degree of either personal or community control seen to be preserved by a given program. They are only noted here, without further articulation.

Further Questions and a Concluding Note

Numerous other methodological questions arise in the struggle to make justified allocations of scarce health care resources. A few of them are:

- What group do we ask to obtain the most applicable values or preferences on any of the various factors discussed in the previous section? Patients with the conditions being evaluated, representatives of the general public or insurance plan members asked to imagine themselves to have the conditions related to the trade-offs being examined, or some other group such as politicians or health care providers?
- Should the aggregate, amalgamated preferences of a society derived from some democratic process dominate allocation decisions? Should those be allowed to effectively swamp out the preferences and values of the individuals who are most affected by prioritizing decisions?

- Should the values that ought to guide prioritizing decisions be thought of as empirical preferences that people in a given society happen to have, or should they be thought of as more objective values that must emerge from a structure of reason that may or may not be reflected in people's actual preferences?
- To what extent should prioritizing decisions be made within the framework of a general normative moral theory, or may they be made in more piecemeal fashion without an overarching moral framework?

Related to this last question, it might be noted that several moral and social theories have been referred to, used, or invoked in the previous description of various issues in the landscape of allocation decisions. Utilitarianism is the most obvious. Other theories are more "contractarian" and refer to the consent (perhaps the prior or hypothetical consent) of those who end up being governed by the policies in question. Still other approaches may be "intuitionist" in asserting basic claims about fairness or equality. It is not the intention of the author of this chapter to claim that any one of these frameworks is better or worse than another. They have been referred to only as a way of bringing to our explicit awareness certain underlying patterns of thought in allocation decisions.

References

Brennan, Troyen A. (1991), *Just Doctoring: Medical Ethics in the Liberal State*, Berkeley: University of California Press.

Broome, John (1982), Uncertainty in welfare economics and the value of life, in M. Jones-Lee (ed.), *The Value of Life and Safety*, proceedings of a conference held by the Geneva Association, Amsterdam: North-Holland, pp. 201–17.

Core Services Committee of New Zealand (1994), *Core Services for 1995/1996*, Wellington: Ministry of Health.

Culyer, A.J., Maynard, A., and Williams, A. (1981), Alternative systems of health care provision: an essay on motes and beams, in M. Olson (ed.), *A New Approach to the Economics of Health Care*, Washington, DC: American Enterprise Institute, pp. 131–50.

Daniels, Norman (1985), *Just Health Care*, Cambridge: Cambridge University Press.

Engelhardt, H. Tristram (1996), *The Foundations of Bioethics*, 2nd edn., New York: Oxford University Press.

Hadorn, David (1991), Setting health care priorities in Oregon: cost-effectiveness meets the Rule of Rescue, *Journal of the American Medical Association* 265 (17): 2218–25.

Hadorn, David (1992), The problem of discrimination in health care priority setting, *Journal of the American Medical Association* 268 (11): 1454–9.

Hall, Mark A. (1997), *Making Medical Spending Decisions: The Law, Ethics, and Economics of Rationing Mechanisms*, New York: Oxford University Press.

Harris, John (1985), *The Value of Life*, London: Routledge and Kegan Paul.

Johannesson, J. and Johannesson, P.O. (1996), The economics of aging: on the attitude of Swedish people to the distribution of health care resources between the young and the old, *Health Policy* 37: 153–61.

Jonsen, Albert (1986), Bentham in a box: technology assessment and health care allocation, *Law, Medicine and Health Care* 14: 172–4.

Kilner, John (1990), *Who Lives? Who Dies? Ethical Criteria in Patient Selection*, New Haven, CT: Yale University Press.

Menzel, Paul T. (1990), *Strong Medicine: The Ethical Rationing of Health Care*, New York: Oxford University Press.

Menzel, Paul T. (2002), Justice and the basic structure of health-care systems, in R. Rhodes, M. Battin, and A. Silvers (eds.), *Medicine and Social Justice*, New York: Oxford University Press, pp. 24–37.

Menzel, Paul T., Gold, M., Nord, E., Pinto-Prades, J.-L., Richardson, J., and Ubel, P. (1999), Toward a broader view of cost-effectiveness analysis of health care, *Hastings Center Report* 29 (1): 7–15.

Mishan, Ezra J. (1985), Consistency in the valuation of life: a wild goose chase? In E.F. Paul, J. Paul, and F.D. Miller, Jr. (eds.), *Ethics and Economics*, Oxford: Basil Blackwell, pp. 24–37.

Morreim, E. Haavi. (1991), *Balancing Act: The New Medical Ethics of Medicine's New Economics*, Dordrecht: Kluwer.

Nord, Erik (1993a), Health politicians do not wish to maximize health benefits, *Journal of the Norwegian Medical Association* 113: 1171–3.

Nord, Erik (1993b), The relevance of health state after treatment in prioritising between different patients, *Journal of Medical Ethics* 19: 37–42.

Nord, Erik (1999), *Cost–Value Analysis in Health Care: Making Sense out of QALYs*, Cambridge: Cambridge University Press.

Nord, Erik, Pinto-Prades, J.-L., Richardson, J., Menzel, P., and Ubel, P. (1999), Incorporating societal concerns for fairness in numerical valuations of health programs, *Health Economics* 8: 25–39.

Nord, Erik, Street, A., Richardson, J., Kuhse, H., and Singer, P. (1996), The significance of age and duration of effect in social evaluation of health care, *Health Care Analysis* 4 (2): 103–11.

Pellegrino, Edmund D., and Thomasma, David C. (1988), *For the Patient's Good: The Restoration of Beneficence in Health Care*, New York: Oxford University Press.

Rawls, John (1971), *A Theory of Justice*, Cambridge, MA: Harvard University Press.

Ubel, Peter A. (2000), *Pricing Life: Why It's Time for Health Care Rationing*, Cambridge, MA: MIT Press.

Ubel, Peter, and Loewenstein, G. (1995), The efficacy and equity of retransplantation: an experimental survey of public attitudes, *Health Policy* 34: 145–51.

Ubel, Peter, DeKay, M., Baron, J., and Asch, D. (1996), Cost-effectiveness analysis in a setting of budget constraints: is it equitable? *New England Journal of Medicine*, 334: 1174–7.

Ubel, Peter, Scanlon, D., Loewenstein, G., and Kamlet, M. (1996), Individual utilities are inconsistent with rationing choices: a partial explanation of why Oregon's cost-effectiveness list failed, *Medical Decision Making* 16 (2): 108–19.

Williams, Alan (1985), Economics of coronary artery bypass grafting, *British Medical Journal* 291 (6491): 326–9.

Williams, Alan (1997), Intergenerational equity: an exploration of the "fair innings" argument, *Health Economics* 6: 117–32.

Further Reading

Daniels, Norman (1988), *Am I My Parents' Keeper? An Essay on Justice between the Young and the Old*, New York and Oxford: Oxford University Press.

Eddy, David M. (1996), *Clinical Decision Making: From Theory to Practice*, Sudbury, MA: Jones and Bartlett.

Gold, Marthe R., Siegel, J., Russell, L.B., and Weinstein, M. (eds.), *Cost-effectiveness in Health and Medicine*, New York: Oxford University Press.

Kamm, Frances M. (1993), *Morality, Mortality*, vol. I, *Death and Whom to Save From It*, New York: Oxford University Press.

Chapter 18

Just Caring

The Challenges of Priority-Setting in Public Health

Leonard M. Fleck

"Explicating the demands of justice in allocating public health resources and in setting priorities for public health policies, or in determining whom they should target, remains among the most daunting challenges in public health ethics" (Childress et al., 2002). This will be the primary challenge taken on in this essay. Our key question is this: What does it mean to be a just and caring society so far as meeting public health care needs is concerned when we have only limited resources to meet virtually unlimited health care needs of all sorts? This is a complex question, so our first task will be to sort out this complexity.

Three working assumptions lie behind our key question. First, we assume that issues of justice need to be addressed with respect to meeting public health needs, that these decisions are not simply a matter of social beneficence (freely given or withheld for any reason at all), and that these decisions also ought not be determined through the morally arbitrary use of political power. The basis for this first working assumption is that we are talking about public health *needs*, which, if a society fails to address them, will have morally objectionable consequences so far as protecting fair equality of opportunity is concerned. Daniels (1985) has argued that we are not morally obligated as a society to pursue "equal health for all," an impossible ideal. But we are obligated as a matter of health care justice to provide access to needed and effective health care for all whose normal opportunity range has been significantly constrained by ill health. Public health, just like expansive public education, has the morally desirable feature of protecting fair equality of opportunity for all. (We regard Daniels's conception of health care justice as a reasonable perspective but not the only perspective for justified judgments of health care justice.) Further, for reasons we explain below, the public nature of these needs means that individuals as individuals will lack the capacity to meet these needs effectively.

Second, the needs we have in mind are truly endless. Hence, we assume that health care rationing and priority-setting are inescapable. Efforts to get rid of waste and inefficiency in the health care system will not magically generate resources that will obviate the need for rationing (Ubel, 2000). Third, public health needs will have to compete with individualized medical needs for resources. That is, as a moral and practical political matter, public health needs cannot be segregated from the rationing issues that are ubiquitous in medicine. Part of the reason for that is the current controversy around the legitimate scope of public health.

Many opinion and editorial writers today tell us that we are faced with an "epidemic of obesity" (Lichtarowicz, 2004). That language is intended to suggest that we are faced with a public health crisis and that government needs to intervene to contain somehow this threat to the health of the public. Others (Epstein, 2003), however, would see this as a massive abrogation of personal responsibility, which personal physicians and their overweight patients need to acknowledge and then effectively address. We will also find in both medical journals (Hogan, 1999) and the popular press references to an "epidemic of violence," followed by a long recitation of statistics documenting a multitude of modes of mayhem, such as the 29,000 firearm deaths in the US in 2003. Often the follow-up commentary will conclude with a call for public health officials to do something. In the past few years, multiple studies have documented racial and economic disparities in health and access to health care, often denouncing the injustice represented by these disparities (Kawachi and Kennedy, 1999; Kawachi, Kennedy, and Wilkinson, 1999; Marmot, 1999; Daniels, 2002). Again, these moral judgments are very often accompanied by a call for public health officials to become engaged and to find ways of reducing or eliminating these disparities (Mann, 1997; Kass, 2001).

No doubt obesity, violence, poverty, and racial discrimination all represent threats to the health of the population. All represent unnecessary morbidity and mortality that in principle could be reduced or eliminated. And if we think of the mission of public health as the reduction or control of threats to the health of the public, then we might well conclude that it is the responsibility of public health officials to do something about obesity, violence, poverty, and racial discrimination. However, this conclusion yields a very unwieldy, very expansive conception of what ought to come under the rubric of public health. The task of Part I of this essay will be to establish some reasonable boundaries around the conception of public health, without which issues of public health justice are impossible to address.

Public health expenditures are typically contrasted with medical expenditures for individual health. In 2004 we spent in the United States about $1.8 trillion on health care, roughly 15.3 percent of our GDP. Only 3 percent of that total expenditure is attributed to public health. We could argue about whether such relatively small expenditures for public health were prudent or imprudent. But that is not our focus. Our concern is whether such limited expenditures represent an injustice, an unfair distribution of either the benefits of our very advanced health care system or the burdens (death/disability) associated with preventable or ameliorable illness and injury. We might concretize the issue this way: If there are disproportionate rates of premature death and avoidable disability among identifiable social groups (the poor, racial or ethnic minorities, other groups that are the targets of discriminatory social attitudes), and if these health disadvantages are properly judged to be matters of injustice, then will considerations of justice require that resources be re-allocated from medical interventions to public health interventions instead? Or, alternatively, would justice be equally well satisfied if medical resources were simply redistributed from the relatively healthy and advantaged (de-funding expensive marginally beneficial interventions) to the disproportionately unhealthy (and in other ways socially disadvantaged), funding other *medical* interventions that were typically effective and cost-worthy? In other words, there would be no increase in public health spending to achieve this goal because re-allocation within the domain of medicine would have been sufficient. This issue will be the focus of Part II of this essay.

In Part III we will address the question of priority-setting within public health. Our core question is this: Are there considerations of health care justice that ought to dictate to some extent what our public health priorities ought to be? If so, what precisely are those considerations of justice? Should the dominant consideration be the Rawlsian concern for the least well off? If so, what criteria should we use for identifying who the least well off are from a public health perspective? Assuming we can provide a satisfactory answer to the prior question, is it in fact possible to target the relevant public health interventions that precisely which we seem to do regularly and easily in medicine generally? Alternatively, should public health priorities be determined mostly or entirely by utilitarian considerations? If so, what is it that we are seeking to maximize across the spectrum of public health needs? Are we, for example, seeking to maximize the number of life-years saved through various public health interventions? If so, does this imply that we are morally obligated to award higher priority to each and every public health intervention that has the promise of saving lives or life-years over any public health intervention that would merely result in the prevention of injury or disability? Further, is this an implication we ought to endorse as a matter of health care justice? Finally, should either cost-effectiveness or quality of life considerations be regarded as morally relevant in determining priorities among public health needs? One recent essay strongly recommends that improving the quality of end of life care should be a high priority focus for public health (Rao et al., 2002). Is this a conclusion that ought to be endorsed from the perspective of health care justice?

I The Scope of Public Health: Challenges and Choices

Considerable controversy exists over what the scope of public health ought to be. To simplify matters, we will distinguish the *traditionalists* from the *expansionists*. The traditional tasks of public health include (1) prevention and control of infectious diseases, such as AIDS, SARS, West Nile virus, tuberculosis, Legionnaire's disease, various sexually transmitted diseases, and so on; (2) prevention and control of food-borne illness, which involves recommending and enforcing regulations aimed at protecting the food supply at all stages of production and distribution;

(3) monitoring the quality of the environment and enforcing environmental regulations to protect the public's health from contaminated air or water, or hazardous waste, or a broad range of other environmental threats; (4) health education and health promotion activities aimed at discouraging behavioral activities that represent serious threats to health, such as anti-smoking campaigns; (5) epidemiological research aimed at generating an accurate assessment of the magnitude and relative risk associated with various threats to public health. What unifies these otherwise apparently disparate activities is that (1) they are all aimed at efficiently and effectively preventing injury, disability or premature death; and (2) the specific activities are seen as protecting what are primarily *public interests* rather than the health interests of individuals; and (3) the coercive powers of government are legitimately employed to achieve these ends.

Some (Epstein, 2003) will argue that health promotion and health education should not be regarded as part of traditional public health. The thought of "obesity police," hanging around doughnut shops only for purposes of apprehending the criminally obese, is frightening. However, neither I nor others (Gostin and Bloche, 2003) have anything like that in mind. To the extent that health promotion and health education are analogous in practice to "public education" they can be fitted under the traditional public health rubric. Our society makes formal public education "freely available" because there is a strong public interest in having a well-educated citizenry capable of contributing to our economic advancement (as well as their own personal well-being). Less well off citizens would not be able to avail themselves of these educational opportunities if they were not "free at the point of service." In theory, individuals can "educate themselves" either in the formal general sense or about health matters. But in practice we might have a less healthy citizenry if we left health education entirely to private and personal initiative and expense. As for the coercion part, our society cannot endorse coercing individuals to shed pounds (given our liberal political commitments), but we can use the coercive powers of government to require all manner of food labeling in order to educate the public about the nutritional value or nutritional risks posed by various foods. This is entirely congruent with our liberal political values. The fact that genuine *public interests* are at stake is most central to what public health is about (as opposed to the more expansive notion of the *social determinants of health*). A reasonable definition of public interests would say that they are interests that each and every citizen has but that citizens as individuals (or even as organized private groups of individuals) would be unable to maintain or protect adequately without the organizational and coercive powers of government. Clean air, clean water, and a safe food supply are all readily seen as satisfying this definition in our contemporary world. Powerful corporations motivated by profit maximization have no reason to pay anything at all to protect air or water quality fouled by their activities, nor do individuals have either the power or the interest to compel corporations to behave in a more socially responsible manner. Though each of us would rationally not wish to see our lives shortened by polluted air or water, none of us would spend most of our resources to achieve such an objective since everyone else would benefit from our efforts without having contributed to underwriting those costs. This is the classic "free rider" problem. Government can use its powers to collect taxes from all to put in place policies and regulations that will compel a level of corporate compliance that could never be achieved by individual effort. Likewise, few of us individually have the expertise needed to assure the safety of the food we consume. And none of us can really protect ourselves through our own efforts alone from infectious diseases. Typically we would have no way of knowing in a timely enough way who might be infected with a serious disease before we ourselves would have been exposed and put at risk. This is what *traditional* public health is about. Then there are the expansionists.

The expansionists build on the core elements that have justified traditional public health activities. Public health regulates and discourages the use of tobacco products because of the inherent dangers to health of tobacco (thought of on the model of food) with manufacturers emphasizing the pleasures of smoking and denying for a very long time the dangers (which few individuals could assess on their own). But someone will point out that smoking is a "voluntary" activity, the point being that public health authorities are not legitimate regulators of the activity since individuals have "chosen" to assume this risk themselves. However, smoking puts at risk third parties who have not volunteered to assume those risks and who are unjustly harmed by the choices of smokers. That restores the (apparent) legitimacy of the public interest claim. I will stipulate for the sake of argument that this is a reasonable claim. However, this line of reasoning launches the expansionist project.

The use or abuse of alcohol represents an individual choice. This fact would hardly warrant public health attention. But the social consequences of alcohol abuse are massive, as represented by drunk driving or excess health costs associated with alcohol-related diseases that are borne by taxpayers or insurance premium payers. And, while alcoholism stretches across all income tiers, poverty or dead-end jobs or a host of other social determinants (corporate performance pressures) create an environment that motivates and supports alcohol abuse. All of this is again intended to suggest both that a public health response is legitimate and necessary and that an individualized medical response is misguided and ineffective because such individualized responses fail to address the deep social determinants associated with alcohol abuse. This very same line of reasoning can be deployed with respect to illegal recreational drugs. Likewise, with some moderate factual adjustments this line of reasoning will (apparently) justify a public health effort to address the "epidemic of obesity" or the "epidemic of violence."

Note that the language of "epidemic" is deliberate, and that the public health expansionists who invoke this notion do not intend this as just a bit of rhetorical excess. The relevant argument might go like this: In the case of the 1918–19 influenza pandemic or in the case of AIDS there is a biological infectious agent that is the immediate cause of illness or death in individuals. But it would be very wrongheaded to believe that that infectious agent was the sole cause or the whole cause of the morbidity and mortality in either epidemic. Complex social factors (ease of worldwide travel, bath houses, discrimination against gays that drives them into a hidden sub-culture, denial of access to the stability of marriage) are also integral factors necessary to explain the magnitude and the precise form of a particular epidemic (and, by implication, the complex social response that will be needed to contain or abort that epidemic). The infectious agent is just one of the causal factors in a multi-dimensional causal schema that results in a particular pattern of morbidity and mortality.

Sometimes no infectious agent is needed to trigger a very complex social process that results in unnecessary morbidity and mortality, as would be the case with obesity or violence or alcohol abuse or a very steep income gradient in a particular society. What is most salient (and warrants a public health response from the perspective of the expansionists) is that there are these persistent social determinants that precipitate and sustain the ill health effects associated with obesity or violence (a fast-paced culture that demands cheap fast food, easy access to cheap guns, a cultural belief system that encourages gun ownership), and these social determinants (and their ill health effects) remain largely unaffected so long as the primary health response involves no more than the medical treatment of affected individuals. What is really needed to reduce substantially the "epidemic" nature of the ill health effects is a comprehensive public health response aimed at those deep social determinants of violence or obesity or alcoholism.

Both Rothstein (2002) and Gostin (2001) are critics of this expansionist version of public health, and I am strongly inclined to agree with them. None of us rejects the rightness or legitimacy of the social goals that these expansionists would like to see achieved. For example, I agree with Daniels (2002) that the steepness of the gradient between the rich and the poor in our society is a serious social injustice, which ought to be remedied. But I do not agree with those expansionists who would see this as a responsibility that ought to fall under the rubric of public health. Gostin (2001, p. 123) provides us with three reasons for this conclusion that I find persuasive. First, this expansivist view would make public health limitless in scope. Virtually every social problem that had any adverse consequences for health would become a matter of public health. Such limitless responsibility would ultimately be counter-productive. This can be readily seen when we consider his second point, namely, that public health officials would have to acquire expertise in virtually every major academic discipline available in order to fulfill such a wide-ranging view of their role. And third, what the expansivist project would require is economic redistribution and social restructuring on a massive scale by officials representing public health. In other words, public health officials would have to take on (to use one example) the task of major tax reform for purposes of improving social justice. This would be a very politically controversial task, far removed from the more traditional, more mundane, largely non-controversial tasks associated with public health. I would put the matter this way: There are numerous domains or dimensions to social justice, i.e., social institutions and practices that might fall far short of the requirements of justice. We have no good reason to believe that a social justice czar should have responsibility for remedying these deficiencies, much less a public health czar. Rather, as a moral and a practical matter, the social and political leaders in those social domains should have that responsibility. This implies an acceptance of non-ideal incremental sectoral approaches to bringing about a more just state of affairs so far as health care is concerned (Fleck, 1987, pp. 165–76). This may well be all that is morally reasonable and politically possible. Gostin and Bloche (2003) make a useful distinction between public health research, which can be legitimately more expansive, and public health practice, which needs to be more constrained in its ambitions. This is a reasonable distinction.

II Health Care Justice and Public Health: When Is Enough Enough?

Daniel Callahan writes: "The best prescription for a healthy population is a good public health system, decent jobs and education, and a prudent lifestyle" (1998, p. 173). He goes on to say that in the future priority for resource allocation ought to go to public health rather than individual health, and that this is the key to a "sustainable medicine." This latter phrase is a term of art referring to the extraordinary and unsustainable pace at which medical care costs have increased in the past 40 years. Roughly, we have seen a tripling of the fraction of GDP allocated to health care in the period from 1960–2004, from 5.2 percent of GDP to 15.3 percent. The majority of those health cost increases are tied to an explosion in life-preserving medical technologies during that period, virtually all of which are aimed at meeting *individual* health needs as opposed to population health needs. Callahan sees this as a moral and political failure. He calls our attention to scientific research emphasizing the "behavioral causes of many illnesses and disabilities" (p. 175) and concludes that our society must demand much more from its citizens in terms of personal responsibility for illness. The appropriate social response to such failure for him is increased investment in public health efforts aimed at disease prevention and health promotion. He also wants to see dramatically increased recognition by individuals "that their personal behavior will significantly determine their lifetime health prospects and that they have a social obligation to take care of themselves for their own sake as well as that of their neighbor" (p. 176).

Callahan wants to see a significant decrease in expenditures on "rescue medicine." From his perspective the bulk of rescue medicine is aimed at rescuing people from their own bad choices (over the course of a lifetime). Rescue medicine tends to be very costly and the benefits tend to be marginal in the aggregate. Callahan attaches moral primacy to the value of social solidarity, which he sees in a health care context as being best satisfied by substantial investments in public health. He writes: "Communal sufficiency will include an effort to help the majority of citizens avoid premature death, and to protect them from epidemics, contaminated food and water, correctable environmental hazards, and the like. Technologies for this purpose should have the highest priority" (p. 204).

Though Callahan does not explicitly make this next point, we could add that this pronounced emphasis on rescue medicine has unacceptable social justice consequences. The prime beneficiaries of rescue medicine are those who are already financially well off and well insured. What we have seen over the past 20 years are rapid increases in the number of uninsured in the United States (about 45 million in 2004), mostly attributable to escalating health costs that prompt employers to drop health insurance as a benefit. These are largely smaller employers and employees who are financially less well off, who will also be less well off health-wise owing to their inability to pay for costly health care if they have serious health problems. The implicit argument here is that a shift of resources to public health investments will result in a more equal sharing by all in the benefits of those investments. The background belief in this argument is that public health expenditures have the morally virtuous outcome of benefiting virtually everyone more or less equally. If we improve sanitation or environmental quality, then everyone enjoys that benefit; no one can be arbitrarily excluded for morally dubious reasons, as with our private health insurance system. And, therefore, putting more money into public health represents a clear moral imperative. It is this last claim that needs some critical moral assessment.

Friends of public health routinely cite the huge population health gains that have been achieved as a result of investments in public health over the past century. These have included childhood vaccination programs, motor-vehicle safety, safer workplaces, control of infectious diseases, safer and healthier foods, healthier mothers and babies (90 percent decrease in infant mortality, 99 percent decrease in maternal mortality), fluoridation of drinking water, and a 51 percent decrease in deaths from stroke and coronary heart disease since 1972 (Centers for Disease Control, 1999). Further, these enormous health gains were achieved with relatively modest investments in public health. In comparison, rescue medicine today benefits far fewer individuals to a much smaller degree at very much higher costs. The implicit moral conclusion is that this state of affairs is fundamentally unjust.

I am not so confident that that moral judgment is unequivocally true. I take as a fundamental moral premise that health care ought to be distributed by a just society in accord with health care need. I am cognizant of the fact that this is only the beginning of a moral argument. Not all health needs are morally equal; priorities need to be established among health needs. Health needs can become unsustainably expansive if they are closely linked to advancing medical technologies (Callahan, 1990, Chapter 2). The health needs that make just claims on us must somehow be linked to the costs of meeting those needs and the effectiveness of available therapeutic interventions. Meeting health needs ought not to be linked either to the ability to pay by individuals who have those needs or to the arbitrary beneficent inclinations of employers, both of which are amply represented in the current United States health care system. The virtue of a commitment to universal health care is that *everyone* has a significant portion of their health needs met without having to be concerned about denial of care due to personal inability to pay or other arbitrary factors. Public health is seen as having this very same virtue.

If infectious diseases are well controlled, if the water supply is fluoridated, then *everyone* benefits and no one is denied those benefits on morally arbitrary grounds. This suggests the moral conclusion embraced by Callahan that a truly just society ought to be investing a lot more in public health and a lot less in meeting the health needs of individuals as individuals. However, that conclusion might have been drawn too quickly.

A number of morally relevant distinctions need to be made among types of public health interventions. To begin with, many public health interventions may have relatively significant upfront costs and very low maintenance costs. Once sanitation systems are put in place or factories are retrofitted to protect air quality the environmental quality gains are sustained for decades at very low annual costs. This has the very desirable effect of reducing to almost insignificant levels the cost per unit of benefit (contrary to much of medicine where the cost of a heart transplant is $180,000 whether we do one thousand or a hundred thousand of them). Further, these interventions may be very effective in terms of dramatic reductions in mortality and morbidity. However, it might also be the case that we are dealing with the proverbial "low-hanging fruit" phenomenon. Future public health interventions might not be able to come anywhere close to achieving these outcomes. Public health interventions will reach the economist's flat of the curve just as readily as other medical interventions. That maternal mortality was reduced by 99 percent over the course of a century (owing to excellent infection control) is clearly morally commendable. But the cost of eliminating that final 1 percent might be exorbitant. Reducing carcinogenic effluents in air or water another one or two parts per billion by controlling factory emissions, thereby preventing ten more cancer deaths per year nationally at an amortized cost per year of $10 million likely represents an excessively costly marginal benefit, especially if we can identify alternative ways of saving a greater number of lives at a lower cost with those same dollars. Given any number of presently unmet health needs of women, even needs that have nothing to do with mortality reduction, those needs might make stronger claims on resources from the perspective of justice than additional maternal mortality reduction or marginal improvements in air or water quality.

The work of Louise Russell is quite salient at this point. She calls our attention to a number of public health interventions that are very inexpensive at the level of individual screening and that appear eminently worthy of funding in terms of the desirability of the goals being sought, for example, reduction of uterine cancer by 93 percent through annual Pap smears for women over age 40, but that might have a very low payoff from the perspective of cost-effectiveness analysis. The cost of such a program is more than $2.3 million per life-year saved. However, if that same screening program is carried out at three-year intervals, then we will still save 91 percent of the potential life-years to be saved and the cost will be around $84,500 per life-year saved (Russell, 2000). A similar story can be told with regard to screening mammograms for women 50–69 years old – what we imagine is a free public screening program aimed at an at-risk group. Screening can be done either annually or biennially. Only a very slight gain in lives saved is achieved through an annual program, again at a very high cost per life-year saved (Russell, 2000). But Russell also points out that false positives are a significant problem with screening mammograms. One study found that over a 10-year period 31.7 percent of women who received biennial mammograms experienced at least one false positive result, with all the additional expense, suffering, and anxiety attached to such results.

The above examples suggest the following reasonable conclusion: No wholesale transfer of resources from the medical side of the ledger to the public health side is warranted if the motivating belief is that this will result in a more just distribution of health care in our society. All manner of public health investments are as vulnerable to being marginally beneficial and non-costworthy as anything that is part of medicine. If, with Callahan, we are inclined to judge that very expensive marginal benefits associated with high-tech medicine generate no just claims, then we ought to affirm the same judgment with respect to public health interventions that yield similar expensive marginally beneficial results.

One book by Louise Russell has the provocative title: *Is Prevention Better Than Cure?* (1985). Our common sense intuition might be to give a quick affirmative answer to this question. Why, we ask ourselves rhetorically, should anyone have to suffer disease or injury if we have the capacity to prevent that from happening? And, if the costs of prevention were very low, and if our preventive efforts were extraordinarily effective, then the answer to our question would be easy and obvious. However, the world is more complex than that. Hundreds of screening tests could in theory be put in place for public health purposes. But it is certain that not all these tests would be worthy of being funded. About 33 percent of HIV-infected individuals in the US do not know they are HIV+. We would like to prevent their unknowingly infecting others. We could identify virtually all those individuals if we tested everyone. Do we have any reason to believe, however, that this would be a wise or just or cost-effective use of limited health care resources? Would we have any guarantee that individuals informed of their HIV+ status would refrain from any behavior that could result in the infection of others? Uncertainty in this regard would clearly diminish the utility of this test. Further, if this screening test cost only $25, universal screening in the United States would cost more than $7 billion per round of testing. Given new infections with each passing day, screening twice per year would be necessary. That would be $14 billion per year. What health care should we give up in order to fund that screening program? We currently spend about that same amount of money for the complex drug regimen used to protect the lives of HIV+ individuals whose immune systems have been seriously compromised. Would it be just to take away all these funds from that sort of "rescue medicine" in order to fund this public health intervention? Further, apart from the money issue and justice issue, could we justify the privacy rights violations that would be required by such a screening program?

Other screening programs for public health purposes would raise other issues. Some screening programs could identify individuals in the earliest stages of a disease process for which we had no effective therapeutic intervention. Depending upon the nature of the disease process and its health implications, such knowledge might still be somewhat beneficial to some individuals, perhaps for life-planning purposes. But, depending upon the cost of such screening and the trade-offs that would have to be made to fund the screening, it might be unjust to offer such a program for such limited and personal benefits. Further, with other screening programs there will be complex causal networks that introduce substantial uncertainty into the practical significance of positive test results. This is very likely to be true in the case of most genetic tests, which will reveal, at most, increased susceptibility to a certain disease process for individuals with a specific genotype. A particular genotype may be associated with an increased risk for various forms of cancer or heart disease, but additional complexly related causal factors (epigenetic or environmental) may be necessary in order to trigger an actual disease process in any individual. From a practical point of view positive test results will have little or no utility, either at the individual or social level. Hence, what would be the justification for the reallocation of social resources for that sort of screening program?

Other potential screening programs undertaken as a public health measure could raise more directly problems of health care justice. Recent medical research (Ehrenstein et al., 2005; Ridker et al., 2005) suggests that it might be desirable to reduce levels of both low-density lipoprotein and C-reactive protein (associated with arterial inflammation) for purposes of reducing heart attacks and stroke. Both can be measured with simple, inexpensive ($55 for the CRP test) blood tests. In this case a therapeutic response exists for elevated levels of either. Specifically, individuals would begin taking statins. But these drugs can easily have costs in excess of $1,200 per year, and they would need to be taken for years and years. Well-insured individuals could readily afford to do this; others who were uninsured or less well off economically could not. If such a testing program were deployed as a public health screening program, the net result, morally speaking, would be a net increase in the maldistribution of health care resources. (Noteworthy is the fact that in 2004 we in the US spent $14 billion on statins.) The already well off would be made better off while the less well off would be no better off. The point again is that investments in public health efforts are no guarantee of a fairer or more equitable distribution of health care in our society. Some public health expenditures can yield more unjust outcomes.

The key question we need to answer is whether we ought to be re-allocating health resources from medicine aimed at meeting individual needs to public health aimed at meeting the needs of all. For the moment we need to consider that question in the context of the actual organizational features of our health care system. The proverbial 800-pound fact that confronts us is that those who are working at "good jobs" all have private health insurance. But we have no practical way of transferring resources expended on marginally beneficial non-costworthy health care in the private sector to the public sector.

Someone might suggest a 10 percent tax on private insurance premiums to be used for public health purposes. That, however, is not a transfer of resources from private health care; it simply represents an addition to overall health costs. This is not intrinsically morally objectionable, but a likely result is that these added costs would prompt employers providing health insurance at the margins to drop health insurance altogether as a benefit, thereby adding to the pool of the uninsured. Apart from that, public health care would need to be paid with public resources.

Assuming we are not free to rob other non-health budget areas, increasing public health expenditures means resources would need to be transferred from the health care programs, Medicare and Medicaid. The problem, of course, is that both these serve largely vulnerable populations that are less well off health-wise and wealth-wise to a large extent. From the perspective of health care justice it looks like we would be taking resources from the less well off and least well off in order to fund broad public health purposes. This is not an outcome that commands moral approbation. Also, it is not unreasonable to ask whether the poor and the elderly who are the beneficiaries of Medicare and Medicaid would (or should) endorse such a transfer of resources. Just so the reader knows in concrete terms what we are asking here, I would note that if we only wanted to raise public health expenditures from 3 percent to 5 percent of total health expenditures, those two percentage points equal $36 billion.

We could argue that we intended to cull those resources from marginally beneficial non-costworthy health services currently provided to the elderly and the poor, which they ought rationally and morally to forego. However, they could then reasonably respond that those recaptured dollars ought to be redirected to what they judged as higher priority health needs for themselves rather than public health needs. This response might not be well received by Callahan and his communitarian allies because it would reflect the individualistic biases of contemporary medicine. But in these circumstances it is not obvious that these biases are open to justified moral criticism.

A case could be made more readily for a shift in resources towards public health objectives and away from expensive marginally beneficial health care if all in our society were part of the same health plan, and hence, more or less equally likely to lose access to health services judged too expensive for the marginal benefits achieved. In that scenario, given wise public health investments, virtually all in our society would be beneficiaries of those public health investments and also at risk to a small degree of being denied those expensive marginal benefits. Some of those denied these marginal benefits would be among the "least well off," but this would not be morally consequential so long as they were not disproportionately vulnerable to those losses, which is precisely the moral problem with any re-allocation of resources away from Medicare and Medicaid.

Perhaps we ought to take another critical observation by Callahan as our reference point for justifying a transfer of resources from medical care to public health. Callahan contends that a very large proportion of what we regard as health needs in our society is a product of irresponsible health choices by individuals (smoking, unhealthy diets, excess use of alcohol, and so on). I will grant for the sake of argument that this claim is largely true. What, practically and morally, ought to follow from that? Should society, for example, devise a system for "punishing" such individuals by denying them access to expensive life-saving or life-prolonging medical resources, thereby generating the savings that would be redirected to public health? Imagine this scenario: An individual has been in a serious auto accident and is bleeding badly. There is a strong smell of alcohol on his breath. A quick blood alcohol test is done to establish that his levels are over twice the legal limit. Would we be morally justified in allowing him to bleed to death right there because he had made an irresponsible choice? And if he has a passenger in his car, equally inebriated and equally injured, do we treat that person as an unfortunate victim (and therefore save that life), or do we treat the passenger as an irresponsible co-conspirator (subject to the same denial of care)? If either of these individuals were able to pay for the life-saving care they needed from their own personal resources, should the care then be provided to them? Under any of these options, would we see such social choices as reflecting a morally defensible conception of what a just and caring society ought to be?

The virtue of this first scenario is that there are relatively tight causal connections between the behavior and the outcome that seem to support strong personal responsibility judgments. But fair judging gets a lot more complicated if we consider smoking and lung cancer or heart disease or emphysema. Perhaps reliable judgments of responsibility can be made for the individual with a 40-year two-pack a day history. But how should we judge the individual who starts with a 10-year two-pack history, quits for a year, then relapses, quits again and relapses again for varying lengths of time over 30 years, faced now with advanced heart disease? Should we judge such a person a recalcitrant sinner (duly denied life-saving health care) or a persevering penitent (deserving the life-sustaining care)? Would even Dworkin's Hercules (1986, Chapter 7) have the rational capacities and moral discernment needed to make a fair judgment regarding this individual's fate?

Then there are all the truly complicated scenarios associated (I suspect) with the vast majority of chronic illness in our society, all the personal failings mixed in inextricably complex ways with family histories and psychological vulnerabilities and genetic happenstance and innumerable social behavioral determinants, cultural and economic, largely beyond individual control or responsibility. Who could fairly judge in each and every individual case whether their ill health was due to a culpable failure of personal responsibility? How would we imagine gathering evidence to support such judgments? Would personal physicians have this responsibility? If so, what would that do to the nature and quality of the doctor–patient relationship? Finally, can we imagine any of these proposals as being congruent with the defining values of a liberal society, even the more constrained forms of liberalism endorsed by most communitarians (Wikler, 1987)?

I am certain Callahan would not endorse any of the scenarios I have laid out here. But he does need to get beyond vague admonitions to individuals to take more responsibility for their personal health especially since his other major concern is with the social determinants of health, which presumably are beyond the control of individuals. Again, there will be critical issues associated with protecting the integrity of our liberal political commitments. It is relatively easy to justify as a public health measure banning cigarette smoking in restaurants or the workplace or various public facilities. These are very low cost initiatives that at least have the just effect of preventing harmful second-hand smoke from adversely affecting the health of non-smokers who have no choice but to be where they are (i.e., their jobs) or who clearly have a right not to be driven by smokers from places in which they have a right to be and a desire to be (i.e., restaurants). These sorts of policies minimally restrict the rightful freedoms of smokers who are typically free to smoke outdoors, where no one else's health is threatened. However, the health gains achieved through these policies, as measured by mortality and morbidity reductions, are likely very modest. Very significant gains might be achievable (in theory) through public policies that banned entirely the sale or manufacture of cigarettes (or alcohol or foods high in cholesterol or other health-compromising substances), but such policies would require a virtually complete repudiation of our liberal political traditions. I cannot imagine a reasonable argument outside the most dictatorial regime that would justify such policies. Our society would have to embrace "maximal healthiness" as some sort of supreme political value, again very much contrary to the value pluralism integral to our political traditions.

In conclusion, I cannot imagine any successful arguments that would warrant any wholesale reallocation of health care resources from medical care to public health. There are considerations of justice, cost-effectiveness, privacy, and respect for our most fundamental liberal and pluralistic commitments that all speak against any such wholesale transfer. The most that we can reasonably hope to justify would be retail judgments of justice regarding public health priorities within public health as it is generally currently understood.

III Setting Public Health Priorities Justly: The Limits of Moral Theory

How should public health priorities be justly established? I would give two answers to this question. First, we need to distinguish national public health priorities from local public health priorities. Second, at both levels there will need to be a predominant role for a certain conception of rational democratic deliberation in the priority setting process as opposed to any one theory of health care justice.

Some public health needs are necessarily national in scope. Most problems related to infectious disease, such as AIDS or SARS, cannot be safely relegated to local public health bodies. Effective responses require national commitment and coordination and resources. Many environmental matters of public health will be like this as well, though not all. Clean air and clean water require a national commitment and national resources. Polluted air and water tend to cover numerous political boundaries, thereby creating an opportunity for diffusion of responsibility to the detriment of all. National laws and standards effectively prevent locally powerful polluters (i.e., factories and jobs) from being used to blackmail local governments with threats of moving elsewhere in the country. Threats such as this can represent significant threats to public health. These are potential injustices that require high priority at the national level. But there may not be that many strong obligations of health care justice that determine public health priorities at the national level. That is, there can be lots of possible orderings of public health priorities at the national level that will not justifiably elicit moral criticism from the perspective of health care justice. In most cases there will simply be too many morally relevant considerations and justice-relevant considerations too complexly interrelated and too dependent upon probabilistic predictive judgments to warrant a single "most just" ordering of public health priorities. Rawls (1993) refers to this complex mix of morally relevant factors that are beyond both our rational and our moral capacities for confident, fine-grained balancing judgments as "the burdens of judgment." This is the social space within which there can be reasonable disagreement. However, if we need a socially acceptable policy or course of action, which is to say persistent disagreement is not socially desirable, then we need to turn to fair processes of rational democratic deliberation to achieve some "just enough" and legitimate set of public health priorities. The practical moral challenge is then to establish morally reasonable deliberative forums.

My suspicion is, relatively speaking, that there will not be that many opportunities at the national level to make grossly unjust choices so far as public health priorities are concerned. If, for example, in the early years of the AIDS epidemic public health authorities at the national level caved in to discriminatory public prejudices and allocated minimal resources to AIDS prevention and education because AIDS was concentrated among homosexuals and black and Hispanic IV drug abusers, then strong considerations of health care justice would rightly condemn that minimalism. At the very least Rawlsian and egalitarian requirements of respect for the least well off would be violated. But if we consider the broad spectrum of public health needs at the national level we may not find that many comparable instances or opportunities for gross injustices of that kind. If we are not quite as diligent and committed to certain levels of air or water quality at the national level, then elevated rates of cancer or emphysema or other health problems are likely to affect more or less equally all income groups, all racial and ethnic groups, and any other grouping of citizens we might imagine. To the extent that the health risks are that widely and indiscriminately dispersed, concerns about health care justice will be minimized.

There are some obvious exceptions to this last generalization. If refineries or smelting plants or power plants represent significant health threats (elevated cancer rates) to those within a two-mile radius of one of these plants, and if those living in that circle are primarily poor and socially disadvantaged and politically powerless, then there will be an obvious injustice that may well require a national policy to remedy (or better, to prevent in the first place). A national policy might be needed because local economic interests may ignore too readily the health risks to those about whom they care little in order to bring the jobs and economic gains to those who matter more (politically). By way of contrast to the national level, at the local level of public health needs, there may be more frequent opportunities for moral criticism of public health priorities. Lead paint abatement would provide a good example. The number of white middle-class children at risk of health problems owing to lead-based paint is negligible to non-existent. This is an environmental problem very much concentrated in older housing in poorer neighborhoods mostly occupied by racial and ethnic minorities. Assigning this sort of public health problem a very low local priority would be open to serious moral criticism as an injustice because, again, those least well off (already with greater than average health problems), those with the least political power, those who are most vulnerable and least able to defend their rights (children), those already targets of deep-seated discriminatory attitudes, are having their basic welfare further reduced by such a choice. The general point I am making here is that at the local level there may be much more need for retail moral vigilance in the setting of public health priorities. I am also saying that this points up the limits of rational democratic deliberative processes for public health priority setting. Some public health needs will have attached to them a sort of moral necessity such that failure to address those needs adequately will justly elicit moral criticism. Most often this will be related to the seriousness of the harm, the nature of the harm, the massiveness of the harm and the social target of the harm (already seriously disadvantaged members of society). No democratic deliberative process can legitimate wrongs such as that.

I have described elsewhere what I believe a just and legitimate democratic deliberative process ought to look like (Fleck, 1992; 1994; 1999; 2002) for purposes of health care priority setting. Among other things, I call attention to what I refer to as "constitutional principles of health care justice" that define the boundaries of the space within which these deliberative conversations must occur. Any democratic deliberative judgment about priority-setting that violated those boundaries would lose its legitimacy as a just outcome. This is a major needed constraint on the deliberative process (Gutmann and Thompson, 2004). Beyond that, one of the most critical requirements will be that these deliberative groups be broadly representative of all those who will be affected by the priority-setting process, most especially those social groups that are least well off and most often excluded from effective participation in democratic politics. This is a very demanding requirement but it is a matter of absolute necessity (Young, 2000). This would be the prime lesson we learned from the Communities of Color dialogue project funded under the National Institutes of Health Ethical, Legal, and Social Implications of the Human Genome Project program 1999–2003 (Fleck, 2001).

Finally, I have been critical in this essay of a number of assertions that Daniel Callahan has made with respect to public health priorities. But there is at least one point on which I believe he is certainly correct. We have likely over-invested in medical rescue and treatment of medical disease because the lives that we save there are visible and individually identifiable. The lives at risk when we consider public health priorities are largely invisible, nameless, statistical lives. They have an abstractness about them that can cause a serious distortion in our capacity to make sound moral judgments in the setting of social health priorities. But when public health failures occur, the deaths and injuries and illness will be attached to very visible individuals. The deliberative process provides a place where public education can occur, where those sorts of common distortions can be corrected so that we collectively make better judgments about health care priorities overall. That is an enterprise worthy of significant social investment.

References

Callahan, D. (1990), *What Kind of Life: The Limits of Medical Progress*, New York: Simon and Schuster.

Callahan, D. (1998), *False Hopes: Why America's Quest for Perfect Health is a Recipe for Failure*, New York: Simon and Schuster.

Centers for Disease Control and Prevention (1999), Ten great public health achievements: United States, 1900–1999, *Morbidity and Mortality Weekly Report* 48: 143–6.

Childress, J.A., Faden, R.R., Gaare, R.D., et al. (2002), Public health ethics: mapping the terrain, *Journal of Law, Medicine, and Ethics* 30: 170–8.

Daniels, N. (1985), *Just Health Care*, New York: Oxford University Press.

Daniels, N. (2002), Justice, health, and health care, in R. Rhodes, M. Battin, and A. Silvers (eds.), *Medicine and Social Justice: Essays on the Distribution of Health Care*, New York: Oxford University Press, pp. 6–23.

Dworkin, R. (1986), *Law's Empire*, Cambridge, MA: Harvard University Press.

Ehrenstein, M.R., Jury, E.C., and Mauri, C. (2005), Statins for atherosclerosis: as good as it gets? *New England Journal of Medicine* 352: 73–5.

Epstein, R.A. (2003), Let the shoemaker stick to his last: a defense of the old public health, *Perspectives in Biology and Medicine* 46: S138–59.

Fleck, L.M. (1987), DRGs: justice and the invisible rationing of health care resources, *Journal of Medicine and Philosophy* 12: 165–96.

Fleck, L.M. (1992), Just health care rationing: a democratic decision-making approach, *University of Pennsylvania Law Review* 140: 1597–636.

Fleck, L.M. (1994), Just caring: Oregon, health care rationing, and informed democratic deliberation, *Journal of Medicine and Philosophy* 19: 367–88.

Fleck, L.M. (1999), Just caring: managed care and protease inhibitors, in J. Arras and B. Steinbock (eds.), *Ethical Issues in Modern Medicine*, 5th edn., Mountainview, CA: Mayfield Publishing, pp. 679–86.

Fleck, L.M. (2001), *Policy Reports and Recommendations: Communities of Color and Genetics Policy Project*, East Lansing and Ann Arbor MI: Michigan State University. Available from the author upon request.

Fleck, L.M. (2002), Last chance therapies: can a just and caring society do health care rationing when life itself is at stake? *Yale Journal of Health Policy, Law, and Ethics* 2: 255–98.

Gostin, L.O. (2001), Public health, ethics, and human rights: a tribute to the late Jonathan Mann, *Journal of Law, Medicine, and Ethics* 29: 121–30.

Gostin, L.O. and Bloche, M.G. (2003), The politics of public health: a response to Epstein, *Perspectives in Biology and Medicine* 46: S160–75.

Gutmann, A. and Thompson, D. (2004), *Why Deliberative Democracy?* Princeton, NJ: Princeton University Press.

Hogan, M.J. (1999), The epidemic of violence in America: what can we do about this public health emergency? *Postgraduate Medicine Online*, 105, #6 at http://www.postgradmed.com/issues/1999/05_15_99/guest_ed.htm, last accessed May 22, 2005.

Kass, N. (2001), An ethics framework for public health, *American Journal of Public Health* 91: 1776–82.

Kawachi, I. and Kennedy, B.P. (1999), Income inequality and health: pathways and mechanisms, *Health Services Research* 34: 215–27.

Kawachi, I., Kennedy, B.P., and Wilkinson R. (1999), *Income Inequality and Health: A Reader*, New York: The New Press.

Lichtarowicz, A. (2004), Obesity epidemic "out of control," *BBC News World Edition*, at http://news.bbc.co.uk/2/hi/africa/3969693.stm.

Mann, J. (1997), Medicine and public health, ethics, and human rights, *Hastings Center Report* 27 (May/June): 6–13.

Marmot, M.G. (1999), *Social Causes of Social Inequalities in Health*, Harvard Center for Population and Development Studies, Working Paper Series 99.01.

Rao, J.K., Anderson, L.A., and Smith, S.M. (2002), End of life is a public health issue, *American Journal of Preventive Medicine* 23: 215–20.

Rawls, J. (1993), *Political Liberalism*, New York: Columbia University Press.

Ridker, P.M., Cannon, C., Morrow, D., et al. (2005), C-Reactive protein levels and outcomes after statin therapy, *New England Journal of Medicine* 352: 20–8.

Rothstein, M.A. (2002), Rethinking the meaning of public health, *Journal of Law, Medicine, and Ethics* 30: 144–9.

Russell, L.B. (1985), *Is Prevention Better Than Cure?* Washington, DC: Brookings Institution.

Russell, L.B. (2000), Cost-effectiveness analysis and screening tests for women, *Journal of the American Medical Women's Association* 55: 207–9.

Ubel, P. (2000), *Pricing Life: Why It's Time for Health Care Rationing*, Cambridge, MA: MIT Press.

Wikler, D. (1987), Personal responsibility for illness, in D. VanDeVeer and T. Regan (eds.), *Health Care Ethics*, Philadelphia, PA: Temple University Press, pp. 326–58.

Young, I.M. (2000), *Inclusion and Democracy*, New York: Oxford University Press.

Chapter 19

Justice and the Financing of Health Care

Stephen R. Latham

Introduction: The Moral Arbitrariness of Health Status

We do not get the health we deserve. Some of us are burdened through short lives with debilitating illnesses, while others live disease-free for a century. Much of our health is simply the result of our brute luck in receiving a particular genetic inheritance, in being born into a particular material and social environment, or in living through particular historical events. And while it is true that certain of our voluntary actions – smoking, for example, or eating lots of green vegetables – have statistical effects on health status, it is also true that statistical generalities do not determine the fates of individual persons. Moreover, our health-affecting choices are themselves products of genetic, environmental, and social factors. The distribution of health appears to be morally arbitrary.

This arbitrariness in distribution is made especially troubling by two further features of poor health. The first of these is the obvious and eternal fact that poor health diminishes quality of life: it is no fun to be in pain, and even pain-free illness can affect our capacities to work, to play, to experience the world. The second feature, equally obvious today but of relatively recent vintage, is that poor health is not unavoidable. It can often be avoided or improved by medical and public-health interventions. Unfortunately, the costs of these interventions are frequently greater than can be borne by those who need them. Thus brute luck gives some people a poor quality of life that only a redistribution of resources can alleviate. What does justice require us to do about this fact?

Justice as a Social Virtue

The topic of this essay is not what ethics requires us to do about the moral arbitrariness of health status, but only what *justice* requires us to do about it. Justice, as a branch of ethics, has no monopoly on questions regarding the provision of health care to those in need, nor even on problems of redistribution. Each of us has certain responsibilities regarding others' health that have no grounding in justice, and some of these may involve redistribution of resources. We may feel obliged to care for our sick parents, even at the cost of some considerable time and money – but it may not be justice that creates the obligation. The physician who lends a hand in a medical emergency may incur costs and risks; in doing so she has perhaps fulfilled a requirement of professional ethics, but not strictly one of justice. Personal obligations of charity may lead us to transfer our resources toward others' health needs; but charity need not be a matter of justice. The specific requirements of justice are those that address us collectively, rather than individually. Justice – in philosopher John Rawls's famous phrase – is "the first virtue of social institutions" (Rawls, 1999a, p. 3). Its central concern is not with how each of us is to be treated by each of us, but with how each is to be treated by all.

Given this "collective address" of justice, it is tempting to conflate the notion of a just society with that of a just government – but that would be an oversimplification. Only some of the social institutions with which justice concerns itself are governmental institutions. Business corporations, the market, the family, the press, and organized religion are all social institutions, and each may contribute to the overall justice or injustice of a given society, though each may operate more or less freely from governmental control. Indeed, the degree of freedom from governmental interference that these institutions enjoy may be a crucial part of what makes any society just.

Libertarian and Conservative Arguments

Some philosophers argue that in a just society, government would never use its taxing power to fund the provision of health care to those who needed it. The taxation used to fund such provision would inevitably be redistributive: people's tax burdens vary in every real-world scheme of taxation, and even a strictly uniform flat-tax would be redistributive because some taxpayers would consume more state-funded health care than others. Libertarians such as Robert Nozick (1974) have argued that compulsory redistributive taxation amounts to forced labor; it involves nothing less than the government's taking some people's hard-earned money and giving it to others.

Another objection to government-funded health care is tied to concerns about the government's inability to specify the content of any uniform health plan, without offending the core beliefs of at least some of its citizens (Engelhardt, 1999). Decisions about the content of a health plan implicate people's deepest beliefs about birth, reproduction, and death. Can a government properly spend tax revenues on medical procedures – abortion, assisted reproduction, assisted suicide, even blood transfusion – that many of its taxpayers sincerely find abhorrent? The supposed evil of redistributive taxation is here compounded by the fact that the funds are used to commit what some taxpayers regard as moral wrongs.

These philosophical arguments against tax-funded health care are often bolstered by arguments about the inefficiency of government service programs. First, a certain amount of waste – what economists call "deadweight loss" – accompanies any redistributive taxation, though the exact magnitude of the loss varies with different methods and levels of taxation. In addition, because they are not subject to the discipline of the competitive marketplace, government service programs are at risk of becoming lazy, bloated, and comparatively unresponsive to their users' needs. They are susceptible, also, to political capture by interest groups that can subvert their missions, or divert their funds. And economists worry that government subsidization causes wasteful overuse of services by consumers who do not bear their full costs. There is strong support for each of these claims in the economic and health-services literature; the empirical argument is not about whether these problems exist, but about their magnitude.

Those who advance arguments about the inequity and inefficiency of government programs do not oppose the provision of health care to those in need. They insist only that health care is best provided by private social institutions – notably, by the market and by charity. Market and charitable transactions are voluntary on both sides, so neither burdens property rights, and neither requires anyone to subsidize activities which they morally abhor.

Reasons beyond non-interference commend voluntary transactions. If property owners enter freely into a series of voluntary transactions through which they trade or dispose of their property as they will, the outcome will be presumptively just, and is also apt to be Pareto-optimal. Unlike forced governmental redistributions, market and charitable transactions increase the utility of the transacting parties. (Otherwise, they would not choose to enter into them.) In addition, competitive markets – including the market for charitable donations – are efficient in that they keep costs down, encourage innovation, and allocate scarce social resources to those within the market who value them most. Thus economic theory supports libertarian principle.

The most obvious trouble with these arguments is that, based on realistic assumptions about the cost of and demand for health care, even the most efficient combination of market mechanisms and charity cannot supply even minimal health care to all of those who need it. Pure market solutions do not provide anything for those who are too poor to enter the market. And modern health care is very, very expensive: only a relentless optimist (like Epstein, 1997) can believe that private charity could cover the costs of health care for the poor, if government did not. This leaves us facing a stark conflict of values. Are liberty and property rights so inviolable that we should permit some citizens to suffer and die from treatable illnesses, rather than force the transfer of some resources to provide for their aid?

Some theorists might accept the idea of liberty and property rights, but permit them to be violated in order to ensure a certain level of society-wide health security. This approach, however, is compatible only with certain relatively weak views of "rights." (Some utilitarian moral theorists, for example, have justified rights in terms of the social welfare they supply, and therefore have relatively little problem with violating those rights for the sake of still-greater social welfare.)

Another, more subtle argument undercuts libertarian objections to redistributive taxation by calling into question the notion of individual property rights on which they rely. When Nozick assimilated redistributive taxation to "forced labor," his assumption – inherited from John Locke – was that each of us has an absolute moral right of ownership in our own body, and therefore also in the fruits of our bodily labor. But, as John Rawls argues, wealth and property are never just the fruits of our own labor (Rawls, 1999a). Wealth depends, for its creation, upon massive amounts of social cooperation. Think, for example, of a successful athlete such as Michael Jordan. It is true that he was a tremendously talented and hard-working basketball player. But it is also true that he did not acquire his basic physical talents through merit, but through brute luck; and that his ability to earn money by exploiting those talents was deeply contingent upon a large number of background societal conditions. He could never have earned his money if, for example, basketball had not been invented, or weren't popular, or weren't televised; or if the rules for athletic sponsorships had been different; or if racial equity in the US had not progressed sufficiently to allow a black athlete to compete. Our wealth is never just the product of our own labor, because our earning ability is socially created. This social condition on our ability to amass wealth goes a long way toward justifying social claims upon some share of it.

As a health-policy matter, the pure anti-government arguments have not stood up against liberal arguments in favor of governmental redistribution. Every developed country engages in redistributive taxation to finance health care. Even in the United States, where libertarian arguments are perhaps most common in mainstream political discourse, massive redistributional taxation subsidizes health care for many – though notoriously not for all – citizens. This political reality notwithstanding, the anti-government arguments about forced redistribution, moral non-neutrality and inefficiency still appear in debates about justice and health care finance. Thus we see conservatives promoting tax-preferred, individually owned medical savings accounts because these supply insurance against medical catastrophe without redistribution. We see libertarians arguing for voucher systems that would allow citizens to choose from among private health plans which could compete on price as well as on health-plan content and ideology. Both groups argue for citizens' rights to "opt out" of the national health plan if they can afford to, and against public funding of controversial medical procedures such as abortion and artificial reproduction. Those who urge that government confine itself to regulating and managing private health-service providers rather than providing those services directly raise the specters of government inefficiency and interest-group capture.

Utilitarian Approaches to Justice in Health Care Finance

Utilitarians believe that moral actions are those that produce the greatest net gains in welfare for all the people they affect. "Act utilitarians" believe we should choose among individual actions by evaluating their welfare consequences, while "rule utilitarians" concentrate on the importance of our adopting those rules whose adoption will tend generally to maximize overall welfare. Utilitarians of either stripe can justify redistributive taxation whenever the loss of welfare to those who are taxed is more than offset by the welfare gains of those on whom the money is spent.

Utilitarianism is the favored operational ethic for policymakers – particularly those who have to deal with fixed budgets. The idea that we are morally obliged to spend our limited resources in ways that do the most good is intuitively appealing. Whenever we compare public-health innovations to one another in terms of the number of Quality-Adjusted Life Years they will produce, we are thinking like utilitarians. Similarly, a utilitarian impulse lies behind rhetorical questions like, "How many children could have been vaccinated with the money we spent on the artificial heart?"

There are, however, some serious problems with using utilitarian theory to discuss the justice of health care finance. First, utilitarianism has difficulty separating "macro" justice issues (e.g., whether public taxation be used to subsidize health care) from "micro" issues (e.g., whether a particular procedure should be covered by a health plan), since the right answer on the macro level depends upon the welfare-sum of all the micro-level decisions taken together. Even rule-utilitarians have this difficulty, since choosing the appropriate general rule involves hazarding guesses as to its effects on welfare in all the particular cases where it will apply. Second, utilitarianism has no reason to regard health care as "special," or as marking out its own sphere for policy consideration. Health care affects welfare, but so do myriad other things. For example, a utilitarian would have no problem with eliminating health-coverage for the elderly if more welfare could be produced by spending the money on noise reduction or computer access or public art. Third, utilitarian theory is unable reliably to compare welfare across persons. Does spending a thousand dollars on pain medication for cancer victims generate more or less welfare than spending that amount on the provision of motorized wheelchairs to persons with progressive neurological diseases? Utilitarian theorists need to be able to answer such questions, but no objective answer seems possible. Finally, utilitarianism considers only overall social welfare, and not the welfare gains or losses that fall upon particular persons. It may therefore justify serious harms to small groups for the sake of securing very small welfare gains to each member of a large group. Utilitarianism has no stable conception of an inviolable right, so anything can be done to, or taken from, anyone, provided only that the result is a net gain in social welfare. A utilitarian could thus justify cutting funds for expensive life-saving emergency care for a few in favor of providing free dental floss to millions.

Rawls's Theory of Justice

John Rawls's work dominates the contemporary literature on justice (Rawls, 1999a). Its appearance gave rise to a late-twentieth-century renaissance in political theory and ethics, including bioethics. It is unsurprising, then, that some of the best (and best known) work on justice and health care claims to be Rawlsian.

Rawls's theory is in the social-contract tradition that reaches back to Hobbes, Locke, and Rousseau. He imagines principles of justice being established by agreement among parties in the "original position" – his version of a pre-social "state of nature." The most striking feature of Rawls's original position is that the parties enter into their bargain from behind what he terms a "veil of ignorance." The parties retain general awareness that they all have different natural endowments and different conceptions of the good, but they are temporarily stripped of any knowledge about themselves, i.e., about the natural endowments or disadvantages they happen to possess, or about what their own conception of the good actually is. This "veil of ignorance" builds a dimension of moral reasonableness into what would otherwise be purely self-interested bargaining. It is meant to guarantee the fairness of the outcome, since each of the parties has an interest in working out rules for social cooperation that will satisfy them when the veil is lifted. To put the matter concretely, the parties must agree upon rules for the basic structure of society that would be equally acceptable regardless of whether they turn out to be male or female, weak or strong, religious or irreligious, a member of an ethnic minority or of a majority.

Rawls argues that, because of their radical uncertainty about their own personal endowments and commitments, persons behind the veil of ignorance will bargain using a "maximize-the-minimum," or "maximin," strategy. This means that they will choose social rules that make the position of the least advantaged person as good as possible. After all, each of the bargainers faces some unknown odds of occupying that very position when the veil of ignorance is lifted.

Rawls concludes that the parties in the original position will agree upon two principles of justice. The first – a principle of liberty – guarantees equal and adequate basic rights and liberties to all. The second places limits on social and economic inequalities. Such inequalities can be tolerated only if they satisfy two conditions: first, they must be "attached to positions and offices open to all under conditions of fair equality of opportunity"; and second, "they are to be to the greatest benefit of the least advantaged members of society."

Imagine a society in which certain priests enjoy great wealth and social status. Imagine, further, that priesthood is the exclusive province of males born into a certain caste. This situation clearly violates the first of Rawls's two conditions on acceptable inequality. Wealth and status are here associated with an office – priesthood – that is not open to all. Neither women nor members of other social castes have the opportunity to compete fairly for the position, or to attain the wealth and status that come with it.

Even when the first condition of "fair equality of opportunity" is met, the second condition permits only those social and economic inequalities that benefit the least-advantaged in society. It permits, for example, paying higher salaries to physicians than to day-laborers, if attracting talented persons into medical work and rewarding them well for their training would benefit the least advantaged in society. But it would cap that salary difference at the point where the inequality no longer served to improve the lives of the least-advantaged.

Rawls's theory itself says nothing about health or health care. He does not even envision the parties establishing a "right" to health care under the first principle, which exclusively addresses political rights. Nor does he envision the parties setting up a program of medical insurance as part of the initial bargain about their fair terms of social cooperation. Indeed, health disparities are not admitted as social or economic inequalities to be addressed by the second principle, in part because to introduce them would greatly complicate our ability to identify "the least advantaged members of society."

The philosopher Norman Daniels first established a place for health care within Rawls's framework. Daniels (1985) argued that poor health was a special problem for justice because of its effect on opportunity. Those in poor health are unable to pursue society's various positions and offices and many doors are closed to them. Daniels therefore reasoned that health insurance is necessary in a just society because it helps secure the fair equality of opportunity demanded by Rawls's second principle of justice. A just society's health insurance program should aim at restoring people to what Daniels terms the "normal opportunity range." Where that cannot be achieved, health coverage should compensate those with diminished opportunities. Public funding should be allocated first to those medical interventions that help people achieve or maintain normal function and the normal range of opportunity.

Daniels's position has attracted a number of criticisms. Some have argued that it commits governments to providing an exorbitant amount of health care. Some have complained that it does not address the problem of the "bottomless pit" – the person whose health problems require a tremendous investment of resources for little gain. Others have worried that Daniels's criteria of "normal human function" and "normal range of opportunity" could be used to discriminate against the elderly, or to ration their care, since a decline in levels of functioning is normal in old age, and elders have already enjoyed most of the normal range of opportunity. Still others fault Daniels's theory for failing to prioritize among scarce health resources. Daniels has repeatedly responded to these criticisms, and modified or clarified his position over time (e.g., in Daniels and Sabin, 2002). More recently, though, Daniels has developed a different Rawlsian perspective on justice and health care. To see why, we need to understand something about the causes of poor health.

Justice and the Social Determinants of Health

In the decades after Rawls first published, medical and public health scientists were uncovering startling new facts about the relationship between health and social status. Studies revealed that poor health is not simply a matter of genetics and germs. It is to a large extent the result of social and cultural conditions, many of which are created by public policy (Evans et al., 1994). Life expectancy, for example, is lowest among the poor, even in affluent countries. Life expectancy is lower among those with low-status jobs. Stress has profound negative effects upon health. Unemployment and social isolation are strongly correlated with poor physical and mental health. Better early childhood care is associated with better health lifelong. Those who report feeling in control on the job have better health than those who report that they are not in control. High educational attainment is associated with better health. Strong social support networks and friendships are associated with better health. There is even some evidence – though there is sharp debate on the matter – that radical disparities in wealth within a society also contribute to poor overall population health.

Correlation is not causation, and one has to be careful not to make unwarranted inferences about the impact of particular social policies upon health status. Nonetheless, it seems plain that almost every area of public policy has at least some impact on population health: education, day-care, income-tax, minimum wage, unemployment insurance, and social support programs. Even transportation and zoning policy have health impacts, since those who walk more frequently enjoy better health than those who drive.

These facts substantially alter the scope of the debate about justice and health care. No doubt medical care is still vitally important to people who are ill. But if their poor health is in part caused by social conditions, then provision of health care begins to seem like too little, too late.

Daniels's central contention is that health care is a special problem for justice because of its relationship to opportunity. Social provision of care is therefore necessary to meet the Rawlsian requirement that positions and status remain open to all under conditions of "fair equality of opportunity." Once the social determinants of health are acknowledged, justice requires us to secure fair equality of opportunity by eliminating the root poor social conditions themselves, rather than by simply treating the poor health they cause.

Daniels has embraced this new position, and has criticized himself and others who focused too much on health care and not enough on health (Daniels et al., 2000). There is an appearance of radicalism in this change from arguing for publicly funded health care to arguing for massive across-the-board policy reforms in the name of securing the public's health. But the seeming radicalism of this new position is not terribly radical as a matter of substance. Daniels has always been a Rawlsian. He believes that the Rawlsian program of justice would, if it were implemented, eliminate many of the social causes of poor health. His move from thinking about health care to thinking about health therefore does not signal a change in the underlying requirements of justice, but only a change in the way in which we think about the relationship of justice to health.

Other theorists have moved in substantially different directions because of the growing awareness of the social determinants of health. Pogge (2002), for example, argues that *retributive* justice, rather than *distributive* justice, requires us to pay for the health care of those in need. According to Pogge, poorly structured societies are responsible for creating bad health, and must compensate their victims for the harm they have wrongfully caused.

The Capabilities Approach

One rival to Rawls has achieved particular importance within the public-health debate: the "capabilities approach" to justice advanced by economist/philosopher Amartya Sen (1999) and expanded upon by the philosopher Martha Nussbaum (2000, 2006).

Sen originally developed the capabilities approach as a method for the evaluation of development programs. His aim was to create an instrument that would allow policy-makers to focus on the real human impact of development, rather than on abstract economic measures (income, productive output) that might not translate into improved quality of life. On Sen's view, there are various things that a person might value doing, or being. These he calls "functionings." "Capabilities" are the various functionings that it is feasible for a person to achieve, regardless of whether that person chooses to achieve them. (One can have the capability, for example, to learn to play a musical instrument, without ever actually doing so.) The "capability set" is the set of all possible functionings from among which a person can realistically choose. As such, it is a measure of a person's freedom. Development programs ought to expand people's capability sets – the range of real options they have for being and doing different things, whether or not they choose to be or do them.

Sen does not supply a clearly identified minimal set of capabilities that a society ought to supply its citizens, nor does he offer any satisfactory account of how different capabilities are to be traded off against each another. Instead, he appeals to a continuing process of public reasoning about such trade-offs. Martha Nussbaum, however, has attempted to transform Sen's basic approach into a full-blown theory of justice. She regards her approach as superior to Rawls's because it can address a number of vexing theoretical issues. Nussbaum contends that there are certain universal natural capabilities that any just society should secure to its citizens. These capabilities are grounded in a notion of a basic and universal human nature, and constitute the prerequisites for living a life that is fully human.

Nussbaum provides a provisional list of the basic capabilities. Some are primarily physical (life, bodily health, bodily integrity); some are mental (ability to use the senses, to imagine, think and reason; ability to develop emotional attachments and responses to other people and things; ability to engage in practical reason); some are primarily social ("affiliation," described as including the ability to live concernfully with others, and to have self-respect and equal dignity with others; and "play," described as the ability to laugh and play with others, and to enjoy recreation). Her list also includes the ability to live in concernful relation with other species, plants, and the natural world; and control over one's environment, which is defined to include both political control (rights of political participation, free speech and association) and material control (including both the ability to hold property and seek employment on an equal basis with others, and freedom from unwarranted search and seizure).

The contrast between Nussbaum's approach and Rawls's is stark. Whereas Rawls sets out to frame the basic institutions of a just society, Nussbaum's core theory says very little about the proper shape of such institutions, and begins instead with what she regards as a substantive account of what any just set of institutions ought to deliver. Nussbaum says comparatively little about political and civil rights, and almost nothing about inequality or resource distribution. She is, however, deeply concerned with the effects of poverty and of unequal opportunity, and concentrates on personal capacities and interpersonal ties that Rawlsian theory does not address.

The capabilities approach obviously supports redistribution of social resources for the provision of health care. A just society ensures that its members can live to the natural end of a full lifespan, and ensures their proper health and nutrition. The capabilities approach is quite compatible with the literature on the social determinants of health, since social capabilities like affiliation, play, and control over one's environment are correlated with good health.

The capabilities approach to justice in the health arena has been embraced by the public health and international development communities. Health workers and researchers use the theory as Sen intended – to measure the progress of a wide variety of interventions undertaken by an array of institutions: departments, state and national agencies, public international organizations, private non-governmental organizations, individual research teams. In such varied settings, the concentration of the capabilities approach on concrete and observable features of human lives is a virtue.

Nussbaum has recently argued for the superiority of the capabilities approach not just on the operational level, but as a matter of theory (Nussbaum, 2006). In particular, she argues that the capabilities approach is better suited than Rawlsian social-contract theory to addressing, *inter alia*, the problems of justice for persons with mental disabilities and of justice across national boundaries. (Her arguments about international justice and health are treated below.)

With regard to mental disability, Nussbaum argues that Rawls's theory systematically excludes those with substantial mental disabilities from the sphere of justice. For Rawls, those who lack the moral powers of reasonableness and rationality cannot be parties to the social contract. Those whose mental disabilities exclude those powers therefore have no standing to bargain about the principles of justice. Rawls leaves the question of their treatment to be dealt with legislatively, as a matter of social benevolence, rather than as a core matter of the just structure of basic social institutions. The capabilities approach, in contrast, defines justice in terms of the capabilities delivered to every person. It therefore gives the mentally disabled a full seat at the table of justice, and places their needs precisely on a par with others', regardless of their inability to engage in social cooperation. Nussbaum has little to say about who, institutionally, has the duty to meet the demands of the mentally disabled for justice, or why.

International Justice and Health

The debate about justice and health care financing also has an important international dimension. The inequality of the distribution of health is painfully obvious on the global scale: life expectancy at birth in Japan is 81 years, in Swaziland, 33. In Angola, 187 infants die for every 1,000 live births; in Singapore, fewer than three.

Most theories of justice are structurally ill-suited to addressing international disparities. That is because theories of justice normally address the question of how members of a community ought to live together. We do not (yet) live in a worldwide community. Contractual theories of justice like Rawls's cast justice as consisting in fair terms of cooperation. Unfortunately, some countries are so poor or politically disorganized as to be unable to bring any promise of cooperation to the bargaining table. Nonetheless, in recent years, theorists of justice have attempted to address international disparities in wealth and resources. These attempts bear on the question of how we should think about redistribution of world resources to those in need of health care.

A number of utilitarian theorists (e.g., Singer, 1985) have argued that morality demands massive redistribution of resources away from wealthy countries and toward poor ones, and away from wealthy persons toward poor ones. If, for the price of my stereo system, I could purchase health care for a child in sub-Saharan Africa, I am morally bound to do so, because the welfare produced in Africa by the transfer will far outweigh my welfare loss. The plain implication is that wealthy persons and countries ought to be transferring massive amounts of wealth to others. There are a number of difficulties with this theoretical approach, however. First, utilitarians have no obvious tools for framing national or other institutional structures through which such international transfers ought to be made. Second, utilitarianism seems too demanding as a moral theory. It threatens to transform everyone into welfare-production machines, unable to pursue their own projects or goals. For example, since preventing a case of river-blindness would undoubtedly give rise to more net welfare than spending the same amount of money on a toy for a child, the utilitarian welfare calculation would seem to demand that I spend my money on health programs in Africa rather than on my child's birthday present. But this leaves me nothing that I can care about, or privilege, over the sufferings of strangers.

Rawlsian theory has developed in a number of different directions to deal with international injustice. Some Rawlsians (Pogge, 1989; Beitz, 1999) have suggested that the original position simply be stretched to include all persons in the world as bargaining parties, and that the principles of justice – including those governing social and economic inequality – simply apply to everyone. This approach obviously requires substantial modifications to Rawls's own view of the theoretical basis for his egalitarian prescriptions.

Rawls himself proposed a two-stage bargain, in which countries, having set their own terms of social cooperation internally, then bargain with one another to set the terms of a worldwide social contract for fair international cooperation (Rawls, 1999b). Rawls's two-stage bargain results in some redistributive international aid, but that aid is not aimed at securing certain levels of health or living conditions for individuals. Instead, the main point of international aid, on Rawls's view, is to assist states to achieve the level of political and economic security necessary to permit them to create stable and just internal institutions of their own. Buchanan (2000), among others, has criticized Rawls for ignoring an immense global basic structure of non-state institutions that stands in need of regulative principles of justice, including redistributive justice.

Nussbaum (2006) has also criticized Rawls's commitment to international resource-distribution as too thin, and has claimed that the capabilities approach is superior in establishing a demand, based in justice, for international redistribution of the resources that will help people achieve meaningful human lives. Her discussion in this area stresses health disparities, and redistribution for the sake of securing health is clearly central to her agenda. But once again, the capabilities approach has little to say about how this redistribution ought to be achieved. Nussbaum does argue (in deliberate contrast to utilitarian theory) that international redistribution should primarily be the responsibility not of persons but of institutions. In doing this, she seeks to avoid the paradox of a capabilities approach so demanding as to cause some individuals to deprive themselves of capabilities in their efforts to provide them to others. But again, she has very little to say about the proper assignment of the institutional duty to meet justice's demand. She is content to say that governments, NGOs, international bodies, and multinational corporations all have their role to play in securing the capability of health to those who need it.

Conclusion

As long ago as 1962, the philosopher Bernard Williams pronounced it a "necessary truth" that "the proper ground of distribution of medical care is ill-health" (Williams, 1962). "In connexion with the inequality between the rich ill and the poor ill," he continued, "we have straightforwardly the situation of those whose needs are not receiving the same treatment, though the needs are the ground of the treatment. This is an irrational state of affairs." In the decades since Williams wrote, much has changed in our understanding of justice, in our health policy, and above all in our medical knowledge. But the "irrational state of affairs" of which he complained persists. That fact stands as one of the greatest challenges to bioethics.

References

Beitz, C. (1999), *Political Theory and International Relations*, 2nd edn., Princeton, NJ: Princeton University Press.

Buchanan, Allen (2000), Rawls's law of peoples: rules for a vanished Westphalian world, *Ethics* 110: 697–721.

Daniels, N. (1985), *Just Health Care*, Cambridge: Cambridge University Press.

Daniels, N. and Sabin, J.E. (2002), *Setting Limits Fairly*, Oxford: Oxford University Press.

Daniels, N., Kennedy, B., and Kawachi, I. (2000), *Is Inequality Bad for Our Health?* Boston, MA: Beacon Press.

Engelhardt, Jr., H.T. (1999), Freedom and moral diversity: the moral failures of health care in the welfare state, in J. Arras and B. Steinbock (eds.), *Ethical Issues in Modern Medicine*, 5th edn., Mountain View, CA: Mayfield.

Epstein, R.A. (1997), *Mortal Peril: Our Inalienable Right to Healthcare?* New York: Addison-Wesley.

Evans, R.G., Barer M.L., and Marmor T.R. (eds.), (1994), *Why Are Some People Healthy and Others Not? The Determinants of Health of Populations*, New York: Aldine de Gruyter.

Nozick, R. (1974), *Anarchy, State and Utopia*, New York: Basic Books.

Nussbaum, M.C. (2000), *Women and Human Development: The Capabilities Approach*, Cambridge: Cambridge University Press.

Nussbaum, M.C. (2006), *Frontiers of Justice: Disability, Nationality, Species Membership*, Cambridge, MA: Harvard University Press.

Pogge, T. (ed.) (1989), *Realizing Rawls*, Ithaca, NY: Cornell University Press.

Pogge, T. (2002) *World Poverty and Human Rights: Cosmopolitan Responsibilities and Reforms*, London: Polity Press.

Rawls, J.B. (1999a), *A Theory of Justice*, revised edn., Cambridge, MA: Belknap Press of Harvard University Press.

Rawls, J.B. (1999b), *The Law of Peoples*, Cambridge, MA: Harvard University Press.

Sen, A.K. (1999), *Development as Freedom*, New York: A. Knopf.

Singer, P. (1985), Famine, affluence, and morality, in C. Beitz (ed.), *International Ethics*, Princeton, NJ: Princeton University Press.

Williams, B.A.O. (1962), The idea of equality, in P. Laslett and W.G. Runciman (eds.), *Philosophy, Politics and Society*, 2nd series, Oxford: Blackwell.

Chapter 20

Judgment and Justice

Evaluating Health Care for Chronically Ill and Disabled Patients

Anita Silvers

Introduction

Three kinds of complex and poorly understood evaluations characteristically affect how health care professionals, and the medical system as a whole, treat individuals with chronic illnesses and disabilities. These judgments are influential, and even insidious, in determining whether people with chronic illness and disabilities will receive care. The evaluations in question affect the scope and goals of the care chronically ill and disabled people will get. They affect, as well, whether what these people need and what is done for them is considered to be health care or some other kind of benefit. Unlike decisions allocating health care to acutely ill individuals, the evaluations in question turn on who the patient is rather than what s/he suffers from.

The first kind of evaluation relates the propriety of providing treatment to the patient's quality of life. Chronic illness and disability are presumed to compromise the worth of any life. Such a presumption prompts questions about the degree of benefit to be reaped from resources expended on individuals who are disabled or chronically ill, compared with what can be gained by directing these resources to unimpaired or curable individuals.

The second kind of evaluation relates the propriety of the patient's receiving treatment to the furthering or frustrating of broader public goals. The health states that call for chronic care do not resolve themselves within a predictable span of time. The needs of patients with chronic illnesses and disabilities for treatment thus can seem interminable and boundless. Special issues of justice arise because chronically ill and disabled people's need for heightened levels of health care is long-term rather than transient.

The main issues in this kind of evaluation are whether such individuals should receive continuing medical care that maintains but does not cure them, and how much must protracted medical intervention mitigate their dysfunction to legitimate their call for care. One place where these issues arise is in cases when persistent global dysfunction is the prognosis for a patient immediately in need of acute care. When a patient presents with severe brain damage, for example, the prospect of long-term care for a person who remains in deficit may weigh heavily. A related question pertains to individuals whose biological deficits chronically reduce but do not devastate their functioning. Ought they to be assigned to the "sick" role, which relieves them of (some of) the usual expectations of responsible citizenship but at the cost of their giving up various social opportunities?

The third kind of evaluation relates the propriety of the patient's receiving treatment to the standpoint from which the treatment is perceived. Patients, physicians, and the public as a whole are united about the desirability of curing acute illness. But chronically ill and disabled patients often rate the disutility of their conditions very differently from how other people do.

Some social scientists have suggested that chronic illness and disability inflect people's experiences in ways that alter their values. They designate as ordinary or routine the preferences and priorities, and resulting values, of people who are biologically species-typical or "normal." But living with chronic illness or disability can alter a person's preferences and priorities, so that a shift to what are designated as adaptive values results. Patients whose values have become adaptive may not agree with other people about the desirability of pursuing cures, and especially about the desirability of submitting to risky interventions in pursuit of cures. Researchers who draw this distinction do not agree, however, as to which perspective – the routine valuations made by physicians, policy-makers, and the public, or the chronic patient's adaptive valuations – should prevail in decisions about allocating health care resources.

The number of people living with chronic illness and disability, and therefore the number affected by the ethics of health care decisions regarding these conditions, is large and is growing. Yet medical ethics has been unmindful of the special problems about medical justice posed by individuals who survive illness and accident but are not subject to full cure. Medical ethics remains absorbed with and by the ethics of acute care, as if doing right by acutely ill patients both sets and satisfies the standard for a just health care system. To correct the mistaken assumption that achieving justice in acute care satisfactorily models just decision-making for other kinds of care, this chapter explores how the three kinds of evaluation to which chronically ill and disabled individuals are subjected – namely, assessing the quality of their lives, adjudicating conflicts between their personal and the public's needs, and assigning priority where their perspectives diverge from those of medical professionals or the public – play out in the ethics of health care for chronically ill and disabled people.

Chronic Illness and Disability

People whose biological condition departs dysfunctionally from the species-typical state are to be found everywhere. When an individual's dysfunction is persistent, and cannot now be cured, the person usually is thought of as being chronically ill or disabled. Such a chronic condition may be stable, or intermittent, or vulnerable to exacerbation, or inexorably progressive. Maintaining the individual's stability, or mitigating or delaying symptoms, often calls for regular medical interventions and/or long-term care.

Being disabled and being chronically ill are not the same. These are two different states, although they often overlap because chronic illness very commonly occasions disability. Nevertheless, some people with chronic health problems are not disabled. Continuing medical treatment may mitigate an individual's biological dysfunction so the person encounters no extraordinary difficulties in executing major life activities, but only as long as, and to the degree that, the individual has access to effective medical management.

The way multiple sclerosis can now be managed is illustrative. Formerly, multiple sclerosis was thought to be episodic, although sometimes marked by the enduring consequences of acute incidents, such as paralysis and visual impairment that do not recede. But MRI technology now has shown that untreated multiple sclerosis usually involves the progressive accumulation of lesions even during asymptomatic periods. Regular administration of interferon or other medication can, however, reduce the occurrence of new lesions and induce old lesions to abate, and may even enable individuals diagnosed with multiple sclerosis to maintain the remittance of symptoms for decades.[1]

Thus, individuals with this biological impairment may be continuously in treatment for their health problems but nevertheless may, thanks to this medical intervention, experience no diminution of their capacity for performing major life activities or the activities of daily living. They may, that is, exhibit no disability at all. HIV infection, diabetes, glaucoma, and sickle cell disease are other examples of biological conditions in which chronic (systematic or episodic) medical intervention can delay, reduce, or prevent disability. Whether or not they experience compromised capability to execute all basic activities of daily living, chronically ill individuals typically rely on long-term treatment relationships with physicians or other medical experts.

Concomitantly, some people are disabled but are not ill. In such cases, the person's ability to execute major life activities is compromised by the consequences of past infection, injury, or other mishap, but the cause of the impairment is not expected to recur. To illustrate, a person in robust health may nevertheless be seriously limited in manual activity because of phocomelia caused by his mother's ingesting thalidomide early in his gestation. Although biologically dysfunctional in some respect, the person's condition does not need further medical intervention or support to have better health or be more well. He is disabled by the disruption of limb development that occurred long ago during his fetal growth, but by no means does this disabling event in his past translate into his being ill now, nor is it appropriate to treat him so.

Disabled people who are not ill nevertheless often have an on-going need for health-care related medications, devices and services that address sequelae of an illness or injury, rather than preventing, mitigating, or curing the illness or injury itself. Their enduring impairments may require durable medical equipment, orthotics and prosthetics, magnifying mechanisms to enlarge printed texts or enhance the clarity of spoken words, or long-term assistance in executing basic activities of daily life. Although a physician's expertise may be invoked, or even required, to document patients' biological conditions as a way of verifying a physical reason for their dysfunction, other kinds of medical professionals, as well as craftsmen and engineers, usually are called upon to manufacture, select, procure, and provide these assistive devices and services.

Individuals who are disabled but not ill often rely on long-term relationships with technicians, vendors, home health care providers, or personal assistants, rather than on the care of physicians, for the support they need to remain functional. Current practice tends to conceptualize such support as falling within the framework of the health care system. There are compelling reasons for doing so, but equally compelling considerations for a change.

Continuity of care is one of the strongest arguments for supposing that the medical system owes support to the disabled. If an individual is owed acute care to save her life from, or to reduce the severity of, illness or injury, it may be supposed that the same individual is owed chronic care for the residual outcomes of the illness or injury, or of the treatment itself. To illustrate, administering antibiotics to a pre-term neonate may fight infection, enabling the child to live, but with seriously impaired hearing resulting from secondary effects of the antibiotics. An argument can be made that what the child needs in future to mitigate her chronic hearing dysfunction should be provided by the same medical system that mitigated her acute respiratory dysfunction, for the same reasons invoked in establishing obligations to provide acute health care.

To think this is to recommend that the evaluative structure of allocating resources for acute care be extended to cover chronic care. But an equally compelling argument may be made against subsuming support for chronically ill and disabled individuals under a conceptual framework primarily meant to propel delivery of acute care. There are fundamental differences between the two situations, and these differences may make addressing the dysfunctions of chronically ill and disabled people as we do acutely ill ones both inefficient and inequitable.

Acute and Chronic Illness: Health Care's Goals

Acute illnesses occur as discrete episodes. Medicine's goal is to intervene so effectively in the short-term that biological malfunction is prevented or removed. As Ronald Amundson has noted, the "sick" role is a kind of social stepping or stopping out, but one that is disadvantageous, inappropriate, or impractical for individuals to assume or be assigned to on a long-term basis. Amundson comments: "the 'sick role' . . . relieves a person of normal responsibilities, but carries . . . other obligations with it."[2]

Separating one's self from society's practical activities so as not to disrupt or distract others from conducting them, and identifying one's good and complying with efforts to exit the "sick role," are among the obligations of individuals whom society identifies as being "sick." When treatment succeeds, the patient leaves the "sick" role behind and her life proceeds as if the acute illness or injury had never been. But when the curative aim of acute care is attained only very imperfectly or not at all, different values – those important to chronic care – move to the foreground of both personal and policy decision-making. In chronic care, medicine's goal is to reach and maintain as adequate a quality of activity as possible, despite the patient's continuing biological malfunction, rather than to eliminate the malfunction. This is not to suggest that chronic conditions should not be cured but that curative care administered to chronic patients does not transfigure or translate smoothly into chronic care.

The questions dominating deliberations about the ethics of chronic illness and disability focus on whether, despite persisting experiences of dysfunction, the patient's life is made worth living, for the patient or for society, over a prolonged period of time. Whether chronically ill and disabled people should remain in the "sick" role is a central issue here, for there are distinctly different perspectives about the advisability of their stopping out from, or instead continuing to execute the responsibilities of, the social world. How we treat chronic illness and disability will be guided by personal and social values related to living with biological malfunction, rather than (as in treating acute illness) by the values related to escaping it. But whether these values are personal or social makes a great difference to how chronically ill and disabled people will fare in obtaining care.

Where, for example, a public policy perspective prevails, life-saving medical interventions may be reserved for non-disabled people whose recovery will return them to full health. For from society's point of view, individuals with untreatable impairments or chronically compromised health may have difficulty achieving sufficient quality of functioning, and at best may require more resources than other people to do so. Or their pre-existing condition may mean that that their life expectancy will be less than what otherwise could be expected for a similar expenditure of resources on an unimpaired or fully curable individual. Giving weight to this kind of social benefit consideration invites the belief that treating chronically ill and disabled people for health problems, even those unrelated to their chronic condition, is a questionable social investment because despite these expenditures they cannot escape the sick role.

From the standpoint of a disabled or chronically ill individual, however, public health care policies that magnify their disadvantages, or that turn their biological disadvantages into social ones, are very likely to appear undeserved and unfair. For one thing, such policies seem inequitably to weigh their lives as being less good than the lives of other people, in regard to the quality of both their personal experience and their capacity for reciprocal social contribution, and therefore to decree that they are less important than other people. Such policies may even be understood to decree that their survival is of less value to the larger group than other people's. At the very least, policies and practices driven by this kind of devaluation limit social opportunities available to the population of chronically ill and disabled people and thus further extend into the social realm the extent to which their biological conditions result in their suffering.

The Population

The causes of chronic illness and disability are many and varied. Some chronic conditions (or at least the disposition to manifest them) – for example, sickle cell disease, cystic fibrosis, achondroplasia in children with an achondroplasic parent, certain kinds of deafness, and schizophrenia – are inherited. Others – for example, phocomelia, achondroplasia resulting from mutation, deafness following fetal exposure to German measles, and Down syndrome – result from alterations during embryo or fetal development. Still others – such as diabetes, traumatic brain injury or spinal cord damage, deafness resulting from administration of antibiotics to a neonate – are acquired after birth. Forethought and preventive action can avoid some of these causes or their sequelae, but others require sophisticated knowledge and technology or favorable social and economic conditions to dodge, still others await further research into their mechanisms, and some may be inescapable, forever beyond our power to remove.

The number and diversity of sources of chronic illness and disability make it unlikely that we can eliminate these conditions. Doing so was the aim of the twentieth century's notorious eugenics programs, implemented both before and after World War II in some of the most medically advanced societies and mainly aimed at ensuring that biologically impaired individuals did not reproduce. The rationale for these programs was that the presence of a minority of chronically ill and disabled people in society impeded the realization of the majority population's full potential by imposing a burden of care. A community in which chronically ill and disabled people could participate was imagined to be one where performance standards had to be lowered to suit the impaired, but a community that excluded them from attempting productive roles yet would be burdened by their presence.

But eugenics programs miss their purported mark of creating an ideally capable citizenry because comparatively little chronic illness and disability is the product of biological inheritance alone. Almost all biological dysfunction arises at least in part from adventitious circumstance, even where individuals are predisposed to manifest the condition. And even where inheritance plays a very large part, dysfunction may be more or less severe depending on circumstance. Consequently, pre-emptive elimination of chronic illness and disability from the population would turn into targets a much larger proportion of us than ever would become symptomatic.

Our better understanding of the mechanisms of biological inheritance suggests that a much larger proportion of the population carries the potential for chronic illness or disability than twentieth-century eugenicists hypothesized. Very likely the majority of us do so. So many more of us would be vulnerable to a eugenicist approach aimed at freeing the health care and other social systems from caring for chronically ill and disabled individuals than the eugenicists of earlier times typically imagined.

The chronically ill and disabled will remain amongst us. As people age, they are more likely to become chronically ill or disabled. In the US, 12 percent of the working age (21–64 years) population is identified by the US Census Bureau as having a disability, but nearly 40 percent of those age 65 or older have a disability. To suggest how numerous chronically ill and disabled people are, out of a US population of approximately 263 million, approximately 90 million US citizens are chronically ill, and approximately 38 million of these have sufficient difficulty with major life activities to be identified as disabled.[3]

Disability and chronic illness are much less common among the young than the old. Nevertheless, in the United States, for example, 30 percent of all children have chronic health conditions or special health care needs. About two-thirds of these children have comparatively mild conditions, such as asthma or chronic ear infections, that require continuing but not extraordinary health care. The others have a chronic condition that calls for special care.[4] Thus, even the very young may be affected by the values that influence the medical treatment of chronic illness and disability.

Given the current rate of onset for diabetes, one in every three children born at the beginning of the twenty-first century in the United States eventually will become diabetic.[5] There is reason to worry about how valuable the health care system will consider their care. In New York City, for example, the incidence of Type II diabetes has nearly doubled in the last decade,[6] but the city's public health system devotes less than $1 million and just a three-person staff to the 800,000 citizens who are diabetic, compared to $27 million and 400 staffers to the 1,000 New Yorkers infected with tuberculosis.[7]

A *New York Times* article on diabetes diagnosed the problem: "Chronic care is simply not as profitable as acute care because insurers, and consumers, do not want to pay as much for care that is not urgent."[8] On this principle, almost all insurers cover the $30,000+ cost of lower limb amputation, a familiar complication of diabetes, and $300+ daily charges for dialysis, but many refuse to authorize $150 for preventative podiatry or pay for more than one blood-testing strip a day.[9] In American health care, according to the *New York Times*, "the real profit is made not by controlling chronic diseases like diabetes but by treating their many complications."[10] One can imagine how shocking a society that balks at low-cost prevention of complications, but eagerly endorses expensive treatment after complications set in, appears from the perspective of those who must suffer the complications.

Adaptive Values

Health care researchers remain divided about whether or not, in the case of people whose chronic illnesses or disabilities distance them from having species-typical experiences and lives, the division between personal and social perspectives is inherently oppositional. And, if so, which of the two perspectives – the singular personal or the collective depersonalized perspective – should prevail in distributing health care resources. There seem to be important inconsistencies, or at least profound differences, between valuation from these two standpoints. These inconsistencies show up when abstract allocation preference models designed by social scientists are made the basis of empirical research projects, and they also are evident in everyday life.

There are well-documented differences between how the public rates lives with chronic illness and disability, and how individuals with chronic illnesses and disabilities rate their lives. It is well known, for instance, that chronically ill and disabled people tend to rate the disutility of their conditions much lower than otherwise similar people who do not have these conditions. Asked whether they would sacrifice some life expectancy to a treatment that significantly reduced their symptoms, less than 10 percent of people with arthritis, severe back pain, migraine, angina, cataracts, ulcers, colitis, and sleep disorder, and less than 20 percent of people with depression, asthma, and chronic bronchitis, agreed. This was significantly lower than the risk people without these conditions supposed would be worth taking to abate the chronic symptoms associated with these diseases.[11]

Clearly, deciding whether living a particular life is worthwhile is perspectival rather than univocal. We each judge how worthwhile our own lives are through a personal lens no other person shares. The policy-maker who claims to feel other people's pain is making a figurative rather than a literal claim, for he surely does not experience their pain as they do. The extensive empirical research on health preferences suggests that "the essential point of the valuation task seems to be whether the task is related to self or others."[12] And, of course, one's knowledge of the texture and the possibilities of one's own life is more immediate, real, and compelling than what one knows about others' lives.

Generally, "once a (chronic) disease is detected, patients change their internal standards to evaluate the situation and the yardstick of what is acceptable and what is not is lowered substantially."[13] Two different explanations of this well-documented phenomenon have been advanced. These diverge from one another in several ways, but mainly in regard to whose standpoint is positioned in the foreground, the individual living with the chronic condition or those who are observing (aspects of) that individual's life.

One explanation begins by hypothesizing that people on the whole are risk aversive, and people who already believe themselves to have been especially disfavored by luck are especially so. Consequently, individuals, and especially chronically ill and disabled individuals, often personally prefer preserving their current capabilities to risking a reduction of capability by gambling that an invasive medical intervention will improve their functionality or quality of life. From the immediacy of a personal point of view the difference between maintaining one's current degree of dysfunction or devolving into even more dysfunction if an invasive treatment fails may be so profound as to be prohibitive. From society's impersonal and abstract point of view, in contrast, the difference between the current degree of dysfunction and a prospective worsening of it may be negligible.

It is the individual with the impairment who actually bears the risk, however, not society as a whole. On the notion that personal consent to the risks of intervention is a cornerstone of medical decision-making, therefore, the individual's perspective should be decisive. If individual perspectives prevail, then we should defer to patients who prefer the risks of living with a familiar chronic illness or disability to the possibly greater risks of living with the unknown sequelae of a failed medical intervention. And we should defer equally to patients who embrace the prospect of escaping disability or illness regardless of the treatment's risk.

But another, more dismissive explanation of why disabled and chronically ill people tend to rate their own lives more favorably than unimpaired people do often prevails. Resignation is a well-known survival technique under objectively distressing conditions. So it may be that chronically ill and disabled people endure the limitations in their lives by deceiving themselves as well as others about the acceptability of their current state, when in reality they are merely resigned to it.

Complacency under such circumstances should not be confused with contentment in regard to them, however. Nor should complacency be countenanced, for to do so distracts us from the desirability of improvement. We want to be sure that disabled and chronically ill people who do not disparage their state are not like the happy slave who, even if he does not pity himself, is in an objectively pitiable condition. At the least, we want to be sure they are not forgoing interventions that would improve their functionality and their quality of life. Further, (some) people's being able to adjust to living with chronic illness or disability should not encourage failures to offer treatment to those who desire to be cured, just as some people's being able to accept living as slaves is no reason for failing to fight slavery.

On this second explanation, then, it is wrong to defer to chronically ill or disabled individuals' preferences for living with, rather than pursuing risky cures for, their conditions. The stronger preferences of non-disabled people for a functionally homogeneous population should prevail. The argument is that a society where everybody functions species-typically is better for everyone, and therefore we should bring each person up to the standard of such a society whenever we can.

Diametrically different understandings of adaptive values drive these antithetical explanations. Adaptive values are the altered assessments that people are said to adopt to accommodate to being chronically ill or disabled. For example, people who claim prospectively that they would rather be dead than lose the use of their legs often have a change of heart if such befalls them. They discover that walking is not essential to their well-being.

From their new point of view, walking is an over-valued activity, one whose prominence is due in part to being privileged by social assumptions about the universality of walking. They find that their flourishing is not dependent on their walking, except to the extent that they are excluded from opportunity because social arrangements presume that citizens can stand and walk. Thus they have altered their assessment of the value of walking, but whether from resignation because they now cannot walk, or from recognition of an earlier exaggeration of the value of walking, is in dispute.

The two explanations of why people's values adapt to the experience of living with disability or chronic illness differ in regard to what notions of a flourishing life they presume. Adaptive values should not prevail if their adoption is motivated by resignation to a deficient level of thriving – resignation compelled by the limitations chronic illness and disability impose – but they should prevail if adopting them enables achieving a fulfilling level of thriving within these limitations. Whether adaptive values should be embraced or dismissed thus turns on whether people genuinely can thrive within such limitations, and also on whether it is desirable to invite or expect people to do so.

If being chronically ill or disabled is incompatible with thriving, adaptive values rest on a mistake. To be mistaken here could be dangerous, for to embrace adaptive rather than routine values might encourage the individuals who do so to settle for flourishing less fully than they might do. In principle, the possible sources of error about adaptive values are two-fold.

Error might arise from mistakes made about the factual possibilities of life with chronic illness or disability, or else from mistakes made in evaluating the badness occasioned by the natural and social limitations of such a life. It is an error to presume that all atypical limitations on life activities are intrinsically bad. Although such limitations may reduce a person's horizons atypically, there is no consensus as to how broad people's realizable opportunities must be to facilitate flourishing. People differ from each other in temperament and desires, and change their preferences and pleasures in accord with altered circumstances and evolving stages of life. The individual who in youth suffers from restlessness and rootlessness but is made comfortably secure by the boundaries aging brings has a life story that is not rare.

What basis we could have for attributing epistemological error in predicting whether a particular person would flourish or fail if chronically limited by illness or disability also is hard to see. Reflection reveals no standpoint from which to describe the experience of being chronically ill or disabled that is veridical. Prior to becoming chronically ill or disabled, people usually have no realistically concrete idea of how they will experience life in this condition. When they think about being treated for illness or trauma, they therefore are drawn to the prevailing acute care conception that the outcome to be desired is full cure. Often they cannot imagine being satisfied absent a capability familiar to them: being able to walk wherever they want, being able to eat whatever they want, being able to remember when they want. That one might be significantly less capable than at present and yet thrive is unthinkable for most people

But a person's speculations about the quality of a kind of life often diverge enormously from how that person experiences that kind of life when actually living it. Consider, for example, how dimly youngsters in their twenties view the prospect of life as a 60-year-old, whereas lived 60-year-old lives often are replete with satisfactions 20-year-olds do not comprehend. Similarly, for a biologically unimpaired individual, a future life with a chronic illness or disability may appear agonizingly disruptive of that person's current approach to life – his pleasures and his plans. Yet, if that same person – now become chronically ill or disabled – tells us that he nevertheless thrives, we neither believe he must be mistaken because he once thought otherwise, nor that he previously must have violated an epistemic standard when he thought otherwise.

Indeed, persuasive evidence that he could flourish in this situation was not available to him before he lived in it. Other people, he knew, had reported their success in doing so. But living with chronic illness or disability is like other challenges people encounter that demand profound alterations to their routine expectations and assessments of life. One cannot predict how successfully one will meet them until one is called upon to meet them.

This observation suggests a way of understanding how the two seemingly incompatible explanations of adaptive values may relate. We should note that, despite the differences in these accounts, particular judgments made under them are likely to converge in certain contexts. This is because, from both perspectives, the positive benefit of having more rather than less capability is a truism.

Those who fear that adaptive values might deceive chronically ill or disabled individuals into ignoring or abandoning a promising course of treatment reasonably oppose adapting only where real promise of successful intervention exists. Concomitantly, those who fear that pursuit of a cure might deceive chronically ill or disabled individuals into vain pursuits of an unattainable future, distracting them from building a desirable here and now, reasonably oppose not adapting only where intervention courts more risk than it promises success.

Different sets of values are not at issue here, but instead differences in applying the same values. Divergent judgments are propelled by differences in the salience of certain kinds of risk rather than from the opposition of dissonant values. Biologically unimpaired individuals who seem to have routine values, and chronically ill and disabled individuals who seem to have adaptive values, actually have the same values but weigh courses of action differently because of different information about the risks and promises involved.

Such a basis for difference in judgment does not entail that one standpoint is veridical while others are mistaken. Even when they generate contradictory judgments, neither routine nor adaptive values rest on a mistake. What is going on is that those whose values have been labeled "adaptive" have access to a different kind of evidence from those whose values are imagined to be routine. What is at issue is whose experience – not whose values – shall prevail.

Personal and Public Perspectives

We have seen that in one of the kinds of evaluation characteristic of discussions about health care for chronically ill and disabled people, differences of judgment turn on different experiences that lead to disparate views about risk. The personal question is whether there is greater potential for loss if the individual attempts to flourish while living with a chronic illness or disability, or whether seeking a cure is likely to result in greater loss. The political question is whether individuals who bear the risk should choose which risk to take, or whether such choices are better assessed based on the prevailing outlooks of the medical or public policy systems.

A similar question arises in regard to another of the kinds of evaluation characteristically at issue in chronic care, namely, the adjudication of conflicts between the patient's good and the public's good. In acute care, the controlling goal is the good of the patient. Ordinarily, the importance of the patient's direct good may be superseded only by appeal to other patients' direct good, and only when competition among patients for care cannot be prevented or avoided. So, for example, medical personnel who must make triage decisions when many patients require attention at once weigh each patient's individual good against the others to decide which one(s) will benefit most.

On the other hand, to sacrifice the good of acutely ill patients to a depersonalized and generalized view of the good would be unethical even if motivated by health-related concerns. For example, every use of antibiotics risks developing drug resistant strains of germs, so restraint should be exercised in regard to prescribing these medications in consideration of the public good. Nevertheless, declining to secure an acutely ill patient's recovery because the diffuse benefit to the public of refraining from using antibiotics outweighs the focused benefit of their use to individual patients clearly is misguided.

Rare instances excepted, considerations of the public good ordinarily are understood as being compatible rather than competitive with acute patients' personal good. When policy permits a patient with active tuberculosis to be hospitalized involuntarily, for example, part of the justification invokes the common good. The warrant for encroaching on a patient's liberty in such cases usually is that the patient is not adhering to the prescribed medication regime and thereby may become a source of a drug-resistant variation of the disease that will endanger the public generally. But this warrant is reinforced by another reason, one that references the patient's personal good, namely, that hospitalization also is the route to the patient's being cured.[14]

In chronic cases, however, there is no similar imperative to align the public good with the patient's personal good. For example, we tolerate profound disconnects between patients' good and the public's good in advancing reasons for the involuntary hospitalization of patients with chronic psychiatric conditions. Although the prospects of a patient's being a danger to himself, and of the patient's also being a danger to others, sometimes converge, more often they do not. Patients disposed to harm or disturb others are likely to be hospitalized continuously for that reason alone, without pretense of their receiving benefit, while it is much more difficult for patients likely to harm only themselves to receive extended care. Further, policy ordinarily calls for the public good to prevail where advancing the chronic patient's personal good is thought to prompt social burdensomeness or harm.

The allocation of rehabilitative therapies constitutes a well-known example of such a conflict. At issue here is whether the patient's good or whether society's good should prevail. From a public perspective, rehabilitation's point is to elevate the patient's functioning to a level where independence and the ability to contribute to others are achieved. Rehabilitation's value to a community lies in turning people who are pathological into people who are normal, or at least transforming dysfunctional people into functioning ones, thereby changing them from burdensome social outliers to productive citizens. Once therapeutic intervention appears unlikely to reach this goal, or bring the patient significantly closer to it, the social value of rehabilitation no longer is in play as justifying the long-term expenditure of health care resources.

From the patient's point of view, of course, continuing therapies initially offered to effect rehabilitation may remain crucial to various aspects of personal well-being. A patient who has "plateaued," and who is not expected to progress even with additional therapy, may still need continued care to deter deterioration, to maintain hope, or for other reasons apart from a full return to productive citizenship. The enduring dependence of chronic patients on medical materials or skills draws their individual welfare into conflict with the common good.

The most familiar kind of stand-off between the personal good of chronic patients and the public good involves competing claims on resources that systematically are decided in favor of the latter. In this kind of case the conflict often is camouflaged by being cast as a choice between competing needs of different kinds of patients, with the chronic patients' needs less of a priority than those of patients who can approach a cure. For example, reserving care for patients who can make progress often is cited as the reason for withdrawing rehabilitation therapy from patients who have "plateaued."

Rehabilitation cases are complicated because of the tendency to permit considerations of economic justice to become dominant in debates about health care justice. So examining a different kind of case – one in which rationing is not an issue – may better illuminate the nature of the more fundamental conflict. For example, current policy that regulates the treatment of chronic pain clearly illustrates the basic process whereby the common good is construed to clash with the interests of chronic patients.

Chronic pain is one of the most common disabling conditions, and the availability of effective treatment commonly is one of the most contentious issues in health care policy. As many as 10 percent of Americans suffer from chronic, disabling pain. About 1 percent of Americans benefit from long-term high doses of medications such hydrocodone (Vicodin), oxycodone (OxyContin), morphine or methadone. "This small group is probably responsible for a large portion of all the narcotic painkillers prescribed."[15]

Like the acute care patient, the chronic care patient's decision about rejecting rather than consenting to treatment – for pain patients the question usually is about being chronically maintained on opiates – basically is a self-regarding one. As in acute cases, there is an obvious impropriety in demanding that chronic patients renounce achieving their own possibility of health or functioning in favor of the welfare of other people. We reject the idea that people are required to make live donations of their kidneys or liver sections, reducing their own capacity for functioning or health to improve someone else's. We reject the idea that people are required to serve as subjects in drug trials to expedite findings that will serve the common good. Why then should chronically living in agony be a price extracted from some people as payment for safeguarding others from temptation? Should we not respect the pain patient's self-regarding reasons for obtaining effective pain control as more compelling than countervailing other-regarding reasons citing the public good?

Parenthetically, coerced other-regarding behavior is neither altruism, nor is it good. Nor is coercing behavior conducive to personal flourishing or, in the long run, to public welfare, except in cases with special circumstances such as that of the non-compliant tuberculosis patient discussed earlier. While we applaud individuals' freely embracing other-regarding sacrifices of their health, we rightly should be reluctant to demand of anyone, especially already vulnerable patients, to agree to giving over in this way. But current discussion of health care justice reveals little in the way of incentive to make policy pursued in the name of the public good consistent with chronic patients' good.

To return to the situation of chronic pain patients, consider the availability of treatment with opiates, which is heavily regulated by law. The value overtly motivating current regulation is to prevent people from becoming psychologically or physically dependent on using these drugs. There is, however, a sub-set of the population for whom such prevention cannot be an overriding value. These are people whose medical need to manage pain is met most effectively, or even exclusively, by opiates, and for some only by large amounts of opiates. Any dependence on opiates such people experience is initiated by medical rather than recreational needs.

The disconnect between personal and public good here occurs because people with chronic pain are a minority. That they are a large minority has not even been acknowledged till recently. For (some members of) this minority, the benefits of access to controlled substances prevail over the detriments, but the case cannot be made for the majority of the population. People not in the portion of the population that needs effective pain management may be attracted to these substances for recreational reasons, and it is this latter group – the larger part of the population – for whose good barriers to the use of these substances are erected.[16]

In principle, of course, regulatory policy meant to achieve public value should distinguish clearly between medical and recreational users of opiates. Nevertheless, difficulties in holding to any such clearly distinctive standard may be inescapable. First, substances distributed for medical use can be diverted to recreational use. "Pain management has become a crime story,"[17] says David Joranson, director of the Pain and Policy Studies Group at the University of Wisconsin. Public policy therefore intervenes with special regulation of these drugs even when they are for medical use. The amount that can be prescribed, and the duration of a prescription, are limited by the state. As a result, physicians and pharmacists are reluctant to prescribe/dispense large quantities of these medications,[18] physicians prescribe lower doses than otherwise to escape notice,[19] and the American Association of Physicians and Surgeons warns doctors against treating chronic pain lest they face years of legal problems.[20]

A second difficulty is the tendency to judge chronic pain patients as if their use of medication is casual, that is, as if they could very well function although in pain. In the same vein, chronic pain patients sometimes are subsumed into the category of addicts because they are likely to be dependent on their medication. The public good as the warrant for obstructing access to opiates often is claimed to align with patients' personal good by protecting them from dependence on these substances. But dependence cannot be intrinsically harmful because many people depend on some medication or other without eliciting moral concern. Patients with HIV infection or multiple sclerosis also are dependent on medications that stave off symptoms. The definitive issue here lies not in the patients' dependence on their medication, but in the fact that members of the general population, and not just the sub-set who are patients with chronic medical needs, may become dependent on it.

The individual good of people who, owing to their biological impairments, need this kind of medication so as to obtain sufficient pain relief to be functional appears to recede in importance when compared to the good of the general population. From a personal perspective, the confidence that a medication will afford relief from one's own pain likely seems more compelling than speculation about that medication's availability tempting other people to use it recreationally. From a public perspective, however, the protection of the as-yet unimpaired is likely to seem paramount. Such ranking of the public good over patients' personal good is common – perhaps even endemic – in regard to health care justice for chronic patients.

Worthy Lives

A sad circularity invited by shifting perspectives clouds reasoning about the resolution of the apparent conflict between chronic patients' interests and the common interest. People suffering from chronic pain may seek medication to be able to function as contributing members of society. As patients they should pursue their own welfare and seek medical treatment so as to function sufficiently well to escape the "sick role." But as responsible citizens they should hold the welfare of others, and the common good, above their own. Thus, their claim to receive care to improve their social participation and productivity is condemnable from the very point of view they aspire to reach.

A core concern has emerged during our examination of evaluations characteristic of contexts centered on chronic illness and disability. Evaluative conflicts seem to be created by who these patients are. Because they are a minority mired in the stigmatized "sick" role, these patients' views of the good characteristically are overridden by majority opinions about the good.

These incurables – disabled and chronically ill people – are systematically distanced from the paramount, and therefore controlling, aim of the health care system, namely, the aim to cure. The common goal is not their goal. Their good is not the common good, for the common good is to be cured, and that is a good from which, in virtue of their chronic condition, they are definitively removed.

The feminist disability activist Jenny Morris describes the far-reaching effect of this displacement on people unable to achieve a cure:

> the only things that can be offered are treatments and cures . . . which prevent us from doing the kinds of things that non-disabled people do because we are not recognized as full human beings . . . As long as non-disabled people retain the power to represent our reality, impairment will always mean at best a cause for treatment and cure, at worst a life not worth living . . . It is this approach which leads to segregation and exclusion – and ultimately to the assumption that our lives are not worth living and that we would be better off dead, or not being born in the first place.[21]

In self-defense, disabled and chronically ill people tend to deform the way they represent themselves in order to lessen the distance with which the health care system separates them from its goals. Morris explains:

> It is difficult . . . and dangerous because, to articulate any negative feelings about our experience of our bodies may be to play into the hands of those who feel that our lives are not worth living. We share a lot with other civil rights movements, but our form of oppression has a unique characteristic: it is not inherently distressing to be Black or a woman or gay, while it may be to experience an impairment . . . But to deny the distressing nature of the body's experience of arthritis or epilepsy, for example, would be foolish.[22]

In Morris's experience, acknowledgement that one's health state is incurably defective is imprudent to express:

> Sensory impairment, motor impairment, intellectual impairments are seen as things to be avoided at all costs. In the face of this prejudice it is very important to assert that anatomy is not destiny and that it is instead the disabling barriers "out there" which determine the quality of our lives . . . Indeed, I worry myself that if we do start talking about the negative aspects of living with impairment and illness, non-disabled people will turn around and say, "there you are then, we always knew that your lives weren't worth living."[23]

As Morris's testimony evidences, people with chronic illnesses and disabilities believe themselves to be subjected to evaluations that embed biases against them based on their kind of health. One response to their concern has been to try to drive a conceptual wedge between impairments and people with impairments. The claim is that to abhor impairment is not to abhor people whose bodies or minds are impaired. But this strategy is far from reassuring, for impairments do not have abstract or disembodied existence.

If medicine aims at eliminating impairment, then health care practice will be shaped by the idea of altering people who are impaired. People with chronic health conditions will find that the system's drive to cure them, rather than valuing care that achieves the highest quality of life for them consistent with their impairments, obscures even the usual cautions against risky medical intervention. Such people will not be convinced that their impairments can be targeted for cure without they themselves being subjected to the treatment. Nor will people whose experience indicates that the premium placed on cure discounts their needs for medical maintenance understand how their incurable impairments can be denied care without they themselves also being deprived of it.

Two important ideas about chronic illness and disability need reconciliation. One is the idea that being unimpaired is more agreeable than being impaired, and therefore the health care system should in general aim for promoting the first state and reducing or eliminating the second. The other is that unimpaired and chronically impaired people are equally worthy, and therefore the health care system should have no aim that results in preferences being accorded members of the first group over members of the second.

Disabled and chronically ill people, at least in Morris's view, would embrace the premise of the former argument, readily acknowledging the defects of their impairments if they could express themselves without fear. But they can do so only if an additional premise that speaks to their situation is supplied. The needed premise must assign alternative or additional aims to health care systems, aims that are pursued for the sake of people who will remain ill or disabled, rather than for the sake of reducing the number of such people by effecting cures. This is not to disparage curing but instead to observe how often curing is not the appropriate aim.

The ideas requiring reconciliation are used to guide choices. The former is a criterion for choosing treatments. The latter is a standard for choosing people. Treatment decisions inescapably are decisions about people. But the criteria for treatment decisions should not become standards for people.

Treatment decisions are how-to-treat choices assessing what is the best care for each patient, not whom-to-treat assessments about which patients to choose. The contexts in which the relevant choices are made diverge sharply from one another. The last formulated choice – deciding which patients to choose – is a triage-type rationing decision acceptable in some acute care emergency situations but not appropriately applied in the context of chronic care.

Conclusion

These observations about keeping assessments in context suggest a reconciliatory approach. The first step is to elevate those contexts that center on chronic care to a prominence that equals the attention afforded to acute care. In doing so, we should recognize that, although patients do transition from one context to another, the same may not be true for approaches to health care justice. An idea of fair treatment developed in and for a system that aims to cure patients so they no longer need care may become distorted when transported into a system that aims to maintain patients with lasting care without curing them.

The second step is to elevate the prominence of chronically ill and disabled people in the context of the latter kind of system so that decisions fully and respectfully further their good, understood in terms of what these individuals themselves take to be their good. The idea that unimpaired and chronically impaired people are equally worthy, and therefore the health care system should have no aim that results in preferences being accorded members of the first group, either individually or collectively, over members of the second, inspires this change. Disabled and chronically ill people will seize on this idea as a way of confronting the currently prevailing forms of evaluation that threaten them.

We should not underestimate the political challenges, at both practical and theoretical levels, facing such a revision of priorities for health care. The primacy now conferred at least initially on acute care patients, including the deference paid to their perspectives on their own good, emanates from the prospect of their being released from the "sick" role, either by regaining health or by ending life. But during the past century, medical progress has altered the prognoses of many kinds of illness and traumas from being fatal to being chronic or to having enduring pathological results.

Rethinking health care justice so that it is more attentive to and inclusive of chronically ill and disabled people calls for better reflecting what medicine now does, and what it still cannot do. Bioethicists are needed to participate in this reconceptualization, but to do so will necessitate reducing the attention paid to the more dramatic ethical issues that arise in acute care. It will mean as well that bioethicists must turn their backs on solutions that work well for acute care and build a different approach on a more appropriate understanding of medicine's goals. Doing so will take us beyond medical conceptualizations to reconsider our fundamental notions of what makes people valuable, both to themselves and to society.

Notes

1 See *Understanding MS* at http://www.understandingms.com/, last visited November 1, 2004.

2 Ronald Amundson, Disability, handicap, and the environment, *Journal of Social Philosophy*, 23 (1992): 105–18 at p. 114.

3 For statistics about chronic illness, see the website *Cure Research*, at http://cureresearch.com/c/chronic/stats.htm, last visited April 2, 2005. For 2003 census data for persons with disabilities, see a website called *Steve Gold's Treasured Bits of Information*, at http://www.stevegoldada.com/stevegoldada/archive.php?mode=Aandid=104;andsort=D, last visited November 1, 2004.

4 Ibid.

5 N.R. Kleinfield, Diabetes and its awful toll quietly emerge as a crisis, *New York Times*, January 9, 2006 at http://www.nytimes.com/nyregion/nyregionspecial5/, last visited January 21, 2006.

6 Ian Urbina, In the treatment of diabetes, success often does not pay, *New York Times*, January 11, 2006, at http://www.nytimes.com/nyregion/nyregionspecial5/, last visited January 21, 2006.

7 Kleinfield, op. cit.

8 Urbina, op. cit.

9 Ibid.

10 Ibid.

11 D.G. Fryback, E.J. Dasbach, R. Klein, et al., The Beaver Dam health outcomes study, *Medical Decision Making* 13 (1993): 89–102. Also see J. Tsevat, E.F. Cook, M.L. Green, et al., Health values of the seriously ill, *Annals of Internal Medicine* 122 (1994): 514–20; F.J. Fowler, Jr., P.D. Cleary, M.P. Massagli, et al., The role of reluctance to give up life in the measurement of the value of health states, *Medical Decision Making* 15 (1995): 195–200; E. Nord, Time trade-off scores in patients with chronic disease. Comparison with the York hypothetical TTO tariff. Paper for the EuroQol Plenary Meeting, Oslo, October 1996.

12 G. Ardine DeWitt, Jan J.V. Busschbach, and Frank De Charro, Sensitivity and perspective in the valuation of health states: whose values count? *Health Economics* 9 ((2000): 109–26 at p. 117.

13 Ibid., p. 116.

14 For example, although public safety was the primary reason for incarcerating Mary Mallon ("Typhoid Mary"), who was believed to be a non-symptomatic carrier of typhoid, the physicians who advised this course of action also argued that the plan would enable them to find a cure for her. See the transcript of the PBS program *The Most Dangerous Woman in America*, http://www.pbs.org/wgbh/nova/typhoid/, last visited October 23, 2005.

15 Sally Satel, Doctors behind bars: treating pain is now risky business, *New York Times*, October 19, 2004: D6, D10 at p. D6.

16 In *Gonzales v. Oregon*, decided January 17, 2006, Justice Kennedy, writing for the majority, emphasized that Congress authorized the Attorney General, acting through the federal Drug Enforcement Administration, to control the recreational use of these drugs, not their medical uses. The decision is found at http://caselaw.lp.findlaw.com/scripts/getcase.pl?court=USandvol=000andinvol=04–623, last visited 21 January, 2006.

17 Satel, Doctors behind bars: D6.

18 Ibid.: D6.

19 Ibid.: D10.

20 Ibid.: D10.

21 Jenny Morris, Impairment and disability: constructing an ethics of care that promotes human rights, *Hypatia* 16 (4) (2001):1–16 at p. 3.

22 Ibid.: 9.

23 Ibid.: 10.

Chapter 21

Justice in Research on Human Subjects

David Buchanan and Franklin G. Miller[1]

Introduction

Justice, like most elemental notions that guide the moral life, is a rich and complex concept, with layer upon layer of interpretation deposited over time. In the modern medical research context, justice concerns have historically centered on fairness and duties to protect individuals from exploitation. Research is unjust if it is conducted without the consent of the participants, deceives them about the conditions of their participation, or unfairly targets or excludes members of social groups. More broadly, principles of justice underlie the social value of biomedical research and the determination of priorities for investment in research. This chapter discusses different ways that justice considerations should govern the conduct of health research.

Principles of justice can be applied at three levels of the social organization of the research enterprise. Starting at the broadest level, we first consider the role of health research in relation to the duties of the state: do governments have a moral obligation to support and carry out research aimed at curing and preventing disease? Second, within the scope of government activities, we examine the issue of fairly allocating scarce public resources devoted to health research, a problem of distributive justice. Finally, we discuss principles of justice within the research setting itself, by examining the justice implications of eight ethical standards that human research must meet. After describing justice concerns at these different systems levels, we illustrate their application in analyzing a controversial case study in detail, the Kennedy Krieger case, where researchers investigated low-cost lead abatement procedures to reduce blood lead levels in children living in public housing in inner city Baltimore.

It is important to be clear from the outset that agreement on a comprehensive unified theory of justice has proven elusive (Buchanan, 1981; Barry, 1989;

Beauchamp and Childress, 2001; Clayton and Williams, 2004). Broadly speaking, principles of justice have two major components: a formal requirement that like situations be treated alike, and different situations differently; and a substantive ideal of the good society, against which current conditions can be compared as a measure of the extent to which justice prevails. These substantive ideals have been referred to as "patterned conceptions of distribution" with respect to rights and resources (Powers, 1998). Different and potentially conflicting ideal patterns (e.g., to each person an equal share; to each according to need; to each according to effort, etc.) have been derived from various ethical theories, including utilitarian, libertarian, communitarian, egalitarian, feminist, Marxist, and others. When faced with incompatible and seemingly irreconcilable visions of just outcomes, groups must often appeal to procedural justice or fair procedures (e.g., democratic majority vote) to resolve their disagreements. We do not adopt a single theoretical perspective here; rather, we try to alert readers to the major schools of thought reflected in our account and to the different positions that different views about justice might take on the issues at hand.

In this chapter, we focus on publicly funded health research in developed liberal-democratic societies. We do not discuss the justice of research in the international context, because it has received considerable attention recently and is deserving of separate treatment in its own right. We also do not address privately funded research, such as that sponsored by the pharmaceutical industry. A number of excellent analyses of the pharmaceutical industry's investment in research have recently become available; the basic theme of these works is that such research is driven primarily by the profit motive, with consequent concerns about corrupting research and exploiting patient-consumers (Abramson, 2004; Angell, 2004; Avorn, 2004). Since the financial investment and volume of health research conducted by private industry now exceeds that of public research in the US (Bodenheimer, 2000; Rettig, 2000), justice considerations in corporate undertakings deserve further attention, but space constraints preclude an adequate discussion of the distinct issues involved here. To set the stage for the discussion that follows, we start with a brief synopsis of the historical rise of justice concerns in modern medical research.

Historical Background

Walter Reed's use of informed consent in his yellow fever experiments in Cuba in 1900 is generally recognized as one of the earliest well-documented examples of the application of ethical principles in conducting health research (Levine, 1986; Berg et al., 2001). There can be little question, however, that it was the horror of the Holocaust and the so-called Doctors Trial at the Nuremberg War Crimes Tribunal that marked the emergence of serious public, political, and intellectual attention to the injustices inflicted in the name of medical research. In the aftermath of the brutal Nazi experiments involving concentration camp inmates, the Nuremberg Code placed great weight on the principle of respect for human autonomy, and consequently, stringent mandates for informed consent and voluntary participation. These principles were subsequently re-affirmed by the World Medical Association in the Declaration of Helsinki in 1964 (World Medical Association, 1997).

Yet, despite these documents, it took newspaper reports in the early 1970s about the on-going US Public Health Service Syphilis Study at Tuskegee – research that began in the 1930s – to provoke sufficient public outrage to force the US Congress to address the ethics of publicly funded health research in a major national public forum for the first time (Jonsen, 2000). In response to the egregious misconduct by researchers at Tuskegee (and other ominous violations documented by Beecher (1966)), the National Commission for the Protection of Human Subjects of Biomedical and Behavioral Research was convened by Congress in 1974 and their landmark Belmont Report issued in 1978 (National Commission, 1979). The Belmont Report provided guidelines for the ethical conduct of health research and still stands as one of the most articulate expositions of the rationale, warrants, and ethical principles that should guide the conduct of health research.

The Belmont Report found two applications of justice principles to be important to the conduct of medical research: the distribution of burdens and benefits should be fair, and equals ought to be treated equally (Kahn et al., 1998). As the reports states (p. 5):

> Who ought to receive the benefits of research and bear its burdens? This is a question of justice in the sense of "fairness of distribution" or "what is deserved." An injustice occurs when some benefit to which a person is entitled is denied without good reason or when some burden is imposed unduly. Another way of conceiving the principle of justice is that equals ought to be treated equally.

And as they continue (p. 7):

> Individual justice in the selection of subjects would require that researchers exhibit fairness; thus they should not offer potentially beneficial research only to some patients who are in their favor or select only "undesirable" persons for risky research. Social justice requires that distinction be drawn between classes of subjects that ought, and ought not, to participate in any particular kind of research, based on the ability of members of that class to bear burdens and on the appropriateness of placing further burdens on already burdened persons.

In the climate of the times, the Belmont Report concentrated on justice considerations internal to the research process, focusing primarily on protecting potential research participants from harm and exploitation (in lieu of other possible considerations or levels of analysis). The recommendations of the National Commission were incorporated into detailed regulations governing research involving human subjects funded by the United States government. These regulations, known as the Common Rule (45 CFR §46, Protection of Human Subjects), specify the requirements of independent prospective review by Institutional Review Boards (IRBs), reasonable estimates of foreseeable risks and benefits, and strict adherence to written voluntary and informed consent, including enumeration of the conditions in which children and adults incapable of providing their own competent consent can be enrolled and the conditions for which informed consent can be waived (Code of Federal Regulations, 1991).

As the effect of these regulations took hold and experience with clinical trials grew, the weight of public moral concerns began to shift from a preoccupation with the risks of participating in research to an appreciation of the potential benefits (Kahn et al., 1998; McCarthy, 1998; Powers, 1998). As the Belmont Report noted, both the risks and the benefits of research must be distributed fairly. Throughout the 1980s, heart disease studies, for example, excluded women from participation on the questionable grounds that the research posed unreasonable risks to the reproductive and childbearing capacities of women. But as a result, the effects of new drugs and new medical procedures on the distinct female biology and physiology were not investigated. Not only were women being denied access to new and potentially life-saving therapies in the trials themselves, but also, outside of the trials, women as a class were being denied information on the risks and benefits of new therapeutic interventions. Then, with the onset of the AIDS epidemic, the dire need for effective treatments led many people to view research participation not as a burden, but as an opportunity to obtain the scientifically most advanced therapies possible. With the change in public attitudes, the focus of justice debates within the research context has largely shifted today to issues of the just distribution of the benefits of research for traditionally excluded groups, such as women, minorities, children, and the disabled. Concerns about subject protection have not been abandoned, but interest in gaining access to the potential benefits of participating in clinical trials has opened the door to new claims upon justice.

The Role of Health Research in Promoting Social Justice

Starting at the societal level, we consider the role of health research in relation to the obligations of the state to improve the welfare of citizens and reduce unnecessary suffering in society as a whole. Do states have a moral obligation to conduct health research? Could industrialized nations that do not provide public institutional and financial support for health research be considered just societies? In the bioethics literature, a great deal of attention has been paid to issues of justice in providing medical care, but much less to the question of a duty to conduct health research.

In the midst of well-established, publicly funded research programs, it may be difficult to see how this question gains purchase. It is important, however, because the ethics of human subjects research has all too often been equated with subject protection, without due attention to the moral considerations that stand in favor of conducting health research. Indeed, a number of serious counter-arguments regarding a state's obligation to conduct health research have been put forth. The classical liberal interpretation of justice, originally articulated by John Locke in the seventeenth century, was concerned primarily with individual rights, especially respect for private property and defining the conditions in which individuals should be able to enjoy the fruits of their labor. This liberal conception of justice thus focused on setting limits on government authority and protecting individuals from governmental interference with their right to pursue their own understanding of happiness (Powers, 1998). One major stream of this school of thought today is represented by libertarian conceptions of justice, best known in the work of Robert Nozick. Nozick (1974) argues that the overriding moral obligation of the state is to prevent violations of individual freedom, and thus, government action is justified if and only if it protects citizens' rights. In the libertarian conception of justice, the state has no obligation to increase the public weal; rather, it performs best by leaving such developments to the free market. Concerted efforts by the government to redress any emergent inequalities stand to threaten the liberty rights of individuals.

Coming at the issue from a different angle, a distinguished founder of the field of bioethics, Hans Jonas (1974, p. 129), has argued, "Let us not forget that progress is an optional goal," and elsewhere (p. 117),

> The destination of research is essentially melioristic. It does not serve the preservation of the existing good from which I profit myself and to which I am obligated. Unless the present state is intolerable, the melioristic goal is in a sense gratuitous, and this not only from the vantage point of the present. Our descendents have a right to be left an unplundered planet; they do not have a right to new miracle cures.

While it would be a mistake to pigeonhole the fertile thought of Jonas, his views on this particular point would find support in a libertarian theory of justice. More recently, Daniel Callahan, founder of the Hastings Center, the US's premier bioethics think-tank, has similarly cautioned against the unbridled pursuit of what he terms the "research imperative," which "stems from the view that medicine has an almost sacred duty to combat all known causes of death" (Callahan, 2000, p. 654). Callahan raises provocative questions about the goals of health research, which he characterizes as an "all-out war on death" (Callahan, 2002, p. 3). He is troubled by what he sees as the current direction of medical research: the ends are narrowly conceived (biologically reductionistic efforts to conquer diseases one at a time until there is nothing left to die from); the achievement of these research objectives will likely exacerbate existing social inequalities (because the high cost of new therapies will be available only to those who can afford it); and the huge financial and psychological investment in the search for miracle cures diverts attention from the social and economic determinants of health and sickness (Callahan, 2003).

Both Jonas and Callahan are concerned that the language of "obligation" can easily be misinterpreted to claim a need for conducting research that would override other moral values. They want to temper the idea of "absolutizing disease" – the single-minded quest to find cures for disease, pursued as if no greater evil existed – harking on concerns that it might be used to justify unreasonable and unwarranted sacrifices, as suggested, for example, in invoking a "war on cancer" or patriotic duties to test new vaccines in the face of bioterrorist threats (Annas, 2002). If societies believe that they have an obligation to conduct medical research, Jonas and Callahan fear that safeguards may be set aside and the ends used to justify the means. In their view, the assertion of an unqualified obligation must be carefully circumscribed, in deference to competing claims on limited public resources intended to improve social conditions, such as education, housing, and employment opportunities.

Jonas and Callahan are right to warn about a research imperative that might ride roughshod over the rights and well-being of research subjects and crowd out the pursuit of other more worthy social goals. However, it does not follow that the support of health research is morally optional for developed, liberal democratic societies. Societal obligations do not have to be understood as absolute or unlimited in scope in order to be considered binding.

The strongest case for a societal obligation to support health research derives from the influential account of justice as fairness developed by John Rawls. Rawls (1971) argues that justice is constituted by three principles: a basic liberty principle, a principle of fair equality of opportunity, and a difference principle. The liberty principle holds that each person is to have an equal right to the most extensive system of equal basic liberties compatible with a similar system of liberty for all. The fair equality of opportunity principle maintains that offices and positions are to be open to all under conditions of equality (i.e., persons with similar abilities and skills should have equal access). It requires the elimination not only of formal discrimination, but also inequalities in occupational opportunity that originate from the "social lottery" (such as the individual's social class background). The difference principle is a measure of just differences in income and wealth, and posits that social and economic institutions should be arranged to benefit the least well off as much as possible.

In a significant extension of Rawls's work, Norman Daniels (1985, 2001) has argued that, if liberal democratic societies have a duty to protect fair equality of opportunity, then they must also have a duty to preserve the normal functioning of individual human lives. By impairing normal functioning, disease and disability restrict the range of opportunities open to individuals; therefore, maintaining and restoring normal functioning are essential for protecting fair opportunity to participate in the social, political, and economic life of society. Based on the principle of justice as fairness, people should have the opportunity to pursue the life plans that it would be reasonable for them to choose were they not ill or disabled. In terms of health research, the principle of fair equality of opportunity points to the need to go beyond those diseases and disabilities that can now be treated, cured, or prevented to address those impairments that could potentially be redressed through further research. Any scheme of justice that regards the state as obliged to make provisions for the welfare of its citizens has ample reason for supporting health research aimed at protecting fair opportunity. To promote this vision of the just society, research to combat a range of diseases merits consideration for government support. Given competing claims among different disease targets, how should research priorities be set?

Justice in Setting Research Priorities

Questions of justice also arise in determining how best to distribute public resources designated for health research. In 2004, the budget for the US National Institutes of Health (NIH) was approximately $28 billion. Because funding comes from taxpayer dollars, fairness in the allocation of these funds is imperative. The mission of the NIH is "to uncover new knowledge that will lead to better health for everyone," but everyone's needs cannot be addressed at once. Whose needs are greatest? How should fair and equitable concern for the health needs of different social groups be determined? What is fair in setting research priorities?

An initial intuition might suggest that there should be a correlation between the distribution of disease burden and the allocation of research funds, with a more substantial share of funding going to those problems that cause a substantially greater burden of disease. But there are conflicting ways of measuring disease burden. Congressional representatives, for example, have complained that there appear to be widely disparate amounts of research funding per afflicted person from one disease to the next, and they have pointedly asked why the NIH spends much more per death from HIV/AIDS than other causes of death, such as cancer, heart disease, or stroke. Callahan, on the other hand, has argued that far too much money is spent on research on the diseases of old age, such as cancer, and that priority should instead be given to diseases that cause premature death (before the age of 65).

In response to these criticisms, the NIH has tried to make its decision-making processes more transparent. A 1997 report, *Setting Research Priorities at the National Institutes of Health*, identified five criteria to guide distribution decisions: (1) public health needs, (2) scientific quality of the research, (3) potential for scientific progress, (4) portfolio diversification, and (5) adequate support of research infrastructure (Institute of Medicine, 1998). Under each of these areas, the report enumerated further sub-criteria; the estimation of public health needs, for example, includes:

- the number of people who have a particular disease
- the number of deaths caused by a disease
- the degree of disability produced by a disease
- the degree to which a disease cuts short a normal, productive, and comfortable life

- the economic and social costs of a disease
- the need to act rapidly to control the spread of a disease.

The *Setting Research Priorities* document declares that all of these criteria are relevant, and conversely, the use of any one of them alone would lead to unwarranted neglect of some diseases. Allocating funding according to the number of deaths, for instance, would neglect chronic diseases that produce long-term disability and high costs to society (such as mental illness and arthritis). Other major factors that influence distribution decisions include the fact that each of the 21 institutes within the NIH receives its own individual appropriation from Congress and that the NIH has been directed not to duplicate research supported by private industry. After Congress has set the individual institutes' budgets, each institute director has primary control over allocating funds internally, although decisions regarding the distribution of funding must be justified to Congress during annual appropriations hearings.

A number of concerns have been raised about both the adequacy and the implementation of these criteria. One major criticism is that the criteria are so general that NIH officials have almost total freedom in exercising their discretion. Common complaints are that decisions are driven more by scientific curiosity than by practical problem-solving, with undue emphasis on basic science over clinical application, and by politically motivated concessions to highly visible, organized advocacy groups. Likewise, several commentators have criticized the skew towards a biologically reductionistic emphasis on molecular and genetic determinants of health to the neglect and exclusion of research on social, behavioral, and environmental factors, factors that many researchers consider much more powerful influences on the health of the population as a whole (Rees, 2004; Rogers, 2004). Both internally and externally, critics have also warned that, due to the many limitations with the quality of various health indicators, these data need to be collected and analyzed more systematically before they can be reliably used for making sound allocation decisions. Finally, there are inherent trade-offs in these criteria that cannot be easily resolved. Rebecca Dresser (2001, pp. 81–2) lists a number of fundamental dilemmas:

> Should the NIH assign highest priority to research on disorders and injuries that cause death, or significant disability? When, if ever, should the agency support studies addressing less serious health problems? How should funding be affected by a prediction that significant advances are unlikely in research on a lethal or seriously debilitating disease? What if studies addressing a less serious condition are believed to have a high likelihood of significantly benefiting people at risk for that condition? . . . When do lesser benefits to the many outweigh greater benefits to the few? . . . in what situations, [does] past neglect require compensatory justice – in other words an "affirmative action" approach to research funding?

In fact, in response to a request from the Congress, a 1997 report by the NIH showed little correlation between NIH funding allocations and the distribution of disease or the costs (to Medicare) associated with 66 disease conditions and the 15 leading causes of death (National Institutes of Health, 1997; Gross et al., 1999). Owing to the many conflicting considerations, Dresser, however, stresses that it would be a mistake to conclude that such empirical findings demonstrate that the distribution of funding at NIH is patently unfair. Different value judgments are involved in comparing differing metrics of disease burden.

Faced with conflicting and seemingly irresolvable value judgments, modern democracies must often look to fair procedures to resolve their disagreements. Daniels and Sabin (1997) describe one such fair process for making controversial allocation decisions, a procedure they call "accountability for reasonableness." Daniels and Sabin developed their proposal to assist priority-setting in medical care settings – specifically, insurers' decisions regarding coverage of particular medical interventions – but their recommendations are directly relevant to setting research priorities. They state (p. 307) that the decision-making process will be perceived to be legitimate and fair if the system has four features:

> One key feature is the provision of publicly accessible reasons, that is, a public rationale, for decisions. A second is that the rationale must constitute a reasonable construal of how to meet the medical [or research] needs of a covered [or affected] population under acceptable resource constraints. A third key feature is that there be mechanisms for considering challenges to decisions that are made and for revisiting those decisions in light of counter-arguments . . . [Fourth], there is voluntary or public regulation of the process to ensure that conditions 1–3 are met.

Regarding the fourth point, public regulation of the process, the NIH has acknowledged that its interactions with the public are "generally weak" and proclaimed the need for more fully engaging the public to redress concerns about the legitimacy and fairness of its distribution decisions (Institute of Medicine, 1998, p. 7). As public input and oversight improve, the quality of deliberations in any such public bodies will, however, still depend on the ability of its members to evaluate the cogency of the rationales put forward. Justice demands that critical questions be posed and alternative criteria, like those proposed by Callahan, be judiciously considered. Setting research priorities has yet to receive the analytical and ethical attention that it deserves. Much more work needs to be done on the systematic assessment of research priorities based on the criteria of accountability for reasonableness.

Justice Concerns within the Research Context

The goal of clinical research is to generate new scientific knowledge for improving the diagnosis, treatment, and prevention of disease. Because clinical research involves the use of human beings, there is an inherent tension between pursuing rigorous science and protecting human subjects. The use of research subjects becomes exploitative when it unfairly exposes them to risks for the sake of science and society

(Wertheimer, 1996). Since exploitation is one of the most fundamental forms of injustice, strong protections for research subjects must be put in place. In a major review and synthesis of the most significant historical documents and ethical codes to date, Emanuel and his colleagues (2000, 2004) have identified a set of eight ethical standards for clinical research. The eight requirements that make research ethical are: (1) social or scientific value, (2) scientific validity, (3) fair subject selection, (4) favorable risk–benefit ratio, (5) independent review, (6) informed consent, (7) respect for enrolled subjects, and (8) community collaboration. Taken together, these eight principles constitute fair terms for inviting human subjects to participate in clinical research. Each provides particular safeguards, and collectively, they specify how exploitation in research can successfully be avoided.

Social or scientific value

Clinical research is designed to answer scientific questions about the etiology, treatment, and prevention of disease. Without a valuable question or hypothesis, a study is not worth conducting. The risks to volunteers in studies lacking clinical or social value cannot be justified, making such research unethical. As the risks of a study increase, the value of the science should be proportionately more compelling. Still, the fact that a study has great potential for producing clinical and social value does not imply that grave risks to research subjects are justifiable.

Scientific validity

To achieve the potential value of clinical research, studies must be designed with sufficient methodological rigor to provide a scientifically valid test of the hypotheses that can contribute to generalizable knowledge. If the design of a study lacks methodological rigor, such that it cannot produce interpretable results or valid data, then it is not worth conducting. The risks to human participants cannot be justified in poorly designed research. It is important to note that tensions between methodological rigor and other ethical requirements give rise to many challenging ethical issues, for example, in the use of placebo controls or deceptive research procedures.

Fair subject selection

Fairness in subject selection typically concerns groups of human subjects regarded as "vulnerable." Certain types of people are considered vulnerable because their characteristics or situation appear to render them less than fully capable of making voluntary, informed decisions about research participation (Levine, 1986). Vulnerable populations include children, because they are dependent on adults and legally incapable of giving informed consent; prisoners, owing to the coercive environment of penal institutions; and economically disadvantaged individuals, who may be subject to undue inducement deriving from payment for research participation.

As a rule, subjects who are vulnerable to exploitation or undue influence should not be targeted for research unless their participation is necessary to answer valuable scientific questions. Fair subject selection, on the other hand, also concerns not arbitrarily or unjustly excluding people from research participation. For example, concern about undue inducement of economically disadvantaged individuals should be balanced against concern for avoiding unjust discrimination and depriving them of the opportunity to receive appropriate payment for research participation (Buchanan et al., 2002; Pace et al., 2003).

Favorable risk–benefit ratio

Risk–benefit assessment is ethically required to judge whether the risks to which participants are exposed are justified by the benefits anticipated from proposed research. Three dimensions of risk are relevant to risk–benefit assessment: probability, magnitude, and duration of harm. Thus, three questions must be addressed in assessing the level of risks posed by a study. First, what are the chances that the research interventions will produce various harms to the participants? Second, how serious is the potential harm from the study interventions? Third, how long is the potential harm expected to last if it occurs?

Achieving a favorable risk–benefit ratio requires that research risks must be minimized as much as possible. The Nuremberg Code states, "The experiment should be so conducted as to avoid all unnecessary physical and mental suffering and injury" (Annas and Grodin, 1992). The requirement to minimize risks does not mean that risks must be eliminated, for that would make almost all clinical research impossible to conduct. Risks must be minimized with respect to the task of answering valuable scientific questions by means of scientifically valid methods (a point that illustrates how the ethical requirements of clinical research must operate in tandem). Study designs should be evaluated to determine if they could be modified to pose less risk to participants without compromising the validity of the study data.

A critical part of risk–benefit assessment involves making judgments about when the risks of a proposed study are too high, regardless of the potential scientific value. The US federal regulations governing research with human subjects, however, provide little guidance with respect to judgments of acceptable risk (Code of Federal Regulations, 1991). The Nuremberg Code, developed in the wake of the concentration camp experiments, states: "No experiment should be conducted where there is an a priori reason to believe that death or disabling injury will occur." Yet, how can it be determined whether the potential value of knowledge to be gained from a given study can justify the risks posed to healthy volunteers? There are no formulas available. The assessment calls for carefully considered and deliberated judgments by research sponsors, investigators, and IRBs.

Independent review

Prospective independent review of research protocols by IRBs was mandated by the US federal government in response to revelations in the 1960s of abuses of research subjects, including healthy volunteers (Faden and Beauchamp, 1986). Self-regulation by investigators was no longer considered sufficient. Independent review is a key procedural safeguard for protecting research participants from the inherent potential of clinical research to compromise the rights or welfare of subjects. Independent review also provides public accountability for clinical research, a process that exposes participants to risks for the good of society. The task of the IRB is to apply the other substantive ethical requirements in their review, modification, approval, and oversight of research protocols.

Informed consent

The purpose of informed consent is to assure that research participation reflects the free choice and self-determination of those who enroll in research. As the term "informed consent" suggests, this requirement includes two basic components. First, prospective research subjects must understand what their participation entails: the nature of the study, the procedures to be administered, the risks and potential benefits (if any), alternatives to participation, and the right to decline or withdraw participation without penalty. Second, subjects must voluntarily agree to participate under those conditions.

Respect for enrolled subjects

Clinical research must be conducted with adequate safeguards to protect the welfare and rights of participants during the course of research. These include procedures to protect privacy and confidentiality, monitoring the condition of research subjects to assure their safety, terminating study participation in the case of adverse events, and informing enrolled subjects about risks and benefits discovered in the course of research or new information reported in the medical literature. IRBs should review and approve written plans to monitor the condition of research participants. Adverse event reports must be prepared by investigators and submitted to IRBs in a timely fashion so that determinations can be made about whether to modify the study design, change informed consent documents, notify enrolled subjects, or stop the research.

Community collaboration

Emanuel and colleagues later added an eighth requirement of community collaboration, in particular, to address concerns about the potential for exploitation in international research conducted in developing countries (Emanuel et al., 2004). According to this ethical standard, researchers should develop a partnership with the community. This includes involving community partners in sharing responsibilities for determining the importance of the health problem; assessing the value of the research; planning, conducting, and overseeing the research; and integrating the study findings into the health care system. It also entails respect for the community's values, culture, traditions, and social practices and assurances that the participants will receive benefits from the conduct and results of the research.

This requirement may also be applicable to health research within developed countries, as we point out in the next section.

Case Study: The Investigation of Alternative Lead Abatement Procedures by the Kennedy Krieger Institute

To demonstrate the relevance and application of justice considerations at the different levels of analysis described above, we present a case study of research designed to determine if more or less extensive and expensive lead abatement procedures can effectively prevent lead poisoning in children living in high-risk environments. This research was conducted between 1993 and 1995 by the Kennedy Krieger Institute (KKI), a children's health facility and research institute affiliated with Johns Hopkins University in Baltimore, Maryland. Two participating families later sued KKI, stating that they were not fully informed of the risks of participation for their children and that KKI failed to inform them in a timely manner of test results. In *Grimes v. Kennedy Krieger Institute*, the Court of Appeals (Maryland's highest court) overturned a lower court's ruling to dismiss and reinstated the families' lawsuits. In August 2001, the Court of Appeals judges issued a scathing 96-page ruling condemning the research (Maryland Court of Appeals, 2001). The judges' remarks made national headlines and spawned a contentious debate about the ethical justification of this research.

The health problems caused by lead poisoning from lead-based paint have been known since the late 1800s. Young children face the most danger from exposure because their growing bodies absorb lead more easily than adult bodies. The most common source of children's exposure is contaminated dust from older homes that contain lead-based paint. Children absorb this dust from their hands and toys through normal hand-to-mouth activity. Over the last 30 years, the Centers for Disease Control (CDC) has regularly revised downward the blood lead level at which lead poisoning occurs, from 60 micrograms (µg) per deciliter of blood in the 1960s, to 30 µg in 1975, to 25 µg in 1985, to 10 µg in 1991 (Ross, 2002). For children 5 years old and younger, lead levels of 10 µg or more have been determined to impair their ability to learn. At higher levels, lead poisoning can cause mental retardation, coma, convulsions, and death.

When the KKI study was being conceived, an estimated 95 percent of low-income housing in identified neighborhoods in Baltimore was contaminated by lead-based paint. Studies at the time showed that 40–50 percent of the predominantly African-American children living in these high-risk neighborhoods had elevated blood lead levels over 20 µg, deemed "moderate" blood lead elevation by CDC standards. But because of the high costs of implementing the recommended standard lead abatement procedure (approximately $20,000 per house), little was being done about the problem.

In the late 1980s, the KKI had tested alternative, less expensive lead reduction methods in empty properties and demonstrated that these techniques reduced ambient lead paint dust by 80 percent or more. They then proposed a follow-up study to determine if the reduction in lead paint dust in housing that had been treated with these processes would result in lower blood levels in children living in houses so treated. The research was approved and funded by the federal Environmental Protection Agency. The study included 108 houses in five comparison groups: three treatment groups that used the new lead abatement procedures, costing $1,650, $3,500, and $6,500, respectively; and, two comparison conditions, composed of housing that had been abated by the city of Baltimore and housing built after 1978 that was presumably free of lead paint. By design, the researchers chose not to include a control comparison of existing housing that had received no abatement procedures, because they felt that it would be unethical to follow children who were being exposed to a known health hazard without remediation, despite the fact this was the condition of the majority of children living in these neighborhoods. The study was designed to collect blood samples at baseline, 6 months and 24 months; children whose blood lead level exceeded 20 µg or whose blood level increased by 5 µg or more were to be referred for medical and environmental attention. The results of the research showed significant reductions in lead dust in all five study conditions. Overall, the blood lead levels of children residing in the KKI-treated homes stayed constant or went down, although there were a few cases of increases.

After the lawsuit was initially dismissed by the Circuit Court, the Court of Appeals sent the case back for trial, issuing a blistering critique that compared the research to the Tuskegee syphilis study and Nazi research on prisoners. The judges called it a callous scientific experiment that put children in harm's way, saying they were being used merely as "measuring tools." The Court's remand focused on three main issues: (1) informed consent, declaring that parents cannot give consent for their children to enroll in "non-therapeutic" research; (2) the duty to warn due to the "special relationship" between the researchers and participants; and, (3) the inadequacies of the Institutional Review Boards' review, referring to the Hopkins IRB as "in-house agents" who were not "as sufficiently concerned with ethicality of the research as they were with the success of the experiment."

Since the judges' ruling, several commentaries on the case have appeared in legal, public health, medical, and bioethics journals. In one of the harshest attacks on the research in the bioethics literature, Spriggs (2004, p. 179) charged that the study lacked any social or scientific value, stating "Nothing in the research suggests that the study would lead to the enforcement of more lead reduction." He concluded (p. 180),

> Knowing how to get rid of lead or reducing exposure was not as much of a problem as getting someone to pay for it . . . the dominant value of the lead paint study seems to be that it is not acceptable for landlords to lose out financially but it is acceptable for children in low income housing to face the continuing risk of lead poisoning.

While the factual merits of the lawsuit have yet to be determined in court, it appears that there may have been inadequacies in the informed consent document and some delay in informing the families about the levels of lead dust found in their homes. Setting aside these important ethical concerns, we want to address the question of whether research of this sort could ever be considered just.

At a societal level, does the government have an obligation to conduct research into finding cost-effective ways of addressing a known, significant health problem? More specifically, does the fact that it is possible to create a home environment free of risk from lead paint indicate that it is unjust to conduct research on the effectiveness of more practical, less expensive means of lead paint abatement? CDC data show that, in 2000–2001, 2.2 percent of all children 1–5 years old in the US, and 9.6 percent of African-American children, had lead levels that were above 10 µg (Meyer et al., 2003). According to the Alliance to End Childhood Lead Poisoning, an estimated 5 million preschool children still live in houses with significant lead hazards. Because the current standard lead abatement process costs approximately $20,000 per house, attempts to enforce housing code regulations on absentee landlords with properties in high-risk neighborhoods typically result in abandoned buildings, which then become "crack" houses and "shooting galleries" for drug addicts, and in resorts to arson to collect on insurance, which displaces families onto the streets. In a society that does not guarantee the provision of safe housing for all its citizens, one might fairly ask about the ethics of *not* conducting research aimed at finding affordable means to improve the safety of the existing housing stock for disadvantaged children.

Drawing on the three-tiered framework described above, we would argue that the state has an obligation to support needed health research because lead poisoning in children causes lifelong disabilities that interfere with the ability of those affected to pursue the life plans that they might choose if they were not so impaired. Even though the technical capacity for complete lead abatement is available, the lack of a social policy commitment to require lead-free housing for all children makes it ethically imperative to find more cost-effective methods to alleviate this serious, widespread public health problem. As some commentators have suggested, the KKI case is analogous in many respects to research aimed at preventing perinatal transmission of HIV through low-dose AZT treatments, research that Kass (2004) has described as "just research in an unjust world." Precisely because available public resources are limited, lead abatement research designed to find more cost-effective methods that would allow improved health for disadvantaged children should also be considered just research in an unjust world.

Within federal health research funding priorities, a good case can be made that such research should have high priority. Lead poisoning affects a large number of people; it produces moderate-to-severe lifelong disabilities; it interferes with one's ability to lead a normal, productive, and comfortable life; and there are significant economic and social costs associated with its sequelae, from school failure, to drug abuse, to teen pregnancy, to participation in violent and criminal activities. Lead poisoning has its greatest impact on economically disadvantaged children – one of the most vulnerable populations in society. When justice is conceived as fairness, governments have an obligation to arrange social institutions to maximize benefits to the worst off.

Turning to the conduct of the research itself, Spriggs claimed that the research had no social value, but, in view of the social and political context in which this research was conducted, this blanket unqualified assertion seems obviously false. The social value of this type of research is based on the reasonable expectation that the less expensive intervention will be implemented to improve the living conditions of disadvantaged groups. Similarly, the Court opined that the research was "non-therapeutic," and hence, children should have been excluded from research that offered no medical benefit. Although it is not clear from the opinion, the Court may have concluded that a study focusing on housing interventions to reduce lead exposure was not "clinical" or "medical," and therefore, not therapeutic by definition. If this is the case, it demonstrates a very limited understanding of the causes of disease, the conditions that put people at risk for developing serious ailments, the benefits of prevention, and the nature of public health interventions to reduce risk. Likewise, the Court stated that "healthy children" were being put in harm's way by the research. But because these children were living in high-risk environments, it would be more accurate to define them as "at-risk," in the same way that ostensibly healthy adults are "at-risk" for developing heart disease from hypertension, smoking, and high cholesterol.

In IRB deliberations, the characterization of risks and benefits is key: the benefits to the participants in this research must be understood in terms of reducing the likelihood of developing lead poisoning. It is important to recognize that the KKI research did not expose children to a more risky home environment than they would have otherwise experienced. This study offered a favorable risk–benefit ratio both in terms of potential benefits to the children by living in safer housing, and in terms of the social value of knowledge to be gained regarding cost-effective means of lead abatement.

Finally, Mastroianni and Kahn (2002) cite the Kennedy Krieger case as a good example of the need for establishing community partnerships in conducting research with any vulnerable populations. If the KKI had gained community buy-in and approval of the research from the outset, the many charges and misunderstanding that have arisen since its completion may have been avoided. Alternately, if the community had not found the proposed research acceptable, then it would have given the researchers pause to reconsider the research design.

In conclusion, justice concerns arise because social resources are limited, and therefore, the burdens and benefits of living in society must be distributed fairly. We have argued that states have an obligation to promote justice through health research designed to achieve fair equality of opportunity and to improve the conditions of those who are least well off. Since the KKI lead abatement study was designed to produce knowledge aimed at benefiting the most vulnerable segments of the population by preventing lifelong learning disabilities associated with a wide spectrum of social pathologies, such health research should have high priority in allocation decisions. Lastly, this research can be conducted in a way that not only does not exploit the participants, but also extends the benefits of research to traditionally underserved groups.

Conclusion

Concerns about justice drive the most basic considerations about the ethics of health research involving human subjects. A firm grasp of fundamental principles of justice is essential for deliberating well and determining an appropriate balance between the two primary moral obligations of health research: subject protection and knowledge generation. Debates about justice in the research setting have evolved from an initial focus on protecting participants from harm and exploitation to providing fair access to the benefits of emerging findings to all social groups. It is concerns about justice that drive current demands for fair and adequate representation of different racial and ethnic groups and age groups, access for the disabled, and an equality of gender representation in determining sample populations and recruitment strategies in new research designs. Notably, justice considerations extend even further, to setting research priorities and understanding more clearly a societal commitment to supporting health research. Vigorous debates about justice will continue to shape discussions about the purposes and methods of health research, with new frontiers opening with respect to global justice, environmental justice, emerging health enhancement technologies, and the social implications of the genetic lottery. Grappling with the tensions between living in a world with gross social injustices and conducting research responsibly is likely to remain an enduring source of ethical reflection and controversy. To serve justice, sponsors, investigators, and research ethics committees must strive to ensure that both the means and the ends of their research contribute to alleviating human suffering, reducing health inequalities and improving the quality of life for all.

Note

1 The opinions expressed are those of the authors and do not necessarily reflect the position or policy of the National Institutes of Health, the Public Health Service, or the Department of Health and Human Services.

References

Abramson, J. (2004), *Overdosed America: The Broken Promise of American Medicine*, New York: HarperCollins.

Angell, M. (2004), *The Truth about Drug Companies: How They Deceive Us and What To Do About It*, New York: Random House.

Annas, G.J. (2002), Bioterrorism, public health, and civil liberties, *New England Journal of Medicine* 346: 1337–42.

Annas, G.J. and Grodin, M.A. (1992), *The Nazi Doctors and the Nuremberg Code*, New York: Oxford University Press.

Avorn, J. (2004), *Powerful Medicines: The Benefits, Risks, and Costs of Prescription Drugs*, New York: Alfred A. Knopf.

Barry, B. (1989), *Theories of Justice*, Berkeley: University of California Press.

Beauchamp, T. and Childress, J. (2001), *Principles of Biomedical Ethics*, 5th edn., New York: Oxford University Press.

Beecher, H.K. (1966), Ethics and clinical research, *New England Journal of Medicine* 274: 1354–60.

Berg, J.W., Appelbaum, P., Lidz, C., and Parker, L. (2001), *Informed Consent: Legal Theory and Clinical Practice*, 2nd edn., New York: Oxford University Press.

Bodenheimer, T. (2000), Uneasy alliance: clinical investigators and the pharmaceutical industry, *New England Journal of Medicine* 342: 1539–44.

Buchanan, A. (1981), Justice: a philosophical review, in Earl Shelp (ed.), *Justice and Health Care*, Boston, MA: D. Reidel Publishing Company, pp. 3–22.

Buchanan, D., Shaw, S., Stopka, T., Khooshnood, K., and Singer, M. (2002), Ethical dilemmas created by the criminalization of status behaviors: case examples from ethnographic research with injection drug users, *Health Education and Behavior* 29 (1): 30–42.

Callahan, D. (2000), Death and the research imperative, *New England Journal of Medicine* 342 (9): 654–6.

Callahan, D. (2002), Ends and means: the goals of health care, in M. Danis, C. Clancy, and

L. Churchill (eds.), *Ethical Dimensions of Health Policy*, New York: Oxford University Press, pp. 3–18.

Callahan, D. (2003), *What Price Better Health? Hazards of the Research Imperative*, Berkeley: University of California Press.

Clayton, A. and Williams, A. (eds.), (2004), *Social Justice*, Malden, MA: Blackwell Publishing Ltd.

Code of Federal Regulations (1991) 45 CFR §46, *Protection of Human Subjects*, Rockville, Maryland: US Department of Health and Human Services.

Daniels, N. (1985), *Just Health Care*, New York: Cambridge University Press.

Daniels, N. (1996), Wide reflective equilibrium in practice, in L. Sumner and J. Boyle (eds.) *Philosophical Perspectives on Bioethics*, Toronto: University of Toronto Press, pp. 96–114.

Daniels, N. (2001), Justice, health, and health care, *American Journal of Bioethics* 1 (2): 2–16.

Daniels, N. and Sabin, J. (1997), Limits to health care: fair procedures, democratic deliberation, and the legitimacy problem for insurers, *Philosophy and Public Affairs* 26: 303–50.

Dresser, R. (2001), *When Science Offers Salvation: Patient Advocacy and Research Ethics*, New York: Oxford University Press.

Emanuel, E., Wendler, D., and Grady, C. (2000), What makes clinical research ethical, *Journal of the American Medical Association* 283 (20): 2701–11.

Emanuel, E., Wendler, D., and Grady, C. (2004), What makes clinical research in developing countries ethical? The benchmarks of ethical research, *Journal of Infectious Diseases* 189: 930–7.

Faden, R.R., and Beauchamp, T.L. (1986), *A History and Theory of Informed Consent*, New York: Oxford University Press.

Gross, C.P., Anderson, G.F., and Powe, N.R. (1999), The relation between funding by the National Institutes of Health and the burden of disease, *New England Journal of Medicine* 340: 1881–7.

Institute of Medicine (1998), *Scientific Opportunities and Public Needs: Improving Priority Setting and Public Input at the National Institute of Health*, Washington, DC: National Academy Press.

Jonas, H. (1974), Philosophical reflections on experimenting with human subjects, in Hans Jonas (ed.), *Philosophical Essays: From Ancient Creed to Technological Man*, Englewood Cliffs, NJ: Prentice-Hall, pp. 105–31

Jonsen, A. (2000), *A Short History of Medical Ethics*, New York: Oxford University Press.

Kahn, J., Mastroianni, A., and Sugarman, J. (1998), Changing claims about justice in research: an introduction and overview, in J. Kahn, A. Mastroianni, and J. Sugarman (eds.), *Beyond Consent: Seeking Justice in Research*, New York: Oxford University Press, pp. 1–10.

Kass, N. (2004), Public health ethics: from foundations and frameworks to justice and global public health, *Journal of Law, Medicine, and Ethics* 32 (2): 232–42.

Levine, R.J. (1986), *Ethics and Regulation of Clinical Research*, 2nd edn., New Haven, CT: Yale University Press.

McCarthy, C. (1998), The evolving story of justice in federal research policy, in J. Kahn, A. Mastroianni, and J. Sugarman (eds.), *Beyond Consent: Seeking Justice in Research*, New York: Oxford University Press, pp. 11–31.

Maryland Court of Appeals (2001), *Ericka Grimes v. Kennedy Krieger Institute, Inc.* no. 128, September Term, 2000, available at: http://www.courts.state.md.us/opinions/coa/2001/128a00, accessed July 17 2006.

Mastroianni, A., and Kahn, J. (2002), Risk and responsibility: ethics, *Grimes v. Kennedy*

Krieger, and public health research involving children, *American Journal of Public Health* 92 (7): 1073–6.

Meyer P.A., Pivetz T., Dignam T.A., Homa, D.M., Schoonover, J., and Brody, D. (2003), Surveillance for elevated blood lead levels among children – United States, 1997–2001, *Morbidity and Mortality Weekly Surveillance Summary*. September 12, 52 (10): 1–21.

National Commission for the Protection of Human Subjects of Biomedical and Behavioral Research (1979), *The Belmont Report: Ethical Principles and Guidelines for the Protection of Human Subjects of Research*, Federal Register Document 79–12065, Washington, DC: Department of Health and Human Welfare, US Government Printing Office.

National Institutes of Health. (1997), *Disease-Specific Estimates of Direct and Indirect Costs of Illness and NIH Support*, Bethesda, MD: National Institutes of Health.

Nozick, R. (1974), *Anarchy, State, and Utopia*, New York: Basic Books.

Pace, C., Miller, F.G., and Danis, M. (2003), Enrolling the uninsured in clinical trials: an ethical perspective, *Critical Care in Medicine* 31 (3): S121–5.

Powers, M. (1998), Theories of justice in the context of research, in J. Kahn, A. Mastroianni, and J. Sugarman (eds.), *Beyond Consent: Seeking Justice in Research*, New York: Oxford University Press, pp. 147–65.

Rawls, John. (1971), *A Theory of Justice*, Cambridge, MA: Harvard University Press.

Rees, J. (2004), The fundamentals of clinical discovery, *Perspectives in Biology and Medicine* 47 (4): 597–607.

Rettig, R. (2000), The industrialization of clinical research, *Health Affairs* 19 (2): 129–46.

Rogers W.A. (2004), Evidence based medicine and justice: a framework for looking at the impact of EBM upon vulnerable or disadvantaged groups, *Journal of Medical Ethics* 30: 141–5.

Ross, L. (2002), In defense of the lead abatement studies, *Journal of Law, Medicine, and Ethics* 30: 50–7.

Spriggs, M. (2004), Canaries in the mines: children, risk, non-therapeutic research, and justice, *Journal of Medical Ethics* 30: 176–81.

Wertheimer, A. (1996), *Exploitation*, Princeton, NJ: Princeton University Press.

World Medical Association (1997), Declaration of Helsinki, *Journal of the American Medical Association* 277: 925–6.

Chapter 22

Ethics of Disclosure Following a Medical Injury

Time for Reform?

Troyen Anthony Brennan

Introduction

Patient safety has arrived as a focus for health care. Few areas of health policy have provoked as much discussion and controversy in the last half decade. With the publication of the Institute of Medicine's quality reports, beginning with *To Err Is Human*, physicians, nurses, politicians, and policy analysts all began to address the problems of iatrogenic injury, errors in medicine and prevention strategies (IOM, 2000).

Swept along with this vortex of discussion has been the matter of disclosure to patients of harm they may have suffered at the hands of the medical care system. The new science of patient safety was built on the insight that medical injuries were really rather common, occurring in as many as 4 percent of all hospitalizations (Brennan et al., 1991). In addition, the insights of safety engineering, and the literature on quality improvement (Brennan and Berwick, 1996), which were imported into medical care, emphasized the importance of honest recognition and analysis of errors. The same sense of openness and honesty obtained from medical ethics. Hence, safety advocates came to a single conclusion, that errors should be openly discussed and the insights from investigations shared widely.

The sunshine aspects of safety engineering threw new light on what had been one of medicine's best-kept secrets. The health care system has responded to medical errors, and especially the injuries they cause, through risk management, that is, doing whatever is possible to ensure that the risk *of a lawsuit* was minimized. The traditional techniques involved quiet investigation and minimal discussion, especially with the injured individual.

The juxtaposition between open discussion and the traditional risk management approach raises interesting issues in ethics. A health care system committed to provider altruism and respect for patient autonomy nonetheless turned a cold eye toward those whom they injured. Fortunately today, safety advocates, fortified by ethical arguments, are trying to turn back the regressive risk management approach, and do the right thing for patients, as we will discuss in this chapter.

The Foundations of Altruism and Autonomy in Medical Ethics

Just as it is difficult to define health law, it is also hard to define medical ethics. There are many different theories of medical ethics (Brennan, 1991). Many are culture-bound, and many reflect a national set of assumptions about the appropriate relationship between provider and patient. Furthermore, medical ethics in a given country can be marked both by influential authors and by local endorsement of particular ideas.

Nonetheless, at least in American medical ethics, we have two very strong and broadly endorsed views about the ethics of medicine. First physicians are committed to altruism. This means that physicians have a fiduciary responsibility and they are morally bound to act for the good of their patients. The doctor's only end is the good of the patient. Second, borrowing from Kantian ethics, in the 1960s American medical ethics absorbed the notion of respecting autonomy and treating patients as ends in themselves: A patient is not a means to an end, but rather the only end.

These commitments to altruism and autonomy had consequences. Of course, autonomous patients want to improve or maintain their health and function. And, of course, physicians are committed to altruism. Together, the doctor–patient team fought disease without concern about external system issues.

Physicians, however, controlled both the supply and demand of health care. They held the strong end of a power relationship and they had a tremendous advantage *vis à vis* the patient in terms of knowledge. This imbalance, coupled with a nearly universal and extraordinarily passive health insurance system (for the middle class and above) helped the medical profession become rich (Starr, 1982). The costs of care, the structure of the institutions in which it occurred, and the nature of the insurance function could be overlooked or dismissed, as the patient (and the physician) were protected by the requisite selfless professional commitment.

While a great many of the aspects of this relationship and the culture of medicine it created have persisted, one part was significantly modified by the early 1980s. The power relationship one can make out in the doctor–patient relationship clearly created the potential for an overwhelming paternalism. The physician was in a position to dictate treatment terms to the patient. Indeed, most of the case law of the period 1940 to 1960 suggested that such therapeutic privilege was both prevalent and correct (Katz, 1984). If the physician did not make decisions on behalf of the irrational patient, very bad things might happen to the patient – hence better to support doctor decision-making.

Katz's great history of informed consent indicates how, at least to some extent, medical paternalism was blunted by the courts. By the middle of the twentieth century, the law of informed consent had moved completely away from its base in battery and instead was a matter largely of negligence, with the weight of professional responsibility couched in the rule of medical custom. Physicians were to provide patients with the amount of information that they believed was prudent. The doctor who was committed to the good of the patient, sometimes had to overrule the wishes of the irrational patient by providing less information than the patient might request or expect.

With the emergence of the civil rights movement, and the Supreme Court's increasing protection of the penumbrae of privacy, the notion of individual patient autonomy began to infiltrate informed consent litigation. As early as the case of *Salgo v. Leland Stanford Hospital* (Brennan, 1991) and certainly by the late 1970s, a patient-based standard had begun to replace the professional standard with regard to the amount of information that a patient might expect. Similar to developments in end of life care and hospitalized patient rights, the individual's right to make care choices began to come out from underneath the profession's prerogatives. Within the decade the principle of patient autonomy was firmly ensconced in medical ethics.

Its hold, however, has never been firm. For example, the patient-based standard in informed consent has been retrenched over the last three decades in response to a variety of pressures from tort reform. Nevertheless, the profession still exercises greater discretion than what is typical in most market encounters. In many ways, altruism and autonomy conflict where the former begins to pass into paternalism. But in some settings, such as we will see with medical injury and disclosure, the principles are greatly aligned.

The Problem of Medical Injury and the Emergence of Safety

Medical errors and the injuries they cause are as old as medicine. Hence the famous Hippocratic admonishment: do no harm. But the culture of medicine has not allowed much open discussion of substandard care and the iatrogenic injury. For reasons far beyond the scope of this paper, medicine generally, and American medicine in particular, preferred to operate with the presumption that routine care was faultless, and that accidents which did occur were rare and preventable.

Two factors figured significantly in this fiction. The first was the professional paradigm of the isolated physician struggling against the patient's disease. Highly trained and morally committed, the professional image would not admit to error as a cause of problems. This model was supported by the dynamics of the doctor–patient relationship as explained by Jay Katz (Katz, 1984). Yet, medical care is provided in the face of tremendous uncertainty. Consequently, diagnoses can be wrong, treatment choices can be incorrect, and interventions, especially surgery, can go wrong. But to admit to that uncertainty would bring troubling doubt to both doctor and patient. So, along the lines of the old joke of a good surgeon who is sometimes wrong but always certain, both doctor and patient proceed under a pretext of certainty. Of course, acceptance of the illusion constrains significant dialogue and precludes the possibility of discussion of avoidable potential injury or errors.

Second, there was a penalty for negligent error, that is, a malpractice suit. The medical profession had long insisted that the professional model of regulation was sufficient for assuring competent practice. This battle had been won over the course of the twentieth century, so that by 1960 all regulation was institutional self-regulation (Brennan and Berwick, 1996). Hospitals controlled hospital oversight, and doctors controlled doctor oversight.

The only uncaptured mode of regulation was the system of medical malpractice. Operated by independent plaintiff attorneys and protected by common law courts, malpractice suits could sanction doctors who negligently caused injury. With the increasing tilt toward plaintiffs on the part of the major state courts in the 1940s through the 1960s, attorneys were able to take advantage of a variety of relatively new doctrines that increased the probability of the suits prevailing. This development spawned more litigation (Weiler, 1990). Physicians, of course, hated tort litigation, and sought ways to obstruct it.

Physicians have been rather successful in that regard. The events in California from 1960 through 1976 demonstrate this dynamic well. The California Supreme Court was the leader in the liberalization of tort doctrine, specifically in product liability, but also in medical malpractice. The decision of *Ybarra v. Spangard*, which corporated *res ipsa loquitur* into tort law, was the best example of the ferment among courts concerned about defendant prerogatives (Havighurst, Blumstein and Brennan, 1999). By the early 1960s the prevalence of malpractice litigation in the Golden State had begun to increase and by the mid-1970s it was reaching crisis proportions for a medical profession accustomed to little outside oversight. The rates of claims, the cost of each claim, and hence the premiums paid by physicians were all rising very quickly.

The well-organized physicians of the California Medical Association (CMA) recognized a crisis and moved in two directions. First, they approached the state legislature with a series of proposals regarding tort reform. Tort reform is a quite neutral sounding euphemism that essentially means changing the statutory law to make it more difficult for plaintiffs to sue. The key to tort reform is to reduce the probability that an attorney will bring a suit on behalf of an injured person.

This requires one more step deeper into tort law. The plaintiff's attorney is the key decision-maker in a suit. The attorney must assess the degree of the patient's injury, the costs associated with that injury, the costs associated with bringing a suit, and the probability of prevailing. This complicated calculus is based on the contingency fee system: that is, the plaintiff's attorney is compensated on a portion of the settlement for the plaintiff. Getting paid is contingent on prevailing. The attorney only brings the suit if the probability of winning is high enough to risk the investment.

The legislature can change the rules to make it more unlikely that the plaintiff will win, or cap the amount of a successful claim and thereby reduce its worth. Both measures would reduce the number of suits because the costs of bringing a claim are relatively stable. For example, if the average severe injury case had provided an award of one million dollars for pain and suffering, a cap could bring that down to $250,000.

The CMA packaged a group of such reforms into the Medical Insurance Comprehensive Reform Act (MICRA) of 1976, which was eventually passed by the California legislature and signed into law (Weiler, 1990). It immediately became a classic bit of legislation and has been widely emulated by states since that time. It is also seen as having fixed the malpractice crisis in California.

The other step taken by the CMA received little press, but was perhaps more far-sighted than the tort reform measures. Taking a cue from turn-of-the-century social reformers who advocated an administrative "no fault" plan for work-related injury (which eventually became known as workers' compensation), the CMA sponsored a large study of medical injury in hospitals. The researchers, led by Don Harper Mills, used teams of nurses and physicians to review over 20,000 medical records of hospitalized patients. They found that 4.65 percent of patients suffered an adverse event, that is, an injury caused by their medical care as opposed to the disease process. They also found that 0.8 percent of people had an injury that was due to substandard care. Thus the number of iatrogenic injuries caused by substandard care was much larger than expected (Weiler et al., 1992). The CMA's reaction to the study findings was understandable. They did not push forward with no fault reform as they were concerned about its costs. Also, they did not allow the results to be published rapidly, as they were concerned about the backlash, especially since they had just managed to get reform enacted that would decrease the amount of tort litigation.

Hence, over 30 years ago, the essential paradigm in malpractice litigation and medical injury was clear: in the face of evidence that the burden of injury caused by the medical care system was vast, the profession nonetheless sought relief from the one uncaptured source of oversight of medical errors, the tort system.

More recent research makes the point that there is far more medical injury than malpractice litigation. The Harvard Medical Practice Study, undertaken in the early 1990s for study year 1984 in New York, and the follow-up Colorado/ Utah Medical Practice Study from the late 1990s both showed that approximately 3 percent of people have adverse events during hospitalization and that 1 percent have an injury as the result of negligence. Furthermore, since both of these studies were random samples, they produced firm estimates of the number of people injured in those states during the specific study year (Studdert, Brennan, and Thomas, 2000).

Using study data, the investigators could also compare the number of medical injuries to the number of suits brought. What they found was startling: there were as many as seven negligent injuries for every suit that was brought. Hence, there is a huge reservoir of potential claims, but only a few lead to litigation. Those cases that do come to litigation are often not based on solid evidence of medical injury. These results shed more light on medical error and its relation to litigation than had previously been available anywhere in the field of accidents.

Yet the studies gained little interest until 2000. At that point, the prestigious Institute of Medicine's quality committee decided to bring the matter to the attention of the public. Extrapolating from these studies to the United States population they reported to the press that between 44,000 and 98,000 people die in American hospitals every year from iatrogenic causes. The fact of medical injury was something that the profession could no longer avoid, and the safety movement was started.

Of course, the issue of patient safety would not have taken hold without a firm base of evidence. Part of that was provided by the original epidemiological studies that had characterized the scope of medical injury and targeted certain kinds of interventions. An equally large part was provided by the development of the notion of safety engineering in health care. Accidents could be prevented if we own up to the fact that they occur, and if we study their conditions so that we can figure out ways to prevent them. Our failure to respond to medical injury derived from our approach to error which in turn was based on the fictions that the profession had accepted, namely, that error does not occur and when it does, it should be either discussed quietly as a singular exception or ignored. In place of that approach, the safety movement requires responding to errors with openness and an aggressive consideration of every error as a lesson to be learned. Unfortunately, medical malpractice still frustrates that approach.

The Ancient Practices of Malpractice Litigation

Malpractice as a sub-field of tort or personal injury law is based on a reasonably straightforward concern for social welfare. Tort doctrine involves four elements of proof. The successful plaintiff must show that there was a dutiful relationship between the tortfeasor and the plaintiff; that there was an injury; that there was negligence on the part of the tortfeasor; and that the negligence caused the injury. In medical malpractice litigation, the dutiful relationship is one between doctor and patient; and the negligence must, according to the rule of medical custom, be defined by an expert doctor. Decisions based on negligence are, therefore, significantly different from administrative no-fault programs like workers' compensation where there is no need to prove negligence.

The social functions of tort law include compensation, deterrence, and corrective justice. By maintaining the fault criteria, and by holding the individual liable for the costs of the injury that he or she causes, corrective justice is thought to suffuse the culture. This is certainly a debatable area of tort doctrine, but is highly defended by the plaintiff's bar.

Of course in health care, the need for proof of negligence and the desire for corrective justice come with a cost. Before a personal injury occurs the doctor–patient relationship is based upon altruistic commitment to the patient's good and respect for his/her autonomy. In most instances, the parties are not strangers meeting at the site of an accident. They are acquainted and even share mutual trust. A tort action sharply transforms the relationship from partners fighting disease to adversaries fighting each other. In most situations, the abrupt change from selfless commitment to fierce litigant is too much for physicians and patients and destroys any pre-existing relationship. We need to keep this factor in mind as we start to think about disclosure.

The second function of tort law is compensation. In theory, the injured person gets uninsured costs of an accident paid for by the defendant. But, as we have seen above, most cases of medical injury do not lead to litigation. And once litigation begins in a specific case, most of the money is spent on the system of litigation rather than as compensation for the injured parties. The best estimates are that as much as 55 percent of the costs are administrative – read lawyers (Studdert et al., 2006).

There is little evidence that personal injury litigation can be justified by its deterrence effects. Theory would have it that the defendant who has been sued will be more careful in the future, and that others will learn from his example. That happy prospect is not easily proven. In fact, a comprehensive review of deterrence in tort law concluded that there was no evidence that deterrence actually occurred. So, while the social function theory is appealing, it lacks supporting evidence (Mello, Kelly, and Brennan 2005).

A review of the history of medical malpractice law, does, however, provide some inherent logic for the entire enterprise. The plaintiff attorney must have a good case to bring because he or she does not get paid without prevailing. As the field began to develop in the middle part of the twentieth century, the litigation was, in most circumstances, solely against the doctor. He (in most cases a male) was classified by common law rules as the "captain of the ship" directing the rest of the health care team. Nurses reported to him as the superior. Hospitals were generally passive, and the charitable immunity doctrine protected the non-profit hospitals from litigation. So, litigation was directed at the doctor.

Before a suit, the doctor and patient are working together, and (in the middle of the twentieth century with medical paternalism at its maximum force) the doctor is leading the patient to health. Once a malpractice suit is brought, the physician is the main (or only) target of an adversarial system that presses hard on the notion of corrective justice. To gain justice, the accident must be corrected by the doctor's payment for the patient's injury. This is the classic model of malpractice that persists today.

Of course, the framework for malpractice litigation has changed. Now hospitals can be held liable, although the development of a notion of enterprise liability has been slowly developing in many states. Also, many layers of insurance now exist for both doctors and employees of hospitals. Yet, none of this has changed the presumptions and assumptions that doctors bring to the proceeding. Even the most recent research on the point demonstrates that doctors do not believe that malpractice has anything to do with improving care. In fact, doctors actually believe that malpractice suits are a very significant impediment to practice; that they diminish the quality of care; and they encourage doctors to retire or get out of practice (Mello, Kelly, and Brennan, 2005). They see negligence suits as random events, and they fail to consider the factors that lead to errors and learn from the events.

Underlying this antagonism and persistent disregard is the fact that doctors still tend to treat any questions about quality and negligence as a matter of moral culpability. Starting from the framework of medicine's altruistic commitment to patient welfare, the doctor sees the claim of injury as a personal failure and as a break in the professional relationship (Hupert et al., 1996). The doctor cannot recover the relationship if the patient sues. Used to success on tests of skill and knowledge, the malpractice claim suggests ineptness because doctors find it hard to accept that there can be errors even in the best hands.

Consequently, the doctor's instinct is to fight and hide. The doctors and their insurers and lawyers are aggressively defensive about possible litigation. They keep records of adverse events carefully sequestered, and peer review protections provide some immunity from discovery. All witnesses are carefully coached on what they say. The events are reviewed by expert witnesses who assist in developing a strategy to defend the case. Often it takes several reviews to find one expert who will provide a favorable report, but given a murky and complicated history, the defense team can usually find one expert who will defend the treatment that was rendered.

These machinations do not take place in full view. In fact, malpractice litigation is usually rather secretive. Doctors do not talk about it, in fact their lawyers instruct them not to do so. Within a medical institution a risk management officer typically manages communication with the patient following an adverse event in an effort to avoid a suit. Risk management is all about managing the risk of litigation, not monitoring and repairing the conditions and procedures that could lead to errors that cause injury

What Do We Disclose Today, and What Will We Disclose in the Future?

Traditionally, then, there has been little disclosure about poor outcomes to patients. We have little reason to believe that much has changed. Indeed, a recent study in critical care units showed that less than 2 percent of charts reveal any information regarding discussion of adverse events with patients (Lehman et al., 2005). While this finding may simply reflect a failure to document discussions, that is doubtful. Given the highly charged nature of such communications, it is more likely that the health care team would have carefully documented what was said in the chart if the conversations had occurred. In any case, there is little evidence that physicians are being more honest with patients today than they have been in the past.

Advocates of disclosure suggest that doctors being forthcoming make patients less likely to sue. The linchpin of this argument is that most patients sue because they think that the doctors have been deceitful – all they wanted was more information and instead they got stonewalled. If the doctors and nurses involved were more open and disclosed the truth of a medical injury, most patients would appreciate their openness and the risks inherent in medical care and, therefore, not sue.

This stance is based on some evidence, but the data are thin. One article that appeared in the *Annals of Internal Medicine* as a case report from the Veterans Administration (VA) showed that a single hospital which had a disclosure policy also had lower rates of suit. However, this case report has not been validated, and it failed to mention that the liability regime governing the VA is quite a bit different from what we find in state common law. There have been similar anecdotal reports from the University of Michigan and other medical centers, but unfortunately, without substantiating evidence. COPIC, the most innovative of malpractice companies, has several new programs that provide for early admission of the fact that treatment did cause injury and for early offers of settlement. These bear watching, but we cannot yet say that there is good evidence that the open approach produces better outcomes.

The principled arguments in favor of the "disclosure movement" come from two directions. One is based in medical ethics; the other issues from efforts to improve patient safety. To illustrate them, consider the following clinical scenario.

> I am the primary care doctor for a patient. He is a 39-year laborer, who supports his wife and four children. He has no health or disability insurance. I have been seeing him as a patient for the past 10 years in the neighborhood health clinic and following his hypertension and hyperlipidemia. Our health center is affiliated with an academic medical center where I am on the staff. We use integrated medical records so I can review his treatment should he be admitted to the hospital.
>
> One morning, he has chest pain on the job and goes to the academic medical center emergency department (ED). His electrocardiogram (EKG), is read as a normal. He is diagnosed with atypical chest pain and sent home. In reality, the EKG was misread and it actually shows a large anterior wall myocardial infarction. (This is not pure fantasy because misreading of EKGs in the ED is a major source of liability.) At home the pain continues. While watching television that evening, he suffers a stroke and is taken back to the hospital. He has an uneventful hospital course, but is left paralyzed on the left side of his body and he cannot return to work. In retrospect, it is clear that the heart attack that was not diagnosed earlier in the day caused his left ventricle to fail to some degree, allowing a clot to form, which was then carried to his brain causing the stroke. In technical terms, a negligent adverse event caused uninsured disability.
>
> What should I as the doctor do? Both medical ethics and patient safety tell me I should be open and honest with the patient, revealing not only the injury, but also that the patient should sue the hospital. With regard to medical ethics, I started the day with an altruistic commitment to the patient's good. Within the context of medicine, I have a deep commitment to deal selflessly with my patients. I should, therefore, expend my professional time and the resources of the medical care system on advancing the patient's welfare. Seen from the lofty principles of medical ethics,

the patient is still my patient at the end of the day, I am selflessly committed to his medical good, and I know there is a compensation scheme available to him. I would help him with his disability applications (if he had such insurance), so why should I not help him gain the compensation due him from the health care system? He is justly entitled to an award from the malpractice carrier. If I am committed to the patient, why would I not simply disclose that a medical injury had occurred, that our medical system was negligent, and that I will help the plaintiff attorney hired by the patient to bring the case? It should be straightforward. Moreover, my assistance in the suit will help to ensure that the administrative costs of preparing the case will be kept under control. The plaintiff's attorney will still take his contingency fee, but with my help, our insurance company will be compelled to settle in a hurry, and will not waste time and money in protracted litigation of the case.

Of course, this scenario rarely plays out for several reasons. First, the malpractice case is rarely so well focused on other doctors. It is often the treating physician who makes the mistake. When the error is our own it is hard to admit the mistake and it is hard to accept that an admission would be compatible with self-preservation. Second, and more important, the malpractice system forces a break in the doctor–patient relationship. Once litigation and the adversarial process begin, the altruistic commitment of the doctor–patient relationship is allowed to be rescinded. Instead, the attorney–client relationship dominates. This may not be appropriate, but it appears to be common practice.

Respect for patient autonomy, exemplified by truth telling, is also sacrificed by this practice. Once the legal process intervenes, disclosure is controlled. Any examination of a set of interrogatories in the typical malpractice case will show that the defending attorney's aim is to have the defendant speak the truth, but not the whole truth, only enough to answer the question without lying. The defendant's communication is totally controlled. The point is that the honesty and altruism of the doctor–patient relationship evaporate once litigation begins. The demands of the legal process trump those of the ethical medical relationship.

Similarly, the aims of the safety movement fade from view in the face of litigation. Presuming that the patient who brought a law suit was not being assisted by the primary care doctor, what would typically have happen in the ED after this event? The negligent doctors would have felt very badly, but they would not have been disposed to talk about the mistakes. Professional embarrassment and a system of quiet oversight well described by Charles Bosk nearly 30 years ago would have ensured that there was little publicity (Bosk, 1980). It is unlikely that any specific changes would be made within the health care system. The doctors involved would be cautioned to be more careful in the future. All subsequent conversations would be regulated by the litigation process, where the less talk the better.

In a culture committed to safety, much would have been different. First, there would be no cover-up. We would acknowledge openly that errors occur and that we have to talk about them if we are going to design appropriate systems to prevent reccurrence. Second, we would study the situation. How was the diagnosis missed? Was it the error of a single person? Should EKGs have duplicate reviews? What time of day and in what part of a shift did it happen? Were the doctors involved over-worked or over-stressed? Was the case presentation atypical? Of course, some of this might have been done in well functioning organizations in the past, but certainly not with a great deal of openness, and certainly errors were not universally treated as opportunities to learn.

A safety approach would also advocate for disclosure to the patient for several reasons. First, the disclosure mandate is the foundation for the honest and open inquiry. If you can tell the patient that an error and injury occurred, then you can certainly share it within the institution. Second, there is the possibility that the patient could have crucial information that could help lead to prevention of future incidents. The patient, in this regard, is a key player in the investigation of what happened and what can be done to prevent a similar error in the future. Insulating the patient by keeping him/her in the dark just eliminates an opportunity.

Although both ethics and safety promote open disclosure to patients, malpractice litigation persists, and it acts as a very strong counter-weight on the important considerations of altruism, honesty, and better and safer patient care. Disclosure advocates are confident that the rationality of their arguments will bring a new accommodation, with or without legal change in the operation of the common law (Leape, 2002). Others, having seen little real progress over the last half decade in safety, are doubtful that change can occur without real reform in the compensation of medical injury (Brennan et al., 2005). The jury is still out, but a review of the vision of reform helps further illustrate the problems with disclosure and the injustices that flow from the *status quo*.

Malpractice Reform: Health Courts

Much of malpractice reform consists of efforts to reduce the amount of tort litigation by reducing the probability that the plaintiff's attorney will make sufficient profit on the case to warrant bringing it. Based on the evidence of the number of medical injuries that occur and the lack of compensation for them, it is clear that this "reform" approach does not move us in the right direction.

The only major alternative to such tort reform is to move away from common law litigation and toward a health court approach, a system that more facilely uses expert testimony and which relies on administrative compensation. Under a health court system the injured patient would apply directly to the hospital for compensation, with or without representation by a lawyer. The application for compensation would be considered directly by a hospital, and if there were no disagreement, the institution would pay the claim. If there were disagreement, the matter would be referred to a health court – an administrative compensation panel that would involve a trier of fact (i.e., someone who is trained in medical litigation), and objective experts with backgrounds relevant to the case at hand. In an expedited fashion, compensation would be awarded. The patient could appeal to a court if not satisfied with the result, but that appeal would be heard on the more traditional arbitrary and capricious standard.

Two aspects of the health court approach would make it much more open to maintaining the doctor–patient trust and commitment, and to promoting safety. First the standard would be directed at an avoidable adverse event rather than negligence. The idea here is that the charge of negligence, necessary for the successful prosecution of a tort, is the point of the sword in terms of the emotional and psychological affect of the litigation on the medical care professions. The concept of substandard care means that the adverse event involved treatment outside the range of expectations for the profession. However professionals can agree that avoidable injuries do occur. "Avoidability" has much less of a sense of moral culpability than does "negligence." Thus it is no surprise that other countries with similar professional mores and common law presumptions have shunned negligence and opted for administrative compensation schemes based on avoidability.

It is hoped that the health professionals involved in an error will have a much easier time disclosing that an injury was avoidable, rather than that negligent care was provided. Indeed the health court system is based on this disclosure. The presumption would be that the health professionals initiate the process with the patient. This approach does work in the Scandinavian countries where over 90 percent of error disclosures are initiated by the doctors on behalf of the patients. In the United States, we can also create sanctions that would be applied to providers who fail to disclose that an injury is iatrogenic. This approach should promote greater openness and safety.

Advocates of health courts can reasonably hope that the application for compensation will not sunder the doctor–patient relationship. The physician, for example, can maintain the altruistic relationship by helping the patient gain compensation for an injury. The commitment to honesty could be celebrated rather than forgotten, and the ethical basis for the relationship maintained. Furthermore, the case would be open so as to allow an investigation into the error. No longer would the cloak of litigation silence fall over the injury. Root cause analyses and eventual epidemiological analysis would really contribute to prevention of similar errors in the future.

The second aspect of health courts that would promote doctor–patient relationships and patient safety is that they would operate on an enterprise liability basis. Modern thinking about patient safety acknowledges that medical care is provided in a complicated system. Nurses and doctors exercise professional judgment and discretion, but their practice can be made safer by systems that help them. For instance, in the case described above, a computerized reading of the EKG may have identified the abnormality and thereby prevented the injury.

Health courts would turn patient safety into enterprise liability. The enterprise would be held liable for the injury and the institution would pay the costs of compensation. This does not in any way lessen medicine's altruistic, professional commitment to the patient. But it does appropriately allocate responsibility for the safety of patients and clinicians who are limited by the system and design of their institutions. In the context of today's complex health care, doctors, nurses, and hospitals have to work together to develop systems that cultivate safety. We cannot rely solely on an individual commitment because when things go wrong, it is frequently not an individual at fault, but rather a complicated process. This is often the way a safety engineer would see the situation, and it is the way we need to have health care professionals think about patient care so that they will be honest with their patients and so that they can develop and implement methods to prevent error.

Thus a health court approach, based on avoidable injury as the compensable event and operated according to the principles of enterprise liability, would help cure many of the ethical and safety-related problems of our current tort-based approach. The conceptual problems of tort law, in particular the manner in which it displaces the appropriate impulses of altruism and honesty, fail both in the provision of just compensation to injured patients and in promoting patient safety. The current malpractice system will never help the majority of people who suffer medical injuries, and it will never help develop prevention strategies of any merit. Thus an ethical profession, one outlined in the recent Professional Charter (Project of the ABIM Foundation, 2002), must support real reform along the lines of a health court. Indeed it will be very interesting to see whether this concept, which is now gaining political steam, will come to fruition. Examining the ethics surrounding medical injury prevention and just compensation suggests that it should.

References

Bosk, C.E. (1980), *Forgive and Remember*, New York: Oxford University Press.

Brennan, T.A. (1992), An empirical analysis of accidents and accident law: the case of medical malpractice law, *St Louis University Law Journal Health Law Symposium* 36: 823–78.

Brennan, T.A., and Berwick D.M. (1996), *New Rules: Regulation, Markets and the Quality of American Health Care*, San Francisco, CA: Jossey-Bass Inc., Publishers.

Brennan, T.A., Gawande, A.A., Thomas, E.J., and Studdert, D.M. (2005), Accidental deaths, saved lives, and improved quality, *New England Journal of Medicine* 353: 541–6.

Brennan, T.A., Leape, L.L., Laird, N.M., Hebert, L., Localio, A.R., Lawthers, A.G., Newhouse, J.P., Weiler, P.C., and Hiatt, H.H. (1991), Incidence of adverse events and negligence in hospitalized patients: results of the Harvard Medical Practice Study I, *New England Journal of Medicine* 324 (6): 370–6.

Havighurst, C., Blumstein, J., and Brennan, T.A. (1999), *Health Law and Policy*, 2nd edn., Mineola, NY: Foundation Press.

Hupert, N., Lawthers, A.G., Brennan, T.A., and Peterson, L.M. (1996), Processing the tort deterrent signal: a qualitative study, *Social Science and Medicine* 43 (1): 1–11.

Institute of Medicine (2000), *To Err Is Human*, Washington, DC: National Academy of Science Press.

Katz, J. (1984), *The Silent World of Doctor and Patient*, New Haven, CT: Yale University Press.

Lamb, R.M., Studdert, D.M., Bohmer, R.M.J., Berwick, D.M., and Brennan, T.A. (2003), Hospital disclosure practices: results of a national survey, *Health Affairs* 22 (2): 73–83.

Leape, L.L. (2002), Reporting of adverse events, *New England Journal of Medicine*, 347: 1633–8.

Lehmann, L.S., Puopolo, A.L., Shaykevich, S., and Brennan, T.A. (2005), Iatrogenic events resulting in intensive care admission: number, cause, and disclosure to patients and institutions, *American Journal of Medicine* 118: 409–13.

Mello, M.M., Kelly, C., and Brennan, T.A. (2005), Fostering rational regulation of patient safety, *Journal of Health Politics, Policy and Law* 30: 375–426.

Mello, M.M., Kelly, C.N., Studdert, D.M., Brennan, T.A., and Sage, W.M. (2003), Hospitals' behavior in a tort crisis: observations from Pennsylvania, *Health Affairs* 22: 225–33.

Project of the ABIM Foundation, the ACP-ASIM Foundation, and the European Federation of Internal Medicine (2002), Medical professionalism in the new millennium: a physician charter, *Lancet* 359 (9305): 520–2.

Starr, P. (1982), *The Social Transformation of American Medicine*, New York: Basic Books.

Studdert, D.M. and Brennan, T.A. (2001), No-fault compensation for medical injuries: the prospect for error prevention, *Journal of the American Medical Association* 286 (2): 217–23.

Studdert, D.M., Brennan, T.A., and Thomas, E.J. (2000), Beyond dead reckoning: measures of medical injury burden, malpractice litigation, and alternative compensation models from Utah and Colorado, *Indiana Law Review* 33 (4): 1643–86.

Studdert, D.M., Mello, M.M., and Brennan, T.A. (2004), Medical malpractice, *New England Journal of Medicine* 350: 283–92.

Studdert, D.M., Mello, M.M., DesRoches, C.M., et al., (2005), Defensive medicine among high-risk specialist physicians in a volatile malpractice environment, *Journal of the American Medical Association* 293: 2609–17.

Studdert, D.M., Mello, M.M., Gawande, A., et al. (2006), Claims, errors, and compensation in medical malpractice litigation, *New England Journal of Medicine*, 354: 2024–33.

Weiler, P.C. (1990), *Medical Malpractice on Trial*, Cambridge, MA: Harvard University Press.

Weiler, P.C., Hiatt, H.H., Newhouse, J.P., Johnson, W.G., Brennan, T.A., and Leape, L.L. (1993), *A Measure of Malpractice: Medical Injury, Malpractice Litigation, and Patient Compensation*, Cambridge, MA: Harvard University Press.

Chapter 23

Pre-existing Conditions

Genetic Testing, Causation, and the Justice of Medical Insurance

Robert T. Pennock

Introduction

Ethical controversies regarding the control of science and technology, especially emerging biotechnologies, are among the most contentious of current issues under public debate. Cloning or somatic cell nuclear transfer (even the terminology is controversial) and stem cell research are hot-button political issues, with presidential ethics advisors, presidents and ex-first ladies weighing in, threatening vetoes, or making alliances with strange bedfellows. Every technical advance sets off a new round of discussion and seemingly intractable disagreement. Similar ethical debates complicate public policy decisions regarding the development, regulation and use of genetically modified organisms, gene therapy, and other biological technologies. Research on creating artificial cells and artificial lifeforms is still too early in its development to have reached a comparable level of public awareness, but these areas will also require that we give careful thought to their ethical implications.

Using the term applied ethics for such deliberation is misleading; anyone who has tried to negotiate such practical ethical controversies knows that simply "applying" ethical theory off the shelf is rarely sufficient. At the very least, resolution of ethical questions caused by advances in science and technology will require close collaboration of both scientists and ethicists. Progress on the controversy about human cloning, for instance, may be possible when scientists, ethicists, and philosophers of science use their relevant expertise to sort through the combination of facts and values that is involved (Pennock, 2001). Progress on these kinds of issues may also be easier when we move from a simplistic, generic question about "the morality of X" to a more fine-grained analysis that frames questions in ways that take into account relevant ethical differences between developing just public policies, recognizing professional responsibilities, and respecting and delimiting the boundaries of personal liberties. In this chapter, I will explore how one may begin to work through such complexities of practical ethics, taking the case of genetic screening technology as an illustration.

As the story is told in newspaper reports from the labs where scientists mine for the gold of genetic knowledge, advances in genetic technology are opening up vast new veins of information about genes that cause disease, bringing us to the cusp of a medical revolution. Spurred by the Human Genome Project, molecular biology has taken on a boomtown mentality. Each week heralds the discovery of yet another purported disease gene. Besides the money being spent by the government, private companies are investing hundreds of millions of dollars to develop genetic tests for disease genes as they are discovered. No one underestimates the vast potential value of the new biological knowledge that is being gained. But the value varies by one's perspective. Health care professionals, for instance, see this technology as providing new and more precise data, opening the possibility of earlier and more accurate diagnosis, and (eventually) possible cures. For individuals, the possibilities of better diagnosis and treatments are the major values, but they also may simply value the increased self-knowledge and the basis it can provide for life-planning. To businesses and insurers, genetic screening technology is of value in identifying and reducing risks and costs (Waldman, 2004). However, as in other cases in which a sudden influx of capital enters an economic system, this new wealth of information may drastically upset an established equilibrium. Revolutions always carry with them the dangers of grave injustice during the transition to a new equilibrium, which is of concern from the perspective of public policy. In this case, the new genetic information threatens to upset the balance that so far has held between our (imperfect) knowledge of our health risks and the system of medical insurance upon which we have relied to protect ourselves from those risks.

As tests that can identify genes associated with diseases proliferate, individuals face a new problem: if they test positive for a disease gene they may find that insurers or employers say they have a "pre-existing condition" and cancel or deny coverage, or reject someone for a job on that basis. As I write this, the German government is considering legislation to permit and regulate limited genetic testing for employees in jobs such as construction and public transportation. The question involves how much of a person's genetic information a potential employer, for example, has the right to know (Tzortzis, 2004). The prospect immediately raised concerns about the potential for genetic discrimination, such as had already been seen under the Nazis and elsewhere. In the United State, cases of individuals being denied insurance by companies because of their genetic risk were among the famous list of cases of genetic discrimination brought to public attention by geneticist Paul Billings (Billings, 1993). A study by the US Office of Technology Assessment in 1992 found that half of all private and non-profit health insurers would refuse coverage to applicants if a genetic test revealed the likelihood of a serious, chronic disease. The same study found that 14 percent of genetic counselors and nurses had clients who had reported having problems about their health insurance because of genetic test results (Sanders, 1993). Health care professionals cannot neglect to inform patients of such potential problems when getting informed consent for genetic testing (Conti et al., 2004). In part because of such problems, President Clinton's failed comprehensive health reform bill had been expected to prohibit the use of any pre-existing conditions clauses (Sanders, 1993). Public concerns about misuse of screening continues to increase, with a 2004 study showing that 92 percent of Americans say employers should not have access to a person's genetic information, and 80 percent say that health insurers should also not have access (Rovner, 2004). From the insurers' point of view, however, pre-existing condition exclusion clauses make good sense and it seems obvious to them that when a genetic test reveals that someone has a disease gene this is a proper reason to deny him or her coverage.

This chapter will focus on the ethical implications for the future of medical insurance of regarding genes in this manner. Are pre-existing condition exclusion clauses (PECECs) in insurance policies just or unjust? In particular, is it just to deny medical insurance to people who test positive for a disease gene on the grounds that it is a pre-existing condition?

I will argue that we cannot make a general pronouncement about the justice or injustice of PECECs; in certain circumstances they are perfectly just. The first section defends the justice of PECECs for the sorts of conditions that have traditionally been excluded under this heading. However, there are both conceptual and moral problems with excluding people who test positive for some "disease gene" under this rubric, and I will argue that justice requires minimally that people not be denied medical insurance on these grounds. The second section provides the framework for this argument. I present a model of the causal relation – the CaSE model – and apply it to show why it is wrong to consider in general the presence of a particular allele (i.e., form of a gene) as being equivalent to having a genetic disease and why, instead, it should be considered in the same light as environmental conditions. This tells us that the argument of the first section does not apply as a valid reason to deny someone insurance on the basis of a genetic test alone. However, it does not show that it is wrong to charge higher premiums if a gene increases risk of disease and this could lead to a situation in which large numbers of people become genetically uninsurable. In the final section I argue from a Rawlsian viewpoint that, as genetic information proliferates, justice will require a change in the system of health care insurance to protect affordable coverage.

Pre-existing Conditions

Originally, when an insurance company declined to insure people with a pre-existing disease condition, that phrase meant that they already had the disease. A miner who was already diagnosed as suffering from black lung disease, say, could not then apply for insurance for that condition. Such PECECs made sense in the circumstances under which insurance organizations arose and on the traditional model of what an insurance policy is.

The contingencies of the world require us always to act under conditions of uncertainty, and medical insurance arose as a way to deal with uncertainty about one's future health. A health insurance policy allows individuals to take financial precautions against the possibility of debilitating illnesses and other maladies without all individuals having to tie up significant portions of their resources saving for illnesses that might never occur. Some fortunate policy-holders wind up never being sick a day in their lives and so never collect on their policies, but such people have no reason to think that they wasted their money. When they bought their policy they were in the same position as others who bought theirs, none knowing what the future would bring. For anyone who was acting prudently it made good economic sense to share the risk with others in a similar predicament.

The advent of mathematical probability and statistics in the seventeenth century, originally developed by Pascal in response to a gambling problem posed him by the Chevalier de Méré in 1654, made such decisions under uncertainty more precise. In 1657 Huygens wrote the first probability textbook, and in 1662 John Graunt published the first set of statistical inferences based in part upon mortality records (Hacking, 1990, p. 16). Such data and mathematical tools allowed an actuary to differentiate people by groups that had differential risks and thus to assign them different premiums – individuals in groups with lesser risk could then pay less than those who fell in groups that had a greater risk. Some people would be required to pay a higher premium than others, but this sort of differentiation seems morally unproblematic. *Prima facie* it fits Aristotle's formal principle of justice, which says that equals should be treated equally and unequals unequally. Furthermore, it looks as though differential risk is the relevant property for the case at hand.

If we think of buying insurance on the model of placing a bet in a gambling game, as early statisticians did and as many people still do, this form of differential treatment does seem just. If several people are placing bets together on what will turn up when a pair of dice is thrown, with the winner collecting the whole pot, then it would be unfair to require the person who bets on snake eyes to pay as much as the one who bets on seven, since the latter has a higher chance of collecting. Instead, because the latter has a six times greater chance of winning than the former, fairness requires that his initial bet be six times larger. Once the differential probabilities of winning are known, mathematical probability lets gamblers calculate what would be fair bets for the different outcomes. Similarly, information about differential risk of illness (or disability, or mortality) among different groups allows the actuary to say that an individual in one or another group has a respectively higher or lower chance of "winning" – that is collecting an insurance payoff by virtue of becoming ill (or disabled, or dying) – and thus to charge them appropriately different premiums.

When we consider insurance in this traditional manner it also seems obvious that the original sort of PECEC was just. To allow John Doe to join the insurance game and receive a policy for a disease that he already suffered from would be like allowing someone to place their bet after the dice had already been thrown and their number had already come up. In this scenario the PECEC simply prevents someone from being a guaranteed winner. Surely it would be unfair to the other "players" that they pay for those who joined the game only after they had already "won." It would be like allowing deceased persons' heirs to sign them up for a life insurance policy *post mortem*.

How does this bear upon the issues raised by the new genetic tests? In a straight-forward way genetic tests reduce uncertainty by providing more information. They allow us to take people who previously would have been classified together in the same risk group and to place them into smaller, more homogeneous reference classes. To ignore the information that genetic tests provide would seem to violate the basic principle upon which insurance works. An insurance company spokesman argues the perspective of the insurance industry this way:

> Insurance is sold to provide financial protection against unanticipated loss. If people who know they will die at an early age are allowed by law to purchase insurance, then they are at an advantage not only over the insurer but over all the other policy hold-ers covered by that company. As a basic principle, insurance is priced so that those at equal assumed risk pay equally for their protection. If that is not the case, the price of all insurance must change.
>
> (Lowden, 1994, p. 1509)

Here the spokesman was focusing on life insurance, but the same point applies to health and disability insurance. Genetic tests function like a peek at the cards. Losses or wins may no longer be unanticipated and if the law were to prohibit insurers from denying coverage to people who are privy to their genetic information this would be equivalent to allowing those individuals to legally cheat the odds.

Of course, in most cases individuals learn the results of a genetic test in settings where it becomes a part of their medical records and thus is accessible to insur-ers. If unfair use of genetic information is going to occur it is thus more likely that it will be individuals who are at a disadvantage *vis à vis* insurance companies. There are already documented cases of genetic discrimination against individuals. Probably the most systematic case of this occurred in the 1970s after some states began to require genetic screening for the sickle cell trait. The original motivation for screening was to provide family planning aid to people with the trait, but a National Academy of Sciences panel noted that it led to a situation in which car-riers of the gene were "denied jobs and charged higher insurance rates without evidence that the trait placed a person at a higher risk of illness or death" (Hilts, 1993). The unwarranted assumption of insurers seemed to be that simply having the gene meant that one had an increased risk.[1] In this case the differentiation was unjust because it involved imposing higher premiums without demonstration of higher risk. However, why would it necessarily be discriminatory to deny insurance to someone who tests positive for a disease gene, assuming that we *did* have good evidence that it increases the risks? The insurance company position is that it is not unjust to deny insurance in such cases on the same grounds as before, namely, because the disease condition was pre-existing.

Despite the apparent reasonableness of this position, I want to argue now that it rests on a couple of important confusions in the notions of "genetic disease," "disease gene," and "pre-existing condition." In brief, there is an ambiguity in the notion of a "pre-existing condition"; having a disease gene is not the same as having a pre-existing disease. Furthermore, I'll argue that there is parity between causal conditions that are genetic and those that are environmental, so that, looking simply at the level of causal interactions there is no reason to say that "the cause" of a disease is "genetic" and not "environmental." In a trivial sense, every disease may be said to have a pre-existing genetic component. One must bring in pragmatic considerations before classifying a disease as genetic rather than environmental. To make this argument I will begin by introducing some general considerations about the causal relation; I'll introduce the CaSE model as a framework for representing causal relations and then apply it to the case of genetic diseases.

CaSE Model of Causation

Causation is an ontic relation – it takes place in the world and involves physical objects, events, properties, processes, and so on. We must distinguish this onto-logical aspect of the causal relation from the way we *speak* about causal relations. When we make causal claims we typically speak of causation as though it were a simple two-place relation. We say things like "Pressing your foot on the brake causes the car to slow and come to a stop" or "Striking a match causes it to light." In the world, however, causation is not so simple. The world is a complex web of intersecting causal processes converging one upon another and diverging again at points throughout space–time. There are other important features of the causal relation (for example, that it involves production and propagation, and that it has an important asymmetry, that it licenses certain inferences) but for our purposes here the critical feature is its web structure – multiple causal factors are required to produce an effect or effects, and those factors themselves are effects with multiple causes.

Ordinarily it does no harm to think of the causal relation as we usually do as the two-place relation "C causes E" with only a single factor as the cause C and another as the effect E. In most circumstances, explaining to a novice learning to drive that "Pressing the brake causes the car to slow down and stop" is all that is required to convey the causal principle. However, the experienced driver knows that it takes more than pressing the brake C to stop the car E, for that may not work if the brake pads are worn, the car is heavily loaded, or the roads are slick. When considering the causal relations involved in stopping when in the car, the driver tacitly takes into account these other relevant factors. Clearly, therefore, more information is required to express the causal relation fully and accurately than is included in the single-factor representation.

A more sophisticated representation acknowledges that it is always a constellation of factors that makes up the causal antecedent. With this approach we may say that the antecedent of the causal conditional contains *multiple independent relevant variables* (that it is MIRVed), and it is their combined force that produces the effect. In the car case, besides the pressing of the brake, the antecedent C would have to specify that the brake linings are not worn, that the tires are dry, and many other relevant factors. For the representation to be complete, the antecedent C would have to contain *all* the factors that are involved in the production of the effect, including negative factors as in the example. Given the effect that I am interested in, such as my coming to a stop in my car at noon yesterday at the intersection of Fifth and Craig, there is a precise answer to the question of what caused it, but that answer is a complex one and requires specification of far more than the mere fact that I pressed the brake.

Having a MIRVed antecedent is more faithful to the ontic relation in that it recognizes equally all the multiple causal conditions that produce the effect, but the approach has a few notable disadvantages. It is rarely practical, since a specification of all the factors could quickly make the representation unwieldy. It also reduces the inferences that one may draw. And it obscures what often appear to be significant differences between the various factors, such as the difference between a triggering cause and background conditions. Also, it does not do as well as the single factor approach in capturing the way we ordinarily speak of causation.

I propose the CaSE model of the causal relation as an alternative representation that incorporates the virtues of both points of view. To accomplish this compromise the model uses a four-place relation in which the pragmatically highlighted factors of "the cause" and "the effect" are placed in their occasioning context or "situation," giving us *Condition C in situation S causes effect E*. This is abbreviated in the acronym "CaSE." The capitalized letters are placeholders for the ontic causal factors and the lowercase "a" stands in for the pragmatic elements (often expressed in terms of alternatives, for example, C rather than C', or E rather than E'). In the CaSE formulation all the factors of the MIRVed antecedent that had resided tacitly in the background in the single factor two-place relation are put in the situation S. So, for example, if we are talking about the striking of a match (C) causing it to ignite (E), then S would include such relevant factors as there being oxygen present, the match being dry, the air being calm, and so on. When precise specification of the factors is not necessary we sometimes think of S as representing assumed "standard conditions."

The CaSE model thus makes explicit that it is actually a combination of factors that causes an effect and it also allows us to isolate a particular factor that is of special interest, as we commonly do in ordinary causal talk. What we label "the cause" from among the multiple causal conditions is a *salient* factor that we choose to highlight because, for instance, we take it to be the triggering factor in standard background conditions or because of our particular interest at the time. More generally, from among the multiple relevant causal factors, the one we choose to call C is based on pragmatic considerations and may change depending upon the question we ask, or the stake we have in the outcome, or the context of the discussion. For example, we are often interested in causal relations because we desire the ability to intervene and to control outcomes and so will typically cite as "the" cause of some given effect that factor that is amenable to our control. In other cases we are interested in unusual or unexpected factors that have significant effects under otherwise standard conditions. For instance, under normal conditions we say that striking causes the match to light. But if striking the match had taken place in what we thought was an air-tight, oxygen-free chamber we would probably say, not that the striking was the cause, but rather that the oxygen that had entered unexpectedly through a faulty valve was the cause. The ontic causal factors that conspired to produce the flame are the same in the two cases; only which of them are taken as "background conditions" and which is taken as "the cause" changes. This *parsing* into cause and conditions is thus a function of pragmatics rather than of ontology.

In an analysis of causation it is also common to distinguish between necessary causal factors and sufficient causal factors. In the match example the presence of oxygen was a necessary factor in the relation that produced the flame. Yet, in the second match example, because of the unexpected leak in what was thought to be an air-tight valve, the introduction of oxygen was a sufficient factor in the relation that produced the flame. This division between necessary and sufficient factors is common. Nevertheless we notice that the oxygen was once cited as a necessary factor and another time as a sufficient factor, though in both cases the list of contributing factors was the same. If the necessary/sufficient division reflected some important ontic difference then it would seem strange that this could happen. Again, the CaSE model suggests that this is a pragmatic difference. In the first example by reparsing the situational factors (i.e., by conceptually "holding fixed" the striking of the match as part of S), the necessary cause (oxygen) is seen to be also sufficient relative to the background situation. In the second example, holding fixed the original set-up, the introduction of the sufficient cause (oxygen) is also recognized as having been necessary for the effect.[2] In this way we have just reversed what was illustrated in the original examples; how we place the emphasis is simply a pragmatic matter.

To illustrate how the CaSE model may represent different pragmatic parsings of causal conditions, let us take a slight variation of Hanson's classic example of an automobile accident at the intersection (Hanson, 1958, p. 54). What caused the accident? In the shop, the mechanics say that the cause was worn brake linings. At the station, the police officers say that speeding was the cause. At town hall, concerned citizens say that a tree-branch that partially obscured the traffic light was the cause. And so on. These persons cite things that were among the necessary conditions in the constellation of causal factors that produced the accident, but which were also sufficient given the "normal" or "default" situation assumed by their constituency. Mechanics assume that people may drive fast and that road conditions will vary, and focus on what is within their power to remedy. The citizens recognize that drivers occasionally exceed the speed limit and sometimes fail to have their vehicles in the best condition, and they seek to eliminate unusual environmental hazards that could bring a worst-case possibility into actuality. Shared context of discussion, shared community assumptions, usually determine quite clearly what is included in situation S. When discussants do not share common assumptions it may become obvious in the course of conversation and they usually take steps to remedy the misunderstanding by making their assumptions explicit.[3] On an informal level, therefore, we see that the four-place relation does seem to be implicitly assumed in our causal talk and that it is brought to the fore when speakers recognize that they are operating with different conceptions of what constitutes standard conditions.

To summarize, the four-place CaSE model holds all causal factors as ontically equal for the production of a given effect, while providing a way to recognize the striking feature of causal talk – that of singling out a particular factor as being of special interest. This acknowledges the multiplicity of factors that are involved in the production of an effect and also, by means of the pragmatic element and the slot for placing those factors one takes to be fixed as the background situation, makes explicit the ways we may highlight one or another of the conditions as "the" cause. It also makes clear that our labeling of some factors as "conditions" and another as "the cause" can change depending upon our interests and pragmatic choices, as can whether a cause is thought of as "necessary" or "sufficient."

CaSE study of "Genetic Disease"

What does this model of causation tell us about the concept "genetic disease" and the notion of a "disease gene"? A quick CaSE study provides the answer. For any given symptom set there are necessarily both genetic and environmental contributing causes. It is not the gene alone, but the gene in some environmental situation, S, that produces some effect. For example, the gene called "patched" is involved in the occurrence of basal cell carcinomas. The gene works by inhibiting cell growth, but if both copies of patched in a single cell are damaged by ultraviolet radiation from exposure to the sun then the cell divides unchecked and a tumor – a basal cell carcinoma – forms (Pennisi, 1996). Furthermore, if we are talking about some particular gene, G, the other genes in the genome would also have to be included in S, becoming, as it were, part of its environment. If G appeared together with a different combination of other genes it might have a completely different effect. The CaSE model helps make it clear that this is as true for so-called "single-gene diseases" like sickle cell anemia as it is for polygenic diseases. In many cases geneticists have no idea what additional factors are necessary for a gene to express itself. For instance, a gene for Hirschsprung's disease – an intestinal disorder – was recently found on chromosome 10 that appears to be autosomal dominant with incomplete penetrance; some people with a single copy develop the disease but others do not (Fackelmann, 1993). A disease symptom set is a possible effect, so whether *G* gets expressed in that way or not will depend upon what happens to be in *S*. These considerations let us draw a couple of important conclusions.

First, it tells us that simply having a particular allele in one's genome is not the same thing as suffering from a disease. To take an extreme example, it would be absurd to disqualify someone from dismemberment insurance on the grounds that they already had the gene sequence that codes for arms, without which they could never lose an arm. Even having the "chalky bone" mutation that weakens bones and predisposes one to fractures only causes that malady under particular environmental conditions, namely, hard and bumpy ones. Furthermore, there is great variability in the occurrence, severity, and course of most genetic diseases. Someone who gets the gene for neurofibromatosis may develop "marked disability of the nervous system, muscles, bones, and skin, while others will exhibit only minor pigmented spots on their bodies" (Gostin, 1994, p. 126). Some people with sickle cell anemia "are seriously ill from early childhood and others show only 'minor symptoms later in life'" (Cranor, 1994, p. 131). Indeed, a gene that is neutral or even disadvantageous in one situation may turn out to confer an advantage in another; this is the essence of what it is to be a pre-adaptation. Because of this possibility, critical in evolutionary development, it is important that we remember that it can be misleading to call something a "disease gene" – an allele that causes a disease in one set of circumstances could in theory turn out to confer an advantage in another. By itself, a gene is not "for" anything, let alone some malady, but produces effects only in concert with the other causal factors in which it is situated.

What this means is that we must disambiguate two senses of the term "pre-existing condition." In the initial argument given in support of PECECs for medical insurance we judged that it was unfair to allow someone to join the insurance pool after they already suffered from the disease (the condition) for which they wanted to be insured. But having the disease condition in this way is quite different from having the causal conditions that predispose one to developing the disease condition. To say that one has a disease gene is just to say that one has a given allele that under certain conditions increases one's chance of getting the disease. It is true that having a disease gene is a "pre-existing condition," but this is so in the latter sense (i.e., a causal condition that in a given situation may develop into a disease) not the former (i.e., the disease condition itself), which was the sense used in the insurer's argument justifying genetic PECECs. Thus, we may not automatically infer that that argument shows that it is ethical to deny someone insurance because they have tested positive for a gene that is a causal pre-condition for developing a disease. The argument uses the term "pre-existing condition" in two different senses and so is not valid because it commits the fallacy of ambiguity. Indeed, as we shall see, if that argument were the basis for exclusion, then no one would qualify for insurance at all unless they didn't need insurance in the first place.

This follows from the second point we should glean from the CaSE analysis, namely, that all diseases are "genetic diseases" and all are "environmental diseases" as well in that all have genetic causes and also all have environmental causes. It makes sense to settle on one aspect rather than the other only relative to other causal factors in the situation. Thus, whether we think of a particular disease as genetic or environmental depends upon which of the occurring causal factors we consider to be the background situation. Again, this is a pragmatic and not just an ontic matter.[4]

Of course, in most cases pragmatic factors will likely tend to one side or the other. We judge individual cases relative to what we take to be a standard set of conditions and for ourselves typically we will do this relative to what we take to be the normal healthy bodily state under the normal range of environmental conditions that we live. There are several ways that we might choose to define the normal healthy state – a statistical norm relative to a population, a functional norm relative to our evolutionary history, or a value norm relative to some standard of preferences – that correspond to different theories of disease. If the diseased departure from this state can be traced to a change in the corresponding "normal gene state," then we are likely to call it a genetic disease. If it can be traced to a change in the corresponding "normal environmental state" we are likely to call it an environmental disease.

The story quickly gets more complicated, however, because there may be other features of the situation that may also be of pragmatic interest and thus change which factor we emphasize. We may categorize cases differently depending upon whether and how we can intervene to prevent or cure the disease. Take hemochromotosis for instance, an adult onset disease that looks like end-stage liver failure and carries with it the risk of pituitary problems and cardiac failure. The gene that is blamed for the disease is an autosomal recessive. However, because the disease is totally treatable by conventional therapy (phlebotemy to draw off the excess iron store) it is not usually thought of in the category of genetic screening problems, but rather just as a conventional illness. On the other hand, as genetic technologies improve and the promise of efficacious gene therapy becomes more of a reality some scientists are beginning to call a genetic disease anything that could be *treatable* with some gene level intervention. These alternative classifications work the same way as singling out one or another causal factor as "the" cause of the car accident depending upon what variables of the situation people's interests take to be fixed and what is under their purview to modify.

There is much more that could be said about the pragmatics of disease classification, but this discussion is sufficient for us to now return to the original question. The foregoing considerations put us in a better position to evaluate the ethical question we originally posed about the justice of PECECs that deny insurance eligibility for individuals who test positive for some disease gene. Is there a moral reason to come down one way rather than the other in fixing the assumed situation and thereby calling a given disease genetic or environmental? For our purposes in considering the justice of exclusion clauses for medical insurance I would argue that the environmental/genetic distinction makes no moral difference in and of itself. The fallacy of ambiguity that we identified in regard to genetic causal pre-conditions would equally apply to environmental pre-conditions. In neither case is having a predisposing causal condition that could cause a disease the same thing as suffering from the disease condition itself. This showed us that at a merely ontic level there is a parity between genetic and environmental causal conditions. The parity extends in other relevant ways as well.

The most important point of parity involves how changing conditions change risks. Of course, having a genetic pre-condition for a disease, D, can make a difference, perhaps even a very large difference, in one's risk of developing D, but this is equally true of environmental causal conditions. Smoking, engaging in certain sexual practices, or living on a flood plain significantly increase one's chances of contracting various diseases and of dying. There is an exact symmetry between genetic and environmental causal conditions in the sense that *either* may raise (or lower) one's risks a little or a lot, depending upon the situation. Thus, if insurance company policy was to have PECECs for any pre-existing causal factor that increased one's chances of some D, then they could insure no one at all. But, of course, this would be absurd since the point of insurance is to take pre-cautions against risks. Driving an automobile, living in a city, or working as a coal miner all increase the chances that one will need medical attention. It would not make sense for an insurer to deny insurance on the grounds that someone had the "pre-existing condition of urban residence" or had already begun working in the mines.

Even in cases in which the risks are extremely high of contracting a disease given some genetic or environmental pre-condition, there may be considerable variability in time of onset, and here too there is parity between genetic and environmental factors. In neither case do we know, as we do when a person already suffers from a disease, whether those factors will develop to the point that the person begins to exhibit symptoms and requires medical care. It can be extremely difficult to predict time of onset of a disease because of the extreme variability of genetic disease, even within the same family (Gostin, 1994, p. 126). Even in cases in which the gene could be shown to cause a disease with certainty, with many diseases one still could not say exactly when or even if the onset would occur. A person with the gene marker for Huntington's or other late onset disease may never collect any insurance for that malady, if only because they may die earlier in an explosion caused by an oxygen leak. Similarly, someone with the human immuno-deficiency virus could die in a automobile wreck before developing any symptoms of AIDS. Even knowing that the effect is inevitable and that it is certain that one could collect on insurance eventually is not in itself a reason to deny insurance because of the variability in time of onset. Everyone is going to die, but that is not a good reason to deny someone life insurance; follow that rule and there would not be life insurance in the first place.

The main conclusion we should draw from this discussion is that genetic and environmental causal pre-conditions are on a par. For that reason, it is wrong to deny someone insurance by counting having a "disease gene" as a pre-existing condition. We have misled ourselves in thinking that there is something critically different about genetic causal conditions. Probably this is because we have begun only recently to be able to identify and understand genes and we still have only marginal abilities to intervene to control them. Genes still seem mysterious. It has not helped that scientists have done little to discourage the popular press in its tendency to speak of genes as though they alone determine our lives. People have developed an attitude that might be described as "genetic fatalism." The fatalistic attitude about genes is unwarranted; it is based on a simplistic understanding of the causal web within which a gene is just one factor among many. This over-generalized view of the power of genes can lead people unjustifiably to conclude that testing positive for "a disease gene" is the same as having a disease.

The second conclusion we can draw is that under the current US system of medical insurance based on the gambling analogy of players freely choosing whether or not they will agree to play, it is acceptable for premiums to reflect differential assumed risk, assessed by a genetic test. *Prima facie*, it is the degree of risk and not whether that risk is introduced by genetic or environmental causes that should make a difference in insurance rates. That is, the morally relevant consideration is not where the causal inputs come from but rather what their known effects are and how information about those inputs allows one to anticipate differential losses. In a fair game of chance the price of the bet should reflect the known odds. That is why the case we mentioned earlier of insurers raising rates for people who tested positive for the sickle cell gene was unjust genetic discrimination, because the premium increase was imposed without evidence that carrier risks were indeed higher. It is fair to charge more when risks are higher, but it should not make a difference that the risk is genetic rather than environmental.

The Future of Medical Insurance

This leads us to look into the future of medical insurance. One implication of the previous argument is that insurers may charge proportionately higher premiums for greater risks, and we know cases in which the increased risks may be substantial. Indeed, if we maintain a complete parity between genetic and environmental factors, we should even allow insurers to deny insurance to people with a "disease gene," not by virtue of a PECEC, but simply because the risks and costs (which can be extremely high for diseases like PKU, Parkinson's or cystic fibrosis) make the policy a bad bet for the insurers. Previously these costs were spread out over everyone who was insured since there was no way to sub-divide the assumed risk group. But with the advent of genetic testing, the new information allows insurers to refine reference classes. Such groups will often be too small to make the premiums affordable to individuals when the costs are divided. With over a thousand genetic tests already available and more being developed every day this will lead to a situation in which a large proportion of the population simply cannot afford medical insurance. As developing genetic technology pushes us inexorably in this direction new considerations of justice arise.

Would it be just to maintain the current system of medical insurance in which only the genetically lucky can afford health insurance? Up to this point we have been considering the question of justice within the current institutional structure of health care. As we look into the future we must consider the possibility that the provision of health insurance will have to be reformed. Putting this another way, it may no longer be proper to judge the fairness of insurance on analogy with placing bets in a gambling game as we did before, taking for granted the current rules of the game. Justice may require that we change the rules.

An argument in favor of this view may be made on Rawlsian grounds. Briefly, Rawls tells us to think of justice as fairness, and proposes a framework – the original position (Rawls, 1971, Chapter 3) – for evaluating the justice of social institutions. What institutional and legal structures would we, as free, equal, and rational people, agree to set up and be governed by if we had to make that choice from under a "veil of ignorance"? That is, what structures would it be rational for us to agree to if we did not know in advance which personal characteristics, values, position in society, and so on we would have in that society?

Naturally, under the veil of ignorance we would be ignorant of the specifics of our genome. We would not know whether we would have genes that confer a high degree of disease risk. Nor would we know whether we would be wealthy enough to afford the high insurance premiums concomitant with high risk under the current system of medical insurance. Given that adequate health is a prerequisite for the pursuit and enjoyment of what one values, health care is a basic good, and it would be in our rational interest to see to it that it was guaranteed to all for such conditions. When we consider the justice of health insurance institutions and rules in light of these considerations we see an immediate reason to question the earlier analogy to the game of chance. We cannot chose not to be born and we cannot chose whether or not to roll the genetic dice. Though the current system looked fair initially, it is unfair from a more global perspective. This conclusion connects with another Rawlsian insight, namely, that issues of justice involve compensating for the inequalities of life's "natural lottery" (Rawls, 1971, p. 74). We would want to be sure that our access to health care was protected, particularly if we should be born with a predisposition for some disease.

This is not to say that we would necessarily decide in the original position in favor of universal health care for all disabilities. However, for genetic risks we have inherited I conclude that it would be in our enlightened self-interest to require an institutional structure that would guarantee coverage.[5]

What we have seen is that the new genetic information may lead to a situation in which health care coverage is not offered to everyone. These changing circumstances may force a reform of current insurance practices.

Conclusion

Once information becomes readily available it will also affect the economy of exchange. New genetic information has already begun to upset the established equilibrium that allowed the current system of medical insurance to work, and something must change if we are to find a viable new equilibrium. Before genetic tests became available, people with a genetic predisposition to some disease still had access to coverage because there was no way to identify their increased risk in advance of its expression; since everyone was in the same state of ignorance no one had an unfair advantage in the insurance game. We are no longer in that situation and, unless we want to leave a large percentage of the population uninsurable, either we will have to change the rules of the game or we will have to start playing another game. As we have seen, this policy issue involves issues of justice and sits squarely in the middle of public morality.

I have not argued here for particular changes in institutional structure. Some philosophers, such as Philip Kitcher (Kitcher, 1996, pp. 135–6), have argued persuasively that in these new circumstances it will be necessary to have universal health care and drop the private medical insurance system entirely, but this is not a foregone conclusion. Perhaps the insurance industry could find a way to offer genetic "as is" health insurance or find a sufficiently broad classification scheme that would allow health insurance to be generally affordable. For this to work it might be that the government would have to institute some industry-wide regulations regarding genetic pre-conditions to maintain fairness for companies. There is already a precedent for such regulations in laws that prohibit differential premiums based on racial classification and legislation along these lines for genetic conditions has already been proposed. Such legislation could be a boon, not just for individuals, but for biotechnology itself (Anon., 1996). Perhaps we would have to move to some mixed system of public and private health insurance. Tom Beauchamp and James Childress, for reasons independent of the genetic considerations we have discussed, have proposed a two-tiered system that would provide a public guarantee of a "decent minimum" of health care and allow for optional private insurance that people can purchase for supplemental coverage (Beauchamp and Childress, 1994, pp. 348–56). Perhaps under the framework of the original position we could decide on a pragmatic norm that could be used to classify diseases and disease pre-conditions. For example, relative to a standard situation, we could agree that diseases resulting from inherited factors should be covered by universal insurance whereas conditions arising from environmental risks that one takes on by choice should fall under the traditional form of insurance.

These and other possibilities will require serious deliberation as we adjust to the availability of new genetic information. In the end, personal, professional, and public ethical perspectives have to work together. Scientists and heath care professionals must be aware of both their research duties and their clinical duties.

As they push the technology forward they must be careful to explain the utility of genetic tests without the loaded "disease gene" terminology, and be sure that patients understand the nature and implications of the information, so they can assess the costs and benefits. Furthermore, a policy must be developed to change (somehow) the rules of the medical insurance game through either legislative or judicial action so that genetic tests are not used unjustly. Minimally, we can conclude here that the practice of denying health insurance to people with a genetic predisposition for disease on the grounds that these fall under PECECs is improper. Justice requires that the current system of health insurance be modified in light of these changing conditions.

Notes

1 In fact, we know that the sickle cell gene has a heterozygote advantage in conferring resistance to malaria, so in some circumstances having the gene actually lessens one's overall risk of ill-health.

2 Of course, we are here speaking not of causes as logically necessary and sufficient, but as physically or productively so, since we are still dealing with ontic causation.

3 As a first approximation we might think of S as a *ceteris paribus* clause – C causes E, *other things being equal*. However, S need not include *all* other things, but just a restricted subset. Specifically it should include those factors that make a difference to, and thus can be taken to be significant in, the production of the effect. The fact that the car in the accident had brake linings that were worn made a difference. The fact that the driver had on a vest with worn lining did not. The former factor gets included in the specification of S. The latter is irrelevant and is omitted. *Situation S should thus include all and only those factors that are causally relevant (that is, actually make a difference) for the production of the given effect E, relative to the factor of interest, C.*

4 Other philosophers have mentioned that there may be pragmatic reasons for picking out a gene in some contexts as "the" cause of a disease. For example, in his useful article on genetic causation Carl Cranor writes, "The fact that a complex set of conditions is sufficient to produce an event does not detract from drawing attention to one of the contingencies as 'a' or 'the' cause for certain purposes. What matters is the context and the purpose and that we do not lose sight of the complexity of the processes involved" (Cranor, 1994, p. 131). What the CaSE model shows is that pragmatic partitioning of causal factors is a general feature of the causal relation that must be recognized for all causal claims, so its application to questions having to do with "genetic diseases" is to be expected.

5 Interestingly, Alexander Lowden, who had argued for the insurance companies' perspective, appears to accept this idea. His concluding argument against legislation that would have limited insurance company's use of test information is that such legislation "will add to the cost of a product that should be available to all" (Lowden, 1994, p. 15).

References

Anon. (1996), Legislative insurance against genetic discrimination is insurance for biotechnology, *Nature Biotechnology* 14 (5): 547.

Beauchamp, T.L. and Childress, J.F. (1994), *Principles of Biomedical Ethics*, 4th edn., Oxford: Oxford University Press.

Billings, P.R. (1993), Genetic discrimination, *Healthcare Forum Journal* 36 (5): 35–7.

Conti, A., Delbon, P., and Sirignano, A. (2004), Informed consent when taking genetic decisions, *Medicine and Law* 23 (2), 337–53.

Cranor, C.F. (ed.), (1994), *Are Genes Us? The Social Consequences of the New Genetics*, New Brunswick, NJ: Rutgers University Press.

Fackelmann, K.A. (1993), Gutsy genetics: hunting down a gene for a children's digestive disorder, *Science News* 144: 174–5.

Gostin, L. (1994), Genetic discrimination: the use of genetically based diagnostic and prognostic tests by employers and insurers, in R.F. Weir, S.C. Lawrence and E. Fales (eds.), *Genes and Human Self-Knowledge: Historical and Philosophical Reflections on Modern Genetics*, Iowa City: University of Iowa Press.

Hacking, I. (1990), *The Taming of Chance*, Cambridge: Cambridge University Press.

Hanson, N.R. (1958), *Patterns of Discovery*, Cambridge: Cambridge University Press.

Hilts, P.J. (1993), Genetic testing can lead to discrimination, science panel warns, *Austin American-Statesman*, November 5: A16.

Kitcher, P. (1996), *The Lives to Come: The Genetic Revolution and Human Possibilities*, New York: Simon and Schuster.

Lowden, J.A. (1994), Genetic testing, *Science* 265 (September 9): 1509–10.

Pennisi, E. (1996), Gene linked to commonest cancer, *Science*, 272 (5268): 1583–4.

Pennock, R.T. (2001), The virtuous scientist meets the human clone, in Charles Blackburn (ed.), *New Ethical Challenges in Science and Technology, Sigma Xi Forum 2000 Proceedings*, Research Triangle Park, NC: Sigma Xi, The Scientific Research Society.

Rawls, J. (1971), *A Theory of Justice*, Cambridge, MA: The Belknap Press of Harvard University Press.

Rovner, J. (2004), Public fear of genetic discrimination grows, *Colorado Health Guide* 10: 1–2, available at http://www.coloradohealthguide.org/Library/CHGNews10.pdf.

Sanders, E. (1993), With gene testing comes fear of insurance discrimination, *Austin American-Statesman*, May 23: A14.

Tzortzis, A. (2004, *Are You (Genetically) Up to the Job?* from http://www.dw-world.de/dw/article/0,1564,1369432,00, last accessed October 20, 2004.

Waldman, L. (2004), The ethical, legal and psychosocial challenges of genetic testing: implications for primary medical care, *Missouri Medicine* 101 (2): 117–20.

Suggestions for Further Reading

Brandt-Rauf, P.W., and Brandt-Rauf, S.I. (2004), Genetic testing in the workplace: ethical, legal, and social implications, *Annual Review of Public Health* 25: 139–53.

Collins, F.S., and Watson, J.D. (2003), Genetic discrimination: time to act, *Science*, 302 (5646): 745.

Ellis, A.M. (2003), Genetic justice: discrimination by employers and insurance companies based on predictive genetic information, *Tex Tech Law Review*, 34 (4): 1071–99.

Fisher, N.L. (2004), Genetic testing and health insurance: can they coexist? *Cleveland Clinic Journal of Medicine* 71 (1): 8–9.

Godard, B., Raeburn, S., Pembrey, M., Bobrow, M., Farndon, P., and Ayme, S. (2003), Genetic information and testing in insurance and employment: technical, social and ethical issues, *European Journal of Human Genetics* 11, Suppl. 2: S123–42.

Holtzman, N.A. (2003), Ethical aspects of genetic testing in the workplace, *Community Genetics* 6 (3): 136–8.

Markman, M. (2004), Genetic discrimination arising from cancer risk assessments: a societal dilemma, *Cleveland Clinic Journal of Medicine* 71 (1): 12, 15–18.

Nedelcu, R., Blazer, K.R., Schwerin, B.U., et al. (2004), Genetic discrimination: the clinician perspective, *Clinical Genetics* 66 (4): 311–17.

Offit, K., Groeger, E., Turner, S., Wadsworth, E.A., and Weiser, M.A. (2004), The duty to warn a patient's family members about hereditary disease risks, *Journal of the American Medical Association* 292 (12): 1469–73.

Partlett, D.F. (2003), Misuse of genetic information: the common law and professionals' liability, *Washburn Law Journal* 42 (3): 489–523.

Shinaman, A., Bain, L.J., and Shoulson, I. (2003), Preempting genetic discrimination and assaults on privacy: report of a symposium, *American Journal of Medical Genetics* 120 (4): 589–93.

Silvers, A. and Stein, M.A. (2003), Human rights and genetic discrimination: protecting genomics' promise for public health, *Journal of Law Medicine and Ethics* 31 (3): 377–89.

Simon, J. (2003), Genetic testing and insurance: an international comparison, *Journal International de Bioéthique* 14 (3–4): 59–78.

Index